INDIKA

INDIKA

THE COUNTRY AND THE PEOPLE OF INDIA AND CEYLON

by

JOHN F. HURST, D.D. LL.D.

WITH MAPS AND ILLUSTRATIONS

GYAN

Published by

Gyan Publishing House
5, Ansari Road
Daryaganj, New Delhi-110002
Phone: 011-47034999, 9811692060
E-mail: books@gyanbooks.com

Distribution Network
gyanbooks.com
India, USA, Canada, UK, Australia, France

ISBN : 978-81-212-6075-6 (PB)
First Published, 1891

2nd Impression 2021

Printed at: Gyan Press, Delhi.

Indika
Author: John F. Hurst

THE WINDOW OF SELIM-SHISTI'S MONUMENT.

From a painting by V. Verestchagin. By permission of the American Art Association.

INDIKA

THE COUNTRY AND THE PEOPLE

OF

INDIA AND CEYLON

BY

JOHN F. HURST, D.D., LL.D.

WITH MAPS AND ILLUSTRATIONS

1891

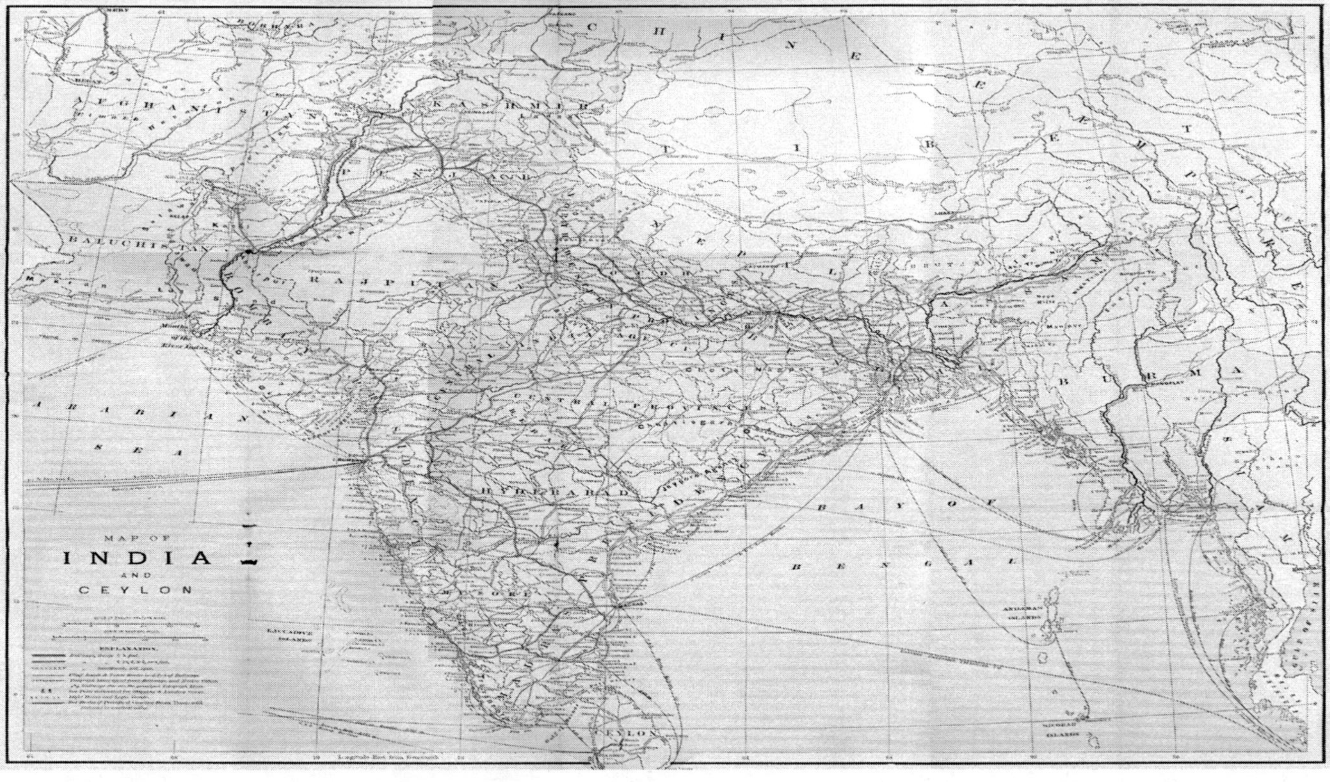
MAP OF
INDIA
AND
CEYLON
AFGHANISTAN
BALUCHISTAN
KASHMIR
RAJPUTANA
C H I N E S E E M P I R E
T I B E T
N E P A L
BHUTAN
CENTRAL PROVINCES
HYDERABAD
MYSORE
B U R M A
ARABIAN SEA
BAY OF BENGAL
ANDAMAN ISLANDS
NICOBAR ISLANDS
LACCADIVE ISLANDS
CEYLON
EXPLANATION

FOREWORD.

The object of the following work is to describe India and Ceylon as they are to-day. But to make clear the existing condition of a country, and to account for it, the past must be constantly recognized. Therefore, at every stage of this work the historical antecedents have been summoned, and made to do duty as interpreters of the existing India and Ceylon. My plan of travel required a journey to nearly all the large places, and to many of the more obscure, throughout the empire. Landing in Bombay, and going across the peninsula to Madras, I proceeded to Ceylon, and went into the interior as far as Kandy, the ancient capital. On embarking from Colombo I landed in India again, this time near its southern extremity, and proceeded northwestward to Mysore. Thence I went to Madras, and there took passage up the Bay of Bengal to Calcutta. After a protracted stay in that place and its environs, I proceeded up the valley of the Ganges, with here and there such digressions as official duties permitted or required. The point where my itinerary brought me most closely to the Himalaya Mountains was Naini Tal, where, one cloudless morning, from Mount Chena, I could see the magnificent panorama of snow-clad mountains which form the southern barrier of Western China. The limit of my tour in the northwest was Lahor, whose minarets look down on the swift Ravi and out towards the valley of the Jhelam. This historic plain was the battlefield on which Alexander the Great won India, his last conquest, and opened its gates for the first time to the western world.

In the United States and Germany I had provided myself with helps for the study of the country and its romantic past. But in Bombay my apparatus was greatly enlarged, and it grew continually during my stay in India. I soon saw that if one desires to understand all that is involved in the Christianization of a land, he must make a special study of the country, its people, antiquities, dead faiths, industries, literature, habits, and political history. It was always a special privilege to meet representatives of the new thought and life of the empire. Every day brought with it something fresh, instructive, and attractive. When the hour came to leave the country, it seemed as if awaking out of a delightful dream. Not until, one February morning, when I was actually on the deck of the *Siam*, and sailing out of the Bombay harbor, with the vessel pointing towards Aden, was the charm broken. There had been a certain subtle and undisturbed joy which came from the environment. Nor could I know the depth and power of the Indian fascination until the ghats back of Bombay faded into the perfect sky and the eye could no longer see the beautiful islands in that matchless bay.

Subjects which simply suggested themselves on the spot have, by later study, grown into large groups. The astounding advance of sentiment in favor of temperance; the spread of the opium trade, and England's responsibility for it; the uprising of the natives, not for another mutiny against their rulers, but for a representative government, in which the governed may share; the multiplication of missionary forces from Europe and America; the steady elevation of the whole body of the Indian people by the extraordinary educational advantages which Macaulay was the hero to inaugurate; the new and abundant literature bearing on India and its manifold life; and the constant trend of the Indian languages towards disuse and oblivion, with the English as the sole speech of the future, are topics now of absorbing interest to readers in every part of the civilized world.

In the plan of the work the personal narrative has been everywhere made subordinate to the general descriptive interest. It has been introduced largely for the purpose of throwing such light on the life of the people of India as might fall to the lot of a guest. Special topics have been treated in the centres which suggested them. For example; the Parsis could be studied to advantage only in Bombay, missions and education better in Calcutta and Serampore than elsewhere; and the Mutiny better in Cawnpore and Lucknow than in places less central, and which had suffered less in that ordeal of blood.

One of the most perplexing questions has been the correct spelling of the Indian proper names. Some, since the first draught of the work, have required a changed orthography. Other names were adopted at first, then abandoned, and finally both necessity and propriety required a return to the original spelling. The word *Marhatta*, for example, has needed to be changed several times, and was finally adopted in its present form—Marhatta—in compliance with the usage of those writers whose authority seems most weighty. The spelling of Macaulay's day is now largely obsolete. The Hugli cannot any longer be written Hoogley. M. Le Bon suggests that the English themselves have taken little pains to arrive at unity in Indian orthography. There are no two Indian maps which adopt the same form for spelling the names of places. Even of cities through which the railway passes, one can find four different spellings—one on the railway map, another in the railway guide, a third in the station itself, and a fourth in the postal indication. While it is not very difficult to identify Cawnpore in Kanhpur, Amritsar in Umritsur, Pondichery in Punduchery, and Conjeveram in Kanchipuram, it is not so easy to identify Tanjore in Tanjawur, Awadh in Oudh, Travancore in Tiruwankodu, and Mandir-Ray in Madras. Thornton's *Gazetteer*, one of the most important works on India, spells the one word *Fath* in eleven different fashions—Futeh, Futh, Futtre, Futick, Futi, Futte,

Futteh, Futtih, Futtun, Futty. Even the colonels of regiments have sometimes been unable to identify the places on the itineraries which the government had placed in their hands. In comparing the official map of the government of Madras there was often no resemblance between the names. On five different maps there were five spellings of one river—Tamrapavni, Tamberperny, Tambaravari, Pambouri, and Chindinthura.*

The present tendency of English writers on India is to approach the Indian spelling. But to this there are exceptions. The pronunciation of Indian words has led to an English spelling. For example, *a* is often really *u*. Hence the custom arose of spelling *Panjab* as if written *Punjab*. The usage of Monier Williams and other recent scholars in writing Panjab has been adopted. The old spelling of *Mahomet* is now rapidly passing away. The latest of the reliable authorities spell it *Muhammed*, and the old *Koran* must now give place to the new *Qurán*.

Throughout the work I have been compelled to balance the orthography, and follow in the path of the safest of the recent guides.† In some instances the usual English method has been pursued. We are not quite far enough as yet to write Kanhpur for Cawnpore, Dihli for Delhi, and Lahknau for Lucknow. The

---

* Le Bon, "Civilisation de l'Inde" (Paris, 1887), p. 477.

† Carter, in his "History of India," published at the Cambridge (England) University Press, takes Hunter as his guide, and says: "Indian names are spelled according to the *Imperial Gazetteer of India*, edited by Sir W. W. Hunter, which represents the system adopted by the authority of the Indian government in 1870. A few names which have acquired popular currency are left unaltered

"The vowel sounds are represented and sounded thus:

a as in rur*a*l and f*a*r.
e as in gr*e*y.
i as in f*i*ll and d*ee*r.
o as in b*o*ne.
u as in b*u*ll and r*u*de.
ai as in l*y*re.

"The consonants are to be sounded as in English, except *g*, *ch*, *s*, *t*, which are sounded only as the corresponding letters in *give*, *church*, *solstice*, *tin*."

diacritical points which are commonly employed to distinguish the long from the short sound of the vowels have, in most cases, been omitted.

For all statistical information my chief reliance has been the full tabular reports issued at Calcutta by the departments of the Indian government. For important suggestions while this work was in manuscript, and for special help during its passage through the press, I am indebted to Bishop James M. Thoburn, of Calcutta; the Rev. Thomas S. Smith, of Jaffna, Ceylon; the Rev. B. H. Badley, D.D., of Lucknow; the Rev. Thomas J. Scott, of Bareilly; the Rev. George H. McGrew, D.D., of New York, and the Rev. Albert Osborn, B.D., of Buffalo, New York.

The title of the work—INDIKA—I derive from the Greek Megasthenes, the first writer to reveal the inner life of India to the western world. After the conquest of India by Alexander the Great, Seleucos Nicator, the founder of the Syrian monarchy, became possessor of India. His hold, however, was very slight, for, while he was consolidating Syria, Chandra Gupta was arousing India and throwing off the despised Greek domination. Instead of a new warfare, there was a compromise between these two rulers. It was a clear case of barter. Chandra Gupta gave Seleucos five hundred elephants as a present, while Seleucos gave the great Indian chief his daughter in marriage. Seleucos sent, as his ambassador to the Indian court at Patna, the learned Megasthenes. The Greek scholar remained there many years, and travelled extensively, and had all the skill in acquiring information which Herodotus possessed in gaining knowledge from the Egyptian priests during his leisurely tours along the Nile. Megasthenes, on returning to Greece, wrote his book Ἰνδικά (Indian Things), which was an account of his travels and observations in far-off India. This valuable work, which contained minute information concerning the land conquered by Alexander, is lost, but such important fragments of it have been preserved by Strabo, Arrian, and Ælian as to give a certain completeness to many of its topics.

While INDIKA is not written in any prevailing interest, it may be said that the publishers have been so kind as to suggest the largest liberty in the treatment of missions. It is hoped that the result will be not only of some aid towards a general knowledge of India and Ceylon, but of such service in making better known the magnitude of the intellectual and spiritual needs of the millions of the people as to awake the largest sympathy of all Protestant people, and to aid somewhat in attracting to the Aryan cradle of our Anglo-Saxon race a hundred missionary, medical, and educational laborers where to-day there is but one.

WASHINGTON, D. C., *February* 9, 1891.

TABLE OF CONTENTS.

LIST OF ILLUSTRATIONS.

LIST OF MAPS.

INDIKA.

CHAPTER I.

THE THREE SEAS TO INDIA.

My path from Europe to India lay through Vienna and the rich wheatfields of the Hungarian plains. At Belgrade the railroad was left behind. The passage by steamer down the Danube is one of the most interesting experiences through which one passes in Eastern Europe, while the rapid gliding through the Iron Gates leaves nothing to be desired in the way of picturesque scenery and historical associations. After a halt at Sistov and Rustchuk, and a detour to Bucharest, the capital of Roumania, Filippo took me in charge for a drive of three days across Bulgaria. His wagon was not the best, while his horses were not equal to the climb up the Balkan heights. We accordingly took buffaloes. They proceeded at slow rate, but finally brought us to the top of the Shipka Pass. Here we took our horses again, and proceeded rapidly down through the rose-gardens of Kasanlik into the romantic plains of Thrace. At Philippopolis I again found a railroad, and proceeded to Constantinople.

A week's rest on the western bank of the Bosphorus, at the home of the Rev. Dr. A. L. Long, proved a good preparation for the voyage to India. The doctor accompanied me on a journey to Troy. On returning to the Dardanelles, I found myself compelled to pay the severe penalty for our luxury of two days' wandering over the Troad by being obliged to take a wretched Russian steamer, *The Tsar*, for Alexandria.

Alexandria was in process of rebuilding after the great fire and devastation in the unsuccessful war waged against the English by Arabi Pasha, whom I saw later in exile on the island of Ceylon. The dust in Alexandria was flying in all directions. Building materials blocked up many of the streets. I was determined to see the city well, and get over the impression of a former visit, in 1871, that there is next to nothing to see in this renowned place. But the second visit was as unremunerative as the first. The traveller should make haste to see Pompey's Pillar, climb a knoll, or get out on a house-top, and see the matchless Mediterranean and the wonderful curve of the coast-line, and then take his leave for Cairo. Many a city has risen and fallen here, but the traces are few and faint. Alexandria is only a memory. Kingsley's "Hypatia" and Shakespeare's "Antony and Cleopatra" help one to bring back its past. The Mediterranean Sea is now the only fresh and beautiful thing for all eyes to rest on. The Alexandrian obelisks and other treasures, so far as they have not been ground into shapeless fragments by the mills of time and war, have gone into foreign hands, to enrich the antiquarian collections of Europe and America.

In Cairo one has a different feeling. He is sure to be rewarded. Its interior location has preserved it from the assaults of navies. It is both new and old. There is, on every hand, enough of the old past to keep fresh the picture of former greatness. Bits of antiquity greet you at frequent intervals. Then, on all the drives, the Pyramid of Cheops stands out in full view, from its place on the plains, in all the calm dignity and majesty of an immortal queen. Shepard's Hotel, in October, 1884, was a busy place. It was the general rendezvous for British officers, high and low, who were about to ascend the Nile to Khartoum, for the campaign against the Mahdi for the rescue of General Gordon. Lord Wolseley had charge of the British army. Every move was a blunder. Gordon was killed. The expedition failed, and it was a piece of the best fortune that the larger part of the British army escaped with their lives. After Gordon's death, his Bible was found and brought back to England, and given to his sister. Its worn appearance tells the story of its faithful use by Gordon during his stay and dreadful siege at Khartoum. The sister, much as she prized it, presented it to the Queen. It was gratefully accepted by her, who, not willing to bury it among her literary treasures in the library of Windsor Castle, had a special cabinet prepared for it, where it now rests alone in the corridor of the Castle, and where any visitor can see its well-worn pages.

The starting of the train from Cairo for Suez brought me face to face with my long Indian tour. In twenty-four hours I was to take the steamer. Suez was reached at nine in the evening. An accident delayed the train an hour. Judging from the volume of hot water falling on the track, and the great escape of steam, and the fright of the throng of jabbering Arabs on the engine, there was a near approach to an explosion of the boiler. How do the Egyptians put out a locomotive fire on one of their

KANTARAH, ON THE SUEZ CANAL.

trains? Easily enough. They go out into the desert, which is only four feet off, and fill their shallow palm-baskets with sand, and pour that on the fire. The smothering is instantaneous. When the fire was out, and I began to resign myself to staying all night out in the desert, a freight-train whistled in the distance, in the rear of our train. It was a pure accident that help was near. The freight-cars came quietly up, put their locomotive to our train, and pushed us into Ismailia. After a ride of two and a half hours farther we reached Suez.

The servant who took me in charge at the Suez hotel was a

pure Arab. He had as beautiful, pearl-like teeth as ever shone between two lips; a round face; eyes dark and soft; and he spoke a "leedle Eengles." He represents a large class of Egyptian natives whom England is bringing up out of the sands, and to whom she is giving a future, though humble at the start. The agent of the Peninsular and Oriental Line, to which the *Sutlej* belongs, met me after breakfast, and told me to be ready in ten minutes to go out in his steam-launch, as my steamer for India had arrived, and was making round the southern end of the canal. I packed up in a hurry, and was soon at the quay. Our little cockleshell, which steered coquettishly between a mass of sailboats, took me to the gangway of the steamer, laden with one hundred and fifty saloon passengers, who had come all the way from England, and would only step ashore in Bombay.

My first and chief concern was to know where my berth was to be. The purser showed me two berths, one of which was half covered by the swinging berth of another man over it, and at right angles to it, and the other was in a darker place in another room. Nothing else, I was gravely informed, was to be had. Each room had three other men in it. I walked the deck, meditating on the thermometer, now about 90° Fahrenheit, and soon to go to the hundreds in the white silence and perfect calm of the Red Sea. I learned that the ship's carpenter would part with his little room, and sleep somewhere else, for a consideration. On examining it, I found it to be greasy, narrow, in a noisy place, and with the hideous ash-pipe from the engine near by. But I was compelled to engage it. I sought the steward, and asked him if he was equal to the task of cleaning it.

"I am your man, sir. My name is Light. I'll put it straight."

He did what he said. He cleaned out every nook and corner, save only the cockroaches. The little room was about seven feet square. There was just space enough to turn around and take two steps. My steward, Light, stretched a canvas frame straight out of my porthole, and stood it at right angles to the ship. Later, when gliding farther southward, between Mecca on one side of us and Berber on the other, and the sea a glassy, steamy caldron, I was thankful to Light for having provided me with the friendly little windsail.

The *Sutlej* glided out of the harbor of Suez at midnight. The water was as smooth as molten glass. On the west, and standing back from the Gulf of Suez, there is a mountain of three precipitous peaks. It rises like a great granite trident. Here Professor Palmer, of Oxford, had been murdered about two years previously. Some years before his fatal visit he had made his tour through the Sinaitic Peninsula, the fruit of which was his masterly work, "The Exodus of Israel." He was now in Egypt for other than archæological purposes. This time he was in the service of the government, helping to promote the Egyptian campaign, probably to purchase camels, or to secure the aid or neutrality of the wild and dangerous Sinaitic tribes. The agent of the Peninsular and Oriental Company, in Suez, knew him personally, and related to me a number of interesting facts concerning him. Among others was the following:

The agent said to him, "You are going to a dangerous place just now."

"Oh, no. I know the people and their language. I am used to their ways. I was there before, you know."

"True enough," replied the agent, "but you did not then have seven thousand pounds sterling with you."

"Oh, I am safe," replied Palmer. And he went straight to his death. He and his few companions were arrested, blindfolded, and hurled down a precipice from the top of a mountain. Several of his murderers were afterwards caught, and tried in Suez. They were all condemned to death. They were then separated, taken to different places, and executed. This method was adopted, no doubt, to avoid an organized attempt at rescue.

As our steamer passed down the Gulf of Suez, both shores became very beautiful. The weather became hotter as we went southward. The ladies gave up their fans, and bore the heat most patiently. The gentlemen put on canvas slippers and gossamer coats. Many of the passengers slept on deck all night.

By one o'clock of the second day we had come into full view of the great Sinaitic range. One observes a ruggedness about its fine lines, and a sudden sharpness and angularity to its varied elevations, which make it different from the entire lower range which leads up to it. Even in the Tyrol and Switzerland such delightfully beautiful and delicate shades to mountain outlines are seldom observed. While some glowing and Turneresque colors could be seen in the sunrise of the Red Sea, the richest shades are in the evening, when the mountains are now fawn-color, now light green, and now shimmering purple and blue. These shades change again and again, according to the angle of vision and the degree of approaching darkness. The stars seem near at hand, as if one could pluck them. The desert is on either side, Egypt at the right, and Arabia at the left.

The children were the happiest creatures on our steamer. One little fellow bore the name of "Ed." He had a brother named "Charley." The boy "Ed" entertained a profound prejudice against his name, and insisted that everybody should call him "Charley," a name he greatly admired. That would make two of one name in the family. I concluded, from the persistency of the situation, that "Ed" would win, and that his parents would be compelled to make a new distribution of names.

Our hottest day was November 3. Everybody gasped for air. The children, however, always magnificent on a journey, never uttered a word of complaint. I looked at them with admiration, and learned patience and silence. We were now far below Egypt and Nubia. Mecca was only sixty miles back from the coast. At nightfall the Abyssinian mountains were all ablaze with the after-glow of the sunset. We passed twelve rocks in the middle of the throat of the Red Sea, which bear the name of the Twelve Apostles. The captain pointed out the smallest and most dangerous, and said it was "Judas." The next morning I asked the first officer,

"When do we get to the Straits of Bab-el-Mandeb?"

He looked at me with surprise, and answered,

"We passed through them at three this morning."

"Then I was asleep," I answered; "and, as we have gone safely, I am quite satisfied."

We had now made the twelve hundred and ten miles of the Red Sea's length, and in two hours should be at Aden. We were skirting along the shore range of the southern coast of Arabia Deserta.

The subjects which interest one are in the ratio of the realm in which we live. When one is in the little world of a ship at sea, such themes become of interest as on shore would not attract a moment's attention. Nothing interested me more than the constant work of the postmaster in handling the mail-matter. I never wearied in watching him. At Suez our chief mail-agent came aboard. His work began at once. The time before reaching

Bombay is none too long for handling the mail and distributing and having ready the immense mass of matter for sending in all directions on arriving in India. In a steamer of the Peninsular and Oriental line on which Professor Monier Williams made a voyage, he says that there were three mail-agents, and that they worked ten hours a day from the time the steamer left Suez. They handled about forty-six thousand letters and thirty-five thousand newspapers, and distributed them in two hundred and fifty mail-bags, and had them all ready on landing at Bombay. He gives the following illustration of one of the difficulties besetting a Peninsular and Oriental mail-agent. A letter was found with this address:

J. Faden
Sapper
Engear
Bromeday.

This letter had been mailed in England, and sent to three Bromleys before leaving the country. At last some mail-clerk suspected that "Engear" might mean India; and so the letter was put into the Indian mail. The London supposition was quite correct. "Engear" did mean India; "Bromeday" did mean Bombay; and J. Faden received his letter.*

Our halt at Aden was brief, but long enough to afford the passengers time to go ashore and stroll along the one street of the old town. The place is believed by some scholars to be the Eden of Ezekiel (xxvii. 23) and the Endaimon of Periplus. The Romans gave it the name of Portus Romanus. All passengers are amused at the remarkable feats of swimming by the little Arabian boys, who paddle out in light skiffs, and dive from them, and pick up coins thrown into the water by passengers before the bits of money can sink to the bottom. The favorite of these clattering and busy little swimmers, who in this way earned their livelihood, is one who has lost a leg, said to have been bitten off by a shark. By far the most of the money is tossed out to him. He is an expert swimmer, and, so far as I could see, his loss of a leg was a positive gain in his struggle for bread.

---

* "Modern India and the Indians," p. 26.

VIEW OF ADEN.

On November 8 we were well out from Aden, and ploughing across the Arabian Sea. We had heavy weather, or what the sailors call a lumpy sea. The northeast monsoon had set in with fury, and the *Sutlej* was tossed about like a presidential candidate. My little room being high, the port was not yet closed. The ladies were not numerous at the table, and those who were present came with a very uncertain appearance. The spar-deck had the look of a hospital. The captain went around in a good-humored way, and told everybody what a rough passage the last one had been. Commend me to physicians and ship-masters for the highest attainments in the language of encouragement and hopefulness. I braced myself in my berth, and read Hunter's "Indian Empire," Isambert's "L'Orient, Grèce, et Turque d'Europe," Muir's "Turks, Greeks, and Slavons," Isaverdenz's "History of Armenia and the Armenians," and the Marquis of Bath's "Observations on Bulgarian Affairs." It was a piece of good-fortune not to run out of reading-matter. My supply of books, some of which I had brought from America, but had gathered the most in Germany, served me now delightfully.

I was told, on the 9th, at breakfast, that the dining-saloon had gotten a drenching about four o'clock in the morning. The people who would not sleep in their rooms, but lay around on tables and seats, were taken by surprise at the incoming flood. But it was only a chance wave. There was none other like it. The weather continued intensely hot. But the kulis pulled the punkhas, and so fanned the few at table with commendable industry.

SITUATION OF BOMBAY ON THE GULF.

CHAPTER II.

ARRIVAL IN BOMBAY.

On nearing the Indian coast there was less motion of the ship. We had come within touch of the land winds, and, though still a hundred miles from Bombay, could tell from the air and the color of the water that the shore was not far away. A beautiful butterfly, borne off from his Indian field, flew about our deck, as if to bid us welcome to his beautiful India. The passengers busied themselves in packing up. They had much to pack, for, except those who had come aboard on the Italian coast, all except myself had been on the ship twenty-five days. A pilot came aboard, bringing with him the Bombay *Times* of the same day. This journal said that Cleveland had been elected president. The first telegrams had insisted on Blaine's election. Neither account was believed to be definite. The result was, that the American residents of India were compelled to wait for the slow mail to know certainly who was elected.

Is there anything, in all one's experience as a voyager, which brings him more joy than the first flash of the Indian coast? It is a revelation, and, so far as I was concerned, the thrill of excitement lasted every day of my stay beneath its palms and within sound of the throb of its silver surf. My first view was under a cloudless sky. The *Sutlej* sailed grandly on. By and by the pearly islands of the harbor sprang out into clear individuality. The steamer slowed up, and we dropped anchor. The suburb of Kolaba bears off to the right, and loses itself in the sea. The lovely Malabar Road sweeps far around to the left, and its jagged rocks at the end mark the garden-wall of the governor's residence. Within this charming curve lies Bombay. Back of the city rise the ghats, or hills, which mark the scene of Wellington's conquest of the troublesome Marhattas. The valleys which divide the background of mountains, and the very mountain-sides themselves, tell the whole story of England's

GREAT INDIAN PENINSULAR RAILWAY, VICTORIA TERMINUS AND ADMINISTRATIVE OFFICES, BOMBAY.

occupation and final possession of western India. Eastern India, though farther away from England, was first securely conquered by Clive. The question then was to overcome and possess the interjacent territory, or Western India. The glove had been thrown out among enemies, and the question was now to fight for the place where it lay. When the smoke of Wellington's last battle rolled away before the incoming breezes from the Indian Ocean, England was mistress, and has ever remained so, over Marhattas and all else.

The hills seemed to come near to us, like friendly hosts before their Indian door, to bid us hearty welcome. Up the ship's ladder, and in clamorous crowds, climbed the native boatmen. The best course in all such cases is to select your boatman early, take the first well-looking one you see, then never change him, or think of doing it. The competition and uncertainty would be distressing and overwhelming. When once you have your boatman, and he has even your lightest rug or smallest piece of baggage, the rest of his craft will let you alone. They consider you engaged.

Many English people came to the ship's side in steam-launches, and climbed up the stepway to meet their friends from dear and far-off Britain. The mail had been long doing its kindly errands, and these friends in India knew the vessel, and almost the hour of her arrival, by which those dear to them would come. Since witnessing the endearing scenes I there saw, I can never associate coldness with the Englishman's nature. Those who do him this injustice should see his Indian welcomes. Here were fathers who had come from some distant part of India, and had been waiting several days in Bombay. They now stood upon the deck of the incoming vessel, and were broken up like very children themselves when they caught sight of their sons and daughters, who had been for years in England, in the schools, or with friends, and were now coming back again to take their place in the old household of their Anglo-Indian parents. Here were men who had been in the civil or military service of the Indian government ever since their youth, and, having served their twenty-five years, and spent a summer's vacation in England, had now come back again to India.

Not one would have said it, had you asked him, that he was returning to India to spend his last years. All Englishmen expect to die in England. But the Anglo-Indian is most likely to die in India. So, when a number of my fellow-passengers went home to England, and looked about the old homes, and greeted the old friends, they saw nothing that was familiar to them. Everything had changed. Not even London, which every Englishman expects to find much the same when he returns as when he had left it, could hardly be recognized as the same London of the elder days. With this breaking up of the old familiarities the Anglo-Indian can hardly find himself at home again in England. He turns his face towards India, after all, as his real home. When October comes, he provides himself with the necessaries of the voyage and engages passage for the land where he has spent his best life. He is more at home there. He is glad to get back. He likes India far better than he had supposed. The little graveyards all over India, from Cape Comorin to Lahor, and even in Afghanistan and Kashmir, tell the rest of the story. His dead and living bind him still to dear India.

These are only a few of the touches of romance that one sees, in spite of himself, as he gathers his luggage together and makes ready to land. But all India is full of them. My right-hand neighbor at the table on the *Sutlej* had been in England for the summer. He had served out his time and had well earned his pension. He had gone back to England, as I should have thought, to spend the remainder of his life. But he could not find his old friends or environment. Hence he came back to India again. His malady was insomnia, and even sweet old England could not give him what he wanted. About two months afterwards, as I was changing trains at Benares, I heard a familiar voice calling to me. It was my neighbor at the table of the *Sutlej*.

"How have you been?" I asked.

"Oh, only fairly well. Can't sleep. I am afraid—yes—it is a serious case." He was giving up.

These were our last words together. Though he cannot sleep, even in India, he will hardly leave it again.

CHAPTER III.

BOMBAY.—TOUCHES OF ITS HISTORY.

LAKSHMI, "OUR LADY OF BOMBAY."

BOMBAY is a fair illustration of the firmness of the Englishman's grasp. This one city represents in miniature the whole history of the English people in the East.

The entire western coast of India was a strong attraction to the Portuguese in the sixteenth century, when their keels were cleaving all seas. Wealth in Hindustan was as powerful an incentive to this discovery and possession as it was to the conquest of South America. The Portuguese aspirations differed totally from the English. The Portuguese cavaliers and naval heroes entered India for conquest, dominion, and wealth. They had historical aims. Every movement was conducted with all the splendor of romance. The English entered India modestly, quietly, and solely for commercial purposes. Bombay, known probably as an excellent harbor, early attracted the Portuguese. They saw a little cluster of native houses, took possession of them, and built more. Soon the town grew into a population of ten thousand.

The origin of the name Bombay is uncertain. The most likely theory is, that the word is a corruption of Malime and Mumbaye—the names of the two ports of the island on which the city now stands. According to Anderson, the second name, Mumbaye, or Momba Devi, was that of an idol, whose temple once stood on the Esplanade of the present city. In fact, a temple and tank of the name of Momba Devi still exist, and rank among the most interesting objects of the present native city. The presumption, therefore, is in favor of the heathen origin of the word Bombay.

The English saw that the town would be a necessity for their commercial purposes, and therefore made several quiet efforts to possess it. But the Portuguese, though deriving little advantage from it, were not willing to part with what might become a valuable centre of trade. The English, however, were already masters in the art of getting things. What could not come as a desired acquisition fell as a wedding-gift into England's hands. On that May morning, in the year 1662, when the princess the Infanta Catharina of Braganza, daughter of John IV. of Portugal, married Charles II. of England, Bombay was presented to England as a part of the beautiful young lady's dowry. This was confirmed by an article in the treaty of June 23, 1661, which reads like a piece of rare satire; for, among other objects of the gift, it was alleged, as one reason, that the King of England might protect Portuguese against the commercial aggression of the Dutch, who were now a third party, disputing the claim of the sea and of the Indian possessions. The treaty reads thus: That the cession is made "for the better improvement of the English interest and commerce in the East Indies, and that the King of Great Britain may be better enabled to assist, defend, and protect the subjects of the King of Portugal in those parts from the power and invasion of the States of the United Provinces."

History utters no voice as to who suggested such a strange and far-off gift. A probable theory is, that the English ambassador was instructed to say to the Portuguese government that Bombay would be an acceptable marriage present.

But, thoroughly desirable as Bombay had been, it was no sooner in the hands of the English government than it was found to be, after all, only a troublesome elephant. It would cost more to take care of it than the little annual income of seven thousand pounds, which was the total annual revenue returned by the indigent and thriftless population of Bombay.

The English government not knowing what to do with Bombay, the king looked about for some one to whom to present the city. The East India Company stood ready to accept it, and did so, in consideration of paying annually into the treasury of Great Britain the nominal sum of ten pounds sterling. This was all that was ever asked, and all that was ever given. No sooner did the Company enter Bombay than it began to take special measures for the improvement of the city and for the encouragement of colonists. For five years the Company promised exemption from customs; made the taxes very low; gave looms to the weavers, to encourage the manufacture of silk and cotton goods; permitted settlers to come, and possess any land not already occupied; and guaranteed the ownership of such land to them. The Company encouraged the Protestant faith, but declared perfect religious liberty to all who would become citizens of the new city.

The result was, that Bombay became the most attractive place in the East Indies, not only to Englishmen, but to people from many lands. Persians came in very large numbers, and made India their permanent home. Also Arabs, the Topazes, or Indo-Portuguese, and, indeed, people from every part of the Eastern world, drifted to Bombay, and combined to build up the city. It was a contest as to which race should acquire the most land and build up the largest business. The strife went on with great animation. By and by the town became a great centre of trade—the hand which received the manufactures of Europe, and, in return, sent back the fine wares of the Indian artisan into the Western world.

But clouds hung over the future of India. This pearl of the sea could not be purchased at the small price which the English had so far paid.

By the year 1682 the population of Bombay had grown to sixty thousand. Such prosperity could not escape the notice of powerful freebooters. The city became an object of jealousy and invasion, on both land and sea. The corsair Seedu, an Abyssinian sailor, was ravaging the ports along the coast, carrying off the people into bondage, and selling them as slaves. Yet he was the authorized tool of the Great Mogul, who was ruling in Delhi and Agra, and was winning new provinces, extending his rule into Northern India, and looking towards the south and west for more booty. The English would not allow Seedu to sell his slaves in Bombay or its neighborhood, and, because of this refusal, the wild rover invaded Bombay. Every house was converted into an arsenal of defence. The place which afterwards became the historical Fort of the city, and was the citadel of the place, was thrown into intense excitement. The whole city caught the wild fever of defence. But the English were powerless, as they soon saw, and what they could not do by strength they achieved by stratagem. They secured from the reigning Mogul emperor, Aurangzeb, an order for Seedu to withdraw from his attack.

So much for danger from the sea. Now came the greater risk from the land. The Marhattas, under the lead of the celebrated Sivaji, saw that the way to hasten the downfall of the Mogul empire was the capture of the English trading settlements along the western coast. Surat, the very centre of English power and commerce, was constantly exposed to danger. Bombay would be safer. As a result, the local government of the East India Company was removed from Surat to Bombay. In the year 1708 the latter city, with its surrounding territory, was made a Presidency.

The efforts of the Marhattas to get control of Bombay were now of the most desperate character. One of their chiefs, Angria, captured an English ship, the *Success.* Clive afterwards appeared on the scene, but just as he was about to lead the English troops against the Marhattas, the Bombay government kept him back, in consequence of a peace which had been patched up between the East India Company and the Marhattas. But he always knew how to find a way to fight when he saw that English authority was in danger. Clive was one of those rare men who was never disturbed at the want of an opportunity. He had the genius to create the opportunity whenever he wanted one. The Marhattas were now convinced of the power of English authority, repudiated Angria, their pirate chief, and joined the English in measures against him. Clive had his suspicions. He knew the Oriental methods. Fighting was resolved on. It was arranged that Clive should lead the land forces, while Admiral Watson should conduct the attack on the corsair fortress, Gheriah. The fortress fell, and became an English possession.

This achievement, largely due to Clive, enlarged the territory of Bombay, and made that city a secure place for the future. It is a singular fact that this work of Clive was a mere incident in his career. He had won three victories in Arcot, which had given Southern India to England, and had now gone home with the prospect of staying. But as the East India Company had new trouble in Bengal, and their authority and possessions were in danger from the French, they entreated Clive to return, and establish English rule against all future contingency. He seems to have seen the danger of the western coast, and to have appreciated the importance to England of making Bombay, its nearest Indian port, secure. At any rate, he went to India by way of Bombay, instead of by Madras, and had authority to use the Company's troops. Having done this most effectively, he went to Bengal, and, in the following year, 1757, fought and won the battle of Plassey.

Bombay now rapidly increased in wealth and population. But the Marhattas were at heart bitter enemies to the English. Even after their power was broken by the terrible defeat at Panipat, they again harassed Bombay, and threatened to destroy it. Back and forth the tide of fortune went with Bombay, as with the English interests in general on the western coast, until 1805, when sufficient territory was secured to the Presidency to make it strong against any inroads from native princes. It was reserved for Arthur Wellesley, afterwards Lord Wellington, to achieve such victories, in 1804, as led to this security, and enabled him to leave India after services inferior only to those of Clive and Hastings.

One would little suspect, as he walks along the Esplanade of the present Bombay, that this large city of eight hundred thousand inhabitants, and covering twelve islands, should have risen to its present wealth and commercial importance out of such small and precarious conditions. One by one the very evidences of the old military character of the place have disappeared. The European quarter occupies what is still called the Fort. The place is covered by a large park, by Watson's Hotel, the Clock Tower, the University Hall, the markets, the Town Hall, the School of Design, and other public buildings. Many of these edifices would be an ornament to any European capital. One sees a freshness and a variety in the architecture of the larger structures of Bombay which have the most pleasing effect. The air is always invigorating in the early morning. I first learned here that, if one will utilize his Indian day, be must begin by five o'clock.

My first stay in Bombay lasted nearly two weeks. Every day was one of exquisite pleasure. Each morning I took a walk, generally varying the direction, that I might see Bombay in its varied humors. One time I strolled along Meadow Street, and saw the shopkeepers from Persia and Kashmir opening their places of business, and getting ready for their day's trade. Another walk was along Rampart Row, where every building and many faces became familiar. At another time I strolled as far up towards the native city as the market, bought a few of the sweet apples from Kashmir, and returned by either the same street or a more circuitous one. Then, on another morning, I walked along the shore of the bay, in the direction of the Grant Buildings and the Cotton Market. I always timed myself by the clock in the Tower, for breakfast came at nine.

The following remark was made to me soon after landing in Bombay:

"Perhaps you thought your war in America, in 1861, did no good? It has done this much for us—it has made Bombay what it is."

I heard afterwards, from various sources, that the interruption of the cotton industry by our war produced such a revival of the production of that staple in India that the wealth and business of Bombay, which was the chief Indian gainer by our calamity, had greatly increased. It was a prosperity unanticipated, which has been rapidly doubling ever since.

During these walks, but especially during my lengthy drives in the evening, I was surprised at the many evidences of individual liberality which I frequently saw. Bishop Heber, when entering Bombay, in 1825, said: "On this side of India there is really more zeal and liberality displayed in the improvement of the country, the construction of walks and public buildings, the conciliation of the natives, and their education, than I have yet seen in Bengal." His reference was largely to the remarkable benefits accruing to Bombay from Elphinstone's administration, from 1820 to 1827. But his tribute to the government would, even thus early, have been equally just had it been applied to the late participation of the natives themselves in their own improvement. Many years ago it was not unfrequently the case that native citizens would found hospitals, and build public fountains of a charitable and beneficent purpose. But in recent years this tendency has assumed large proportions. One can hardly go into any part of Bombay, or out into the suburbs, without being amazed at the magnificent evidences of native benefaction.

THE NATIVE QUARTER, BOMBAY.

CHAPTER IV.

THE FIRST EUROPEANS IN INDIA.

When the Europeans first became acquainted with India, and took a profound interest in the country, is one of the lost secrets of history. It is probable that when Greece began to emerge from its primitive and wild state, there were men who went to India as travellers, lingered in the towns, and after years of wandering came home again and communicated fragments of knowledge to their native country in the West. Others, remembering the humble attainments of their Greek countrymen in the arts and sciences, may have borne back with them some of the precious secrets from far-off India. Were it possible to restore the old conditions of Greece when she was as yet only a disciple at the feet of the elder nations, we might behold in the villages along the shores of the Greek isles, and in the advancing towns of Attica, minstrels grown gray and weary with long journeys, singing, to the groups in the open Greek spaces, of the distant land of India, with its many millions of people, its highly developed arts and industries, and its heroic leaders on many an Aryan battle-field. Many of the descriptions in the Iliad bear unmistakable evidences of Indian suggestion. The striking parallels between the working in metals, the household life and the domestic usages then existing in Greece, and the same conditions in India, as recently brought to light by archæological research, are more than accidents. They prove a high and common paternity.

The first important records by the Greeks concerning India which have come down to our times are by Megasthenes, Nearchus, Herodotus, Ctesias, Arrian, Strabo, Quintus Curtius. Diodorus Siculus (B.C. 55) and Strabo (B.C. 54), as geographers, gave minute and accurate information concerning India. But Arrian was the first great narrator of Indian life and history. Yet he was only a borrower. He utilized the works of his seniors in history—Megasthenes and Nearchus—to excellent advantage. The works of these two writers have been lost; and Arrian, in his description of Alexander's campaign in India, has gathered up from the journals of these two writers such fragments as reconcile us in a measure to the oblivion of the precious records of which he made full use.*

It was not the usage of military leaders in ancient times, any more than in the modern, to enter upon a long campaign without accurate knowledge of the countries through which they needed to march on their path of subjugation. Alexander, when he crossed the Bosphorus into Asia, and began his great campaign, undoubtedly supplied himself with all the records then in existence, and secured all possible help from those who had visited India. The ancient leaders were consummate masters in the art of acquiring information useful towards success. Here Alexander displayed as much skill and was as industrious in acquisition, as he was brave in person and fertile of resource in the enemy's presence. It was only after his victories in India and his death, and the hopeless breaking up of his broad empire, that the communication between Greece and India was frequent. The doors opened by his great army have never since been closed. That the European knowledge of Indian wealth and of the resources of the soil was accurate, may be seen in the description of the country by Dionysius:

> "To the east a lovely country wide extends,
> India, whose borders the wide ocean bound;
> On this the sun, new rising from the main,
> Smiles pleased, and sheds his early orient beams.
> The inhabitants are swart, and in their locks
> Betray the tints of the dark hyacinth.
> Various their functions: some the rocks explore,
> And from the mines extract the latent gold;
> Some labor at the woof with cunning skill,
> And manufacture linen; others shape
> And polish ivory with nicest care;
> Many retire to rivers' shoal, and plunge
> To seek the beryl flaming in its bed,
> Or glittering diamond. Oft the jasper's found
> Green, but diaphanous; the topaz, too,

* Crawfurd, "Researches Concerning Laws, Theology, Learning, and Commerce of Ancient and Modern India," vol. ii., p. 225.

A STREET IN BOMBAY.

Of ray serene and pleasing; last of all
The lovely amethyst, in which combine
All the mild shades of purple. The rich soil,
Wash'd by a thousand rivers,
Pours on the natives wealth without control."

AN EVENTFUL AFFRONT.

One day, while Alexander was in India, there appeared at his tent-door a native Hindu prince. His manner was friendly, and he seems to have expressed a willingness to serve Alexander, hoping, of course, to escape the rigors of the new Greek master. He was treated coldly by the mighty conqueror from the West. As a result his pride was wounded, and he withdrew without formality. If we may judge from his subsequent career, from the very moment of his departure he declared revenge on the Greeks. He visited native rulers, raised a great army, placed himself at the head of it, and by one victory after another became the instrument of breaking up the unity of the Greek rule in India. The name of this chief was Chandra Gupta. The Panjabi viceroy, who represented Alexander after his death, was driven out of the country by Chandra Gupta. Seleukos, however, one of Alexander's generals, endeavored to regain hold on India, and again invaded the country. What took place proves that Seleukos found his task very difficult. His conquest was formal rather than otherwise. Whatever the cause, a new element came into the conflict. Seleukos gave to Chandra Gupta his daughter in marriage. In addition, he ceded to the powerful prince all the provinces east of the Indus which had been conquered by the Greeks, on the slight consideration that the Indian ruler should send to Seleukos an annual gift of fifty elephants. This was the ignoble end of the great Alexander's conquest of India—fifty elephants to a Syrian king!*

At the time of Alexander there existed in India one hundred and eighteen separate kings. No slavery was tolerated. The men were brave and the women chaste. Honesty prevailed, and no lock was needed on any door. The Indian did not lie, and no

* The best work we have met with on the early communication between Europe and India is Macpherson's "History of the European Commerce with India." London, 1812.

one ever thought of accusing him of it. The Brahmans (Brachmanes) were the priestly and the scholarly class. The farmers were exempted from war and public duties. Fabrics of various kinds were manufactured. The Brahmans made forecasts of rainfall to guard against famine, and "the philosopher who errs in his predictions must observe silence the rest of his life." *

Megasthenes divided all India into eight castes: philosophers, husbandmen, shepherds, artisans, soldiers, overseers, councillors, and assessors.† These castes, however, must not be regarded as the inflexible divisions of modern times. The growth of the present wretched system of social and religious differences was not even sanctioned by the earlier Vedas. This evil is only one of the many proofs in India of the fact that any system, lacking divine authority, really gravitates downward.

Recent studies on the origins of philosophical thought are bringing out the fact of an important parallelism between the Indian systems and the philosophical structures of Greece.

There are, unquestionably, Oriental elements in Pythagoras and Plato, and other Greeks; and the view formerly prevailed that India was the great source from which the great Greek thinkers derived large portions of their speculative philosophy. But the most recent investigations prove that, in this department, India was the borrower from Greece. The path by which the sciences reached India is not yet fully determined, but it is most likely that it lay through Bactriana, which had a large Greek population, and derived its culture from the northern country. The most ancient Hindu works of astronomy, as those of Varahavinra, who lived in the 6th century, frequently employed Greek terminology, and refer to the Greeks.‡

It is strongly claimed by the most philosophical of all the recent European writers on India, M. Le Bon, that India derived all its great theoretical sciences from Arabia and Greece. He holds that the mathematical works of Aryabhata, of the fifth century, and those of the celebrated Brahmagupta, of the sev-

---

* Megasthenes, "Fragmenta" (Ed. Didot), in "Fragm. Histor. Græc.," vol. ii., p. 426b.

† "Ancient India as Described by Megasthenes and Arrian," Calcutta, 1877, pp. 42 ff.

‡ Le Bon, "Les Civilisations de l'Inde," p. 548.

enth century, are only borrowings from Greece.* But we regret that this author does not furnish his proof. We are compelled to hold, for example, that the Hindus originated instruction by apologues, and the decimal notation by nine digits and zero. Colebroke says that in algebra the Greeks were behind the Hindus. The early Hindus knew that the square of the hypothenuse of the triangle is equal to the squares of the sides containing the right angle. They divided the circumference of the circle into three hundred and sixty equal parts, and each into sixty others, which is the same as our division into degrees,

CARPET-WEAVING.

minutes, and seconds. The Hindus conceived the year to consist of three hundred and sixty-five days, five hours, thirty minutes, and forty seconds. This division differs only $1\frac{33}{100}$ from the new solar tables of Delambre.† Abu Fazl declares that the arts and sciences of his country were three hundred in number. Chemistry was cultivated with rare skill and success. The science of medicine was carried to a high degree. The Hindu legends say that one of the fourteen precious ratnas, or precious

* "Les Civilisations de l'Inde," p. 549.

† Royle, "Lecture XI., On Arts and Manufactures of India," p. 343.

things which the gods are believed to have produced by churning the ocean with the mountain Mandaran, was a learned physician. Even the way in which the Hindus met Alexander when he invaded their country, proves their advancement in the art of war. They led against him a disciplined army of thirty thousand infantry, with elephants and war-chariots.*

* Martin, "Progress and Present State of British India," p. 3.

SILK-AND-GOLD EMBROIDERY ON SILK, PERSIAN.

CHAPTER V.

THE ANGLO-SAXON IN INDIA.—HISTORICAL ANTECEDENTS.

On landing in Bombay one immediately becomes deeply interested in the novelty of the Oriental types. Even while in the Levant, it is natural to imagine one's self already in the

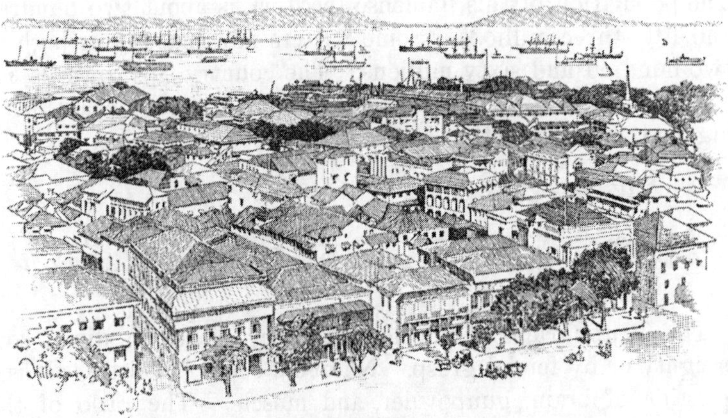

OVERLOOKING THE CITY OF BOMBAY.

Eastern world. Yet the first scenes in Bombay are so peculiar, so utterly unlike anything in Asia Minor, Syria, or Egypt, that the traveller is convinced at once that now, for the first time, he is really in the East. After a few days, when the Indian costumes, modes of life and business, and the wonderful mixture of races become somewhat familiar, the mind wanders back into the past, and the question arises, "How has all this come about? Why is the intrusive Anglo-Saxon also in India? What is he doing here? How long does he intend to stay, and what does he expect to be the outcome?"

The manifold ownership of this great country is one of the marvels in the world's history. Is there any land which has had more masters than this? The history is one long tragedy. For thirty centuries India has been compelled to pay the painful penalty of possessing the fatal gifts of wealth and beauty. She is the Lorelei of all the ages. She has attracted the conqueror from afar, but, with only the Anglo-Saxon exception, invariably dealt him ruin when once within sound of her siren voice.

The whole of India is one immense God's acre of dead civilizations and forgotten races. The area of the country is one million five hundred thousand square miles. From Karachi in the west to the eastern borders of Assam in the east the distance is eighteen hundred miles. From the northern boundary of the Panjab to Cape Comorin, in the south, it is also eighteen hundred miles. The population of this immense territory is about two hundred and fifty-three millions. Some writers now place it as high as two hundred and sixty millions. The country tips towards the east, the range of hills, or ghats, on the western coast being higher than that on the eastern.

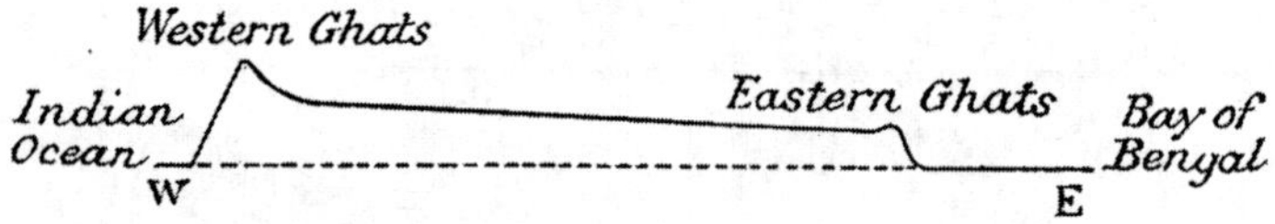

The Briton rules this whole territory, either in direct sovereignty or by feudal grasp. Numbers count but little. It is a question of brain, gunpowder, and muscle. The ratio of the ruler to the subject is no longer a secret. There are in India one hundred and forty thousand Englishmen, civilians and soldiers. Out of this number there are nine hundred members of the Covenanted Service. These last are the administrators of the government of all India. Less than a thousand men, therefore, Britons all, govern two hundred and fifty millions of Indian natives. No questions are asked. Each class well understands the other. England rules far India more easily than near Ireland.

The first appearance of India in the general and prominent history of nations was when the Aryans conquered and ruled the country. They, far off as they seem to us, were only later comers into the attractive valleys of the Ganges and the Indus.

From the Aryan to the Englishman the path has been long, and many have walked in it. The Mohammedans, or Persian Moguls, the Portuguese, the Dutch, the Danes, the French, and then the English, have each stepped upon the golden shore, and claimed the land for themselves.* But they have all dropped aside, excepting only the Anglo-Saxon. This man, of inevitable destiny, coming latest and profiting by the mishaps of all his predecessors, has caught the secret of staying. He is now as much at home in Madras as in Piccadilly. He sits at the table of Watson's Hotel in Bombay, and eats his curry and rice, and slings his gun across his shoulder for a day's hunt around the waters of Surat, with a couple of kulis to follow his every step with such collected air that one would think this latest master had discovered the country and invented all its industries. India is already

THE "LAKSHMIDAS KHIMJI KAPAD BAZAR," A CLOTH MARKET IN BOMBAY.

and permanently Saxon. Scratch a Hindu and you reach an Englishman. What is the Hindu but the Aryan who first established himself in India, say five thousand years ago? What is the Anglo-Saxon but an Aryan who settled in Europe and began the central chapters in the world's general history? He is the same Aryan, whether on the banks of the Ganges, the Weser, the Thames, the Seine, or the Hudson. When the Anglo-Saxon went to India, in the person of wild Robert Clive, it was only the Aryan going back to the old homestead, as Alexander did

* Lethbridge, "Short Manual of the History of India," p. 244.

over twenty centuries ago. When the German Ziegenbalg went to Tranquebar with his printing-press, and Carey went to Serampore with his open Bible, it was an Aryan visitation, to renew acquaintance with long-separated kinsmen. It was good advice which Hafiz, the Persian poet, born in the original Aryan home, gave to his brothers who had suffered from violent hands. It were well if the conquered India of these last days would bless the hand which offers gifts better than the sword.

"Learn from Orient shell to love thy foe,
And store with pearls the hand that brings thee woe;
Free, like yon rock, from base vindictive pride,
Emblaze with gems the wrist that rends thy side.
Mark where yon tree rewards the stony shower
With fruit nectareous, or the balmy flower.
All nature calls aloud, 'Shall man do less
Than heal the smiter and the railer bless?'"

PRIMITIVE SILVER JEWELLERY OF DINAJPUR, BENGAL.

CHAPTER VI.

INDIA IN HISTORY.

I.—THE ORIGINAL INHABITANTS.

THE first inhabitants of India of whom we have even the most vague traces bear no general name, but are grouped under the general term of non-Aryans. They consisted of three great stocks: the Tibeto-Burman tribes, which came down into India

LORD CLIVE.
(From the painting in the Government House, Calcutta.)

from the northeastern gateway of the Himalayas, and still cling to the eastern ranges; the Kolarian tribes, which also entered by the same gateway, and still live in the hilly northeastern region; and the Dravidian tribes, which entered by the northeastern gateway, and drifted southward, and whose posterity still occupy the southernmost part of India.*

If we may judge by the rude remains of these elementary tribes, war was their chief occupation. Some of them were wild savages. They were not acquainted with the use of metals, and their rough flint weapons and agate knives are now to be found in the Narbada valley. They did not use letters, or even hieroglyphs. The only works we have from them are upright slabs and the places where they interred their dead. They were succeeded by others, who were also ignorant of the use of metals, but hunted and fought with stone implements of nearly the same character as the early Scandinavian weapons, which we can see in endless variety in the museum in Copenhagen. Still later we come to the mound-builders, who knew the use of metals, fought with iron weapons, understood the manufacture of earthenware, and wore ornaments of gold and copper.

The duration of this long non-Aryan period is uncertain. There were many grades of intelligence, however, some of the tribes being in a state of abject slavery, while their masters were intelligent, and knew the power of civil government. The earliest non-Aryans seem to have had no religious rites, while the latest, who held the country at the time of the great Aryan invasion, had a religion, believed in the future, and adorned their dead with gifts, raiment, and ornaments. In this they gave proof that they believed their dead would attain to a future life. That these non-Aryan inhabitants of India were brave and patriotic, and knew the value of their country, is abundantly attested by the great Indian epics, which describe the long struggle of the Aryans to conquer India. Though no authentic history has come down to us concerning this mighty war of races, and we are compelled to rely solely on the mythical poetry of the epic writers, it is not likely that bloodier battles were ever fought than those which resulted in the possession of India by the Aryan invaders. The conquerors, if we may believe the Vedic hymns, loathed their enemies, whose lands they were striving to overrun. They called them Dasyus, or "slaves." They declared them "noseless," or flat-nosed, "disturbers of sacrifices," "gross

* Hunter, "Brief History of the Indian People," pp. 32 ff.

THE DUKE OF WELLINGTON.

feeders on flesh," "raw eaters," and "without gods and without rites."

When the aboriginal tribes were conquered, they either fled to the mountains or became serfs to the Aryan lords of the soil. During all subsequent ages some of these aboriginal tribes have kept their languages and dialects, and have preserved a certain measure of individuality. But they have remained the most abject part of the population of India. The servitude which was the outcome of the great Aryan struggle has left its permanent impression upon them.

II.—The Great Invasions.

India has been the world's Eastern battle-field. The invasions have been on a vast scale, and are the real measure of the great foreign estimate placed upon the value of the land and the treasures of the people. The great invasions, with two exceptions, by Asiatic forces, have been eleven in number:

1. The Aryan Invasion.
2. Invasion by Sesostris, King of Egypt, B.C. 1308.
3. Persian Invasion by Darius Hystaspes, B.C. 518.
4. Invasion by Alexander the Great, B.C. 327.
5. The Scythian Invasions, B.C. 100–A.D. 500.
6. The Tartar Invasion, B.C. 126.
7. The Invasion of Mahmud of Ghazni, A.D. 1001.
8. The Invasion of Tamerlane, A.D. 1398.
9. The Invasion of Babar, A.D. 1526.
10. The Invasion of Nadir Shah, A.D. 1739.
11. The Invasion of Ahmad Shah al Abdali, A.D. 1761.

III.—The Great Aryan Invasion and Conquest.

The Aryans first appear in history as an advanced and growing race in the upper table-lands of the southerly districts of Central Asia and Turkestan—probably the Pamir plateau and the region surrounding the sources of the Oxus.* Their home was Bam-i-Dunya, the "Roof of the World." But this land, though broad and beautiful, was not near enough to the sun, and the soil too unyielding, for the great genius and boundless ambition of its occupants. The Aryans began to colonize, not as peaceful migratory bodies, but as armed hosts, marching boldly forth for the possession of fairer fields and for the blood of all who stood in their path to possession. The sparks from this metal, carried to white heat, flew off with amazing rapidity. Each one carried destiny with it. They fell upon three continents.

The first outgoing host took a westward path, and on its way founded the great Persian empire. It then reached Europe, and, finding it wild and disorganized, set to work to bring it into shape and within the grasp of law. It created the history of the classic and modern world. It founded the Greek republics, built and governed Rome, occupied Spain, produced the Teuton race, converted Gaul into France, and peopled and moulded Britain into its present shape and history. The Anglo-Saxon was thus the di-

* Williams, "Modern India and the Indians," p. 148.

rect offspring of Aryan ancestry. The roots of the most familiar words spoken by Harold and his soldiers who fell at Hastings before the Normans, had floated all the way along the Persian pathway, and still live in the Sanskrit taught by Brahman pundits beneath the palms which fringe the banks of the lower Ganges. Wherever these Aryans went towards the setting sun they carried victory, law, organization.

Another Aryan body, or possibly a part of the larger one moving westward, struck a southwestern path, and Egypt was its miracle.

But these great movements did not exhaust the Aryans of the homestead. There was a portion of the race which thought it best to take its chances by going towards the rising sun. They pressed down through the Afghan passes upon the plains of the Indus and the Ganges, caught the aroma of the plants and flowers of India, and set vigorously to work to conquer the country. They pushed onward as by a spell of enchantment. The very air seemed to give them the spirit of conquest. The wealth which they took in battle was enormous. No aboriginal armies could stand before them. They halted in the Panjab, and founded settlements along the banks of the Saraswati, a small river between the Jamna and the Satlej. Here they became famous. It was in this territory, including the North Behar of the present Hindustan, that the Aryans created the rich Sanskrit language, produced their immortal bards and sages, and developed that wealth of poetic literature which must forever hold a firm place in the family of the world's great epics. This is the country which bears the name of Brahmarshidesa, the Hindu's Holy Land. It is his Palestine. He thinks of it with the profoundest reverence, because of its association with the most heroic deeds of his immortal ancestors. The Aryans here organized a government, and possessed houses, chariots, mailed armor, ships, and merchandise. The government was patriarchal. The tribal chief was priest.

But even here these Aryan masters found the field too small. The farmers put on their weapons and marched farther into Hindustan. They did not know when or where to stop. On they went, dropping off colonies, organizing governments, appointing satraps, and then conquering new regions. Finally, they subjugated nearly the whole of the broad India of to-day, extending from the Arabian Sea on the west to the bay of Bengal on the east, and from the Himalayas in the north to Cape Comorin in the south. They gave their whole land the name Aryavartta, or the Land of the Aryans.*

Nation after nation went down before these victorious Aryan armies. Many were so thoroughly conquered that their identity seems to have been lost. The northern nations which fell before them bore the generic name of Dasyus. The southern may be grouped under the broad term of Dravidians, who extended down to Cape Comorin.

IV.—The Brahman Supremacy.

The ascendency of the Brahmans, or the priestly caste, was the first period during which we observe approaches to a settled government of the Aryan race in India. The long process of civil organization gave evidence of all the great qualities which distinguished the Aryans on their first battle-fields in India. This process continued about fifteen centuries, or from B.C. 2000 to B.C. 543. It was in this time that the Vedic hymns were composed. The earlier Vedas tell of the Aryans in the first stage of their conquest and government in the extreme north-west. The later Vedas bring the Aryan race farther southward, not only conquering their foes, but establishing a permanent government on the banks of the Ganges.†

BRAHMA.

The Rig Veda, a collection of one thousand and seventeen short poems, and containing ten thousand five hundred and eighty verses, reveals the first Aryan civilization in India. The family was presided over by the father, who was the priest,

* Lethbridge, "History of India," pp. 137 ff.

† Hunter, "Brief History of the Indian People," pp. 46 ff. Fergusson and Burgess say that the Brahman ascendency continued to the middle of the third century before Christ ("Cave Temples of India," pp. 12, 13). But this position is unquestionably untenable, because of the earlier rise of Buddhism, B.C. 543.

while the chief of the tribe was father and priest to the tribe. The king was elected by the tribe. Women were held in high honor, and noble ladies and queens became the authors of some of the most beautiful hymns. There were various craftsmen, such as blacksmiths, coppersmiths, goldsmiths, carpenters, and masters in other trades. The Aryans had towns and villages, and used chariots and cavalry in battle.

Four divisions, or castes, arose—the original source of the present caste system of the Hindu race. The first caste was the Brahmans, or priests; the second was the warriors, the fighting companions of the king; the third was the agricultural class; and the fourth was the Sudras, or conquered non-Aryans, who were serfs. The Brahmans became the highest class, and have remained so until the present day. They were not only the priests who preserved the sacred writings, but the makers and teachers of the law, the poets and the men of science. The two great epics of this period—the Mahabharata and the Ramayana—were composed by them. The former, which comes down to B.C. 1200, tells of the Aryan conquest and settlement in northern India. The latter describes the Aryan conquest of southern India. There are other epics of inferior grade which come down to a time approaching the Christian era. They describe the legends of the gods more than the actual exploits of the Aryan heroes.

The long line of kings professing the Brahman faith cannot be definitely traced, since it is impossible to detect, in Hindu chronology, where fable ends and history begins. Saha-deva was king at the time of the Mahabharata war. The thirty-fifth king in succession from him was Ajata-Satru, who murdered his father, Brinbasara, and whose reign witnessed the birth of Buddhism.*

V.—The Buddhist (Religious) Supremacy.

B.C. 543–A.D. 1000.

The dynasties professing the Brahman faith ruled India without serious obstacles until the rise of Buddhism, about B.C. 543. The greatest ruler who openly espoused the system of Buddha with a view to establish and propagate it, was the celebrated

* Pope, "Text Book of Indian History," p. 39.

Asoka, king of Magadha, or Behar. He was converted to Buddhism about B.C. 257, and made his government one immense machine to propagate his faith. Kanishka, a king of the Scythian line, was also a zealous Buddhist. He convened the fourth great Buddhist council, A.D. 40. The celebrated Siladitya, of the seventh century, was a zealous advocate of Buddhism. He called the fifth great council, A.D. 634.

VI.—The Greek (Political) Supremacy in India.

B.C. 327–161.

The Greek episode in Indian history is of profound significance. For ages there had been no direct intercourse between the Aryan wanderers in Europe and their kinsmen in India. Each, widely separated in the world, was working out its destiny. The two groups were strangely alike, however, whether studying astrology on the plains of Delhi, or rearing the matchless Parthenon at Athens, or building on the banks of the Tiber a city destined to rule the world. Each scion of the Aryan family was intense in its search for truth, for framing law, for occupation of the land, for the government of men.

Greece was fragrant with Indian associations. The brothers, long separated, seem to have maintained a subtle sense of relationship. The mythology of Greece, coming from the Aryan hearthstone, could not be unlike that of India, emanating from the same place. The ancient Hindu pantheon is strangely similar to, and often identical in name with, that of Greece. The Latin word for heaven (*coelum*), coming through the Greek, is believed to owe its origin to the Indian mount Kailas, which rises to the enormous height of thirty thousand feet!* It cannot be doubted that whenever a Greek conqueror arose above the surface of his times, and thought of further conquests, he had his hope of India. The wealth which it was known to possess, the abundance of its natural products, and the variety of its climate, made it an object of military ambition. Alexander the Great was the first European successful enough to realize the dream of Indian conquest. When he led his army from the

* Pocoke, "India in Greece" (London, 1832), p. 68. This author has exceeded all others in tracing the wonderful parallel between Greece and India in religion and language.

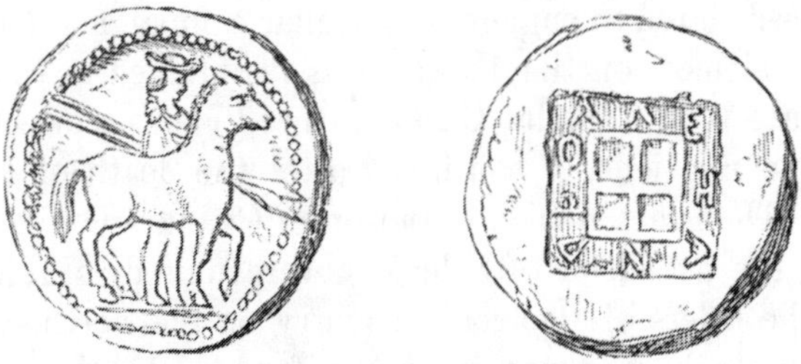

SILVER COIN OF ALEXANDER I.

Dardanelles southward and then eastward, and never rested until he reached the bank of the Indus, it was the visit of one Aryan brother to another, after many centuries of separation. It was warfare, but it was that of brothers.

In B.C. 327 Alexander the Great entered India and began his campaign for its conquest. He had no doubt studied the country in the writings of Hekataios of Miletos (B.C. 549–486), Herodotus (B.C. 450), and Ktesias (B.C. 401). He was determined that his sword should conquer India. He reached Orthostaana, the modern Kabul, capital of Afghanistan, and planned for a campaign of triumph. He divided his army into two great columns. Taking one himself, and putting the other in charge of his most trusted subordinate, they came down through the Khaibar and other difficult passes, and spread out their army on the plains of the Panjab in the hottest season of the year. Taxiles, Abisares, and Porus ruled over a large part of the Panjab. Porus, the ruler over three hundred cities, met Alexander with 4000 cavalry and 50,000 foot. Alexander fought him and won the battle of Jhelam in April or May, B.C. 326. His victory cast all northwestern India at his feet. Alexander built here two cities, one south of the Jhelam, and the other on the north. The one on the south was called Nikaia, and is identified in the ruins of the present Mong. The city on the north, which the conqueror called Bukephala, after his favorite horse, was built on the site of the present Jalalpur.*

Alexander's men refused to proceed farther into the interior. He accordingly followed the Indus down to the sea, and then upward through "the burning Gedrosian deserts of Biluchistan," to his Persian capital, Susa. After Alexander's death the

* Lethbridge, "Short Manual of the History of India," pp. 163 ff.

dream of Indian conquest by the Greeks was dissipated. No later Greek dared to engage in a similar campaign. The slender hold of Seleukos on the Panjab was maintained in the form of an alliance with Chandra Gupta, rather than as a direct control. The same relationship continued after the death of these two rulers. The great Asoka, grandson of Chandra Gupta, and Antiochus, the grandson of Seleukos, were united as allied kings. Later, the rulers of Bactria, a country on the northwest of the Himalayas, whose government was founded by the Greeks, invaded India with desperate energy. The Greco-Bactrian kings combined much of the genius of the Greek with that of the Hindu. They penetrated farther into India than Alexander had carried his sword, and between B.C. 181 and 161 reached as far eastward as Oudh and as far south as Sind and Cutch.

But these conquests never assumed the form of a regular government. The invasions were not followed by direct and permanent results in the form of laws and dynasties. The Indian, on his own soil, was always too strong for the Greek away from home. In an indirect way there remained traces of Greek culture. The Greeks bequeathed to India a higher knowledge of astronomy than it had ever possessed. The architectural remains of Buddhist temples built before the Christian era show the influence of the Greek builder, while the sculptures of the Indian artists which have survived to this day prove the refined taste of the Greek. Constant additions are made in the Panjab to the archæological treasures emanating from this period of Greek influence. The Bactro-Greek coins in use in India were numerous, and are still coming to the light. In this field Prinsep has been the most industrious gleaner.*

While Alexander's stay and that of his successors from both Syria and Scythia was brief, it is now a matter of knowledge that the Greek letters and language were understood in northern India and in Kabul as late as the second century of our era. The lately discovered coins furnish the incontestable proof. It need not surprise if, later, other monumental remains will confirm the same fact on a much larger scale.†

---

* Compare his "Indian Antiquities." 2 vols. London, 1858.

† Gardner, "The Coins of the Greek and Scythian Kings of Bactria and India in the British Museum," p. liii. London, 1880.

VII.—The Scythian Invasion.

B.C. 100–A.D. 500.

Not far from the original home of the Aryan race, on the border land of Persia and northwestern India, a great body of warriors united and set out in search of conquest. They have passed into history as Scythians. They speedily put an end to the Bactro-Greek kingdom, and marched down through the great northwestern pass into India. Wherever they found traces of the Greeks they obliterated them, and on the ruins of the Bactro-Greek colonies in the Panjab they reared a great kingdom. This was about the beginning of the Christian era. The celebrated Scythian, King Kanishka, became a zealous Buddhist, carried on great wars, and consolidated an empire extending from Agra and Sind in the south to Yarkand and Khokand north of the Himalayas.*

Strong efforts were made by the native Indian kings to break up the Scythian kingdom, and drive the hated people out of the country. King Vikramaditya, in B.C. 57, was the most celebrated of the Indian opponents. He was distinguished for wisdom in the council, for profound learning, and for heroism in the field. Salivahana, in A.D. 78, followed him in patriotic warfare. But both were unsuccessful. The Scythians were reinforced by new arrivals. For five centuries the strife went on, and it was only about A.D. 500 that the Scythian kingdom was broken up, and the Aryans already in India were permitted to continue their rule over the country.

VIII.—The Hindu Supremacy.

A.D. 500–977.

The rule of the native Hindus in India continued about five hundred years. During this period there were wars, great and small, between competing kingdoms, with occasional invasions from the northwest. The land was seldom, if ever, at peace. The boundary-lines of the kingdoms constantly varied with success or defeat in warfare. In the northwest of India the territory was governed by Rajput princes. They ruled the country

* Hunter, "Brief History of the Indian People," pp. 80 ff.

along the valley of the Indus and the upper waters of the Jamna.* The great central north, the classic theatre of the Aryan period, had its capital at Kanauj. The northeastern country, comprising the lower valley of the Ganges, or much of the present Bengal, from Behar down to the mouth of the Ganges, was under the control of three powerful dynasties in succession—the Vidyu, the Pala, and the Senas—the last of which defied all opposition until overrun, finally, by the Mohammedan conquerors, A.D. 1203.

The Vindhya mountains, which run east and west across India, dividing the northern from the southern half, were occupied chiefly by the fragments of the rude aboriginal tribes. On the west, near the coast of Bombay, was the powerful kingdom of Malwa. Southern India was covered principally by the four great kingdoms of Chera, Chola, Pandya, and Vijayanagar. Here was the powerful abode of the aboriginal or Dravidian population, who still speak for the most part the Tamil language. The kingdom of Pandya had its capital at Madura; Chola, at Combaconum and Tanjor; and Chera at Talkad, in Mysore.

LOTA (DRINKING-VESSEL), OLD BRASS, HINDU.

There have been no kings, outside of China, whose dynasty was of such long continuance as these. Their protracted existence is attributable to remoteness from the points of invasion. The Pandya dynasty numbered one hundred and sixteen kings, and extended, approximately, from the seventh century before Christ down to A.D. 1304. The Chera kingdom had a dynastic line of fifty kings, and Chola one of sixty-six.

The most modern of the four Hindu kingdoms was Vijayana-

* Hunter, "Brief History of the Indian People," pp. 100, 101.

gar, or Narsingha. It existed from A.D. 1118 to 1565. Its capital "can still be traced within the Madras district of Bellary, on the right bank of the Tungabhadra River, where there are to be seen extensive ruins of temples, fortifications, tombs, and bridges, haunted by hyenas and snakes. For at least three centuries the kingdom of Vijayanagar dominated over the southern part of the Indian triangle." * It was one of the descendants of the royal family of this kingdom who granted to the English the site of Madras, in 1639, and thus laid the foundation of the British empire in India.

No general description of the kingdoms and rulers of India at this period can present an adequate picture of the real state of the country. While there were large kingdoms which had been able to perpetuate themselves for many centuries, there were many smaller ones which defied all the power of the larger ones to conquer and absorb them. The following are the ancient Hindu states, large and small, of this period. Our list begins with the north and closes with the south:

1. Magadha.
2. Malwa.
3. Gujarat.
4. Mewar.
5. Kanauj.
6. Benares.
7. Mithila.
8. Delhi.
9. Ajmir.
10. Marwar.
11. Sind.
12. Kashmir.
13. Pandya Kingdom of Madura.
14. Chola of Kanchipuran.
15. Sera of Travancore.
16. Balala of Dwara Samudra.
17. Warangal.
18. Pacthun—Salivahana.

IX.—The Afghan or Mohammedan Dynasties in India.

A.D. 996–1526.

The whole Mohammedan period in India extends from the first successful inroad by Sabaktigin, A.D. 996, down to the break-up of the Mogul empire through the capture of Delhi by Nadir Shah, in 1740. But the Mogul empire, because of its peculiar history and specific name, while thoroughly Mohammedan, deserves separate treatment. The Afghan rulers began their conquests A.D. 977. They were succeeded by the Mogul emperors, the first of whom, Babar, by the second battle of

* Hunter, "Brief History of the Indian People," p. 116.

Panipat, founded the Mogul empire, which lasted two hundred and twenty-two years, and astonished the world by its achievements alike in war and peace. The Afghans did not occupy merely the territory now known as Afghanistan, but were a group of fierce and powerful tribes inhabiting the mountain regions of Ghor, and other great stretches of territory bordering on Kabul and Persia.* They were originally fire-worshippers, but, having been conquered by the Mohammedan warriors, became zealous propagators of Islam. They loved warfare. They looked upon India as their proper field of battle, and gave themselves no rest until they had crossed the Indus, planted their banner on the walls of ancient Delhi, and founded dynasties which furnish a catalogue of thirty-four kings.

There are four classes of Mohammedans in India. 1. The Sayyids, who claim to be of the family of Mohammed. 2. The Moguls, descendants of the Tartar conquerors of India. 3. The Pathans, or Afghans, whose title is Khan. 4. The Shaiks—all who do not belong to the three former divisions.

There were seven Afghan dynasties which invaded and ruled India:

		A.D.
I.	The Ghaznivides	996–1152.
II.	The Ghorians	1153–1206.
III.	The Slave Kings	1206–1288.
IV.	The House of Khilji	1288–1321.
V.	The House of Tughlak	1321–1412.
VI.	The Sayyids	1412–1450.
VII.	The House of Lodi	1450–1526.

The history of these royal families is not surpassed for daring, for wisely planned campaigns, for contrasts between lowly origin and great honor, and for all the varieties which enter into bloody warfare. Mohammed of Ghazni, descended from the slave Sabaktigin, ruled thirty-three years, invaded India seventeen times, and spent twenty-five years in fighting. He laid the foundations of the Afghan rule in India. The great Mogul chief, Changiz Khan, whose broad empire extended from the wall of China westward to the Volga, began an Indian invasion A.D. 1217, but was stopped by the Indus, and never reached Delhi. Tamerlane (Timur Lene) invaded India, reaching Delhi in 1398.

* Pope, "Text-book of Indian History," pp. 50 ff.

HINDU CARVING—BLOODTHIRSTY GOD BHAIRUB.

His massacre of the population of Delhi is one of the most cruel and bloody deeds even in the dark annals of Indian warfare.

Among the characteristics of this period was the light in which each invader looked upon the rule founded by his predecessor. No sooner was one invading dynasty founded than it became a bitter struggle to contend, on the one hand, against the native Hindu population and patriotic chiefs, and, on the other, against other invaders, who came in from the northwest, and proposed to take possession of the country and occupy the throne. Delhi or Agra was always regarded as the one object of conquest. Either, as the case might be, was the royal city, and he who took either Delhi or Agra was conqueror and ruler. Thus Delhi or Agra was the seat of government for three hundred and twenty years, or from 1206 to 1526. Further, while some of the rulers were revengeful and bloodthirsty, others were humane, fond of learning, and promoted the arts of peace. But the latter class was small. The peaceful ruler was only an occasional star in the black and ill-boding Indian firmament. As the throne was generally won by blood, it was necessary to retain it by the same means.

TAMERLANE.

Women often played an important part, as they have always done in Oriental life, whether in camp or court. With all the subjection of woman by the Qurán, the Mohammedan conquerors found all their courage and ingenuity taxed to outwit the counter-schemes of gifted women. Only once, however, did a woman reach the throne of Delhi, and rule in her own name. This was Raziya, who reigned from A.D. 1236 to 1239. She was clad in tunic and cap, like a man, and daily sat on her throne, and administered justice to all who applied for it. A chief rebelled against her rule, defeated her in battle, and took her prisoner. But she conquered him at last by winning his affections and marrying him. A rebellion of her nobles, however, put an end to the joint-rule of herself and her husband.*

X.—The Mogul Emperors.

A.D. 1524–1857.

The Mogul empire furnishes the most romantic and dazzling picture in the history of Asiatic dominion. Six of the rulers were among the most gifted of any land who ever held a sceptre. For many centuries the supreme effort had been to retain the rule won by violence. Even after the Mogul domination had

* Pope, "Text-book of Indian History," p. 66.

begun, the struggle for the displacement of the emperor was often violent and unnatural. The rebellion of the son against his father, and the seizing upon the throne, and the imprisonment of the father in a palace, were characteristics of this wonderful dynasty.

The history of the Mogul empire consists of two general periods. The former extends from the conquest of Lahor by Babar, A.D. 1526, to the beginning of the decline, A.D. 1707. This was the brilliant period of rise, expansion, and splendor. The second period consists of a steady and fatal decadence, from A.D. 1707 to A.D. 1857.

Babar, the founder of the Mogul empire, was, on his father's side, the sixth in descent from Tamerlane the Tartar, and, on his mother's side, from a Mogul connected with the tribe of Changiz Khan. His real name was Zahir-ud-din-Mohammed—"The Light of the Faith." He assumed the title of Padshah, a Persian word signifying king. This term became the permanent title of the Mogul emperors. So soon as he had developed his marvellous qualities as a warrior he was called Babar, the Lion—the name by which he has always been known in history. He succeeded his father as king of Ferghana, on the Jaxartes, and when forty-four years old, or A.D. 1526, he came down into India at the head of his mighty hosts—

> "Like Indus, through the mountains came down the Muslim ranks,
> And town-walls fell before them as flooded river-banks."

THE GREAT MOGUL EMPERORS.

		A.D.
I.	Babar	1526–1530.
II.	Humayun	1530–1556.
III.	Akbar	1556–1605.
IV.	Jahangir	1605–1627.
V.	Shah Jahan	1627–1658.
VI.	Aurangzeb (or Alamgir I.)	1658–1707.

THE LESSER MOGUL EMPERORS.

		A.D.
VII.	Shah Alam I.	1707–1712.
VIII.	Jahandar Shah	1712–1713.
IX.	Farukhshir	1713–1719.
X.	Rafi-ud-darajat	1719–Feb.
XI.	Rafi-ud-daula	1719–May.
XII.	Mohammed Shah	1719–1748.

		A.D.
XIII.	Ahmad Shah	1748–1754.
XIV.	Alamgir II.	1754–1759.
XV.	Shah Alam II.	1759–1806.
XVI.	Akbar II.	1806–1837.
XVII.	Mohammed Bahadur	1837–1857.

These two groups of Mogul emperors differ from each other in all the great qualities which distinguish the wise and mighty ruler from the weak and cruel occupant of the throne. While the first six were distinguished for great ability as military leaders and civil administrators, the last eleven, with rare exceptions, were marked by all the inferior characteristics of a declining imperial line.

A striking parallel in European history is furnished in the Carlovingian dynasty. Pepin, who laid the foundation of the broad Frankish empire, may be properly compared with Babar, the founder of the Mogul empire. Charlemagne, the son of Pepin, has his parallel in Akbar, whose reign was by far the most brilliant of all the Mogul rulers. The Mogul line, however, continued strong, and worthy of its founder, much longer than the Carlovingian. The three successors of Akbar were great rulers, while those of Charlemagne declined in mental quality and moral force until they became only impotent and formal instruments of government, always at the mercy of the Papacy or intriguing courtiers. When the brilliant reign of the six Mogul rulers terminated with Aurangzeb, and the new and feebler group began with Shah Alam I., the Mogul empire was strikingly similar to that of the Frankish empire under Charles the Fat. With the Mogul empire as with the Frankish, it was only a question of time when the great fabric, created and consolidated by genius, should fall to pieces through weakness in the representative of the government.

The aggregate reigns of the greater Mogul emperors amounted to one hundred and eighty-three years. In all the history of hereditary rule there is no instance where a reigning family possessed its original strong qualities during such a lengthy period. There are instances where a family has been represented by several richly endowed members. The house of Napoleon Buonaparte is remarkable for the large number of gifted members. American history, as is proved by the family of John

Adams, is not without similar illustrations. But the great Mogul dynasty founded by Babar has no equal in the annals of men in the rare combination of long reigns and capable rulers. These men retained many of the rude and fierce qualities which distinguished the family while yet obscure, far beyond the north-western boundary of India. They never became thoroughly Indian. But some of them acquired strong Indian tastes, and all learned how to govern the Indian mind, and attach soldiers to them by ties stronger than life itself.

The colors in this wonderful picture of Mogul rule are very vivid. The conquests take the first place. When the central government was established in Delhi and Agra, each emperor endeavored to rule over a realm larger than that of his father. No danger was too great for an emperor to engage in. Even single combat was not shunned. The leading of a forlorn hope was the pastime of a Mogul emperor. One, for example, at the head of a desperate force of three hundred, faced a strong body of hostile troops, fought like a lion, gained a brilliant victory, and saved his army and his empire.

All the six great Mogul emperors were fearless on the battle-field. Such an example was of incalculable influence over an army. The soldiers of each Mogul emperor acquired a marvellous fearlessness, and gained the popular fame of invincibility. Wherever the Mogul rulers went they carried victory with them. Not satisfied with conquering all the foes along the valley of the Jamna and the Ganges, they became masters of the northern half of India. They even looked beyond, for victory in the south. They crossed the midway barrier of the Vindhya Mountains, burst down into the plains of the southern half of the inverted Indian pyramid, and swept all opposition before them. Some of the Hindu thrones, which had defied all enemies from time immemorial, now fell before them like creations of a day. In due time all India, with merely nominal exceptions, lay in their power. From the vale of Kashmir in the north to Mysore in the south, they ruled with skill and a firm grasp. The waters of the Bay of Bengal washed their eastern boundary, while the surf of the Indian Ocean beat against their western coast. Foreign rulers heard of the splendor of the Mogul court, and sent nobles as ambassadors, with rich gifts and long-drawn flatteries.

The way the Mogul rulers governed their remote possessions was peculiar, though a wise, and perhaps the only successful method. They placed governors or princes in possession of the tributary thrones, and gave them almost supreme power. Annual tribute had to be levied for the general treasury. But frequently the native prince would rebel, and, at the head of a large army, assert his independence. Then the Mogul army was needed to put an end to the mutiny. The emperors, therefore, were nearly always on the march. Their chief palace was the tent, far remote from the jewelled walls of the palaces of Delhi and Agra. The real court, therefore, like that of Cæsar, Constantine, Charlemagne, and, to some extent, of Charles V., was not in settled capitals, but itinerant, on the battle-field or the line of the long and hazardous march. The constant study was either to crush a rebellious army or to add a new province to the great empire.

While war was the chief occupation of the six great Mogul emperors, it was far from being all. Akbar was fond of literature, understood Sanskrit, and undertook literary enterprises. He openly expressed profound sympathy with other faiths besides the Mohammedan. He founded a new and second Mohammedanism, which he called the "Divine Faith." He studied Hindu works of science and religion, and took pleasure in discussions between Brahman priests, Mohammedan teachers, Sikh gurus, and Roman Catholic priests. In these scientific and latitudinarian tastes Jahangir was a devoted imitator. He was an Oriental Frederick the Great. He published his own memoirs.* At his court he gave cordial welcome to scholars at home and of foreign lands, and was as generous in his patronage of religions as of the sciences and arts. By some he is supposed to have been as much a Christian as a Mohammedan. He carried a rosary ornamented with figures of Christ and the Virgin, and permitted two of his nephews to espouse the Christian faith. Probably neither faith gave him great concern, except as a helpful instrument for government or conquest. Both Agra and Delhi were distinguished as centres of learning and art. The great observatory near Delhi is a present witness to the profound attention given to astronomy.

---

* "Memoirs of the Emperor Jahangir, written by himself, and translated from a Persian manuscript by Major David Price." London, 1824.

TOMB OF THE EMPEROR AKBAR AT AGRA.

The most enduring effect of the Mogul rule is to be found in the architectural monuments still existing in the northern half of India, and to some extent in the Nizam's dominions in the south. The Taj Mahal, built by Shah Jahan, at Agra, on the banks of the Jamna, is not only the most splendid mausoleum in existence, but the most beautiful structure in the world. The Pearl Mosque, by the same emperor, is a house of worship, in white marble, which is not surpassed in the beauty of its proportions and the skill of its workmanship by any religious edifice known to architecture. The Great Mosque of Delhi is a wonder in stone, distinguished for the boldness of its plan, the splendor of its material, and the vastness of its proportions. The Palace of Delhi, with its Peacock Throne and far-reaching

HINDU GOLDSMITH.

courts, its baths and fountains, its surrounding buildings in marble and other fine stone, is still the wonder of India. No one can be said to have seen India unless he has entered the majestic portal of that palace and lingered amid its blaze of Oriental glory in marble softened by arabesques of precious stones.

Beyond the magnificent architectural remains, the permanent effects of the Mogul rule are few. No appreciable impression was made on the scientific status of the people. There does not seem to have been an increase of taste for popular education. Great schools do not appear to have been organized. Learning was regarded rather as the ornament of the court than a beneficent means for the elevation and development of the millions. The great body of the people never saw in these Mohammedan rulers, their armies, or their courtiers qualities sufficiently admirable to make them prefer to renounce their faith and adopt that of their conquerors. The Hindu population never fell to the small number of the Mohammedan, and to this day for every four Hindus there is but one Mohammedan.

Aurangzeb, the last of the great emperors, left an empire which no ordinary hand could rule. The old Hindu spirit was discovering a new opportunity for reassertion, and the bonds which held the empire together were growing looser and feebler every day. Six of the eleven emperors succeeding Aurangzeb were powerless in the hands of a general, Zulfikar-Khan, while the remaining five were the mere puppets of schemers. The empire was now only a name. Long after England conquered India she permitted the descendants of the Moguls to retain a nominal sovereignty over the country. The last scion of this degenerated line took part with the Sepoys in the mutiny of 1857. When England crushed out the mutiny, this feeble remnant of a once proud dynasty sat a prisoner at Delhi, within the palace walls of his mighty ancestors, to receive sentence of banishment. He died in Rangoon, on November 11, 1862, and was buried on the day of his death. The Mohammedans, with all their pride of history and faith, paid no attention to the event.

XI.—The Marhattas.

A.D. 1650–1818.

In the year 1577 there was, in the service of the Murteza Nizam Shah I., a native prince by the name of Maloji. He was commander of a body of cavalry. He had a certain prestige among his associates, because he was a scion of the ancient family of Bhonsla, which had descended from the royal house of Udipur. This man was the ancestor of the line of great Marhatta leaders, who won some of the most remarkable battles in the history of the world, who founded a broad but unsteady kingdom on the ruins of the Mogul empire, and who were the most violent and intrepid of all the enemies whom England had to conquer on its thorny path to the dominion of India. The Mogul empire received its death-blow from the intrepid and revengeful warriors whom the descendants of Maloji awoke as by the wand of a magician. Who were the Marhattas, and what was their signifi-

VIEW OF THE TAJ MAHAL FROM THE GARDEN.

cance in history? They represented the elder Hindu race, ground down by the long dominion of the Mogul rulers. It now reasserted itself, and determined to break the power of their empire. It was the old patriotic fervor again flashing out after the long darkness.

The name of the Marhattas is derived from the country where they arose—Maharashtra, the Great Kingdom. It comprises the hilly region of Central India, extending from Nagpur, in the east, to the western coast, and running along the coast from Cambray down to Goa. Never did a more rugged race of warriors start out in search of thrones. In the early Mohammedan invasions they fought, in an obscure way, against the foreigners. But later, when the Mohammedans became rulers of North India, the Marhattas became brave soldiers in their armies and wise civilians in the administration of the government.

ROBBER CHIEF, KACHAR.

Shahji, the son of Maloji, was born A.D. 1627. He was the real founder of the Great Marhatta power. He distinguished himself by brilliant achievements on many fields of battle. He prepared the way for the wonderful military triumphs of Sivaji, one of the greatest warriors of history. The career of Sivaji abounds in romance. Through the quiet teaching of a Hindu preceptor, his mind became early imbued with a desire to drive the Mohammedans out of India. He took delight in the mythology of his people, and regarded himself of royal blood and worthy of a great throne. His imagination revelled in the prospect of a mighty empire. He was not taught the refinements of even a general education, and never learned to write his name. A firm faith in his own religion, and an intimate knowledge of all the resources of Oriental warfare, were his sole acquirements when, with a fearless spirit, he went forth for empire. When only nineteen years of age he captured the hill-fort of Tornea, near Puna, and thenceforward war to the knife was his meat and drink.

Sivaji was outwardly friendly to the Mogul emperor, but

sought the first opportunity to betray his interests. In his march to power, no falsehood or treachery was too base for him, if he could gain new territory. While his own hands were red with the blood of his enemies, and he did not hesitate to slaughter a strong foe in private, he was humane to his captives taken in war. His method in warfare was that of the freebooter. He stands out as the greatest raider of whom we have any account in history. He had a large army at command, which burst down from its retreat in the Western Ghats, crushed proud and victorious foes, captured large booty, fled quickly back again, and waited its time for another destructive demonstration. His soldiers were planters in seed-time; then they left for bloody warfare, and only came back to be reapers in harvest. At all other times they were on horseback, with deadly weapons, ready for any daring enterprise.

AN OUTCAST HINDU, BERAR.

Sivaji assumed the title of Raja, or King, in 1664. In the following year he joined the Mogul armies against the independent state of Bijapur, but afterwards rebelled, and gained new power by victories in the Karnatic.* He was fearless in battle, and a master in Indian subterfuges. No scheme was too intricate to escape his adroitness. For example, he secured admittance to the house of his enemy, Shayistah Khan, by a mock marriage procession. But his turn came at last to lose. The fortunes of war turned against him. He died A.D. 1680.

With the death of Sivaji, and that of his feeble son Sambhaji, the line of Marhatta kings died out. But the Marhatta power still continued its warfare for dominion. The line of Sivaji was succeeded in 1718 by the Peshwas, an hereditary office originating with an able Brahman minister of the court of Sambhaji. The Peshwas now began to organize and build up the Marhatta confederacy, with Puna as the capital. Great aggressive wars were carried on, and, of all the forces which triumphed over the decaying Mogul empire, the five Marhatta powers, with the Peshwa at their head, were the most conspicuous gainers.

* Mackenzie, "Romantic Land of Hind," p. 257.

The English first came into conflict with the Marhattas in 1775, when a war was waged with them for seven years. The Marhattas had an intense hatred of the English, and seemed to regard them as their powerful competitors for the control and government of India. They had with them, as their allies, the great Haidar Ali and the Nizam. Under the wise administration and careful planning of Warren Hastings, the English, while not directly victorious, were saved from hopeless disaster. The Treaty of Salbai was acceptable to all parties, for all alike were glad to rest from arms.

But the Marhattas were steadily gaining, and during the last quarter of the eighteenth century they made great advances. By the beginning of the nineteenth century the Marhatta confederacy numbered forty millions of citizens, and extended from Delhi in the north to the Kaveri in the south. It possessed an army of three hundred thousand men, unsurpassed for daring in the annals of warfare. The French combined their interests with the Marhattas, believing this to be the best way of destroying the English domination in India. It required four great wars, covering a period of forty-four years, or down to 1819, for the English to completely conquer and possess the Marhatta country. Lord Wellesley, Warren Hastings, and Generals Lake, Munro, and Pritzler immortalized themselves, and reflected new glory on the English name, by the victorious part they took in this great and triumphant struggle.

Almost all traces of the Marhatta rulers have passed away. In Gwalior, Indore, and Baroda the only scions of this once great power now remain. They rule by native princes with only the semblance of authority, but are closely watched by English Residents, and are harmless. Never did a power which had arisen to such great possessions, or had achieved such memorable victories, and presented such able chiefs, decline and die with so few traces of moral greatness. Their one great aim was conquest, plunder, and the Mogul thrones. Not one Marhatta ruler can be found who possessed those high moral qualities which took pleasure in educating, refining, and making happy the people. One has only to see the condition of India—a poor suffering prisoner in the hands of a bloodthirsty army of freebooters, to measure both the timeliness and the beneficence of the English coming.

XII.—The Europeans in India.

THE PORTUGUESE.

For many centuries there was but little intercourse between India and Europe. While the invasion of Alexander the Great had awakened in Greece, and in the more advanced European centres west of Greece, an interest in the farther East, this interest had long since died out. The collapse of the Greek Republics and the Roman Empire made India a sealed book to Europe until the revival of commerce towards the close of the Middle Ages.

The first direction in which this new spirit of discovery and commerce manifested itself was the search for India by an ocean pathway. Columbus had no other thought, when he lost sight of the coast of Spain, than to reach India by a westward course. He even carried with him a letter to the great Khan of Tartary. Indeed, Columbus died with the full belief that the new land he had discovered was the East Indies, which he had set out to reach.

The first traveller in modern times to penetrate India was the celebrated Venetian Marco Polo, whose experiences there excited universal attention in Europe.

The Portuguese, however, were the first modern discoverers both to reach India and to take possession of a portion of the country. No sooner had Portugal risen to great importance as a nation than it took a profound interest in the discovery of distant lands. Prince Henry, son of John I. of Portugal, and his queen, the English princess Blanche of Lancaster, lived on the coast, that they might see the outgoing fleets. Henry promoted enterprises for distant seas, and of him it has been sung,

> "The Genius, then,
> Of Navigation, that in hopeless sloth
> Had slumbered on the vast Atlantic deep
> For idle ages, starting, heard at last
> The Lusitanian Prince, who, heaven-inspired
> To love of useful glory, roused mankind,
> And in unbounded commerce mixed the world."

Madeira was discovered in 1420, the Cape de Verde Islands

in 1460, and the Cape of Good Hope in 1486. The Portuguese were thus slowly finding their way down the coast of Africa, and getting ready to reach the distant shore of India. This great end was reached by Vasco da Gama, in 1498, when he dropped anchor at Calicut, on the southwestern coast. He was the discoverer of a sea-route to India around the African continent. This one act put the whole trade between Europe and the East into the hands of the Portuguese, who retained it a long time.*

Cabral arrived in 1500. In 1503 Alfonso Albuquerque, the greatest name connected with the Portuguese rule in India, arrived at the head of three expeditions. His mind was less devoted to commerce than to conquest.† Two years later, Francisco da Almeida arrived, with a large fleet and fifteen thousand men under his command. He was the first Portuguese Governor-General and Viceroy of India. From A.D. 1500 to 1600, the Portuguese had the undisputed right of European trade with India. They had stations extending from Ormuz, at the Persian Gulf, all the way down the Indian coast to Ceylon, and far across to Malacca and the adjacent islands. They had thirty factories, and a coast-line of twelve thousand miles. Their vessels plied through all the neighboring seas. Their soldiers were famed for bravery and skill. Their Jesuit missions, with Francis Xavier at their head, achieved a record which made them the pride of Rome and of every true Roman Catholic throughout the world.

Towards the latter part of the sixteenth century, or in 1580, the Portuguese kingdom was united with that of Spain, and Spanish interests now predominated. Portugal lost abroad as well as at home. Through the English and the Dutch, who were now in India, and carrying on an extensive trade, the Portuguese trade declined.

All that now remains of Portuguese power in India are Goa, Daman, and Diu, with a population of half a million, and a territory of four hundred square miles. Nearly all the Portuguese are of mixed blood, half Indian and half Portuguese. About

---

* Lethbridge, "History of India," pp. 245 ff.

† Macpherson, "The History of European Commerce with India," p. 24. London, 1812.

twenty thousand of these half-breeds are in Bengal, and thirty thousand in Bombay and the environs.

THE DUTCH.

The Dutch followed the Portuguese to India. So soon as Holland threw off the Spanish yoke her people turned their attention to maritime discovery, and commerce with remote lands. They endeavored to find a way to India by sailing around the northern coasts of Asia and Europe. Failing here, they tried the route around Africa. Houtman was the first Dutchman to reach the Eastern seas, A.D. 1594. Commercial relations were established with the Archipelago. Collision with the Portuguese soon took place, and the Dutch were everywhere masters. They expelled the Portuguese from the Molucca Islands. This brought on a war between the two nations. The Dutch were victorious. They expelled the Portuguese from Amboyna and Tidor in 1605, and, until superseded by the English, controlled the commerce of the Eastern seas. In 1610 the Dutch founded the colony of Batavia; in 1640 they drove the Portuguese out of Malacca and took possession of it; in 1656 they took Ceylon from the same rulers, and became masters of a rich trade with that island; and in 1660 they took Nagapatam from the Portuguese, and established an important settlement there. The other Dutch settlements in India were at Sudras, Pulicat, and Bimlipatam, all of which fell into English hands before the close of the eighteenth century.

THE DANES.

The Danes possessed two settlements in India, both of which have become immortal in the missionary history of the world. One of these was Tranquebar, in South India, and the other was Serampore. Tranquebar has become famous throughout the world as the most thoroughly Christianized territory in India. Here labored the first missionaries to India — Ziegenbalg, from 1706 to 1719, and Fabricius, from 1739 to 1791. Schwartz, also, made Tranquebar his home for eleven years. Serampore, in the north, became the centre of the gigantic operations of Carey, Marshman, and Ward. Both these settlements were sold to the English in 1845.

THE FRENCH.

The French organized East India Companies as early as 1604. But they had their eye on India at a much earlier date. From the fourteenth century they had dared to roam over all known seas. In 1365 the people of Dieppe had establishments in Senegal and on the coast of Guinea. Canada, Brazil, and India followed in rapid succession. Colbert was largely instrumental in promoting settlements in India. Mazarin, when about to die, said to Louis XIV.:

"Sire, I owe you everything, but I acquit myself fully by leaving you Colbert."*

It can be truthfully said that Richelieu and Colbert directed the splendid colonial enterprises of Louis XIV. French interest in India was probably augmented by the travels of Tavernier, a jeweller of Paris, who was born in 1605. He made no less than six journeys to India for the purchase of precious stones, and published interesting accounts of his observations.†

The first important French settlement in India was at Surat, a little north of Bombay. This was the humble beginning of a scheme which developed into a gigantic French undertaking for the establishment of an Indian empire. We next hear of the French in the south, where they captured two settlements from the Dutch, and built the important city of Pondicherri. The Dutch, however, captured all three places, but lost them again by the Peace of Ryswick, in 1697, when the settlements were restored to the French.

The two greatest names in connection with the French rule in India were Bourdonnais and Dupleix. The former was master of the naval forces, while Dupleix commanded the land troops. Dupleix was the first to see that India could be conquered only by domestic dissension. He saw that there was no unity, and that to array the native kingdoms still further against each other was the key to the conquest of the whole country.‡ Clive, later, caught Dupleix's secret, practised upon it, and by it gave India to Britain.

---

* Henry Bionne, "Dupleix," p. 3. Paris, 1881.

† Ball, "The Diamonds, Coal, and Gold of India," p. 2.

‡ Holmes, "A History of the Indian Mutiny," p. 3. London, 1883.

There was no harmony between Dupleix and Bourdonnais. Each achieved great victories, but neither utilized the genius or success of the other. They met, on July 8th, 1746, and Bourdonnais addressed these words to Dupleix:

"We ought to regard one another as equally interested in the progress of events, and to work in concert. For my part, sir, I devote myself to you beforehand, and swear to you a perfect confidence."

Whichever was to blame, the result was no "concert." Madras was captured from the English by the French, but Bourdonnais afterwards allowed them to ransom it by paying a large price. The great French opportunity was thus lost. The English reaped every advantage. Bourdonnais returned to France, was regarded as a traitor, was thrown into the Bastille for three years, and died in 1753 of a broken heart.

Dupleix now remained in India, and was supreme in the management of French interests. He enjoyed temporary success. Madras was recaptured, and the French flag floated again from Fort St. George. The name of Dupleix became renowned in India and throughout Europe. But Europe had something to say. The Peace of Aix-la-Chapelle restored the new French possessions to England, and Dupleix was again compelled to adopt new measures to bring back French prestige throughout India. Having early learned the art of arraying the Indian princes against one another, he now again exercised his skill in this difficult department. He espoused the cause of one chief against another, put upon the throne only those whom he could control, and became the king-making Warwick of all India. The troops of France fought side by side with Indian troops, and always the outcome was new territory to the French. The French party was triumphant at nearly every court. But after 1751 a great change took place in the cause which Dupleix was defending.

Lawrence had charge of the English forces, but his great executive officer was Clive. The two worked in perfect harmony. Wherever the English fought they won. They had, indeed, well learned from the French how to manage the natives of India. The second siege of Trichinopoli, in 1752, where the English were victors, terminated the career of Dupleix. He left India for France in 1754. He died in poverty, and without honor, in Paris, in 1764.

The French cause was continued with persistence by Lally, who arrived in 1758. But it was too late, even had he possessed the qualities for successful warfare. The English put an end to all hope of French dominion in India by their victory at Wandewash, near Madras, in 1759. Lally returned to France, and was beheaded in 1766. Three years afterwards the French East India Company came to an end.

THE ENGLISH.

While India was originally entered by the English for commercial purposes only, warfare of the most heroic and devastating character has been necessary to gain and to hold the country. Malleson's estimate is low, that from 1746 to 1849 England has fought twelve decisive battles in order to win and to hold India. The great stages of English supremacy in India are the following:

I. A.D. 1600–1746.—The first interest awakened in England concerning India seems to have arisen from Thomas Stevens, of New College, Oxford, who went to Goa in 1597, and whose travels were afterwards published in England. Other travellers followed him, such as Storey, Newberry, Leedes, and Fitch. These men carried a letter from Queen Elizabeth to the Mogul emperor, Akbar. The first practical effect of the reports concerning India took shape in the British East India Company, which was incorporated by Queen Elizabeth on the last day of the sixteenth century, or December 31st, 1600. For nearly a century and a half, or from 1600 down to 1742, we find this great Company gradually assuming larger proportions, getting important concessions from the native rulers, growing wealthy, raising an army to defend its commercial interests, acquiring large territorial possessions, and, in wisdom and enterprise, far surpassing all other European claimants for supremacy in India. The East India Company was really a nation, without the name or the formality.

II. A.D. 1746–1759.—This was the period of English struggle and final triumph. The time was brief, but it was occupied in bloody and bitter warfare. The southern half of India was one great battle-field. The French and English were the leading contestants, and the conflicting interests of native princes were used by each of the foreign powers only to aid its own cause. England's triumph left the southern half of India in her possession. The scene of war changed, during the last years, to the north. Clive, who had saved the south, returned from England to save the north. Four other great names were associated with him in giving final triumph to English arms and administration —Watson, Coote, Forde, and Warren Hastings. The Black Hole tragedy, in Calcutta, awakened the wrath of Clive and all the English to such an extent that bitter vengeance was sworn.

This was in 1756. The battle of Plassey was fought June 23d of the following year. The Indian chief, Siraj ud Daula, had 68,000 soldiers, and an immense train of artillery. Clive had but 900 European troops, 2100 Sepoys, a few Portuguese, and only ten pieces of artillery. He called a council of war. Thirteen of his officers voted against a battle, and seven for it. Clive withdrew to a grove near by, reflected on the emergency, threw the judgment of the council to the winds, and fought and won Plassey, the most momentous of all the struggles of England for rule in India. Many thousands of native troops were slain, but the English loss was only twenty-two killed and fifty wounded. This battle gave northern India, and therefore all India, to the British crown.

III. A.D. 1759–1818.—During this period the English were engaged with frequent hostile forces of the native troops. The Marhattas more than once threatened the English supremacy. Even a more difficult task was the organization of the civil administration. The East India Company was the actual government. England, as a government, did little more than hold the Company to a strict accountability.

In 1774 a thorough change was made in the general administration. Hitherto the governments of Bombay, Madras, and Calcutta had been independent presidencies. But in 1773 the Regulating Act was adopted, by which a governor-general was appointed for all India, and the three presidencies were united by a Supreme Council and by a Court of Judicature. This new arrangement for the civil government of India has continued, with minor changes, down to the present time. The ecclesiastical establishment in India was organized in 1813, by which a bishop of Calcutta was appointed, with an archdeacon, and later a bishop, in the capital of each presidency. Middleton was the first bishop, and Heber, Wilson, and Cotton were his worthy successors.

IV. A.D. 1818–1857.—The supremacy of England was now apparently complete. But there were three important requirements on which the permanence of English rule depended. The first was the safe and wise introduction of reforms; the second was the annexation of contiguous territory and the absorption

WARREN HASTINGS.

of its threatening population into submissive subjects; and the third was the ability to conquer one of the most appalling and widespread mutinies known in modern times. All these requirements were fully met by the wisdom, justice, and unsurpassed heroism of the statesmen and the soldiers who represented England in the administration and authority of her Indian affairs. During this period of about forty years the army in India was engaged in no less than six military expeditions, which, in several instances, assumed the magnitude of formal warfare. The eastern frontier was threatened by the Burmese demand, in 1818, for the cession of Chittagong, Murshidabad, and Dacca. The result was a war, which began in 1824, and was successfully terminated in 1826 by the cession of an important part of Burmese territory to England, and the pledge of the Burmese government "to maintain the relations of amity and peace between the two nations."

In 1852–53 a second war with Burma was carried on, which resulted in the firm establishment of British power over, practically, the whole of Burma. Since then, in 1887, a third war with Burma has been waged, by which the immense territory of Burma has been formally annexed. England has thus become practically the ruler of India to the Chinese frontier. A war with Bhartpur was conducted in 1826, the result of which was a complete success. Sind, a dependency of Kabul, was conquered in 1843 by Sir Charles Napier. The Amirs, who had governed it, were brought as exiles to Benares, and put on a pension. The valley of the Indus was now in the full possession of the English. The war for Sind, however, reflects no credit on the English name. "The feeling then prevailed," says Pope, "and posterity will deliberately confirm the opinion, that the war was unrighteous. It is the one annexation upon which the English nation can look with no satisfaction." *

FISHERMAN, SUNNI MUSSULMAN, SIND.

* "Text-book of Indian History," p. 386.

It became apparent that the great gateway through Afghanistan must be kept secure against invasion. Russia was planning, by interference with the native populations, and holding them in sympathy, against English security in India. In 1845 the first Panjab war broke out, and in 1848 the second. The result of the bitter conflict was favorable to England, and in 1848 the Panjab, which has ever since formed the extreme northwestern province of British India, was annexed.

It is difficult to measure the magnitude of this brief period of warfare. It was war to the knife. The natives showed no mercy whenever they had the English at advantage. But the English were equally brave and daring, while their experience of over a century in combating native troops gave them an acquaintance with their methods which proved of infinite aid. In the short space of three years, 1843–46, the English fought not less than eight great battles, and completely annihilated the three armies of Sind, Gwalior, and the Panjab, numbering 120,000 men. Oudh, a native state which had been under English guardianship since 1801, was annexed, by direct order from the home government, in 1856. This whole period was interrupted by few military reverses, while such advances were made as caused the British power to be an object of dread by every native prince, either within or without the boundary-lines of British India.

V. The Mutiny.—So rapid and profound had been the recent advancement of the British rule in India, that it became clear to the native mind that unless some great and sudden method of resistance should be adopted, it would soon be too late for the natives to regain any control over the country. The mutiny of 1857 was the practical outcome of this widespread apprehension. No sufficient cause for it can be found in the English dealing with the natives. The lenient spirit had increased steadily. The governors-general had been considerate. The argument that native officers and privates had, in some instances, been underpaid, was only a pretext. The real cause was the determination of the natives, strengthened and inflamed by the remaining scions of the old princely and royal families, to overthrow the supremacy of England, and re-establish the native power. Had they succeeded, it is safe to say that India would to-day be little better than what it was during the Marhatta carnival of blood.

One day in January, 1857, a Laskar in Calcutta asked a Sepoy to give him a drink out of his lota, or water-cup.* The Sepoy was of high caste, and refused indignantly to grant the request, since to allow low-caste lips to touch his cup would violate the traditions and prejudices of his caste. When the Laskar saw this he replied that the British government was at that time making cartridges of the grease of cows and hogs, and that native lips would have to be polluted by biting off the ends of the cartridges when loading their English guns. The soldier was still more indignant. He told this piece of news—whether true or not is not known—to others, and it soon spread into far circles. That there was force in this argument of the greased cartridges being an offence to the caste prejudice of the Hindus, can be seen in the later fact that, in a regiment of native troops, out of ninety men only five would touch the cartridges.†

A peculiar system of correspondence was adopted. A soldier was sent to a military station with a lotus-flower in his hand. This he presented to the chief native officer, who in turn presented it to a soldier. This soldier handed it to another, and this one to a third, until every soldier had held it in his hand. The last soldier to receive and hold it took it to the next station, where the same process was gone through. There was profound silence. But all understood the deep and dreadful meaning. The significance was death to every Englishman.

The way of reaching the non-military masses was by sending out six little cakes of unleavened bread, called *chapatties*, to the chief man of a village.‡ He received them, and sent out six others to the chief man of the next village. But little, if anything, was said. Yet here, too, every one understood the profound meaning—a great struggle was about to come, and every native must do his duty. The religious element was aroused. Priests went through the country, quietly preaching a crusade against the English rulers.

There were three stages in the mutiny. The first was the time of doubt, which lasted from the outbreak at Berhampur, in March, 1857, to the siege of Delhi. The second was the decisive

---

* Holmes, "A History of the Indian Mutiny," pp. 81, 82.

† "Parliament Papers," vol. xxv., p. 333. 1859.

‡ "Story of the Indian Mutiny," p. 21.

event, the siege of Delhi, in September, 1857. The third was the conquest of the non-military population, in the province of Oudh, closing in January, 1859.

The whole history of warfare and insurrection does not present a picture of more bloodthirsty and cruel deeds on the one hand, and of more intrepid bravery and innocent suffering on the other, than in this brief rebellion of the natives of India against their English rulers. The war was confined chiefly to the northern half of the Indian triangle. But there was unrest in every part of the country. The English did not know whom to trust. War was in the air, from the mountains all the way down to the Cape. Over the northern half of India the armies of the insurgents swept like a besom of destruction. They held in their hands the very rifles which had been given them, and whose use had been taught them, by the English. From Calcutta in the east to Lahor in the west, the tide of warfare ebbed and flowed with varying success. The three hot centres of the mutiny were Cawnpore, Lucknow, and Delhi.

Nana Sahib was the leader of the mutineers, and Sir John Lawrence, Sir Henry Lawrence, Sir Henry Havelock, Sir Colin Campbell, Sir James Outram, and General Neill were the leaders of the British forces. The native forces massacred, in cold blood, men, women, and children. At Cawnpore the butchery of the little English contingent, with the families, surpasses all power of description. At Lucknow the English were besieged in the Residency, and every day they were dying from hunger, stifling heat, and the shot of the enemy. Havelock hastened to the rescue. He and Sir James Outram entered the city with but two thousand men, while the enemy numbered fifty thousand.* Luck-

STATUE OF SIR JAMES OUTRAM.

* Dutt, "Historical Studies," vol. ii., p. 393.

now was saved, but the cemetery of the Residency tells the sad story of the enormous number of the English who died during the struggle. Havelock died of dysentery in November, 1857, and his body lies in a garden near where he gave his life to his country. He met death with that Christian confidence and grandeur which had distinguished his remarkable career. He lay upon a rude bed, on the ground, in his tent, ministered to by his devoted son only. Among his last words were:

"I die happy and contented. I have for forty years so ruled my life that when death came I might face it without fear."

Of him it was said at Rangoon, by Campbell, the general commanding, when informed that the enemy was approaching one of the English posts:

"Call out Havelock's saints; they are never drunk, and he is always ready." *

For death, too, Havelock was ready. Taking his whole career together, no name stands higher on the long roll of England's great commanders than that of Havelock. As a Christian soldier, he shares with Gordon the highest place in the group of men who, in the nineteenth century, have reflected honor on the English name by a rare combination of religious fervor and martial daring.

Several important results were reached by the suppression of the great mutiny. One was the termination of the complicated relations between the English government and the East India Company. The last renewal of the charter granted by Parliament was in 1853, for only such period as the government might see fit. The number of directors was reduced, their patronage for appointments to the civil service was taken away, and appointments for offices were henceforth made dependent upon the principle of open competition.† In 1858, however, Parliament transferred, after long debate, the whole administration of India to the Crown, and the East India Company ceased to exist.

A second great result was, that England learned by the mutiny that her government of India was henceforth to depend on Christian principles. There was no longer any public sympathy

* Holmes, "A History of the Indian Mutiny," p. 424.

† Hunter, "Short History of the Indian People," p. 211.

with the false religious traditions and prejudices of the natives. The earnest Christian spirit of Havelock and the Lawrences convinced the world that the highest military quality is consistent with a deep religious experience. The patriotic spirit of

THE RESIDENCY AT LUCKNOW.

the missionaries in this critical time was remarkable. The massacre of missionaries and their families was a part of the great price which England paid for her complete victory over the mutineers.

A third great result attained by the suppression of the mutiny was the profound and universal conviction among all the natives that all further attempts to conquer England in India were out of the question. The mutiny had been made with unsurpassed energy, and it had utterly failed. No one of judgment in India now imagines that another effort for independence can ever be made, even under the most favorable circumstances.

VI. THE QUEEN'S PROCLAMATION, on assuming the government of India, was issued November 1, 1858. It has been called the Magna Charta of Indian rights. Complete amnesty was granted to all inhabitants of the country, except those who had taken direct part in the murder of English people. These few words are sufficient to declare the spirit of the entire proclamation: "We hold ourselves bound to the natives of our Indian territories by the same obligations of duty which bind us to all our other subjects."

For the princes who had remained firm to England during the mutiny the Order of the Star of British India was instituted, and many natives were rewarded in its different grades. The Sanad, or Patent of Nobility, was issued, by which the one hundred and fifty-three feudatories of Britain in India were constituted nobles of the British empire.

The great representative of English authority at this time was Lord Canning, the first viceroy. His measures were of the most conciliatory character. He was much abused by the large English element who advocated retaliatory measures, and the sobriquet of "Clemency Canning" was a favorite term. But his unpopularity lasted for a brief season only. The true judgment of history is that but for the very course which he adopted the peaceful government of the millions of India, from that time to the present, could never have been achieved.

VII. SUBSEQUENT EVENTS.—Since the mutiny the development of the administration of the government has been wise and rapid. Nothing seems to have been neglected to cement the different parts of the country and to elevate the condition of the people, excepting only the treatment of the questions of opium and intoxicating liquors. Queen Victoria was declared Empress of India by the special management of Lord Beaconsfield, the premier of the time. Lord Ripon, the viceroy from 1880 to 1883, attempted a series of reforms calculated to give larger liberty to the native aspirations. The repeal of the Vernacular

Press Act removed the last restraints on the free discussion of public questions.* Lord Ripon's scheme of local self-government has opened the way for a new era of political life to the natives of the country, while his appointment of an Education

THE MEMORIAL WELL AT CAWNPORE.

Commission has resulted in a great advance of popular education. Lord Ripon, though a Roman Catholic, enjoyed the favor and confidence of the whole body of Protestant missionaries.

* Hunter, "Brief History of the Indian People," p. 216.

The natives regard his administration as peculiarly favorable to them, and showed their appreciation of his services by popular demonstrations of remarkable magnitude and heartiness. The administration of his successor, Lord Dufferin, which lasted from 1885 to 1888, was wisely conducted. Its most important political event was the accession of Burma to the empire of India. But the most far-reaching event was the founding of a movement by the Countess Dufferin for the supply of Medical Aid to the Women of India.

MARCO POLO.

CHAPTER VII.

THE NATURAL DIVISIONS OF INDIA.

INDIA is known to its inhabitants, not as India, but as Bharatavarsha, or Land of King Bharata, the great ancient ruler of the Lunar dynasty.* It is mentioned in the Book of Esther as one of the one hundred and twenty-seven provinces of the son of

SOPOR, HIMALAYAS IN THE BACKGROUND.

Darius Hystaspes. It is cut off from the great central zone of Asia by the Himalaya Mountains, or Abodes of Snow. This range extends a distance of fifteen hundred miles, and has an unbroken water-shed of eighteen thousand feet in height, extend-

* Dutt, "Historical Studies and Recreations," vol. i., p. 34.

ing from the gorge of the Brahmaputra in the east to the gorge of the Indus in the west.* The width of the Himalaya range is enormous. This mountain region far excels in size the whole Alpine range. The entire width of the Alps, measured from Lake Thun to the plains of Lombardy, is about seventy-five miles, while a line drawn across the Himalayas, from Simla due north, measures four hundred miles.†

It has been truly said that "along the entire range of the Himalaya there are valleys into which the whole Alps might be cast without producing any result that would be discernible at a distance of ten or fifteen miles." Here rise great mountain systems, now culminating in peaks higher than any thus far known to men, and now extending in great snowy lines, with immense glaciers stretching down in all directions. Mount Everest rises 29,002 feet above the sea, or 12,000 feet higher than Mont Blanc. Three other Himalayan peaks are nearly as high—Kinchinjinga (28,156 feet), Chumalhari (23,929), and Dhawalagiri (26,826). General Strachey declares his expectation that many mountain-peaks will be found which will measure between 25,000 and 30,000 feet, and that some peaks will be discovered which will measure more than 30,000 feet in height.

The Himalayan Mountain region furnishes the water supply for India and Burma. The streams pour out from the glaciers, and, gathering strength from many mountain tributaries, roll down from the lofty heights at from eight hundred to twelve hundred and fifty feet of descent per mile. Beyond the snowy crests of the Himalayas lie the broad plateau and the chain of Kuen-luns, running parallel with the Himalayas, which separate Tibet from India. The Himalayas and the Kuen-luns, with the table-land between, form one gigantic mountain system, of an average width of five hundred miles and two thousand miles in length. Such an immense mountain region has no equal on the face of the earth. Few of the peaks have been ascended, while many of the valleys have never been trodden by human feet. Here rise not only all the great rivers of India, but of all Asia. The rivers which run through the Chinese empire and Burma rise in the east, while the rivers of India, and, to some extent, of Persia, rise in the central and western regions.

* Smith, "The Geography of British India," pp. 1 ff. † Ibid., p. 20.

KOTTIAR, CEYLON.

South of this great range lies British India. It covers an area of 1,577,698 square miles, and supports a population of over 250,000,000 people. The distance from the Himalayas down to Cape Comorin is about the same as from Iceland to Spain. The distance from Bombay to Calcutta is the same as from London to Naples. The following table, from Behm and De Stein's statistics, will show the relation of the population and area of British India to other large countries:

	Square Miles.	Square Kilometres.	Population.
British Empire	8,036,007	20,090,019	303,512,568
British Indian Empire	1,494,310	3,845,186	253,140,886
Chinese Empire	1,609,876	4,024,690	280,000,000 (estimated)
Tibet and E. Turkestan	4,725,500	11,813,750	29,800,000
Russian Empire	8,281,200	21,703,002	88,018,530
Turkish Empire	2,494,520	6,236,300	23,119,800
United States, N. A.	3,708,976	9,272,448	50,438,960
Netherlands, with N. India	679,378	1,985,183	27,320,469
Persia	658,828	1,647,070	4,400,400

The following table will furnish a picture of the kingdoms and republics of Europe, contrasted with the great provinces and states of India:

INDIA.	Square Miles.	Population.	Population.	Square Miles.	EUROPE.
Bengal..........	203,437	69,133,619	37,672,000	204,177	France.
Assam..........	55,384	4,908,276	25,968,286	58,320	England and Wales.
British Burma...	87,220	3,736,771	29,702,656	89,005	Great Britain.
Andaman Islands.	3,285	30,000	150,000	4,200	Cyprus.
N. W. Province, with Oudh...	111,086	44,851,542	28,437,091	114,296	Italy.
Panjab..........	221,749	22,712,120	37,839,427	240,942	Austria-Hungary.
Bombay..........	191,847	23,396,045	20,974,411	219,260	Spain and Portugal.
Ajmir..........	2,710	460,722	936,340	2,866	Hesse.
Baroda..........	4,399	2,154,469	1,506,531	5,851	Baden.
Rajputana.......	130,994	11,005,512	27,278,911	137,066	Prussia.
Central India....	89,098	9,200,881	29,702,656	89,005	Great Britain.
Central Province.	113,042	11,505,149	28,437,091	114,296	Italy.
Berar..........	17,728	2,672,673	2,846,102	15,992	Switzerland.
Haidarabad......	80,000	9,167,789	29,702,656	89,005	Great Britain.
Madras..........	150,248	33,840,617	16,625,860	182,750	Spain.
Kurg..........	1,583	178,302	349,367	1,526	Brunswick.
Mysore..........	30,500	4,186,399	3,734,370	30,685	Scotland.

Beginning with the base of the Himalaya Mountains and looking southward, we have three distinct ranges of mountains distributed through India. One is the great Vindhyá, or "Hunter" range. It runs six hundred miles from east to west, or from Neesuach to Sasseram; and three hundred miles from north to south, or from Agra to Hoshangabad. This immense Vindhyá plateau separates the great valley of the Ganges from the Dekhan. It is the "middle land" of the Aryan conquerors, and it is here, in the jungles and mountain fastnesses, that are still preserved the most undisturbed specimens of the pre-Aryan races. The aboriginal tongues are still heard here, and we can well imagine that, with the exception of some Sanskrit words and an element which has dropped in from the surrounding vernaculars, one can still hear the same speech which was spoken by the inhabitants of India long before an Aryan had found his way down through the Afghan passes, or a single line of a Veda had been chanted along the valley of the Ganges.

The Satpura, or "Seven Towers" range, lies south of the

Vindhyá, and runs parallel to it, extending six hundred miles westward to the Arabian Sea, and having a width of one hundred miles.

But the most important range of mountains south of the Himalayas is the Sahyadri, or Western Ghats. They run along the western coast from the Tapti River to Cape Comorin, a distance of one thousand miles. They are intersected by passes, which, seen from the coast, present the appearance of a sierra or comb. The eastern coast is flat, and the western is elevated. Every important river, therefore, rising in the heart of India is thrown eastward, and empties into the Bay of Bengal. The average height of this range is three thousand feet. There are variations in the general direction. While the general trend is along the coast, there are scarps in different directions, and now and then lofty cones, which shoot up almost perpendicularly from the plain. Along the east coast there are occasional elevations, but not enough to affect the general geological character of the country.

Each section of India has a mountain region for a refuge for Europeans during the summer. The plateau of Puna furnishes a delightful summer resort for the citizens of Bombay. The southern people have only to betake themselves to the plateau and ridges of Mysore and the Nilgiris for a cool and bracing atmosphere. Those living along the valleys of the Jamna and the Ganges, and elsewhere in the north, can find refuge from the heat by going to the Vindhyá range, or, which is best of all, by going to the many resorts in the Himalaya Mountains. Simla, because of its being the summer resort of the viceroy and his council and court, is the most fashionable of all the summering places, and, while Calcutta is nominally the capital, it can really boast of the honor for only about four months of the year, while Simla possesses it the remaining eight months. India is really governed from this magnificent summer retreat.

The rivers of India are among the most remarkable in the world. We begin with the eastern or Burmese group. The Irawadi has two sources in the Himalayas, separated by a day's journey. This river is a mile broad while yet eight hundred miles from the sea. It divides into two rivers before it reaches the Bay of Bengal. The Tsit-Toung (Sittang) has a breadth, in the Shwe-gyeen district, of from seven to eight miles, but narrows again before reaching the Bay of Bengal. It drains an area of twenty-two thousand square miles. The Salween is a narrow and rapid stream, flowing south of the Chinese province of Yunan.

The Brahmaputra, or "Son of Brahma," rises in the great Tibetan table-land, and flows a distance of 1800 miles, finally emptying into the Bay of Bengal at its head. The basin which it drains has an area of 361,200 square miles. It is navigable a distance of eight hundred miles from the sea, and in volume, agricultural facilities, and commercial advantages it ranks next to the Ganges and the Indus, as the third Indian river in value to the empire. The Ganges, "The River," is eldest daughter of Himavat, "The Lord of Snow." It is the sacred river of the Hindus, who call it "Mother Ganga." Venerable temples mark its rise among the glaciers of the Himalayas, and keep guard along its banks until it pours its vast waters into the Bay of Bengal. Its main course is 1680 miles in length. It loses its identity before reaching the sea. It begins to form its great delta while yet 240 miles from the sea. It divides into the Megua and the Hugli rivers, through which it passes its vast volume of water to the sea. The fertilizing power of this one river, and its relation to the life and commerce of India, beggars all description. It has no parallel in the world's life-bearing streams. "From the source of the Ganges in the Himalayas," says F. G. Carpenter, "to its mouth in the Bay of Bengal, it has a fall of more than two and one half miles, and as a fertilizing bearer it surpasses any river on the face of the globe. Egypt is the gift of the Nile. You could lose Egypt in these plains, which are the gift of the Ganges. The mighty Nile, with its unknown source, does not carry down as much water as this holy river of the Hindus, and its maximum discharge, at a distance of 400 miles from the sea, with many of its tributaries yet to hear from, is one third greater than that of the Mississippi. Where the Ganges rises, bursting forth from a Himalayan glacier, it is 27 feet wide. It falls 3500 feet in the first ten miles of its course, and it has an average depth of 35 feet 500 miles from its mouth. Its delta is as wide as the distance from New York to Washington, and hundreds of mouths run from this width back into a sort of a parallelogram for 200 miles more, where they unite. The water of the Bay of Bengal is discolored for miles by the mud

THE LAST VOYAGE. A SOUVENIR OF THE GANGES.

(From the painting by Edwin Lord Weeks.)

brought down by the Ganges, and the whole country is fertilized by it.

"The water is the color and thickness of pea-soup, and the silt or mud is so rich that these vast plains use no other fertilizer. The crops are harvested by pulling the stalks out of the ground. No cows or horses are allowed to pasture in the fields, and their droppings are mixed with straw and mud, and then dried and used as fuel. In this Ganges valley Nature is always giving, but never getting. Every atom of natural fertilizer save this Ganges silt is taken from the soil. Still the land is as rich as guano, and it produces from two to four crops every year. About Calcutta the alluvial deposit is 400 feet deep, and an experiment was lately made to get to the end of it. A well was sunk, but at the distance of 481 feet the auger broke. At this point the end of this rich soil had not been reached.

"The amount of fertilizing material brought down by the Ganges has been lately estimated, and scientific investigation shows that some distance above the point where it unites with the Brahmaputra its yearly burden is the enormous amount of 355,000,000 tons. A thousand-ton ship is by no means small, and a fleet of 350,000 such ships could not carry this burden. The average freight-car is thirty-four feet long, and it takes a strong car to carry fifty tons. Suppose our freight-cars to be each sixteen feet longer than they are. Load upon each car fifty tons of this fertilizing mud, and it would take a train of more than seven million such cars to carry the yearly fertilizing output of this great river. If these cars were on a single track, the track would have to be 67,400 miles long. It would reach twice around the earth, and leave enough cars over to run two continuous trains through the centre. The most of this silt comes down during four months of the year, and if there were daily fleets of 2000 ships, each containing 1400 tons of mud, during these four months they would just carry it.

"But this is the work of the Ganges alone. It is five times as much as is carried by the Mississippi to the Gulf; and farther down the river, where the great Brahmaputra joins it and flows out into its hundred mouths, the silt output is still greater. During the rainy season alone the river here carries out enough silt to load 13,000 ships, with 1400 tons each, every day for four months. During this rainy season this whole delta of the Ganges is covered with water to the extent of about thirty feet.

You see only the tops of trees, and the villages which are built upon the hills, and the river farther up the country is diverted by canals from its course to every part of these vast plains. The best of the wheat is irrigated, and the water, being allowed to lie upon the land, drops this fertilizer and enriches it."*

The Indus, or Abba Sin, "Father of Rivers," rises in the same great general Tibeto-Himalayan range. It has a course of 1802 miles, and empties into the Arabian Sea. The great Five Rivers —the Jhelam, Chenab, Ravi, Beas, and Satlej—pour their waters into the Indus. The Indus has brought fertility to a vast sandy region, and has created the province of Sind as completely as the Nile has produced Lower Egypt. Its mouths are numerous, and frequently change. They extend a distance of 120 miles along the coast.

We now come to the rivers which run through the centre and southern part of India, and which take their rise in the central and southern mountains. The Narbada separates Hindustan proper from the Dekhan. It is fed mainly by tributaries from the southern side of the Vindhyá range, drains a basin of 36,400 square miles, and empties into the Arabian Sea north of Bombay. The Tapti runs parallel to the Narbada, drains an area of 30,000 square miles, and can boast of one hundred and eight sacred shrines along its banks. The Mahanadi, or "Great River," runs through the Central Province, and empties into the Bay of Bengal, having a drainage basin of 43,800 square miles. The Godavari rises within fifty miles of the Indian Ocean, and runs eastward across the peninsula, and empties into the Bay of Bengal. The Kistna, or Krishna, runs in the same general direction, and also empties into the Bay of Bengal. It has a drainage of 94,500 square miles. The Kaveri also crosses the peninsula eastward, drains an area of 28,000 square miles, and empties by two mouths into the Bay of Bengal.†

There are but few lakes in India proper. But there are many, which are very beautiful, in the Tibeto-Himalayan plateau. Among these are Manasaraur and Rahhas Tal. On the Pamir steppe, or "Roof of the World," is Pamir, or Victoria Lake. It is fourteen miles long, and gives birth to the Oxus River, flow-

---

* Correspondence of the *New York Times* (June, 1889).

† Medlicott and Blanford, "A Manual of the Geology of India," p. iii.

ing westward, and to the Aksu, which flows eastward. Pang-king is a series of saline lakes which extend a distance of one hundred miles. The Runn of Kutch is a great salt marsh of about 9000 square miles in area, and is one of the chief sources of the salt supply of India. Palti, Chonito-Dong, Dalguchu, Tengri-nor, Bulcho, and Koko-nor, "Blue Sea," are all situated in the northern Himalayan plateau. In the southern Himalayan plateau are

A SALT-WELL, KUTCH.

the beautiful Kashmir lakes, Srinagar and Manasbal, and Nular, Konsa Nag, Naini Tal, the Six Lakes of Sikkim, Sambhar, Lonar, Nakhi Talao, Amber, Nal, Chitka, Kolar, and Pulikat. Many of the tanks, receiving the waters from rivers and rainfalls, are so large as to compare favorably with natural lakes. The great tank at Haidarabad, in the Dekhan, would be readily taken in America for a natural lake.

CHAPTER VIII.

ANIMAL AND VEGETABLE LIFE.—MINERALS.

India comprises all climates. The uplands along the base of the Himalayas remind one of the temperate regions of Europe and the United States, while the southern part of the peninsula is as thoroughly tropical and luxuriant as the West Indies or the Molucca Islands. The animal life derives its varied forms from the many Indian climates. In Zerai and Assam the elephant still runs wild.* The dense jungles are their favorite home. The wild elephants are caught and tamed, and used for bearing burdens or adding to the dignity of petty chiefs or the Anglo-Indian nabob. In the old sculptures there can be seen magnificent elephants forming an important part in imperial processions. The same fondness for elephantine display still exists in India. On great occasions a line of elephants, richly caparisoned in purple and gold, is still considered a necessary factor in a vice-regal or princely procession.

The lion, long the king of the Indian forest, is now rapidly disappearing. The south is still the home of the tiger. This animal is getting more timid of late, because of the inroads made upon his species by English sportsmen and because of the progress of agriculture; but the species known as the "man-eater" is still dreaded, because of his terrible ferocity Hunter gives the following account of the depredations of four of these animals: In three years one man-eater killed 108 people; another destroyed 80 people in one year; another was the dreaded pest of 30 villages; while a fourth, in 1869, killed 127 people, and for many weeks closed up a great road to all travel.

Chamois, chevreuils, bears, wild dogs, wolves, and other animals of this class, are to be found in the north, and to some extent in all parts of India. The panther, hyena, jackal, croco-

* Le Bon, "Civilization of India," pp. 57–68.

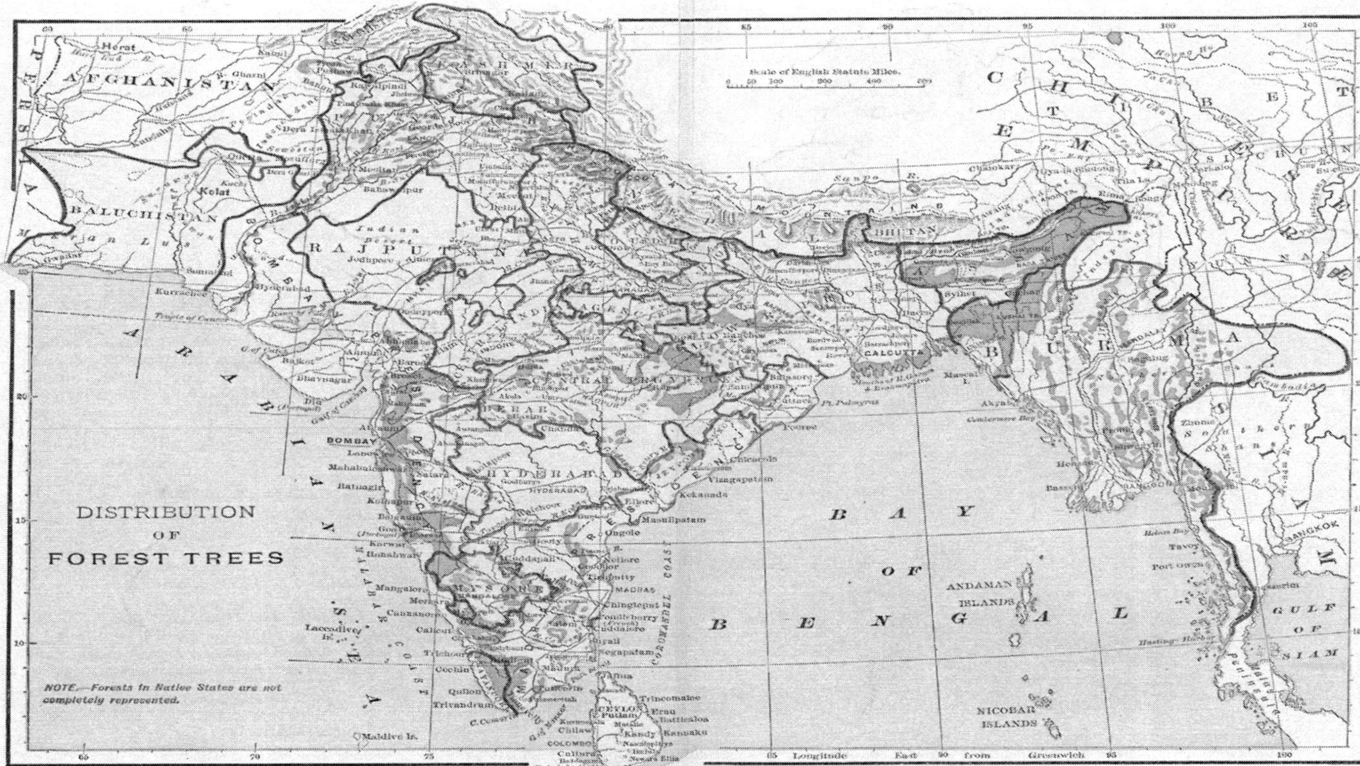
DISTRIBUTION
OF
FOREST TREES
NOTE.—Forests in Native States are not completely represented.
Scale of English Statute Miles.
Longitude East from Greenwich
PERSIA
AFGHANISTAN
BALUCHISTAN
RAJPUTANA
CENTRAL PROVINCES
HYDERABAD
MYSORE
BHUTAN
BURMA
SIAM
CHINESE EMPIRE
TIBET
CEYLON
BOMBAY
CALCUTTA
MADRAS
BANGKOK
ARABIAN SEA
BAY OF BENGAL
GULF OF SIAM
ANDAMAN ISLANDS
NICOBAR ISLANDS
Maldive Is.
Laccadive Is.
MALABAR COAST
COROMANDEL COAST
Malay Peninsula
Herat
Kelat
Kurrachee
Jodhpore
Bhavnagar
Ratnagiri
Kolhapur
Belgaum
Karwar
Honahwar
Mangalore
Cannanore
Calicut
Cochin
Quilon
Trivandrum
C. Comorin
Trincomalee
Batticaloa
Kandy
COLOMBO
Point de Galle
Negapatam
Cuddalore
Pondicherry
Chingleput
Nellore
Ongole
Masulipatam
Kokanada
Vizagapatam
Chicacole
Pooree
Balasore
Sylhet
Akyab
Bassein
Tavoy
Port Owen
Zimmé
Pt. Palmyras
Tropic of Cancer

dile, and alligator are frequently met with. The rhinoceros is to be found chiefly in the marshy islands of the Ganges delta. In some instances the wild beast roams unpleasantly near the homes of quiet citizens. For example, Travancore, says Mateer, is a land whose capital is surrounded by the primeval forests, where the elephant, tiger, and wild ox roam unchecked near the

NATIVES FELLING TIMBER.

Brahman official or Sudra noble who lectures on modern science and writes the English language as well as any of us.*

The most numerous of all animals in India is the cobra. It is regarded as sacred, and represents one of the powerful attributes of the god Vishnu. The cobra glides into the most private places. A newspaper lying on the grass in the courtyard of an Anglo-Indian for a day or two may be found to cover a cobra.

* "Native Life in Travancore," p. 8.

All classes of people in India soon learn the stealthy habits of this monster, and observe proper precautions against it.

The government offers liberal rewards for the slaughter of dangerous animals. But, in spite of stringent preventive measures, the destruction of human life by them is still deplorably large. The latest official returns (1886) present the following dark picture of the loss of life from the destructive animals of India: During the year 1886, in British India, 24,841 persons were killed by wild beasts. Of these, 22,134 were killed by snakes, 928 by tigers, 222 by wolves, 194 by leopards, 113 by bears, 57 by elephants, 24 by hyenas, and 1169 by other animals, including scorpions, jackals, lizards, boars, crocodiles, buffaloes, mad dogs, and foxes. In the same year 57,541 animals were destroyed by wild animals; but in this case the proportions are quite different, for, while snakes were responsible for the deaths of eleven twelfths of the human beings, they only killed 2 in every 57 animals, tigers and leopards doing the greatest damage. Tigers show 23,769, leopards 22,275, wolves 4275, snakes 2514, hyenas 1312, and bears 758. In the case of both human beings and animals the destruction appears to be on the increase; in the former case the number is higher than any one of the previous ten years, and in the latter it is third in ten years in point of numbers killed. At the same time the numbers of wild beasts killed and the rewards paid for that purpose are increasing. In 1886, 23,417 wild beasts were destroyed, and 417,596 snakes.

Sheep are raised for both meat and milk. The Hindu shares with the Jew an abomination for pork. The great streams abound in fish. Monkeys are numerous. In Cawnpore, Lucknow, and Benares they have their own way, and in some instances they have to be removed because of their remarkable fecundity. Parrots and birds of all varieties of rich plumage abound. The Hindus regard many birds as of great value to them, because they destroy insects and rapidly remove all decaying vegetable matter.*

The flora of India presents a picture of marvellous richness and variety. Great gardens, as in Allahabad, abound in roses of many species. In the mountains of Khari there are two hundred

* Balfour, "The Agricultural Pests of India," London, 1887.

SLEEPING TIGER.

(From the painting by Barye.)

and fifty varieties of orchids. The Indian sun develops an ordinary plant into remarkable growth and productiveness. Wheat, maize, rice, and millet belong to the chief cereals which support life. For it must be remembered that the Hindu lives on vegetable food. It is safe to say that millions of the Hindu people never taste animal food from the cradle to the grave. The valley of the Ganges is the greatest harvest-field of India. Its soil is as rich as the valley of the Nile, and is kept fertile by the constant bringing down from the mountains of matter essential to the growth of the cereals. Three crops a year on the same soil are frequent.

Cotton now belongs in the front rank of products. The fibre is not so good as the finer American varieties, but is improving constantly, and the export is a fine source of national revenue. The current native manufacture of cotton goods is now becoming disturbed by the manufacture of Indian cotton by the mills of Europe, and by sending back the stuffs to India, where they are furnished cheaper than the natives, by their simple weaving, have been in the habit of supplying them. Tobacco and jute are produced in large quantities. The tobacco of Trichinopoli is famous throughout India.

Coffee was introduced into India on a large scale by Wallich & Gordon, in 1823, and is now very industriously cultivated on large plantations.* Tea is produced to a larger extent than in any other country except China. The great Himalayan tea-gardens in India were begun from seedlings sent to Calcutta from China by Gordon in 1835.† Opium, which is strictly a government monopoly, is mostly cultivated in the valley of the Ganges, in Panjab, and Rajputana. Indigo, betel, and quinine are important products.

The spoliation of forests is common in India. Great reaches of rich timber-land have been stripped of trees by the natives, generally to get ashes for fertilization. Much of the forest-land is still in private hands, and therefore the government is powerless to prevent its devastation. In the Central Provinces 35,000

---

* Hall, "Coffee Planting in Ceylon," p. 296; also, Royle, "Essay on the Productive Resources of India," p. 185.

† Lees, "Tea Cultivation, Cotton, and Other Agricultural Exports in India," p. 43.

square miles are owned by private individuals, while the government owns but 20,000 square miles. In Bengal the landed proprietors hold from 40,000 to 50,000 square miles of forest-land, while the government owns but 11,754.* The sal (*shorea robusta*) and the teak (*tectona grandis*) are the two great varieties of trees for all general purposes. The teak is a magnificent wood for durability. No wood seems to be more nearly indestructible. The average life of a ship in the English navy is twelve years; but a vessel built of teak will last fifty years and upwards. The famous old *Lowji Castle*, a merchantman of a thousand tons' burden, which ploughed the Eastern seas for three quarters of a century, was built of teak. This wood is the principal material for building throughout India.

In the higher lands the oak, the pine, and others of the more familiar trees of England and the United States, flourish. In the plains, and extending down to the Cape, the banyan and the mhowa abound. In seasons of famine this last-named tree has furnished, by its flower, the only food for the sustenance of multitudes of people. The bamboo, the iron-tree, and the fragrant sandal are important woods, and flourish luxuriantly.

The most frequent and characteristic tree is the palm. Its graceful fronds wave everywhere, up to the very base of the Himalayas. But the paradise of the palm is in Southern India and Ceylon. It has many varieties. The fronds and bark mark the individuality. The talipot, the areca, the palmyra, the sago, the cocoanut, and the toddy palms are prominent varieties. Ferguson says that the palmyra palm alone can be used for five hundred different purposes.† Others reckon its uses at about a thousand. Under favorable circumstances the cocoanut-palm sends out its spikes of blossoms every month, and is well-nigh a perennial bearer. In Ceylon the cocoanuts are plucked green when designed for immediate use. The vendor sells you one, and with a large knife cuts off the top. Unless you are careful, the creamy juice will fly all over you. The fruit is soft, like jelly, and very palatable. The juice of the young cocoanut is called "illaoreer," or "young water," "young juice"—"youngster," one might say.

Each tree is very prolific, and is highly prized by all who have

* Schlich, "Review of the Forest Administration in British India for the year 1882–3," p. 1. Simla, 1884.

† "Information Regarding Ceylon," p. 5.

LION AND BOA-CONSTRICTOR.

(From the water-color by Antoine Louis Barye.)

the good-fortune in life to possess one. The man who owns a plantation of palms is regarded as well-to-do in the world's goods. The palmyra bears an annual crop of from five to eight clusters of fruit, and from twenty to thirty nuts in each cluster. In the cocoanut, while the nut is the valuable part, the husk and the shell are utilized. The husk is the material from which coir-fibre is manufactured. Ropes are made from it, which are used for fishing-nets all over the world, because they are never rotted by salt-water. It is beaten out, after being soaked for months in salt-water. In the palmyra the nut is inedible except when less than half grown. In each palmyra-nut there is a rich orange-colored juice, which is a favorite drink. A wild date-palm yields about a hundred and eighty pints of juice a year; each tree produces seven or eight pounds of sugar annually.* The cocoanut thrives best near the sea, or within reach of salt air.

Bishop Fowler gives the following excellent description of the Singhalese palm:

"One is constantly delighted with the variety and beauty of the palm. It seems to supply all the native wants. If he can climb (in this he approaches the skill of the monkey), he has food and shelter at hand. A young native puts his feet against the tree, and hooks his hands about it, and walks up it with ease and velocity; or, slipping his feet into a loop of rope a foot long, he clasps the tree with his feet thus held together, and leaps up three or four feet at a time.

"The cocoanut-palm is at home in this climate. It probably came over from Southern India. It prefers sandy sea-shores to inland soils. It seems to float, like the British flag, in all warm seas, and to root in every beach it touches. Even to the coral islands of the Indian Ocean floating cocoanuts have attached themselves, and are now covered with forests of these trees. The trunk is bare for forty or sixty feet, when it unfolds into a rich feathery crown or plume of long leaves, eighteen to twenty feet long. Every part of this tree is utilized. It is the centre of many industries. The tree is also especially adapted to the climate as a shade tree. One sees the houses or bungalows along the sea-shore completely shaded by these and other varieties of palms; yet the under space is open and clear for the free circulation of air. These

---

* Drury, "The Useful Plants of India," p. 330.

palms draw themselves up as slimly and high as possible, trying to hold their needed umbrellas over the heads and homes of man without obstructing his vision or his breath. A few of the uses of this palm may be catalogued. The fibre is made into mats, ropes, cords, clothes, brushes, brooms, hats, and stuffing for cushions instead of hair. The fruit also produces valuable oil as well as food. It is expressed in the most primitive fashion. It is used for cooking and for light (non-explosive). Four nuts to a person is sufficient for a meal. The milk is like some New York milk, more like water than milk. It is sweet, clear, and cool. For a very small coin a native went (walked or ran) up the tree, selected some nuts, picked them, took them in his teeth, came

PANTHER DEVOURING A GAZELLE.

(From the bronze by Antoine Louis Barye.)

down as he went up, trimmed off the coarser shell down to the white meat, then stuck in his knife, when the milk spirted up two feet above the nut. The palm is a patent refrigerator, for the milk hanging in the broiling sun keeps sweet and cool. The shells are made into spoons, cups, and other things. The milk is made into *toddy*, vinegar, and sugar. The leaves are valuable for thatching houses and for being braided into mats, hats, and coats. The undeveloped leaf, cut out of the heart of the tree, is used as we use cabbage. The brown fibres of the leaves are made into sieves and nets. Many drugs are made from the tree.

"The leaves of the palmyra and of the talipot palm supply

the Hindus with paper. One of the curiosities offered to the traveller, and greatly tempting him to buy, is the 'Hindu Bible,' written on these leaves. One is much interested in the kitul palm. It grows to its full height, fifty or sixty feet, before it blooms. Then it begins to unfold its flower at the top. The flower is long and hangs down like a horse's tail, and is ten or twelve feet long. Then another flower unfolds in the joint below, and so on down, till all the leaves are pushed off and the tree dies." *

The mineral wealth of India is not sufficiently developed to enable us to determine either its rarity or its extent. Iron has long been known to exist in great quantities. Among the earliest traces of human life are the rude iron implements forged far back in the aboriginal times. Copper and gold exist, and have been utilized from immemorial times. Coal is found in immense quantities. The river-basins furnish the great supplies, which are every year making the country more independent of England for fuel. The area of Indian coal measures is the fourth in size of all nations:

Godavari and affluents	11,000	square miles.
Sone	8,000	" "
Sirguja and Orissa	4,500	" "
Assam	3,000	" "
Narbada and affluents	3,500	" "
Damodar	2,000	" "
Rajmahal	300	" "
Unsurveyed	2,700	" "
Total	35,000	" "

Comparison with other countries having the largest coal measures:

United States	500,000	square miles.
China	400,000	" "
Australia	240,000	" "
India	35,000	" "

India is very rich in salt. There is a range of mountains in the Panjab called the Salt Range, in the upper waters of the Indus, which furnishes an inexhaustible supply of salt, and is a government monopoly. Rubies, sapphires, topazes, and emeralds abound,

* Correspondence of the *Christian Advocate* (New York, March 28, 1889).

but not as in former times. The diamond is now a rare thing in Indian mines. Amethysts abound in the Aravalli Mountains. Rock crystal abounds in the Narbada Valley. The agate, the carnelian, and the onyx are frequent in Gujarat. Rajputana abounds in magnificent marbles, as rich and varied as is furnished by the quarries of Russia.

GANGA SAGAR (WATER-VESSEL), BRASS, JHELAM.

CHAPTER IX.

THE GOVERNMENT OF INDIA.

The form of the English government of India is complex. It is the outgrowth of great wars and long and laborious legislation. There have been two distinct historical stages. The first was an individual government, or the rule of the East India Com-

EARL LYTTON.

pany, from A.D. 1600 to 1857. The second has prevailed from 1857 to the present, and is the government under the sovereign. The change from the East India Company to the present control of the Queen was made by direct act of Parliament. It was the result of the Sepoy rebellion, when it became clear that, to hold India, there must be a direct responsibility of the government itself.

The system is duplex, the general supervision being in England, but the real work being done by the local government in India. The supreme head of authority is the British sovereign, who is at the same time the Empress of India. But the practical English government of India is vested in the Secretary of State for India, and the Council of Fifteen Members. They administer the home business, such as the engagement of officers for the various departments of civil administration, the payment of pensions, the provision of funds for Indian expenditure in England, negotiations with the railroad companies, the purchase of supplies for Indian administration, and many other matters belonging to the English authority over India. The Secretary of State for India, at Westminster, is vested with almost supreme power. He is the real representative of the sovereign. He can even veto any legislative enactment or administrative arrangement of the Viceroy and his Council in India. But his course is marked with conservative care, and he takes his counsel largely from the local Indian government.

Let us now look at the government of India in India itself. At the head stands the Viceroy, who is called, in a business sense, the Governor-General of India. He is appointed by the Queen, at the nomination of the existing ministry. His term lasts five years. The late Viceroy, Lord Dufferin, was appointed through the nomination of Gladstone. The present Viceroy, Lord Lansdowne, was nominated by Lord Salisbury. The capital of India is Calcutta, where the Viceroy lives in the great Government House, and with almost regal surroundings. His summer capital is Simla, in the Himalaya Mountains. He has a council of six ordinary members, besides the commander-in-chief of the Indian army and the lieutenant-governor of Bengal. The six ordinary members of his Council are appointed by the Viceroy himself, are confirmed by the crown, and hold office five years. This is the Supreme Council.

The Viceroy has also a council for making laws, known as the Supreme Legislative Council, composed of the members of the Supreme Council and nine others, five of whom must be non-official.

The Supreme Council has charge of the finances of India, controls the subordinate or provincial governments, and can amend

LORD LANSDOWNE.

or annul any orders or proceedings of those provincial governments. The Supreme Legislative Council has in hand the making or change of laws which apply to India as a whole, but leaves the local legislation to the provincial legislative bodies. It is not necessary that the Governor-General's Council consist of Europeans only. For example, a few years ago one of the members was a prominent Mohammedan lawyer of Calcutta, and well known throughout India. He went to Europe, and actually married a Christian wife.

There are five provincial governments: Madras, Bombay, Bengal, Northwest Provinces, and Panjab. Each of these governments is fully equipped, having civil officers, judicial officers, and authority to collect revenue. The governor of Madras is appointed by the crown, holds office five years, has his capital at Madras, and has a council of three. The government of Bombay is constituted in the same way as that of Madras, with the city of Bombay as the capital. The government of Bengal is administered by a lieutenant-governor, with a legislative council of twelve members. The lieutenant-governor is appointed by the Viceroy, and holds office five years. Calcutta is his capital. The Northwest Provinces and the Panjab are, each, under a lieutenant-governor, appointed for five years.

The Church of England in India.

The English government makes ecclesiastical provision for the Indian empire. There are five bishops, one of whom is the Roman Catholic bishop of Bombay; three arch-deacons; and one hundred and eighty chaplains, besides registrars, clerks, and other minor officers. The bishop of Calcutta is the metropolitan, or head. Madras, Bombay, and the Panjab have each a bishop of the Church of England. Of the one hundred and eighty chaplains, the majority are of the Church of England, but a few are of the Church of Scotland. The annual cost to the treasury of India for keeping up the ecclesiastical establishment is one hundred and sixty-four thousand pounds sterling.

The Government and Education.

There is no compulsory education in India. Each presidency has its college and graded schools throughout the country, according to the needs of the population. There are ten inspectors-general, or directors of public instruction; four hundred and fifty inspectors, sub-inspectors, and deputies; and about six thousand principals, professors, head-masters, and teachers of all grades. Many of these positions are held by natives, but the higher appointments are usually filled by Europeans. The annual cost to the empire for keeping up the educational establishment is one million pounds sterling, while the receipts from fees and other sources only reach about one hundred thousand pounds sterling.

The Army.

During the government of India by the East India Company the army for India consisted of a large force, both native and English, but not forming a part of the regular army of Great Britain. The present arrangement is, that no English soldiers are enlisted for special service in India. But there is a large body of them in India all the time, though they constitute a part of the regular army of Great Britain. For their support the English at home do not pay a shilling. India must pay the

BENGAL LANCIERS.

whole bill for all her soldiers, whether European or native, and even meet the expenses of transportation between England and India. One third of the regular army of Great Britain, therefore, does not cost the English tax-payer anything. The average strength of the Indian army is one hundred and eighty thousand, exclusive of officers. Of this number sixty thousand are European troops. The annual cost of this force is sixteen million pounds, of which twelve millions are spent in India, and nearly four millions in England. Heavy ordnance, shot and shell, and small arms are supplied to the Indian army from England, but gunpowder, cartridges, bullets, clothing, and similar necessaries are manufactured in India at the government factories. Horses for cavalry service are mostly brought from Australia. England takes good care to make the people of India share in providing for any war, at home or abroad, which she may carry on.* If there should be a war between England and the United States, and our country should be invaded by the English army, we might expect native Hindus and Mohammedans to be a prominent contingent in the invading force. Then, too, India would pay the bill for sending her own troops to our shores. While England has an empire in India, not less than the Roman at its greatest extension, she rules India by Indian troops, and pays them with Indian money. There are but 65,000 British soldiers in India, while the native troops number 135,000.† There were more Sepoys than Europeans at the siege of Arcot and the battles of Plassey and Buxar. This immense Indian empire, which is now made to pay its own bills, was won to England at the very time when she was losing the thirteen American colonies which became the United States. One of her very agents for winning India was Cornwallis, who delivered his sword to Washington, and surrendered the struggle for further possession of the American colonies.

THE POLICE.

The police force of India was systematically organized about 1860. The model is that of Great Britain. Each presidency has its separate establishment, under the control of inspectors-

* Hunter, "England's Work in India," p. 13 ff.

† Seeley, "Expansion of England," pp. 178–191.

general. The total general police force is as follows: Two hundred and sixty district superintendents and their assistants; one thousand and fifty inspectors; two thousand two hundred and fifty sub-inspectors; fourteen thousand head constables; and ninety thousand constables. These are under the charge of six inspectors-general, and twelve assistant inspectors-general. The annual cost of keeping up this system is two million three hundred thousand pounds sterling.

Medical System.

The medical system of India is kept up largely by the general treasury. Hospitals provided by private beneficence are as yet few, but are on the increase. The present medical establishment is the outgrowth of the arrangements made by the old East India Company. Every principal station, or seat of government offices, has a medical officer, with a dispensary and a staff of assistants. Where necessary, there is also a hospital. All persons, Europeans and natives alike, are entitled to the gratuitous use of these provisions. Medical colleges are established by the government in many of the principal cities and towns. But all these arrangements are insufficient for the great needs of the people. The missionary societies are supplementing the efforts of the government in a remarkable degree. But for their aid the sufferings of the women and children would be incalculable.

WATER-VESSEL, COPPER-TINNED, OLD KASHMIR WARE.

CHAPTER X.

THE FEUDAL STATES.

It is an error to suppose that England is ruler of all India. There are certain native states which have never passed under the English crown, and it may be centuries before they will be compelled to do so.

The reasons are many. Among them, and chief of all, is the old friendship of certain native rulers for England. In the long

NARAYAN HITTI, THE PALACE OF THE MAHARAJAH, AND RAJ GURU'S TEMPLE.

conflict in which England was engaged for the conquest of the country there were always native princes who, with their troops, fought under the British flag. The most of the soldiers who fought with Clive at Plassey were native Hindus. Whatever the promises made, the fact remained the same—Clive, Cornwallis, Wellesley, and all the rest were shrewd enough to oppose native troops by native troops. Motives of interest were not wanting. The land had no peace. The many native rulers were at war with each other, and when England proposed to share in the fighting there were natives who rejoiced in the opportunity of help in slaughtering their foes. When Clive conquered he displaced one opposing prince by putting a friendly one, who had helped him to victory, on the throne. From the very beginning of English rule there have been friendly native princes.

England has respected this friendship. The native rulers who have stood firmly to her interests, and have aided her in adjusting her government to the conditions of the country, have never lost their thrones. The attitude towards the government on the part of the native princes, when the mutiny of 1857 broke out, was the most critical feature of the great convulsion. The northern part of India was in hot rebellion. In the south, however,

ENTRANCE GATE TO THE MAHARAJAH'S PALACE, INDORE.

there were friendly princes, who had closer acquaintance with English power and a higher appreciation of English justice. They joined their cause to that of England herself. Had England depended entirely on her own troops, she must have lost her empire. She not only found friendly allies in the south, but some of her bravest soldiers were the native troops which had come to her through her conquests. For example, the Kashmir state and the protected Sikh states furnished some of the bravest and most loyal of all the troops who fought for the suppression of the mutiny.

Of all the native princes who stood firmly beside England in

REIGNING KING, IN COURT DRESS. NEPAL.

the greatest crisis of her Indian history, the Nizam, whose territory bears the name of "The Nizam's Dominions," in the Dekhan, was the most important. His territory is the largest of all the native states. Its area is equal to that of Maine, New Hampshire, Massachusetts, Rhode Island, Connecticut, and Maryland. The Nizam's prime-minister at the time of the mutiny was Sir

ROYAL PALACE, BHATGAON.

Salar Jang. He was wise and of broad view. He held his high office about twenty-five years, and was practically the ruler of the country all the time. He advised the cordial support of England in her struggle against the mutineers. As a result, when the mutiny was overcome the Nizam was more firmly seated on his throne than ever. Had the Nizam and his subjects thrown their influence and the weight of their army on the side of the natives, it is likely that the mutineers would have succeeded, and secured control of the whole country. The loyalty of the Nizam's Dominions was the breakwater against the general tide of rebellion in the north, extending from Delhi in the west to Calcutta in the east.

After the death of the Nizam, and during the minority of his son, the same wise man directed the regency. The son of that Sir Salar Jang is now the prime-minister of the present Nizam. The young Nizam is following closely in his father's footsteps, as a friend not only of England, but of all the progressive movements which have had their origin since the beginning of the English supremacy. Once, while inspecting a list of ready-made appointments, he dealt a severe blow to the native prejudices by saying: "In my opinion, it is my duty and that of my government to protect the right of my people. It is not, however, my desire to select natives of my dominions for employment irrespective of their qualifications. Preference should be given them when they are found to be qualified for positions in the public service, but, in cases where their attainments are not equal to the required standard, the services of outsiders must be procured."*

The liberal policy of the English government towards these native states may be seen in the one fact that, when railroads are built through them the native treasury is not charged with the expense. It is a question, indeed, whether in any department of English administration more wisdom has been shown than in the careful and considerate treatment of the native rulers.

It must not be supposed, however, that England is not watchful of the conduct of all the native princes. She always provides an English Resident, who lives near the native court, and watches every movement. He is the medium of communication between the native government and the British government of India. In Haidarabad, for example, I found the English Resident living in a palatial home, with beautiful and extensive grounds. The business of this English gentleman is to preserve loyal relations on the part of the Nizam's government. Every important movement, not only in Haidarabad, but all over the Nizam's dominions, is watched. The Resident's business is to observe and report. In addition to him there is a great English camp at Sikandarabad, five miles distant. It is the largest body of Brit-

* For an excellent description of the native states of India, see Pearce, "History of India," pp. 227 ff. On the number and magnitude of the native states of India, see Appendix.

A NATIVE PRINCESS AND HER SUITE. NEPAL.

ish troops in Southern India. They, in case of insubordination to the English government, could be on the spot in an hour's time, and quell the uprising instantly. The presence of the English Resident and the proximity of the troops, all of whom are commanded by British officers, furnish a picture of the peculiarly effective and original way which England has found by experience needful to preserve actual control over all the native populations of India.

The native states furnish a certain annual tribute to the British government, and have no share in an outward policy. They exist, and enjoy the illusion of an independent political life. One of the great concerns on the part of the princes has been the right to name a successor in case of the absence of a son. In 1858, however, the English issued a decree by which a native prince can adopt a successor, according to the Hindu or Mohammedan usages. This measure was brought about largely through Lord Canning, who was governor-general at the time.

The native states will diminish, and in time disappear. Some rulers have chosen to give up these merely nominal thrones and receive a pension from the English government. But England is very patient, and so long as no trouble comes she has little to say. She keeps aloof from local strifes, and leaves to her Resident the giving of needful advice, which is generally regarded as final. Nearly all the native princes are in hearty sympathy with Western life. They are fond of making the "grand tour" to England, and learning all about the country which has so strangely extended itself to their native India.

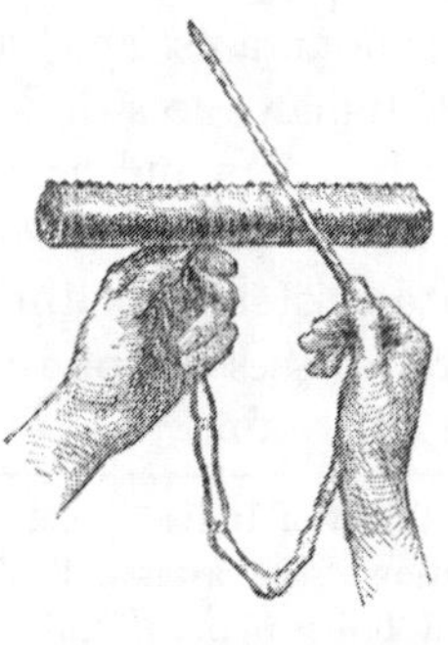

MUSICAL INSTRUMENT USED IN DEMON WORSHIP.

CHAPTER XI.

THE WILD TRIBES OF INDIA.

The wild tribes of India are beginning to come in for their share of European study. They stand in the same relation to the great races of India that the American Indians occupy in relation to their Anglo-Saxon conquerors. They are the first-known occupants of the soil. The Aryan conquerors took possession of all the desirable country, captured the towns and cities, seized upon the arable land, and either made serfs of the conquered foes or drove them off to obscure places. Only a few of the stronger races, by bravery and withdrawal, managed to preserve a separate existence. For example, the Khonds, of the Central Provinces, continued to lead a measure of independent life until A.D. 358, and were first thoroughly subjugated by the Rajputs.* The Bhils, the Kols, the Oraons, the Nagas, and many other fragments of the first-known races of India, now subsisting on unnatural food, and the gross denizens of the jungles and marshes, are but the fragments of tribes, old and numerous, which were strong and fearless when the gifted Aryans came down from the northwestern table-lands, and had the daring, even before their work was complete, to write epics of their achievements. Those early Northern aboriginal tribes—so says the "Rig Veda"—bore the names of Dasyus, Rakshasas, and Asuras, or Pisachas. One chief, for example, Sambara, lived forty years upon the mountains, and ruled over one hundred strong cities. As the Indian races of Mexico, which were conquered by the Spanish invaders under Cortez, were compelled to flee to the mountains and to the more secluded places, and who thus kept up a separate existence for three centuries, so the only safety of the conquered possessors of India lay in withdrawing to the jungle and the mountain.†

* Rowney, "The Wild Tribes of India," pp. 14, 140.

† For a minute enumeration of the castes and tribes in India, see Kitts, "Compendium of the Castes and Tribes found in India." Bombay, 1885.

These tribes, the oldest blood of India, may be grouped as follows:

I.

TRIBES OF THE CENTRAL PROVINCES.

The Khonds.
The Brinjarís.
The Bhowrís.
The Tarímuks.
The Korawars.
The Bhatus.
The Mudikpurs.

II.

TRIBES OF WESTERN INDIA.

The Bhíls.
The Kols.
The Grassias.
The Kattís.
The Kattaurís.

III.

TRIBES OF RAJPUTANA.

The Mairs and Mínas.

IV.

THE DESERT TRIBES.

The Sodas.
The Kaorwas.
The Dhattís.
The Lohannas.
The Rebarris.
The Sehraes.
The Thori.

V.

KOLARIAN AND OTHER RACES IN BENGAL.

The Kols.
The Sontals.
The Oraons.
The Paharís.

VI.

MINOR TRIBES IN BENGAL.

The Karwars.
The Puttuas.
The Sauras.

VII.

TRIBES OF THE MADRAS PRESIDENCY.

The Khonds.
The Todas.
The Eriligaru.
The Karubarus.
The Soligas.
The Niadís.
The Gypsies.

VIII.

THE FRONTIER TRIBES.

The Baluchís.
The Pathans.
The Mizíras.
The Bunnoches.
The Murwatís.
The Afrídís.
The Momunas.
The Sevatís.

IX.

TRIBES OF THE NORTHERN FRONTIER.

The Bhotís.
The Khasias.
The Boksas.
The Tharus.
The Limbus.
The Murmís.
The Vayus.
The Kerantís.
The Lepchas.
The Butíahs.
The Mechís.
The Kochís.

X.

TRIBES OF THE NORTHEASTERN FRONTIER.

The Akhas.
The Duflas.
The Míris.
The Abors.
The Mishmís.
The Khamptís.
The Singphos.
The Nagas.
The Cacharese.
The Míkirs.
The Kukies.
The Cossyas.
The Garos.

XI.

TRIBES OF THE EASTERN FRONTIER.

The Júmias.
The Shindus.
The Khumeas.
The Kus.
The Mrus.
The Khyens.

Between the wild tribes of India and the great fixed Hindu population there are important differences. This might be expected. The tribes have changed but little, except as influenced by slight contact with Europeans, but more especially by the labors of Protestant missionaries. If one wishes to know what kind of people occupied India before the Aryans swept down into the great Gangetic Valley, he has only to visit the naked Hill-men of to-day. The following are among the differences between the wild tribes and the Hindus:

1. The Hindus have division of caste. The aborigines have no caste.

2. The Hindu widows do not remarry; the widows of the aborigines do remarry, mostly taking the younger brothers of their former husbands.

VEDDAH.

3. The Hindus venerate the cow, and abstain from beef; the aborigines feed on all flesh alike.

4. The Hindus abstain from intoxicating drinks; the aborigines delight in them, and even their religious ceremonies are not complete without them.

5. The Hindus prepare their own food, and take only what has been prepared by a higher caste; the aborigines partake of food prepared by any one.

6. The Hindus do not shed blood habitually; but no ceremony of the aborigines is complete without the shedding of blood.

7. The Hindus have a caste of priests; the aborigines select their priests out of those particularly skilled in magic, sorcery, or divination, or in curing diseases.

8. The Hindus burn their dead; the aborigines mostly bury their dead.

9. The Hindu civil institutions are municipal; those of the aborigines are patriarchal.

10. The Hindus have known letters, science, and the art of

writing for more than three thousand years; while the aborigines are now, at least, illiterate.

Among the more advanced of the primitive tribes are the Santals and the Khonds. Many remains of non-Aryan tribes are found in the Anamalai Hills, in the southern part of the presidency of Madras. Among them are the Puliars, the Mundaoers, the Kaders, and the Nairs. In the Central Provinces

THE DASERA, OR ANNUAL SACRIFICIAL FESTIVAL OF THE GURKHA REGIMENTS IN INDIA.

the non-Aryans form an important part of the population. The Khonds are the most important stock. In Orissa there are the Juangs, or Patuas, "leaf-wearers." The Akas live in Assam. The Bhils are the most important race of a large group of non-Aryans living in the mountains separating North from South India. The languages of these wild tribes bear no resemblance to the Sanskrit, which was the language which the Aryans brought with them. Many of the missionary societies have begun work among these rude tribes, and have met with great success. The Gypsies can not be reckoned an aboriginal Indian tribe. But the testimony is strong that they appear early in India, if, indeed, they are not of Indian origin. They first come to light in Indian history among the marshes bordering on the Indus.*

The wild tribes have developed some of the most persistent and bitter violators of the laws. Many of them know very well that their fathers were the original possessors of the soil, and have always cherished the most relentless antipathy to both Hindus and Mohammedans. The Bhils, until made to feel the pressure of English rule, were a fair example of the lawless class. They pursued an original method of operation. They levied a tax on a community, and, unless it was promptly paid, carried out their threat of death or mutilation.† For example, a note was found one day dangling about the neck of a village idol. It had been secretly placed there. It read as follows:

> "From Mohun Naik
>
> To Bhola, Patel of Keepra Kaira.
>
> "The moment you receive this note you must bring rupees 500, which are due to us. If any delay occurs we will put your people to death, cut off their ears and noses, and help ourselves. Let this be well considered."‡

We can well imagine that this was "well considered," and that the demand was promptly complied with.

The conquered race is always at the feet of the conqueror, not only to smart under his lash, but to partake of his vices. The Indians of the American colonies, and later of the United States, became intemperate through the practice of the new-comers of selling them intoxicating liquors. Few vices known to the Anglo-Saxon have been kept aloof from the American Indian. Precisely the same scourge has come to the native races of India. The English have supplied them with "fire water." It is not likely that there is one important hill tribe in all India which has not been placed at the mercy of the liquor-seller or the extortionate money-lender.§

---

* MacRitchie, "The Gypsies of India," pp. 2, 8.

† Rowney, "The Wild Tribes of India," pp. 211, 217, 218.

‡ Ibid., p. 25. § Ibid., p. 211.

CHAPTER XII.

RAILROADS.—CANALS.—TELEGRAPHS.—POSTAL SYSTEM.

The growth of the Indian railway system has been rapid. The first road was begun in 1849, and eight trunk lines have been completed, which unite all parts of the country. The government began the construction by a wise method of guarantee. It was supposed, at the beginning, that, owing to the poverty of the people, the railroad could not be made to pay expenses. But the government saw the necessity of the railway system, not only from a military point of view, but as a means of national development. Accordingly, it was resolved to guarantee a minimum interest, or dividend, on all capital subscribed. With this good offer the capital for all proposed railways was immediately

A BRIDGE OF SHOPS, SRINAGAR (KASHMIR).

taken in England. Only a few natives have taken shares. In 1882, out of a total of 64,321 registered holders of Indian railway shares or stocks, only 317 were natives of India. But the natives are doing the main work. Of the 197,748 persons employed on the working lines in 1884, only 4069 were Europeans, and 4250 were Eurasians, while 189,429 were natives. Within a few years the Indian government has taken even a more direct share in the construction of smaller or branch roads. It is building them at the expense of the state, and pays for the construction out of the current annual revenues.

The railroads of India are of two classes—the Guaranteed and the State Railways. So far as we can safely compute, from the latest statistics, there are now about sixteen thousand miles of railway in India. About twelve hundred miles of new railway are added every year. The authorities of the different roads are about establishing, in the Hill Country, sanitaria for the children of Europeans in the service of the railways.*

Rapid as is the progress of the railway system in India, we see to-day only the crude beginning. The time is rapidly approaching when the entire land will be covered with a network of railway lines, and when a close connection with Europe will be established. The old palanquin is rapidly passing away. In time it will be as rare, except in the Nilgiri Hills and the Himalayas, as in Surrey. The Anglo-Indian will be content with more modern means of locomotion, instead of being borne slowly over the country, and being compelled to listen to such nocturnal strains from unwilling and perspiring palanquin-bearers as the following:

"Oh, what a heavy bag!
No, it's an elephant.
He is an awful weight.
Let's throw his palkee down;
Let's set him in the mud;
Let's leave him to his fate.
No, for he'll be angry then;
Ay, and he will beat us then,
With a thick stick;
Then let's make haste and get along,
Jump along quick!" †

Frequent trains will, in due time, traverse the distance between India and Europe, and instead of there being only a weekly mail, as now, by the Peninsular and Oriental steamers, a train will arrive in India every day, bringing a large number of passengers and the latest mail from the whole Western world.

The present extension of the European system of railroads towards the Indian interior warrants this anticipation. Railroad extensions already in progress, from Russia eastward and from India westward, when completed, will make the interval only a

* Mackenzie, "How India is Governed," p. 51 ff.

† Eden, "India, Historical and Descriptive," p. 115. (Lond. 1876.)

matter of eight hundred and fifty-seven miles, over which a railway can be built at a cost of less than four million pounds sterling. Marvin says that the present indications are that the gap will very soon be only two hundred miles; that already some of the gates of Herat are in the Postal Union, and that a letter can be sent by the Russian ambassador from London to Alikhanoff at Pul-i-khisti for a penny.*

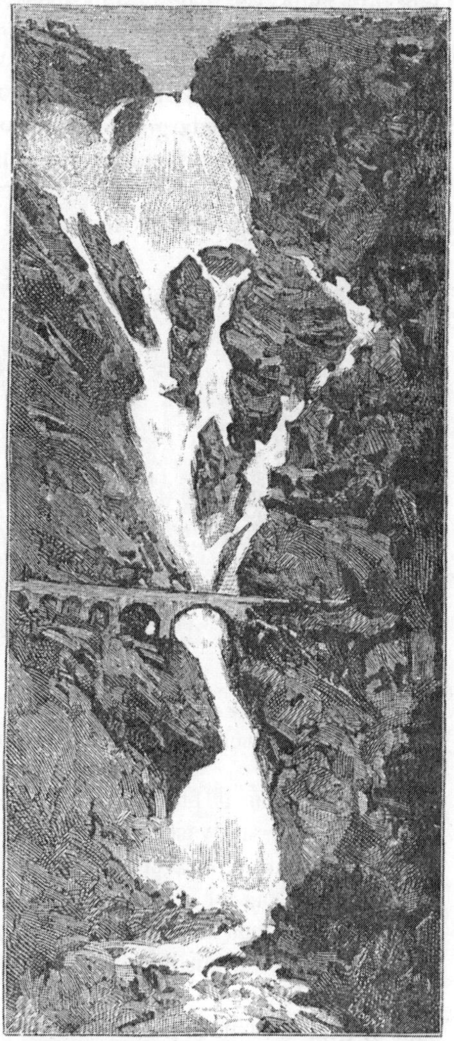

"THE OCEAN OF MILK" WATERFALL AND THE RAILWAY VIADUCT, ON THE WEST-OF-INDIA PORTUGUESE RAILWAY.

With a fair allowance made for detentions arising from the collision of English and Russian interests, it can hardly be more than eight years before the line will be unbroken between Calais and Calcutta, and that the Governor-General of India will receive his mail eight days after leaving the London post-office.

The government has been equally attentive to the construction of canals. During the supremacy of the native rulers as much was done for irrigation as could have been expected of men whose chief business was warfare. Many of the present canals are made to serve

* "The Russians at the Gates of Herat," Amer. ed., pp. 157 ff.

the double purpose of bearing produce and articles of merchandise and of irrigating the fields. The wells in some villages are sunk for drinking purposes, but the great mass of the tens of thousands of village wells are mainly for irrigation. Irrigation had already been in use, but the present government has developed into larger proportions what it found. It has renovated or enlarged the old works, built new irrigating canals, and overcome difficulties which no preceding government could have surmounted.* The Ganges Canal, which is seven hundred miles long, and catches up half the volume of the water

BARABUIRA LOCK, ON THE KENDRAPARA CANAL.

of the Ganges as it bursts forth from the mountains, and distributes it over the vast region lying between the Jamna and the Ganges, is the greatest irrigating stream in the world.†

In Madras, out of a total of twenty-two millions of arable acres, four millions are artificially irrigated.‡ In the Northwest Provinces, one million five hundred thousand acres are under irrigation, and produce seven hundred and seventy-five thousand tons of grain. This is provision for six millions of people.§ In 1882 there was a total of twelve thousand seven hundred and fifty

* Temple, "India in 1880," p. 248.

† Murdock, "India's Needs," p. 23.

‡ Strachey, "Finances and Public Works of India," p. 177.

§ Ibid., p. 179.

CROSSING A STREAM.

miles of irrigating ducts throughout the empire. By the present date the number of miles must be about fifteen thousand. In 1880 the acreage under irrigation was six million three hundred and ten thousand. This area is constantly increasing. Since 1823 the amount of money expended by the government for canals has reached twenty millions of pounds sterling.* The revenue arising from all the irrigating works amounts to five per cent. on the capital invested.†

The telegraph system is keeping up with the railway. All the larger places are connected by telegraph. The government owns all the lines, except those in possession of the railroads, which

* Smith, "Student's Geography of British India," p. 34.

† Buckley, "The Irrigating Works of India," p. 189.

also open their wires to the public for use along their own lines. The usual rate for messages is high—two shillings for every six words. The annual expenditure on the Indian telegraph establishment is about five hundred thousand pounds sterling, and the average receipts about three hundred and fifty thousand pounds sterling. This leaves an annual deficit of one hundred and fifty thousand pounds sterling as an annual charge on the imperial revenues.*

The postal system is as nearly perfect as anywhere in the world. It is a rare thing for a letter to be lost. A merchant of Calcutta, having a large correspondence, told me that for promptness and faithfulness in delivery no praise was too high. My letters from Europe and America followed me from place to place, and were often so marked by frequent changes at post-offices that the address was nearly illegible.

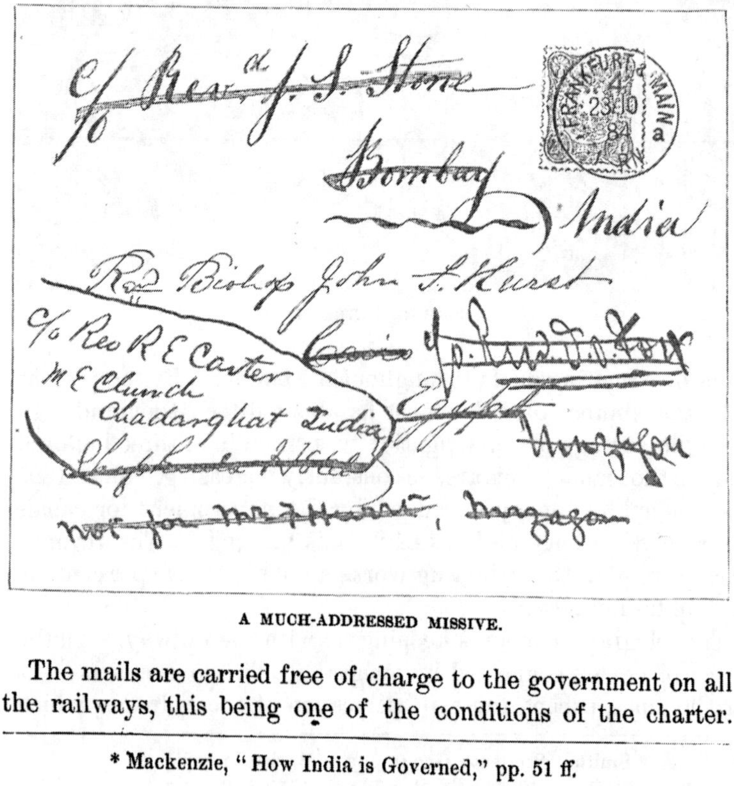

A MUCH-ADDRESSED MISSIVE.

The mails are carried free of charge to the government on all the railways, this being one of the conditions of the charter.

* Mackenzie, "How India is Governed," pp. 51 ff.

The annual expenditure for the postal department is about one million pounds sterling. The annual deficiency in meeting this sum is about one hundred thousand pounds sterling.

A PUZZLING POSTAL-CARD.

CHAPTER XIII.

THE PARSIS OF INDIA.

MY first view of the Parsis was on the steamer *Sutlej*. A number of them took passage at Aden for Bombay. A portion of the forward deck was assigned to them, where they spread out their bedding every night, and gathered it up in the morning. They were well clad, intelligent, affable, communicative, and of fine features. I observed that their more prominent buttons were of solid gold, and, singularly enough, were the smaller gold coins used in the United States. I had several conversations with these Parsis, when our subject was generally their religious opinions.

This contact with only a few members of this strange community made me fully prepared for a larger view of the great Parsi population of Bombay. Every day my admiration for this people, saving only their false religion, increased.

Throughout India there are probably 80,000 Parsis. Of these about 70,000 live in the presidency of Bombay alone, and 50,000 of these live in the city of Bombay. They form a class by themselves, separated socially from both the Christian and Hindu populations, and thoroughly independent of all other classes.

Why are these Persians in India? The question will strike any studious stranger frequently, as he sees the important place which the Parsi community occupies in the commerce and general advance of the country. Yet the proper answer lies far back in the past of both India and Persia.

The Parsis are the descendants of the Persians who were driven out of their own country, in the eighth century, by the Mohammedan conquerors. Khalif Omar was the first Mohammedan chief to invade Persia. He was victorious, and dealt destruction on every hand. Violent persecutions were organized against the conquered people, who fled before their cruel masters. They reached the mountain region of Khurasan, or the outlying deserts, and remained about a century. But here, too, they were persecuted. Some, however, continued to occupy Yezd and Kirman, where they still linger in a wretched condition of ignorance and poverty.* Professor Westergaard, of Copenhagen, visited this poor Parsi community in 1843, and found the majority in a wretched state, oppressed and unfairly taxed by the Persian government. No complete copy of the Zend Avesta existed among them, though there were a great many copies of the Khorda-Avesta, and a few of the Vendidad and Yasna. These Persians have no opportunity to rise above the lowest life, and, in order to support themselves even scantily, become gardeners.

A large number of the conquered Persians, however, instead of fleeing to the mountains and desert, took refuge in the island of Ormus, at the entrance of the Persian Gulf. But there was no peace even in this retired place. They finally succeeded in getting a few boats, and, embarking on them, set sail for the Indian coast. They could have remained in Persia, had they been willing to adopt the Mohammedan faith. But the religion of Zoroaster had too strong a hold on them. They would not sacrifice one of its tenets. They preferred exile to another religion. In India they were cautiously received by the Hindu prince Jadi Rana. From this little colony has sprung the wealthy and strong Parsi population of India.†

This was in the year 716. The prince was afterwards favorably impressed by their appearance, and gave them full liberty to reside and practise their religion in his province of Sanjan. They enjoyed three centuries of quiet, during which time they were reinforced throughout the Gujerát region. When the Mohammedans from Persia, in their march of conquest, finally reached India, and set up the great Mogul empire in the valleys of the Ganges and the Indus, the Parsis were again in great danger. They feared the cruelty of the same hand which had conquered them at home, and had made them exiles forever from their native country. They allied themselves with the

---

* Monier Williams, article in *Nineteenth Century*, March, 1881 (American edition).

† The best sources of information concerning the Parsis are the "Essays" of Monier Williams; Haug, "Essays on the Sacred Language, Writings, and Religion of the Parsis" (London, 1878); and Karaka, "History of the Parsis," 2 vols. (London, 1884).

Hindu chiefs, and yet both Hindu and Parsi were conquered, and, as a political and military force, went down beneath the all-powerful Mogul chiefs. But they scattered, led quiet lives, engaged in commerce, and were permitted to preserve their faith. So soon as the English came to Western India the Parsis hailed them as the hope of the country. From that day to this they have admired the English rule in India, and have been its warmest supporters in all the dangers which have threatened the hold of Britain on her Indian possessions.

BRASS ORNAMENTAL CHAINS, MODERN GUJERÁT.

That the Parsis have been an important factor in the development of the country during the last two centuries is owing entirely to the coming of Europeans. Their relation to this new element was at once prompt, close, and valuable. No sooner did people from Portugal, France, and England arrive than they saw the wealth of the Parsis, their capacity for business, and their perfect reliability in all commercial matters. The wealthy region of Surat early invited trading companies; and as this was the original home of the Parsi immigrants, these companies from Europe entered into relations with them, and thus each party derived great advantages from the other. This was the beginning of the amazing commercial prosperity of the Parsis. While employed by the companies from Europe they laid the foundations for their own strong future in India. All the factories represented by foreign nations in Surat employed Parsis as their chief brokers, and could not have carried on their great operations without them. They were able to accommodate differences between the companies and the native rulers which otherwise would have proved fatally disastrous. In 1660, for example, Rastam Manak, the chief broker of the English factory in Surat, by a personal audience with the Mogul emperor Aurangzeb, at his palace in Delhi, not only caused the removal of obstacles which the Hindu nobles were now placing in the way of the English, but secured a gift of land for building a factory and the freedom from duty of all imported goods.

The large settlement of Parsis in Bombay occurred just before the King of Portugal gave the island to the English as a marriage dowry to Catharine, the bride of Charles II. of England. From this time they enjoyed a new and broader life. They now had their first open field in India, on a perfect equality with the people of all other nations. While loyal to the country as an English possession, their future depended less upon any political relations than upon their capacity in commerce. Here has been the department to which they have steadily adhered for two centuries, and to-day they stand at the head of the business of Bombay, and have the profound respect of every class.

The Parsis have their sects—the Shenshais and the Kadmis. The former are in the majority. This division arose about one hundred and fifty years ago, when a Persian priest named Jamasp arrived in India, and found that his co-religionists differed from their brethren of Iran in their calculation of time by a full month, and in other minor points relating to their "liturgy." Serious disputes arose in consequence, which ended in the formation of the two sects—the Shenshais adhering to their own views, and the Kadmis adopting the opinions imported by Jamasp—and thus agreeing with their Persian brethren. The difference lies in their computation of time and in some slight variations in the forms of prayer.*

One can easily recognize the Parsi wherever he meets him. He uses a dress different from his ancestors in Persia. His is a half-way costume between the Hindu and the European. He wears a loose garment of cotton, flannel, or silk, extending from his neck to a few inches below his knees. Many are now wearing light trousers—a late innovation. The round, dark, high hat, rising like a small cylinder, but without brim, is the head-covering of the men. The ladies dress very becomingly, and are distinguished for their jewels and rich robes. They differ entirely from the Mohammedan and Hindu women in the high and honorable estimate which the Parsi men place upon them. They, with their children, often accompany their husbands in afternoon drives out on the Malabar Hill and in other directions. Their equipages are richly appointed. One sees, also, many of the ladies driving out on afternoons along the Queen's Road, with as much style as though their spirited horses were whirling them through Hyde Park. The ladies wear a loose robe, and do not cover the head. With them, not less than with the men, the tendency is towards the adoption of European dress. They are getting to take their meals sitting in chairs instead of, as formerly, upon the floor. The household usages are gradually conforming to those of the English. They are very fond of many lights at home, and their rooms are hung with so many lamps that, at night, one can always distinguish the Parsi house.

The most notable features of the Parsi population of Bombay are their rise to great wealth, their present control of the internal commerce of the country, and their vast trade with China and Japan. Frequently, when a Parsi has risen to eminence and wealth, his son has continued his business with equal success, and entered upon all the official dignities of the father. Many prominent families, such as the Patels, the Benajis, the Modis, the Kamas, and the three brothers of the "Readymoney" family, have become synonyms for commercial success and probity. Many of them trace their origin far back to their first days in India, when their fathers were fugitives from Mohammedan

* "Journal Royal Asiatic Society," No. VIII.; "Indian Calendar for the Year 1872," pp. 46, 47.

A PARSI OF BOMBAY.

oppressors; and some of them make a leap still further back, into Persia, their original home. In originating an important trade with the farther Asiatic ports, in ship-building, in railroad contracts, in the new and now immense cotton trade, and in supplying the army with provisions, they have not only given satisfaction to all classes, but have placed themselves in the first rank of the merchant princes of India.

Their benevolence has been commensurate with their growth in wealth. There is nothing which a Parsi more enjoys than giving freely to a needy cause. His heart seems to be in his hand. He is touched by an appeal to his sympathy, and rich and poor alike give freely, according to their ability. Some of the largest and most beautiful charities and educational institutions of Bombay have been established by them as direct gifts to the country. The Benevolent Institution, founded by Sir Jamshidji Jijibhai, consists of a group of male and female schools. This gentleman was the first Parsi baronet created by England, in recognition of his many benevolences and his sterling character. The Alexandra College, for Parsi ladies, was established by Manikji Khurshidji. Many of the studies pursued in European schools are in the curriculum. When one sees such an institution as this, with all the appliances of an English educational establishment, it cannot be surprising that the higher Parsi classes should be rapidly adopting European ideas and usages.

Vikaj Merji raised, at great expense, a dam across the Banganga River, with other similar works, to shut out the salt-water tides, and thus make a large district in the Bombay presidency productive, because of the irrigation now first made possible. Mr. Dinsha, said to be the wealthiest Parsi in Bombay, has established many charities among his own people, and also in the general interests of the country. In 1883 he donated a hospital for the treatment and cure of horses, placing it under the charge of the Society for the Prevention of Cruelty to Animals. He has also established charitable dispensaries in Bombay and several places in Gujerát; caused wells and tanks to be dug in Puna, Ahmadnagar, and other places; founded charitable schools, libraries, book-clubs; provided means for poor students to receive a liberal education; and built a hospital for lepers in Ratnigiri. Sir Kavasji Jahangir Readymoney made it his special duty to alleviate the sufferings of the poor. Hospitals, lunatic asylums, dispensaries, the great building of the Elphinstone College, University Hall, and the Puna Engineering College are only a few monuments to his princely liberality. Mr. Khurshidji repaired and extended the Chaupati asylum for the aged and blind; established free dispensaries in Bombay and other places; erected the Industrial School at Surat; and built one of the handsomest ornaments to Bombay—the Flora Fountain.

One of the most beautiful of the charities of Bombay is its sanitarium for the poorer Parsis, founded in the suburb of Colaba by Mervanji Panday. I took special pains to visit this remarkable institution one evening, as the setting sun found me far out on the Colaba Point, where the spray dashes wildly up into one's face, and the sea breeze is constant the year round. My friend said: "Now let us stop, I want to show you something."

We then entered a large building. It was divided into small rooms, but to each was attached a section of the broad veranda, which extends around the entire building. There was a brightness and airiness about the rooms, and surrounding the building, that made the premises exceedingly attractive. It was an institution for convalescents, founded by a Parsi. Whenever an invalid is declared able to be removed, he can be taken to this place, which is directly upon the sea, and where the air is always fresh and invigorating. No provisions are taken. But the invalid can take with him his entire family, and establish himself there, and the domestic group can live as cheaply as their taste or necessities require. There is no embarrassment whatever. I saw some invalids, and watched their children playing about them, and could detect in the appearance of the family the pressure of a life of poverty. It is certainly a generous impulse which gives this home by the sea to the sick among the poor of Bombay.

One of the most remarkable features of the charity of the Parsis is, that as a rule it takes place during life. If done by bequest it is the exception. The Parsi wants to see the growth of his work. He measures his benefactions by the rule of his business. He looks for development, and when an emergency arises he wants to meet it, and wishes to see perfect security before the vultures tear his spent body to pieces. I have never seen such extensive charities grouped within so narrow a compass as among these Parsis of Bombay. There seems to be no limit to their humane plans. The example has been set, and there is no probability that there will be decline in this magnificent spirit.

One must admit that the inscriptions on the benevolent institutions, such as buildings and fountains, are very lavish in praise of the donors. Many words are employed, far more than a more quiet Western taste would admit. Moreover, I have been told that much of this benefaction comes from a love of admiration, and possibly from an eye to business. But I am not here speaking of motives. One must approve the results, whatever be the impulses. Even supposing the causes somewhat selfish, is it not better to found a school or asylum for the poor, or some other humane institution, from an imperfect motive than not to do the good work at all?

But the charity of the natives of India is by no means confined to the Parsis. The native Hindus and Mohammedans are sure, on acquiring a fortune, to give away part of it to objects of charity or public usefulness. All the cities, and the very roadsides in the rural regions, furnish beautiful memorials of the spirit of charity among the natives of India.*

The Parsis, perhaps largely as an outgrowth of their attention to education, have exhibited a great fondness for literature. Some of this community have distinguished themselves as authors, and their works have received foreign recognition. The Rahmunai Mazdayasnan Sabha, or Religious Reform Association, consists of a body of men who aim to elevate the social life of this community, and to restore some of the forgotten features of the system of Zoroaster, by the publication of works throwing light on the early history and doctrines of the Parsis. Their first issue was Sorabji Shapurji's work on the "Origin and History of the Zend-Avesta," which has been followed by many others, all thoroughly scholarly works, and almost our sole source of information on many accessories of the Parsi history and doctrines. Dastur Peshotanji has published a Pahlavi grammar and other important works. In this ancient language lie buried some of the greatest Persian literary treasures, and it is no wonder that Parsi scholars are endeavoring to bring them out of their long obscurity. The Pahlavi was the ruling Persian tongue during the Sassanian dynasty. Dastur Jamaspji has issued four

* Temple, "India in 1880," p. 128.

volumes of his Pahlavi Dictionary. Dastur Hoshangji Jamaspji has given to the public the texts of an old Zend Pahlavi Glossary, an old Pahlavi Pazand Glossary, and the Arda-Virofi-Nama. To Ervad Kavasji Kanga we owe Gujeráti translations of the Vendidad, the Khorda-Avesta, and even an English translation of Anquetil du Perron's account of his visit to India. The most learned Life of Zoroaster in literature has been written by Kharshedji Rastamji Kame. He has founded a periodical, the *Zarthoski Abhyas* (Zoroastrian Studies), which aims to introduce into India the fruits of German scholarship in the line of Oriental subjects.

The *Bombay Times*, now the *Times of India*, and the best paper in the western part of the country, if not of all India, owes its existence largely to the enterprise of Framji Kavasji. Karaka's History of the Parsis, a work which has been of great service to me in the examination of this strange people, is by far the best account we have of these Indian descendants of the ancient Persians. Some of the Parsi publications appeared in Bombay, but it is not uncommon for them to see the light first in London. Haug, in giving an account of the Zoroastrian studies among the Hindu Parsis of our day, devotes an important section to this description, in which he pays a high tribute to their scholarship and candor.*

The present Parsi faith is the system of Zoroaster. Monotheism lies at its base. Haug says: "The leading idea of his theology was Monotheism; that is, there are not many gods, but only one. The principle of his speculative philosophy was Dualism; that is, the supposition of two primeval causes of the real world and of the intellectual. His normal philosophy moved in the triad of thought, word, and deed." This idea is confirmed by the realistic statement of Herodotus: "The Persians have no images of the gods, nor temples, nor altars, and consider the use of them a sign of folly. This comes, I think, from their not believing the gods to have the same nature with men." All the Parsi writers are emphatic on this point of Monotheism. They claim that, before the appearance of Zoroaster, there were tendencies among his people to idolatry, but that the entire effort of

* "Studies in the Sacred Language, Writings, and Religion of the Parsis," pp. 54–62.

his life was to counteract them. The present Parsis, basing their doctrines on the most ancient writings of their ancestors, believe in the resurrection of the body, future life, immortality of the soul, and rewards and punishments. They reverence the sun, fire, water, and air. They pay such devotion to fire, that, to a stranger, they seem to regard it as a proper object of adoration. But their scholars repudiate the supposition, saying that they only regard fire as a manifestation of Deity. Karaka, speaking for his co-religionists, says: "God, according to the Parsi faith, is the emblem of glory, refulgence, and light; and in this view a Parsi, while engaged in prayer, is directed to stand before the fire, or to turn his face towards the sun, because they appear to be the most proper symbols of the Almighty." My Parsi fellow-voyagers, on the steamer *Sutlej*, performed their morning devotions at sunrise, and always took care to turn their faces to the east when making them. One cannot see the minute attention of any Parsi to fire, and his keeping the sacred flame always burning in his temples and home, without firmly believing that the regard for fire amounts to devotion. It seems to be, in their sense, an original divinity rather than a simple emanation.

The Zend-Avesta is the prime source of the Parsi theology and moral system. It abounds in monstrosities, and to sift them is no easy task. Mitchell has done this successfully,* though his work has not the scholarly completeness of the very important work of Haug,† to whom European scholars are most indebted for a survey of the whole range of the Parsi sacred books. Mitchell says that we can find in the Zend-Avesta all three systems—Monotheism, Dualism, and Polytheism. Every thing good in creation is, by its precepts, held to be worthy of worship. The following prayer, offered on the last day of the month by the devout Parsis, certainly favors the largest idea of the plurality of gods: "We sacrifice to the eternal and luminous space. We sacrifice to the bright garonma (heaven). We sacrifice to the sovereign place of the eternal weal. We sacrifice to the Chinvat bridge, made by Mazda. We sacrifice to Apam Napat, the swift-horsed, the high and shining lord, who has many wives. We sacrifice to the water made by Mazda, and

---

* "The Zend-Avesta and Religion of the Parsis." London, n. d.

† "Essays on the Parsis." London, 1878.

holy. We sacrifice to the golden stall, homa. We sacrifice to the enlivening homa, who keeps death far away. We sacrifice to the pious and good Blessing. We sacrifice to the awful, powerful, and wise god. We sacrifice to all the holy gods of the heavenly world. I praise, I invoke, I meditate on; and we sacrifice to the good, the strong, the beneficent Fravashis of the holy ones."

In the Parsi theology there are spirits good and evil, who fill all space. The water expressed from the homa plant is the chief article of sacrifice. The ancient Persians sacrificed animals. Herodotus says that Xerxes sacrificed on the site of Troy "a thousand oxen, while the Magi poured out libations in honor of the ancient heroes." * But all animal sacrifices have long since ceased. The ceremony of offering the homa is performed not only in the fire-temples of the present Parsis, but in their private houses, twice a day. Great attention is paid to bodily purity. Ablutions are frequent. The touching of a dead body is regarded as especially defiling. The moment life is extinct the body is supposed to be possessed by the fiend Nasu, who can be expelled only by bringing up a white dog. The dog immediately sends the demon back to hell. Each day of the month is consecrated to a special divinity, and has its own formal prayers.

The Zend-Avesta has some good teachings, which contrast strongly with other Oriental faiths. For example, it ascribes no immoral acts to the object of worship; sanctions no immoral acts as part of its worship; none of its worship is marked by cruel acts; it exhorts its believers to contend against all productions of the evil principle; and declares its faith in the final triumph of the good over the evil. On the other hand, in the Zend-Avesta there is no idea of the fatherhood of God, of the heinousness of sin, of expiation, of salvation from sin, of guilt consequent upon sin, of divine comfort in sorrow, of the divine purpose in bereavement, and of self-denial and self-sacrifice.

In the religion of Zoroaster there is large place given to the dog. The Avesta devotes a whole division to a description of his excellences, and the light in which he is placed leads inevitably to the conclusion that the dog is, in the Parsi mind, a sacred animal. During the recitation of the funeral address the

* Book vii., p. 43.

face of the deceased is exposed three or four times to a dog's gaze. In some mysterious way, this animal is supposed to be a guide to the departed to the final heaven, and to guard against the approach of evil spirits on the way thither. Haug says: "A man who touches a dead body, the contagious impurity of which has not been previously checked by holding towards the corpse a peculiar kind of dog, is said to be at once visited by a spectre representing death itself; this is called 'drukhsh nasush,' or the destructive corruption. . . . It is called the 'four-eyed-dog,' a yellow spot on each side of its eyelids being considered an additional eye. He has yellow ears, and the color of the rest of his body varies from yellow to white. To his eyes a kind of magnetic influence is ascribed."

A PARSI CHILD.

The Avesta assigns special sanctity to the house-dog and the shepherd's dog: "To kill one of either is a crime of grossest character. Sweetness and fatness will never return to the place where it has been committed until the murderer has been smitten to death, and the holy soul of the dog has been offered a sacrifice for three days and nights, with fire blazing, with the baresma tied, and the homa uplifted." *

If any Parsi kill a water-dog or otter (udra), he must be unmercifully punished, for the reason that this animal is believed to contain the souls of a thousand male and a thousand female dogs. The perpetrator, to atone for his crime, must receive ten thousand lashes with a horsewhip, or kill ten thousand animals of the bad creation, such as snakes, mice, lizards, or frogs, and carry ten thousand loads of wood to the sacred fire.

Next to their splendid homes and the large public buildings

* Vaud, xiii., pp. 167, 172.

which the Parsis have built and given to Bombay, the Towers of Silence are the most notable reminder of them in the city. They are large circular structures of heavy black granite, in an elevated part of the suburban city. Here all the Parsi dead are disposed of. There are five of these towers, standing in a group on a hill a hundred feet high, and rising above the palms and cypresses which grow in beautiful stateliness about them. The better way is to take them on returning from the drive out to Malabar Hill. The carriage-way is magnificent, built at the expense of a Parsi, Sir Jamshidji Jijibhai, who also donated one hundred thousand square yards of land on the north and east sides of the towers. The view becomes wondrously beautiful as one ascends, for it embraces the great sea-front of Bombay and the suburbs on either horn of the brilliant crescent. On reaching the end of the drive you ascend a flight of eighty steps, where there is a notice—"None but Parsis may enter." But the Parsi secretary gave me a permit, which allowed me to walk at leisure about the beautiful grounds and among the flowers, and take one of the many convenient seats, where the marvellous view can be enjoyed without disturbance. But no permit allows one to enter either of the towers. Not even a Parsi can do it. He would be defiled without hope of purification. The entrance of a bier is a frequent occurrence. I did not see one, and therefore must trust to Eastwick's description: "A bier will be seen carried up the steps by four Nasr Salars, or carriers of the dead, with two bearded men following them closely, and perhaps a hundred Parsis in white robes walking two and two in procession. The bearded men, who come next to the corpse, are the only persons who enter the tower. They wear gloves, and when they touch the bones it is with tongs. On leaving the tower, after depositing the corpse on the grating within, they proceed to the purifying place, where they wash, and leave the clothes they have worn in a tower built for that express purpose."*

The body is borne up a flight of steps into the opening leading into the mysterious interior of the tower. I was shown a model of a tower, by which I could see the internal construction, although I was not permitted to examine a real one. The largest tower is two hundred and seventy-six feet in circumference

---

* "Hand-book of the Bombay Presidency," pp. 141, 142.

and twenty-six feet above the ground. There are three series of fluted grooves, which constitute the stone flooring of the tower. They diminish in size as they approach the centre. The outer circle is for the bodies of men; the second is for those of women; and the third, being smallest, is for the bodies of children. The descent towards the centre of the tower is gradual, and the grooves where the bodies are laid conduct the water to the centre, which is a great circular pit or well. Just as soon as a body is laid in the tower the bearers return, and the many vultures, which are always flying about or resting in the trees, in expectancy of a feast, pounce down upon it and tear the flesh rapidly from the bones. There are from five hundred to a thousand of these vultures, and the human body is their chief food.

PARSI TOWERS OF SILENCE.

They strip a body in about an hour, so that nothing is left but the skeleton. After the bones are completely dried beneath the tropical sun the carriers go in, and with tongs take them to the pit in the centre, and cast them down. There they soon decompose, a process probably hastened by strong chemicals. From the bottom of the pit there are pipes which connect with deep outstanding wells, which are underlaid with thick strata of charcoal. Through this bed the water finds its way, purified, into channels leading out into the sea.

This method of disposing of the bodies of the dead is a fundamental part of the Parsi faith. That vultures should destroy the lifeless body has been from time immemorial a usage, and no Parsi would think of burial or cremation. The reasons which are given by the community for their method were once presented to Monier Williams, who, when visiting the Bombay Towers of Silence, asked Nasarvanji Bairaniji, a high ecclesiastical officer, why such a method of destroying the body was resorted to and adhered to with such fidelity. He received the following reply: "Our prophet Zoroaster, who lived three thousand years ago, taught us to regard the elements as symbols of the Deity. Earth, fire, water, he said, ought never, under any circumstances, to be defiled by contact with putrefying flesh. Naked, he said, we came into the world, and naked we ought to leave it. But the decaying particles of our bodies should be dissipated as rapidly as possible, and in such a way that neither Mother Earth nor the beings she supports should be contaminated in the slightest degree.' In fact, our prophet was the greatest of health-officers, and, following his sanitary laws, we build our towers on the hills, above all human habitations. We spare no expense in constructing them of the hardest materials, and we expose our putrescent bodies in open stone receptacles, resting on fourteen feet of solid granite, not necessarily to be consumed by vultures, but to be dissipated in the speediest possible manner, and without the possibility of polluting the earth or contaminating a single living being dwelling thereon. God, indeed, sends the vultures, and, as a matter of fact, these birds do their appointed work much more expeditiously than millions of insects would do if we committed our bodies to the ground. In a sanitary point of view, nothing could be more perfect than our plan. Even the rainwater which washes our skeletons is conducted by channels into purifying charcoal. Here in these five towers rest the bones of all the Parsis that have lived in Bombay for the last two hundred years. We form a united body in life, and are united in death."

Of the effect of this communication on Professor Williams, and the impression derived from a second visit to the towers, in the same year, 1876, he gives the following testimony: "My second visit has confirmed me in my opinion that the Parsi method of disposing of dead bodies is as perfect as anything can be in a sanitary point of view. There is no spot in Bombay where the breezes appear so healthful as in the beautiful gardens which surround the towers. Nothing during all my travels throughout India, from Cashmere to Cape Comorin, has instructed me more than my two visits to the Parsi Towers of Silence."

This may be quite true, and yet it is hard to forget the loathsome scene of hungry vultures ready to swoop down upon the body of a dead person the moment it has been left alone in the Silent Tower, and glutting themselves upon such prey. I have brought home from India the memory of these hungry and waiting vultures as one of the most repulsive pictures which I ever gazed upon. One cannot help thinking of such an unpleasant scene, with all its associations, much longer than of the beautiful gardens in which the Towers of Silence stand, and the rare and varied scene of the city and the sea and its outlying emerald islands.

There is nothing of which the typical Parsi is prouder, next to the creed he gets from Zoroaster, than of his historical traditions. He loves to think of his old kings, Cyrus, Cambyses, Darius, and all the rest, when the world quaked beneath their armies. He remembers with peculiar joy the time when Persia's eye dared to look upon even Europe as a fit field for conquest, and that his own Xerxes fought the Greeks in the Bay of Salamis and within sight of Athens. His favorite study, as we have seen, deals with the past. His people, though exiles, regard themselves as the banished descendants of a race of warriors and heroes, who made immortal many a battle-field of old Persia and of the lands she had the prowess to invade. Even after defeat by the Mohammedans their fathers were not willing to die without a struggle, and Moore tells only the simple truth when he says of them, when only a shattered army,

> "But none, of all who owned the chief's command,
> Rushed to that battle-field with bolder hand
> Or sterner hate than Iran's outlawed men,
> Her worshippers of fire."

That the Parsis of to-day, now that the light of science is breaking upon them, should be making inquiries into the genesis of their faith and the almost lost threads of their history, is a most significant fact. They have found many things to astonish them. The old Pahlavi literature has revealed to them many doctrinal crudities which the better minds would gladly ignore as authority on worship and creed, and which are deviations from the severer code of Zoroaster. But these candid inquiries can only result in good. They will suggest the striking contrast between the conglomerate Parsi religion and Christianity, while the contact with European Christians will constantly lessen the prejudice against the Christian religion, and make the Parsis more accessible to the Gospel. In the plane of moral ideas, they stand so far above the Hindus that we must regard them as occupying a midway position between Christianity and Buddhism.

We cannot but believe that the Parsi, as he studies more closely the differences between his own faith and the Christian, will, in due time, come to accept the latter. It must be admitted, however, that the Parsis have proven very inaccessible to the Gospel. It is said, that of all the Christians in the presidency of Bombay, not more than a dozen are from the Parsi community. But Mitchell, who has studied the prevailing tendencies among the people during his residence in Bombay, has a hopeful view of their Christian future. He says: "The immense disparity between Christ and Zoroaster is dawning, we believe, on that interesting people, the Parsis of India. They have been clinging to their ancient faith from a feeling of nationality rather than of religion—from tradition more than conviction; but immense changes are certainly at hand. But we believe that, as the Magi from the East, who probably were Zoroastrians, hastened to lay their gold, frankincense, and myrrh at the feet of the new-born Redeemer, so, ere long, the Parsis will in all probability be the first of Eastern races to take upon them, as a race, the easy yoke of Christ."

CHAPTER XIV.

A SAIL TO THE CAVE-TEMPLES OF ELEPHANTA.

THE most charming excursion from Bombay is the sail to the island of Elephanta. The gliding out of Bombay harbor, past the shipping, and in full view of the many picturesque islands which lie out in the mouth of the bay, is an experience at once delightful and novel. The semi-circular mountain-range forming

ENTRANCE TO THE CAVES OF ELEPHANTA.

the magnificent background of Bombay appears altogether different from what it seemed when seen from the deck of the incoming steamer. Our little steam-launch, provided by my thoughtful host, Mr. Fido, made rapid way through the shipping, and in due time brought us out into the sweep of the Indian Ocean. We soon finished our six miles to Elephanta, and were ready to drop anchor. Then we entered small boats, and drew up to the long, narrow pier by which the visitor makes his landing on the island. Here we were met by a group of boys, offering for sale some hanging-birds' nests, petrifactions, little marine curios, and other articles gathered on the island and about its shore. My investments on this occasion were confined to the hanging-birds' nests. On leaving the pier we ascended a flight of one hundred and eighteen steps. Then our path went through a shaded way. After a walk of a quarter of a mile we reached the bungalow of the superintendent of the caves, who is a retired English officer. He was very courteous, went with us to the temples, and took with him his drawings of the reliefs, together with an excellent book on the history of the caves. Here I heard my first narrative of the Indian snakes. The predecessor of the present superintendent, likewise an Englishman, was one day sleeping in his chair, beneath the shade of the palms near the bungalow. His hand was hanging from the arm of his chair, and must have been near the ground. A cobra crawled along, and bit the hand. The sting caused the man's death in a few hours.

The first view of the vast cave-temples is a most pleasing surprise. The great portal bursts suddenly upon the eye. The vegetation, which is as luxuriant as in Ceylon, crowds from the hills down to the edge of the temples. Shrubs and vines in great profusion hang over the entrance, and surround it on all sides with a rich and varied drapery. There is, first of all, the great façade to the main temple. It is supported by two immense pillars and two pilasters. These make three entrances to the temple. The great temple itself is one hundred and thirty feet long, and one hundred and twenty-eight feet broad. On either side there is a large chapel. The temple proper has immense supporting columns, twenty-six in all, with sixteen pilasters. The temple, and even the columns and statues, are cut out of the solid native mass of porphyry.

A peculiarity of every part of the structure is the variety of the architecture. The columns vary in size, ornamentation, and separating distances. Even the height differs slightly, the distance from the ceiling to the roof ranging from fifteen feet to

THE CAVES OF ELEPHANTA.

seventeen and a half feet. Some of the pillars are fluted and others square, and many are surrounded by ornamental fillets. The capitals are overhung with graceful leaves. The pillars are connected by beams, which give unity to the whole interior. In addition to the main temple and the supporting pillars, there are two smaller rooms, probably designed to contain the utensils and other belongings of the service.

These immense spaces in the solid rock are the real wonder of the caves of Elephanta. The sculptures form remarkable reliefs upon the walls. All the figures are of colossal size. The day when they were hewn by many hands, in the remote times, was one for great objects. Only the gigantic and preternatural were aimed at.

The cave-temples of Elephanta, Karli, Ellora, and other places did not proceed from one common religious movement, nor did they take their origin in the same period. The Indian cave-temples belong to two classes—Buddhist and Brahmanical. Those of Elephanta were tributes to the Brahmanical worship. Around one chapel, on the outside, are figures of doorkeepers, resting on dwarfs, a picture of high-caste Hindus trampling upon the low-caste. The principal mural figure is the three-faced image of the Hindu triad. It is only a bust, and yet is nineteen feet high. It represents the original Hindu divinity, in his three personal characters, as Brahma, Vishnu, and Siva. These three are manifestations of Brahm in his relation to man and the world. The central face, with an exquisitely carved jewel on the breast, represents Brahma as the creative principle. That on the right, as one stands in front of the colossal bust, represents Vishnu, the preserver of life, holding in his right hand, as a fit emblem, the lotus in full flower. The face on the left is that of Rudra, or the destroyer. He is quietly smiling on the cobra di capello which winds around his arm and is looking savagely upon his face. There are two figures at the portals here, both of them over twelve feet high. They represent doorkeepers.

VISHNU.

In another compartment, on the left of the three-headed Siva, are figures of Siva and his wife Parvati. All these are of gigantic size, and illustrate the sacred mysteries of the Brahmanical faith, such as the marriage of Siva and Parvati; the birth of Ganesh, the eldest son of Siva; Ravan, the demon king of Ceylon, attempting to remove Kailas, the heavenly hill, to his own kingdom; the destruction of the sacrifice of Daksha, the son of Brahma, born from the latter's thumb; Bhairava, an incarnation of Siva, to oppose Vishnu's incarnation as Narsingh, the man-lion; and, last of all, Siva as an ascetic.

A CHAPEL IN THE GREAT CAVES OF ELEPHANTA.

These various figures, all of which are carved with great care, have been badly mutilated. Some writers attribute the wanton mutilation to the Portuguese, who, it is claimed, found the temples in perfect condition. But no author, not even the painstaking Wilson, has been able to furnish the proof that the charge is well-founded. The date of these particular excavations is supposed to range between the eighth and twelfth centuries of our era. They form a part of the great aggressive system by which the Brahmans sought to propagate their faith throughout

India. The mould has gathered on the walls here, and in some of the spans of the temple the water has oozed down from the roofs and covered the floor. Even with the powerful rays of the Indian sun to dry it, the water filters through the rock above so fast, and falls to the floor in such quantity that the walking is anything but pleasant.

The ornamentation of some of the figures is most elaborate. In the female statues and reliefs one sees a calmness of feature,

SIVA, THE DESTROYER.

an ease and simplicity of the whole countenance, which make many of them singularly attractive. The ideas which lie back of all are abhorrent in the extreme; but the way in which the sculptor has wrought out his plans is different. He has sought to make these incarnations of the great Siva pleasing to the worshipper, that he might be won to them, and to higher adoration. Before any of the existing Indian temples above ground were made, we may well suppose these great cave-temples were hewn out of the solid rock. If Hindus did the chief work—and there is no doubt they did—they must have had the assistance of

Greeks and Bactrians.* The delicacy of the work shows the steady chisel and trained eye of the Greek, while the figures themselves, and the ideas which they symbolize, belong to the fundamentals of Brahman theology.

No finer picture of the passing away of the old, and the coming in of the new, in India, can be presented than in this scene at Elephanta. Here are immense spaces, cut out by patient hands in the elder days, with all the reliefs and statues which wealth, labor, religious zeal, and the long years could command. Probably the hills in the neighborhood were adorned with other important structures, either beneath them or upon their slopes. But, if so, they have long been overgrown and concealed by the wild vegetation, and especially by the rich creepers which everywhere abound. Possibly there are excavated temples hereabouts whose very existence has not been known to any one for centuries. Our guide, the English superintendent, showed us a remarkable inscription which he had very lately discovered beneath the mould on the ceiling of one of the larger halls.

Niebuhr, in the last century, was the first to take back to Europe the news of the marvels of the strange temples of Elephanta. Since then much light has been thrown on their meaning. But the faith which the excavations and their imagery suggest is in rapid decline. The conquering Christian nation has taken charge of the ruins, and provides a man to exhibit them, as an object of only antiquarian interest. Out in the beautiful roadstead lie the vessels from the many ports of that same nation, stopping here for a time, and then going to Australia or China or Southern Africa, or homeward to the little island which rules at its antipodes. One turns away from such a reminder of a dying creed, with all its savage monstrosities, with hope to the new. That one little Christian chapel, on Grant Road, in Bombay, has richer associations and larger possibilities than all the cave-temples of India.

When we had carefully examined all the antiquities of Elephanta we wandered down towards the water's edge. The ladies of our company had anticipated our wants by bringing a substantial lunch, as there is no provision on the island for the accommodation of strangers. Our provisions were spread out

* Wilson, "Religious Excavations of Western India," p. 12.

beneath the fronds of a friendly palm. Here we were fanned by the gentle breeze from the sea, and had before us the wonderful scene, in the distance, of Bombay, the supporting Ghats in the far background, and, near by, the islands which throng the bay. As the evening drew on we entered our little boats and rowed out to our launch, in which we glided back to Bombay.

LOTA (DRINKING-VESSEL), SILVER INCRUSTATION ON COPPER, TANJOR.

CHAPTER XV.

THE CAVE-TEMPLE OF KARLI.

THE surprises in stone greet the traveller in India on every hand. The farther back the massive temples take us, the purer becomes the faith which they represent. The inevitable tendency of all false faiths is towards a darker depth. I had no suspicion of the strong Indian illustrations until I had seen the temples themselves, in both Northern and Southern India, and studied the times which produced them. The eldest—as well those cut from the mountains as those constructed of quarried stone—prove that the gross and grotesque Hindu paganism of these later days is only a vile lapse from the early and better faiths. There is not an ancient temple in India which does not reveal the fact that the idolatry of to-day is the vile progeny of a once purer and more intellectual religion. The debasement of the modern idolatry beneath that of its ancestry is a picture presented in stone from one end of India to the other. The truth forces itself on the mind, in that country as well as throughout the East, that a false faith is unable to rise a single step, and that it is compelled downward by a law it cannot resist, give it never so many centuries to make the effort.

Of this downward tendency of false faiths the cave-temples, wherever one sees them, are most striking examples. The monks of Albania and other regions between the Adriatic and the Ægean seas dug out many a cell in the early Christian days, and honeycombed great regions, where they spent their lives, and where they were laid away when the monotonous life was over. Then, in Egyptian Thebes, for centuries the great Pharaohs hewed for themselves sepulchres under the mountains, where they and their loved ones could lie as splendidly in death as they had lived along the plain. But India stands alone in converting the mountains into spacious temples. The Hindus have adorned these temples with all the wealth of massive and yet

INTERIOR OF TEMPLE HEWN FROM THE ROCK

careful sculpture which distinguished the Aryans before their gross idolatry.

The Karli cave-temple is of the same general class as those of Elephanta; but it is very different in construction. Not even excepting those of Ajanta and Ellora, it is by far the finest Buddhist cave-temple in the country.* To reach it, one takes the

THE KAILAS—CAVE-TEMPLES OF ELLORA.

train from Bombay and goes nearly a hundred miles eastward, on the general line to Calcutta. The road soon ascends, and the air becomes rarer and more bracing. Many a view from the car window reminds one of the Swiss scenery about Meyringen, while the well-tilled vales suggest as fine fields as ever a patient Hanoverian won from Harz boulders, or the phlegmatic Olden-

* Temple, "India in 1880," p. 28.

burger from Frisian bog. The train makes a long climb, until at last you overlook the broad and picturesque Marhatta region, where Arthur Wellesley won his spurs, and began to find his path towards Waterloo. Up these very mountains he drew his supplies, and awaited his reinforcements before marching on Puna, and adding another dominion to the English sceptre in India.

The town of Khandala stands at the height of the range, and its pure air attracts many of the easier citizens of Bombay to spend the summer. It is a beautiful place, well shaded with palms, and having magnificent roads. From Khandala to the Karli cave-temple we had a ride of five miles on horseback. We had some difficulty about horses. Our message, sent out two days before from Bombay, seemed to have had no result. A halt of a half-hour brought three horses, however, and we were soon in rapid motion. It was not long before we were compelled to leave the carriage-road, and take a path through the fields towards the range of mountains on our left. By the time we were getting accustomed to the meanderings of the road we had to give up our horses and begin climbing in downright earnest.

Now a climb in India, even to see its finest temple-cave, is no small task. Only a month before, in Egypt, I had climbed the pyramid of Cheops, with the help of three propelling and provoking Arabs; but that labor was slight compared with the much shorter climb up to the portal of the Karli cave-temple. It was on a day late in the Indian November, but my white pith helmet, with folds of light cloth coiled about it, and then a double umbrella of gray cloth and white cotton within, were a poor defence against the sun. My genial companions, the Rev. Mr. Fox and the Rev. Mr. Hard, had been long enough in the country to endure almost any number of sunbeams which might fall on them, and yet I noticed that, when we reached the cool and shaded vestibule, and threw ourselves down on the first broken stones we saw, and looked up into the face of the colossal stone goddess, who sat on an elephant of stone and bade us welcome, my friends were glad enough to rest.

The temple walls, and every part of their adorning sculpture, are hewn out of the stone mountain. Were there no pagan deities in stone, no reminders of any early worship, and were the country any other than India, one would take this wonderful structure for a superb cathedral. Not many serious changes would need to be made in order to convert it into an English minster. Fergusson says that "the building resembles an early Christian church in its arrangements, while all the dimensions are similar to those of the choir of Norwich Cathedral." * The nave is one hundred and twenty-four feet long, forty-five feet broad, and forty-six feet from floor to ceiling. There are aisles on either side of the temple, separated from the nave by octagonal pillars. The capital of each pillar is crowned with two kneeling elephants, on whose backs are seated two figures representing the divinities to whom the temple is dedicated. These are of beautiful features, as, indeed, are all the representations of deities in the Karli cave-temple. There is nothing of that repulsive sculpture which one sees at Puna and in the modern Hindu pagodas in the south. I saw no figures which were in part human and in part beast-like. Each was true to its class, from vestibule back to altar. Now the altar and the place where it stands keep up the resemblance to a Christian church. Behind it there are seven pillars, which separate it from what, in a church, would correspond with the choir. There are, altogether, thirty-eight columns in the temple. The grandest is the large lion-pillar in front, which has sixteen sides, and is surmounted with four lions.

All this great recess has been cut from the solid rock, which seems to be nothing softer than porphyry itself. The statuary is massive relief, and consists of figures also cleft from the rock, like Thorwaldsen's lion in Lucerne. The great pillars are chastely proportioned columns, both base and capital proving that they have not been introduced, but, like all other stone portions of the temple, have been cut from the solid mass of which the whole mountain consists. They are part and parcel of flooring and ceiling. There is an outward porch, or vestibule, fifty-two feet wide and fifteen deep, and on the heavy molding above there are figures of a man, a woman, and a dwarf. All this, too, like the whole spacious temple itself, has been patiently cut from firm rock.

The only thing which is not of native rock is a wooden cover-

---

* "Rock-cut Temples of India," p. 27.

ing or ceiling. This has been the puzzle of all the toilers in Indian archæology, and they seem to-day to be no nearer a solution of the difficulty than when they began. The entire immediate covering of the temple is of teak, a native wood, almost the only one which resists the white ant and every Indian insect. As you look up, and take in the whole nave, it reminds you at once of the inverted hull of a ship. The cross-timbers and the boards have that appearance, and yet the more one examines the whole of the wooden umbrella, and compares it with the rest of the temple, the more exact is its correspondence with the stone of which all the rest of the sacred building consists. The finishing of the wood-work is of the same style as that of the stone. As to the reason why the wood was put above this wonderful cave-temple, no one can answer. The ceiling was already of stone, and many a foot beneath the roots of the trees which waved on the mountain-top. Nothing could add to the massive and attractive character of the whole. It is not likely that this wooden covering was added later, long after the work was finished and the temple had been used. On the other hand, Thomas, Burgess, and Fergusson, the best searchers among the antiquities of India, began their interpretation of the Karli temple by supposing the wood to be a later addition. But after their examination, more closely conducted, they concluded it was put there at the time the temple was excavated from the mountain-side. Fergusson's reasoning, that "the design of the ceiling is repeated in stone in all the niches in the temple front," seems to settle all doubts. Why may not that ceiling, made of adamantine teak, have been placed there as a shield against dampness? I believe this to be the correct solution. Rain from May to October is abundant throughout Lower India, and water would trickle down through crevices in spite of every precaution. In the cave-temples of Elephanta, where there is no wooden umbrella, every floor is at least damp, while some are wet, and even shoe-deep in water. But the floor of the Karli temple is perfectly dry. Not a drop of water could fall from any part of the ceiling. Should dampness collect, and even become a slight stream, the water would find its way down the sides, without dampening the whole floor.

But who knows when this, the Karli temple, was built? This is another question which none have been able to answer. Of

VESTIBULE OF THE GREAT CAVE-TEMPLE AT ELLORA.

the various interpretations of its origin, hardly any two can be found to agree. There is, however, a general belief that the excavation was made before the beginning of the Christian era. Bird says he found an inscription there which reads, "Of the twentieth year of Datthama Hara, otherwise called Dattagamini, King of Ceylon, B.C. 163." But there is no trace of an inscription now, so far as our eyes could see, and therefore the accuracy of Bird's statement cannot be tested. The inscription, at all events, may have been put there by some Christian anchorite or priest. For no Hindu would think of giving a Christian date to such a magnificent memorial of the early and heroic days of his people. Perhaps Burgess is as satisfactory and precise in his interpretation as we can hope from any one, when he says, "We shall probably not be far wrong in placing the excavation of these caves anterior to the Christian era."

Another of the uncertainties is, that no one has yet been able to decide by what class of people the temple was built. But for the Oriental reliefs, such as elephants and other figures peculiar to the East, it might well have served for an early Christian church. But these features preclude the idea that it was ever intended for this purpose. All the reliefs of deities do not help us towards deciding whether the Brahmans or Buddhists made it. One thing is sure, that the idea of excavating the very mountains in order to erect beautiful temples is of very early origin, and that these cave-temples of India sprang into perfection at the very beginning of their history. In no part of the land is one to be found which betrays an apprenticeship.

After leaving the Karli temple and inspecting a few minor excavations, we made a circuit around the shoulder of the mountain. We could then see that the place where the temple was made had been wisely chosen for defence. The mountain itself was a protection, had there been no ascent. And as to beautiful scenery, no sacred building could have a more charming location. The worshipper in the Karli temple, whether in ancient or later times, could stand in the vestibule of his fane and look down the valley and enjoy a scene of enchanting beauty. The valley lay at his feet like a piece of beautiful tapestry, while either mountain-side seemed to hang as a rich drapery of darker hue. Should war come, as it often did, he knew that little harm could happen to his temple. For it was a recess, and, break what they might, the savage soldiers could not do much real damage to a simple excavation. Besides, it would be no easy task to draw their battering implements up the steep acclivity. A strange army, also, would never see the temple or know of its existence; for in a few hours, by timely preparations, rock and earth enough might be brought together to conceal its very vestibule from the valley below. Indeed, only during a few reaches in our path hither could we see the entrance at all, so carefully was the spot chosen to prevent notice from the passers-by in the valley. This security must have been a prime motive in hewing out cave-temples. The land has always been rent with warfare. The whole story of India, from the time of Alexander's invasion of the Panjab down to the adjustments of English possession, is a flame of violent war. Not a vale or mountain is without its epic of bloodshed. Religion has come in for its share of interest; for in many of the wars the idolatries of sects and teachers have added to the frenzy. Wholesale massacres have played their part, and crimes to which there are no names have been planned in places of barbaric splendor and perpetrated on the innocent millions.

But the better day is coming for India's coral strand. It has come.

BUDDHIST SUPPORT FROM THE GANESA GROTTO NEAR CUTTACK.

CHAPTER XVI.

PUNA, THE MARHATTA CAPITAL.

Of all the Indian cities, not one more fully illustrates the transition from the old to the new, and the very burial of the old in the new, than Puna. Nor is there a place which better proves what the Englishman can do with the Hindu's prostrate possessions—namely, to take up a dead and hopeless capital, and, bringing in the large outlying territory, clothe the whole with a beauty and thrift of which the Hindu had never dreamed. The old Puna, with all its death and desolation, has been surrounded by the English with a framework of beautiful homes, spacious hotels, large and imposing public buildings, fine residences, and gardens worthy of any land.

The old city is not very ancient. It owed its first importance to two considerations. It was chosen by the Marhatta chiefs as the capital of their empire, and its elevated position gave it a perfect atmosphere. The city lies on the plateau of a mountain range. It became the capital of the Marhatta kingdom in 1750. When that power began to decline, the importance of Puna as an English military station grew rapidly. Schools for engineering and other departments of military science were established.

SLICING LEMONS.

Many retired officers have chosen Puna for their final residence, and the presence of their families creates an attractive and cultivated society. This is largely increased in the summer months by people from Bombay, many of whom have their country residences here. It is the Orange Mountain of Bombay. The city numbers about one hundred thousand inhabitants; but the closely packed native city is entirely separated from the English portion. The British residences are in the midst of large grounds, and have all the air of comfort which prevails in the homesteads in England itself. The English churches are richly decorated. The spacious memorial tablets are eloquent of English bravery, and are beautiful tributes to the strong ties of affection which the long distance from Britain has made more intense. There are, in the St. Paul's Church, tombs to Morris of the Balaklava charge; to Stuart, and many others who fell in the mutiny; and to Frankland, who fell in Persia. There are others in memory of personal friends, who either here or elsewhere in the Dekhan have found their grave in India. St. Paul's was dedicated in 1825, by Bishop Heber. In the old cemetery in East Street there are some neglected monuments. Here, in this place of rank vegetation and general neglect, lies the dust of the gifted Maria Jane Jewsbury.

The native city is divided into seven quarters, which are named after the days of the week. An ancient palace, now a ruin, is in the Saturday quarter. It is enclosed by a wall one hundred and eighty yards square. Out in the suburbs, and on an eminence, I visited the ancient Fort, where many a tragedy has been enacted. The doors are covered with iron spikes, to make the entrance as nearly impossible as lay in the power of the rulers. From the terrace here, in 1795, the young chief, Madhu Rao, because he had been insulted by his prime-minister, cast himself down, and died of his injuries two days afterwards. However, the most of the violence in this fort has been involuntary. The annals of the place are written, every page, in blood. Near the Fort is the street where Marhatta offenders were put to death by being trampled upon by elephants. This was a common mode of getting rid of troublesome subjects. Its only objection was its publicity. The native princes generally chose more retired methods. But, in any case, they did not stand long on the order of their deadly doing.

The ride out to Parvati, a lofty hill crowned with a group of temples, is the most interesting excursion in the neighborhood of Puna. The road leads past the Hira Bagh, or Diamond Garden, where one sees some tombs to other Englishmen, who here found

A REVIEW OF NATIVE INFANTRY AT PUNA.

their last resting-place. Among the most noticeable is that to Cornwallis Harris. The main temple at Parvati was built by the peshwa, Balaji Baji Rao, who ruled from 1740 to 1761. He died of chagrin, after the defeat of his army at Panipat. The traveller, to reach the temple, must pass beneath a filthy bridge, after which he ascends a long flight of broad stone steps. When the Prince of Wales visited Parvati he rode up these steps on an elephant, and it is the favorite way of reaching the height. I was disinclined to adopt it, however, from a wish to put off my elephant ride in India as long as possible. There is a silver image of Siva in the temple. Those of Parvati and Ganesh are said to be of gold. There are smaller temples surrounding the larger one, the whole forming a most pleasing architectural group. From the Moorish window, on one side of the surrounding wall, Baji Rao watched his army as it struggled for victory, and saw at last his kingdom go down with the close of the fatal day.

ACROBAT ON HORSEBACK.

A flight of steps leads to the top of the wall. Here the view is of surpassing beauty. The distant outlying mountains form a charming landscape. Twelve miles off is the memorable Singarh, which was captured by Tanaji Malusrai in 1670. In other directions are Chakan, Saswad, Jijuvi—each the scene of noted military encounters. The valleys, traversed by streams, wind along between the mountains. Towering palms stretch out their fronds on hillside and in the vale, while the mango and other trees furnish a picture of luxuriance which I feasted upon with rare delight. At our feet lay the city of Puna, its larger buildings and entire outline being clearly in view. The whole is a study. Here reigned and died the last of the Marhatta rulers in India. His palaces are ruins, and are now visited only by the curious tourist. The Englishman is here, building wisely and ruling justly, and fairly blotting out the old memories of cruelty and blood by all those improvements and institutions which find their real genesis in his higher Christian civilization.

CHAPTER XVII.

THE NIZAM'S HAIDARABAD.—A NATIVE CITY.

There are two Haidarabads in India. One is in the north, near the Indus, and is the capital of Sind. The other is in the south, and is the largest city in the great territory known as the Dekhan. It is the capital of the Nizam's dominions. The southern Haidarabad is the more famous of the two, and has played an important part in the history of India for two centuries. Just here, at the battered gates of this southern Haidarabad, begins the whole history of European empire in India. The great Nizam-ul-Mulk died. A war of succession broke out. The French interfered. The flames of war spread everywhere. The English, who never see fighting without a wish to participate, took part here.* The end was what we see to-day—the English queen the Empress of India.

OFFICER OF THE NIZAM'S GUARDS, HAIDARABAD.

The Nizam is prince of the country. The population subject to him amounts to about ten millions. He has a personal income of fifteen million dollars.

The prime-minister in office at the time of my visit was Sir Salar Jang, the son of that extraordinary Sir Salar Jang who was premier at the time of the mutiny, and proved himself to be a firm friend of England. The son gives promise of following closely in his father's footsteps. The Rev. Dr. A. W. Rudisill thus describes his personal appearance: "He is very tall, with grace in his every step. He has fine, silky, jet-black hair,

* Seeley, "Expansion of England," p. 203.

delicate skin, sharp features, a pear-shaped head, with the large end of the pear up."

Long before reaching Haidarabad I noticed that the country was dotted in every direction by huge masses of dark rocks. Some were mere boulders, while others were sharp and conical, closely resembling the parti-colored sandstone cones along the Yellowstone Falls. Some of those in the vicinity of Haidarabad rise abruptly amid the cultivated land, their sharp needles point-

THE RESIDENCY AT HAIDARABAD.

ing jaggedly into the air, as though no attempt in all the centuries had ever been made to get rid of them. The Hindus have a way of accounting for every natural irregularity, and they explain this rocky phenomenon by the theory that the Creator, after completing all the rest of the world, had a great many shapeless fragments left over, for which there was no use, and so he tossed them all down in the country around Haidarabad.

Several times during my week in this place I strolled out to a hill, a confused pile of these bare rocks, quite beyond the suburban residences. This is "Tipu's Lookout." It rises fifty feet above the plain. A flight of steps is cut into one side of the chief granite mass; but I generally succeeded in missing them, and so had to pick my way by a very uncertain path. From the summit of Tipu's Lookout one enjoys a view of the country for many miles around. The more prominent object is the gloomy old Golconda fort in the west, with the massive tombs of the Kutub Shahi kings in the foreground.

The garden of the Nizam is public. It was within five minutes' walk of my place of entertainment, the house of the Rev. Mr. Carter. I never tired of wandering through its labyrinths, enjoying its delightful fragrance, and examining the endless variety of the plants. Every art which these cultivators of flowers in India have arrived at by the experience of centuries is here employed, by rich designs in colors, by succession of flowering shrubs, and by a happy combination of large shrubs and the smaller plants. All the more delicate plants are in pots, and need to be watered every day. There are six millions of potted plants alone, to say nothing of the multitude of larger ones. Watering is the great business of the laborers. To do this properly a large force must be constantly at work. The garden has walks of all kinds—straight and in curves. Little surprises came to me every time I sauntered here, though I thought I had seen the garden well at my first visit. There are miniature lakes, jaunty belvederes, laughing nooks, now a bit of jungle and now a broad and beautiful open space, where the distant view is enchanting.

The city of Haidarabad, with its outlying suburbs, has a population of three hundred and fifty-five thousand. Of all places in India it is the most turbulent and unsafe. This curious condition of things has come about because of the hostility between the two ruling classes of the population. These are the Hindus and the Mohammedans. But many other faiths and nations are represented in this strange city. In the brilliant days of the Mogul empire in the north, when the emperors ruled all India from Lahor, Delhi, and Agra, they fearlessly marched far to the south and conquered the country. They established subordinate princes in Golconda as a capital, which was later abandoned as a residence. Haidarabad was then laid out and built to take its place. The ruling prince was the Nizam. He, like his fathers, was a Mohammedan. But his subjects were for the most part Hindus. The latter, naturally enough, have always been secretly hostile to the Mohammedan conqueror and his descendants, and every now and then there is a violent outbreak of the old hatred.

Haidarabad is still walled, and it is not always safe for a foreigner to walk through the streets without an escort. I was re-

STREET VIEW AND CHAR MINAR, HAIDARABAD.

peatedly cautioned against entering the gates and strolling even into the nearest bazaar. Only the week before my short sojourn an outbreak had occurred, when nine persons were killed in the general uproar. This particular conflict came about in a peculiar way. The Nizam, years ago, called to his aid an Arab prince, the Sultan of Aden, with his army of several thousand troops. He promised a certain payment, which was high. The prince came hither, at the head of his troops, and settled in Haidarabad. But the pay was not forthcoming. The Nizam had other uses for his fifteen million dollars' income. The debt increased, and, though the prince was very wealthy, he wanted his money. His troops shared with him the sense of injustice, and that made them overbearing, and ready at any time to commit deeds of violence. It was a conflict between imported Arab troops and the native soldiers and population of the Nizam. The outbreaks generally lead to tedious trials in court, and, in the case of the trouble which occurred the week before my visit, the Arab prince was found guilty, fined heavily, and expelled the country for a number of years. So far as I could learn, there was no justice in the verdict. The whole affair appeared to me to be only an Indian method of getting clear of a troublesome neighbor and an uncomfortable debt. As this piece of summary procedure took place in the interval between the death of the senior Sir Salar Jang and the accession of his son to the premiership, we may infer that it is a fair specimen of native Indian justice.

THE NIZAM'S STATE COACH, HAIDARABAD.

CHAPTER XVIII.

GOLCONDA.—AN ELEPHANT RIDE.

DURING my week in Haidarabad I had two opportunities for an elephant ride. The first was a mere stroll in a suburb, and around the walls of the Nizam's garden. The howdah, or saddle, was comfortable, and my elephant was as calm and obedient as a used-up Syrian horse. I found myself on a level with the tops of many of the native houses. But this was a mere promenade compared with the more stately ride on one of the court elephants. Three were furnished for our little company. Our plan was to ride through Haidarabad, inspect its chief buildings, and then go out into the country and make a visit to Golconda.

To Mr. Henry Croley I was indebted for such special courtesies as made this second ride the most remarkable excursion during my stay in India. He is the author of the "Geography of the Eastern Peninsula," and during his residence in Burma was the tutor of the Delhi princes, the last scions of the great Mogul dynasty. Mr. Croley is now inspector of schools in the Nizam's dominions, and has passed successfully through all the stages of violent jealousy and opposition, and is firmly established, by his successful management of the department of education, in the favor of both the Nizam and his cabinet. He is only second in authority in educational work in the Nizam's dominions, the director of public instruction, Gyed Ali, being first.

Mr. Croley made application to the court for elephants, and a permit to examine the city and visit the ancient fort of Golconda. For two days there was no answer to the request; but a satisfactory one finally arrived, couched in all the epithets of Oriental courtesy which both the Hindustani and Arabic languages convey:

"ROYAL COMMAND.

"An order has been issued for the 26th November that Bishop Hurst and his party will visit the tombs of Golconda, and that he may see the place.

"For this reason, all government servants and peasants (or civilians) shall see and provide that no trouble or molestation shall occur to the gentleman and his party.

"If the gentleman written above, and the party referred to, require help or assistance in any way, I hereby issue an order that the same be furnished.

"It is done. 24th November.

"The writing is finished.

"Written, 5th Shair Safar.

"1302 Hijra.

"Concluded in the blessed city of Haidarabad."

In addition to this general order there was another, communicated by the prime-minister to Mr. Cunningham, the First Assistant English Resident. It provided for the means of conveyance, and read as follows:

"HAIDARABAD, DEKHAN, 24*th November*, 1884.

"MY DEAR MR. CUNNINGHAM,—I have signed and now return the pass for Bishop Hurst to visit Golconda.

"Two elephants have also been ordered to be at the city gate at 7 o'clock on Wednesday morning.

"I will let the Nawab Bashir ud Daula know of the bishop's desire to visit the Jahan Numa, and unless you hear to the contrary you may count on necessary orders having been given.

"Believe me, etc., SALAR JANG.

"(True copy.)

"MOSES HUGHES, Extra Assistant Resident."

Two elephants were furnished, well caparisoned, and provided with a strong guard. I have never seen a larger elephant than the one to whose lofty back I was assigned. If I may judge from its enormous size, it might well have been the great one which had belonged to the senior Sir Salar Jang. The name of that famous beast was Khudadad (that is, Deodatus, God-given), reputed to be the largest elephant in all India. Put on my elephant's back a spacious and elevated howdah, and then add to that the distance to the top of my cork helmet, and one has converted a man into a conspicuous feature of the Indian landscape. My howdah was rich in tinsel, but it leaned obstinately to one side. I was told that this augured no ill, as all the straps were tight. But there was a sense of discomfort with every step of the great beast. A number of gentlemen rode on the same elephant with me, and as we had no clatter of wheels to disturb us, our social intercourse was as undisturbed as if we had been sitting on a group of chairs in the Nizam's palace. If people accosted us with unsavory epithets, they never went so far as to interfere with our progress. Perhaps the guard, with the courtly trappings of our elephants, produced a cautious respect.

Haidarabad has thirteen gates. We pass through one and over a bridge which spans the Musi River, and are now, in due

SIR SALAR JANG, THE ELDER.

procession, making a straight course through the main street of the city. All the lesser animals, with the throng of pedestrians, get out of our way. Our elephants seem to have all rights, and care for nothing. They pass steadily along, and in due time I get accustomed to the sag of my howdah.

The general architecture is not inspiring. With the exception of a few public buildings, such as the mosques and the palaces of the nobles, there is but little architectural merit. Nearly all the edifices were erected in troublous days. Hence the substantial character of all the massive teak-wood gates and wickets, over which are quarters for a guard or small garrison. Every now and then we pass a spacious bazar. The best of these are the Cloth Bazar, a handsome row of buildings facing an ornamental garden containing fountains and great tanks, and the Arms Bazar, where one can see old and new armor of every kind, and form some conception of the bloody work these people have been doing for two centuries. The people whom we pass in the streets present the most warlike appearance of any civilians whom I ever saw. All the inhabitants of Haidarabad carry a weapon of some kind, while the military classes go armed up to their very eyes. It is the custom of the upper classes to pay a visit to each other or to the Nizam with an unaccoutred dagger stuck in the girdle, or a sword suspended from the gold-lace belt which the majority wear. Servants and attendants copy the formidable adornments of their masters.

The mixed nature of the population is very striking. All the ruder nations and tribes which have drifted into India, or have been produced on the soil, are represented. Here is a semi-military Arab, with a perfect arsenal of weapons in his kamarband, or waistband. An Arab chief in his palki, or palankeen, is escorted by a surging and tumultuous crowd of his retainers, firing off muskets and shouting out the wonderful titles of their august master as they pass along. Next comes the Seedee, with his broad, black negro face, who is more fearful to behold than an Arab villain. The Rohilla, with slow and dignified step, may next be seen; his huge bell-mouthed blunderbuss, without which in Haidarabad he is never seen, is as distinguishable as himself. The Pathan, the Afghan, the Persian, the Bokhariat, the Georgian, the Parsi, the Dekhanese, the Sikh, and the Turk, with many others, may be seen passing along, and making way for our magisterial elephants. We now reach the Char Minar (Four Minarets). It is the heart of Haidarabad. Four streets diverge from it. Each of the four minarets is one hundred and eighty

AN ELEPHANT RIDE.

feet high. Above the arches are a couple of rooms, used as a madrasa and masjid (school and church). No one is allowed to ascend either of the minarets, for they look down on the Nizam's palace. The Char Minar was erected A.D. 1591, by Mohammed Kuli Kutub Shah. He built it in honor of God's favorable answer to the prayers of some holy men in a day of a fierce pestilential scourge. In 1756 Bussy and his troops occupied it and the gardens around. It is the "scandal point" of the idle loiterers of Haidarabad. Writers of petitions and letters are squatted around on the steps, plying their trade, just as one used to see in great abundance in the Neapolitan market-places. Near by is the Mecca Masjid. This mosque is a quadrangle of three hundred and sixty feet square. Its roof is supported by fifteen arches. During the festivals from eight to ten thousand worshippers meet under the two huge domes. Abdula Kutub Shah began it, and Aurangzeb, the great Mogul emperor, finished it. Within the mosque many of the princes lie buried.

We made only two or three halts while passing through the city, but, for prudential reasons, did not dismount. Having emerged from the gate of the city at the farther end of the main thoroughfare, we turned to the right, and took the road skirting a massive wall. We had a special permit to visit the Jahan Numa, one of the principal palaces of Haidarabad. As we were now away from the warlike throng of Haidarabadese, we dismounted, and began a ramble through hall and gardens. The Jahan Numa belongs to the family of one of the chief noblemen, Bushir-ud-Dowlah. Having gone through some buildings connected with the palace, but shielding it largely from public view, we came into a large court, which seemed to have been used for soldiers, both horse and foot, and the retainers of the prince. At the farther end of the court we came to a staircase, and entered the main rooms of the vast palace. Here were spacious halls, covered with carpets and rugs of many ancient and curious designs. The furniture was richly carved. Some of it was of dark old Indian woods, but a portion was of European and later origin. I was struck by the odd contrivances to amuse the members of the princely household living here. Here were clocks of fantastic workmanship, and at every convenient corner there were automata of the quaintest possible construction. All were in motion, and so contrived as to amuse by doing unexpected things. For example, I saw the figure of a grenadier, whose sole business it was to swallow miniature fish. There were instruments for performing musical freaks. Stuffed birds

MIR ÁLAM LAKE.

could be seen everywhere, grouped into all possible combinations, so as to make the scene as nearly lifelike as possible. I visited many other palaces in India afterwards, and learned that it was an ancient usage of the kings and noblemen of Hindustan to employ the most accomplished artists in curious mechanism, whose sole business it was to contrive and construct odd and unheard-of devices of this kind to please the ladies of the Indian courts. In the old days their time hung heavily. There were many women to be pleased, and they had their jealousies, and could be best appeased by having their fancy charmed by the sight and sound of these curious devices.

Having finished the halls of the palace, we ascended a staircase, and came out upon a beautiful and fragrant garden. My first thought was that the rooms which we had just left were immediately below us, and that the garden we were now in was on the roof of the palace. In other words, I supposed myself to be in a hanging garden. But on examination I saw that the garden was really only on a level with the roof, but was supported by a terrace so raised as to give the visitor the impression that he was walking over the palace roof. This too was evidently only a device to bewilder the guest into still greater admiration at his environment. This garden contained flowers of rare beauty and fragrance, and was laid off in exquisite designs. Having left it, we wandered through the grounds in the rear. Here we came into a labyrinth of pleasing and curious construction. It served its purpose, as I soon learned by getting lost in it. Always expect the Indian to do his work differently from the rest of the world. This labyrinth was not of the same order as the one in the Palmengarten in Frankfort-on-Main, or the less pleasing one in the outlying grounds of Hampton Court, but it served its purpose far better.

CHAPTER XIX.

THE FORT AND TOMBS OF GOLCONDA.

We now remounted our elephants and proceeded on our way around the wall of Haidarabad. Our excursion was only to end with the four-mile ride out to the celebrated fort and tombs of Golconda. But we had not proceeded long on our road around the wall before we found carriages in waiting. Our friends whom we had left behind had imagined that we would be thoroughly tired of the elephants, and would be glad to exchange them for comfortable carriages. In this they were quite correct. An elephant ride to Golconda in the torrid sun would not only have occupied the entire day, but would have been, to me at least, a dangerous experience. Happy is he who lives in a country where it is not the highest discourtesy to decline the offer of the largest elephant belonging to the court of the prince. Our mammoths doubled up their spongy feet and dropped down with us. We were soon taking a little stroll on terra firma, and then entered the welcome carriages.

Golconda has an old, old history. Haidarabad, with all its years, great population, and bloody history, is young in comparison with the dead city whose acropolis rises from the plain three miles in the distance on our left. The blocks of black granite which lie scattered over the country here lose their individuality, and form an immense cone, on the apex of which stands the grim fort of old and rich Golconda. The fort is still surrounded by its crenellated stone wall, three miles in circumference. It has eighty-seven high bastions at the angles, on which are still the ancient Shahi guns, some of them with their breeches blown out from service in half-forgotten wars. The bastions are built of solid blocks of granite, either cemented together or bound with iron clamps. Many of these blocks are of colossal size and weight. The average thickness of the bastions is from fifty to sixty feet.

A NARROW ESCAPE.

On the sides of this towering acropolis, and enclosed by the great wall, Golconda was built, the streets running at all possible angles, and crossing each other at unexpected places, the whole forming as complete a zigzag as one can find in the older parts of Genoa. I suspect, however, that all the buildings which this ancient wall enclosed were connected either with the army or the court, and that the general population of Golconda lived in the plain surrounding the rocky heights. It was the Indian way to call the place a fort where the palace and all its dependencies were situated. The army was always the needful support of royalty, and must be near at hand. Hence the homes for officers and the quarters for soldiers had to be within reach. The entire group of buildings, with the many additional structures for servants and all the belongings of palace and army, was called the Fort. It was the combined home of the king and his army, and large space was needed for such a population. It was, indeed, the kingdom in miniature.

The Golconda fort was the most remarkable elevation in all the region of Haidarabad. Its high wall concealed all parts near the base of the hill; but other buildings and towers and palace ruins rose above these, until the open and airy tower, with graceful balconies and broad parterres, crowned the very summit and commanded a broad and beautiful view. I had no hope of being able to visit this mysterious place at first; for in Eastwick's "Guide to the Madras Presidency" I had read these discouraging words: "No person is ever permitted to visit the interior of the fort unless the Nizam himself should go there, and, as that seldom or never happens, the persons who can describe the details of the fortification are few or none." But Mr. Croley was fully equal to the emergency. With his other permits he had secured the all-important one to go within the very fort itself, and see every part of it, and stay as long as we might choose. On reaching the gates the chief of the guard, all of whom were accoutred with old-time Indian weapons, advanced to meet us. Mr. Croley drew forth our high-sounding permit.

The warder made low obeisance, and flung wide open the creaking and battered gates, and bade us enter. The very sight of those old portals made one shiver. They were of teak-wood, and nearly covered with iron knobs, and bristling with rude and heavy spikes, enough (and much to spare) for resisting the attack of any number of assailing elephants. We now left the carriages, and began a steep climb to the top of the hill. The scene was one of decay and filth. The very streets up and down which great royal processions had moved, and queens and princesses decked in jewels had been borne in glittering palanquins by human hands, were now neglected, and reeking with wretched odors. On the way up we passed many battlements. It was fort within fort. We saw piles of fragments of palace walls; decayed mansions, where still beautiful sections of the delicate jalousies told the story of former splendor and social elegance; and heavy guns, which had grown rusty in their long silence and disuse. On our right we saw an immense piece of masonry—a chambered wall with granite substructures—the whole covering a catacomb of fabulous dimensions. Here lay the buried treasure of Golconda in the old times, when the kings revelled in untold glory, and their very names were symbols of heroism and wealth throughout India. What this treasure consisted of is not well known, but most probably it was in jewels and gold. These were buried somewhere in these far-down vaults, and only the Nizam, with possibly his premier, knew their exact whereabouts. He had a diagram of the catacomb, and knew where to go with his diggers, who were probably blindfolded when in sight of the treasure. When treasure was taken out, the place was walled up again, that all trace of the locality might disappear. It is believed, according to the best information I could derive, that vast wealth is still stored here, which is at the service of the Nizam when his revenue from regular sources gets scanty. I noticed that there had been recent openings in the solid masonry, but could not tell whether they had been caused by making repairs or for outlets for the concealed treasure, and again walled up.

The "mines of Golconda" are a pure myth. The diamonds and other precious stones discovered near Cuddapah were brought here for sale, and were readily purchased by the rulers and their wealthy court. They were cut and polished here, and were regarded as equally good with gold as permanent treasure of the realm. The burial of them for future emergency gave the popular impression of a mine.

The vegetation of this wonderful climate was the only cheering object which we passed in our climb to the top of the acropolis. Graceful palms grew in the midst of spaces where once had been brilliant palace halls. Miniature lakes, which must have been as pearls, were now only filthy excavations, overgrown with weeds and become the haunt of hideous reptiles. All the vines known to the tropics grew in luxuriance, and wound themselves about parapet and balcony, and over the rude huts where the soldiers sleep.

By and by we reached the topmost point, and came out upon a broad esplanade, and looked off into the vast distance. This

SWIMMING-DRILL OF ELEPHANTS.

was a part of the king's palace—his promenade and outlook. The picture was one of indescribable beauty. The December sky was cloudless and the air perfect. The sense of lassitude had passed away. We had fairly forgotten the fatigue of the elephant ride and the climb up the steep way to our final lookout. On one side was the entire city of Haidarabad, with its palaces and forts, and without the walls the green zone of English homes and churches and the smiling and fragrant gardens of the Nizam. Nine miles on the east side lay Sikandarabad. Towns and villages, great rectangular tanks, large enough for lakes, conical hills of black rock, lofty palms, graceful minarets, shooting up towards the sky, and, above all, the great domed tombs, still glittering with rich porcelain adornments, where rests the dust of kings and noblemen in the plain at our feet, formed a panorama entirely different from anything I had seen, or could hope to see, in India.

This was the rich Golconda of nearly four centuries ago. For an unknown time a village had lingered in filth and obscurity around the base of the rocky cone. In 1512 the Sultan Kuli Kutab Shah declared his independence of the prince Mahmud Shah Bahmani, who ruled over the entire country. Mahmud's soldiers were strong, but Kuli's were still stronger and more successful. The latter built in this plain and on the hill his capital, and hoped to found here an imperishable throne. But pestilence, probably caused by lack of pure water, frequently invaded the place. It became a very den of disease. The treasures of his home sickened and died without apparent cause. In 1589 a successor resolved to remove the capital, and hence he began to build Haidarabad, which has served that purpose ever since. During the entire time since then, however, Golconda has been held as a fort, and has been carefully kept up as a military stronghold and treasure city.

The history of Golconda, even when it ceased to be the capital, is a piece-work of singular romance. It is not unlikely that the kings still came out from Haidarabad, and spent many a quiet hour on this lofty place, and enjoyed the bracing air. But the doom of the past made all its associations gloomy. Haidarabad, in time, took precedence over Golconda. The fame of the new residence extended into all the Oriental countries. The Shah of Persia once sent hither his ambassador with a crown studded with rubies, and other valuable gifts, who in return took back with him gold cloth and other Indian treasures. The Nizam of Haidarabad made war on his neighbors, absorbed their territory, and even invaded Bengal. This was too strong a power in the south to allow the great Mogul rulers of the north to feel secure. The Emperor Aurangzeb marched hither at the head of his great army, and with his immense engines of war attacked the fort, captured it, and made the royal family prisoners. This was the beginning of a new order. The present Nizam, as a successor to the old Mogul line, rules over this one fragment of the now dead empire of the Mogul rulers of the north—the greatest of Indian dynasties since the days of Alexander.

Our luncheon was spread out in the balcony of the Fort, and we could enjoy the view during our whole stay. On returning to the gate we found our carriages waiting, and then proceeded to visit the celebrated tombs of the kings.

An Indian tomb is unlike any memorial structure in the

ELEPHANTS ON THE MARCH.

Occident. When a wealthy or royal Hindu or Mohammedan wished to build a tomb in memory of his beloved dead, he took care to make it large—a great building of solid stone or well-burned brick, covered with durable cement. Or, as in many cases, the whole might be of solid marble, with inlaid colored stones. The dead were buried in a vault below, but on the floor directly above it was the ornamental tomb, which in finish varied according to the taste and skill of the architect and the amount of gold put into his hands.

Take one of these Golconda tombs as a type. That of the sixth king, Sultan Abdulla Kutab Shah, may be regarded as a fair specimen. There is a broad base, nearly a hundred feet square. Above this on every side are arches, beneath which one passes into the broad and unbroken hall where the one or several tombs are. Here is a tomb of black stone, consisting of five decreasing plinths, which are engraved with favorite extracts from the Qurán, and an epitaph recalling the astounding virtues of the king. Directly above rises a dome of fifty feet in height. There are stairways leading through the walls to the balconies above, where one can look down upon the square hall below, or, as in some cases, out upon the surrounding country. Much of the exterior of some of these tombs is covered with porcelain tiling. The colors, though fused into the cement by an art now lost to India and the world, are as bright as though laid on only yesterday. They dazzle the eye in the glowing sun. They may be simply inscriptions from the Qurán or graceful arabesques from old Persian designs. Some of this exquisite tiling has fallen, but enough still remains to tell how even a rare combination of bright colors was made to do its good part towards beautifying and making cheerful the exterior of these memorial places of the dead.

The largest and most magnificent tomb of all is to the fourth king, Mohammed Kuli. The eight plinths abound in incised quotations from the Qurán. From the base of the building to the top of the ornament which rises above the dome there is a distance of one hundred and eighty feet. There are galleries and corridors in both the lower and upper stories. The colored tiles filling the distance between the stone-work on the exterior walls are exceedingly rich. From places where the tiles had fallen I could see the way in which the artists had taken pains to secure them in their places. Spikes with hooks on the ends had been driven into the walls. The tiles, being perfectly ready, were laid in a bed of fine mortar, and the blocks, in this plastic condition, were placed upon these spikes, and pushed back into the general surface, and left to harden. The hooked ends of the spikes, being surrounded with the hardened mortar, held the tiles in place. That the workmen did their work well, the still remaining bright tiles on many of these tombs, after the waste and wear of three centuries, furnish ample proof.

There are many of these tombs at Golconda. They vary in size, and are in all degrees of preservation. Some are ruins, but the most are in good condition, and great pains are taken to keep the corridors and halls and even the approaches well swept. The white domes rise in all directions, and form such a picture of splendor in memory of the dead as is found nowhere else even in India. It was an old Indian taste that nature should do its part towards the adornment of the God's-acre. The friends of the departed took care that gardens should wind about the tombs, where, amid the beauty and fragrance of rich vegetation, they could sit at will and linger by the day in sight of the resting-place of their loved ones. So to this day there are rich gardens surrounding these vast tombs. They bloom on—the only bright picture in this dark landscape of decay and death.

It is one of the strange vicissitudes to which a royal tomb can come that an English family can go and occupy one, by special permission, during the summer months. That they are the coolest structures in all this region no one can deny. The tomb proper occupies but small space, while the great hall in which it stands is clean, has small rooms at its sides, and is well adapted for a comfortable home for a family. Mr. Schafter, one of the gentlemen in our little company who visited the fort and the tombs, informed me that he and his family had occupied one of these better tombs during the whole of the preceding summer, and had found it a most delightful lodging-place. The idea that they were living in the burial-place of the dead had no disturbing effect whatever on his household. His family seemed never to think of it. But I soon found that in India one soon gets accustomed to things which at home the very mention of would seem preposterous. I found in Lucknow that one of the principal houses permanently occupied by one of our lady missionaries was a tomb. The sarcophagus occupied the centre of a room, and figured only as a piece of superfluous furniture in Miss Blackmar's really beautiful home.

Before leaving Haidarabad I had intimated to Mr. Schafter that I would like to purchase some specimens of ancient armor. He gave notice to some retail dealers in the Arms Bazar that a customer might be found, should they choose to bring some specimens of their wares to his bungalow. The hint was quite sufficient. Early in the morning, almost before I had finished my coffee, several of these dealers came within Mr. Schafter's compound. They were laden from head to foot with all manner of early Indian or Arabic weapons. What they could not carry on their shoulders they had packed in bags and bundles, and, when they had unloaded themselves, they not only covered a good part of the veranda, but also the parlor floor, with their murderous wares. They had brought enough of their ancient treasures to make a respectable museum. The typical American searcher for bric-à-brac would have gone wild at such a scene. Here were a woven shirt of iron, great steel bows, short swords for thrusting, daggers with curved blades and double edges, raw-hide shields, and many other fine specimens of armor now no longer made. The sword-hilts were profusely inlaid with gold and silver thread, while the blades bore figures of rich arabesques, either burned in or cut with great skill. All were of a make for dealing sure and savage blows. The weapons were irresistible. They came, I saw, and they conquered. Some of the more curious in many departments I bought. After making my selection I had to beg Mr. Schafter to tell the men to pack up and be off. I began to fear for the reserves in my letter of credit. I sent my collection by private conveyance to Bombay to await my sailing day, two months later. It is now safely stored in the Indian corner of my library in Washington.

NECKLACE, ENAMEL ON SILVER, SEMI-BARBARIC HILL WORK, FROM KANGRA, PANJAB.

CHAPTER XX.

WAYS OF INDIAN TRAVEL.

THERE is no country where there is such great diversity in the methods of travel as in India. The inventive faculty seems to have gone wild, in all times, in devices to make transportation both possible and easy. In the plains one finds one class of conveyances, and in the hill country another kind. Yet these are strangely

TRACK-LAYING NEAR BHOPAL.

mixed. In the interior the surprises are numerous, and, away from the railroads, it is difficult to anticipate what sort of conveyance will be brought before your door for a long journey. But the railway is the certain method of land travel for the future. The native Hindu, when he takes his seat in a third-class carriage, seems to be supremely happy. He appears as though just awakened from a sleep of ages.

There are three classes of Indian railway-carriages—first, second, and third. The doors are at the sides, the carriage being divided into cross sections, as in European countries. Each section of the third class holds about fourteen people, the seven on one seat facing the seven on the other. The second-class sections are about ten feet long, divided by three seats parallel with the track. Each seat can hold four people, but I have seen no case where a whole second-class compartment has been able to accommodate more than four or five persons for a night ride. The first-class compartment is about the size of the second-class, but has only two seats, which run along the two sides of the car. These seats are broad, and have leather upholstering. Above each there is a folded frame, which lets down at night and becomes a bed, just over the regular seat, like the upper berth of a Pullman or Wagner section. Some of the first-class cars have a seat running across the end of the compartment. I noticed that this was often avoided by travellers. But I always had the best sleeping on it, and was therefore glad to get it.

The first and second class carriages are furnished with a toilet-room, and in some cases with a bath-room. But there are no towels or brushes, or even soap. Neither is there any carpet, or even a shred of oil-cloth, on the floor. The main compartments, however, of both the first and second class, have oil-cloth covering for the floor. But there is no attempt made to keep it clean.

At one end of some of the third-class carriages there is a small compartment, with seats for about eight persons, which is "for Europeans only." That means it is not for the barefooted and half-naked natives. It has hard seats, but otherwise is not uncomfortable. If you and your travelling companion can secure that between you, and will spread out your wraps on the seats, you can have a good night's rest. As to the springs of the carriages, they are all alike uncomfortable. There is a jar and sudden jerking, which I found on all the lines. Hence it is much more difficult to preserve your axis of vision, in both reading and writing, than in the easy German carriages, and our still more easy American. But I managed to catch up a good deal of lost time on even these trains, by resting my eyes more frequently, and so avoiding a strain.

On some roads there are separate carriages for ladies and gentlemen. When a man and his wife are travelling they must each take a separate compartment. One day a gentleman and his wife came into a first-class compartment and took seats. I came afterwards, and took my seat also, and wondered what the result would be from a lady taking a seat in the gentlemen's car. I did not have to wait long, for the conductor came to the door and

KOTTIAR CANOES PASSING ROUND ISLAND.

informed the lady that there was accommodation in the *zenana* carriage for her. She left in great disgust, and her husband had to stay with me. Of course, the two were strangers in India. Otherwise the husband would have escorted his wife to the ladies' carriage, and then looked out for himself in one where only gentlemen could ride.

Children do not travel much in India. At any rate, I saw but few of them on the trains. They are left at home, in the care of servants.

Nothing being furnished in the matter of bedding, how to spend the night with any comfort becomes a serious question when one has an all-night ride, or perhaps a thousand miles, before him. You must take your own bedding, and when you are ready to retire you unroll it over your seat, and then betake yourself to dreams. On reaching Bombay the Rev. Dr. Fraser was considerate enough to supply me with a *bichauna*, or travelling outfit for sleep. It was well that he did, for I should never have thought of taking all the things he put at my disposal. First of all, there was a pillow of cotton flock, which I found necessary to supplement my India-rubber pillow which I had brought from New York, and had used everywhere on sea and land. Then came a light quilted counterpane, of Kashmir origin, and then a thick padded quilt or comforter. To these were added sheets, and such other things as one needs to complete a railway bed. All this was rolled up into a great bundle, and duly strapped. It was, indeed, a most formidable *impedimentum*, of size enough to frighten any one except an Anglo-Indian. But I did not have too many wraps. On the contrary, my good friend, the Rev. C. L. Bare, of Shajahanpur, added another thick covering to all the rest, as my journey through the Northwest Provinces to Lahor was bringing me within reach of the cold night air from the Himalayas. Just as I write these lines, they lift their icy peaks off to the right in wild and broken forms. They are now taking on the evening rose tints, and the deepening shadows tell of the great chasms which no plummet has ever fathomed. The air comes down across the plains, and makes one shiver long before the sun has set. But this is India, the land of inexplicable contradictions, and yet of many a bright and beautiful harmony. Even at the base of its pyramids of everlasting ice you must protect your head, especially the back of it, against the straight rays of this terribly sure-shooting sun.

But the office of the *bichauna*, or bundle of bedding for travel, is not over when you have finished your railway ride. It goes with you to your lodging. The presumption is, that wherever you are a guest the hostess will see that your bed is supplied

RATTAN BRIDGE ACROSS THE TEESTA, FIVE THOUSAND FEET ABOVE SEA-LEVEL.

with ample furnishing. But that is not always the rule. Often the servant takes your bedding, and puts it on the bed of the room where you are to sleep—not that there is not a plenty of such dry-goods in the house already for a guest, or even for several, but because it is presumed that you are used to your own bedding, and may prefer to have it. In many of the homes where I was entertained I saw only the bed frame, with cotton bands running across it, and lengthwise, to support the sleeper and his wraps. The spring-mattress is not yet the rule. Having gone out of my room afterwards, and then returning, I missed my *bichauna*. What had become of it? I looked again, and yet in vain. Who took it off? Had a petty thief slipped in by the back-door, and taken away my property? Not at all. Honesty reigns here among servants—except only as to pocket-knives and scissors. One gentleman told me, at his house, that I might leave anything on my table but those two bright things. They must always be cared for by yourself, and so concealed.

But the *bichauna?* While I was out of my room the bearer had come in, unstrapped and unfolded my bedding, and spread it all out on the bedstead of my bedroom. So I was to sleep on it that night, and all the remaining time when I should be in the house as a guest. I grew strangely attached to this bedding. How could I ever give it up? Though it was of immense size, and was supplemented by other parcels, it had lost its inconvenience. I naturally became an expert in making my own bed, for I had to do it every night spent on the railroad. At first it was very awkward work. With all my efforts the things would not lie smooth. But in time they took their place more easily. I blew up my rubber pillow hastily, was less particular as to when the last pillow-slip had been to the *dhobi*, as everybody in India calls the washerman; and learned to handle my quilts *en masse.* The next morning much less time was needed to strap up the bed-clothing. I was soon ready for the anticipated halt, and to be greeted at the station by the good missionary, who had a programme for work to be done in twenty-four hours that ought to occupy at least forty-eight.

The railroad travel is revolutionizing the whole country. If, out of the two hundred and sixty millions of natives of the country none would patronize the railroad, because to ride on these would break their caste and ruin their souls, what use would a railroad be at best? It was at first a grave question whether the travel would pay. But the Hindu is a most adaptable creature. Where can his elasticity be equalled? His theology told him at the outset that he must not ride on the cars. But that theology is a flexible affair, and can fit the last necessity with the greatest ease. He suddenly took to reading his eldest Vedas, and there he learned that Brahma was to have an eighth incarnation, some time in the far future. Behold, the time has come. It is George Stephenson's railroad! Hence the Hindu now rides whither he will. He is making fewer foot pilgrimages, and goes on the train. The eighth incarnation is a paying investment. Any Brahman may buy a ticket from the dog-paws of an Englishman, and flaunt his robes against an American, and yet keep his caste intact. The trains, therefore, are nearly always full. The thousands who are constantly going upon a pilgrimage to some shrine or other, or taking their brass jars to Allahabad or Benares, in order to worship in a sacred temple, and bear away some of the precious Ganges water to their far-away homes, are almost countless. The stations are packed with these pilgrims. By night and day one sees them. They swarm like locusts. They can sleep anywhere, and live on two cents a day. Often, in the case of a *mela*, or religious fair, or on the sacred days in special temples, the railroads are overpacked. An English gentleman, Mr. Howard, of Allahabad, told me that on the decennial pilgrimage of Hindus to the junction of the Jamna and the Ganges, there are millions who come, and while the most walk all the way there and back, sometimes a distance of thousands of miles, there are hundreds of thousands who take the trains. The trains from the main line to the *mela* grounds run every five minutes, and yet these people crowd in with such persistence that there is no withstanding the pressure. This same gentleman informed me that he had seen the railroad officers stand with great bamboo rods, and beat away these pilgrims, pounding them over the head and shoulders with all their might, in order to keep back the dense crowd from overwhelming the train.

The pilgrims and ordinary natives take the third-class carriages. But the Europeans are taking to them very rapidly. When Bishop William Taylor was making his four years' evangelistic tour through India he began the custom, among the

Europeans, of riding in the third-class cars. It was not considered respectable to adopt that humble means of travel. He was asked:

"Why do you ride in third-class cars?"

His quick reply was,

"Because there are no fourth-class cars."

Ever since then—so I was told—it has been respectable for Europeans to ride in any class.

The travel in India is the cheapest I have ever known. The average cost on the third-class is one half a cent a mile, the cost on the second-class is one cent and a half a mile, and that on the first-class is three cents a mile.

One has little trouble with his baggage at the stations. As soon as the train stops he has only to go to the door of his compartment and call out, "*Kuli hai?*"—which means, "Is there a

A PAIR OF BULLOCKS USED FOR CARRIAGES.

porter about?" The question is answered by one or, more likely, a half-dozen barefooted natives.

Two *kulis* generally handled my baggage, the *bichauna* requiring one and the loose luggage another. They caught up my baggage, and carried it easily and carefully. In all my journeys I did not see a *kuli* drop or injure a piece of luggage. They handle your things as delicately as though each piece was a precious stone model of the lace-like marble Taj Mahal. There is little destruction of baggage anywhere in India. The pleasure of pounding travellers' trunks into pulp is a department of advanced Western civilization, which, no doubt, will reach India in due time.

The railway stations are supplied with good restaurants. The four regular meals, in common use in the domestic life of the Anglo-Indians, are carefully looked after by the railway authorities.

One of the most noticeable characteristics of Indian railway travel is to be found in the beautiful stations themselves. In the southern half of the empire they are kept more neat and beautiful than in the northern. Some of the railroads offer prizes for the best-kept and neatest station on the line. One road offers annually three prizes, one being 150 rupees, another 100 rupees, and a third 75 rupees, or $60, $40, and $30 respectively. I found the station-masters in the Dekhan persistently competing for the prizes. The effect of such encouragement is marvellous.

Some of the stations are pictures of rare beauty. There are plants along all the roads and paths leading to them, while flowering shrubbery is everywhere made to add beauty to the scene. Then in the station, and about its outer walls, there are plants growing in large jars. Many of the plants are of rich flower, and it is not difficult to see that there is a studied effort to have a succession of flowering plants, so that the traveller, so soon as he alights, can be greeted by them. The beauty of even the little country stations is amazing. Take obscure Karli as an example. It would be difficult for any one to bring more beauty out of the same area than the Eurasian in charge has developed from his little bungalow and its narrow enclosure. In another station I observed that the master had an antiquarian taste. He had filled his waiting-rooms with veritable antique furniture, such as the English must have brought out in the early days of the East India Company. Such curious tables and chairs, with griffins' claws, and other things to match, would set a *bric-à-brac* maniac doubly crazy. Along all the lines the restaurant tables are generally burdened with flowers. Even when there are no flowers, one sees a few sprigs of fern, or something else, which shows that the growths of the garden and the fields are not forgotten. In some of the obscurest parts of Calcutta I saw the windows of the poorest people smiling with a burden of plants. The blaze of flowers is everywhere. India deserves to share with the German Fatherland the beautiful and fragrant empire of flowers.

The trains do not enter the native Indian city, but stop in the English suburbs. The typical Indian city consists of three parts. First of all comes the old native city, where the streets are narrow, the houses truly Oriental, and the bazars flash out all the splendor, gayety, and filth of the Eastern life of five centuries ago. The old city may be the original one, or stand on the site

AN UNEXPECTED DANGER.—AN ENGINEER'S PREDICAMENT IN INDIA.

of it; but most likely it is only a late parvenu descendant of the first historically known city. For example, there have been six well-known and clearly identified Delhis. That of to-day is only the last survival of innumerable wasting wars. In Lahor, where I am now writing in a dark and quaint old house, there have been at least four different cities, all of which can be easily identified by the separate types of ruins. Outside of this original Indian city there is a belt of new houses, with large compounds or grounds, and well protected by high walls. This is the English part of the city, and has grown into existence since the English captured the country. No Englishman thinks of living in the close native city. He always has his home in the outer belt.

Now, it is in this outer belt that you always find the railway. I have seen no railroad, so far, which runs into the ancient native city or halts right by it. That would be neither business nor policy—and the Englishman has an eye to both. The English part of the Indian city is where most business is conducted, and is the city of the future. Last of all comes what is called the Cantonment, which here is always pronounced *Can-toon'-ment.* This is where the soldiers are; for the English soldiers must still guard the country. England took India by the sword, and must still hold it in the same way. The Cantonment is the outmost circle, the guarding enclosure, of the entire city.

The hotels of India are conducted by Europeans. They are few in number compared with the many travellers. For example, there are but two large hotels in Bombay, though there are many of smaller grade. The guest pays for meals and lodgings, according to the "American plan," and his charges are about four dollars a day. The hotel accommodations at the stations, even in the case of large towns, are of a kind peculiar to India. Refreshments are supplied at the station, where the restaurant is generally well kept and the supply of provisions is generous. There is variety as to the sleeping accommodations. The native does not want much accommodation. He drops over, goes to sleep, and never thinks of the circumstance of a great bedstead. But for Europeans the case is different. They have no fondness for the floor. There are sleeping provisions made for them by having cots or bed-frames, sometimes quite a number in a room, or in small rooms with low divisions, the travellers' own bedding supplying all further need. Where there are no bedrooms at the station, there is generally near by, a "rest-house," where the traveller can take his bedding, spread it out, and come to the station for his meals. At Bassein, for example,

CROSS-COUNTRY TRAVELLING IN INDIA.

the only place I found for sleeping accommodations was in a rest-house about a quarter of a mile from the station, while in the station itself there was ample provision for meals. In Madura, which has a population of fifty-two thousand, I saw no hotel. In the railway station there is an excellent restaurant, while across the street from the railway there is a very comfortable rest-house. These rest-houses are provided by the railway company, and the restaurant is also under the same management.

In some instances there are hotels, owned by the government, in the centre of the larger cities. While in Jaipur I stopped at one of these places, the *dak-bangla*. Here the accommodations were excellent and the prices moderate. I copy this bill, as a specimen of this particular part of a traveller's life in India:

No. 783.

Two Gentlemen Dr.

To BISHUMBER NATH,

Proprietor, "UNITED SERVICE HOTEL." Established 1865.

DELHI, AGRA, AND JEYPORE. STATE DAK-BUNGALOW.

1885. ☞ *It is particularly requested that the amount should be paid on presentation of Bill.*

				Rupees.	Annas.	Pies.	Rupees.	Annas.	Pies.
Jan.	28	To	2 Small Breakfasts	...	12	—			
		"	A Light	...	2	—			
		"	1 Cup Tea	...	6	—			
		"	2 Dinners	3	—	—	4	4	—
		"	1 Hot Bath	...	...	...	...	2	—
		"	Carriage to Train	...	...	...	1	—	—
		"	Room 1 Day, or Occupation fee	...	...	...	2	—	—
							7	6	—
		"	Carriage-hire for the Country	...	...	...	4	—	—
			Total Rupees	...	...	...	11	6	—

Delhi, Agra, and Jeypore. E. E. Received Payment with thanks,

Jan. 28, 1885. W. Abbott, Manager.

CHAPTER XXI.

MADRAS.—PAST AND PRESENT.

On arriving at Madras, by the early morning train, I found the atmosphere in a steamy, misty condition. There had been a terrific monsoon, which had uprooted trees and torn down many native huts. The sun, which had now come out clearly again, was rapidly drying the earth, and producing a suffocating air. This, however, lasted only a day or two, though at no time during my stay was the atmosphere of Madras as exhilarating as in the upper Dekhan. After passing through pools of water and among uprooted banyan-trees, we reached the delightful home of the Rev. Cecil M. Barrow, M.A., Principal of the Doveton College, who, with characteristic Anglo-Indian hospitality, had invited me to be his guest for a week. In no place in India was I made more thoroughly comfortable than here. This gentleman and his excellent lady had been long in India, and to their accurate knowledge of the country and its people I have been a great debtor.

The buildings of the Doveton College are situated in the rear of Mr. Barrow's dwelling. He is known to literature for his superbly annotated edition of Shakespeare's "Henry V.," and for various text-books which have grown out of his experience as a teacher. Mrs. Barrow, who has the same tastes as her husband, and has a minute knowledge of the better productions of English literature, gave me a cordial welcome, and made me quite forget, for the moment, my far wanderings. Mr. Barrow has done more to introduce into India the rich training of Oxford than any other gentleman whom I met in the country. By a happy accident—or was it only a yielding to my infirmity?—the rooms assigned me included Mr. Barrow's working library. My bed was in the middle of it, almost within reach of the masters in all literatures. To add to the kind services of this excellent family, when I left Madras for Ceylon, Mrs. Barrow supplied me with a letter of introduction to the Messrs. Ferguson, of Colombo, which opened the way to sources of unexpected enjoyment on the island, and to a study of its history and conditions, which otherwise I should have been entirely without.

Here, in the Presidency of Madras, was the beginning of the English possession of South India. A small strip of land along the coast, six miles long and one mile wide, was bought by the East India Company for six hundred pounds a year. The Rajah of Chandragiri made the sale, and conveyed the property in a title-deed engraved on a plate of gold.

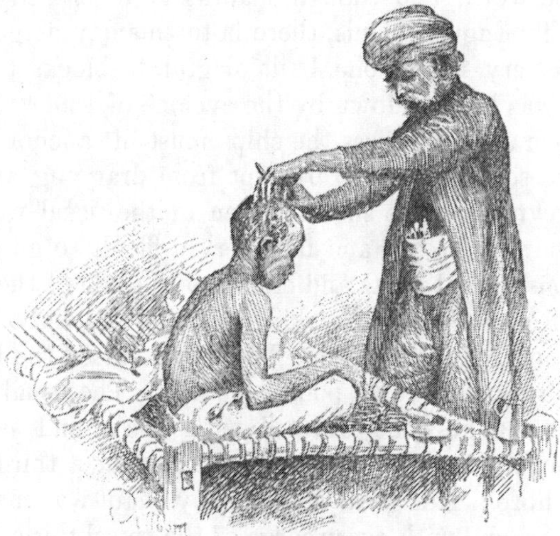

HINDU BARBER, MADRAS.

There are three sections of Madras. Vepery is the part where the English population reside. The houses are large, retired within spacious grounds, and thoroughly comfortable. There is a gateway in the enclosing wall or railing, on which, as a rule, the name of the resident is found. These houses are so far apart as to present the idea of country homes, but it is the way the English have learned, by their long experience in India, to be most comfortable. The grounds are the "compound." You are protected from the noise and dust of the thoroughfare, there is ample space for the children and for promenading, and for additional buildings. Most missionaries find it necessary to conform to the same rule. The quiet compound is universal. The missionaries are, for the most part, as much removed from the native quarter as though they did not live on the same hemisphere.

The next section of Madras is Blacktown, where the bazar, the stores of all kinds, and the offices are situated. Here, whenever they can be crowded in, are the lodging-places of the native population. The third section, fronting the sea, is devoted to the various kinds of government buildings. In the midst of this last class is St. Mary's Church.

The Madras population is about four hundred thousand. The entire coast is perhaps more swept by cyclones than any part of the Asiatic world, and though Madras is an old city, and has long been in English hands, there is to this day no good breakwater. A very strong one, built of granite blocks twenty-five feet long, was broken down by the cyclone of 1881. The result is, that when a storm arises the ships must lift anchor and stand well out to sea, in order to be kept from dragging anchor and being thrown upon the shore. Even in the usual weather the surf is generally heavy, and it is very difficult to go out in the queerly constructed boats and climb up the side of the vessel.

When I was about embarking here for Colombo I hired a boat, manned by eleven men. The waves tossed the boat high, and then dropped it correspondingly low. The usual boat here is built of mango-wood, caulked with straw, and sewed with strings of cocoa bark. The steamer lay about a third of a mile from the shore. Her great and lengthy chain was made fast to an iron buoy, and with every surge of the vessel this chain would tighten and be lifted out of the sea, or sink proportionately below it. My rowers were going to row deliberately over this chain. "What," thought I, "would be my fate should the chain tighten as we cross it? It would pitch our craft far into the air." I remonstrated, begged the men to row around the buoy —any course but the one on which they were bent. But they would not vary a whit from their line. It was the shortest way to the steamer. They watched their chance, when the chain was deep in the water, and so we shot safely over it. Now was an opportunity for drawing a long and free breath. By and by we reached the vessel's side.

But now came a new difficulty. The tossing of the waves brought our small boat high up along the stairway, and now dropped it as far below the lowest step. There is often here, I was informed, a rise and fall of twenty-five feet, so that one can easily imagine that there must often be a long pause before he can step easily and safely from his boat to the ship's ladder. Formerly, ladies had to be tied firmly in chairs, and lifted or lowered, as the case might be, from the yard-arm of the vessel. In my case the operation was most tedious. Up and down our boat went, and I chose to await my opportunity to step on the ladder. The officer on the steamer's deck shouted down to me:

"Now's your chance!"

"Not yet, so far as I can see," was my reply.

He waited impatiently, and showed plainly that, as I was about the last passenger to come on board, I had better be hurrying a little. By and by our boat came to a halt on a plane with the foot of the stepway, and I escaped from my shaky prison, and walked easily up to the deck.

TAMIL GIRL.

But my baggage? I had a very large and heavy trunk, with far too many books in it. Then came smaller parcels, together with my great *bichauna*. I determined not to witness the operation of getting that trunk on the deck. To all appearance the chances were that it would soon be at the bottom of Madras harbor. Some Madrasi jugglers were performing on deck for the amusement of the passengers; and other natives, in most scanty robes, were selling boxes of sea-shells and other curios. I went to the knot of spectators, and resolved to be patient, not knowing but that I should hear a splash, and then be informed that my trunk had been unfortunate. My eyes were on the jugglers' tricks, but my mind was on my treasures in the trunk. The time seemed long. But by and by there was a big buzz at the gangway. A troop of natives had dragged my trunk up the steps, and placed it safely on the steamer. Poor perspiring fellows! They had well earned their money. In due time the smaller baggage was brought up safely, and placed as a guard around the ponderous trunk. If I had my Indian experience to go over again, I would take all my belongings in bags, however great the number, and leave all the trunks at home.

In and about the government buildings were planned, in the last century, the great arrangements which led to the conquest of Southern India. The Fort was taken and retaken again and again, by French and English, when Dupleix and Bourdonnais and Lally conceived the magnitude of India's future, and were intent upon conquering the land for fair France. The keys of the Madras Fort were the keys of empire for the whole of India. It was a proud day, the 10th of September, 1746, when Bourdonnais, in the name of the King of France, received those keys in surrender from English hands. Both French and English knew that this was the key to all Southern India. Hence, twelve years later the French were defeated on the same spot. Then came, in 1769, Haidar Ali, at the head of his victorious army, and dictated terms of peace. The English were threatened on every side. It seemed as if they would soon be driven out of India.

There now came in a new factor. There sat at a plain desk in the Writers' Building a youth fresh from England—"Bob Clive." He was destined to eclipse all others in connection with England's conquest of India. Born in Shropshire, England, in 1725, he landed in India when only eighteen years of age. His parents sent him out in the East India Company's service, not knowing what to do with him at home. He became a clerk, and pretended to keep accounts and make out bills of lading. Suddenly the idea of India's future importance to England aroused him. The same thought, however, possessed Dupleix, the brilliant Frenchman, who applied it to his own country, and saw in the India of the future a great Oriental France. Clive saw for England what Dupleix had earlier seen for France. If India was desirable for France, why not for England? Clive formed a resolution to do his part to outwit and outfight Dupleix, and make India an English possession. His despair forsook him. He had twice attempted to shoot himself, but his pistol failed to discharge. He shut up his ledger, never to return to it again. The young man now became a soldier, enlisting first as an ensign. He entered into friendly relations with the commanding officer at Madras. Then began the long duel between him and Dupleix, along the Madras coast, for the possession of all India.

A HINDU YOUNG KULI WOMAN, MADRAS.

He entered on his military career as a commissary, with the rank of captain, under Major Lawrence. He came out of it the conqueror of India for England.

Clive was a new character to India. The French were in alliance with the natives. In due time Clive learned the native tricks, and caught the secret of dividing tribes. His methods were unscrupulous, but he justified himself on the ground that he was dealing with Indians, and must practise their own usages. His memorable answer, when afterwards charged at home with appropriating the vast wealth of native rulers, shows the bent of his mind: "When I remember my opportunity I am surprised at my own moderation!" It was during Clive's second visit to India that he fought the battle of Plassey, near Calcutta. Had he failed here, the French would have held the country, and all the fruits of the victories in the south would have been lost. But Clive won here, as everywhere else.

The Fort at Madras contains, in addition to its stores of military material, the large rooms in which all the old records are kept, and the governor's reception-room, sixty feet in length. In the Arsenal there are some curious relics of the old conflicts for the possession of the country, such as Dutch and French flags; two great helmets belonging to defeated native chiefs; a brass mortar, shaped like a tiger ready to spring upon its prey; the little iron cage in which Captain Armstrong had been kept a prisoner seven months in China; tiger-headed guns captured at Seringapatam in 1792; the six keys of Pondicherri, taken in 1778; a bloody projectile, which, when once blown out of the cannon, opens into a double-bladed sword, of nearly six feet in length; leather petards, with straps to fasten them to a gate, and many other objects known only to relentless Indian warfare.

St. Mary's Church is a fitting companion to the Fort. England's triumph in India has been due as much to her religion as to her sword. This historical Christian temple contains tablets to officers and others who have taken noble part in the conquest of India. But there are other tablets, to wives and children, reciting their virtues, and telling the ever old, and ever new, story of broken English hearts far off from home.

Madras is not without its American associations. Standing out at a distance from the Fort there is a tomb, with a square base and a pyramidal tower. One tablet contains a brief account of the marriage of Elihu Yale, who was governor of Madras, to the widow of Joseph Himers, a member of the council. She was ready for Yale's overture, and married him five months after her former husband's death—so narrates this inscription. The history of Yale is remarkable. He appeared afterwards in America, and settled in New Haven. His first gifts to a college there were larger, and perhaps earlier, than Branford's, when the latter gave his library in these words: "I give these books for founding a college in Connecticut." At any rate, the college was considered more indebted for its permanence to Elihu Yale than to any one else, and hence has borne his name ever since.

Another American association is here called up. Close to the Fort, under a stone canopy, is Chantry's magnificent statue of Cornwallis. From his surrender to Washington at Yorktown that officer went to India, and really retrieved there the prestige he had lost by the failure to subdue the American colonies.

The great drive in Madras is on the beautiful road along the beach. Here, in the late afternoon, the English residents take their airing. Many of the equipages are very handsome, with a full supply of liveried servants and outriders. The air from the sea is cool and delicious. The ladies, in the carriages, call for their husbands at their places of business, and the family take the evening drive together. When the drive is over they return home for dinner, which is as late in beginning as it is slow in ending.

TABLE OR STOOL, IN COARSE OLD SILVER.

CHAPTER XXII.

MY MADRASI HOME.

A Madrasi home, occupied by an English family long in the country, is a type of the English residences everywhere in India. There is, however, this single exception—the grounds are larger, and the house more retired, than I had elsewhere seen.

The first story of my Madrasi home was occupied mostly by servants, and the family have little to do with it. By a broad stairway you ascend to the upper veranda, where the family spend most of the time. This veranda is immense—one hundred and fifty feet long and about fifty broad. There are chairs and lounges scattered here and there, nearly all made of open rattan-work, and of the fine designs peculiar to the East. They have taken shape, most likely, from old-time Indian models, but have undergone some English adaptations. The rocking-chair appeared here as a regular institution. Here, on this veranda, were little tables, where books and newspapers lay. The latest London *Times* was just twenty-four days old. The ladies sit here and sew or read, as they choose. If there is any breeze at all, it is sure to sweep past this veranda, and those who recline in the easy-chairs can catch it. The drawing-room differs little, except in higher ceiling and broader spaces, from an American parlor. All the hangings are light, and every window is protected by Venetian blinds. The thick American curtain, which hangs before the window, and keeps out the sunlight and the sweet breath of the sky, is not known in India. The bedroom is large and airy. Insects, like all forms of life, abound in India, and minute precautions are taken against them in the Indian home. My bed, for example, is placed in the middle of the floor, and consists of the very lightest frame imaginable. Pains are generally taken to have the legs of the bedstead stand on glass or metallic rests, to prevent insects from finding an easy ascent. My table is a broad mahogany one. It is a luxury to have room in which to lay out your books and papers! No wonder the Indians use mahogany. Their white ants find it too hard and distasteful to burrow through. Racks for clothing are not against the wall, but stand out in the floor. Clothes-presses, and other places for concealing your clothing, are avoided. Everything is done to prevent the insects from concealing themselves in your garments. Crickets abound, and if one is not careful they will ruin his new coat the first night he gets it from the tailor's. Everything must be kept not only as secure from the prowling and climbing insects as possible, but ought to be shaken out before being put on.

I was as much amused at the crows of Madras as at any one feature of its animated life. They are very tame, and as wise

LITTLE INNOCENTS ABROAD.

as any that ever pulled up an Ohio farmer's corn, and then knew how to keep at a safe distance from his gun. They fly into any part of the Madrasi home, and caw away at one as if he were the East India Company and the stranger only a Frenchman. They perch over the door in the transom while the guest is at breakfast, and wait impatiently for him to eat his last spoonful of rice and curry and his last plantain. The moment the persons who have been breakfasting are gone the crows swoop down on the table, and pick up anything they can find, and are off with it. The servants have to watch them all the time, to keep dishes designed for the table out of their grasp. They are especially fond of the kitchen, and have to be watched, as remorseless depredators, all the time.

My host, Mr. Barrow, on whose broad piazza the circumstance happened, in the presence of his family, told me the following story of two crows: His dog, a white fox-terrier, lay on his fore-paws, gnawing a bone. A crow wished the bone, and came down and stood beside the dog and began to peck at him. The dog snarled, but was not to be cheated out of his bone. He held it firmly, for experience had taught him that it would take its flight the moment he lost his grip. The crow saw that he was unequal to the task of getting the bone, and so he disappeared. In a short time two crows appeared upon the scene. One sat before the dog and the other behind him. The one in the rear pecked the dog violently; and when the attacked quadruped wheeled round to resist his assailant the crow in front caught up the bone and sailed off with it. Of course, the other crow had no further motive for remaining, and the two flew away in company to enjoy together their ill-gotten gain.

But the crows of Madras are not confined to homes. They are church-goers. The Sunday morning I worshipped in the Black Town church they were present in full number and speech. They cawed uninterruptedly during parts of the service. They sat on the rafters and along the spaces in the upper weather-boarding which had been left open for ventilation. As there was nothing for them to eat, and never had been, I have not yet learned what induced them to come, except simply to be ready in case some edibles should be forthcoming. Nobody paid the slightest attention to them. Every one was used to their consummate impudence. As the fatigue of my long railroad ride had taken away my voice completely, my kind host, Mr. Barrow, took my place in the pulpit. The denominational landmarks undergo a wonderful diminution in India. There is always brotherhood on the front line. One has to get even as far away as to the Christianity in a pagan land to see the full beauty of Christian unity.

There are flowers in abundance about my Madrasi home. They are planted in pots, and fill up all available spaces. You see them in their bright and delicate tints, caught from the equatorial sun, in the recesses of the verandas, on the doorstep, along the balconies, out on the sward, and wherever there is the space to put them. Large flowering shrubs adorn the compound, and relieve the scene of verdure. The varieties are mostly Oriental. Excepting roses, I saw few specimens with which I had been familiar in the Western lands. Some trees are fragrant with their blossoms, and the aroma reminds me of that of orange flowers more than of any other variety.

The meals are differently timed from those of one's earlier and Occidental life. I had become somewhat accustomed to the revolution while on board ship, coming to Bombay. In India itself there is the same new arrangement, only everything has a greater emphasis. For instance, the curry of India itself has a sting to it of which I had not a suspicion before. Your eating in this country is based on the necessities of the climate rather than on the humors of the people or the force of fashion. For example, you must rise early in the morning, or you will do but little through the day. The time when the average American business man gets to work, say nine o'clock, or somewhat later, is about the hour when the Anglo-Indian expects to be really through with his morning's labor, and, indeed, well on towards his day's task. My host rises about four, and by eight or nine he has done the larger part of his day's work. The first meal you take is the *choti-hazari*, or little breakfast, which consists of a cup of coffee, or, more frequently, Indian tea, and a single slice of toast or buttered bread. The code requires you to take this as the first thing, and to do no work whatever until you have had your *choti-hazari*. You are now ready for work at your desk, in literary labor, or anything else which does not require you to leave your house.

If your duties make you leave your house for a place of business elsewhere in the city, you do not go thither before nine o'clock at the earliest. When endeavoring to secure a ticket for the steamer to Ceylon, not a single responsible clerk in Binny's office could be found before ten o'clock; and this, too, on the sailing-day of the steamer.

It is in the early hours, before the sun is high, and even before he is up, that you must do your walking. There is danger of sunstroke to an unaccustomed head without careful guarding, even very early. Judge Muir, of Bombay, told me that he regarded the sun as having its most dangerous power before seven in the morning. You must wear your pith helmet, and also take your white umbrella, no matter how soon you start for your walk, lest the sun do damage before you get back.

Breakfast is in order any time from ten until one. It is the most flexible Indian meal. On the steamers the regular hour for it is one. In my Madrasi home it was at eleven. It is simply the mid-day meal, and whenever it does come one is safe in calling it breakfast, or the French *déjeûner;* although Anglo-Indians generally speak of it as *tiffin.* It consists of about four courses; frequently beginning with soup, and always concluding the main dishes with rice and curry. It is simply a small dinner, served in *table d'hôte* style. There is no mixing of dishes. When the steak and potatoes are handed around, and you have finished that course, your plate and knife and fork are removed, and you are served with others for the next course. If there are six courses, you have each in succession, and only one or two articles served at a time. I did not find that fruit is used to begin a meal with, but is always brought in at the close. Flowers are often put on the table—not a trim bouquet, but simply a bunch of loose flowers, as though caught up in a pleasing hurry, after the manner of Nature's charming negligence.

The meats are much the same as with us—beef, mutton, and fish being the staples. Teal is a favorite game in Madras. Fruits are the loose-skinned orange, the plantain, and the pomegranate. Grapes do not prosper, and are scanty. Apples come from the upper country, as the lower lands in India do not produce them. The best I have seen in India were in the great fruit-market of Bombay. They were beautiful in color, but too sweet to be palatable.

Throughout India there is a prevailing silence after breakfast. You are expected to take yourself away. People who have little to do can remember that they rose early, and that now they can sleep awhile, and make up for lost time. In offices, and business places generally, there is a universal pause for *tiffin.* Many mercantile houses are entirely closed, and I found some inconvenience in small business matters because no one was to be seen, and I had to go back again later in the afternoon. About two o'clock there is a stir again, and matters move on briskly until six o'clock, when dinner may come; or it may be half-past seven, or even later.

Dinner is the Anglo-Indian's great stand-by. Whatever else suffers, his dinner must come, and he is not going to hurry from it. It, like the *tiffin*, is always served in the *table d'hôte* style. It begins with soup, then come the fish, meats, and vegetables, in due order. The rice and curry must come at the last. You do not eat it with the fork alone, but with the spoon and fork together. I was told, very soon after landing, that I must not fail to conform to two things—never use the word "sir" in conversing with clergymen, and always eat my rice with both spoon and fork, the spoon in my left hand and the fork in my right. Of course, I was careful of both pieces of advice. The shunning of the word "sir" seems to have some reference to the servants,

A STRIKING SPECTACLE.—ILLUMINATION OF THE SURF.

who use it in addressing their Anglo-Indian employers. It is a suggestion, not of equality, as with us, but of the difference between the upper and lower social orders.

The dinner lasts a good while. Nobody has any motive for hurrying. The day's work is done, and the longer it is spun out the fuller the conversation. When dinner is over the family and their guests go out upon the veranda and take easy seats. The more space one can occupy the better. There is plenty of room everywhere—no crowding, lofty ceilings, great wicker chairs.

One of the peculiarities of the country is the *pankhas*, or fans, suspended from the ceiling. These are short hangings, generally of stiff brown linen, about a foot wide and often many yards long, according to the space you wish to have fanned. The frame, for instance, on steamers, is the length of the tables. A thin rope is attached to it, and is run through a hole in the wall, or runs over a wheel, and a servant outside pulls it, and you are fanned. You sit right under it, and the fanning goes on all the time, while the poor fellow who is pulling the rope by which you are fanned is sweltering away in the next room, or even at a greater distance.

You see the *pankha* everywhere. No house is without it. When you call, even before you have doffed your helmet and rubbed away the perspiration, you find yourself fanned. The swinging thing goes on all the time you are in your friend's house. In the hot season these fans often go all night, right over your bed. Multitudes of Anglo-Indians could not sleep without being fanned all the while. They would well-nigh suffocate. All the counting-houses have them. Not a bank in the country, or a steamer-office, but has them swinging away, *kulis* pulling them back and forth. Poor fellows, they often go to sleep; and even then they swing them back and forth. I saw one sleeping in a Bombay bank, and yet his hand tugged away at his work. Sometimes, when they get utterly worn out, they will tie the rope to one of their feet, and pull away with that until they have rested their arms.

When I first saw a *pankha* in a church it struck me as a most amusing arrangement. But I soon became accustomed to even the ecclesiastical *pankhas*. In one of the English churches in Madras there are not only *pankhas* for the entire congregation, but for the clerk and reader, and right over the pulpit, for the preacher while he is preaching. You see few individual fans. People think that as much caloric is evolved by using one as there would be without it. Strangely enough, no one has as yet invented a machine for fanning. The man who does it will liberate from monotony scores of thousands of *kulis* who are tugging at these ropes and fanning their Anglo-Saxon conquerors.

CHAPTER XXIII.

COALS TO AN INDIAN NEWCASTLE.

ONE of the most curious of all the recent phenomena of Hindu thought is an American reinforcement of Buddhism. Madras seems to have been a chosen Theosophic centre. I had not been in India a day—indeed, I had not landed as yet—before I heard from Anglo-Indians concerning the doings of Madame Blavatsky and Colonel Olcott. That is the order in which these now notorious names are usually presented.

In 1875, the Theosophical Society was founded in New York. Its objects, as stated in the "rules," were declared to be: "1. To form the nucleus of a universal brotherhood of humanity, without distinction of race, creed, or color. 2. To promote the study of Aryan and other Eastern literature, religions, and sciences, and vindicate its importance. 3. To investigate the hidden mysteries of nature and the psychical powers latent in man."

Colonel H. S. Olcott and Madame Helen B. Blavatsky were founders of this society. Olcott, of New York, had been an officer in the Civil War in America, and seems to have long been a firm believer in spiritualistic operations. Blavatsky, the author of "Isis Unveiled," was the daughter of Colonel Hahn, of the Russian Horse Artillery, and quondam widow of General Blavatsky, Governor of Erivan, in Armenia, during the Crimean War.* These kindred spirits regarded India as a fair field for the display of their genius, and for their double crusade to overthrow Christianity and to substitute for it an eclectic Oriental system.

They arrived in India in February, 1879, and began their work in Bombay. They declared themselves the representatives of a

---

* B. H. Badley, D.D., article, "The Rise and Fall of Theosophy in India," in *Christian Advocate*, New York, April 21, 1887.

large religio-philosophical society in New York, and solicited the attention and co-operation of cultivated natives of India. From Bombay they went to Madras. Here they made the real beginning of their success in India. They met an educated native, Damodar K. Manalankar, who had some money, and was therefore especially attractive. He entered into relationship with them. *The Theosophist*, designed to be the organ of the new movement, was established. It published reports of meetings, gave information of the objects of the Theosophic apostles, published accounts of the remarkable phenomena accompanying the work of the leaders, set forth the great advantages which would come to India by accepting these special doctrines, and flattered the pride of the natives by telling them that they had, already, much of the very essence which these people had come to India to reveal once more. The Coulombs, a family destined to play the important part of an exposure of the whole of this precious nonsense, cordially co-operated with Blavatsky, Olcott, and Company.*

Blavatsky and Olcott next went to the north, and established themselves in Simla. This being the summer seat of the government, should they succeed in this important political and social centre, they could hope for great things throughout the country. Here they gained a very important disciple—A. P. Sinnett, the editor of the *Pioneer*, the leading daily of India, published at Allahabad, and author of a work on "Occult Science." The system was here expounded at great length. The two chief apostles of the new world-faith had the help of various spirits, who were members of the Tibetan brotherhood spoken of as Mahatmas. But these two people were not particular about the origin of their belief. Buddhism seems to have furnished the principal element, but all the old and dying religions of India were drawn upon at will. Olcott became a Hindu among the Hindus, a Buddhist among the Buddhists, a Mussulman among the Mussulmans, and a Zoroastrian among the fire-worshippers—praising up every system of religion except Christianity, though himself a professed Buddhist.†

---

* "The Theosophical Society," by Rev. Arthur Theophilus, Madras, 1882, p. 18.

† *The Theosophist*, May, 1882, p. 191.

The War on Christianity.

Of the intense opposition of this mongrel faith to Christianity, we may judge by the following declarations: "Trinitarianism may supersede religions that are inferior to it, such as devil worship and various forms of gross idolatry; but it will never supplant a pure monotheistic faith, seeing that it is hampered not only with the clumsy theology of a Father, a Son, and a third person, being one and the same God, but also with the doctrine of incarnation." In another place, Christianity is thus scoffed at: "It is a scheme of thought which throws reason and logic overboard altogether, and rests its claims entirely on sentimentality; it is a religion, in fact, fit for women and not men." Olcott speaks of Shem, Ham, and Japheth as "the mythical sons of the imaginary Noah." Of the Biblical chronology he says: "When the ancient historical mines of the Egyptian hieroglyphs, the Sanskrit Shastras, and the Assyrian tile records were once opened, antiquity was pushed back *countless centuries*, and the Biblical chronology fell to pieces."* Of the missionaries in India, he says that they are "lazy, ignorant, and good-for-nothing." He says of Christendom, that it "shows her real principles in her Armstrong guns and whiskey distilleries, her opium ships, sophisticated merchandise, prurient amusements, licentious habits, and political dishonesty."†

These apostles of Theosophy were careful to visit the mission fields, and to counteract, so far as they could, the work of the apostles of Christ. So soon as they became known as opponents of the Christian faith, many of the educated natives gave them a hearing, hired halls for the *séances*, and welcomed them within their doors. I know of one place where there was such eagerness to hear them, and for the honor of entertaining them, that, on their arrival at the railway station, there were seven equipages in waiting, competing for the privilege of taking them to native homes as honored guests. Many of the larger cities in the north were visited, such as Calcutta, Lucknow, and Allahabad. Everywhere there was great flourish of trumpets,

---

* "Farewell Address in Patcheapper's Hall."

† "The Whole Truth about the Theosophical Society," p. 21.

and the success of Blavatsky and Olcott in propagating their opinions was heralded in all directions.

The Absurdity Exposed.

But a marvellous change came over the calm progress of this revived pagan wisdom. In Madras the Coulombs, who had been the chosen intimates and friends of the two apostles of the ancient Theosophy of the Hindus. There seems to have been a disturbance of the friendly relations of the Coulombs and the apostles, even while they were living together in such apparent unanimity. But Blavatsky and Olcott went to Europe, and, whether the money for the Coulombs gave out, or whatever be the cause, this much is true, that the Coulombs exposed the Theosophic trick. Madame did the least shrewd thing in all this propagation of her notions when she went away from Madras, and left her papers scattered about in confusion, and left the Coulombs in possession of her private letters, in which she explained and gave directions for constructing the entire machinery of the esoteric Theosophy.

In Madras there is published the *Madras Christian College Magazine*, a monthly of about one hundred octavo pages. It is an excellent serial, and not only possesses great value for its light on Indian topics, but on general evangelical and theological themes. In September, 1884, it startled its readers by an excellent piece of literary enterprise. It secured the whole mass of the correspondence of Blavatsky with the Coulombs. There was no mistake as to the evidence. It was too direct to be gainsaid. The writing of the letters was in the exact hand of the author herself, and an expert has recently published an excellent pamphlet, in which he gives a report of each of the letters, and shows by peculiarities in the handwriting the genuineness of the published correspondence. His painstaking report covers the whole case, and would serve as an excellent model for all similar attempts to determine the genuineness of any manuscript.

We now come to the letters themselves. The editors of the magazine say: "We have weighed the responsibility and resolved to take it up. After satisfying ourselves by every precaution that the sources of the following narrative are genuine and authentic, we have resolved, in the interests of public morality, to publish it."

Madame smokes cigarettes, and her cigarette papers play an important part in all her scenic displays. In many cases, her method is to take a cigarette paper, mark it in some way, or tear off a corner in a peculiar line, and then, by her occult forces, despatch this paper to some remote place, where her deluded votaries find it. Here is a specimen letter, written from Madras:

"Last night, Sunday, I wanted to show my friends a phenomenon, and sent a cigarette tied up with my hair, to be placed opposite Watson's Hotel (Bombay), in the coat of arms, under the Prince of Wales's statue, under the horn of the unicorn. Captain Maitland had himself chosen the town and named the place. He spent thirteen rupees for a telegram to Police Commissioner Grant, his brother-in-law. The latter went the moment he received it, and found nothing. It is a dead failure, but I do not believe it, for I saw it there clearly at three in the morning. I am sorry for it, for Captain Maitland is a Theosophist, and spent money over it. They want to tear the cigarette paper in two, and keep one half. And I will choose the same places, with the exception of the prince's statue, for our enemies might watch and see the cigarette fall and destroy it. I enclose an envelope, with a cigarette paper in it. I will drop another half of a cigarette behind the queen's head, where I dropped my hair the same day, or Saturday. Is the hair still there? and a cigarette still under the cover? Oh God, oh God! What a pity!

"Yours faithfully, H. P. B."

On a slip of paper accompanying the above, the following was written:

"Roll a cigarette of this half, and tie it with H. P. B.'s hair. Put it on the top of the cupboard made by Nunbridge, to the farthest corner near the wall on the right. Do it quick."

Now the one great thing revealed by this letter was, that all the details are arranged beforehand. No wonder the Theosophy succeeded for a time. To convince the believers, or persons whom it is hoped to make believers, in this alleged occult faith, great events must be brought to pass. A thing must be done with a slip of paper, and instantaneously the paper, or whatever it is, must be found a thousand miles away. Of course, when the other slip has been previously sent away, and the object already deposited, it is very easy afterwards to say, "Go and find it." Naturally enough, it is found.

One of the chief forms of impressing the people was to declare the unknown and the unknowable. These strolling persons claimed that they could write down a request for a thing, and in a few minutes receive an answer from the far-off Tibetan

Kut Humi. A person might lose a brooch, but, by proper representation to Madame and Colonel, Kut Humi would instantly reply that it was under a certain tree, and that it could be found there. Of course, with such distinctness of reply, such specific response, the result was always satisfactory. Still they did some wondrous things, and some mysteries which their jugglery has brought to pass have not yet been solved. Madame, in one letter, is very anxious that something should happen in Bombay to convince the sceptical. In another, she expresses her anxiety that Jacob Lasoon, a man of immense wealth, living in Puna, should become a disciple; for, in that case, he would give ten thousand rupees to repair the Theosophic headquarters. In another she writes to Madame Coulomb: "I beg you to send this letter (here enclosed) to Damodar in a *miraculous* way. It is very important." Of a certain attempt to play a handkerchief trick, she wrote: "I believe the handkerchief is a failure. Every one here is anxious to see something. My hair will do well on the old tower in Siam, or even in Bombay. Select a good spot, and write me at Amritsar *poste restante*. . . . Have you put the cigarette on the cupboard of Nunbridge? Do something for the old man, Damodar's father."

These tricks were of such thin disguise that it would seem impossible to deceive any one. Everything was arranged in all details, either by mail or telegraph, and the curiosity and inquiry of those whom it was desirable to deceive were gradually led along the desired line, and to these individuals were suggested just the things they asked for. Hence the trick succeeded. But there were cases when things have had to be done with more despatch than even the post or telegraph furnish. Then, by adroit prearrangement, Kut Humi dropped his divine answers down through crevices in the ceiling. M. Coulomb was the engineer-in-chief of this part of the apparatus, but in all cases Madame Blavatsky wrote the answer to the questions of inquirers. Here is a bright and cheerful letter, written after the success of an important scheme:

> "It is just post time, my dear. . . . Yes, let Srinavas Rao prostrate himself before the shrine, and whether he asks [anything] or not, I beg you to send to him this reply by Kut Humi, for he expects something. *I know what he wants.* To-morrow you shall have a long letter. Grand news!
>
> "Thanks, H. P. B."

Now this Srinavas Rao was a native judge, in the employ of the English government; and we have the picture of a man of no little prominence among his fellow natives publicly lending himself to these creatures, and prostrating himself at their shrine.

These Theosophists were very shrewd in trying to manipulate

WEST GATE OF THE VISHNU TEMPLE, AT CONJEVERAM, NEAR MADRAS.

the wealthy and influential. Their gospel was not to the poor. Here is what Madame writes about the scheme to practise upon the credulity of a very distinguished native: "I am told that Dewan Bahadur Ragunath Rao . . . wishes to place something in the temple. In case he should do so, here is Christofolo's answer. For God's sake arrange this, and we are triumphant." In another letter this same effusive woman writes: "You must read the key of the scheme to me. Do it by the underground way." Here is a case where she will not trust even the Colonel himself to look into the shrine. She must be the sole manager of the innermost mysteries of the grand modern Theosophy. In one of her letters she even calls him a "muff." In another letter she gets angry with everybody, and uses such profane language as a hardened Malay sailor would fairly shiver to employ.

The Effect of the Exposure.

The editor of the magazine in which these letters were published raised a tremendous storm. His enterprise was worthy of London or New York. But he astounded his readers by saying that he had made public only a very small part of what was in his possession, and that he was ready to give more, whenever he might choose. The public officials and society gentry, from among the natives who were named in the correspondence, were highly incensed. They would have brought suit in the courts, but this would only have rendered them ridiculous to a still greater degree. Dr. Hartmann, a dupe of the Theosophic pair, rushed into print, to show that Madame and Colonel were really very good people, and that they possessed a wonderful amount of truth. But he was, as the sequel showed, a very poor advocate. He let out what he knew concerning the stage trickery of the whole matter. It turned out, according to his confession, that the shrine had secret passages, holes in the walls, and all possible contrivances for carrying on a piece of gigantic and systematic fraud.

To this published account of the minor deception of the Theosophists, I must add a fact which I derived from an honored missionary of the Church Missionary Society, now engaged in work in India. He says that one of his most inquiring native members, hearing that Madame and Colonel were about to visit his city, asked him, his pastor, if he would advise against his going to one of their *séances*. The pastor, believing that no harm would come to the man, for he was a shrewd observer, made no objection. The man went, and had an interview with Madame. All at once she started into a rhapsodical abstraction. She claimed that the spirits were singing and playing. "Don't you hear them?" she asked of this gentleman, whom she regarded as only an unsuspecting native. "Yes," he answered, "I hear the music." Now the music which he heard was none other than an ordinary music-box, whose varying tunes happened to be quite familiar to the visitor's ears. This instrument was concealed in the folds of Madame's dress. The trick was hardly well enough concealed to deceive a child. In this case, it not only satisfied this member of the missionary's church that the travelling couple had nothing new to offer, but, his experience becoming finally known, prevented any success from their stay in that important city.

The Deception Acknowledged in England.

As to the effect of the publication of the correspondence, in the *Christian College Magazine*, on the adherents of this new paganism, there was a falling away of some, while others cried out persecution. The leaders went so far as to deny the genuineness of the essential parts of the correspondence, but the proof was too positive. Mr. Gribble, the expert employed to examine the correspondence, reported that "the letters [to the Coulombs] contain scarcely any interpolations at all, and what there are are of harmless character." Madame declared that she would prosecute the *Christian College Magazine*. But she did not do it. This failure on her part was most serviceable to her cause, for then the proof would have been furnished in the courts that she wrote every word of what had been made public.*

But while the legal results were not reached, the same moral end was gained—one which resulted in the total failure of the whole movement in India. The adventurers appeared in England. Blavatsky, Olcott, Sinnett, and Company presented themselves before the Society for Psychical Research in London. This society is presided over by Professor Balfour Stewart, F.R.S., and it determined to sift the affair to the very bottom. The representations of the appellants were duly recorded and printed. The society then sent out to India an expert, Mr. Richard Hodgson, B.A., "who investigated the phenomena. He found that all were explainable by such tricks as sliding panels in doors, trap-doors in ceilings, and other forms of deception, and pre-

---

* *The Pioneer*, Bombay, January 28, 1885.

sented his report to the society, which plainly showed the would-be reformers were simply impostors." *

Mr. Hodgson, after having examined many witnesses, returned to England, and the committee of the Psychical Society made the following report:

"1. That of the letters put forth by Madame Coulomb, all those, at least, which the committee have had the opportunity of themselves examining, and of submitting to the judgment of experts, are undoubtedly written by Madame Blavatsky; and suffice to prove that she has been engaged in a long-continued combination with other persons to produce by ordinary means a series of apparent marvels for the support of the Theosophic movement.

"2. That, in particular, the shrine of Adyar, through which letters purporting to come from Mahatmas were received, was elaborately arranged with the view to the secret insertion of letters and other objects, through a sliding panel at the back, and regularly used for this purpose by Madame Blavatsky or her agents.

"3. That there is consequently a very strong general presumption that all the marvellous narratives put forward as evidence of the existence and occult power of the Mahatmas are to be explained as due, either (*a*) to deliberate deceptions carried out by or at the instigation of Madame Blavatsky, or (*b*) to spontaneous illusion, or hallucination, or unconscious misrepresentation, or invention on the part of the witnesses.

"4. That after examining Mr. Hodgson's report of the results of his personal inquiries, they are of opinion that the testimony to these marvels is in no case sufficient, taking amount and character together, to resist the force of the general presumption above mentioned. Accordingly they think it would be a waste of time to prolong the investigation."

Of Madame Blavatsky the committee thus speak:

"It forms no part of our duty to follow Madame Blavatsky into other fields. But with reference to the somewhat varied lines of activity which Mr. Hodgson's report suggests for her, we may say that we cannot consider any of these as beyond the range of her powers. The homage which her immediate friends have paid to her abilities has been, for the most part, of an unconscious kind; and some of them may still be unwilling to credit her with mental resources which they have hitherto been so far from suspecting. For our own part, we regard her neither as a mouthpiece of hidden seers, nor as a mere vulgar adventuress; we think that she has achieved a title to permanent remembrance as one of the most accomplished, ingenious, and interesting impostors in history."

Colonel Olcott is thus described by Mr. Hodgson:

"The testimony of Colonel Olcott himself I found to be so fundamentally at variance with fact in many important points that it became impossible for me

---

* Badley, article "The Rise and Fall of Theosophy in India."

to place the slightest value upon the evidence he had offered. But in saying this I do not mean to suggest any doubt as to Colonel Olcott's honesty of purpose. In short, my lengthy examinations of the numerous array of witnesses to the phenomena showed that they were, as a body, excessively credulous, excessively deficient in the powers of common observation, and too many of them prone to supplement that deficiency by culpable exaggeration.

"It would in truth be impossible to reproduce all the palterings and equivocations in the evidence offered to me, or to describe, with any approach to adequacy, how my personal impressions of many of the witnesses deepened my conviction of the dishonesty woven throughout their testimony."

The Society for Psychical Research received the report, and adopted it, and this ended the matter. It had taken great pains, examined witnesses in India, and reached its conclusion without difficulty. The result in India was what might be expected. The New Theosophy had been weighed and found wanting. It soon lost all support, and is now remembered among the dead substitutes for Christianity which Christendom itself transported to India.

We now come to the question, Why this new vagary in India? What does it mean? I answer, that the antagonism of some Hindus and Brahmans to Christianity makes them ready to accept any help against it, and causes them to make sacrifices to introduce any form of opposition. On the other hand, many have lost faith in their old religions, and do not know what to do. They stand on the fence, and are looking for some place of refuge.

The readiness with which educated natives welcomed this miserable deception is the most lamentable feature of the whole matter. One after another was deluded. The flattering correspondence and printed documents overwhelmed them. It must be remembered that all India abounds in natives who claim sympathy with the new, and the newest, science. They are avowed Hindus or Mohammedans, but they hold that their faith should take on new accretions, and accommodate itself to the latest learning. They will have nothing to do with Christianity. They are out at sea. They are not willing to accept Christianity, and yet the old faith has lost all hold on them. They see the King's march. They hear His voice. They tremble at His approach. They know the certain triumph of Christianity. But they will stay its march as long as possible. They will throw logs in its path, and, if they cannot find logs, they will cast straws in its

16

face. These people hail anything with gladness which serves their purpose of opposing the Christian faith. Some of them would muster into their service any infidel books which Christian lands have produced, and make a great cry against the divisions of Christianity. Hence such men spread abroad the writings of Paine and Ingersoll, which have already found their way into several of the Indian tongues. Then, Hindu and Mohammedan opponents of Christianity never grow tired of finding some new force to employ against it. Therefore, when Blavatsky and Olcott became known as opponents of the Christian faith many of the natives gave them a cordial reception.

Money the Probable Cause of the Esoteric Crusade.

Two theories have been advanced to account for the invasion of India by Blavatsky and Olcott. One is that Blavatsky is a secret Russian agent, who has chosen this way of getting sympathy and support for a later Russian invasion. I cannot see any real support for this view, though some good grounds for it have been presented. The most probable of all causes is, that money lies at the bottom of the entire matter. I have no doubt that the wealth of India has produced the invasion of this American Theosophy, and that it was to get an easy and large livelihood that these people spent their time in India. Many of the natives are nobles, and roll in wealth, drawing great pensions from the government, their ancestors having been thus bought off from their thrones by England in Clive's day. Some of them are capable and brainy in all things but religion. It is no wonder that, in the general break-up of the old conditions in India, the gold of the Hindus should excite the itching palm of adventurers, even in England. The Coulomb correspondence abounds in shrewd financial measures. Blavatsky, in one of her letters to Madame Coulomb, swears prodigiously at a certain native for giving her only two thousand rupees when he ought to have given much more. Now that is eight hundred dollars, a pretty neat sum for the new esoteric wisdom! Yet she was manipulating for a much larger amount, and so failed in her great object. The published correspondence shows a careful planning for larger lodgings, servants, and everything necessary for a great domestic establishment. Not only must halls be rented, but ample funds for wide propagation be piled up.

The Missionaries not Disturbed.

The manner in which the missionaries of India treated this delusion was superb. To see Christianity at its very best one must visit a far-away mission field, and watch its representatives in the presence of a new and attractive enemy. They observed a calmness and equipoise which were simply magnificent. The Lucknow *Witness* and the Bombay *Guardian* came out in strong protests, and said, in substance, "Wait awhile; this is a deception; give it time, and it will kill itself. We have no fears of the result." So soon as the exposure came, all the Christian workers had a sense of relief, not that they had ever once doubted the sequel, but that they had been embarrassed by the difficulties which presented themselves to the natives by such a mysterious imposition from the civilized West. But when the exposure came the case was immediately reversed. The native mind was attracted anew to the open methods and moral purity of the Christian missionaries, and to the cause which they represented.

SURAHI (WATER-VESSEL), MODERN KASHMIR WARE, COPPER-TINNED.

CHAPTER XXIV.

CEYLON.—COLOMBO BY THE SEA.

Of all the tropical scenes which delight the voyager in the Orient, nothing exceeds the beauty of the eastern coast of Ceylon when seen from the steamer coming from Madras. Every mile of the way from Point de Galle to Colombo brings a new enchantment. The whole sweep of vision, from the breaking surf along the shining coast to the mountain-peaks, abounds in rich and strange scenes. Every vale and granite buttress furnish a new surprise. The Singhalese are not content to go moderately into antiquity for heroes. They begin at the beginning. There is a reef running all the way from India across to Ceylon, which lies just beneath the surface, and shuts off all important navigation. This is called Adam's Bridge. Not only does the bridge bear his name, but the fifth highest mountain is called Adam's Peak. But Adam's name is a frequent one in the island. Why not? The general tradition is, that when Adam was driven out of Paradise this Singhalese paradise was his next home.

Long before I reached Colombo (*corumbu*=harbor), or could see where it sits, like a queen on her throne, with the sea as her kingdom, Ceylon presented the appearance of a mountain in the sea. This, however, is only a sea effect. The area covered by mountains is not over one fifth of the whole island. But the mountains are so abrupt and beautiful that they seem to predominate over the level country. The island rises in towering masses from a zone of unsurpassed luxuriance, the brightest gem in the sunny Indian Ocean. Its bays, precipitous shores, tangled jungles, and jutting rocks make a picture of tropic splendor which no pen can describe. The most of the land skirting the northern third of the coast is covered with dense jungle. The southwestern plain is far more fertile, and produces every fruit known to the tropics. The highest mountain is Piduru Talagala. It is over eight thousand feet high. But there are several other peaks, such as Kirigalpota, Totapelakanda, and Kuduhugala, which are of nearly equal height. These mountains, with the sea sweeping in upon the shore, and sending its spray high up the granite barriers, present a strangely beautiful picture.

A CATAMARAN.

One gets new ideas of English pluck when he gets at the antipodes and the equator. Look at this Colombo harbor. The

English needed a safe place for their immense commerce; spent £4,000,000 to get one; and, to make the wild sea behave itself, stole five hundred of its turbulent acres. The result is the splendid harbor of Colombo.

All at once the *Dacca* makes a graceful curve in her course, and the domes and spires and bright houses of Colombo, beautiful queen of beautiful Ceylon, burst like an apparition upon the view. You are fastened to the deck. Everything is new. Nothing is wanted to make the picture at once unique and memorable. Heber's

> "Spicy breezes
> Blow soft o'er Ceylon's isle"

are not a poetic fancy; they are a truth which a near catching of a Singhalese breeze confirms. You can stand on the deck of your vessel to-day and take in the spicy breath from the aromatic shrubs along the coast. The burden of the air is a dense perfume. Miss Jewsbury, too, was right, and is still as right as forty-five years ago, when she touched her harpstrings and sang,

> "Ceylon! Ceylon! 'tis nought to me
> How thou wert known or named of old,
> As Ophir, or Taprobane,
> By Hebrew king or Grecian bold.
>
> "To me thy spicy, wooded vales,
> Thy dusky sons and jewels bright,
> But image forth the far-famed tales—
> But seem a new Arabian night.
>
> "And where engirdled figures crave
> Heed to thy bosom's glittering store—
> I see Aladdin in his cave,
> I follow Sindbad on the shore."

Like Sindbad, I, too, went ashore. This was no easy task. My hold had to be firm and my foot steady as I went down the ladder of the *Dacca*. When once in my little boat, it bobbed about with fearful uncertainty. The men pulled heartily, and in due time I reached the shore.

One sees the story of Ceylon in Colombo. Here are traces of the Portuguese conquest; still clearer, however, of the Dutch, and, latest of all, of the English. Here are the stages of Ceylon's ownership. Six centuries before Christianity a prince

A STREET IN COLOMBO

from Northern India, Vijaya by name, came hither and conquered the whole island. His rule was long; and then came a succession of kings of Ceylon, who reigned until 1505, when the Portuguese sailed into Colombo, or where it now stands, and built a fort. Their object was half commercial and half political. Next came the Dutch sailors. They were traders. What cared the Dutchman for rule, if he could only treble his florins? He came to Ceylon in 1602. Those old Dutch graveyards still tell the romance of his stay. They remind you of the inscriptions in the God's Acres along the Passaic and the Mohawk. The Singhalese never took a fancy to the Portuguese; for the latter meant, not trade alone, but ownership, and a change in the succession. Hence the Singhalese welcomed the Dutch. The Portuguese were driven out, after eighteen years' warfare, by the Dutch and natives. This was in 1658; and from that year to 1796 the Dutch predominated.

Then came the English, who were invited in to help put an end to the cruelty of the Kandyan kings, the Dutch now having lost interest in the island, and not disturbing themselves by looking after its government. Since 1796 the English have ruled Ceylon. Their control has been paternal, strong, and elevating. With their rule there has been a constant advance in the evangelization of the people. Singularly enough, before the landing of the English—and for this we take Mr. Ferguson as authority—there was not a carriage-road in the whole island. All the ways were rough and sandy. But England began to build good ways, not only for military purposes, but for all industrial and commercial uses. Over these she first hauled gunpowder and then the Bible. It is a singular fact that the stage on the road from Colombo to Kandy, the ancient capital of the island, which began to run on February 1, 1832, was the first mail-coach in the whole continent of Asia.

My first walk was along the shore. Here I found a magnificent road, as hard as granite, and raised quite out of the reach of Neptune's spray. The material is laterite, or decomposed gneiss, of a dull red color. The road is broad and beautiful, with the sea to the right and the city to the left. I had but little disposition to examine the city, such was the fascination of this wonderful promenade. Here the people come out in the evenings, and walk up and down the enchanting place, and forget the cares of the day. The sea-breeze never rests, and the sea itself presents a variety which makes the picture always new and welcome. The Museum is far out in the suburbs. You leave the buildings of the city, and reach the suburban homes, with the great compounds and courts, and then enter the public gardens. After a few curves in the road, I reached the Museum. One expects, as a matter of course, to find many marine curiosities and monstrosities; but I had seen enough of them elsewhere in India to satisfy my taste for natural history. Every hour you spend indoors when in Ceylon is a punishment. You want no house. You revel in the broad expanse of Nature and her thousand perfumes. Even a stroll through the Museum of Colombo was a necessity rather than a pleasure. Its antiquities are its chief treasure. For a continuous history of a great length Ceylon is equal to the Roman empire. One can read it, as it winds along from century to century, without finding any hiatus. It is positively monotonous to go over one hundred and seventy Singhalese kings and as many queens and not misplace one. In the Museum there are magnificent stones, with earlier inscriptions, which date back into the centuries when the world was young, and could write its letters and chip its stones only rudely. The Buddhistic memorials are grotesque enough, and, best of all, they are authentic. It must not be forgotten, that of all places under the sun Ceylon is the best in which to study this Buddhistic system. Buddha, driven out of India, and thrice conquered and stamped into the very dust, took sweet revenge by halting here in Ceylon. Here is where the system has been studied, and with a fiery analysis. Its emptiness has been found out in its very home. Spence Hardy, the Wesleyan missionary, has turned it inside out, and made it reveal its inherent wickedness, and has told the world its story in his three works, the best of all being his "Eastern Monachism."

But it is no wonder the Wesleyans have loved Ceylon as a mission field, and bearded the Buddhistic lion in his very den. Yonder, in the offing, the grand Coke, with enough fire in his brave heart to set all India ablaze, gave up his spirit, and the Indian Ocean still sings his requiem. The Wesleyans have always kept his burial-place upon their sailing-charts. Faith always keeps up with its dead.

HINDU TEMPLE, COLOMBO.

Visit to the Exiled Arabi Pasha.

After leaving the Museum I went to see Arabi Pasha. It was he who led the native Egyptian troops, a few years ago, against the English. He did not lose his head when taken prisoner, but, instead, was sent an exile to Ceylon. "Take nothing for grant-

ALONG THE SHORE, CEYLON.

ed" is a good motto for the traveller. On our way to his house we were met by a party of English ladies and gentlemen, who said to the Rev. Mr. Fox and myself, "It's no use. You can't see him. He is asleep." We thanked them, but drove on. In twenty minutes we were sitting in his veranda, beneath his palms, fanning ourselves in mid-December. We had a pleasant reception from Arabi's son, who bade us wait only a few minutes, when his father would receive us.

The son has an indescribably sad face. He is tall, has lost an eye by the universal Egyptian opthalmia, and in his manner and expression seems to say, "I am an exile's son; but I will stay with my father." Arabi, the father, has a tall and muscular body, and inclines to corpulence. His eye is far-seeing, and inclines to look downward, as if to rest. He talks with hesitation about his campaigns, and would rather pass over them altogether, but is quick to discuss the future. His heart is with his native Egypt. He wants the country to rule itself. Can this be the man who burned Alexandria, who caused assassination to run wild both there and elsewhere, and who came near conquering the English army? So far as appearances go, he is the man. But the safer solution is, that he was obeying the sultan's orders —that he had received hints from Constantinople, and that he was following them to the letter. If not, then why did the sultan prevent him from being put to death, and ask the English to make only an exile of him? This is one step. The next will be his return to Egypt at the same sultan's wish. Then we shall hear again Arabi's cry, "Egypt for the Egyptians." He is ready again for fight, and thinks of the hour when his exile will end.

WILD HOG OF INDIA.

CHAPTER XXV.

THE ENCHANTÉD ROAD TO KANDY.

Think of a railroad amid the tangled and varied wonders of Ceylon. Yet here is one from Colombo on the sea to the ancient capital, Kandy. For the first fifteen miles the road is nearly level. But then it begins to climb. Soon you are far above the sea and the housetops of beautiful Colombo. The steady climb continues more than three hours. The view becomes more entrancing every minute. When Mrs. Browning had her dream of her sweet distant island, did not Ceylon float before her vision?—

> "Hills running up to heaven for light
> Through woods that half-way ran!
> As if the wild earth mimicked right
> The wilder heart of man."

The scenery grows wilder, of deeper tints, and more richly tropical. The surprises intoxicate and bewilder. Great boulders lie out on either hand, and hills, which grow into mountains, can be counted by the score. But boulders and hills and mountains are all different in Ceylon from those of any other land. The wealth of vegetation, which becomes a drapery to all things, gives an entirely new character to every rock, whether standing alone or combined with a mountain-chain. Here, for example, is a great jagged rock, a hundred feet in diameter, scarred and gashed by the storms and shocks of ages. But the vines have thrust themselves into its deep lines and climbed over its rugged points, and fairly smothered every angle with their delicate and dallying fingers, so that one would think the hard rock was only placed there as a support for a tropical vine.

But this is not all. Shrubs have found their way into the crevices, and pushed their roots deeply down, and now their broad and ample branches flash out over the mossy shoulders as rich scarlet and yellow blossoms as ever borrowed color from the sun near the equator. Even the palms seem to take special pleasure in getting close to the rocks, then flinging their great fronds right out over the gray granite, as much as to say: "How dare you take up so much space? Make way, or I will cover every inch of your impudent face with my big leaves, and drive you into perpetual oblivion."

The Singhalese Palms.

The palms along this wonderful road are the very kings of trees. They are the chief feature, next to the mountains themselves, of the unparalleled landscape. They have the same general trunk—long, graceful, slender—but, like men, exhibit amazing differences when one comes to examine them minutely. The fronds always tell the story of individuality. You see the talipot palm, the areca palm, the sago palm, the cocoanut palm, the toddy palm, and I know not how many others. Each has its large class of uses, and there is hardly any limit to its applications.

The palms abound everywhere along this enchanted road to Kandy. They run along both sides of the road. They climb well up the mountain-sides, and run down into all the valleys. No doorway seems complete without one, to throw down its welcome shade upon all who enter it. No home is too stately or too poor to be without it. It is the cosmopolitan fruit of beautiful Ceylon. It hugs closely the railway track, grows in plenty far away from any house, bends over the thatched roof of the farmer, as if for protection, lets the gray cattle come and lean against it; and now and then, when still young, drops its fronds so low down that a child can play with them and swing by them. In some instances they form a vista, and as you drive under them, as we did in one case, they are found to have thrown out their branches to meet one another, and to have interlaced, and to have made so thick a shield that only an occasional fleck of sunshine could be seen on the red and perfect road.

Coffee and Tea.

No one can number the whole catalogue of plants and trees which we pass on this single ride of seventy miles from Colombo to Kandy. Up on the hillsides the cinchona-tree abounds, and is now an important branch of culture, but only on Euro-

THE GIANT INDIA-RUBBER TREES OUTSIDE THE PERADINIA GARDENS.

pean estates. The Singhalese seldom try any product of the tropics without succeeding in their undertaking. The coffee-tree has, almost alone of their sources of revenue, failed them to some extent of late. A fungus, or leaf disease, has appeared, and so injured the harvest that, within the last few years, there has been immense loss to the coffee-planters. This disease of the coffee-plant in Ceylon, in connection with similar losses to the sugar-planters of the Mauritius, led to the suspension of the Oriental Bank Corporation a few years since.

Several substitutes for the coffee-plant in use in Ceylon have been attempted. One of these is the Liberian coffee, introduced from Western Africa. It has been only partially successful; but there is hope that in time it will make some amends for the failure of the Singhalese coffee-tree. Now the cinchona-tree is one of the substitutes for the coffee. Large tracts of land are planted with it, and many great hillsides are covered with it. In the distance, the cinchona orchard has the appearance of a lemon or orange grove. There is the same deep green, and the trees stand about the same distance apart. The main difference is that the cinchona appears to be a smaller tree.

Tea-gardens abound. The tea-plant is becoming the general substitute for coffee, and is destined to become far more widely cultivated, as it thrives at a much greater range of elevation. The cinchona is chiefly successful as a supplementary crop on coffee or tea plantations.

Rice.

But the favorite plant is rice. When it is growing, it is always called "paddy." Buckle says that caste, oppression, and high rents come from eating rice. In reply, it may be said that the native sons of Ceylon and India indicate no less fondness for rice after having renounced paganism than before adopting the Christian religion. Of Indian rice—and we may assume the same of that of Ceylon — Hunter reports that two hundred and ninety-five different kinds are known to the peasant.* The Singhalese have solved one problem, how to make their rice climb mountains and come down on the other side. But then the mountains must not be over

* "Statistical Account of Bengal," vol. vii., pp. 234, 237.

four thousand feet high, for the rice cannot thrive at a greater altitude.

Rice must always have abundance of water. The seed must soak in the wet earth, and the green spires must shoot up through the shallow pools. Ceylon has its lakes and rivers, and it is easy enough so to divert their waters from the very top of its mountains that they can be made to irrigate any spot on the whole island, however high the patch of land. Now there is no such thing as irrigating a mountain-side in any other way than by terraces. The land must be flat in order that the water may lie an equal depth everywhere. Hence, the entire side of the mountain is a succession of beautiful terraces. The water comes into the top section or terraced lot, and from that it descends by channels and by an outlet into the one below, and thence into the lower, until the scores and hundreds of beautiful terraces are supplied with water enough to make the rice fairly bound into beauty and a bountiful harvest. These terraced fields are not prepared loosely or irregularly. It would seem that great care is taken to arrange the terraces that the effect might be pleasing to the eye. But, on inquiry, I learned that the Singhalese and the Tamils have little or no sense of beauty, and that the beauty of their landscape is largely due to the economy of space, labor, and water, and, above all, to the wonderful powers of nature.

If a hillside of one hundred acres is to be put in rice, the most careful plan is made to divide it into terraces, and to arrange them in relation to each other. The result is, that when the work is over, and the sowing is done, and the rice is out in its emerald dress, you find yourself gazing upon as beautiful a piece of agricultural art as your eyes ever saw.

Then, suppose you are looking at twenty of these hillsides at once, dropping down towards the plain at different angles, and of all possible shapes and sizes, and every one covered with rice terraces. The borders are resplendent with a growth of green grasses, and cheerful streams sing their way outward and seaward in a thousand directions, while great palms and wild vines interrupt the scene, and form the border lines in this picture of enchanting beauty. The wonderful luxuriance of the heart of this strange Ceylon is a perpetual surprise. You wonder how trees can grow into such gigantic shapes, and how each growth can produce so many flowers and so much fruit.

THE GREAT BANYAN-TREE, ON THE ROAD FROM COLOMBO TO MOUNT LAVINIA HOTEL.

Wildness of Nature.

But we are still climbing this wonderful hill. At no moment, however, is there any release from the sweet bondage of this perfumed and dazzling scene. You are fairly overwhelmed with every new mile in your upward road. Each moment there is something new and strangely fascinating. Rich as the vegetation is in Southern India, and especially on the plains about Madras, and on the fertile table-lands of Mysore, there is not an acre in all India which compares with Ceylon in productiveness and a certain lawlessness of color and vegetation. One sees so much which he never thought of seeing, that he becomes surfeited with the prospect. It is like looking at too many Guido-Renis in the same gallery.

I was thoroughly tired by the time I reached Kandy—not because of the journey itself, but because of Nature's extravagant display of plants and flowers and fruits. My eyes and sensations were overtaxed. Then, where there is neither flower nor fruit, Nature seems to take a special delight in winding wild vines in all possible directions, in making them spring to every branch and rock, and get ready for a loftier leap. Many of these vines, when they had exhausted all the supports they could find, just jumped out desperately into the air; and there they hung and waved and nodded their smiles down upon us, as much as to say: "Just give us more trellis, and we will wander out on larger paths into this Elysian air."

We have now reached the Kandy station. Here are tall people, the giants of this isle of dreams and history. Neither Dutch nor French nor English ever conquered them. Their spears have been very weavers' beams. The English would not be here to-day, with their good rule and even justice, but for the cruelty of the native king, whom the wise native chiefs asked English help to rid them of. The English were waiting. They are heroes of an opportunity. Here they stayed, and are now as firm here as the granite sides of the isle itself. A *bandy*, or little carriage, is waiting for us, to drive us to the Queen's Hotel. Things are reversed here. You see the opposite of what you wait to see. The women do not wear combs, but the men do. So our driver, a pleasing native, has long hair, twisted into a firm knot on the top of his head, and held by an artistic comb of tortoise-shell. The wearing of combs by the Singhalese men is said to have been introduced by the Dutch ladies, in the time of the dominion of Holland, who insisted that if their household servants would wear long hair, they should also wear combs.

Our driver of the large comb helps us to our seats, and soon we are whirling past the trim houses and beneath the long arms of the welcoming palms of this old, old Singhalese capital.

SINGHALESE WAITER

CHAPTER XXVI.

KANDY AND ITS WONDERS.

THE impression one forms of Ceylon from his view of Colombo undergoes a thorough revolution when he gets to Kandy, the ancient capital. Colombo is the busy and commercial seaport which monopolizes nearly all the trade of Ceylon. It is a thriving place, and takes on a European coloring as rapidly as if it were within gunshot of Liverpool. It is the stopping-place for vessels around the Bay of Bengal, the Chinese and Siamese ports, Japan, and Australia; and then, again, on their return westward, for all the ports which are entered by means of the Suez Canal. From the harbor of Colombo there go, probably, more products for the acre into the great world than are grown under any other sky. From any seed you let fall in Ceylon you may expect that your plant will grow higher, become more fragrant, have a deeper color, and be more prolific when the reaping comes than any you have ever let fall elsewhere. Kandy is seventeen hundred feet higher than Colombo, and lies back in the silences of Ceylon, where life moves more slowly, and the native spirit has no sympathy with the nineteenth century.

In Kandy, whether one will or not, the mind will go back to the Lake region in England. You find a calm and quiet beauty, a freedom from strain and stress, a cluster of hillsides which throw down their beautiful face into the mirroring lake at their feet, a sweetness in all the pulsations of the air, and a universal friendliness between all Nature and its lord, which bring up Grassmere, Windermere, Derwentwater, and their spirits—Southey, Wordsworth, Coleridge, and all the rest of the Cumberland immortals. Even the hostelry of Kandy, the Queen's Hotel, suggested to me immediately the Keswick inn. The whole reminder was pleasant enough at first. But too much of such resemblances is not good. You can less easily resign yourself to the novelty of your new environment. You lose the new by recalling too intensely the old.

The story of Kandy is the history of Ceylon.* It is Asia in miniature. Ptolemy and Pliny mention it, and call it Anuro-

THE GIANT BAMBOOS IN THE PERADINIA GARDENS, NEAR KANDY.

grammum. But it then disappeared entirely from history, and only came again to the surface in the fourteenth century, during

* Tennent is the best authority for the history and condition of Ceylon. For all practical purposes, Ferguson, "Directory of Ceylon," is ample.

the reign of Prakrama Bahu III. It was he who embellished Kandy, surrounded it with all the sanctities of the Buddhist faith, and erected a temple to the Sacred Tooth of Buddha. The possession of this relic, spurious as it is, together with the countless jewels which are stored away in the many shrines about the great and smaller temples, has made Kandy the Canterbury of the whole Buddhist world. With the year 1505, when the Portuguese first landed in Ceylon, Kandy became a coveted prize for the ambitious schemes of every European nation which aimed at Asiatic conquests. The Portuguese, not satisfied with enriching themselves with the trade of Ceylon, resolved on planting Roman Catholicism firmly throughout the island. The Jesuitism which became rooted in Bassein, Goa, and other places along the western coast of India struck directly for the heart of Ceylon. It failed in every case, but kept up a warfare which lasted a century. In 1602 the Dutch traders came; and, as they proposed to attend strictly to business, the Kandyan king, Kunappu Baudara, gave them a cordial welcome. The Dutch united with the Kandyans in repelling the Portuguese. In 1672 the French came, and the Dutch assisted their good friends, the same Kandyans, to repel them. So M. de la Haye, having been beaten in his attack on the Point de Galle, was glad to find his way from the Isle of Spices at any cost. Last of all came the English, in 1763, who began to manage most wisely for the possession of the island. The Dutch evacuation of Kandy took place in 1796, and in 1798 England sent her first governor, Lord North, afterwards the Earl of Guilford, who took formal possession. Ever since then the Union Jack has floated over the whole island.

Ceylon is not connected with the Indian government. It is ruled directly from London, and is the first of the crown colonies under the Secretary of State. It has a local governor of its own. With him are associated a legislature and an executive council. The legislative council is composed of official and unofficial members, the former being government officers, the latter the representatives of the different populations of the island, appointed by the governor from candidates nominated by their respective constituencies. The official members are in a decided majority, and are bound to vote at the dictation of the governor whenever he may so require. The government is, therefore, autocratic, and the unofficial members can only express the voice of the people by moral pressure on the government.

Kandy, though many times attacked, has never been conquered. The real Kandyan is a mountaineer. He lives from two to five thousand feet above the sea, loves his hills with an idolatry equal to his veneration of Buddha, has all the robustness of the Scotchman, is tall and well-knit, and, as history well proves, is a master in using his mountains as a safe defence. In no part of Asia have I seen such fine specimens of well-formed men among the natives. They might safely be taken by any Angelo as models for sculpture of the human form.

TEA-PICKERS IN CEYLON.

Just a few rods from the Queen's Hotel you step up to the broad and beautiful walk which surrounds the celebrated Lake Maha, or Lake the Great. This wonderful sheet of water is the heart of Nuwara, or the Great City, as the Singhalese love to call their beautiful Kandy. It was the work of an early rajah, and is as beautiful as the crystal image of Buddha off yonder in one of the shrines. It is bordered by a low parapet of stone, indented like a castle wall, and has a beautiful islet in the centre, from whose trees the vines and branches hang down into the lake itself. No boats ply upon the lake, and no one is allowed to fish in it. It is simply a crystal setting in the centre of the charming city, where people may walk at will, by day and night, along its gravelled margin.

I shall not soon forget my night ramble along this enchanted body of water. The moon never shone more brightly. It was in the full, and almost eclipsed the brightest stars. It lighted up the farther hillside, and threw down into the lake the shadows of the villas that climb up to the very top of the mountain. The Temple of the Sacred Tooth was lighted up, there being service that evening, and one could see, reflected in the lake, the entire outline of the strange building, the lights from many a window and archway, and the coming and going worshippers. Once again, after returning to my lodgings, I went back to the esplanade surrounding this matchless sheet of water, and walked up and down, in every direction, almost asking myself whether this was dream or reality. The air was laden with fragrance. There was no ceasing of these delicious pulsations of the air at nightfall. And yet they are not to be defined. The perfume of roses fairly filled the whole place; but there were so many other flowers, of equal perfume, which competed for the sway, that one could not tell which predominated.

The Temple of the Sacred Tooth of Buddha shows how far idolatry can go when it once sets out on its absurdities. Nature has nothing to do with suppressing superstition or destroying faith in grim images in wood and stone. The fairest sky and most beautiful scenery beneath it say nothing against even so gross a corruption as a great temple to even the spurious tooth of a spurious god. The temple and the many dependent buildings about it are at the farther end of the lake. One can descend the sacred steps and walk down the stone way to the water's brink. There they stand, the Sacred Tooth Temple in the midst, and the rest only as accessories to it. Happy the Buddhist who can once look upon that pyramid which he calls his most sacred temple. Wherever he lives, far up under the shadow of the Himalayas or across in Burma, it is all the same. This temple is his Paradise. The Buddhist kings of all lands send costly presents to it, as they have been doing for ages; and these many shrines are very jewel-boxes, which the wealthy, the strong, and

COFFEE-PLANT AND BLOSSOMS.

the beautiful, from great distances, have overburdened with their most precious stores. All the things which the Buddhist regards as most sacred cluster here.

THE BUDDHIST LIBRARY.

There is an octagonal building, which hangs near the temple front, on the bank of the lake, as a bird's nest against a tree. This is the Library. Can there be anything like it in all the world? It contains two thousand precious manuscripts, on *olas*, or prepared leaves of the talipot palm. Paganism, with all its ignorance, professes to be built on books. There is nothing a

Buddhist thinks more of than his records. They confirm him, however weak they are, in his wildest faith. These manuscripts are in long leaves, and slide along up and down two connecting strings. The outer parts of each manuscript are protected by cases, some of which are of richest workmanship. Here is one of ivory, whose fine miniatures must have taken a lifetime to make. Another is of solid silver, with reliefs which would add to the fame of a Benvenuto Cellini. Here is another, with a gold intaglio on a background of silver. Still another is of some fragrant wood, which defies all time to destroy its perfume. It is literally covered with gold arabesques, fixed so firmly that one would think the gold had been burned into the very fibre of the wood.

The finest manuscript and case I saw were from Burma. The ground-color is a rich and soft yellow tint. On this the letters are inscribed in gold and black, each leaf, or palm-sheet, being in itself a triumph of art. The characters are in Burmese. But there are manuscripts in other languages—Tamil, Pali, Singhalese, Telugu, and all the others that have for centuries been beating about the walls of this Asiatic Babel.

Strange to say, there is one alcove in this unique collection entirely devoted to English works on Ceylon. But one finds nothing among them which strikes at the pagan root. Look as carefully as you may, for example, you will see no trace of Spence Hardy's "Eastern Monachism." I have the good authority of Mr. Ferguson, the publicist of Colombo, for saying that no book approaches it as a reliable source for the understanding of Buddhism.

Temple of Buddha's Tooth.

I visited the Temple of the Tooth at the time of the evening service, half-past six. Worshippers were crowding in. Each went first to a fountain within the temple wall, where he poured water on his feet and hands, and then bought flowers from vendors who stood near by with baskets laden with them. These flowers are, first, the rich and fragrant champac, or frangipani, the flower of the temple-tree, and, second, the blossom of the ironwood, or na-tree. They are all white, with a slight dash of pink. Their perfume fills all the sacred spaces. The air hangs heavy, and surfeits one with the combined fragrance. On advancing to the outer court, whose entrance is guarded by two broad pillars, I ascended the temple steps, and reached an outer veranda. Here I saw a series of rude frescoes on either side, descriptive of the torments of the Buddhist hell. Of the hopelessly lost, by far the larger part were women. You then come to the veranda which immediately surrounds the great temple itself. To the left is a small shrine, where there are several images of

ENTRANCE TO BUDDHIST TEMPLE, KANDY.

Buddha, the chief of which is the one made of a single block of crystal. The cabinet enclosing it consists of combined silver and ivory, curiously wrought, and in a style well worthy of the early Italian workers. To enter the main temple, where the sacred tooth is, you have to pass two pairs of huge elephant-tusks, which serve as portarii on either side of the steps by which the worshipper ascends the stairway to the awful sanctuary. You now go through a doorway, the whole frame of which consists of three parts, a smaller frame, then a larger one outside of it, and the largest outside of that. One is of ivory, minutely wrought, and evidently very old, having grown very dark by age. Another is of solid silver, covered with a sheathing of gold. By this last doorway you enter the dark and mysterious *sanctum sanctorum* of the whole Buddhist faith. There is first a silver table, which stands before the shrine, and awaits the worshipper's gifts. You look through iron bars, and behold a gilded shrine, shaped like a bell. This is a mere covering for six other shrines, of decreasing size, one within the other. All are of solid gold, with rubies, pearls, emeralds, and other precious stones. Here are Oriental cat's-eyes incrusted into gold and silver. The two smallest of these shrines are covered with squarely cut rubies.

The sacred tooth, invisible in these days, is contained in the smallest of all. Burrows, the best living authority on this relic, saw it, and says of it: "It is an oblong piece of discolored ivory, tapering to a point, and about one and one fourth inches in length, and half an inch in diameter at the base. It is not the least like a human tooth, and more resembles that of a crocodile or large pig." Inside the large shrine there is also kept a large collection of jewels, the most of them once the property of the early nobility and rajahs of Kandy. One of the most precious relics, always excepting the bogus tooth, is a sitting figure of Buddha, carved out of a single emerald. But great precious stones and pearls of fabulous size are the order here. Their very splendor becomes distressing. One is glad to get out and stroll along the beautiful lake, and see in its deep bosom the shadows of God's patient stars.

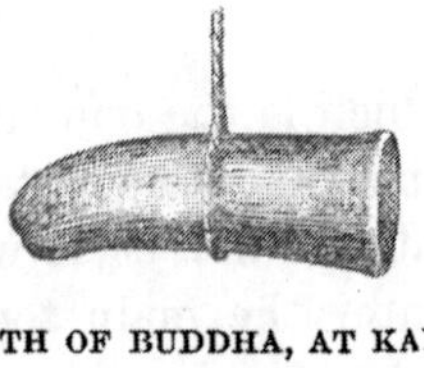

TOOTH OF BUDDHA, AT KANDY.

CHAPTER XXVII.

THE PEARL FISHERY.—MADURA AND ITS TEMPLE.

On leaving Ceylon for the mainland, I took steamer for Tutikorin, a town of ten thousand inhabitants. This place was long celebrated for its pearl fishery.

Cæsar Frederick visited India in 1563–1581, and tells us that the fishing began in March or April, and lasted fifty days. "During the continuance of the fishing," he says, "there are always three or four armed foists or galliots stationed to defend the fishermen from pirates. Usually the fishing-boats unite in companies of three or four. These boats resemble our pilot boats at Venice, but are somewhat smaller, having seven or eight men each. I have seen of a morning a great number of these boats go out to fish, anchoring in fifteen or eighteen fathoms water, which is the ordinary depth along this coast. When at anchor they cast a rope into the sea, having a great stone at one end. Then a man, having his ears well stopped, and his body anointed with oil, and a basket hanging to his neck or under his left arm, goes down to the bottom of the sea along the rope, and fills the basket with oysters as fast as he can. When it is full he shakes the rope, and his companions draw him up with the basket. The divers follow each other in succession in this manner, till the boat is loaded with oysters, and they return at evening to the fishing village. Then each boat or company makes their heap of oysters at some distance from each other, so that a long row of great heaps of oysters is seen piled along the shore. These are not touched till the fishing is over, when each company sits down beside its own heap, and falls to opening the oysters, which is now easy, as the fish within are all dead and dry. If every oyster had pearls in it, it would be a profitable occupation, but there are many which have none. There are certain persons called Chitini who are learned in pearls, and are employed to sort and value them according to their weight, beauty, and goodness, dividing them into four sorts. The first, which are round, are named Aia of Portugal, as they are bought by the Portuguese. The second, which are not round, are named Aia of Bengal. The third, which are inferior to the second, are called Aia of Kanara, which is the name of the kingdom of Bijanagar, or Narsinga, into which they are sold. And the fourth, or lowest kind, are called Aia of Cambaia, being sold into that country. Thus sorted and a price affixed to each, there are merchants from all countries ready with their money, so that in a few days all the pearls are bought up, according to their goodness and weight." *

The pearl fishing of Tutikorin has now passed away, because the oysters, except of an inferior kind, no longer grow along the coast. Pearl oysters still grow on the Singhalese coast, but if a tourist wishes to buy pearls, and be sure of what he is getting, he should not select Colombo, but some place in Europe or the United States, for his purchases.

Tutikorin was my nearest point for finding a railroad and taking a train for a visit to some of the most ancient and celebrated Indian temples.

The *Nerbudda* was about to sail for Tutikorin, and I took passage by her from Colombo in the afternoon. The sea was high, and we were in the region of sunken reefs and many a shipwreck. People avoid this route, so far as they can, but this was my only opportunity to visit the region south of Madras. On the day following the departure from Colombo we came in sight of the Indian coast. Off in the distance there lay the wreck of a magnificent steamer. She had run on a hidden reef some months before, and was now forsaken, and would in time disappear beneath the waves of this treacherous sea.

"How shall we land?"

"Oh," replied the captain, "we shall not venture much farther in. We shall soon cast anchor, and the little launch will come out and take you all ashore."

This was no pleasant news. I had never seen, in all the East, a launch that I would be willing to trust myself to in such a heavy sea and at such a distance from the shore. We dropped anchor eight miles from the coast. By and by we saw a little

* Kerr, "Voyages and Tramps," vol. viii.

bobbing speck—the launch in question—emerging from a tongue of land beyond which Tutikorin lay along the coast. It was coming out for us. As it came clearly into view I could see its tossings more clearly. By and by the dwarf came up to our side, and was fastened to the *Nerbudda*. We had many passengers, mostly natives, who were scattered over our deck in heterogeneous masses. They, too, wanted to land, and meant to take the launch as well as ourselves. The officers had little control over them. They dropped down rapidly into the launch, and seemed to me to fill every part of the frail craft. I must either follow them or depart with the steamer in a different direction, and thus spoil all my plans.

I took the risk, and went down the rickety stepway into the launch. We were soon cast loose, and bobbing and rolling up and down in the wild waters. We passed near the great wreck, and moved on towards the land. Those were eight venturesome miles. There was no room for a comfortable seat, and I therefore had to stand and hang on by any support within reach. By and by we came within the lee of the land, and the water grew smooth. In due time we landed. The question now was, when was the train to leave—the only one in twenty-four hours?

"Immediately," said the captain of the diminutive launch. I was one of the first to step ashore. Two *kulis* caught up my luggage, and hastened towards the railway station. But I had the disappointment of seeing the train move out just as I reached the station. I was too late. Therefore I had to adjust myself to a halt of twenty-four hours. I found a humble hotel, where I took a bath, and made myself as comfortable as the circumstances would admit. In the afternoon I strolled through the bazar, and visited one of the Jesuit churches—one of the many planted, either directly or indirectly, through the labors of Xavier around this coast.

When I was buying my ticket the next morning for Madura, the station agent was kind enough to say:

"Don't you know there is cholera in Madura?"

"What, real Asiatic cholera?"

"It's real Asiatic cholera, and nothing else," he answered.

"I have not heard it before," I replied. "I landed only yesterday from the steamer *Nerbudda*, and have had no news of any kind. Many deaths?"

"Oh, no. Nothing compared with last year. Five thousand died during the season. Only about ten die a day just now, and we don't consider that anything."

I mused a moment on the mortality of ten cholera patients a day in a place of fifty thousand, and then asked: "Do you think it safe to go?"

"I can't answer that. It all depends."

Two facts now came to my relief. One was, that few people in India think cholera contagious. There are no separate hospitals for such cases, cholera patients being put in the same wards with patients suffering from fever and other diseases. The other fact was, that two weeks before, when I was in Puna, there had been a cholera case in the native bazar, and yet I had a most pleasant ride through that part of the city, and had suffered no harm, and saw no alarm anywhere. The truth is, nobody thinks of cholera as any more likely to happen than any mild disease. Dr. Waugh told me afterwards that cholera prevailed more or less in all Indian towns, but that nobody minded it. It might be next door, but it frightened no one. It is very necessary to watch its beginning, and then manage it, as you can, with care and caution. Another is, to take care of one's diet. This must be said, however, that when cholera does come, and its first stage is neglected, the collapse is very sudden.

Taking all things together, it did not seem much of a risk to spend my intervening day, before meeting an engagement at Bangalore, in Mysore, in making a halt in Madura, and using my only opportunity to see the famous pagoda, or temple, there—the largest, not only in India, but in the world.

The Temple of Madura.

Long before reaching Madura one can see the great towers which rise above the pagoda, and dominate not alone the city, but the whole surrounding country. In many of the Indian cities the temple is in the suburbs, and even completely alone in the country, having been left by the population drifting far out in other directions. But this is not the case in Madura. The pagoda is in the very heart of the old city. The bazars lead directly towards it, and overflow into it. It is the city in miniature, with its dirt, ill odors, poverty, wealth, superstition, and infamous idolatry. All the surging tide of tradesmen flows towards and about it. No adequate conception of an Indian temple can be formed from any European illustration of sacred places. Perhaps the Troïtska Monastery in Russia, where many cathedrals are grouped around one central sacred place, making the whole a very Canterbury, is as near an approach to an Indian temple and its spaces as can be found anywhere west of Asia.

While the object which gives Madura its chief celebrity in these modern days is its vast temple, in the ancient times its university was its grand attraction. Its fame as a seat of learning spread far and wide. I doubt not that its lecture-halls attracted students from all parts of the Oriental world. The heritage of the city was a rich grouping of intellectual, political, and social power; for Madura was none other than the capital of the kingdom described by Ptolemy as the Regio Pandionis. In the third century the university shone as the literary centre of all India. From that time on, for ten centuries, or until the thirteenth, when the

TEMPLE AND ROYAL SEPULCHRE, MADURA.

Persian Mohammedans invaded India, and Delhi became a competitor, the university of Madura reigned without a rival as the most splendid seat of Hindu science. From the meridian of Madura the longitude in Hindu geography was calculated, as in English geography the longitude is determined from Greenwich.

The examinations required to enter the university were rigid. A broad system of popular education prevailed, and the late Mr. Bell's effort to establish education for the native masses was only a revival of a long-forgotten Hindu law. In those days every Hindu parent took his child to school when five years of age. This regulation seems to have been not only a law, but so deeply fixed as a duty, that the Hindu associated with it certain religious observances. A ceremony was used in introducing the boy to his schoolmaster and the other scholars. His name was publicly recorded. A prayer was publicly offered to the image of Ganesh, the Hindu god of wisdom, imploring his help to enable the child to grow in wisdom.*

The girls had all the privileges of the boys. No social barrier stood in anybody's way of getting a university education. Caste, with its later iron rules, never entered the portals of the Madura university. The degraded pariah had equal privileges with the first-born son of a prince. One day a pariah and his sister applied for admission, and they were both received. Time brought great changes with the two. The man became the president of the university, and is known to posterity as the learned Tiru Valluvan. He retained the president's chair until his death, and became the author of the "Kural," a poem still held in high esteem by all Hindus. This work contains his thirteen hundred aphorisms, and is the oldest, as it is the most revered, work in the Tamil language.† It is a moral and didactic poem, abounding in beautiful and true sentiments. A standard edition of the "Kural," with English translation, grammatical analysis, and critical commentary, has lately been published in Madras. This edition, a high compliment to a pagan masterpiece, is the work of a native Christian minister.

Tiru Valluvan's sister vied in progress with her brother. She

---

* "The Oriental Annual," 1836, pp. 29 ff.

† Markham, "Travels in Peru and India," p. 416.

is known as the renowned Avvei, a celebrated poetess in Tamil verse.

All traces of the university are now gone. The pagoda, or temple, is the great object of interest. There are conflicting opinions as to its antiquity. It is probable that the place itself was regarded sacred, and was the site of a temple long before a city was built here, and that the city grew out of the temple, and all about it. The immense structure gives clear evidence of its own antiquity. It was built in the third century before the Christian era, by King Kula Shekhara. It is evidently a case where this city, the capital of a large territory, has sprung into life from religious associations. Some parts of the pagoda are modern, and were built by Tirumal Nayak, in the first half of the seventeenth century. But one can easily distinguish the newer from the older. The effect, throughout, is one of great and undisturbed antiquity.

The pagoda space is an immense parallelogram, extending 744 feet from east to west, and 847 feet from north to south. The area is enclosed by a light wall, flanked at various points by nine colossal towers. These towers are of peculiar structure, all after the same model, and so disposed towards each other as to form a symmetrical combination. Each constitutes a gateway for entrance from different sides of the wall. As you enter you find yourself passing through a great open corridor. The *gopura* is shaped like a tent, and on every side is ornamented with carvings. These represent the fabulous doings of the god Siva and his wife Minakshi, and ascend in lessening rows, or stories, until the apex is reached, which is sharp and curved, and reminds one of the general form of an old Roman galley. The colors of these *gopuras* are very rich, and, in the case of several, shine like fine tiling, or even gay enamel. The blue is especially rich, and is fairly dazzling in the bright sunlight. While Siva is the god to whom the temple is supposed to have been dedicated, the more frequent representations of his wife, Minakshi, prove her to have been the favorite of the people.

The Scene in the Madura Temple.

Two gopuras constitute the great entrances. Through one of these I went, followed by a crowd of about fifty ill-clad beggars. They held high carnival as they passed around and against me, and called for alms. I noticed many sleepers in the darker corners, in various parts of the temple spaces. They lie in every position. It seems a habit of the Maduran, when he gets thoroughly tired in his tent, or in the bazar, to drop into this temple and fall down for a good nap at the feet of Siva or some other idol, for Madura is a spot which for ages has been held strangely sacred by the Hindu worshipper. Having passed through the *gopura*, and completed the passage of the great corridor, one sees just the beginnings of this wonderful temple. There stretch out before you great reaches of passages and halls, and, still farther, corridors in all possible directions. But for my safe guide, who added to his other duties the good one of keeping off the crowd of ragged and starving and ill-smelling beggars with a stout bamboo rod, I should have lost my way at once. At your right you see an immense hall, the Hall of One Thousand Columns, which extends far away until it is lost in dark and distant spaces. But, beyond it—for I came back that way—there is a special temple sacred to the ruling god, Siva. At your left are vendors of images, sweetmeats, toys, and various other articles, which, for some reason, are permitted to be sold within the sacred walls. The men who sell them are squatted over the floor on mats of palm, with their wares about them. Think of a seller of small wares, in a temple, sitting or standing, with his goods arranged on a counter or row of shelves! Such a thing would be with us preposterous beyond measure. The drift is downward. No Hindu will stand if he can possibly drop on the floor. He doubles up his legs under him. That is his normal position. He may be talking with you this moment, and as much interested in standing or walking as any one. But a sudden change comes over him. Down he drops, and no boy ever closed the two blades of a jack-knife more quickly than the Hindu doubles himself up, either on the temple floor, or at the side of the street, or in his own doorway. And there he can sit by the hour, nay, the whole day, and be as calm as the serene face of Buddha himself.

Perhaps these sellers in the Madura pagoda have some ancestral claim on the favor of the authorities, by which they receive the privilege of spreading out their wares in the holy place. Over your head there flies about a flock of doves. They are sacred, and woe to the hand that would hurt a feather on their sweet heads! The worshippers feed them. It is a sacred privilege. Yonder, to your left, three sacred elephants are feeding, and frisking their trunks about as if they really knew that they were picking up great wisps of straw and hay within the Hindu's holy place. But I must hasten, or their priestly keepers will loosen the chains of one of them in a trice, and have the mammoth dropping down on all fours, and pulling me up on his back, to take an elephant ride through this labyrinth of marvels. Imagine the absurdity of an elephant ride on a temple floor! Yet that is what you can do here, and take a long promenade, and never have him repeat his pathway. But by going through this first doorway I get away from the vendors and the importuning elephants, and pass out of sight of the Hall of a Thousand Columns and its great, interminable spaces. Here one is in a corridor nearly two hundred feet long, with pillars groaning beneath a wealth of sculptured images. Now comes a brazen door. The frame is vast and heavy, and is entirely surrounded with brazen lamps, all of which are lighted during the *Tailotsava*, "the oil festival."

DETAIL OF A PILLAR OF THE HALL CALLED PUTHU MUNTAPAM, MADURA.

Monier Williams happened to visit the Madura pagoda at the time of the "oil festival," and thus describes the wretched scene: "A coarse image of the goddess Minakshi, profusely decorated with jewels, and having a high head-dress of hair, was carried in the centre of a long procession on a canopied throne, borne by eight Brahmans, to a platform in the magnificent hall, opposite the temple. There the ceremony of undressing the idol, removing its ornaments, anointing its head with oil, bathing, redecorating, and redressing it was gone through, amid shouting, singing, beating of tom-toms, waving of lights and cowries, ringing of bells, and deafening discord from forty or fifty so-called musical instruments, each played by a man who did his best to overpower the sound of all the others combined. At the head of the procession was borne an image of Ganesh. Then followed three elephants, a long line of priests, musicians, attendants bearing cowries and umbrellas, with a troop of dancing-girls bringing up the rear.

"No sight I witnessed in India made me more sick at heart than this. It presented a sad example of the utterly debasing character of the idolatry which, notwithstanding the counteracting influences of education and Christianity, still enslaves the masses of the population, deadening their intellects, corrupting their imaginations, warping their affections, perverting their consciences, and disfiguring the fair soil of a beautiful country with hideous usages and practices unsanctioned by even their own minds and works." *

You are now introduced into a darker corridor, and then again into a broad and pillared space, where the columns are sculptured, being cut through and through into figures of dancing gods, like Krishna when he played his flute to the shepherds. You now look out upon a little sheet of water with a miniature temple in the middle of it. This is the Lake of the Golden Lilies. Near by it is the little chapel where Queen Mangammal's subjects starved her to death in 1706, having placed food so near that she could see and smell it, but not taste it. We now enter another department of the temple; above there are stone images, up around the pillars, in all corners, and hanging down over you wherever you go near walls or archways. These images are not grave and majestic, but, in the main, grotesque, bacchanalian, in fantastic attitudes, and often combining the bodies of man and beast. They represent, for the most part,

* "Religious Thought and Life in India," part i., pp. 442, 443.

the escapades of Siva. Every now and then one comes to a shrine where worshippers lie prostrate before it, and remain motionless for a long time. No one knows how long it has taken these poor dusty pilgrims to reach this sacred place. Perhaps they have been three months on the journey. They come from the very base of the Himalayas or the borders of Tibet, and, now that they have reached the end of their pilgrimage, would die with a happy heart. There are several gold-plated images, veiled from view, which represent the god Siva or his wife in some part of their marvellous career. The representations in stone, both of men and the brute world, are frequent everywhere. Elephants, horses, cattle, and every kind of animal held sacred in the Hindu mythology, are cut out of stone, and made to portray the supposed divine attributes of Siva and his wife. Here, too, are the very *vehanas*, or great chariots, plated with gold, in which the god and his wife are taken out on special days in the year to ride. Besides these, there are silver litters, which serve the same divine purpose on other days.

One grows weary of the procession of splendid but gross images and idols in this vast space. Now you are out for a time in the open air, where a vacancy has been left in the roof, and the beautiful sky throws down its blessed sunlight upon this terrible picture of idolatry. But very soon you are brought again under the shadowing and lofty ceiling, and, before you are aware of it, you are almost lost in a dark labyrinth of sculptured pillars, black idols in gold wrappings, dusty and absorbed pilgrims, cheerful doves, and the constant crowd of men and boys who follow you, either to sell you their sweets, or beg for your loose *pice*. All at once you come out from a corridor to the marble steps of a miniature lake. Be careful now. Only the real Hindu dares to step down into its waters. For every drop is sacred, and must touch only the skin of Siva's children. Over the calm surface the towers stand as gay sentinels, from century to century. Turning again, you must look carefully, or you will tread upon a sleeping form, which has dropped in from the hot air and let fall its burden, and eaten its rice, and now rests an hour. There is a mother, with a nose-ring so large that it hangs down over her mouth, and she must eat through it or starve. Her ankles are encircled by heavy silver anklets, cut like serpents. Her toes are glittering with jewelled rings.

She has led her child up before an image of Siva's wife, and is explaining what it all means. Poor woman! Little she knows the truth. The One Name above all others she has never once heard. Here is a dwarf, who stands beside a shrine, and holds out his withered hand for an *anna*. Here, in a place where the statuary has given way to the wear of ages, are workers in stone, who are making new pillars, with sculptured flutings, to take the place of the old. All the work, every stroke of mallet and chisel, must be done right here, where everything is holy, and Siva smiles calmly down upon the labor.

After inspecting the temple, I went to the great hall which Tirumal Nayak, the builder of the modern parts of the pagoda, also built. He reigned from 1621 to 1657. The hall was erected by him as a temporary lodging-place for Ganesh, the chief idol of the temple, which was taken hither from the temple each year for ten days. The hall measures three hundred and thirty-three feet in length, and one hundred and five in width. It required twenty-two years to build it, and cost five millions of dollars. The gate tower has door-posts of single blocks of granite sixty feet high. In this great pillared hall there are statues of the king and his six wives. When this wonderful structure was finished, the king conducted his queen, a princess of the house of Tanjor, to see it and admire its splendor.

"Has your father," asked he, "of whose greatness you so often tell me, any building in his dominions like this?"

"Like this!" exclaimed the queen; "why, the sheds in which he keeps his cattle are finer."

The king threw his dagger at his wife. It hit her in the hip, and caused her death.*

The palace of Tirumal Nayak, at Madura, stands among the foremost in massive grandeur among the royal residences of India. Some of its great courts are now used for offices of administration and law. The vast corridors, the wonderful domes, the rich carving in stone, combine to make this building one of the most remarkable pieces of architecture in existence.†

---

* Russell, "The Prince of Wales's Tour: a Diary in India." New York ed. (1874), p. 274.

† Temple gives it the first rank ("India in 1880," p. 38). Fergusson, in "History of Architecture," presents an account of this palace, p. 381.

Over the great chamber which is supposed to have been Tirumal's bedroom there are four holes through the roof. Through these are said to have been suspended four hooks, which supported Tirumal's cot. One large hole is alleged to have been made by a thief, through which he descended on the chain supporting one corner of the king's bed, and stole the crown jewels. Tirumal, as the story runs, offered an hereditary estate to the thief if he would come, voluntarily, and restore the jewels, adding that no questions should be asked. The thief appeared, and restored the jewels. The king asked no questions, but—decapitated the thief.

If such were the habits of one king, what must have been those of many others of that long unbroken line of one hundred and sixteen Madura kings, extending from the fourth century before our era down to modern times!

SARASWATI.

CHAPTER XXVIII.

THE TEMPLE FORTRESS OF TRICHINOPOLI.

From Madura I took the train for Trichinopoli. Throughout this whole southern portion of India there are abrupt hills, which rise almost perpendicularly from the plains. These peaks, like those near Haidarabad, are not wooded mountains, but bare rocks, and sometimes single boulders, of immense size, and standing on end. They are the offshoots of the Nilgiri Hills. Tall shrines they are, Nature's great sentinels, keeping watch over Southern India. They have been used from time immemorial by robbers and warriors for keeping in awe the surrounding country. In the far-back, barbaric days, the kings built their houses upon them, which, as with the castles on the Rhine and Danube, served the double purpose of palace and fortress.

Each of these great hills has a history, if one only knew it, which combines all the features of an Indian Iliad. Sometimes the top is so shaped that it is difficult to ascend it, much more to build upon it. Besides, there is often, in addition to the fortress, a diminutive temple, with a passage up to it, grooved out of the solid granite. In India, the combination, under the same roof, of the temple and the secular building is not infrequent. It seems to have been the original purpose, in the remote Hindu days, to give sanctity to a stronghold by combining with the place a temple. He has a keen eye who can tell, in such a case, where the secular ends and the sacred begins.

Here in Trichinopoli, the temple forms a brotherhood with a great fortress. The whole group is at once the abode of old-time warriors and imaginary deities. How could a king give up a fort where the most sacred associations were combined with every atom of the glistening rock beneath? All the early record is gone with the flood of faded memories which the new age has swept away. In the case of Trichinopoli, only the story since the first half of the eighteenth century is known, and that is written in blood. The magnificent site of the fortress has been its fatal endowment. Not even the sacred character of the temple, which is a vital part of the whole vast structure, has made an arrow or cannon shot the less.

The Hill.

The hill of Trichinopoli, on which the great fortress stands, is the highest, most picturesque, and most associated with important historical events, of any abrupt hill in Southern India. Around it many a great army has battled for dominion long before the Portuguese and later Europeans dared to touch foot upon the fields of Hindustan. Many of these contests between the native warring tribes having passed into oblivion, the broken sculptures in the temple that clings about the fort are the only pens which describe the narrative of the hot battles in the distant days. When the Europeans came, and began to contend for the mastery of India, one of the first things they did was to choose sides between contending Indian armies, led by brave kings and *nawábs*, and between the two to walk into possession and power. The land lying at the base of Trichinopoli was contested for many times before Clive appeared upon the scene. In fact, the whole history of the place is a story of unbroken warfare, from 1736 down to 1801, when the French and natives marched down and the English marched up. This place was next in importance to Madras, as a strategic point towards the final occupation of the country by the English. Clive saw this, and while Major Lawrence was really the immediate commander, it was owing to Clive's desperate bravery and unwearied diligence that the French were defeated here, and the entire country, save a few still lingering French spots, became an English possession. The victory of Trichinopoli made possible the victory of Plassey.

Trichinopoli was a necessity to the English possession of all Southern India. In the midst of this plain, with its rapid river and the thick jungle along its banks, and these venerable temples, which might be counted by the score, Lawrence and Clive solved the problem of English rule in the Eastern world. Without the combinations and triumphs south of Madras, it would not have been within the range of possibility to establish the rule of the Saxon either in the North or the South.

As one leaves the plain and begins the ascent of the hill, he passes, on the left, the Tappe Kulam, a great tank of about two hundred and fifty feet square. It is of stone, and is surrounded with houses. In the centre is a beautiful miniature temple. In one of the houses on the border of the tank Clive lived when engaged in military operations here. At the door of the particular one which is supposed by several to have been his residence are two kneeling elephants, cut in stone, each over five feet high. This may have been, at one time, a Hindu temple.

Nothing is wanting to this immense fortress, either for nature or art, to make it impregnable. First of all is the immense moat, thirty feet wide and twelve feet deep, which surrounds the outer wall. Then comes the wall itself, which extends two thousand yards from east to west and twelve hundred yards from north to south. This wall is eighteen feet high, five feet thick, and is flanked by great round towers. Then comes an open space of twenty-five feet in width. After this we have a second wall, running exactly parallel with the outer one, and protecting the fortress in all directions. On the inner wall the greatest dependence was placed. It was built to resist any force that might get through or over the outer one. This inner wall is thirty feet high, and of great width at the base. It grows narrower as it ascends, but its top is ten feet broad, the parapet being of solid stones. There are loopholes for guns on every side. Every foot of the way, from the bank of the Kaveri River below to the very corner of this marvellous fortress, has been hotly contested.

No historian can tell the full story of the blood that has been shed and the races that have fought upon this very spot. Let us review a few of these deadly passages at arms within the last one hundred and fifty years. In the year 1736 the widow of the late reigning raja admitted a few soldiers into the fortress, in order to pay over a little tribute, which they were collecting from various parts of the Karnatic. They seized the place, and the queen was made prisoner. Soon the tide turned, and the Marhattas captured the place in 1740, and killed Dost Ali. Within ten years both the French and the English appeared upon the scene, and now it was a conflict between native rulers and foreign invaders. It long lay in doubt which native prince would come out best, or which people, the English or the French, would go down in the general crash. The English took sides with the Marhattas, and the French allied themselves with the rulers of the Karnatic, whose army was led by Chanda Sahib. In 1752 Major Lawrence, who led the English and the Marhattas, defeated the French and the Karnatic troops, and marched up the hill and took their quarters in the fortress.

But the fighting was not over. The Karnatic soldiers and the French still lay near. Clive, who was Lawrence's best fighter, went off with a body of troops to deal another blow to the enemy. He was shot, but not fatally; and though he lost much blood, he was not too weak to give orders, to capture prisoners, and to secure a decisive victory to the English arms. But it was of short duration. The French had skilfully formed an alliance with the Marhattas. But Lawrence, with Clive as his powerful helper, defeated them all in 1753. Soon, however, affairs took an adverse turn. The native princes and their army, who to-day

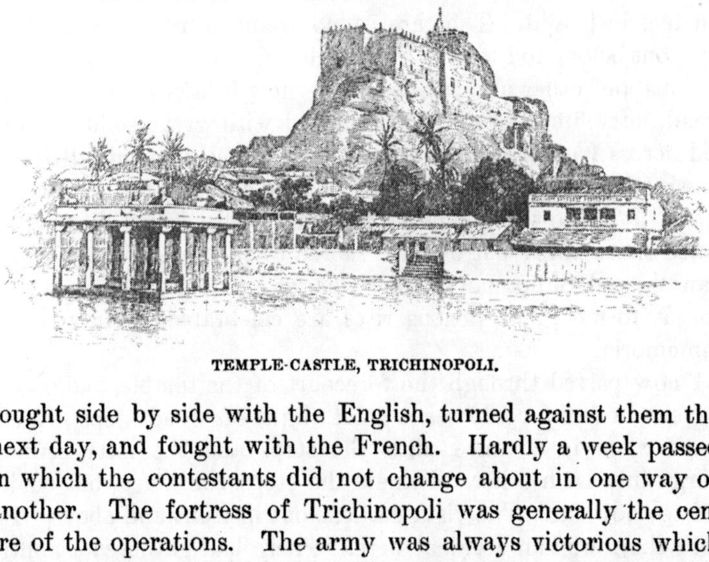

TEMPLE-CASTLE, TRICHINOPOLI.

fought side by side with the English, turned against them the next day, and fought with the French. Hardly a week passed in which the contestants did not change about in one way or another. The fortress of Trichinopoli was generally the centre of the operations. The army was always victorious which could win this great height. The first victory, however, lay with the English. The Nawábs of the Karnatic, who had forfeited their claim to English sympathy because of their final allegiance to the French, had to give up their great fortress in 1801. Since this time the Union Jack of England has floated from its lofty granite crest.

The temple fortress of Trichinopoli has a double dedication to the god Siva and the fortunes of war.

The Ascent to the Temple.

The entrance is through a great and high gateway of carved and polished stone. One must look high, and not hurry, if he would enjoy the rich carving of this magnificent entrance. The doors are gone now. The ill fortunes of war have shattered them, no doubt, and only the broad passage through the great doorway itself is all that speaks of the immense doors through which conquering and conquered kings have many a time passed in procession. There is not a stone beneath one's feet that has not fairly swum in the blood of Indians long before any stranger from Europe arrived and contended for the wealth of the priceless land. The doorway is covered with immense slabs of solid stone. On either side are pillars, each one a single stone of eighteen feet in height. They are of no architecture known to Europe, but belong to the early Jain style, where the capitals abound in lions and other animals. We are now in a covered passage, broad, lofty, impressive. It is vaulted with great solid stones, laid across from side to side, and we can see them in all their massiveness. We come next to the forecourt of the temple of Siva. It is now sadly neglected, and there is but little evidence of worship; but on days sacred to the gods Siva, Parvati, Ganesh, and Subramanya their images are taken out, a procession is formed, and various rites are celebrated, as from time immemorial.

I now passed through the forecourt of the temple, and, looking out in front, could see a great flight of broad steps, which rise far out in advance, until the steps and the lofty ceiling merge into each other. I knew the steps continued, but could not see how far. The vista darkens out in front and above. In 1849 there was an accident here. There had gathered a multitude from all parts of the country to worship Ganesh on the day sacred to him. From some cause the dense throng became frightened, and lost all control of itself, and the people tumbled down the great stone steps, one over another, and became a tangled and crushed helpless mass. When relief came, five hundred dead bodies were taken out of this great passageway. The ascent of this stairway is not easy. The steps are high, and their inclination is abrupt, and they are two hundred and ninety in number. They are painted in red and white stripes. The impression which one has, as he ascends them, is that he is passing up through a solid rock. He is, in fact, climbing a great hill, beneath an ascending archway, over great stone stairways, with only now and then a landing. Up again I had to go, and still keep going, and wondered when the end would come, and I could see the bright blaze of the Indian sunlight again. I had had no such sensation since, years ago, I climbed slowly up through the secret stairway cut through the solid rock of Sorrento, from the shore of the Mediterranean to the house on the cliff in which Tasso had lived, and from which one sees Capri, Ischia, Castelamare, and all the enchantments of the Bay of Naples.

This great passageway served two purposes. It was once the entrance into the temple, and the only pass by which an army could ascend to the fort which crowns the crest of the colossal boulder of Trichinopoli. At last we came to a halting-place. Here was a temple. It is not spacious, but abounds in images of the Hindu gods and other symbols of false worship. The altar was covered with offerings of rice and yellow flowers. I now turned to the right and came out into the free air once more. I was now where man never built or carved an image from stone.

I stood on the solid, native rock, towards whose bald and flinty face I had been all the time toiling, and yet hardly knowing it. But I had still a higher point to reach. Fifty-seven gentle steps have been cleft from the bold surface of the rock to prevent the feet from slipping and the wind from whisking one away. It is no easy thing to walk up them. I would much sooner try my chances again by a climb up Mt. Washington, from the side of the Crawford House, and lie flat on the boulders when the wind is high. There would at least be some chance of finding one's self again, should the wind pick one up and waft him away. But to slip here, on the rock of Trichinopoli, brings one down—where shall I say? On the roof of some far-down shrine, or, more likely, on some uncovered peak of the lower rocks, or, most likely, into some green-covered and slimy tank, with its sleepy fish and lazy bathers, and which has not been cleaned out since Clive's besom swept all India. What with the fiercely-blowing wind and the direct and intense heat of the Indian sun, although in mid-December, I hardly knew what to do. But my umbrella had to come down lest it might waft me away. I stopped to catch breath and a new foothold, and then started for the farther way.

A slippery path was this, but I was thinking what it must have been when it was drenched in blood, and the living and the dead were hurled from this awful height, when Saxon and Indian struggled, hand to hand, and inch by inch, on this awful Hindu rock, and helped to decide the fate of all India for all time. There is no spot in all this wearying upward path, either over the lower stones which man has lifted into place for worship or over the firmer ones which nature has reared into higher service, which has not been contested for by hot blood and beneath a blazing sky and merciless sun.

Just now, when I was comforting myself with the thought that I had about reached the top of the temple fort, I discovered that I had only made a turn in the rocky path. I had yet to enter a deep staircase, cut into the solid rock, and consisting of twenty-six more steps. Up these I went, and, crowning the whole, there was still the Mandapam; and failing in reaching it, and taking refuge from the heat and the wind beneath its canopy, I was glad to rest awhile, and let my turbaned guide drop down in a corner and catch a nap, and wait my time. He was losing nothing by the stay. Few people, I was told, ever came to the fort to ascend it. They knew the fatigue too well. Happily, I was ignorant of the ordeal.

But one thing no one could know who had not ascended the highest point—namely, the wonderful view of the surrounding country. The eye ranges over an immense expanse, some fifty or sixty miles in diameter. Here lay at my feet the hottest battlefield of Southern India. On every hand the Indian tribes, with the French and English, as later and upstart combatants, have struggled for the possession of the whole country from Madras down to Cape Comorin.

The plain of Trichinopoli is even, and only broken near at hand by the abrupt hills which rise like cones from the surface. The Golden Rock stands out like a great pillar against the southern sky. Eastward are the French Rocks, once a bulwark of the French in the last century, when they hoped to save India to their rule. Out towards the north, like a thread of silver, sweeps and curves the Kaveri River on its way to lose itself in the Bay of Bengal. Along its banks is the sacred island of Srirangam, with bright pagodas shimmering in the blazing sunlight, through the dense jungle that enwraps all the works of man. Away to the northwest is the Tele Malai mountain range, rising two thousand feet above the plain, while far off to the north, as the crow flies, the Kale Malai Mountains tower four thousand feet. To the east the Pache Hills bound the wonderful horizon. There is, then, on nearly every side, a framework of hills, varied and broken, yet blue and picturesque. Within this setting there is the city of Trichinopoli, with temples standing over all the plain, towering trees, old forts, a winding river, many small streams, dismantled forts, patches of thick jungle, villages by the score, and many wayside shrines.

You are in a new world. The Orient is everywhere prominent. But it must not be forgotten that the Englishman is here. Out on the Bay of Bengal, to the east, his steamers glide through the waters. Yonder, like a spider's thread, his telegraph runs, all the way from Ceylon to Calcutta, and, for that matter, to Westminster Hall. Away off in the distance, in that cheerful compound, there is a newspaper, published by him, and in his own language, and for his own people. Down that narrow lane, as you can plainly see with your glass, is a company of red-coats, who do not know the Hindustani, except to give orders to their servants and soldiers. Theirs is the Queen's English, and nothing else. They live in India to keep the country in English safety. The conquered Hindus are their hewers of wood and drawers of water. Then the presence of the Englishman means more than the mere soldier. He stands out in front of the missionary and the missionary's Bible, and none dare touch either. Verily, the times are changed wonderfully since Judson was not permitted to stay in Calcutta and preach the Gospel for fear of disturbing Hindu prejudice. Well for the world he did not! He went across the Bay of Bengal, unrolled his flag, and hence the Burmese Christianity of all time to come.

CHAPTER XXIX.

THE SRIRANGAM TEMPLE.

From the great Temple Fort of Trichinopoli I drove three miles to the Srirangam temple. In India some pleasing myth generally underlies the ancient temple. That which gave rise to this wonderful structure of Srirangam may be taken as an illustration of the whole class. Rama had a powerful chief, Vibhishana by name, who lived in Ceylon, but had been long from home, and was now about to return. As a parting gift, and in recognition of his great services, Rama presented him with a golden image of Vishnu. The only instruction was, not to lay it down until he reached home. But the journey was long, and Vibhishana must have some rest by the way. Besides, he could not think of passing the great sacred tank of Srirangam without bathing. So he handed over the precious idol to an attendant, charging him to hold it upright, and by no means to let it leave his hand. But the idol was heavy, and its owner was long in the bath, and hence the follower let it rest upon the earth a moment. It was too late. The image could not be raised by both hands. There was not power enough even in Vibhishana's hands to stir it a hair's-breadth. Hence a shrine had to be built over it, and a great temple, and finally a group of temples, whose fame has gone out into all the Brahman world. The general design of the immense structure is to repeat in stone, for human view, the Vaikuntha, or seven series of quadrangular courts which constitute the heaven of Vishnu.

I was a little disturbed by the cabman bringing his horses to a sudden stop; but I soon found that all vehicles must stand far outside of the innermost temple. It was clear that to walk through the great spaces would require much time and no little exertion beneath the blazing Indian sun, whose rigor I had recently tested by my climb to the summit of Trichinopoli. I passed through an immense *gopura*, or towered gateway, each side of which is lined with pillars. Everywhere I was struck with the magnitude of the stones and the minuteness of the carvings. Many stones are forty feet high. The roof of the high tower consists of horizontal slabs of fabulous size and weight. Having gone through several of these gopuras, and examined many carvings, each differing from all the rest, I reached a stairway, by which I ascended to the flat roof of the principal temple, and walked all over it.

Here, for the first time, I could see the plan of this wonderful structure. First of all is the great outer wall, which encloses a space no less than 2475 feet wide and 2880 feet long. Outside of this the profane city lies, with its homes, bazars, industries, poverty, pollution, and whatever else enters into the curious make-up of a great Indian city. Inside this wall there are temples, towers, and halls of all sizes, from the little secluded spot where only a dozen can conveniently bow to Vishnu to the great Hall of a Thousand Columns. But there is a singular order. Within the outer wall, after a due interval of a broad way, there comes a second, and then a third wall, until you reach the most holy place. Each square is entered by four lofty gateways, whose ceiling is painted in bright colors, and whose outer towers rise, in the shape of a pyramid, to a height overlooking the entire group of buildings, and visible at a great distance before reaching the city. Every step, from the outermost to the innermost wall, is towards the holy of holies. Every new quadrangle brings into view some new group of sculptured marvels—all minute, barbaric, combining the brute and the human form in various ways, and all representing the legendary deeds of Vishnu.

When you have entered the innermost enclosure, you stand near the holy of holies. This is the last spot where any but a Hindu may stand. Not knowing the limit of the proprieties, I stepped beyond the proper line, and was immediately obstructed by a crowd of ill-kempt Hindus. The idol crown is covered with diamonds, while emeralds and rubies abound in great number. There are idols of gold, covered with jewels. Even the toes are set off with rings of gold studded with precious stones. There are, also, chains of gold, which have the peculiarity that they are as flexible as cord, an art of working gold long practised in this venerable city as a special industry. There is also a large bowl of solid gold, besides long chains of gold coins.

Perhaps the most remarkable carvings are in the Hall of One Thousand Columns. Each column is a monolith eighteen feet high. Here is a single row of pillars, a front row, where the statuary is so combined with the pillar that it is the pillar itself. For example, here is a column in the shape of a horseman. His horse is rearing, being frightened by a tiger. This tiger is a savage beast, rampant, and attacking both rider and horse. The horseman, who is a hunter withal, is thrusting his spear into the very vitals of the tiger. Besides these figures, there are also men on foot, the attendants of the divine rider, who have shorter weapons, and are stabbing the tiger with great impetuosity. Now all these figures are combined into a single pillar. The whole is a colossal piece of open-work. Think of what must be the effect of a whole row of such marvels. There is not a particle of relief. Each detail is a reproduction of the living form. It is like witnessing a great hunting-scene in a Singhalese jungle. Then, too, each column differs from all the rest. For it is a characteristic of Hindu art to repeat nothing. Each of these figures relates to the legendary history of Vishnu, and is minutely described in the Vedas.

It was never meant that all within the great outer wall should be silent, and only belong to the temple service. On the contrary, while all within that enclosure is strictly sacred, there is really a town, if not a veritable city, within the wall. But all must be sacred. Here are priests in great number, whose offices relate not only to the service, but to keeping the building in order. They are of all grades, from the highest Brahmans, springing from the brain of Brahma, to the lowest sweepers, each order being defined from ancient times, and sacredly preserved. They all sleep within the wall, and gather sanctity from their duties. Besides these there are other classes, writers and what not, who have something to do with the temple, and whose services are paid for out of the old endowments. The dancing-girls live here. They, too, are very liberally paid out of the same endowment. Their very costume, and their golden bangles, anklets, necklaces, toe-rings, and other ornaments, some of which have the addition of precious stones, tell the story of the wealth by which they are supported. Monier Williams relates that one of the Tanjor girls informed him that she had been recently robbed of jewels valued at twenty-five thousand rupees. Here, too, are the sacred elephants, which must not eat a single straw that is not sacred to the worship of the divine Vishnu. Great, sleek fellows they are. They are taught all manner of priestly tricks, even to the deft putting out of the trunk to take a two-anna piece.

These buildings have not grown suddenly to their present number or proportions. They have been added from time to time, according to gifts from far and near. The fame of Vishnu is as wide as the Brahman faith, and that an image once belonging to him should exist has attracted generous sacrifices from the pious during many centuries. The poor, who could give but few rupees, have had single carvings made here, as their sacrifice. The rich have filled a hall with sculptured pillars, and so paid the price of some great sinning. Kings have reared walls or towers, or caused a series of statues to be erected, and thus have quieted their conscience after many a score of black crimes. Queens and fair ladies of distant courts, in those barbaric days before a Portuguese dared to turn his pinnace towards India's coral strand, took off their brightest diamonds and most dazzling amethysts, and bore them, in person, long distances, and, on bended knees, presented them as offerings to the image itself, for its crown or its robe or ornaments. When the fitful life was about to end, many a niggardly hand relaxed its grasp upon its gold, and spent the last days on earth in finding the way to Srirangam, and laying on Vishnu's altar a gift of treasure and flowers for rearing a sculptured colonnade, or endowing the support of a dozen dancing-girls for the temple, or even adding another temple to the already tangled and crowded group.

"No sight," says Williams, "is to be seen in any part of India that can at all compare with the unique effect produced by its series of seven quadrangular enclosures formed by seven squares of massive walls, one within the other — every square pierced by pyramidal towers rivalling in altitude the adjacent rock of Trichinopoli. The idea is, that each investing square of walls shall form courts of increasing sanctity, which shall conduct the worshipper by regular gradations to a central holy of holies of unique shape and proportions. In fact, the entire fabric of shrines, edifices, towers, and enclosures is supposed to be a terrestrial counterpart of Vishnu's heaven (Vaikuntha), to which his votaries are destined to be transported." *

* "Religious Thought and Life in India," p. 448.

There are seasons when long pilgrimages are made to the Srirangam temple. The fame of its image is so far-spread and so deeply seated that many thousands come from every quarter of India, and even from British Burma, to fall in reverent adoration before the recumbent image of Vishnu.

The great day of the year is the 27th of December. If the pilgrim has reached the temple on this day he may count himself privileged far beyond his fellows in all the Hindu world. As he enters the great outer gateway he begins to be affected by the splendor of the scene. Then he advances, and passes through another, and still another, until he is fairly overwhelmed by what his eyes behold. He finally reaches the innermost adytum. This is Heaven's Gate, and he is there on the only day of the year when even the priestly hands of the highest Brahmans may open it. This must be done, too, at four o'clock in the morning, long before the dawn has shot across the Bay of Bengal, or smitten the gay enamel on the lofty gopuras. The recumbent image of Vishnu must not be disturbed. Nor could it be, according to Brahman faith. But in these lands there is always an easy way to get out of an impossibility. Another image can be made; and there is enough wealth in the hands of dying misers and cut-throats to cover it over with priceless gems. So that image, when once the narrow portal is unlocked, is borne out by the priests, and held aloft for the multitude to behold.

Every foot-sore pilgrim of the fifty thousand, or possibly a hundred thousand, is now happy. It is his first glimpse of Heaven; for has he not entered the Gate? Just behind the great image there are eighteen other images, of Vaishnava saints, brought along by the priests. Then come the priests, in great number, chanting in wild and plaintive notes the old hymns of the Vedas. With the chanting is the tumultuous music of the sacred bands, which have come from distant shrines to help their brothers here to swell the welcome of heavenly minstrelsy. The celebration being constantly varied in scenic display, the attention of the pilgrims is intense throughout. Some are very aged. Others have come with life just opening before them. But all have the same poor belief—this is heaven on earth to every worshipper. His sins of the past are all gone. He has bathed in the sacred tank of Srirangam, and gone through the narrow portal with his gift to the priests and offerings to the idol, and may now go down into his own grave, or back into the sinning world, or let the car of Jagannath roll over his prostrate body. It is all the same. He has even already passed through Heaven's Gate, and beheld with his own poor, human eyes, the Heaven of Vishnu.

AFTÁBA (WATER-VESSEL) SIYAH KALAMKARI, MORADABAD.

CHAPTER XXX.

A RUN INTO MYSORE.

Several friends stood on the platform to give me a cordial greeting as the train entered the Bangalore station. Bangalore is the capital of the province of Mysore, a large district constituting the intermediate land between the Bombay Presidency of the northwest and the Madras Presidency of the southeast. One finds here, as everywhere in India, the traces of terrible havoc. Cornwallis, who gained in India the prestige he lost by his surrender of the American colonies to Washington at Yorktown, fought bravely in this period. But, long before his day, the struggles between native princes had been of the most deadly character, and the cruelties in time of peace had been of the most refined and secret type.

A BRAHMAN OF MYSORE.

Mysore, in its general grouping, belongs to the Madras Presidency. It owes its name to Mahesh-asura, the buffalo-headed demon slain by the consent of Siva, the tutelary deity of the royal family of the province. In the time of the old Mogul rule in the north, permission was given by the court of Aurangzeb to Chikka Deva, the Mysore chief, to hold sway alone and to sit on an ivory throne. The greatest native fighter, however, of this region was Haidar Ali, who rose from the humblest station, filled all India with the fame of his deeds, and was the most powerful of all the native chiefs with whom the English had to contend in their contest for India. He passed rapidly from one country to another, until he had brought Mysore under his dominion. He allied himself with the French, in the hope of defeating the English. But the latter, conquering both, succeeded in bringing Mysore into subjection. Its present native Maharajah is permitted to rule on precisely the same plan

ELEPHANT-CATCHING IN MYSORE, IN A KEDDAH CONSTRUCTED BY ORDER OF THE MAHARAJAH IN HONOR OF THE VISIT OF PRINCE

as the Nizam, farther north, because of the friendly relation of the dynasty to the English government during the mutiny of 1857.

Mysore is distinguished for its immense forests, which have long been infested with furious wild beasts. A lady, long resident in India, told me that in her childhood her father had a coffee plantation here, and the family were often compelled to ascend trees at night, where hammocks were swung and other precautionary arrangements made for a safe night's lodging, because of the dangerous wild beasts. The Macaulay family had its representative here. Dr. Macaulay, an uncle of the historian, was a physician in the region, and shared with the other Anglo-Indians the dangers and trials of the wild life of the country. Rice thus describes one of these Mysore forests: "Trees of the largest size stand thickly together over miles, their trunks entwined with creepers of huge dimensions, their massive arms decked with a thousand bright-blossoming orchids. Birds of rare plumage flit from bough to bough; from the thick woods, which abruptly terminate on verdant swards, bison issue forth in the early morn and afternoon to browse on the rich herbage, while large herds of elk pass rapidly across the hill-sides; packs of wild dogs cross the path, hunting in company, and the tiger is not far off, for the warning boom of the great *langur* monkey is heard from the lofty trees. The view from the head of the descent to the Falls of Gersoppa is one of the finest pieces of scenery in the world."

ROLLING TEA.

There is no better picture of the English transformation in India than Mysore presents. As one now rides through Bangalore, for example, he sees the many evidences of a beautiful and growing Christian civilization. Large and highly ornamented compounds, in the midst of each a delightful English home, surround the entire place. The spaces are broad, as one might well imagine, for the site of the entire city. English and native, it is thirteen square miles, or about the area of London. It stands three thousand feet above the sea-level, and from any exposed point the views are very picturesque.

Bangalore is the centre of a system of very successful missionary operations. The Mohammedan population is scanty, and the Hindu numbers about ninety-five per cent. The Wesleyan missions are prosperous. I made a call on the Rev. Mr. Hudson, the superintendent, and found him a most courteous Christian gentleman, thoroughly acquainted with the whole field, and wisely adapting his methods to conquer rapidly the dying faiths of this polyglot native population.

The Rev. William Arthur, of England, author of "The Tongue of Fire," was in early life a zealous missionary in this country. His "Mission to Mysore" is one of the most accurate and suggestive accounts of Christian work in any land, and has done much to reveal to English Christians the need of increased attention to missionary operations in India. There is probably no missionary now laboring in Mysore who is more successful than the Rev. Henry Haigh. I had the pleasure of meeting him just before I sailed from Bombay, and conferring with him as to his work. He is an eloquent preacher, a cultivated gentleman, and is devoted to India as a field for evangelistic work. He was good enough to come out to the steamer *Siam* when I was about sailing, and his hand was one of the last I grasped before losing sight of the India coast.

An American Hero.

Six years ago, while spending a Sunday in the town of Berea, Ohio, I made a call upon an aged man and his wife, who lived in great simplicity, and who denied themselves a luxurious home that they might give their wealth to Christian purposes. Yet his generous hand had founded the Baldwin University in Berea, had built up the La Teche schools on the banks of the

Red River, in Louisiana, and here, in Bangalore, had founded the beautiful Baldwin schools. Broad is the empire over which the generous heart waves its sceptre of fine gold. As I went from one room to another of these schools, and saw the children who were being moulded into a symmetrical and elevated life by their instrumentality, under the care of the Rev. Mr. Richards, I could not help thinking of the vast good which the plain man of Berea was doing on the other side of the planet. He has since gone to his reward, but the harvest from his good deeds has only just begun.

Mr. Richards accompanied me to the large and handsome buildings where some of his own students, with many others, were about to pass their examination for entrance into the Madras University. That fine institution has arrangements for its examinations throughout the presidency and in Mysore by which students passing in the schools through which they have gone can enter the University without further formalities.

DRYING TEA.

The examination day, December 1, 1884, was a fête day among the schools of Bangalore. On entering the large grounds surrounding the handsome Central School building, young ladies, in holiday attire, were promenading among the palms and flowers. Young men were in groups. All were intent upon the coming ordeal. They all had the air of young people who had done their work well, and were only waiting for the bell to ring them to their desks. The examinations were conducted in writing, with a paper for each student. I have before me a copy of these papers, which would serve well to stand beside similar papers for entrance into any university. Map-drawing, physical geography, Indian history, physics, Latin composition, English history, and other topics had to be treated at sight by the students. Here is a specimen of poetry, "Sunset at Benares," which had to be paraphrased:

> "The shades of evening veil the lofty spires
> Of Kasi's gilded shrines! A *twilight* haze
> The calm scene shrouds. The weary boatmen raise
> Along the dusky shore their crimson fires,
> That tinge the *circling* groups. As day retires
> The lone and long-deserted maiden strays
> By Gunga's stream, where float the feeble rays
> Of her pale lamp—but lo! the light expires!
> Alas! how cheerless now the mourner's *breast*,
> For life hath not one charm. Her tears deplore
> The fond youth's early doom, and never more
> Shall Hope's sweet vision yield her *spirit* rest!
> The cold wave quenched the flame, an *omen* dread,
> The maiden dare not *question*—he is dead."

I visited a tea-drying establishment, for this is one centre of the important tea industry of the whole country. India is constantly increasing her culture of tea, and the English here regard it as superior to that of China. The machinery is very elaborate, and many hands are employed in the Bangalore house.

The great garden of Bangalore is a very attractive object. It covers a great space, and requires a long time to examine any one of its chief departments. One finds nowhere in the world, perhaps, such an endless variety of orchids as here. They have been caught up in the jungles, brought to this place, and developed into exquisite colors. From here they are sent out into all lands. The palms, and all the larger and smaller shrubbery known to the endless Indian flora, can be seen here, until one wearies at the very wealth of color and perfume. The scent of the roses on that December morning burdened the air. In this garden there is a department for seeds. Indeed, it is the chief point of distribution of flower-seeds throughout India. The superintendent was kind enough to place in my hands about forty varieties, for distribution to American friends.

My guide-book had told me that the Maharajah's palace was not open to the public. But I had long since learned to take nothing for granted in travelling, and I found by experiment here that an application for admission was all that was needed to open the front portal and all the halls for a leisurely inspection. This is a new building, of great dimensions, and of fine architectural proportions. It would be an ornament anywhere in London, and would throw Buckingham Palace quite into the shade. There are but few traces of Indian furnishing, and none of Indian architecture. The native princes are quite in love with everything English. Nowadays, when they build a palace and furnish it, they forsake Hindu models. The new Bangalore palace has carpets from France and England, heavy furniture from London, decorations by European artists, and the more ornamental furniture from Paris. The outlook from the great

DESPATCHING TEA BY CART TO THE RAILROAD.

central tower is broad and enchantingly beautiful. Each of the lofty heights in the far distance has its own story of adventure and of final English triumph, while the plains below are full of the evidences of those fine agricultural operations which the English are everywhere introducing into India. The Englishman in India has solved one problem well—what next to do when he has put his sword into its sheath. He has gone to work to make the people like himself, and their land like his own England.

The Bangalore Museum is very rich in memorials of the former times in Mysore. No attempt has been made to make it tell the story of general Indian history. Here are slabs from ancient palaces, one from Tipu's, in particular, with its twelve suggestive Persian distichs. Many of these slabs are of great size, and their still perfect carvings make them precious reminders of times before the Englishman had landed in India. There are fine geological specimens, an ornithological department, and a most interesting series of industrial products. Among the most attractive objects were the great copper plates whereon laws and sacred writings had been engraved long before the age of books. Nowhere in India did I see such perfect specimens of the early metallic books of India as here in Bangalore.

The Old Fort.

The Old Fort, where palace and fortress once stood together, is now a complete ruin. Its history is that of old Mysore under barbaric native rule. Here are great earthworks; battered walls; massive towers in decay; audience-halls, now vacated save by the bats, moles, and the intruding tendrils of immense creepers; tanks where the ladies of the court used to while away the languid hours in fishing; rickety balconies, where kings were wont to sit in state, and were fanned by gayly dressed and nodding servants; banqueting-halls, now silent and filled with offensive odors; and, last of all, the prisons where Tipu and his predecessors used to confine their unfortunate criminals, while out in front of the largest balcony stretched the broad space where the poor unfortunates were executed, as a special pastime for the brilliant court. This fort received its fatal blow in 1791, when Cornwallis captured both palace and prison.

There are several beautiful churches in Bangalore. In one of them, All-Saints', there are many tablets to officers and to members of English families residing in Bangalore.

The Methodist Episcopal Church has two houses of worship in Bangalore. In one of them we held an evening service. After the service my friends accompanied me to the train, The next morning I came once more in sight of the palms of Madras.

CHAPTER XXXI.

THE SYRIAN CHRISTIANS IN INDIA.

THERE are three well-defined stages of evangelization in India.* The first was the propagation of the gospel during the apostolic period of the Christian Church. The second dates from the Portuguese invasion. Only five years after the discovery of America by Christopher Columbus, Vasco da Gama, after receiving absolution for himself and his crew, as though they were all going to die, set sail from the Tagus to find a new way to the Indies. Columbus had failed to find a western path; Vasco da Gama would see what he could do towards finding an eastern. Ten months afterwards he cast anchor off Calicut, and planted the Portuguese flag on Indian soil. This was the beginning of the long chapter of the Portuguese in India. The third stage of Indian evangelization was in the early part of the eighteenth century, and was inaugurated by the Danes in the interest of the Protestant Church. This Danish movement was the first Protestant mission, not only to India, but to any pagan country.

There is abundant ground for supposing that the gospel reached India during the most primitive period of the Christian Church. An early tradition declares that the apostle Thomas founded the first society on the coast of Malabar, and was martyred at a place called Mailapur. Pantænus, Dorotheus, Hippolytus, Philostorgius, Gregory Nazianzen, Jerome, Theodoret, and Gregory of Tours, authors covering the period from A.D. 190 to 595, attribute the spread of the gospel to India directly to the labors of that apostle. This early testimony has later support. Those modern travellers to India who long preceded the founding of the Jesuit order and the coming of Xavier to Goa declare that they found a Christian Church existing on the Coromandel coast, and that its members believed Thomas to have been its founder.

---

* Hoffmann, "Die Epochen der Kirchengeschichte Indiens," Berlin, 1853.

Marco Polo, in 1220, says that both Christians and Saracens held Thomas in great reverence, and made pilgrimages to Maaba, the province in which his body was supposed to be interred.*

In more recent times such careful travellers as Buchanan and Bishop Heber favor the view that prevailed throughout the entire early period of the Church, and which has a strong support in the existing Christian societies, that the apostle Thomas was the first preacher of the gospel in the Hindu peninsula. Heber says, "I see no good reason for doubting; there is as fair historical evidence as the case requires that Saint Thomas preached the gospel in India and was martyred at a place called Mailapur.† Buchanan says that "we have as good authority for believing that the apostle Thomas died in India as that the apostle Peter died in Rome."‡

The most valuable of all authorities for this view is in the statement of Professor Wilson, who says that "we need not be much at a loss for its identification [Mihilaropya with Mailapur], as the name approaches sufficiently to Mihilapur, Meliapura St. Thomé, where our records indicate a city of some consequence, in the beginning of the Christian era, as the scene of the labors and martyrdom of Saint Thomas, occurrences very far from invalidated by any arguments yet advanced against the truth of the tradition."‖ If one takes all the evidence into consideration, the balance seems to be in favor of a very early Christian Church in India, and of the apostle Thomas as its founder. There is nothing improbable in this conclusion. The means of locomotion in the time of the Roman Empire were not unfavorable to long journeys. Life was quite as secure as in recent days. Paul was much safer in his journeys through Asia Minor than any European traveller would be to-day. When the persecution broke out in Jerusalem, and the Christians were compelled to leave, it would not be unreasonable that the apostles should distribute the accessible territory among themselves. If to Thomas was assigned Persia, it would only be a question of months when he could reach there; and, having organized the Persian Church, it would require but a short time to go farther,

---

* Book iii., ch. xviii.

† "Journal," vol. iii., p. 212, 4th ed.

‡ "Christian Researches," p. 134, 5th ed.

‖ "Transactions of the Royal Archæological Society," vol. i., p. 161.

following the drift of commerce, and come southward to the head of the Persian Gulf, and find his way far down the Indian

SANDSTONE DOORWAY, MULTÁN.

coast. Such a journey would not be more difficult than Burton's in Arabia, or Vambery's in the uplands of Northern Asia, or Thomas Coryat's walk, in the seventeenth century, all the way from Jerusalem to Ajmir, and who spent but two pounds and ten shillings for the entire journey.*

Whether Thomas was the founder of the Church in India or not, this remains certain—that by the time of the Council of Nicæa, in the year 325, Christianity had so far advanced as to be represented by a bishop in that most important conference of the early Church. The name of Johannes, Bishop of India Maxima and Persia, stands as one of the subscribers to the Nicene decrees.

By whomsoever founded, Indian Christianity took the later Nestorian type. This was due to its relations with Persia, where the monophysite vagary carried the people with it. When the Mohammedan faith arose, and Christianity was swept away from Persia, the Indian Church was left to fight its battle alone, and the fact of the existence of Christianity in India passed away from the knowledge of the chroniclers of the Church. It was only when travellers of modern times penetrated India, and made report of what they saw, that the existence of Indian Christians became known. Is it any wonder that they should have lost nearly all traces of their original character? The real wonder is, that they have not been entirely obliterated.

The condition of the Syrian Christians is very pitiable. They are superstitious, and have all the infirmities which have come from neglect for fifteen centuries. They have absorbed, unconsciously, many of the weaknesses of the false faiths which have surrounded them. For example, they are firm believers in astrology. An astrologer lives in each village, and a horoscope is procured immediately on the occurrence of a birth. Regeneration in baptism is firmly believed. A remarkable fondness for Scripture names is entertained—probably an inheritance from the days of the origin of the community. The New Testament names are preferred. But many are so altered from their original form as to be hardly recognizable. Peter, for instance, has become Poonen; Joshua, Koshi; Paul, Peili; Zechariah, Tarien; Alexander, Chandy; and John, Lohanan.†

* For an excellent summary of opinions on the apostolic founding of the Indian Church, see Kennett's "Thomas the Apostle of India," Madras, 1882. There is a unique and excellent bibliography of the subject on pp. 29–32. We also recommend, especially, Whitehouse, "Lingerings of Light in a Dark Land." London, 1873.

† Mateer, "Native Life in Travancore," pp. 159, 160.

CHAPTER XXXII.

VOYAGE FROM MADRAS TO CALCUTTA.

There is no direct line of travel along the eastern coast of India. The land lies low, and is swept by frequent storms. The towns are small, and the industries and products are not sufficiently large to warrant the frequent halting of steamers at any point. This section alone, of all India, is still largely unchanged by modern civilization. The railway line to Calcutta runs nearly back to Bombay, and then strikes eastward to the terminus at Calcutta.

I found a comfortable room on the steamer, and several American passengers. One of the more noticeable gentlemen was the brother of the Bishop of Ceylon. I had been informed, in Colombo, of an amusing incident connected with the bishop's administration. Ceylon, like India, has its State Church Establishment—the Church of England. When the present bishop entered upon his duties in the Ceylonese diocese he determined to limit the pretty active operations of the Church Missionary Society, and such other societies of the Church of England as ask but few questions of the bishops, but go on zealously with their evangelistic operations. The Singhalese bishop, I was told, was not pleased with what he saw in his new diocese, and, wherever he could, he quietly disposed of some of the parish clergymen, and all others who could not be controlled, and he put in their places men of his own choice. No little friction was excited, but there was no help except in submission. The already mooted question of the disestablishment of the State Church in Ceylon now received new attention. It was rumored that even the governor favored the measure. The bishop was alarmed, and called upon the governor, when substantially the following brief conversation followed:

"I understand you are favoring the disestablishment of the Church of England in Ceylon," said the worthy bishop.

"Why should it not be done?" was the laconic reply.

"Reason enough. Do you not see that many of the older parochial incumbents would be thrown out of their livings? It would be a very hard procedure to turn adrift men who have been spending many years in the island, and have done important service to the Church. It would be unmerciful."

"Oh, I don't think," responded the governor, "that any large

BLACK PAGODA, KANARAK.

class of these worthy people would be affected by the measure. You have already gotten rid of very many of them, and those remaining are so few that the evil would not be widespread."

The established Church of India arose out of the ecclesiastical arrangements of the East India Company, which supplied a few chaplains for important points. Of this number was the immortal Henry Martyn, whose brief but brilliant life has been an inspiration for missionary effort throughout the Protestant world. Heber, Wilson, and others, who as bishops have represent-

LADIES' CROQUET MATCH ON THE PROMENADE DECK.

ed the Church of England in India, were men who combined great learning with rare wisdom in the prosecution of their work. But, for that matter, many of the men who have served as missionaries in India, from whatever Protestant Church they have gone, have been examples of superior gifts and heroic endeavor.

There is a Disestablishment Society in active operation in Calcutta. This is the outgrowth of a desire on the part of many to see the control of the Church by the government terminated. Both natives and Europeans belong to it. The movement is the more important because, when successful, there will be an end to all government complicity with the support of heathen temple service. Some of the governors-general have shown as much sympathy with the various religious bodies operating in India as with the Church of England itself. For example, about 1865, when Sir John Lawrence was governor-general (1863–69), and was at Simla, the summer capital, he saw a few plain Moravian missionaries who were at work in Tibet, far to the north, and were in Simla for a short time. He inquired carefully into their work, and asked them if they wanted anything. Their answer was, "Candles." By his special order he had a great quantity made for them, and sent them to their remote mission in Tibet, a journey of thirteen days beyond Simla.

The weather during my voyage to Calcutta was good, and in every way favorable to reading and writing. The passage lasted four days. When we came in sight of the lowlands at the mouth of the Ganges, which here takes the name of the Hugli, there was an unusual stir among both sailors and passengers. It was a question whether we could pass the bar, and especially the "James and Mary" shoals. Posts, on which the state of the tide could be seen by registers, gave us little encouragement. The fear was, that we should have to wait twelve hours below the city before ascending the river. But all would be well if we could only cross the "James and Mary." I was told that a vessel of the name of *James and Mary* had once been lost here, and had given its name to the bar. But another account of the origin is that of Hunter, who says that as in Hindi *jal* means water and *mari* means fatal, the two words mean the *fatal water*.

One of the peculiarities of running on these shoals at the mouth of the Hugli is, that there is no hope of either the vessel or the people in it. The river bottom has the character of a quicksand, which, with the rapid current, whirls the vessel bottom upward. Everything disappears. When the *County of Stirling* was grounded on the Falta Sand, she disappeared in eight minutes. The danger of grounding is all the greater from the frequent changes of the channel. The deep water of to-day may be shallow to-morrow. Hence the gauges of the tide are by no means reliable, except for a brief time. It is usual, when there is any fear of grounding, for the sailors to stand ready, axes in hand, to cut away the masts and rigging, and use other violent expedients to keep the vessel from turning bottom upward. I could not view the anxiety of our pilot and the

MONOLITHS AT KANARAK.

officers, and the readiness of the sailors for a casualty, without a degree of nervousness. There was no attempt on their part to conceal the danger of the moment. We crossed the "James and Mary" safely, however, but I was told with only an inch to spare.

As you ascend the Hugli there are broad stretches of beautiful land, rich with the fertile soil brought down from the distant mountains. The currents have left these great patches, over which the keels used to plough their way. The ploughman still turns up the shanks of wrecked and forgotten vessels. This delta of the Ganges spreads out beyond all others in the world. It begins to form two hundred miles from the sea, and is twice as large as that of the Nile.

The scene on nearing the dock in Calcutta is lively beyond description. Here are England and the East in strange intermixture. There is a broad space where carriages of all possible degrees of excellence and worthlessness are in waiting. The Calcutta papers had announced that our steamer was late, and would not be up until the next tide, but even this did not prevent many Anglo-Indians from coming down to greet their friends from dear England. My home during my stay in Calcutta was with the Rev. Dr. (now Bishop) J. M. Thoburn and his charming family, who gave me a cordial greeting and made every hour of my week beneath their hospitable roof a real delight. Here I received fresh news from my family in Geneva and a large supply of late American newspapers.

I was put to work at once. On Saturday morning came a lecture, or expository Bible reading, in the church of which the Doctor was pastor. But my busy day was on Sunday. If I have ever done harder work in one day than on my Sunday in Calcutta, I cannot recall it. Christmas was near at hand. First of all, at 7 o'clock in the morning, came an address to the Sunday-school. Then, at 8.30, came a sermon in the Dhurrumtolla church, to the immense congregation which attended the ministry of Doctor Thoburn. At 4 P.M., I went to the Bengali service, which was under the Doctor's general pastoral care. At 6.30 I preached again to the Dhurrumtolla congregation, and ordained two men to the ministry. At 8.30 I attended the Seaman's Bethel, which was one of the Doctor's agencies for reaching the large seafaring population of Calcutta. This was my fifth service for the day, with the thermometer among the nineties.

In intellectual appearance, in culture, in a profound and breathless interest in every part of the service, I have never seen this congregation in the Dhurrumtolla church surpassed. It is a busy street through the week—say, like Canal Street in New York, or Cheapside in London—and yet people in Calcutta make no question as to where the church is which they wish to attend. The equipages before the church, at the time of the morning service, were so numerous as to make it difficult to cross the street from the parsonage. It is only in the United States that the drift of population empties a church in the busi-

DECK GAME ON P. AND O. STEAMER.

ness part of the city. Even in England, nobody cares that Saint Paul's is at the very heart of London trade, and that Paternoster Row empties into the churchyard, and that the entire ellipse is filled with small shops. The church is there, and that is enough. It is precisely the same in India. It does not matter if the church is in the midst of native houses and petty shops. It is the service of which the religious Anglo-Indians think, and no questions are asked as to where the church is situated. The lesson is one which we, in the United States, should learn, and be quick to put into practice.

SILVER FILIGREE JEWELLERY OF CUTTACK.

CHAPTER XXXIII.

LORD DUFFERIN IN CALCUTTA.

The city was in great commotion for several days because of the approaching public entrance of Lord Dufferin as Governor-General of India. The Queen is called Empress; but such is the power of the chief British civil officer that his word is really supreme. England rules India, not on the Thames, but on the Ganges.

The Governors-General have been of two classes: those who

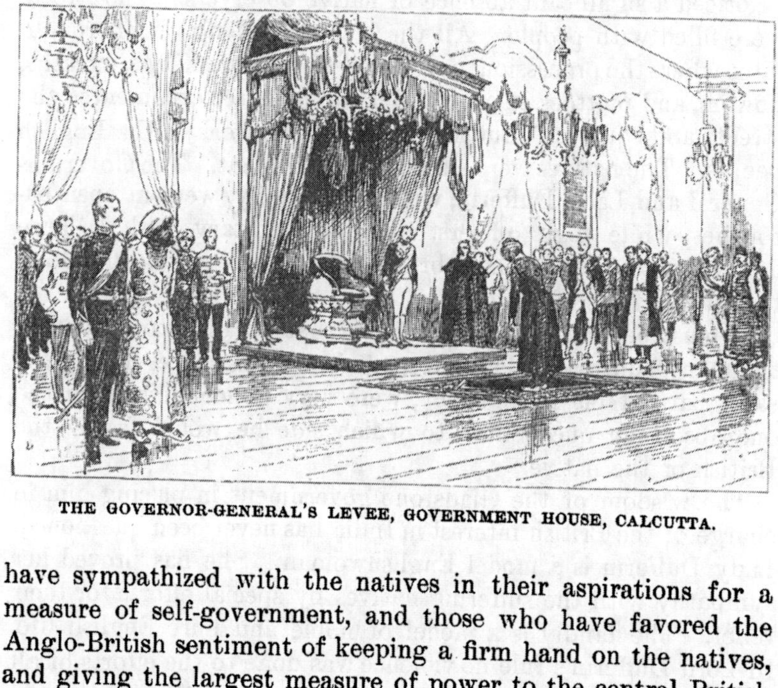

THE GOVERNOR-GENERAL'S LEVEE, GOVERNMENT HOUSE, CALCUTTA.

have sympathized with the natives in their aspirations for a measure of self-government, and those who have favored the Anglo-British sentiment of keeping a firm hand on the natives, and giving the largest measure of power to the central British rule. Lord Ripon, who had just been recalled, was the favorite of the natives. He had done a great deal to strengthen their hopes for a larger share in the government, and was regarded throughout the land as their friend and champion. When he was about to leave the country the native population of many cities turned out *en masse* to do him honor. Most flattering addresses were made to him, valuable gifts were presented, and every mark of high appreciation was bestowed upon him.

I was expecting to find that Lord Ripon's having ceased to be a Protestant, and adopting the Roman Catholic faith, had produced its effect upon the sympathy of the Protestants of India. But such was not the case.

It was a serious question what kind of a Governor-General Lord Dufferin would prove. The natives were distrustful. They were going to wait before joining in the general jubilee. The British residents, therefore, had the ceremonies in their own hands. On the day when Lord Dufferin was publicly received I noticed a significant absence of native observers. The streets were filled with people. All the balconies along the thoroughfares where the procession moved were thronged. Flags, wreaths, flowers, and mottoes of every jubilant character ornamented the streets and squares. But it was largely the work of the English people. The natives were either absent or silent. The Governor-General and Lady Dufferin, with their family, were in open barouches, while high officers, civil and military, with a large detachment of soldiers as a brilliant escort, moved slowly along the chief streets of the city.

It must be said of Lord Dufferin that all his expressions, in the many addresses which he made in various places during the early part of his incumbency, were very noncommittal on the one absorbing question as to which side he would favor—the British or the native.

The wisdom of the Gladstone government in placing him in charge of the British interest in India has never been questioned. Lady Dufferin is a model Englishwoman. She has proved her sympathy with the suffering natives by special efforts for their relief. The family is a model of noble and pure English life. In Lord Dufferin's rule no violence was done to the efforts of all Christians to advance the cause of the gospel throughout the country.

I learned in Athens, later, a pleasant fact in illustration of

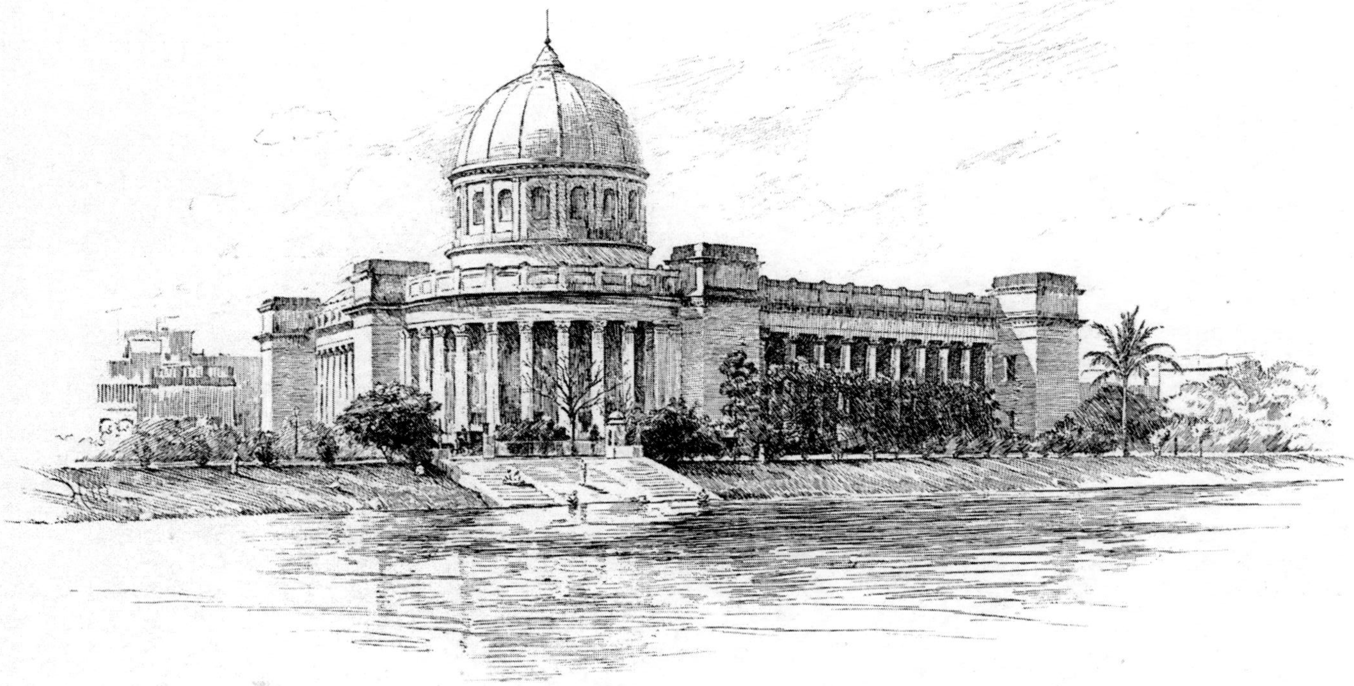

GENERAL POST-OFFICE, CALCUTTA.

Lord Dufferin's accomplishments as a linguist. Dr. Schliemann informed me that he had in his possession a copy of an address in modern Greek delivered by Lord Dufferin in Athens, and composed by him for an important public occasion. I was assured that it was delivered by the speaker with great correctness, and without any help from his manuscript.

AFTABA (WATER-VESSEL), COPPER-TINNED, FROM PESHAWUR.

CHAPTER XXXIV.

PICTURES OF CALCUTTA.

I HAD no little difficulty in securing permission to visit the Government House. The American Consul told me plainly that he had little hope of obtaining the permit, and I thought him disinclined to make even an effort. But a merchant, Mr. Fred. W. May, informed me that he believed it possible, and without further trouble to the American representative. He invited me to accompany him directly thither. We were met at the portal by a guard, who promptly gave us permission to enter the ante-room. Here a Eurasian member of the household arranged a time for us to come again, and receive a reply to our application. At four o'clock we returned, and were at once admitted to see every part of the palace of the Governor-General.

The building stands in the midst of a beautiful space, half garden and half park, of six acres in size. Its foundation was laid by Lord Wellington, in 1799. It is of immense size, with great colonnades and lofty stepways on each side. Of the general proportions of the interior halls and chambers one can easily judge from the size of the breakfast-room alone, which is thirty-two feet wide and one hundred and fourteen feet long. The walls are richly ornamented with portraits, while busts are lodged here and there in convenient nooks. The statue of Wellesley, who was Governor-General from 1798 to 1805, greets the visitor immediately on entering. There are statues and busts of many others of the past representatives of English power in India, such as Lord Cornwallis, Warren Hastings, Lord Teignmouth, the Earl of Minto, the Earl of Ellenborough, Viscount Hardinge, and the Earl of Elgin.

The Queen's picture is in the throne-room. In the middle of this central spot of English power in Asia there is a most significant object. It is the gilded chair of the conquered Tipu. Portraits of many native princes of the past days hang upon the

HIGH COURT, AND STATUE OF SIR CAVENDISH BENTINCK, CALCUTTA.

walls. From one of the windows I saw Lord Dufferin, engaged, with a few friends, under the ample fronds of palms, in a lively game of lawn-tennis, the favorite game of the English all over India.

The most interesting church in Calcutta is St. Paul's Cathedral. It is a modern building, begun about fifty years ago, and of the Gothic style, with adaptations to the Indian climate. Including the buttresses, its length is two hundred and forty-seven feet. It stands in the midst of a beautiful lawn, where tropical trees and a rich variety of flowering plants make a most charming picture. Here, at every step along the nave, are all the evidences of true English affection on the one hand, and, on the

EAST GATE, GOVERNMENT HOUSE, CALCUTTA.

other, of England's undying memory of her sons who have fallen in her service under the Indian sky. Memorial tablets, of all sizes, and executed with exquisite art, abound on either hand. Here are tablets to Sir Henry Lawrence, Bruce, Goodricke, Earl Canning—who died in London in 1862, four months after leaving India—Agnew, Anderson, and many others. Everywhere one is reminded of the sad fate of whole families during the Mutiny. For example, here is a tablet to Captain Gowan. His remains, with those of his wife and infant son, all butchered by the mutineers, lie here in a common grave.

I was greatly interested in the magnificent library of the late Bishop Wilson. It is located over the porch, and was presented by the bishop to the public. But little use, however, seems to be made of it now. It is probably open only to members of the parish, and must be consulted on the spot. It contains many works of general interest, to which few accessions appear to have been made in the last two or three decades. It is rich in Oriental authorities, and especially in the languages and literature pertaining to the country. It is well classified, and in bindings and general appearance is the best preserved of any library which I saw in India. But all libraries have a hard fate in this climate. The white ants burrow into the choicest books, and have to be hunted down and destroyed without mercy. They honeycomb any literary treasure, and leave it standing a mere shell. They will also nibble off the coloring on the linen covers, and leave them as white as before they went to the dyers. I brought from India a work, once blue, whose back had been so industriously eaten by these insects that it would be difficult to tell what had been the original color. The Madras climate is most severe of all on books. A gentleman there, who was going to leave the country for England, told me that he would not dare to leave his books on the shelves, for the dampness alone, in the rainy season, would ruin them. The ants would destroy what the mildew might spare. He had but one thing to do—pack his books in air-tight boxes, and leave them in as dry a spot as he could find. In the two bookstores in Madras which I visited I noticed that nearly all the works, excepting only the most recent arrivals, had been foxed throughout by the all-pervading moisture.

Bishop Wilson's library is only one of many which one finds in India. The English houses abound in rich and rare works. At Mackenzie's auction-rooms, in Calcutta, there are often sold very rare literary treasures. Two of these, works of great worth, were bought by Mr. Fred. W. May, and given to me for the library of the Drew Theological Seminary. Private libraries have been brought over from England with the owners from the early days of the East India Company; and while some have been scattered, many remain, and the number is enlarged by new arrivals. The Anglo-Indians are readers, and great lovers of literature. Public libraries are founded which would do honor to a large English city. For example, the library of the Bombay Asiatic Society, which was founded by Sir James Mackintosh, contains 100,000 volumes.

Home of Keshub Chunder Sen.

The home of the late Keshub Chunder Sen is a centre of great interest to every student of the revolt of the native Hindu mind against the old polytheism. I found no difficulty in gaining admission to the Lily Cottage. This was the residence of Keshub Chunder Sen, the late founder of this most recent approach of Hindu paganism towards Christianity. His son, a handsome and intelligent young man, admitted me on presentation of my card. The Lily Cottage is a quiet and beautiful home. An

BIRD-HOUSE.

open sward, all smiling with flowers, surrounds it. In the ground floor there is the publishing-house, where the master's books are for sale, and where accounts are kept. The printing-office is in a low building, apart from the residence. The walls of the hall and stairway are hung with pictures. Then, on reaching the second floor, there are still others. They had been collected by Keshub Chunder Sen himself, as ornaments to his cottage. Not one among the number showed the least sympathy of the seer with the Hindu faiths. They were simple engravings, or prints in cheap colors, and all of them the outgrowth of Christian thought. Here, for instance, were Cruikshank's familiar engraving of the "Evils of Intemperance;" another, of "Sir Joshua Reynolds and his Friends;" and in the middle of the wall of the principal room a picture of Jesus. In many places, on the tables and in the corners, were souvenirs of travel, which the careful hand and quick eye of the master had caught up as adornments for his home.

On my saying to the son that I supposed the work of his father would be continued by him, he answered, sorrowfully, "All we can do." He led me into the room which Keshub Chunder Sen's mother had occupied, and where she breathed her last. The grandson informed me that it was his father's favorite place in the house. I might have known it without his telling me; for the Hindu reveres his mother until the day of her death, and then she is his patron saint. During life she never ceases to be a mother, whatever the station to which her son advances or the age which he reaches. When she dies, hers is the only image that remains undisturbed for all the years in the innermost sanctuary of his heart. In a letter written by Keshub Chunder Sen to Max Müller on the death of the latter's mother, he thus speaks of a mother: "Who on earth so good as a mother? We in India regard our parents, and especially the mother, as *sakshat pratyakshadevata!* . . . a mother's love who can repay? A mother's memory no loyal son can forget. Alive or dead, we honor and revere her spirit." *

The room in which Keshub Chunder Sen died remains just as it was when his spirit left its tabernacle. No hand is allowed to touch his books or little pocket possessions and trinkets.

* Max Müller, "Biographical Essays," p. 145.

THE MAIDAN, OR ESPLANADE OF CALCUTTA.

Every one of the family who enters must step as carefully as though he were entering a holy place. The remains of the master lie in the trim yard, and are guarded by beautiful flowering plants.

A NATIVE BUNGALOW, CALCUTTA.

CHAPTER XXXV.

FORT WILLIAM AND THE BLACK HOLE.

Fort William formerly stood on the spot where the present post-office building is, but, after the battle of Plassey, Clive thought best to remove it to the river-bank. The new structure, an irregular octagon, was finished in 1773. It is of great strength, and is surrounded on the land side by a wide and deep fosse, which can be flooded immediately from the Hugli in case of need. The six hundred guns, and capacity to hold ten thousand men, make the Fort a most formidable place of defence for the city. In connection with it are St. Peter's Church (Church of England), St. Patrick's Chapel (Roman Catholic), the Soldiers' Institution and Garrison School, the Arsenal, and the Military Prison. Since Clive's day but little has been needed to preserve the strength of this great fortification, except to continue the plan which he made.

Of all the military reminders of the time of Clive, the Black Hole is the most memorable. Until very recently, the exact site of this place was not known to any one. The very traces above ground had been so thoroughly obliterated that nothing was left on which to base a plausible conjecture. I was informed by the postmaster of Calcutta that, in making excavations beneath the post-office, in 1882, the masons had come across the precise walls which enclosed the famous prison. There is now a small square, of dark stone, beside the right-hand wall of the post-office, as you stand in front of it, which covers the precise spot. There is a monument near by, which, including base and obelisk, is forty-seven feet high, and bears on one side the names of many of the one hundred and twenty-three Englishmen who were suffocated in this wretched place on the night of June 20, 1756, and, on the other, the English revenge which became the sequel. The latter inscription reads as follows:

"This horrid act of violence was as amply, as deservedly revenged on Siraju'd Daulah, by His Majesty's arms, under the conduct of Vice-Admiral Watson and Colonel Clive, Anno 1757."

Here, on this little spot, was perpetrated the foul crime upon innocent Englishmen which awakened Clive's wrath, nerved him to make one final effort for English supremacy in India, and which resulted in the decisive battle of Plassey. This wretched den, the famous Black Hole, was but eighteen feet square, with only very small openings for light and air. Only twenty-three of the prisoners were found alive the next morning.

BOATS AT LOW TIDE ON THE HUGLI RIVER.

CHAPTER XXXVI.

A RAJAH'S HOME.—THE BOTANIC GARDENS.

When I was finishing a busy day, in company with Mr. May, we stopped at the house of a rajah, on a side of Calcutta which I had not visited before, and quite removed from the English residences and places of business. The magnificent home of a native Hindu prince is always a place of interest. The fact that such a thing exists, is of itself remarkable. The English have had matters their own way, and, like Clive, could easily have absorbed all the wealth of the country. On the contrary, they have been just and moderate. Many of the native noble families are to-day drawing large pensions from the general treasury. Every now and then one comes across a scion of one of these old Indian noble or royal families, whose wealth is very great, and seems to have been undiminished by all the political convulsions of his country. The English respect for native rights in India is one of the most remarkable illustrations of political justice in history. It is as far above modern Spain's treatment of her colonial possessions, or ancient Rome's procedure in relation to her conquered provinces, as Christianity is above and beyond either ancient or modern paganism.

Of this rajah's home in Calcutta, I found no mention in the guide-books, and should not have known of its existence but for the knowledge which Mr. May had of every part of the city. The entrance from the street is large, and unguarded by servants. There is a large circular court, with a pond for marine fowls and fishes. In the trees there are parrots and other tame birds, of gay plumage and in great numbers. In cages there are wilder birds, but all rare, lazy, and very beautiful. Ostriches and pea-fowls saunter about the grounds in their own leisurely way, and with something of an observant air. None seemed to be disturbed by our approach. The Hindu kindness to animals gets them, everywhere, into quiet habits and a sense of safety. Children are not permitted to disturb them.

Our cards at the door of the great mansion secured us prompt admission. The furniture was rich, and mostly in European style, but there were some old pieces of elaborate Indian workmanship. Marble ornaments, rich floors, finely wrought wainscoting, and tall mirrors were on every hand. The rooms were in part in suites, and in part located singly, as quiet nooks for conversation and retirement. Some of the larger halls and chambers were in process of new decoration.

In India much of the work of embellishing, and even of the more solid decoration in stone, is done by artists who come to the house, and do not labor in the distant workshops. The marble-cutters, instead of finishing their objects away from the house, do it on the spot where they are to be used. It is no short task, therefore, to put a native house in order in India. Wood and stone are brought to the place in the rough, and the workmen carry out their plans under the eye of the owner of the house. In this rajah's house was all the litter of a great Florentine marble workshop, and yet the finished rooms were kept as clean and neat as though no chip had ever fallen from a block of stone. Here was work going on in fine mosaic, the artists, no doubt, having come from Agra for the special purpose. Then for the other kinds of stone-work there were workmen who had probably come from Italy on the special

SPINNING.

errand, and would only return after many months, or even years, when the contract should be completed. There were many servants and overseers, some of them clad in picturesque Oriental costume.

The grandson of the rajah, a courtly young gentleman, conversed with us a few minutes, and then withdrew. The intelligent attendant who had received us at first was in no haste, but gave us ample time to examine this immense building, with all its appointments, and the surrounding grounds. On leaving the place, with its quiet and splendor, and entering again the busy native street, it seemed as though I had been in a different land, so near are the old and the new in India.

One thing astonished me—the apparent modesty of the wealthy native. If he had an ostentatious spirit, it was hard to detect it. He said nothing in praise of his rare birds, or fine mosaics, vast halls, or the immense boa-constrictors, which wind about or sleep in the meadow behind the close wire fence. He simply stood at a distance, or left a servant with us, and only bowed his head in acknowledgment of any words of appreciation we might say concerning any beautiful or surprising collection.

My last day in Calcutta gave me an opportunity to run some risk, and to hurry to such an extent as no one ought to think of beneath the Indian sky. The ladies of the families of the Rev. Dr. Thoburn and Mr. May had arranged for an excursion to the Botanical Gardens, on the west bank of the river. The ride was a long one, and to return in time to catch the only train for Serampore and get back from the latter place on the same day was no easy task. But the attempt had to be made.

These gardens are the finest for botanical purposes in India. They were laid out a century ago, and have been superintended by accomplished botanists ever since. They cover nearly three hundred acres, and abound in all the trees and plants, arranged scientifically, known to the tropical climates. Every step is a surprise. On entering, an avenue of Palmyra palms runs off to the right, while opposite to it is another of mahogany-trees. The broad main drive takes one past a group of casuarina-trees, up whose trunks are fine specimens of climbing palms, and then into the Palmetum, or palm plantation. Then come the wonderfully beautiful flower-garden and the orchid-houses.

The road now ascends. Far ahead, where it seemed to terminate, I observed a tall, wide, and graceful group of what appeared to be independent trees. My friends said nothing as to what the group really was until we were just upon it. They had an object, I suppose—to surprise an unwitting stranger.

A SERPENT-CHARMER.

It was not many trees, but one, the Great Banyan Tree, or *Ficus Indica.* No banyan in India approaches this one in size. Here was a central trunk, fifty-one feet in girth, which had shot itself high up into the air, while its branches had drooped to the ground and taken root, each one becoming itself a trunk.

There are one hundred and seventy of these smaller trunks, many of which have grown into large size. The process of cultivating this tendency of the banyan to multiply itself is highly interesting. A slender root-like shoot is thrown out from the lower side of one of the branches, and grows rapidly downward. Its lower end terminates in a small tuft of delicate rootlets, ready to strike into the ground as soon as they reach it, but at the same time presenting a tempting morsel to any goat which may pass under the tree. For the double purpose of protecting from the goats the slender stem which is to develop into a huge trunk in a few years, and also of encouraging its growth, it is encased in hollow bamboo and fastened to the ground. It very quickly finds its way down the dark little cavity in the bamboo, and when once it becomes rooted in the earth its career is fairly begun, and it becomes the one hundred and seventy-first trunk in the vast system called the banyan-tree!

All the falling leaves of the great banyan had been gathered up. Not a waste branch was to be found, and the whole area of eight hundred feet in circumference was as clean as a sward in the Central Park. One can walk about among these pillars without bending his head to escape drooping branches, while the arches above consist of as graceful curves as were ever left by the hand of Erwin of Steinbach. To reach Serampore, we had to drive hastily through the gardens and take the shortest road back to the railway station. Now running against heavily laden carts, now against a slow-going wagon, and now rubbing up against a quiet knot of scantily clad natives, there was no telling what would be the result. But our Hindu coachman was equal to his task. No violent Russian driver could surpass him in speed. We reached the train in time, and were now gliding along the banks of the Hugli towards Serampore, my last excursion in Calcutta.

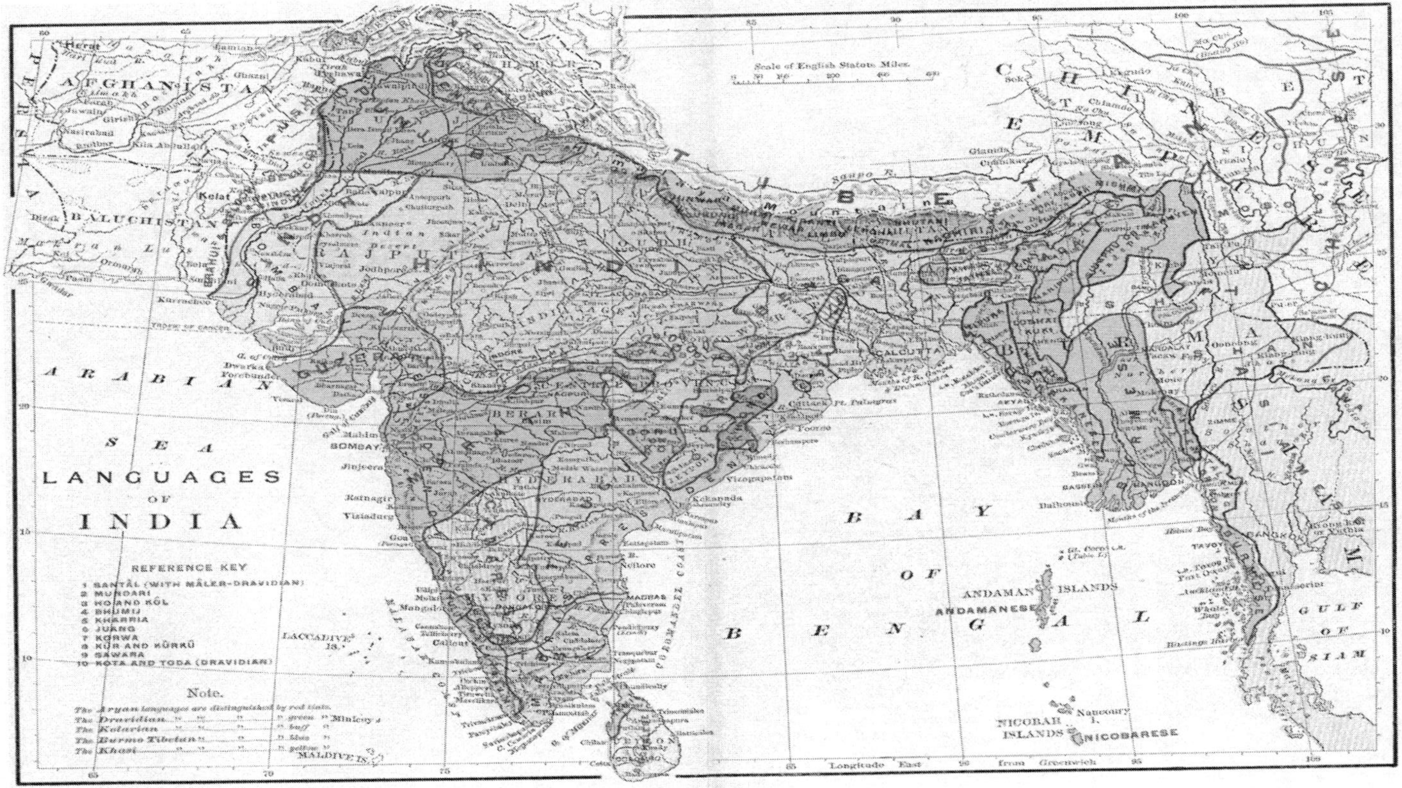
LANGUAGES
OF
INDIA
REFERENCE KEY
1 SANTÂL (WITH MÂLER-DRAVIDIAN)
2 MUNDARI
3 HO AND KÔL
4 BHUMIJ
5 KHARRIA
6 JUANG
7 KORWA
8 KÛR AND KÛRKÛ
9 SAWARA
10 KOTA AND TODA (DRAVIDIAN)
Note.
The Aryan languages are distinguished by red tints.
The Dravidian " " " " green "
The Kolarian " " " " buff "
The Burmo Tibetan " " " blue "
The Khasi " " " " yellow "
Scale of English Statute Miles.
ARABIAN SEA
BAY OF BENGAL
GULF OF SIAM
AFGHANISTAN
BALUCHISTAN
RAJPUTANA
HYDERABAD
BERAR
BOMBAY
CALCUTTA
LACCADIVE IS.
MALDIVE IS.
ANDAMAN ISLANDS
ANDAMANESE
NICOBAR ISLANDS
NICOBARESE
Longitude East from Greenwich

CHAPTER XXXVII.

POLYGLOT INDIA.

THERE are about one hundred and fifty languages and dialects spoken by the natives of India;* but there are seven chief languages. These have arisen by a process of crystallization, the atoms gravitating into masses. The English is the language of the government and of the higher education. The Persian was introduced by the Mohammedan conquerors, and is still the literary language of all Mohammedans. The Sanskrit is the old and classical language of the Brahmans and other Indo-Asians. The Baluchi lies beyond the northwest frontier, while the Burmese dialects are spoken on the east side of the Bay of Bengal.†

It is difficult to tell where a language in India ends and a dialect begins. From every great general language, as a common trunk, there have sprung out separate branches which serve as dialects. Some of the dialects are mere corruptions, and yet are spoken by so many people that they have all the importance of a separate language. Of the one hundred and fifty languages, at least twenty are cultivated and are spoken by many millions. The remaining are uncultivated. Of the uncultivated, about sixty are spoken in one region alone—namely, the hill ranges of Nepal, Bhutan, and Assam. Each range of hills has its language, and each valley its dialect.‡

---

* Beames, in his "Comparative Grammar of the Modern Aryan Languages" (p. 107), claims one hundred languages for India, the rest of the tongues being dialects. Le Bon declares that if one wishes to be understood in every part of India, before he goes thither he must know two hundred and forty languages and three hundred dialects!

† Caldwell, "The Languages of India, and their Relation to Missionary Work," pp. 4, 5.

‡ The best source of information on the native languages of India with which we are acquainted is Hodgson, "Essays Relating to Indian Subjects," 2 vols., London, 1880.

These many languages and dialects are due entirely to the variety of race. Every great invasion was the signal for foisting a new language upon the country. It would seem that when the invasion was made by an army of mixed race and language the result was the introduction of a variety of new languages. The amalgamation of these languages with those already in India produced in turn new languages, which in time assumed a fixed character.

There are two great linguistic groups: the Aryan and the Dravidian.

I. The Aryan Languages.—The principal members of this group are:

1. Hindi and Urdu, or Hindustani......	spoken by	100,000,000	people.
2. Bengali..	"	39,000,000	"
3. Marathi..	"	17,500,000	"
4. Gujerati..	"	9,500,000	"
5. Panjabi..	"	12,000,000	"
6. Kashmiri..	"	1,000,000	"
7. Sindhi..	"	2,000,000	"
8. Oriya..	"	7,000,000	"

The Hindustani, or Urdu—that is, Camp Language, the language of the camps of the Mogul emperors at Delhi—is not regarded by philologists as a distinct language, but only as a dialect of Hindi with the admixture of Persian. But it has all the magnitude and importance of a separate language. It is the linguistic result of the Mohammedan invasions of the eleventh and twelfth centuries, and, except in rural Bengal, is spoken by many Hindus in North India, and by the Mussulman population in all parts of India. Next to English, it is the official language of the government. It is commonly written in the Arabic or Persian characters.

The original Aryan has long ago died out. Its great development was into the Sanskrit, which has disappeared except as a dead language. This is the rich storehouse in which the sacred writings of the Hindus are to be found, and is reverently studied and taught by the Brahman priests. The Hindi and Urdu, or Hindustani, is spoken in the Northwest Provinces—Rajputana, Panjab, and others; the Bengali, in lower Bengal; the Marathi, in Bombay and the Dekhan; the Gujerati, in Gujerat, and also serves as the commercial language of all Western India; the

Panjabi, in Panjab; the Kashmiri, in Kashmir; the Sindi, in Sind; and the Oriya, in Orissa. All the languages of this group are more or less Sanskrit in structure as well as vocabulary.

II. The Dravidian Languages.—These are the surviving languages of the six Dravidian races which lived in the extreme southern part of India before the Aryan invasion.* The word Dravidah designated the country occupied by them. When the region was invaded by the Aryans, the Dravidians proved themselves foemen worthy of their enemies. When they were conquered the languages refused to die, and, as the Anglo-Saxon language refused to yield to the Norman tongue, so these Dravidian languages still live, and are to this day the speech of many millions.

The four great Dravidian languages are:

1. Tamil	spoken by	15,000,000	people.
2. Telugu	"	16,000,000	"
3. Kanarese	"	9,000,000	"
4. Malayalam	"	4,000,000	"

The Tamil is the language of the Karnatic, from Madras to Cape Comorin, and also of Northern Ceylon. The Telugu is spoken in the lower basins of the Kistna and Godavari rivers. The Kanarese is the language of Mysore and the contiguous districts northward; and the Malayalam is spoken in Travancore and the rest of the Malabar coast.

There are two semi-cultivated Dravidian languages: 1. Tulu, spoken by 300,000 people; 2. Kurg, or Kodagu, spoken by 150,000 people. There are five entirely uncultivated Dravidian languages: the Gond, spoken by about 2,000,000 people; and the four Kolasian languages (Santali, Kol, and others), spoken by about 3,000,000 people.

There are many dialects which it has been difficult to classify. The perpetual tendency is now in a double direction,—to discover and analyze the language, and then to absorb. The history of all nations proves that in proportion as a people acquire unity of government the varieties of language undergo a decline. Ideas permeate the whole body as never before. The differ-

* Monier Williams, "Modern India and the Indians."

ences in words and pronunciation observable in the English counties are rapidly disappearing by virtue of more frequent communication between all the people of Britain than was formerly the case. Since the unification of the German empire the long prevailing differences in accent and other departments of language between the North and the South have undergone a decided diminution.

In India the same rapid process of compression is going on. The hill tribes are brought into more frequent intercourse with the great body of the natives, and each language is losing its identity by the force of absorption. India abounds in scholars from Europe, who are searching at the hearth-stone of the Aryan race for the solution of ethnological and philological questions, while the missionaries are penetrating the most concealed tribes, and constructing grammars and dictionaries for them, and translating the Scriptures for their benefit.

A PALANQUIN.

CHAPTER XXXVIII.

THE BATTLE OF THE ENGLISH WITH THE INDIAN LANGUAGES.

When the first English trader connected with the East India Company arrived in India, he brought with him many words already native to the doomed races. The story of kindred blood was repeated in the speech. The living roots of the language of the native of Britain were found to be not only akin to, but identical with, those of the native of India.

The cradle of both languages was the same. Beside the English and the Sanskrit, stood the Zend, which was the early language of Persia. To these came the Greek and the Latin. Here, therefore, are five languages, which have stretched from the Bay of Bengal to the Hebrides, yet all bearing the same general features.

We have only to consult the following table to see the brotherhood of these tongues. As the column of English words is of pure Saxon origin, it represents the whole Teutonic family:

Sanskrit.	*Zend.*	*Greek.*	*Latin.*	*English.*
patri	paitar	patír	pater	father
bharátri	bartar	phratra	frater	brother
duhitri	dughdhar	thugatír	——	daughter
aswa	aspa	hippos	equus	horse
nâman	nâman	onoma	nomen	name
tára	stâre	astír	astrum	star
upari	upairi	uper	super	above (upper)
dwi	dwa	duo	duo	two
tris	thris	tris	ter	thrice
shat	khsvas	ex	sex	six
tishtami	histami	histími	sto	stand *

Look at our English word *mouse.* Where did it come from? Trace the little animal far back, to his original little bed, and we find him in a Sanskrit home. The path is easy: in the Old

* Bopp, "Comparative Grammar."

High-German, he was *mues;* in the old Slavonic, *myse;* in the Latin, *mus;* and in the Sanskrit, *mush.*

The Buddhists and the Brahmans have each a favorite theory for accounting for the antiquity of the Sanskrit. The latter hold that the Sanskrit is the divine language; that it was never spoken by any race before the Brahmans spoke it; and that it is the language of intercourse in the crystal palaces of heaven.* The Buddhists, on the contrary, claim that the Pali is the original language; that it was the vernacular of the country in which Buddha lived; that their sacred books, the Pitakas, are written in this original language; and that it is sometimes called the Magadhi. The grammarian Kachchayans thus speaks of it: "There is a language which is the root [of all languages]; men and Brahmans spoke it at the commencement of the Kalpa, who never before uttered a human accent, and even the supreme Buddhas spoke it; it is Magadhi."

These theories as to the original language of India are in conflict. Neither is correct. Neither the Sanskrit nor the Pali is original. Hardy says: "The Buddhist must, therefore, submit to the same humiliation as the Brahman, and confess that the language of his sacred books is derived, and not original; and that it comes to us from the same source as the dialects spoken by the nations of Europe."

The Brahman is more nearly correct, however, than the Buddhist. The Sanskrit is older than the Pali, and the latter is related to the former as the Italian is to the Latin, and the modern Greek to the Greek of Homer. Besides, as Hardy proves, the modern forms in Pali are similar to those of Italian. For example:

Latin forms, as modified in Italian.			Sanskrit forms, as modified in Pali.		
perfectus	becomes	perfetto.	muktas	becomes	mutto.
factus	"	fatto.	saktas	"	satto.
aptus	"	atto.	suptas	"	sutto.
objectus	"	oggetto.	abjas	"	ajjo.
somnus	"	sonno.	sabdas	"	saddo.

The conclusion of Dr. Muir concerning the antiquity of the original languages of India appears more nearly correct than any other: that the Sanskrit, Zend, Greek, Latin, and Saxon

* R. Spence Hardy, "The Sacred Books of the Buddhists," pp. 12, 13, 17.

are sisters—daughters of one mother, whose name is no longer known, and who died in giving them birth; that the races of

ON A RIVER STEAMER.

men speaking these languages are descended from one common stock; that their ancestors lived together in some country beyond Hindustan, and spoke one original language; that they separated at different times and in different directions—the forefathers of the Hindus southward and southeastward to India; the ancestors of the Persians to the south; and the ancestors of the Teutons to the north of Europe, and those of the Greeks and Romans to the south. Those who remained longest together in the early home were the Persians and the Indians, and their languages, as well as the people, bear the strongest resemblance to each other.

There is not a more touching piece of romance in all the wild legends of the East than we see just here—the coming back of a far wanderer to see his long-lost brother. "The dark and dreamy Brahman," says Hardy, "and the pale and practical European, once chased each other under the shade of the same tree, and lived in the same home, and had the same father, and spoke to that father in the same language; and though the difference is now great, both in outward appearance and mental constitution, not more certainly do the answering crevices in the cleft rock tell that they were once united, than the accordant sounds in the speech of the two races tell that they were formerly one people; and this unity is proclaimed every time that they address father or mother, or call for the axe, or name the tree, or point out the star, or utter numbers." *

The close connection between the Aryan people and the Sanskrit language is very clear. The poets of the great epics of India regarded themselves as Aryans, and spoke of their heroes as Aryans. The very word Arya was used to designate the India of remote times—Aria-bhumi or Aria-désa. The Singhalese dictionary preserves it undisturbed: Arya, "noble, excellent, of respectable lineage." The modern name used in the East to designate Persia is Iran, and Hardy ventures the suggestion that Erin may have derived its name from the still more luxuriant East.

When the Europeans of the sixteenth century entered India, and began that career which has resulted in the possession of the country by the British, the languages presented a remarkable picture. They were divided into the Aryan and the non-Aryan. The Aryan group, with the Sanskrit for its basis, was

* "The Sacred Books of the Buddhists," p. 15.

the language of literature and all advanced thought. The non-Aryan group consisted of the fragments of the primitive language of the people, before the pale Aryans came down from the northwest as conquerors. When the Dutch came to Ceylon, the Portuguese to Goa and Bassein, the Danes to Serampore, and the English and the French to many points along the eastern coast, there was no difference in the classification. The strangers from the West brought with them languages whose basis was the same as that of the Aryan tongues of India. The English Bible, Shakespeare, and Milton possess the same linguistic foundation as the Hindu "Mahabharata." In length, the Hindu epics are the largest in literature. While the "Æneid" of Virgil contains less than ten thousand lines, and the "Iliad" of Homer less than sixteen thousand lines, the "Ramayana" is forty-eight thousand lines long, and the "Mahabharata" is contained in two hundred and twenty thousand lines.

The Sanskrit language, which was the speech of the Aryan ancestors, not only is now a dead language, but was dead two thousand years ago. It speaks only through the memorials which it treasures in the fundamental parts of the great modern tongues. In India it does not occupy as large a place in the intellectual life of the people as the Latin does in Europe and America. The very science of Sanskrit grammar is recent, for Pánʹiní must be reckoned as its father.* The works originally written in Sanskrit which have survived the shock of wars and the innumerable social convulsions which have swept over India are claimed to be not less than ten thousand.†

One of the most striking proofs of the steady battle of the English against all the Indian languages is in the larger use of the Roman characters. The constant tendency of missionary literature is towards the disuse of the native alphabets. Many books are now published without any recognition of the characters of the vernacular. This procedure familiarizes the native with a Western alphabet; and this, of itself, is an important step towards the abolition of the old language. It is already far more common in India to publish, in Roman characters, works in the

* Crawford, "Researches concerning the Laws, Learning, Commerce, etc., of Ancient and Modern India," vol. ii., p. 163.

† Weber, "Indische Studien," 2 Bde., Berlin, 1850. Especially good in Sanskrit studies and comparative languages.

local languages than in Germany to substitute the Roman characters for the old Gothic. But sooner or later, in Germany as well as in the Eastern countries, it will be a rare occurrence for any work to appear in any but the Roman characters.

The missionaries, however, do not by any means encourage this radical transformation. They are conservative in their dealings with native tastes, and introduce as few foreign elements as possible. But they know that the change is inevitable. The second generation of native Christians will probably make but little use of the ancient characters.

The very moment that the Europeans were sufficiently settled in India to become permanent residents, the fate of many of the languages was sealed. Every native language of India is entirely on the defensive. The fact that the English language is that of the government is the most potent factor in familiarizing the natives with it, and in making it attractive to them. The English language has been taught in the schools, and to largely increasing numbers, for at least a century. From the universities there go out annually great numbers of young people, who use the English language fluently, having pursued their entire course of study in it. Indeed, many of the more highly educated natives are growing ashamed of their own languages. The missionary literature is, for the most part, in the native tongues. But the people know that it consists very largely of translations from Christian works, and is printed and distributed by persons speaking chiefly the English language. Missionaries like Carey and Marshman have contributed greatly towards the revival of the study of the Sanskrit and other early tongues of India. But this has been done for the purpose of understanding languages once spoken, to gain light upon the origins of the country and its literature, but with no more view to continue the use of a native language than did Felton of Harvard aim to revive the actual use of Attic Greek when he pressed its study.

While the few great languages of India will hold sway for many years to come, the smaller languages and dialects will gradually die out, and leave only the larger. These larger ones will then in time lose their hold.

The India of the great future will speak only the English language.

CHAPTER XXXIX.

HUMORS OF THE INDIAN LANGUAGES.

One of the most striking evidences of the coalescing of the languages in India can be seen in the many English words which the native servants now use instead of the equivalents in their own languages. The pronunciation is somewhat astray, but one can easily detect the proper English word. There is a large class of such English words which the natives use even in conversation with each other in their own vernacular. To such an extent has this habit grown, that they do not think of the mixed quality of the language which they are using. The English, such as it is, flows out with equal ease with the native words. The constant tendency is towards an increase of the English, and a corresponding decrease of the native tongues. The displacement of the vernacular is a process now so advanced as to be regarded irresistible.

The following English words, as constantly used and pronounced by natives, are sufficient to illustrate the large class to which they belong. They have been kindly furnished me by Mrs. N. Monnelle Mansell: *kitlee* for kettle; *towelee*, towel; *kaffee* (the correct Arabic), coffee; *deesh*, dish; *mees*, mince; *haush*, hash; *silput*, slipper; *putloon*, pantaloon; *kot*, coat; *buckus*, box; *Markeen*, American; *is-kule*, school; *jografee* (this is the correct Hindustani), geography; *buk*, book; *nib*, pen; *tick-us*, tax; *boatl*, bottle; *is-'late*, slate; *is-'tation*, station-depot; *post-offeece*, post-office; *commeetee*, committee.

On the other hand, there are many words of the native languages which, because of their ease in pronunciation, their brevity, or some peculiar force of meaning, are used by the English instead of corresponding words in their own language. If an Englishman or American in India has occasion to use the word note, referring to a brief open letter, he never fails to say *chit.* I received such an English note one day from a native gentleman of Calcutta, which closed in these words: "I hope you will excuse me for giving you a chit only." He possibly supposed that *chit* was an English word, and might well have drawn that inference because of its common use by the English people all over India.

Here is a sentence which exhibits, and I think fairly, the extent to which much of the English of India borrows from the native Hindustani. It was written by Mrs. Mansell, whom I requested to write a brief note, with such admixture of foreign words as Europeans in India would use to each other: "I have talked with many missionaries about the native Christians. The *matlab* of their *bayán* was about this: They are often, perhaps usually, very *kachchá* at first, and many of them remain so for years, and indeed always. But many of them are very *pakká*. Our converts are generally in such poverty that it is necessary to *parwarish* them to some extent in giving them *naukarí*, or otherwise making their *bandobast!*" The Rev. G. H. McGrew, D.D., received one day the following *chit*—clear enough to him, but not to an Occidental not yet in India:

"REVEREND SIR,—Brother H. Wilson wishes the company of yours and Mrs. McGrew to be present in the Tamásha of Katputli, and oblige
"Yours obediently, MASEH CHARAN."

If you are sufficiently helped at table, it is not expected that you will say, "Thanks, no more," but, "*Bas!*" If your servant is desired to hurry, you call to him, "*Jaldí!*" If you wish a school-boy to keep quiet, you say, "*Chup.*" If you wish a carriage, you order a "*gárí.*" When one is pleased with any result, and would naturally say, "All right," in India approval is expressed by one word, "*Thík.*" You would hardly say "thing," but simply "*chíz.*" Instead of talking about a suit of clothing, you would simply say "*kaprá.*" You are no sooner in Suez, or even on a Peninsular and Oriental steamer just leaving London for an Indian port, than the regular midday meal is called "*tiffin.*" It comes from the Portuguese, but is now already domesticated in the English language. Everywhere one knows the word *almaira* to indicate a closet or clothes-press. The word "go-down" is a corruption of a Portuguese word, *godám*, meaning storehouse or magazine. It is a very familiar word, and is heard throughout India, alike from natives and Indo-Europeans.

Any stranger in India, who goes through the country on even a very hasty tour, finds himself constantly absorbing these convenient words. By the time he is ready to leave the country, they have become familiar to him, and he uses them even in preference to his English, French, or German.

The native in India, when conversing or corresponding with a European, is generally quite able to make his English clear. It may not be idiomatic, but serves its purpose notwithstanding. Here is a note which Miss Lore, then a medical missionary, received from an anxious patient: "Please send per bearer the powder for Robert, and the medicine for me as you promised. Also write the directions. Not only my heart palpitates, but the appetite is poor. No proper indigestion—and sleeplessness—and all these things are very troublesome."

There is another side to this picture—namely, the blunders constantly made by the English in their use of the Indian tongues. We hear but little of them. The natives hear them, but the blunders do not see the printed page. Only now and then they come to light. For example, Rev. N. L. Rocky reports the following: Mrs. Blank to-day asked her husband to send the servant to her. So he gave the order: "The madam is a necessity to you. Go." Another, an invalid, was advised to use strong beef-tea. Here is his order to the cook: "Here, cook, get a powerful ox and make me tea from it." What must the servant have thought on receiving such an order?

CHAPTER XL.

THE AGONIES OF ENGLISH STYLE.

One is constantly reminded, when hearing cultivated natives converse in English, of the stately and ponderous rhetoric which they employ. It is easy to imagine one's self sitting with Johnson in "The Cheese," off the Strand, and hearing him dilate to Goldsmith on the completion of the last signature of the great Dictionary. The words are devoid of the new touches of the present century. The masters of a century, or even of two centuries ago, have supplied the natives with a large measure of their vocabulary. Pope is still a favorite. Long since, when the first English schools were established in India, the ruling models in style at the time were promptly inaugurated in India. In some cases, these have continued to the present time. A writer in *Macmillan's Magazine* thus reports his conclusions when present at an examination of a government English school in Bengal: "The class was engaged on 'The Deserted Village.' Each scholar read a few lines, and then gave a paraphrase of them in the most grandiloquent and classical English. I sat aghast at the flowing combination of epithets which came so naturally to their lips; not knowing at the time that the natives who have been brought up at the government schools, having learned our language from Addison and Goldsmith, use on all occasions the literary English of the last century. The passage before us was that beginning,

> "Ill fares the land to hastening ills a prey."

One youth at the bottom of the class, on being asked for a definition of what Goldsmith meant by unwieldy wealth, amused me by replying, 'Dazzling jewels, and plenty—too much elephants!'" Woodrow holds that the ignorance of passing events in Europe, on the part of government teachers in India,

GOING HOME FROM THE BALL.

is very great. He says that the Europe which they know is only the Europe of Addison and Goldsmith.*

AN ODD BOOK.

I cannot furnish a more characteristic evidence of the difficulties of the natives in dealing with the English language than in the following extracts from "The Memoir of Onoocool Chunder Mookerjee, by his admiring nephew Mohindronauth Mookerjee," the second edition of which was published in Calcutta in 1876. The author, it may be said, is a teacher of history in the Shambazar High-Grade English School, and author of "The Effects of English Education upon the Native Mind."

"Let me hold my *Penna* after a few months to write the memoir of the individual above-named: but *quid agis?* if any one put me such a query, I will be utterly thrown into a great jeopardy and hurley-burley. * * *

"By dint of nude energy and perseverance he erected a vantage ground above the common level of his countrymen; nay stood with the rare, barring few on the same level with him, and sat arrayed in majestic glory, viewing with unparalleled and mute rapture his friends and admirers lifting up their hands with heartfelt glee and laudation for his success in life.* * *

* "Bengal Instruction Report," 1855–56, Appendix A, p. 50.

"It was the *bonton* to carry that study much beyond the point which would have sufficed for the purpose of business or official intercourse. * * *

"In the course of two years from the inchoation of his Persian education, he was able to read such books as *Alif Lyala*, *Fasana-Ajahib*, *Galbasanaoor*, *Hatemtaie*, *Bagabahar*, *Golistan*. * * * Shall I not, therefore, be justified to say on the strength of the *supra*statement, that it was undoubtedly a sign of becoming great, and that little Mookerjee was a genius undoubtedly, though he did not show anything supernatural in his college life? * * *

"I have heard from a gentleman who was one of his form-fellows that little Mookerjee never had a snip-snap with any of his college boys. * * *

"It is well known that boys cannot bear the sight of any one of them sitting still or busy with his books when they themselves are to jump over the moon. * * *

"But this singular sheepishness—so ungraceful in a boy—endeared little Mookerjee to all his teachers. * * *

"The progress made by little Mookerjee at school, though not very gairish, was nevertheless of a most solid character. * * *

"When the Lad ascended a few steps, he received a severe blow on his head, which rendered him impercipient for a few moments. * * *

"His father died when he was very young, and the large estate, which he had bequeathed to his children, was gradually squandered away by his eldest brother in unfortunate blind bargains and speculations. * * *

"There are innumerable examples of children possessed of competent means for education remaining beetle-headed for ever. * * *

"His education was not imperfect, nor of an ordinary nature, but what is optable in every enlightened age. * * *

"Each, as he left the magistracy, gave him a certificate testifying to the excellence of his character and his *cui bono* in the post he held. * * *

"He therefore felt himself planet-struck when Hurrish Chunder, after making mention of the Howrah Nazirship, requested him to provide Onoocool Chunder with a better employment. * * *

"None can be great *Impromptu!* * * *

"His determination surmounted every difficulty, for *omnia vincit labor*. * * *

"It is impossible to describe the oblectation with which he contemplated this change in his position. * * *

"The product of the system of patronage which must have benefited the late Justice in no ordinary *quantum* in the early part of his career as a Vakeel. * * *

"It was thus that Onoocool Chunder soon gained the plerophory of the Mooktears. * * *

"His first business, on making an income, was to extricate his family from the difficulties in which it had been lately enwrapped, and to restore happiness and sunshine to those sweet and well-beloved faces on which he had not seen the soft and fascinating beams of a simper for many a grim-visaged year. * * *

"At this time Onoocool Chunder's study embraced the deep and awful hour of midnight. * * *

"Wealth rather served to bring into full play qualities of heart which poverty had either wholly or partially kept snug. * * *

"*Tempus edax rerum*, and on Sunday, the 5th of June 1864, Judge Onoocool Chunder's mother 'shuffled off this mortal coil.' * * *

"Onoocool Chunder celebrated his mother's *shrad* with an ungrudging heart.

"Mookerjee feared that if Mr. Ghose opens the case first, he might play the deuce with it. * * *

"He argued this question, with capacious, strong, and laudable ratiocination and eloquence. * * *

"The Hon'ble Mookerjee did nill the offer politely. * * *

"No client would solely rely on their *cui bono*. * * *

"Now Hon'ble Mookerjee was once again thrown into the peck of troubles. * * *

"He was attacked with a doloriferous boil which was operated by Dr. Nilmadhub Mookerjee (his family Doctor and kith and kin). * * *

"He remained with his family and felt himself much emendatory in his health. * * *

"This was the first time (and in the case of the Hon'ble Mookerjee), that we see a Pleader of the High Court taking a seat in the Bengal Legislative Council, solely by the dint of his own legal weapon and he was an *au fait*, and therefore undoubtedly a transcendental lucre to the Council. * * *

"The selection in Justice Mookerjee was most judicious and tip-top. * * *

"He rose step by step to the *ne plus ultra* of fame and distinction, to the amazedness of the public at large, and men of his profession. * * *

"The hope which he so long hatched at last yielded him what he hankered after, and in seven league boots, 'True hope is swift and flies with swallows' wings'—and he might have justly said—*Veni, vidi, vici!* The law-study to which he had devoted so long his midnight hours, with indefatigable ardour and the zeal of a martyr, yielded him fruits most sacchariferous and wished for—*position*, *respect*, and *wealth*. * * *

"Since he joined the Native Bar down *ad finem* of his career as a Pleader, he had one and uniform way of pleading. He made no gairish of words, never made his sentences long, when he could express his thoughts in small ones. He never made his sentences periphrastic when he could do it in an easy way. He was an eloquent speaker, but made no raree-show of it. Never he counterchanged strong words with the Pleaders or Barristers of the other party. In defeating or conducting a case, his temper was never incalescent and hazy. He well understood the interest of his client, and never ceased to *tussle* for it until he was flushed with success, or until the shafts of his arguments made his quiver void. He was never seen to illude or trespass upon the time of the Court with fiddle-faddle arguments, to prove his wits going a-wool-gathering, but what he said was nude truth, based upon *jus civile*, *lex non scripta*, *lex scripta*, etc., and relative to his case and in homogenity to the subject-matter he discussed, and always true to the points he argued.

"Having first expounded before the Court the anatomy of his case, he then launched out on the relative position of his client with that of the other, pointing out the *quid pro quo* or bolstering up the decision of the Lower Court with his sapience and legal acumen and cognoscence, waiting with quietude to see which side the Court takes in favourable consideration, knuckling to the arguments of the Court, and then inducing it gradually to his favour, giving thereby no offence to the Court. Justice Mookerjee very well understood the boot of his client, for which he would carry a logomachy as if his wheel of fortune depended upon it. * * *

"An unparagoned gentleman he was. * * *

"On multitudinous occasions when the hope and affiance of the clients of Justice Mookerjee *toto coelo* suspended on his pleading, and he was absent from the Court on account of some sickishness, he even on such days came and pleaded their causes when they importuned him to do so.

"Of all the learned walks of life that of a Pleader or a Barrister is the most difficult to win laurels in. A Doctor with his badge and his braggardism for profoundity in Pathology, Ætiology, Nosology, Materia Medica, Regimen, Chirurgery, Surgery, Toxicology, Chemistry, Alchymy, Zoology, Zoography, Anatomy, Comparative Anatomy, Comparative Physiology, or any *logy* that exists in the category of Science (but I should never finish this memoir, and you would feel yourself worried, if I were to attempt to tell you all of them, it will be *quantum sufficit* to say that boldly), can give cremation, sepulture, etc., to as many number of men as he likes, and at the same time can fill his coffer—a Civil Servant is as sure of getting his desired object as soon as he passes his examination—and *pseudo* is the engineer. * * *

"What Mooktear should volunteer to allow him to send up a pilot balloon ? * * *

"If at the persuasion of a tried Pleader, a Mooktear gives him a case, and if unfortunately he loses it, he is at a discount, or fortunately if he wins it, he is *valeat quantum valere potest* as the Mooktear thinks: and lack-a-daisy!—a Mooktear has so much to do with such a profession! But in additum to this, there are other Gordian knots—such as if he is an obtuse, and has an inaudible *voce*, a blunt memory, a beetle-head, or if he is hot-headed, a stuttering speaker, and irrespective of other things that mainly and importantly stand in requisition to constitute one as veritable Advocate in the accurate sense of the expression. * * *

"His elevation created a catholic ravishment throughout the domain under the benign and fostering sceptre of great Albion. His friends—(for persons were sure to be his friend with whom he had talked for a few moments), hailed this budget of news with heart-felt and infinite joy.

"The Hon'ble Mookerjee did bleed freely, but he was not a leviathan on the ocean of liberality, nor he was a *Hatem* or a *Bolee* of his age, but on—whose like we may and should expect in an individual of his *status* and emolument: and the mode of assignment of his charities was to such men, as we truly wish and recommend, and exsuscitate enthusiastically. He used to give monthly something of his *Gooroo* or (spiritual guide), for the support of his family—to his *Poorohit* apart from what he used to get in every *Purbun*,—to four Bramins who remained at his house and had no other source of income—to many of his ignorant kinsfolks whom he would not suffer to drudge in an humble sphere—to many relicts who had no hobbardy-hoy even to support them, and had no other source of sustenance left to them by their consort—and to many unfriended and helpless children to countenance them to tread the path of education in Medical and other Colleges and Schools: These were his regular and peremptory or *tranchant* menstrual distribution, which they do get still after his demise from his sons, who have been submonished by him on many occasions to do so. * * *

"There are many Bramins now, who, after having perpetrated heaps of the lowest dregs of vice, would go and bathe once in the Ganges and then nurture the thought—that they are now *saintlike*, and thus having a faith in that stream, as the one having the power to absterse one's heart from sin, they will go on committing sin till they pop off, or till their doomsday. * * *

"He knew that *vice* should be met with punition, and *virtue* with guerdon.

"Once for the same unsociable conduct or rather *insouciance* he having received a vituperation from his cousin Baboo Gopal Chunder, for not receiving his friends with those things, when his friends were sitting engaged in tittle-tattle with him for more than an hour. * * *

"When a boy he was filamentous, but gradually in the course of time he became plump as a partridge, and so much so, that he weighed himself two *maunds* and three and half *seers* on Monday the 10th of April 1871, and many able doctors said that he will very soon be caught by palsy; but to put him on guard it was required that he should take some physical exercise,—which he used to do since that time. He was neither a Brobdignagian nor a Liliputian, but a man of mediocre size, fair complexion, well shaped nose, hazel eyes and ears well proportioned to the face, which was of a little round cut with a wide front and rubiform lips. He had moulded arms and legs, and the palms of his hands and feet were very small and thick with their proportionate fingers. His head was large, it had very thin hairs on it; and he had a moustache not close set, and a little brownish on the top of his upper lip.

"Even on going to see a *Nautch* or something of the like, I have never seen him in a dress fine as a carrot fresh scraped, but *esto perpetuum* in Pantaloon and in satin or broad-cloth *Chapkan*, with a *Toopee* well quadrate to the dress. But for the last two or three years he was constrained to veer his national *Dhootee*, even when at home, for Pantaloon, and this is ascribable simply to the fattening of his belly, to suppress which and to guard against further corpulence, on being advised by his doctor. * * *

"Which will cause him to be absent from the Bench for that day,—and who knew the EVERNESS! * * *

"All the well-known doctors of Calcutta that could be procured for a man of his position and wealth were brought,—Doctors Payne, Fayrer, and Nilmadhub Mookerjee and others: they did what they could do, with their puissance and knack of medical knowledge, but it proved after all as if to milk the ram! His wife and children had not the mournful consolation to hear his last words, he remained *sotto voce* for a few hours. * * *

"The body was removed, and consumed to ashes according to our Hindoo rites and ceremonies. The house presented a second Babel or a pretty kettle of fish. The night came on, and with its gradual advance, all cry of sorrow was hushed in the house, and every one therein was at last buried in deep slumber, being made weary with weeping and wailing. Now, my dear reader, give a loose to your fancy—what ghastly aspect the house presented! It was as if dreary and desolated but for a man. The hall, which was decorated most tastefully with paintings and valuable articles of furniture, which made it an object of gaze a few hours ago, was most harrowing to the sight, being deprived of its legitimate ornament—the presence of that individual from whom it desumed its beauty. But where is he—the Hyperion of his house—the pride of his countrymen—and an object of love and admiration to his friends? He is gone—and gone forever from this world! The grim and inexorable death (as we say) has taken him in an evil hour and caused a great bereavement to our country! But has death any preponderance over such a great and good man? Yea I know it has! * * *

"What becomes of this spiritual is a *pons asinorum*. * * *

"When the Hon'ble Onoocool Chunder Mookerjee left this earth, all wept for him, and whole Bengal was in lachrymation—and more I shall say, that, even the learned Judges of the High Court heaved sighs and closed it on its Appellate and Original Sides." *

A native student of the Madras University handed in to C. M. Barrow, Esq., the Principal of Doveton College, an examination paper which contained the following definitions of vice and beauty:

"*Vice.* Whatever may be the vices, they still have outwardly some mark of virtue.

"*Beauty.* Some girls buy the powder at bazaar to rub their faces with it, so that they may look more beautiful. By so doing, old men also appear young, which is a work of miracle in nature, and those who desire to be beautiful wore curled, snaky hair of another woman who is dead. They who wear most of it are heavy physically and morally light."

The same student gave the following definitions of Greek characters:

"*Nestor:* One of the Greek historians who followed the Greeks to Troy during the Trojan war. He is a serious man.

"*Alcides:* The patronymic name of Hercules, who says that he may be beaten by his page if they were to play at dice.

"*Erebus:* The god of the lower regions, who allowed the wife of Orpheus to get out of hell, being induced by his singing."

---

* The difficulty of getting a copy of the rare little work from which the above extracts have been derived has been very great. The Rev. Dr. Rudisill, of Madras, could only get a sight of it, and was good enough to send me some extracts. But the book still remained a necessity to me. Dr. Harvey, of Calcutta, had the good fortune to get one. This he sent to Mrs. Cyrus W. Field, of New York, who in turn placed it in the hands of a mutual friend, Rear-Admiral D. B. Harmony, of Washington, through whose favor I have been able to make the above selections.

The Rev. A. D. Rowe reports the following questions and answers given in an examination:

"Question. What is a 'dapper man'?
Answer 1. A man of superfluous knowledge.
Answer 2. A madman.
Question. What is a democrat?
Answer 1. Petticoat government.
Answer 2. Witchcraft.
Answer 3. Half turning of the horse.
Question. Define 'Babylonish jargon.'
Answer 1. A vessel made in Babylon.
Answer 2. A kind of drink made in Jerusalem.
Answer 3. A kind of coat worn by Babylonians.
Question. What is meant by a Lay Brother?
Answer 1. A Bishop.
Answer 2. A step-brother.
Answer 3. A scholar of the same godfather.
Question. Define the expression, Sumpter mule.
Answer. A stubborn Jew.
Question. What is a bilious-looking fellow?
Answer 1. A man of strict character.
Answer 2. A person having a nose like the bill of an eagle."

A candidate for examination writes, asking for marks high enough for him to pass:

"*To the Humane Examiner:*

"*Sir*,—Knowing that I shall be plucked in this branch, I am writing an application to show your favor to me. I am a poor man, son of a poor family. But you may say, that as I have not worked every particular sum, how can I show favor towards you? But the reasons. I have passed in the three other days; and I know not why I cannot work these sums; perhaps God is on my opposite side, or my fortune is bad. If you give me ten marks then that will be sufficient for me. If you do not show me this favor I shall lose my whole year. You see distribute pice (money) to poor which is of great labor; but this is of very petty labor, so give me the above-mentioned marks.

"From your most obedient servant." *

The old Persian teacher of the Rev. Mr. Rocky, a missionary of the Methodist Episcopal Church, wrote the following sympathetic letter to his clerical pupil, who was suffering from rheumatism:

"*To* REV. ROCKY, *Clergyman of Bijnor:*

"*Sir*,—It gives me anything but great sorrow to hear that you were stricken

---

* Wilkins, "Daily Life and Work in India," p. 44.

with palsy. I, praying to God and attending to the Sunday-school, wish your sound health and your visit to Bijnor again with welfare. I also pray that . . . may give you a perfect health; and may you with your family live long with prosperity.

"M. Sham Lal and I are praying for the enjoyment of your family; attend to your school from ten o'clock to three. The number of the students is fifty, but the average of daily presence is forty.

"I most respectfully beg to state that you will be good enough to inform me of your welfare, together with your family's, and the state of sickness whether there is somewhat slightness or not. With kind regard to Mrs. Rocky and good love to the young clergyman.

"Awaiting for a sooner reply.

"I have the honor to be, sir, your most obedient servant,

"F'AZL ILAHI.

"Dated, 1*st January*, 1887."

The envelope was addressed in Urdu character, in all the flattery and prolixity of the truly Oriental style:

"To the destination Lucknow, to Padre Sahib the missionary having gone or to the home of the minister Lucknow in the presence of the treasurer of generosities, Honorable and Rev. Mr. Rocky, most worthy, may he ever be blessed, let this letter arrive and if the Rev. Sir may not be in Lucknow, then may it go to the presence of Mrs. R., and if both may not be in Lucknow, then to the destination Moradabad to the assembly of ministers in the presence of his Reverend Sir Mr. Rocky let it be delivered. An answer is urgently required."

Here is a letter received by the Rev. A. D. Rowe from an admiring native:

"*Most Honorable Reverend*,—I hear that you are high and noble man, and there are none but you. As I am always engaged in business, I never made your honor's visitation.

"I pray your honor regarding a thing, viz.: My priest came from Trichinopoli, that is to say Sreerangam. If your honor please favor me your kindness. I shall be obliged to request you. My Priest is richest. The people say by usage that he is born to God, and also that he is the Son of God. He will not return to Guntoor until thirty years; but I cannot sure say that I can alive until he comes. My main prayer is to only photograph him upon the photograph. If your honor allow me to come to your presence, I shall be obliged to come to your presence. I request you only this assistance but none other.

"Your most obedient scholar, M. V. R * * * *

"17*th March*, 1875."

The following is from a faithful Madras servant to his master and mistress, temporarily absent from home:

"*Honored Sir and Madam*,—Rather I have good news to inform you, Sir, that your shee-goat Nany brought forth two babes last evening; one is male and the other is female; one is the black and the other is a white-spotted one; so I am trying my best to take care of them taking much pains from the dangers come to happen, that is the neighboring dogs and guanas frequently come to devour them, which is prevented by my lovely attendance and sleeping near them at night. Sir, please give the information of this intelligence to Madam." *

I have been kindly favored by Brigade Surgeon Robert Harvey, M.D., Professor in the Medical College of Bengal (Calcutta), with the following additional specimens of the native use of the English language:

When Sir Mahadar Rao addressed the little boys of the English school at Indore, after descanting on the full advantages of obtaining an English education, and on the treasures of European civilization, and reminding them that they were heirs to traditions and philosophies old before England was heard of, he gave this piece of advice to the little fellows: "Equally avoid the iconoclastic impulses of unbridled speculation, and a blind idolatry of a superannuated order of things!"

A Bengali, being rudely jostled by an Englishman at a railway station, used this indignant remonstrance, "Is this your vaunted English jurisprudence?"

The following question in English history was asked in an examination paper: "Who was Cromwell?" The answer was: "Cromwell was a bad man who slew his king with repeated beheadings, and on his deathbed was heard to exclaim, 'Oh, Cromwell! Cromwell! had I but served my God as I served my king, he would not have deserted me in my gray hairs.'"

In ethnology this question was laid before a student: "Who are the Bhils?" (an aboriginal tribe in Rajputana, very turbulent, mostly armed with bows and arrows). Answer. "The Bhil is a black man, only not so hairy. He carries archers about with him, with which he shoots his enemy and throws him in the ditch. By this you may know the Bhil."

In geography, a question was: "What are the chief feeders of the Brahmaputra?" The answer proved to be from another department than geography, but was, nevertheless, correct in its way: "Alligators!"

In justice to the natives of India, it must be remembered that

* *Our Youth*, No. 90, p. 189.

in English schools, in both England and the United States, we have frequent evidences of the deplorable results of teaching, or, possibly, of the original infirmity of the pupil. When one takes into account the short time the Hindu has been at work at the English language, and the difficulties he has had to meet in mastering it, his success has been satisfactory. If he has gone to our classics of the eighteenth century, we must not criticise him too severely. His intimate acquaintance with English slang proves him to have kept wide awake. Some of the Hindu authors have acquired an excellent style. The apostles of the Somajes have written as though on the Thames or the Back Bay. Their opponents have met them with weapons equally polished. Ram Chandra Bose's "Brahmanism" is a clear and strong *exposé* of the emptiness of all Hindu substitutes for Christianity.

The educated Hindu is getting familiar with the charge that his style is stiff, Johnsonian, ponderous. But he is not disturbed by it. He adheres to his literary divinities. When Mr. Bose was in the United States, in 1884, his attention was called to the somewhat stately idiom which he sometimes used in ordinary conversation. "In England and America," he answered, "you learn English from your servants and children in the street, but in India we get our English from the pages of Addison and Johnson."

WESTERN ENTRANCE OF FORT GEORGE, MADRAS.

CHAPTER XLI.

EDUCATION.

How England would deal with old civilizations, and how she would adapt her own educational methods to the exigencies of the many millions of India, was an important question. Her relation to that land was entirely different from that to any other. Elsewhere, as in America and Australia, she had to begin from nothing. The people whom she found were aborigines, and had done nothing for themselves or the world. But when she became ruler of India she had a different task. She found a land where arts and sciences had thriven for many ages. The keenest dialectics had been practised in the far-famed University of Madura, while the astronomical calculations of the savans of Delhi could well take their place beside the triumphs of Western physicists. There is no astronomical ruin in the world which equals in grandeur the masonry of the old Observatory which one passes on the road from new to old Delhi. The architectural triumphs of ancient India deserve to stand beside the Pantheon in many of the fundamental principles of pure style. The great national epics of the Ramayana and Mahabharata belong to the same Aryan family as the Iliad. The grammar of Panini is a triumph of philological skill. Few prime-ministers of Western kings have done such service to their nations as did the Emperor Akbar's Brahman premier, who not only wrote the "Ayin Akbarry," but regenerated the finances of the Mogul empire.*

The East India Company was purely a trading association. But so numerous were its agents that a domestic and social life sprang up in due time. It was not a colony, but a population. The proportion to the natives was small, but it was the small number which carried mastery with it. Trade, however,

---

* Laing, "Lecture on Ind-European Languages and Races," quoted from "Indian Year-Book," 1862, p. 116.

was ever uppermost in the eye of the trading association. The Company drifted gradually into politics. To secure safe commerce it was compelled to build and buy. This involved the necessity of defence. There must be a military protection. But such protection needed to be vigorous. The Saxon arm struck right and left, and neither native, Dane, Dutchman, nor Frenchman was spared.

By and by the alternative arose—the Englishman must either leave the country or own it. He had no thought of leaving. His island in the West was dear to him, but it was small. He had acquired a firm liking for the Indian sky, and for what smiled and bloomed beneath it. He preferred to own the country. He had to choose between owning it, or dying in it, or leaving it. He chose the first. The process was long, but he succeeded at last. His grasp is now passing from the force of steel to the stronger muscle of thought. His present great problem is education. He is sure to solve it rightly, and to build up a population like himself. Some of England's greatest battles, when she comes to fight again in Europe, will be won by the aid of native-born soldiers from India.

The Educational Beginnings.

When Warren Hastings began to organize the country after the English model, educational measures came in for a full share of attention. From that time to the present it has been one of the most difficult questions to answer—how far to educate, and what to teach, and what degree of compulsion to employ.

The first methods were extremely cautious, perhaps wisely so. But there must be no disguising the fact that too much concession was made to the Hindu and Mohammedan taste. First of all, both classes of the native population were opposed to any thorough education. With them, the less the better. The Hindu hostility was not so intense as the Mohammedan. Great scholars, whatever their faith, who had emerged above the surface of the prevailing ignorance were respected and almost adored. But the mass lay in ignorance. To get an education was regarded by the prince and the noble as too hard work for their children. Where the native training was at all above the merest rudiments, it took the line of the false theology. The priests were the teachers, and the science was gross mythology and legendary history. The schools were near the famous temples, and the priests taught in the shaded cloisters of the monasteries or beneath the fronds of palms in sacred groves. Any private teaching was conducted in an easy way in the homes of the noble or princely classes. The time to stop teaching was decided by the pupil's wish rather than the teacher's judgment.

This was the rule in the long Hindu ages, before the Mohammedan came down through Afghan passes into the valley of the Ganges. When he had gained a footing, he, too, did noth-

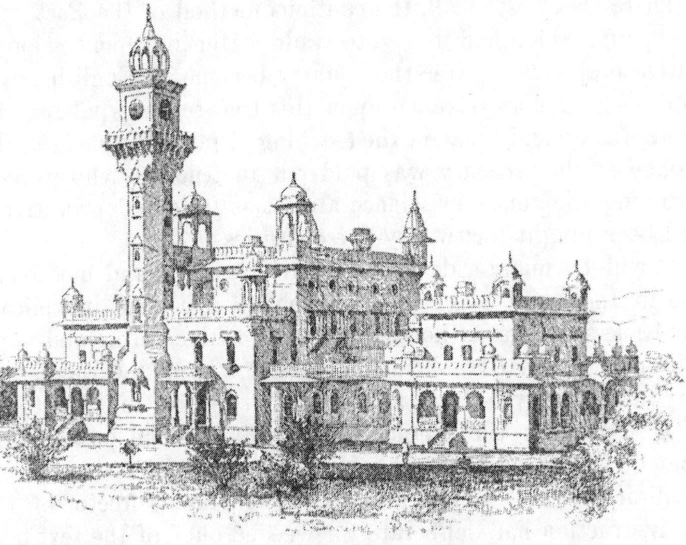

MAYO COLLEGE, AJMIR.

ing for popular education. He had gained his literary laurels by applying the torch to great libraries, and had no interest in more than one book, his Qurán. But some of the Mogul emperors had a taste for learning, just as their Moorish brothers in faith in far-off Spain. They patronized the highest science, and gave all honor to their renowned scholars. They created in India buildings for a privileged few, where they might acquire the best-known science, after the model of those in Baghdad and Ispahan.* But this was a close atmosphere. The beau-

* Temple, "India in 1880," p. 138.

tiful contagion never penetrated the masses. The priests taught young men, in the precincts of the mosques enough of theology to take their place in the service.

But until the English ruled the country it never entered any one's thoughts that education was the nation's affair, and was everybody's privilege. How to get at the mind of two hundred millions of people, and set it to work, and make it burn for an education, is not the triumph of a day or a decade. The successive stages by which India was placed on the highway towards an education are easy to note.

There was, first of all, the cautious method of the East India Company, which had its eye to trade. Hence its concessions to native prejudice. After the country became an English possession there was an advance upon this time-serving policy. But there was no real break in the teaching of false knowledge. The money of the treasury was paid out to teachers who were instructing the youth in science almost as false and primitive as had been taught for twenty-five centuries.

It will be many a day before the text-books and methods in use in India will cease to give proof of a certain inexplicable tenderness of the authorities towards native faiths and superstitions. The native of India does not respect the Englishman any more highly because he shows a disrespect for Christianity or a respect for the religions of the East. The probability is that he secretly despises the man who does violence to his own civilization. But as late as 1861 the Bombay Director of Public Instruction had deliberately "weeded out" of the text-books of that Presidency everything Christian. He characterized any reference to revealed religion as "sectarian" allusions. The Madras Director of Public Instruction published a volume, as a text-book, bearing the title of the "Tamil Minor Poets." In one place we find, in this precious volume for the youth of India, the following kindly advice as to how to pray to Ganesh: "Milk, sweet honey, syrup, and grain; these four mixed together will I give thee. Do thou, O majestic, noble, elephant-faced one, thou holy jewel, grant me the three kinds of Tamil common in the world." In another place there is an injunction to worship Vishnu, in these two words: "Serve Vishnu." Shiv must, however, have the same honor: "No misfortune can overtake those whose minds are ever intent on the praise due to Shiv."

In the following we have a direct teaching of pantheism: "He will not make any distinction, saying, I did this and he did that;" "This is not and this is." But in his state of perfection it will be true of him that "He himself is that (meaning God)." Here we have fatalism and transmigration: "Each must enjoy the fruits of his actions done in former births according to what Brahma has written (on the forehead). O king, what shall we do to those who are angry with us? Though the whole town together be opposed to it, will destiny be frustrated?"

There is no apology for the reading of such errors from native authors in the schools of India. It is the teaching of the old and gross idolatry and other errors by Englishmen, who are paid for their work out of the treasury of the empire. The apology offered is, that these are only reading-lessons from the early native authors, and are not intended to teach idolatry. The argument used is that in Christian lands the works of pagan authors are used, and yet there is no intention to teach the old Greek and Roman mythology. But this beautiful piece of sophistry has been triumphantly exposed by the declaration that no one now believes in the pagan mythology of Horace and other writers, while the children in the schools of India are surrounded by the false faiths which are encouraged in their text-books, and they and their parents are firm believers in them.*

A still more notable illustration of the support of Indian polytheism by the English rulers, through the dread of still causing offence, is to be seen in the aid given by the government towards the support of the temples and their priests. The Bombay Missionary Conference, in 1871, protested to the English government that the number of idol temples and shrines in the Bombay Presidency alone amounted to twenty-six thousand five hundred and eighty-nine, and that these received a support from the treasury and other sources under government control much larger than the number of churches in Great Britain receiving government support. These memorialists declared that seventy thousand pounds sterling were spent annually by the government in the Bombay Presidency for the support of heathen worship, while the annual expense to the

* "Indian Year-Book" for 1862. Madras, 1863, p. 156.

government for the support of idolatry in the Madras Presidency is nearly eighty-eight thousand pounds sterling.*

Now, in justice to the British government, this must be said: That there has never been a deliberate attempt made to encourage and perpetuate the idol worship of India. England had to take the country as she found it. What should she do in relation to the most troublesome of all questions—the faith of the nations? It was a question of method. She found that certain revenues had, for many centuries, been set apart for the temple service. She resolved to continue this system, not permanently, but for a time. As might have been foreseen, the concession was too great. It involved fundamentals. The Christian government of England was immediately placed in a false position, and the policy of conciliation necessarily led to still further concessions. An indignant public opinion at home arose to meet the emergency. The protest was loud and deep. The demand for a thorough reform was made. From the very moment when the sentiment in England arose in all its majesty, the policy in India underwent a change. While there are still some remains of the old system, the trend is to abandon every trace of English sympathy towards the false faiths of India. All dread of offending the polytheistic prejudices of the natives of India is passing away from the representatives of English authority. The time will soon come when in neither school-book nor temple will there be any evidence that the Englishman in India has any fear of the open and positive teaching of Christianity.

Macaulay's Educational Plan.

Macaulay, the preacher's son, did more towards placing the education of India on a proper basis than all the titled statesmen who had preceded him. He issued a Minute against the teaching of false science and false history.† It is a low calculation to suppose that there are now at least 2,000,000 of Hindu children in schools who would not be there but for Macaulay's Plan. Through him, for the first time, the Thames flowed to

* Lyall, "Asiatic Studies," p. 278.

† Temple, "India in 1880," p. 139 ff. For valuable help in our information on education in India, we are indebted to Chapter VIII. ("National Education") of this work, the fruit of the author's thirty years' experience in India.

India. The collapse of the old system had come at last. Thomason, the Lieutenant-Governor of the Northwestern Provinces, was the first English representative to take steps towards a system of education of the peasantry. But the despatch of Sir Charles Wood (afterwards Lord Halifax), in 1854, was a formal prescription of a system of public instruction, "which is," as Temple says, "regarded as the Magna Charta of national education in British India."

The government grants an annual aid to education amounting to eight hundred thousand pounds, or one fortieth part of

DALY COLLEGE, INDORE.

its available revenue. But this only represents a formal allowance. There are other directions in which the government aids education, and Sir Richard Temple, who supposes that the government aid likely reaches two millions of pounds. But he says that even this is a "small sum for so great a country."

It must be admitted that the whole tone of popular education in India has been largely influenced by the high position taken by the missionaries. The influence of Carey, Marshman, and Ward in Serampore was felt not only throughout India, but throughout the Oriental world. Their own mastery of the learning of the Hindus, and their use of it afterwards as an agent for the propagation of the Gospel, gave them an incalculable influence in determining the educational policy for the millions of India.

Next, perhaps, to the influence of the first missions in Bengal, was the revolutionary measure of Duff, of Scotland. His great distinctive policy was to do all his teaching through the medium of the English language. He foresaw that his language must inevitably become the speech of the whole land, and he began to prepare for it by making it the medium of all instruction in his college in Calcutta. His reading and exposition of the English Bible lesson were daily cannon-shots at all the old faiths of India.

In addition to the schools affiliated to the universities, and the many in grade beneath them, there are normal schools and institutions for instruction in art, engineering, and all the departments of natural science. Latterly, the universities are granting degrees in science—a movement which is highly important in its bearing on the breaking down of the old and false science which has prevailed in the country from time immemorial.

In order to get at the best method of popular education, the English rulers had two plans open before them. One was, to begin with the lowest classes, and, by providing good schools and in vast numbers, to reach the uppermost strata in society; the other was, to begin with advanced schools at the top of the social scale, and let the educational process be downward, until the whole body was educated. This was called the "filtration" scheme. It was adopted, as being the most promising. But it failed.* The masses were untouched. Its failure proving itself complete, the other end of the scale was adopted. Schools were provided in great numbers for the poor and most ignorant. The influence was felt immediately by every class. The change of method took place in 1854, and from that time to the present, the work of popular education has been steadily advancing.

I had conversations with professors in schools of all grades, not only in the larger cities, but in the more provincial places. They were mostly gentlemen of European birth and education,

---

* Statement exhibiting the "Moral and Material Progress and Condition of India during the year 1881–2" (Government Document, 18th No.)

and had brought with them all the ease, gentleness, and refinement of the Western scholar. They brought with them their libraries, and all the attachments for every ray of new light which might be shot across from the centres of learning in Germany, France, and England. Nothing fresh and eventful which had been announced in a university of Germany, or in Oxford or Cambridge, needed more than a few weeks to be as well known in India as at home. The scholar from Europe soon finds himself at home in such an atmosphere. And why not? He is in the other England.

The rate of increase in the use which the natives make of the great facilities now afforded by the government schools is very gratifying. The Bombay Presidency can speak for all. During the last decade the Hindu and native Christian students have doubled, while the Mohammedan students have nearly trebled. Under the head of "others" the advance has been more than three hundred per cent.

This revelation proves one thing completely—that the casteless people are now reached. It is a magnificent triumph, second only to Plassey. Compulsory education has not yet entered into the region of possibility. The deeper question is, how to get rice enough to keep soul and body together. When the channels for labor are sufficiently deep, and the government has made it possible for every man to spare his children from the labor into which they are thrust at a premature age, the question of compulsory education will be easy to settle.

CHAPTER XLII.

THE HIGHER HINDU SCHOOLS.

WHAT are the Hindus doing for their own education? In all India there is no great central institution founded by a native, or a number of them, compared with the great Mohammedan University of Aligarh. But there are schools of very high grade which the Hindus have established, and are constantly strengthening. They have been prompted to this new measure in great part by the example of the government and the missionary societies. The far-sighted Hindu is not willing that his children shall be entirely in the power of Christian teachers. He sees what the Christian college and university are doing, and that they are every day acquiring new power. He, therefore, proposes a counteracting force. He has already set before himself the task of founding schools to his own liking. He takes those of the government and the missionaries as his models, and is not inclined to be far behind them in establishing educational institutions where his children, whatever becomes of their faith in later years, shall, at least in their youth, be safe from direct Christian teaching.

Calcutta is the centre of this important native movement. The beginning was made in 1879, when Vidyasagur, the Hindu reformer, opened the Metropolitan College in Calcutta. No foreigners were connected with it, nor was the government asked to furnish even a grant-in-aid.* In 1881 two other colleges were established—the City College, founded by the protesters against Keshub Chunder Sen, and the Albert College, founded by Sen's brother. Shortly afterwards the Ripon College was founded by Surendro Nath Banerjea. With the exception

---

* The best account I have met with concerning this new educational departure of the Hindus is by the Rev. K. S. Macdonald, M.A., in the *Free Church of Scotland Monthly* for February, 1886. To this I am indebted for a large share of the information contained in the present chapter.

of the Albert College, these colleges teach all the studies up to the B.A. examination, and contain as many students and pass as many examinations as the Presidency College. Fees are charged in these colleges, but they are smaller than those required by either the government or missionary colleges. Free scholarships are given to promising students, in addition to what they may have earned by competition.

In Burdwan, a large town sixty-six miles northwest of Calcutta, there is another Hindu college of the same general character. It was founded by the late Maharajah, and is supported

THE CATHEDRAL SCHOOL, BOMBAY.

by funds given by him. No fees are charged. In fact, "several boys, in consideration of their extreme indigence, are found in money, besides being provided with free tuition." The college was affiliated with the Calcutta University in 1882, and its course of instruction covers not only a liberal English education, but two years in the University. In addition to the Anglo-Vernacular Department—that is, the collegiate school and the college proper—there are also a girls' school of six classes, taught by two ladies and professors; a Bengali school, taught by three professors; a Persian school, taught by a Mohammedan professor; and a Sanskrit school, where "Sanskrit logic, with all its accessories," and "Sanskrit rhetoric in all its ramifications," are taught. The whole annual expense of this large establishment is only two thousand pounds sterling a year. It is simply a small slice out of the fifty thousand pounds sterling which the Maharajah set aside for religious and charitable purposes out of his total annual income of two hundred thousand pounds sterling.

No religion is directly taught in the college at Burdwan. But the spirit is Hindu. The education is open to all classes alike. Hindus, Mussulmans, Jains, and Christians are admitted on the same terms of free tuition. In 1885 there were seven hundred and seventy-three students in attendance, of whom seven hundred and eleven were Hindus, fifty-nine Mohammedans, and three "other religionists." The location, in Burdwan, is such as to make the school very influential. It is on the Grand Trunk and East Indian Railway, which connects Bengal with the Northwest Provinces, Oudh, and the Panjab. All the traffic with the Central Provinces, Bombay, and Rajputana passes through it. In addition to these advantages, it has all the social power of being the seat of the Maharajah, the richest nobleman of Bengal.

Now, what is remarkable about this college is the freedom with which it welcomes Christian discussion. Mr. Macdonald relates that on one occasion he went to Burdwan for the double purpose of addressing the railway officials on temperance and the students on the theological subject of "Substitution and Mediation." The temperance lecture was attended by only a few, and they were not enthusiastic; but the lecture to the students was so largely attended that the three doorways were crowded, and the entire audience expressed their obligation by a vote of thanks. Mr. Macdonald reciprocated the cordiality by promising to return, on a future day, and speak on "Jesus as the God-appointed Substitute and Mediator."

It is difficult to tell what will be the future of this attempt of wealthy and cultivated Hindus to educate their young people. The indications are that great good will come from it. Without question, the most of these schools have sprung from the reformatory and advanced thinking in the torpid mass of Hinduism. There is not only a spirit of freedom of religious instruction, but of sympathy with Christian civilization. The most of the warm adherents to the old system of Hindu faith see very clearly how much India owes to Christianity, and the fact stares them in the face that all the science of the times, which is lifting India out of its pagan past, is the gift of the Christian West. When students go out from these Hindu schools, where the very text-books are of Christian authorship and the professors have been taught in the government and missionary institutions of learning, they will carry with them an unconscious Christian influence. Their very education will be proof of what Christianity can do for India.

The great significance of the native Hindu college lies in the fact that it is a transitional movement from the old to the new. If not positively Christian, it is at least in that direction. It is one section of the general break-up of the old conditions.

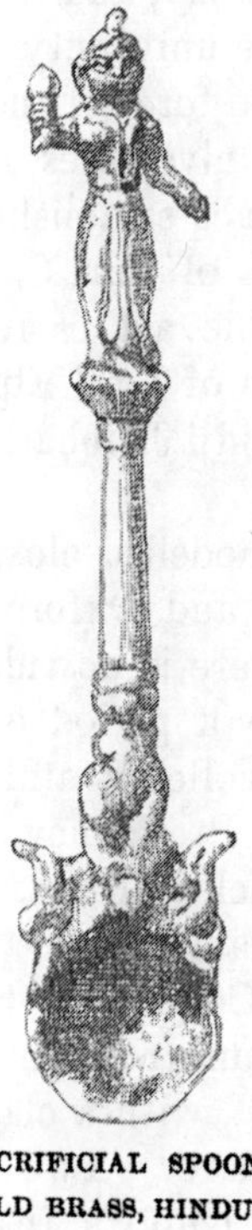

SACRIFICIAL SPOON,
OLD BRASS, HINDU.

CHAPTER XLIII.

THE UNIVERSITIES OF INDIA.

THE British government for India has been prompt and wise in its measures to introduce a thorough university system. There are four of these, the universities of Bombay, Calcutta, Madras, and the Panjab. The acts of incorporation establishing the universities of Calcutta, Bombay, and Madras were passed in 1857. The act incorporating the university of the Panjab was adopted in 1869. The great moral force of the original acts of incorporation establishing these universities may be seen in the names which they bore. The act establishing the University of Calcutta contains the names of Earl Canning, Bishop Wilson, and Dr. Alexander Duff. The act establishing the University of Bombay bears the names of Lord Elphinstone, Bishop Harding, Dr. Harkness, Sir Jamshidji Jijibhai, Jagganath Sankersett, and Dr. John Wilson.

The universities are modelled closely after the great English examples of Cambridge and Oxford. In Madras a period of study is required, but there is no rule as to the place of study. In Calcutta and Bombay a period of study is required in any one of the recognized colleges affiliated with the university. Of these, in the Bombay Presidency there are seven in arts, four teaching up to the Bachelor of Arts Examination, and three up to the Previous Arts Examination. Three are government colleges—the Elphinstone College, in Bombay (recognized 1860), the Dekhan College, in Puna (recognized in 1860), and the Gujerat College (recognized 1879), with a class studying up to the Previous Examination standard. Two are missionary institutions —the Free General Assembly's Institution (recognized 1861), and St. Xavier's College (recognized 1869). The Rájarám College (recognized 1880) is maintained by the Kolhápur State, and has been raised from a school to an Arts College for the purposes of the Previous Examination. In the year 1881 the Baroda

THE UNIVERSITY OF BOMBAY.

College was recognized in the Faculty of Arts for the purpose of the Previous Examination. In addition to these there are three others—the Government Law School (1860), the Grant Medical College in Medicine (1860), which has since 1881 been recognized for the purposes of the Second Examination for the degree of Bachelor of Science; and the Puna Civil-Engineering College, in civil engineering (1865), which has since 1881 been recognized for the purposes of the First and Second Examinations for the degree of Bachelor of Science.

In Madras there are altogether forty-two recognized institutions—twenty-five teaching up to the First Arts Examination, of which five are connected with missionary societies; thirteen teaching up to the Bachelor of Arts Examination, of which three are connected with missions; two in law, one in medicine, and one in engineering. In connection with the Calcutta University there are forty-three colleges teaching up to the Bachelor of Arts standard, of which fourteen are connected with the different churches, twenty-six teaching up to the First Arts Examination, fifteen in law, one in medicine, and two in engineering—in all eighty-seven affiliated institutions.

The Panjab University did not at first possess the power to confer degrees. This was due to the less advanced character and extent of education in the Panjab. The degree conferred would have been of an inferior character, and would thus have lessened the value of the Indian university degree in general. But in October, 1882, it was raised to the regular rank of a university by being clothed with power to confer degrees. A university in the Panjab has difficulties which neither of the other three has. Not only is education less advanced, but the native languages still possess a stronger hold. Hence, the special objects of the Panjab University were declared to be:

"(1) To promote the diffusion of European science as far as possible, through the medium of the vernacular languages of the Panjab, and the improvement and extension of vernacular literature generally;

"(2) To afford encouragement to the enlightened study of Eastern classical languages and literature; and

"(3) To associate the learned and influential classes of the province with the officers of government in the promotion and supervision of popular education."

The above are the special objects of the institution; but at the same time every encouragement will be afforded to the study of the English language and literature; and in all subjects which cannot be completely taught in the vernacular, the English language will be regarded as the medium of examination and instruction.

The institutions affiliated to, or aided by, the Panjab University College are, the Oriental College, Lahor; the Law School; the Medical School; the Government College; and a number of aided schools scattered throughout the Panjab.

The government of each University is vested in a board of Fellows, who represent the highest culture and governmental positions in the land. Some are natives and some Europeans. The affairs of the University are conducted by a syndicate, elected from among the Fellows. The business of this syndicate is proposed by the Faculties, which consist of persons elected from any of its members. I have before me the report of the syndicate for the year 1886–1887. It is a model of minute and thorough statement, both educational and financial, of the successful operation of the Indian universities.*

It must be remembered that the government is a most liberal donor to the schools under the patronage of the missionary societies. It not only makes generous grants to them, but cultivates them, and even charges higher fees for attendance upon its own schools than is charged by the missionary schools. Indeed, the missionary bodies are even represented in the Senates of the three great universities. There is no distinction made in the receiving of students. The course is fixed, and natives of any faith are as free to come as the sons of Europeans.

The number of colleges and other higher institutions affiliated with the universities is constantly increasing. In round numbers there are, to-day, one hundred colleges and five hundred high-schools connected with the four great universities of India. Two millions of the natives of India are now in attendance upon the higher Anglo-vernacular schools and are devoted to the study of the English language. In the various Calcutta colleges alone there are two thousand students.†

---

* For Tables on University Education in India, see Appendix, Nos. IV. and V.

† Macdonald, in *Free Church Monthly*, Sept. 1, 1885.

CHAPTER XLIV.

AFTER THE COLLEGE—WHAT?

NOT all the students in either the government or the missionary colleges become Christians. No religious conditions are required. The student may be a Christian or not; if he is diligent, and obeys all the regulations of the school, he has every privilege, and, if he pass through the prescribed university course, he receives his degree. Calcutta is without question the principal educational, as it is the political, centre of the entire country. Those who have been students in its colleges and university may be considered a type of the alumni of similar institutions of learning throughout the empire. It is computed that in the small area of Calcutta and its suburbs—six miles by one and a half—there are twenty-eight thousand alumni who have completed their curriculum in the five Christian colleges, the two government colleges, and the three non-Christian native colleges.

A native college must be understood to be a college where neither proprietor, professor, nor student is a foreigner. There are about two thousand who are alumni, or students, of the Calcutta University, and there are one thousand youths besides who are studying up to the matriculation examination of the university.

The English language is the medium employed in all these institutions for securing an education. It was a hard battle to introduce the system, but Duff fought bravely, and won, and no one thinks of going back to the old method of studying science through the medium of the native tongues. Macdonald says: "This process of educating the natives through the medium of the English language has been going on for the last fifty years with an ever-increasing impetus. Originating in Calcutta, it has spread all over the country, until there is not a town or village which has not been more or less affected by it. There are colleges affiliated to the Calcutta University in almost every town of importance throughout the province of Bengal. And side by side with all these colleges are large first-class schools or academies, and in the smaller towns and larger villages are Anglo-vernacular schools, almost all of which teach up to the matriculation examination. There is thus scarcely a village of any importance throughout the country in which English is not taught, and from which the cleverest boys are not drafted for some neighboring college to receive a university education."*

Now, what becomes of the Indian alumni of the college and university? Of the many who finish the curriculum, but a small fraction are Christians, or have positive Christian sympathies. If the graduates number thousands in Calcutta alone, what must be the total number throughout India? It may not be wide of the mark to suppose that there are in all India not less than forty thousand natives who have graduated at some school of high grade, and that ten per cent. of the number have passed the university degrees. What is the position of these men to-day? Are they looked upon by the natives with suspicion or aversion? Not at all. They enjoy the highest respect, and are the recognized leaders of native thought. Mr. Macdonald declares that, after they leave school or college, scarcely any of them come under any Christian influence; and that they will not attend the vernacular preaching of the Christian missionary in the bazar, or in the village, or by the wayside. Very few of them have access to any Christian literature except in the vernacular, and that, from various causes, they will not read.

Yet this is the class which is to rule the thought of the India of to-morrow. Already they are, and more are yet to be, the judges, lawyers, magistrates, professors, teachers, orators, physicians, engineers, merchants, authors, and journalists. All the subordinate branches of government, the administration of justice, the training of the young, the trade and commerce of the empire, are to be directed by them. "The courts of law and justice, the government and merchant offices, the telegraph and telephone offices, and the railway stations are already filled by them. Female education is also very largely, if not almost altogether, in their hands. Social reforms and the legislation of the

---

* *Free Church of Scotland Monthly*, Sept., 1885.

country are most powerfully influenced by them. They are at the inception and carrying on of every political agitation that convulses the country. As a class they are at least as clever, intelligent, and intellectual, and as well educated, as the average Englishman, or even Scotsman. They are, as it will be easily seen, the natural leaders of the dense, teeming millions of their poor, ignorant, down-trodden, and despised countrymen. They are the authors of almost all the modern vernacular literature that is scattered broadcast over the country, and which is daily read to the illiterate peasant and ignorant villager. In Calcutta alone they have as daily papers, in the English language, the *Indian Mirror* and the *Amrita Bazaar Patrika*, both of them of much influence and wide circulation; but of still greater influence are their weekly papers—the *Hindu Patriot*, the *Bengalee*, *Reis and Rayyat*, the *Indian Echo*, the *Bengal Messenger*, and the *Liberal and New Dispensation*—all written, owned, and managed by these same educated natives. Besides, much of what appears in the *Calcutta Review*, the *Statesman*, and *Daily News*, periodicals edited by Europeans, is written by them."

It is a serious question: What of the faith of this large number of educated and powerful native Hindus? Are they what they were, in this respect, before they crossed the college threshold? Not at all. As they have progressed towards an education their old religion has lost its grasp. They still practise the outward rites of their old religion, because they desire to please their family and friends, and the formal casting off of the ancestral faith would break all the bonds which unite them to their home. But the old religion has no further charm. The very language, the potent English, through which they have received instruction, has a charm which the native tongue can never again possess. They look upon any Indian language as a thing of the past, and the faith as a doomed one. They are indifferent towards all religions. They talk freely on theological subjects, attend lectures of visiting scholars from the West, and frequently Christian services when some distinguished preacher from abroad conducts them.

The missionaries are now taking special pains to interest these educated natives. They recognize their power, and that the future of India lies in their hands. Mr. Macdonald gives the following gratifying report of the special efforts now going on in

Calcutta to complete the evangelization of the educated young Hindus:

"A Christian literature specially adapted to their need is being prepared—leaflets and small tracts are distributed in large numbers among them, and books, large and small, specially suited for them, are imported into the country from home, and sold to them or lent among them. Some of them are encouraged to visit the missionaries in their own houses, and these and others are visited by the missionaries. Lectures and addresses are prepared for their special need, and delivered in suitable localities. Meetings, got up by themselves for social, literary, and moral purposes, are attended by missionaries, and by speech and conversation effort is put forth to guide their minds to the truth. Advantage is specially taken of their open-air gatherings in some of the squares of Calcutta to bring them together to listen to Christian evangelical addresses, accompanied by the offering of prayer and the singing of hymns alike in the English and the vernacular languages to European or Hindu tunes.

"For the last five years this has been done systematically and perseveringly in Beadon Square, which is situated in the centre of the native quarter of the town, and is laid out as a garden, with gravel walks, clumps of flowering shrubs, and large plots of grass. On one of these plots almost every evening, but especially on Saturdays and Sundays, will be found one or two missionaries, with two or three native converts, surrounded by a pretty large company of educated young men, numbering on the Sunday evenings, on an average, three or four hundred, and sometimes amounting to as many as five or six hundred—all men, not a woman ever among them. Sometimes, however, a good sprinkling of little children accompany their fathers or brothers. These men are, many of them, students of our colleges—a larger number ex-students, including representatives from almost all the subdivisions to which we have above referred.

"The meeting generally commences by the singing of a Christian hymn by two or three native Christian boys, who with praiseworthy perseverance attend these meetings with the view of helping in the service of song. Thereafter one of the brethren present mounts the small platform and offers up a short prayer in the hearing of an attentive and solemn audience.

Another brother offers a short evangelical address, extending over ten to twenty minutes. Then another hymn is sung; another address is delivered; followed by a third hymn and a third address; and if it be a moonlight evening, as many as four or five addresses are delivered before the meeting closes—the audience standing on the grass attentively listening for two or three hours at a stretch, if the speaking be good and no counter-attraction has interfered to draw away the audience.

"Since these meetings commenced five years ago, many thousands of the educated young men of Calcutta have heard the gospel freely proclaimed; and earnest, fervid appeals have been made to them to be reconciled to God through Him who is himself the way, the truth, and the life. That these proclamations and appeals have not been in vain is seen not only in the few who have openly acknowledged Christ as their Saviour, in the larger number who in the course of conversation admit not only the truth of the Christian religion but their own hope of salvation through Christ, but in the still larger number who take a pleasure in attending these meetings, and hearing of Christ and his salvation, night after night, week after week, and even month after month."

The methods thus employed to give a Christian direction to the educated young men of Calcutta are having their influence throughout India. The various missionary societies have a keen appreciation of the importance of this special work, and are adapting themselves to it with a skill and energy worthy of Martyn, Carey, and other founders. Already some of the most brilliant and successful missionaries are from this very class of natives—men who went into the college as Hindus, but to-day are leaders in Christian work. Take the educated natives out of all the missionary bodies now at work in India, and the hands on the world's missionary dial would move backward many a year. The current has set in. The time will come when the Christian Church of India will be in the hands of natives, and in their hands because the European and American missionary will not be needed. If Indian Buddhists planted their system in China and Tibet, why may the day not soon come when Indian Christians will go far and wide, and plant the gospel in the regions longer belated in their pilgrimage towards the truth?

CHAPTER XLV.

ENGLISH WRITERS IN INDIA.

THE more prominent bonds connecting England with India have always been military and commercial. But there are also literary associations which have played no small part in the great drama of English supremacy in Hindustan and Ceylon. In the early operations of the East India Company there was now and then an Englishman combining keen literary taste with an eye to commercial advantage, who helped in both ways to weld the chain which has finally brought India within the enduring control of his little island in the West. The English tradesman, pure and simple, was not even the first revealer of the boundless treasures of India. This was the work of the scholarly traveller. He was the pioneer who wandered over the country, lingered at those splendid courts, and came home with the story of the industries, the gorgeous architecture, the unrivalled jewels, the flora, and the exhaustless soil. His marvellous accounts stirred the commercial mind, and induced the English capitalists of three centuries ago to undertake the forming of great enterprises in the East. Sir Thomas Roe, not content with exploring the Amazon on our Western Continent, never gave a pause to his long pilgrimage until he reached the court of the Great Mogul. The very moment when that traveller—the first Englishman to behold the splendor of the Peacock Throne of Delhi—touched the marble floor of the greatest palace in the East, and breathed the perfumed air of its audience-hall, was full of fate to that mighty empire. From that time onward England's eyes were never turned away from the wealth of India.

The second incident was the formal opening of trade between England and India. The reigning Mogul had a beautiful daughter, who was dangerously ill. Boughton, who played at both surgery and diplomacy, cured the princess. His price was the privilege of the English to trade in Bengal. It proved to be the largest fee in all the annals of medical science, for the first result was the great development of English trade in all India. The final result was the downfall of the Mogul Empire through the double means of British commerce and arms.

The East India Company never displayed greater skill in the management of its affairs in India than in its selection of men. Many of its civil servants were skilful with the pen—an ability which served in good stead after they had become domesticated in India. Warren Hastings was hardly less as a literary character than as a civil administrator. His wide reading, his delightful style, his abiding interest in the antiquities of India, then new to Europe, gave him a prominent place in the group of English statesmen who knew how to enjoy with equal ease the delights of literature and the absorbing engagements of civil rule. His communications to the home government were masterpieces of statecraft amid difficulties which seldom fall to the lot of the English Governor-General in India. Only recently has his voluminous correspondence with his wife come to light. In 1872 a large number of letters and other unpublished matter fell into the possession of the British Museum.

The correspondence with Mrs. Hastings has been carefully edited, and grouped into three series. The first comprises the letters written from Calcutta in 1780. The second consists of letters conveyed secretly in quills while Hastings was at Chunar. The third comprises letters relating to Mrs. Hastings's voyage to England, and her husband's doings until he followed. The whole of this correspondence displays great tenderness, a constant thinking on his wife by Hastings, and a regard for a wife's affection and esteem which is not surpassed in the whole domain of domestic correspondence. In the first series, the minute circumstances connected with the duel between Hastings and Sir Philip Francis are related. Here the Governor-General speaks with that great delicacy of feeling and careful concealment of everything calculated to disturb his wife which place this portion of his correspondence in a place quite apart from the ordinary familiar writing of notable characters. In reading such of these letters of Hastings to his wife as have so far come to light, one cannot help forgetting Burke's terrific arraignment of his Indian administration, and remembering only that tender domestic fidelity which knew no disturbance during the volcanic period when Hastings controlled India, and gathered up the loose threads which lay scattered everywhere as the result of Clive's conquest. Gladstone has not been more successful in making the Homeric age a special study than was Hastings in abstracting himself from his long mortal conflict with Francis, and in studying the peaceful themes of India's past and future. Macaulay thus paints his picture: "The conqueror in a deadly grapple, sitting down, with characteristic self-possession, to inform Dr. Johnson in a letter about Sir William Jones's Persian Grammar, and the history, traditions, arts, and natural productions of India."

Concerning the official communications of Hastings from India on the political affairs of the century, Macaulay further says: "Of the numerous servants of the Company who have distinguished themselves as framers of minutes and despatches, Hastings stands at the head. He was, indeed, the person who gave the official writing of the Indian government the character which it still retains."

Sir Philip Francis, still the most probable author of the "Letters of Junius," led a checkered life in India. He had been connected with the War Office in London, and resigned in 1772. In the following year he was appointed a member of the Council for India. An American cousin wrote him the following letter:

"I have perused the Regulation Bill carefully, and am of opinion that it will answer all your purposes effectually. It gives you vast power and a vast salary. But how did you get this appointment? It is miraculous to me that a man should resign his office in 1772, and in 1773, without any change of ministry, be advanced in so very extraordinary a manner.

"Your merit and abilities I was always ready to acknowledge, sir, but I was never taught to think much of Lord North's virtue and discernment; his treatment of you has in some measure redeemed him in my opinion."

His preparation for civil service had been excellent. Educated at St. Paul's school; then serving in turn as clerk in the office of the Secretary of State; as secretary of General Bligh in the expedition to the French coast, resulting in the destruction of Cherbourg; as secretary to a special embassy to Lisbon; and again as clerk in the Secretary of State's office, he acquired a useful experience, and gradually became absorbed in the professional study of political science and the Constitution and laws of England.

Francis then served eighteen months as amanuensis to William Pitt, Earl of Chatham, and afterwards, for nine years, served as chief clerk in the War Office. He was now ready for India; or, for that matter, for almost any place of political importance within the gift of the government.

As the vessel which bore Francis and the other members of the council up the Hugli, to Calcutta, it was expected by the strangers from afar that the royal salute of twenty-one guns from the batteries of Fort William would be given them. But, alas, the number was seventeen.* Hastings had taken great care that the royal salute should not be given. Francis was disgusted. His pride was wounded. When he met Hastings the reception was cold and formal. He took no pains to conceal his sense of injury. A few ounces more of gunpowder would probably have made them cordial friends. But now there could be no friendship. This first affront laid the foundation of that bitter hostility of Francis to Hastings and his administration, sharpened the pen of Francis for invective and satire hardly less keen than one finds in the "Letters of Junius," and led to a duel between the two in India which resulted in the wounding of Francis and that trial of Hastings by the House of Commons which shook all England and her distant colonies.

SIR PHILIP FRANCIS.

Francis indulged in all the license and splendor which his position, salary, and skill in gaming permitted. It is said that he paid a rent of $60,000 a year for his house, employed 104 servants, and had his grand dinners and balls. But all the while he

* Busteed, "Echoes from Old Calcutta," p. 55.

watched Hastings with an eagle eye. Never has the Indian mail carried back to England more violent attacks on a governor-general than those of Francis against Hastings. During all the first years of his stay in India he underestimated the genius of his foe. Hastings triumphed in the end. His pen, and that endurance which "resembled the patience of stupidity," triumphed over the malignity of the temper and the ambition and the venomous pen of even Philip Francis.

The relation of Francis to Madame Grand belongs to the social history of India, France, and England. This woman was one of the most beautiful and fascinating of her times. She combined all the winning charms of her French origin, her English training, and her Indian home. Her maiden name was Werlée. She was born November 21, 1762. The place of her birth was Anjengo, in the Danish settlement of Tranquebar, on the Coromandel coast. She married a Frenchman, Grand, when she was less than fifteen years of age. She and her husband lived in Calcutta. Francis established relations with her, and a long trial resulted, which attracted the universal attention of the Anglo-Indian people, and gave occasion to more gossip and scandal than any one event in the later history of India.

Madame Grand went to France, where Talleyrand met her. He was fascinated by her, and was compelled by Napoleon to marry her at twenty-four hours' notice. There was no trouble in securing a divorce from Grand before the marriage. He was still in India, living on the money which Francis had paid him. Madame de Rémusat thus describes her: "She was tall, and her figure had all the suppleness and grace so common to women born in the East. Her complexion was dazzling, her eyes of the brightest blue; and her slightly turned-up nose gave her, singularly enough, a look of Talleyrand himself. Her fair golden hair was of proverbial beauty." Her beauty was long a favorite social theme in Paris. Her history was against her, but her personal charms created an empire quite her own. Talleyrand took her with him to Vienna at the time of the Congress of Vienna, where her Oriental tastes and peculiarities astounded the nobles and their families. One of the diplomats remonstrated with Talleyrand on account of some performance of his capricious wife. The only answer which Talleyrand made was, "But, my dear sir, what do you wish me to do? My wife is such a beast!"

The Princess Talleyrand was not distinguished for scholarship. The following story flew like wild-fire through Paris. We give it as told by Napoleon to O'Meara at St. Helena, in 1817:

"I sometimes asked Denon (whose work I suppose you have read) to breakfast with me, as I took a pleasure in his conversation, and spoke very freely with him. Now all the intriguers and speculators paid their court to Denon with a view of inducing him to mention their projects or themselves in the course of his conversation with me, thinking that being mentioned by such a man as Denon, for whom I had a great esteem, might materially serve them. Talleyrand, who was a great speculator, invited Denon to dinner. When he went home to his wife, he said, 'My dear, I have invited Denon to dine; he is a great traveller, and you must say something handsome to him about his travels, as he may be useful to us with the Emperor.'

"His wife, being extremely ignorant and probably never having read any other book of travels than that of Robinson Crusoe, concluded that Denon could be nobody else. Wishing to be very civil to him, she, before a large company, asked him divers questions about his man Friday. Denon, astonished, did not know what to think at first, but at length discovered by her questions that she really imagined him to be Robinson Crusoe. His astonishment and that of the company cannot be described, nor the peals of laughter which it excited in Paris as the story flew like wildfire through the city, and *even* Talleyrand himself was ashamed of it."

It is but fair to say, however, that Talleyrand himself afterwards denied the truth of the story, but in doing so he told another one which was quite equal as an illustration of Madame's sublime ignorance. This notable woman died in Paris in 1835, and was interred in the Cemetery of Mont Parnasse. Her picture by Zoffany hangs on the walls of the College at Serampore, while Gerard's more celebrated portrait adorns the Louvre.

There is hardly any notable event in Anglo-Indian history with which English literature has not some immediate connection. Even the Black Hole tragedy has its intimate associations. That is the best known of all the individual crimes perpetrated by a native of India on English people. Calcutta was captured from the English by the native troops under Siraj ud Daula (Lamp of the State), the Suba of Bengal. The later opinion of those best able to judge the conditions of the times is to the effect that the young Hindu commander was not responsible for the imprisonment and suffocation of the English people in the Black Hole, but that subordinate officers were the real perpetrators of the tragedy.

J. Z. Holwell was one of the few surviving prisoners. He became the historian of the tragedy, and afterwards erected a monument to the memory of his murdered fellow-countrymen. Holwell, when a boy, was educated at Richmond, and arrived as surgeon's-mate in an Indiaman, in Calcutta, in the year 1732. He learned Arabic in Arabia, and soon displayed his scholarly tastes by becoming intimately acquainted with the customs and antiquities of India. He returned to England, wrote on Indian topics, and in 1751 returned to India as 12th member of the perpetual Zemindar and Council. Being in Calcutta at the time of the capture by Siraj ud Daula, he was confined with others in the Black Hole. His health was shattered by the sufferings of that awful night. He returned to England. He again went to India, and, for a short time, succeeded Clive as Governor-General of the country. He retired in 1760 from his Indian service.

J. Z. HOLWELL.

Holwell's history in India was that of a man who seems to have been aroused to intense mental activity by the historical and literary wealth of the country. The very air about him inspired him to earnest research. His "Narrative of the Black Hole Tragedy" was an exhaustive monograph, and is the best original source for the proper understanding of that blackest chapter of Anglo-Indian history. But Holwell's study of India led him into larger fields. He inquired deeply into the religions of the people, their architectural achievements, their usages, and their far-distant history. His principal works are his "Mythology, Cosmogony, Fasts and Festivals," and "Interesting Historical Events Relative to the Province of Bengal." He was probably one of the best collectors of ancient manuscripts and other literary treasures in India, at a time when the European craze for Oriental literary treasures had not as yet made them scarce in India. But his rich gatherings were lost at the capture of Calcutta. In addition to his elaborate books, he wrote monographs on various Indian topics, and contributed largely to awaken in England a literary interest in India. His fame spread to the Continent, where he was recognized, even more than in England, as an author of great worth. Voltaire says of him: "This is the same Holwell who learned not only the language of the modern Brahmans, but also that of the ancient Brahmans. It is he who wrote most precious memoirs on India, and who translated sublime specimens of the first books written in the sacred language. We owe much to this man, who has only travelled to instruct. He has revealed that which has been concealed for ages. We exhort any one who wishes to be instructed to read attentively the ancient allegorical fables—the primitive sources of all the fables which have prevailed in Persia, Chaldea, Egypt, and Greece, and have found their home amid the miserable hordes of barbarians, as well as among the greatest and most flourishing nations. These things are more worthy of the study of the wise man than the quarrels of some dealers about muslin and dyed stuffs."

Holwell survived his night in the Black Hole forty-two years, dying in England in 1798. While he reached the ripe age of eighty-seven, it was not an exception in his family. His mother lived to be 102 years of age, and then did not die a natural death, but was burned in her bed, having on the same day, as the family tradition goes, "danced a minuet with her grandson on the occasion of the anniversary of his birthday."*

Anjengo, the same town in France which gave birth to Madame Grand, was also the birthplace of another woman celebrated alike for her beauty and her relation to English literature. This was Eliza Draper, the wife of a Bombay civilian. She was beloved by the celebrated Abbé Raynal, who

* Busteed, "Echoes from Old Calcutta," pp. 38, 39.

wrote of her that Eliza's name would forever rescue the insignificant Anjengo from oblivion.* But her place in English literature is that of Sterne's Eliza. Of her personal charms, Forbes, in his "Oriental Memoirs," says: "A lady with whom I had the pleasure of being acquainted at Bombay, whose refined taste and elegant accomplishments require no encomium from my pen."

An important movement in India in the latter half of the eighteenth century was the founding of the periodical press. The first newspaper established in the country was *Hicky's Gazette*, which began its history on January 29, 1780, and soon took its place as an organ for the representation of the large Anglo-Indian colony in Calcutta. The freedom with which it discussed social topics made it a great power. It was not discreet, and often wandered into forbidden social paths. The *India Gazette* of 1789, for example, contained an editorial congratulating its readers on the fact "that the pleasures of the bottle and the too prevailing enticements of play were now almost universally sacrificed to the far superior attractions of female society." †

Hicky's Gazette was the parent of a large number of newspapers and periodicals, not only in Calcutta, but in other parts of India. These periodicals, which had grown into a very respectable number by the year 1830, became the medium by which young Englishmen of literary tastes made their acquaintance with the public. It appears that many a man in both the military and the civil service, on going to India, first discovered his own literary spirit in his adopted country. London was too far away for him to reach the public through its periodicals. The editors near at hand were less critical, permitted much larger liberty in the discussion of social and other topics, and were much less exacting as to style and matter. Of the style of the romances written in India by the English at that time, the beginning of Parker's "Oriental Tale" may be considered a fair illustration:

"Joseph, a duwaat (ink-stand), filled with the blackest ink of Agra, and 40,000 new Persian cullums (pens). Good! A fresh chillum; saturate the

---

* Busteed, "Echoes from Old Calcutta," p. 262.

† Laurie, "Sketches of Some Distinguished Anglo-Indians," p. 179.

tatties with Goolaub, scatter little mountains of roses, chumpah, and baubal blossoms about the room; bring me a vast serai of iced sherbet, pure juice of the pomegranate, you understand, and now here goes!"

This was a mere introduction. The beginning of the "Oriental Tale" proper, was as follows:

"The snakes were prodigiously lively—thermometer stood precisely at 138° Fahrenheit in the sun, but was some degrees lower in the shade. There is an uproar! A tiger and a buffalo, coming to drink up the last quart of water which lies in a little patch of marsh, have got themselves into a sufficiently absurd situation: a playful boa has embraced them both. He—poor good-natured creature, quite unconscious of their dissatisfaction, has judiciously wrapped his tail round a pretty extensive clump of teak-trees, and with the spare end of his body is uncommonly cracking the ribs of his companions, which go off like so many muskets, and otherwise preparing them in the most approved manner amongst boas for his supper. I said the snakes were prodigiously lively."

The *Calcutta Literary Gazette*, established about 1835, and edited by D. S. Richardson, was ably conducted. The editor himself became known in Europe as the author of "Literary Leaves," "Home Visions," "The Ocean Sketches," and the "Selections from the British Poets." Macaulay, during his residence in Calcutta, was so pleased with this last work that he drafted a plan for a similar book of selections from the British prose-writers, but never completed his undertaking.

The *Bengal Annual* of 1833 was a great favorite with ambitious young Anglo-Indians. It had a list of fifty contributors, and there seemed to be no end to the enterprise and daring of those young and aspiring tyros in literature in the far-off land of their adoption. It can hardly be doubted that many a writer expected to reach the British public at home by a successful use of his pen in the adventurous journals of India. Many of the works on Indian topics, and, indeed, on subjects of general character, were first treated in the Indian periodicals, and afterwards appeared with a London imprint. For example, Parker's "Oriental Tale" first saw daylight in the *Bengal Annual*, and was published in his collected writings in London under the title of "Bole Pongis." His "Draught of Immortality" and other poems had been issued in London as early as 1827. Torrens's "Remarks on the Scope and Uses of Military Literature and History" was published first in the *Eastern Star* in 1846.

As we read the large lists of works now constantly appearing from the press of Allen, Trübner, Chapman, and other houses in London, it is difficult to tell just what has already seen the light in the *Calcutta Review*, the *Christian College Magazine*, and other periodicals of India. Still, this question of literary birth is hardly ever inquired into very closely, either in Europe, America, or India.

The military authorship of Anglo-Indians received early attention, and has grown with remarkable rapidity. Since the conquest of India by Clive, and its solidification by Hastings, there has grown up a wealth of books on the military fortunes of the country which would constitute a vast library in itself. The expeditions to Afghanistan and to Burma, the Sikh War, the Sepoy Mutiny, and, indeed, every military movement in the country, have awakened a spirit of historical investigation which has taken shape in large works. Some of them are not only treasures of history, but even of archæological research. The conquest of the Panjab has not only been treated in a military point of view, but that country, having been the scene of Alexander's conquest, the old Greek relations have been discussed, and points of identity between Hindu and Greek civilization established. These works have become a part of the permanent treasure of the world's literature.

Many of the great campaigns have been treated by the leaders themselves. Havelock wrote "The Campaigns in Ava," Neill wrote a history of the First Madras European Regiment, Sykes wrote valuable notes on Ancient India, and Phayre wrote on the Burma Race. The important writings of Sir John W. Kaye—such as his "Essays of an Optimist," "History of the War in Afghanistan," "Life of Lord Metcalfe," "History of the Sepoy War," "History of the Administration of the East India Company," and "Lives of Indian Officers"—show how strongly the literary spirit has prevailed among the military leaders who have established English supremacy in India.

To the military treatises of the country belong also books describing the industrial and social life. We do not believe a single industry has been forgotten. Men who have conducted large tea and coffee plantations have written on each subject. No study of cotton culture would be complete without consulting the works of the Anglo-Indian writers. Special antiquity, such as the architecture of the temples, has been treated with scientific thoroughness, and new light has been furnished by Fergusson and other patient English inquirers. The best writers on all these themes have not been mere tourists, but, like Sir William Jones, have had such sympathy with the country as only residence imparts. Their duties, either as civilians or soldiers, confined them often to one locality, where the history, or some other interest of the place, set them to thinking and writing. India owes to England not only a good government, the introduction of Western civilization, the freedom for the propagation of Christianity, but

RESIDENCE OF MACAULAY.

also the revelation of India to itself and to the great Western world.

From Macaulay's connection with India we have the two most brilliant papers on that country which have been written—namely, the essays on Clive and Hastings. The relation of the Macaulay family to India did not begin with the going of Thomas Babington Macaulay as a member of the Council in 1834, and his remaining there four years. His father, Zachary Macaulay, had been a merchant in India and returned to England. The uncle of the historian had lived on the western coast of India. An aged lady of Madras told me of the insecure life of himself and his children, and proved it by the fact that they often slept in couches lodged in the branches of the trees of the plantation, as the only refuge from the prowling beasts of the forests.

In Calcutta I had a conversation with Mr. Andrews, who had been a familiar aid to the historian during his stay in Calcutta, from 1834 to 1838. The reverence with which he spoke of his employer, and of his kindness to him, and the methods of his daily life, was exceedingly beautiful. Of all the memories of Mr. Andrews I doubt not that those of his daily service to Macaulay will remain the most cherished. The residence of Macaulay was one of the most attractive in Calcutta, and is now the Bengal Club-House. The Club is a delightful resort. The rooms are spacious and beautiful. The tables are supplied with the best periodicals from every part of the world.

William Makepeace Thackeray was born in Calcutta. The Armenian School is pointed out as the house where the great novelist first saw the light. The family had long been associated with India. In January, 1766, the *Lord Camden* sailed from England for Calcutta. There were on board eleven men who were to do service in India as writers in the East India Company. One was Ray, the son of Lord Sandwich, and subsequently distinguished as a Bengal author. Another was William Makepeace Thackeray, the grandfather of the novelist. This elder Thackeray was one of the four employed in the Secretary's office. He seems to have given satisfaction to his superior, for in the following year the president informed the Board that he was in need of an assistant as cash-keeper. Thackeray was appointed to this office. The Register of St. John's Cathedral, in Calcutta, contains an entry of his marriage to Miss Amelia Webb, January 13, 1776. The family became permanent residents of that city. The father of the novelist seems to have been of no special prominence. He was buried in the North Park Cemetery, Calcutta, where his tombstone is still to be found.*

The Armenian School is a plain building with a commodious balcony. The structure is old and well worn. As I passed it I could not help going back, in memory, to September, 1857, when I saw Thackeray for the first and only time. It was at a rail-

* Busteed, "Echoes from Old Calcutta," p. 207.

way station in Paris, and I was going out to spend the day among the royal tombs of old St. Denis, the Westminster Abbey of France. As my travelling companion and I were taking in that world of contrasts and contradictions which one sees to perfection in a Paris station, a man was borne in upon a litter by friendly hands. He was an Englishman taken suddenly and seriously ill, and was on his way to his home in London. A tall, gray-haired, square-faced Englishman had just bought his ticket,

BIRTHPLACE OF THACKERAY.

and was about to enter the cars. Just then he caught sight of this poor, helpless brother man. He went to him, bent over him, made inquiries as to his disease and where he was going, and did not leave him until he had encouraged the gentleman by kindly words, had given him a slip of paper containing the address of a London physician who had cured him of the same disease, and had bidden him a brotherly good-bye. I never learned who the invalid was, but the good Samaritan was none other than the full-grown man who first saw the light in this humble place in Calcutta. Who could witness such a scene of sympathy and real tenderness, and afterwards call Thackeray's heart cold and cynical?

"He was a Cynic! By his life all wrought
  Of generous acts, mild words, and gentle ways;
His heart wide open to all kindly thought,
  His hand so quick to give, his tongue to praise.

"He was a Cynic! You might read it writ
  In that broad brow, crowned with its silver hair;
In those blue eyes, with childlike candor lit,
  In the sweet smile his lips were wont to wear."

* * * "If he smiled
His smile had more of sadness than of mirth,
But more of love than either, undefiled,
Gentle alike by accident of birth,
And gift of courtesy, and grace of love;
When shall his friends find such another friend?"

Thackeray was always a roamer. His going, when young, from Calcutta to London was but the beginning. He was no sooner at home than he was ready to leave again, for fresh material for new creations. But the simple London home was always first and last in mind. His great heart tells its own secret at the end of "The White Squall" ballad:

"I thought, as day was breaking,
My little girls were waking,
And smiling, and making
A prayer at home for me."

The cemeteries of India tell many a romantic story, by the bare mention of names, of the close relation between that country and the writers at home. In a cemetery at Puna there lies buried the celebrated African traveller, Sir W. C. Harris, who died October 9, 1848. He was author of "Wild Sports in the West," and "Highlands of Ethiopia." In All-Saints' Church, in Bangalore, there is a tablet to Lieut.-Colonel Sir Walter Scott—we believe a son of the great Wizard of the North—who died at sea February 8, 1847, aged 46. Only recently a son of Tennyson has died at sea on his return from India.

In the North Park Cemetery of Calcutta there is a black marble slab containing the inscription—

In Memory of
The Honourable
ROSE WHITWORTH AYLMER,
who departed this life March 2d, A.D. 1800.
Aged 20 years.

What was her fate? Long, long before her hour,
Death called her tender soul by break of bliss,
From the first blossoms to the buds of joy,
Those few our noxious fate unblasted leaves
In this inclement clime of human life.

This name calls to mind the most romantic period of the life of Walter Savage Landor. Landor left Oxford in 1797. He spent some time on the Welsh coast, where he made the acquaintance of Lord Aylmer's family. An attachment sprang up between Rose, the daughter of Lord Aylmer, and young Landor. One day she loaned him a book from the Swansea Circulating Library. It was a romance, by Clara Reeve. Here he found an Arabic tale which so profoundly impressed him that it suggested his first great work, "Gebir," which contains the Sea Nymph's memorable description of the "sinuous shells of pearly hue." This poem by Landor was greatly enjoyed by Shelley. But even before Shelley enjoyed it Southey had written of it the following words: "I would go a hundred miles to see the anonymous author;" and "There is a poem called 'Gebir,' and written by God knows who, sold for a shilling; it has miraculous beauties." *

The attachment between Rose Aylmer and Landor grew stronger. But an event occurred which separated the two. Rose went to Calcutta, to visit or live with her aunt, Lady Russell, wife of Sir Henry Russell, who was at the time a judge in Calcutta, and afterwards became chief-justice, and, later, a baronet. Landor, in his poem, "Abertawy," indicates both her unwillingness to go and his own sorrow at her departure:

"Where is she now? Called far away,
By one she dared not disobey,
To those proud halls, for youth unfit,
Where princes stand and judges sit.

* Busteed, "Echoes from Old Calcutta," p. 335 ff.

Where Ganges rolls his widest wave
She dropped her blossom in the grave;
Her noble name she never changed,
Nor was her nobler heart estranged."

In March, 1800, the Calcutta *Gazette* contained the following account of her death:

"On Sunday last, at the house of her uncle, Sir Henry Russell, in the bloom of youth and possession of every accomplishment that could gladden or embellish life, deplored by her relatives and regretted by a society of which she was the brightest ornament, the Honble. Miss Aylmer."

The death of Rose Aylmer saddened Landor to such an extent that it gave a sombre tone to much of his writing. A little poem to "The Three Roses" commences as follows:

"When the buds began to burst
Long ago with Rose the first,
I was walking, joyous then,
Far above all other men,
Till before us up there stood
Britonferry's oaken wood,
Whispering, 'Happy as thou art,
Happiness and thou must part.'"

In another poem he sketches an incident of their idyllic life at Swansea. They could find no convenient seat. Landor constructed one by plucking up some thorn rose bushes, for which he had to pay the penalty of a severe scratch:

"At last I did it—eight or ten—
We both were snugly seated then;
But then she saw a half-round bead,
And cried, 'Good gracious, how you bleed!'
Gently she wiped it off, and bound
With timorous touch that dreadful wound.
To lift it from its nurse's knee
I feared, and quite as much feared she,
For might it not increase the pain,
And make the wound burst out again?
She coaxed it to lie quiet there,
With a low tune I bent to hear;
How close I bent I quite forget,
I only know I hear it yet."

The death of Rose in far-off Calcutta was a great blow to Landor. Here is only a part of his famous elegy:

"Ah, what avails the sceptred race?
Ah, what the form divine?
What every virtue, every grace?
Rose Aylmer, all were thine.
Rose Aylmer, whom these wakeful eyes
May weep, but never see,
A night of memories and of sighs
I consecrate to thee."

Charles Lamb was so delighted with the tender words that he wrote Landor: "Many things I had to say to you which there was no time for. *One*, why should I forget? 'Tis for Rose Aylmer, which has a charm I cannot explain. I lived upon it for weeks."

Henry Crabbe Robinson wrote to Landor of a visit to the Lambs, as follows: "I have just seen Charles and Mary Lamb living in absolute solitude at Enfield. I found your poems lying open before Lamb... He is ever muttering Rose Aylmer." Landor survived Rose sixty-four years. Shortly before his death, in Florence, a young Englishman appeared in the old singer's presence and handed him a letter from Lord Houghton (Monckton Milnes). It was the coming of "the youngest to the oldest singer that England bore." The young man afterwards wrote the following beautiful tribute:

"And thou, his Florence, to thy trust
Receive and keep,
Keep safe his dedicated dust,
His sacred sleep.
So shall thy lovers, come from far,
Mix with thy name,
As morning-star with evening-star,
His faultless fame."

Just now the most striking literary bond between England and India is Rudyard Kipling. He was born in Bombay on December 30, 1865. His father stands at the head of the School of Art in Lahore. Young Kipling, like many English boys born in India, was sent to England to be educated. It was at "Westward Ho," a watering-place named after Charles Kingsley's novel, that he was educated.* Kipling returned to India, and very early gave evidence of remarkable literary ability. He became connected with the editorial staff of the *Pioneer*. He published short stories in the Anglo-Indian periodicals. In time small volumes appeared in India—"Departmental Ditties," "The Story of the Gadsbys," "Studies in Black and White," and "Under the Deodars." Since then have been published his chief works, "Plain Tales from the Hills," and also "Soldiers Three," "The Courting of Dinah Shadd, and Other Stories," and the "Phantom 'Rickshaw." Tales not in these volumes are appearing in the periodicals, and the young author's ill-health is the penalty he has had to pay for his rapid authorship. His works have produced a remarkable impression. The brevity of his stories, the rapid movement, the unfailing humor, the knowledge of camp-life, the cynical treatment of society at Simla, and familiarity with the grotesque qualities of the native character, place Kipling high above all writers in the English language who have revealed the lighter shades of India to the Anglo-Saxon peoples. The strong Indian coloring which is found in all his pages is a new and welcome element in our common English literature.

RUDYARD KIPLING.

* Andrew Lang, "Biographical and Critical Sketch," in American edition of "The Courting of Dinah Shadd, and Other Stories," pp. vii–xii.

CHAPTER XLVI.

THE RELIGIONS OF INDIA.

I.—Brahmanism.

Brahmanism is that system of religion which was taught by the Brahmans, or priestly caste, who predominated over all other castes of the Aryan conquerors. Even the kings were subordinate to the Brahman priesthood. To the Rig Veda, or old collection of hymns, were added later three other service books.

LAMA PRIESTESS, NORTHERN INDIA. (LAMAISM IS AN AMPLIFICATION OF BUDDHISM.)

The four Vedas were expounded by the Brahman priests, and were declared to be the "Wisdom of God."* These were poetical works, and to each was added a Brahmana, or prose work, explaining the sacrifice and duty of the priests. The Brah-

* Hunter, "Brief History of the Indian People," pp. 50 ff.

manas, with the four Vedas, constitute the sacred writings of the Hindus—the Sruti, or "Things Heard from God." The Vedas are the inspired psalms; the Brahmanas, the theology, or body of doctrine; and the Sutras, afterwards added, the "strings of pithy sentences" regarding laws and ceremonies. Still later additions were made: The Upanishads, treating of God and the soul; the Aranyakas, "Tracts for the Forest Recluse;" and the Puranas, or "Traditions from of Old." None of these have the force of inspiration, but are of high authority, as Suvriti, or "The Things to be Remembered." The Brahmanism of to-day, as a religious system, does not rest on the ancient Vedas, but upon the later scattered and so-called sacred writings.*

The Brahmans had a long conflict with the warrior caste before gaining supremacy. They renounced all claims to the government, and, while not asserting the right to be kings, they held that they had sprung from the mouth of the Creator, and were superior to all other human beings. They aimed at spiritual distinction.

What is the result? They have survived all the revolutions of three thousand years. The Brahmans of this day are the unbroken line of descendants from the original Aryan conquerors of India. While the royal lines have risen and fallen, and disappeared, the Brahman still lives in the affection, and almost divine veneration, of the people. In mental and physical development they are the finest specimens of the Hindu type in existence. The Brahman can be distinguished from all others by his figure, fair complexion, intellectual features, and scholarly tastes.

The Brahmans, among their own caste, taught the unity of God, but left the people to accept the "four castes, the four Vedas, and many deities." Brahma was Creator. Vishnu was the second person of the trinity, and Siva the third person. The many gods in the Hindu pantheon are the diverse and varied manifestations of Vishnu and Siva. The Brahmans wrought out a system of philosophy, and arranged its doctrines in six schools —Darsanas, or Mirrors of Knowledge. They studied astronomy, medicine, music, and law. Their two great epics, the Mahabharata and Ramayana, are among the most remarkable produc-

* Rowe, "Every-day Life in India," p. 36.

BURNING PILE OF THE LATE MAHARAJAH TUKAJI RAO HOLKAR, INDORE.

tions in the whole history of literature. The Brahmans spoke and taught the Sanskrit language, but the common people spoke a simpler form of the same language, or the Prakrit language. The Sanskrit became in time a dead language, but was the sole language of the sacred writings.

II.—Buddhism in India.

B.C. 543—A.D. 1000.

The historical position of Buddhism is a revolt of the Aryan races against the growth of caste distinctions.*

The dynasties professing the Brahman faith ruled India without serious obstacles until the rise of Buddhism. The King of Kapilavastu had a son, Gautama Buddha, who was meditative and sympathetic. He left his father's palace, withdrew to a cave, sent his horse and jewels back to his father, cut off his long hair of the warrior, put on the rags of a beggar, and preached the new faith of human brotherhood and equality. He gave up his beloved wife and only son, and, with his five disciples, became a wanderer in the jungles.

This sacrifice of his domestic ties, made when Gautama was thirty years old, is the central fact of the great Buddhistic faith. It is embalmed in the sacred writings as the Great Renunciation — the most tender and beautiful part of all the writings of the ancient Indian world. Edwin Arnold, in his "Light of Asia," has furnished the best translation in any modern language. Gautama spent six years in severe penance. No self-mortification was too severe. He searched for peace of mind, and, like St. Francis of Assisi and Ignatius Loyola of the later years, regarded torture and self-abnegation as his only pathway to mental calm. But still he had no peace. He concluded that he had taken the wrong way. He now gave up all his penance, came out of his cave, and began to preach a better life to the people. His five disciples forsook him. He was left alone, and, while sitting under a fig-tree, in the new peace which had come to him, it is said that demons brandished flaming weapons about him. This was his Great Temptation, and out of it he came unscathed, and with a clear view

* Kunte, "The Vicissitudes of Aryan Civilization in India," Bombay, 1880, p. xxii.

of duty, and was ever afterwards known as Buddha, "The Enlightened." *

Buddha now appeared as a public teacher, in the Deer Forest, near Benares. The people gathered about him in great numbers. Women and lowly men were his first disciples. In three months about sixty professed his faith. He sent forth his preachers with these words: "Go ye now, and preach the most excellent law." During the four months of the rainy season he stayed at his little hut in a bamboo grove, and preached to the multitudes who came to hear him. They were from every class—the rich and the poor, the wise and the ignorant, princes and beggars. During the remaining eight months of the year he wandered throughout Northwestern India, preaching his doctrines with intense energy. He went back to his father's palace, not to rule, but to convert.

Buddha had gone out as a prince, and now came back as a beggar preacher, with shaven head, coarse raiment, and the beggar's bowl in his hand. His aged father received him kindly, and listened to his message patiently. Buddha's son, whom he had left an infant, was now a full-grown man. He adopted his father's faith. The fond wife, who was still alive, was fascinated by the new doctrines, and became one of the first nuns in Buddhistic history.

Buddha was a public teacher about forty-four years. He died under a fig-tree, when eighty years old, B.C. 543. He divided his last night between preaching and comforting a weeping disciple. Among his last words were: "Be earnest, be thoughtful, be holy. Keep steadfast watch over your own hearts. He who holds fast to the law and discipline, and faints not, shall cross the ocean of life, and make an end of sorrow. . . . The world is fast bound in fetters. I now give it deliverance, as a physician who brings heavenly medicine. Keep your mind on my teaching. All other things change. This changes not. No more shall I speak to you. I desire to depart. I desire the Eternal Rest" (Nirvana).

Thus lived and died the man who founded a religion, which, with all its absurdities, has the largest number of adherents in the world professing any one faith. Its history abounds in anoma-

* Hunter, "Brief History of the Indian People," pp. 65 ff.

lies. One is that, having ruled India for centuries, it was at last expelled from the land which gave it birth, and its multitudes of disciples are to be found in Ceylon, Tibet, China, Japan, and the other Oriental countries to which its tireless missionaries have borne it.

TEMPLE OF JAGANATH, AND BAZAR.

The doctrines of Buddha were few and simple. He found the Brahmanic caste in all its fulness and iron inflexibility. He did not teach disloyalty to the Brahman priesthood, but respect for it. However, he declared that Brahmans are not mediators between God and man, but that real caste consists in moral quality. Men are divided according to their merit. Salvation is open to all alike. We do not gain divine favor by offering sacrifices, but by living pure lives. Misery here, in this life, is the result of sin in a former life. We gather, or shall gather, only what we sow. The highest future joy is eternal calm. Self-control, kindness to all men, reverence for the life of all the brute creation, were the three fundamental doctrines of practical Buddhism.

When Buddha died, five hundred of his followers met in a great cave near Patna and formed the First Council of Buddhism. Their object was to collect and formulate the great master's teachings. They chanted his whole system, arranging it in three divisions—Buddha's words to his disciples, his code of discipline, and his system of doctrine. The Second Council was held a century later (B.C. 443). Its object was to settle disputes which had arisen among the Buddhistic followers.

Now came the period of the popular expansion of this remarkable faith. It extended all over Northern India, quietly supplanting Brahmanism in every class of society. For two centuries it continued its quiet work of gaining disciples and securing a strong hold on the popular mind. It was now, however, on the eve of its greatest expansive effort in India. Asoka, King of Magadha, or Behar, became a convert to Buddhism, about B.C. 257. He was the Constantine of his times, and established the new faith throughout his broad empire.

Asoka turned all his power as a ruler towards the propagation of his new faith, and made it the religion of his state. He dotted his broad kingdom with eighty-four thousand Buddhist monasteries, and the land is known to this day as Behar, the Land of the Monasteries.* He is said to have supported sixty-four thousand Buddhist priests.† At one time he sent off five hundred Buddhist priests to convert Tibet. His measures to make his faith the religion of the state were successful, and show at once the skill of the ruler and the zeal of the reformer. In the year 244 B.C. he convened at Patna the third great Buddhist

* Clough, "From Darkness to Light: A Story of the Telugu Awakening," p. 281.

† Hunter, "Brief History of the Indian People," p. 69.

Council. One thousand elders constituted this august body. Heresies had arisen, and these were now corrected, and Buddhism received that form which it has ever since retained.

Asoka issued his decrees, and engraved them on rocks, in caves, and on pillars of granite. Some of these great graven pillars still remain, as in Delhi and Allahabad, and are among the most striking and venerable of all the memorials of the ancient world in any country. He had a special Department of Religion and Justice, whose functions were to protect the purity of doctrine and to provide means for the propagation of the faith. His monasteries were made the centres of religious zeal. The great monastery of Nalanda alone served as a glowing fire for distributing Buddhist zeal far and wide. It sheltered ten thousand monks and novices of the eighteen Buddhist schools, who here studied all the sciences known to the Eastern world, such as theology, medicine, law, and philosophy, and were supported by the royal treasury.

Asoka collected the sacred books into a Canon of Sacred Scriptures, and caused them to be written in the Magadha language, the vernacular of his kingdom. This is the version which still prevails among the Buddhists of Southern India, Ceylon, Burma, and the Eastern Archipelago. He sent out missionaries through every part of his dominions, and, not stopping within his own country, he sent them far beyond, into other lands. He regarded himself as the divinely appointed agent to spread the faith throughout the world. All lands and languages, all classes of people, must be visited, and the doctrines expounded, and the multitudes persuaded to accept the doctrines of Buddha. But no violence must be used. The sword must never be drawn from its scabbard. All men must be treated as brothers. The beggar was as good as the chief. If he lived better, then he was better. Asoka, however, did not limit his kindness to human beings. While he established hospitals for his fellow-men, he did the same service for beasts. His whole kingdom was one vast Society for the Prevention of Cruelty to Animals. He issued an edict providing a system of medical aid for beasts. For the stranger and the traveller he made ample provision. For the pedestrian he planted shade trees and dug wells along the highways. His one thought was the welfare of his people and their beasts, but that this universal welfare was only to be brought about by the propagation of Buddhism.

The last great Buddhist Council was held under the Scythian King Kanishka, about A.D. 40. The sacred writings were revised, and it is this version, or the Northern Canon of Buddhism, which still serves the disciples of Buddha in Tibet, Tartary, China, and Japan.

At no time, however, was the religion of the Brahmans completely conquered. It was simply superseded for the time by one and then another ruler who were devoted Buddhists. When the Brahmans gained a little power they pursued their opponents with bitter persecution. They destroyed the Buddhist monasteries, tore down the temples, and mutilated the sculptures. There is, however, no record of a general war of extermination of the Buddhists. But the opposition was steady and long-continued, and the issue lay long in the balance. Sometimes the two faiths approached each other, a result brought about by a spirit of compromise in the ruler. For example, King Siladitya called a general council A.D. 624. His object was to extend Buddhism, but he made a great demonstration of catholicity by erecting on the first day a statue of Buddha; on the second, one of the Brahman Sun-God; and on the third, one of the Hindu Siva. Buddhist doctors disputed with Brahman doctors, and the Buddhists with each other.

Buddhism in India had now reached its zenith. About A.D. 700 it rapidly declined, and by A.D. 800 Brahmanism was restored to its old place. The Buddhists seem to have been rent by internal feuds, and their downfall as a great religious body in India is mainly attributable to that cause. So rapid was its decline in India that, by the tenth century, it was well-nigh obliterated. Kashmir and Orissa, lying far removed from the centre of knowledge and influence, were the only regions which continued true to the teachings of Buddha. By A.D. 900 only a few traces of it could be found anywhere in India. But Buddhism, while driven out of the land of its birth, has gained a firm foothold in other lands. Never did a prophet in his own country find so numerous a following in other countries. His followers number to-day five hundred millions of human beings, or forty per cent. of the population of the world.* It

* Hunter, "Brief History of the Indian People," pp. 70 ff.

should awaken the most serious thought of every believer in Christ that the Buddhists are by far the most numerous religious body on earth. From Afghanistan in the west, its empire extends northward and southward, until it reaches Japan. Hardly less than three hundred languages and dialects are used by its devotees, in which to adore the memory of Buddha and proclaim the brotherhood of man. From the ice-huts of northern Tibet down to the palm-groves of Singapore on the equator, its people imitate the holy calm of the founder of their faith, and sing with ecstatic fervor the Great Renunciation. While the only part of

THE TEMPLE YARD, CONJEVERAM.

India proper which still retains the Buddhist faith is Burma, the easternmost part of the empire, some of its fundamental qualities have incorporated themselves into the very fibre of the Indian character, and can be clearly seen in the Hinduism of later times.

"The noblest survivals of Buddhism in India," says Hunter, "are to be found, not among any peculiar body, but in the religion of the whole Hindu people; in that principle of the brotherhood of man, with the re-assertion of which each new revival of

Hinduism starts; in the asylum which the great Hindu sect of Vaishnavas affords to women who have fallen victims to caste rules, to the widow and the outcast; in that gentleness and charity to all men which take the place of a poor-law in India and give a high significance to the half-satirical epithet of the "Mild Hindu." * The large part of the Buddhist population of India, leaving out Burma, is in the Presidency of Bengal. It consists of about one hundred and sixty-seven thousand people, who dwell in the districts contiguous to Burma, and in the remote valleys of the Himalayas. One of the most significant features of the permanent effects of Buddhism in India is to be found in the fact that the English government, in providing public instruction for Burma, made the ancient Buddhist monasteries the basis of its new system.

III.—Hinduism.

Hinduism is the direct outgrowth of Brahmanism, but having accretions from Buddhism and other faiths. It is the prevailing popular religion of India to-day. The religion of Brahma was a system of calm spiritual pantheism. The Hindu religion is based on the worship of the personal deities Siva and Vishnu, who are the emanations of Brahma. Here is a large field for divisions and sects. There are five sects of Hinduism:

1. Worshippers of Siva (Saivas).
2. Worshippers of Vishnu (Vaishnavas).
3. Worshippers of the female personifications of divine power, regarded as the wives of the deities (Saktas).
4. Worshippers of Ganesh or Ganpati as god of luck or good-fortune (Ganapatyas).
5. Worshippers of the sun (Sauras).

While these are the great general groups of Hindu believers, there are various subdivisions. For example, there are worshippers of demons and spirits; of heroes and men; of ancestors; of animals; of plants and trees; and of natural objects, such as the sun, moon, rivers, rocks, and stocks. †

The complex character of the Hindu system can therefore be clearly observed. While Brahmanism is its key-note, the tones

* "Brief History of the Indian People," p. 74.

† Monier Williams, in "Religious Life and Thought in India," gives an excellent account of the Hindu sects and their doctrinal system.

are so numerous and varied that it is difficult to separate or enumerate them. There is no fixity in the system. In fact, it is not a system, but a string of beliefs, often heterogeneous and contradictory, which have been gathered up during the slow passage of three thousand years. "It is next to impossible," says Barth, "to say exactly what Hinduism is, where it begins, where it ends. Diversity is its very essence, and its proper manifestation is sect—sect in constant mobility." *

Political changes have left their impress on this multiform thing which passes by the name of Hinduism. European thought has not been without an impress upon it. Monier Williams very appropriately calls it "a complex congeries of creeds and doctrines, which in its gradual accumulation may be compared to the Ganges, which receives its tributaries from every side, bears them on over a vast area of country, and finally resolves itself into an intricate Delta of tortuous streams and jungly marshes." The same author further says: "Nor is it difficult to account for this complexity. The Hindu religion is a reflection of the composite character of the Hindus, who are not one people, but many. It is based on the idea of universal receptivity. It has ever aimed at accommodating itself to circumstances, and has carried on the process of adaptation through more than three thousand years. It has first borne with, and then, so to speak, swallowed, digested, and assimilated something from all creeds, or, like a vast hospitable mansion, it has opened its doors to all comers; it has not refused a welcome to applicants of every grade, from the highest to the lowest, if only willing to acknowledge the spiritual headship of the Brahmans and adopt caste rules. In this manner it has held out the right hand of brotherhood to the Fetish-worshipping aborigines of India; it has stooped to the demonolatry of various savage tribes; it has not scrupled to encourage the adoration of the fish, the boar, the serpent, trees, plants, stones, and devils; it has permitted a descent to the most degrading cults of the Dravidian races; while at the same time it has ventured to rise from the most grovelling practices to the loftiest heights of philosophical speculation; it has not hesitated to drink in thoughts from the very fountain of Truth, and owes not a little to Christianity itself.

* "The Religions of India," pp. 153, 154.

"Strangest of all, it has dissipated the formidable organization which for a long period confronted Brahmanism, and introduced doctrines subversive of sacerdotalism. It has artfully adopted Buddhism, and gradually superseded that competing system by drawing its adherents within the pale of its own communion. In this complex quality of Hinduism one can easily see an element of both strength and weakness. The Hindu believer can change his method of defence with all the expertness and suppleness of an acrobat. Beaten on one line, he can betake himself to another. If he tire of one series of beliefs, he may find rest under another. His system has all the advantage of a banyan-tree. If a little too much exposed to the sun beside one trunk, he can betake himself to another, for the light and shade are constantly changing with the circuit of the sun. On the other hand, as a resisting force, Hinduism has all the serious disadvantage of a want of unity. Its forces are everywhere divided. Some of its adherents stand at opposite poles. There is a large body of Hindus at the present time who have no faith whatever in their own system. They expect it to die, and know that the hour of death is only a question of time. This want of solidarity and unity will account in a measure for the success of Christian missions among the Hindus. The harvest has been far greater than among the Mohammedans, whose system has the one advantage of unity." *

The division of the Hindus into castes is endless. The writers on the subject get lost in the mazes of its enumeration. Dr. Wilson, of Bombay, only carried his work on "Caste" to two volumes, when he was interrupted by death, and then had not exhausted his description of one caste. Sherring declares that under the general Brahman caste there are eighteen hundred and eighty-six separate subdivisions. But the caste system, as now existing, is no part of the ancient Aryan civilization. The Vedas never taught it.†

IV.—Jainism.

The Jain system stands midway between Buddhism and Brahmanism. It originated about A.D. 600, and declined after A.D.

---

* Monier Williams, "Religious Life and Thought in India," pp. 57, 58.

† Wilson, "Indian Caste," vol. ii. p. 116.

CAR, SIXTY FEET HIGH, USED FOR THE BRAHMA FESTIVAL, CONJEVERAM.
(DRAWN BY THREE THOUSAND MEN.)

1200. It seems to have arisen out of a spirit of accommodation, by which a common ground of harmony could be arrived at. It was formerly believed to be an offshoot of Buddhism, but it is now proven to have been of independent origin.* The Jains

* Kaye, "Christianity in India," p. 125.

lay great stress on certain saints, whom they advance to an importance even superior to their gods. They retain the Brahman arrangement of caste. Their chief saints are twenty-four in number, and are called Tirthankaras. These, by their self-discipline, have crossed the ocean of human existence, and belong to a rank superior to the gods.

The principal territory in which the Jains have prevailed has been Gujerat and Kanara.* In the eleventh century they were persecuted in Madura, their leaders impaled, and the religion in that locality finally broken up by Kuna Pandiyor. They are to be found, however, here and there in many parts of the country. They have always been distinguished for their literary taste. Some of the richest contributions to Tamil literature have been the work of Jain writers. That language owes a large measure of its refined quality to Jain authors.

On the general religious life of the country, however, the Jains have been of little influence, and have always occupied the place of an obscure, but most highly respectable, sect. They are not confined to any one locality, but are scattered all over the country as merchants, ship-owners, goldsmiths, and other tradesmen.†

"The Jains possess," says Temple, "many fine structures in different parts of India. The adherents of the Jain faith occupy the summits of the forest-clad Parasnath, which overlooks the plains of western Bengal, and of Abu, which stands as a lofty outwork of the Aravalli range. Their religious stronghold in the present time is on the heights of the solitary Satrunj Mountain, near Palitana, in the peninsula of Kathiawar. The numerous cupolas, obelisks, and spires, often bright with the whitest marble, seem to pierce the sky. The shrines are laden with the weight of gorgeous offerings, sent by the wealthy members of the sect from almost every populous city in the empire. From the terraces of the edifices, half temples, half fortresses, is to be seen an extensive view of the rich plains, once studded with historic cities, of which the names alone survive, even the sites being untraceable."‡

---

* Pope, "Text-Book of Indian History," pp. 41, 42.

† For an excellent account of the Jains, see Pocoke, "India in Greece," Appendix, p. 370 ff.

‡ Temple, "India in 1880," p. 31.

V.—Mohammedanism.

The religion of Mohammed was introduced into India by military force. Very shortly after the conquest of Arabia, and the adoption of the Quran as the scriptures of Mohammed, the zealous advocates of the new faith looked towards India as a fit field not only for the propagation of the faith, but for political empire. The establishment of the great Mogul empire was the practical instalment of the Mohammedan faith as the great religion of the country. But no measures were adopted for the suppression of the Hindu worship. The temples were profaned, and much violence shown during the period of conquest, but the existing religions were tolerated. At no time was there any great break-up of the Hindu worship. The prevalence of Mohammedanism never existed apart from political power. Wherever a Mohammedan prince ruled, his religion was supported, and gained a measure of strength. But the religion has never gained a strength commensurate with the political importance of Mohammedan rule in India. At the present time there is about one Mohammedan to every five Hindus. The Mohammedans are at the present time more difficult to reach by Protestant effort than any other class of Indian people.

VI.—The Sikhs.

This sect arose from a disposition to harmonize Mohammedanism and Brahmanism. It was founded by Nanak, who was born near Lahore in the year 1469, and died in 1538. He was originally a Hindu, but renounced idolatry, and his "idea was to bring about a union between Hindus and Mohammedans on the common ground of a belief in one God." The elements of his faith are to be found in the teachings of Kabir, whose fundamental thought was the unity of God, and that every man should submit himself to a spiritual guide (Guru), and remain in complete subjection to him through his whole life. Nanak developed the fundamental principles of Kabir's system, and his followers called themselves Sikhs, or "Disciples," in acknowledgment of their dependence on their pastors or Gurus.* So soon as one looks closely into Nanak's principles, it becomes clear that they were

* Monier Williams, "Religious Thought and Life in India," p. 158 ff.

more pantheistic than monotheistic. Brahma, called by the special name of Hari (same as Vishnu), is the author of all being. He does not create, but evolves out of himself. He is thus an expansive force, and the expansions are really manifestations and essences of himself.

Nanak was the first great Guru of the Sikh sect, and he was succeeded by nine others. These ten Gurus gave firmness and power to the entire sect, each Guru adding some new force and giving some new direction to the strange sect. A remarkable change occurred within the close body of the Sikhs. From being a merely religious communion, whose home was in the extreme northwest of India, they developed a singular capacity for organization, social power, and military strength. The Mogul emperors became alarmed. The Sikhs had been in the most friendly relation with the Mohammedan rulers, and it was known that the cardinal principle of the Moslem faith was also claimed to be theirs—namely, the divine unity. But no sooner did the Sikhs begin to organize as a strong military body than the Mogul empire regarded them as seditious, and sought to suppress them. The most bitter hostility now prevailed. The Mogul soldiers were used to conquer and scatter them. But it was of no avail. The Sikhs lived on, and fattened on the decaying carcass of the Mogul empire.

The fourth Guru, Ram-das, saw the necessity of a religious centre, and purchased the tank called Amritsar, or Lake of Nectar. Here he taught the Sikh doctrines, and attracted large throngs of devout followers. Later, Amritsar developed into a city, and the Golden Temple in the tank or lake became the sacred altar of the Sikh community. Arjun, the fifth Guru, compiled the first Sikh bible—the Granth, or Book. The ninth Guru, Teg-Bahadur, developed remarkable military qualities. The Mogul emperor, Aurangzeb, saw his power, captured him, and so tortured him that the Guru persuaded a fellow-captive to put an end to his sufferings. But the emperor failed to overpower the sect. It became more bitter than ever.

The tenth Guru was Govind-Singh, the son of the ninth Guru. This man became a great military leader. He gave to the whole Sikh sect a martial quality. He converted it into a vast and fearless army. He resolved on national independence. He abolished caste, and declared the perfect equality of all men.

He adopted certain regulations for the uniting of his people into a solid military force. He added the name Singh (Lion) to their other names; the hair must be worn long; a sword, in token of perpetual hostility to the Mussulmans, must always be carried; they must wear short trousers, and never use tobacco; each disciple must be admitted by a certain baptismal rite called Pahul; and an oath must be taken never to mix with certain excommunicated persons, nor worship idols, nor bow to any person except a Sikh Guru, and never to turn his back upon a foe.*

War became the one passion and employment of the Sikhs.

NARENDRA TANK, PURI.

They acquired territory, and in time the whole Panjab came under their dominion. As the Mogul empire declined they rose in power. No braver soldiers ever fought on an Indian battlefield. Their weapons, to this day, are among the most formidable implements of warfare ever forged. The weapons of the Gurus were believed to be holy, and were even worshipped. Under the tenth Guru the sect assumed a decidedly Hindu coloring. Many of the Sikhs of this day adopt caste, wear the Brahminical thread, keep Hindu festivals, observe Hindu

* For an excellent account of the Sikhs, see Ludlow, "British India," Appendix C, vol. i. pp. 296 ff.

ceremonials, and even present offerings to idols in Hindu temples.*

As the English gained power elsewhere in India, it was essential that the Panjab be conquered and occupied, as it controlled the Afghan passes into India. The Sikhs had long held that province with an iron hand. The way they treated invaders was a warning to all who might be rash enough to engage in the same venture. In 1751 it had been separated from the Mogul empire, and conducted its affairs according to its own will. The name Sikh was synonymous with a brave and victorious soldier. The English came into conflict with the Sikhs in 1808, but the latter were not thoroughly conquered, and the Panjab added to the British dominions in India, until 1849. The wars for the possession of the Panjab were very costly, in life and treasure, to the English.

The great final conflict for the possession of the Panjab was fought between the English and the Sikhs at Gujerat, near Nazirabad, the scene of the victory of Alexander the Great over Porus. The Sikhs had risked everything on this one battle, and they lost all. Among the great spoils in this final battle was the Koh-i-nur—Hill of Light—then the largest diamond in the world. It had passed from one Sikh ruler to another, after a long history of inheritance. Now it is a part of the royal regalia of England, and is worn in a brooch by Queen Victoria at her levees. It has been so cut down that now it is the fifth in size, though far the most brilliant.

VII.—The Religions of the Hill Tribes.

The Hill Tribes of India practise a worship of the grossest character. Some of them are so degraded as to have almost no religion at all, while others make a near approach to either the Hindu, Mohammedan, or Buddhist faith, and still others combine certain parts of both Hinduism and Mohammedanism. In many cases it may be said that these aboriginal tribes present as striking a contrast with the great religions of India—Hinduism and Mohammedanism—as the faith of the American Indians with the Christianity of their European conquerors.

Of the tribes of the Central Provinces the Khonds are the chief.

* Monier Williams, "Religious Thought and Life in India," pp. 177, 178.

They are of very ancient origin, as their name is mentioned in the Puranas.* Some of the Khonds have become mixed with the surrounding people, but there is a large class of unmixed Khonds.

PRINCIPAL GROTTO OF KANHERI.

These worship a common deity called Burra Deo, or other names, which is believed to be a representation of the sun. In former

* Rowney, "The Wild Tribes of India," pp. 2, 14 ff.

times human sacrifices were offered to him, but more recently the sacrifice is an image made with straw or other similar materials. Other deities venerated by them are representations of the moon and stars. But there are no temples, the places of worship being spaces in the open air, enclosed by circular walls of loose stone, while the objects worshipped are represented by two or three large stones stuck upright and smeared with oil. The Bhíls worship objects representing the sun and moon. They adore their ancestors, the tiger, and the infernal spirits. The faith of the Kolis is a very near approach to Hinduism. The Kattís recognize the sun as their chief divinity, their worship consisting of simply looking at the sun and invoking his favor.

The Kols, who live in Bengal, believe in a supreme being named Sing Bonga, who is represented by the sun. The moon is believed to be his wife, and the stars his daughters. There is a large number of local and sylvan gods, but no images are made of them, neither is there any worship beyond sacrifices. The Sontals also worship the sun-god, and venerate the spirit of Bora Manjee, a deceased and canonized chief. The Bagh-Bhoot, or tiger-spirit, is another object of reverence, and several tribes worship the living tiger. The Oraons recognize the sun as their supreme deity, but do not pray to him, on the ground that he does not send evil. Ghosts, sorceries, and witchcrafts, as with most of the wild tribes, are a part of the popular faith. The Pahariahs, while believing in a sun-god as the supreme being, accept individual tutelary deities. They believe in a future state and transmigration of souls.

In the Madras Presidency the Khonds are a leading native race. They worship the sun and the earth, as well as subordinate deities — such as rain, spring, wealth, the chase, war, boundaries, and judgment. The Todas worship a god who is represented by a rude stone. Of the Niadís the only thing known of their religion is that they sacrifice to a female spirit yearly. In the Northwest Provinces are the Limbus, who affect the Hinduism of the Nepal, but really have their own gods and goddesses, and a supreme deity. The Bhutías are for the most part followers of Buddha, or the Llama. In the Northeastern Provinces are the Abors, who worship sylvan deities; the Khamptís, who are Buddhists; and the Nagas, who worship a plurality of deities.

Missionary labor has already been inaugurated among the Hill Tribes, and with good success. The Santals and Kols have been a special object of labor by German missionaries. Henry Baker has labored among the Hill-men in Travancore, where there is now a community of two thousand Aryan Christians.* The Oraons have been successfully reached. As long ago as 1871 there were twenty-one thousand Christians among them.†

* Mateer, "Native Life in Travancore," p. 79.
† Caldwell, "The Languages of India," p. 7.

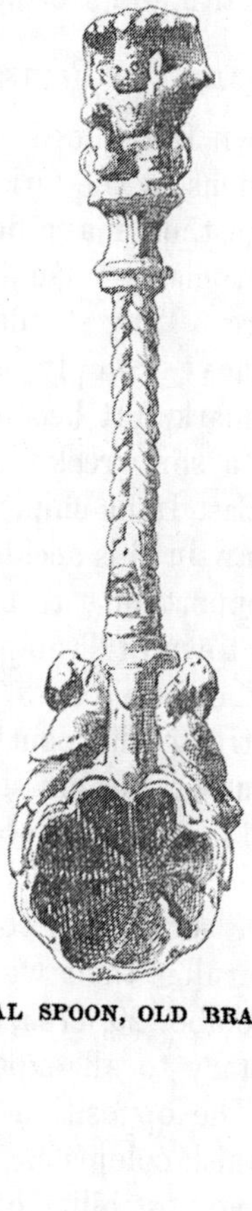

SACRIFICIAL SPOON, OLD BRASS, HINDU.

CHAPTER XLVII.

PROTESTANT MISSIONS IN INDIA.

WHILE India has attracted the commercial and military spirit of the West, its great spiritual needs have not been less potent in attracting the evangelist. The beginning was simple and obscure, but abundant in faith and sacrifice.

ZIEGENBALG AND PLUTSCHAU.

Tranquebar, a little town 180 miles south of Madras, was the cradle of Protestant missions in the Orient. That the missionaries from Denmark began their magnificent work here belongs to the region of religious romance. On July 9, 1706, Ziegenbalg and Plutschau landed here. Why should they come to this obscure and insignificant place? Simply because Tranquebar was a little possession of Denmark. It became a Danish settlement through the accident of a shipwreck. In 1618 Rolant Crape, the captain of a Danish East India ship, was shipwrecked here.

The King of Tanjor saw in this accident an advantage. Believing it to be a good opportunity to show a kindness to the Danes, he made over the town of Tranquebar to Crape, and the Danish flag floated over the little fort of Tranquebar. Frederick IV., the Danish king, instructed his court preacher, Dr. Lutkens, to take measures for sending out missionaries to Tranquebar, which early grew into an important colony. Bartholomew Ziegenbalg and Henry Plutschau, who had been students in the University of Halle, were summoned to the Danish court, and received directions concerning their work. They sailed in the *Sophia Hedwick* on November 29, 1705, and arrived at Tranquebar July 9, 1706. Contrary to all expectation, their reception was far from cordial. The opposition did not come from the natives, but from the Danish colonists. The latter told the missionaries that there was no possibility of their succeeding. This seems to have been a hope rather than a belief. The colonists wanted no missionaries. They gave the two missionaries no reception into a house, but left them all day in the tropical sun, first outside the town gates and then in the market-place. But Altrup, the secretary of the colony, afterwards secured them a lodging-place in his father-in-law's house.

The missionaries immediately began to learn Tamil and Portuguese. In five years Ziegenbalg finished the New Testament in

CREMATION-GROUND AND SACRED SHRINES OF PASHUPATI.

Tamil. By 1719, the year of his death, he had translated the Old Testament as far as Ruth. Schultz, who arrived the same year, resumed the work and finished it. This man went to Madras and translated the whole Bible into Hindustani.* The first converts in Tranquebar were five slaves. These were baptized in May, 1707. Then came schools and churches. Such

* Badley, "Indian Missionary Directory," 3d ed. Calcutta, 1886.

was the beginning of the Protestant efforts for the evangelization of India.*

Schwarz.

Schwarz, who was destined to prove an inspiration to the cause of missions the world over, arrived in Southern India in 1759, and, without waiting for a critical knowledge of the Tamil, began at once with a few words and in broken speech. Between the beginning of his work and the end there lay a period of forty-eight beautiful and consecrated years. If we consider all the qualities which constitute a sublime missionary life, the career of this man is almost without a parallel in missionary history. In calm and patient labor, in the confidence which he inspired among even the heathen who refused his message, and in the results of his work, he stands first in the lengthening catalogue of immortal missionaries.

With the death of Schwarz, in 1798, the first period of Protestant missions came to an end. The difficulties had been numerous, and of such magnitude as to terrify any spirits less brave than the heroes who made the first Protestant attack upon the dense mass of Hindu paganism.

Carey, Marshman, and Ward.

Kiernander, the first Protestant missionary in Bengal, was invited thither by Clive. But the arrival of William Carey in Calcutta, in 1793, began a new era, not alone in Indian missions, but in the history of universal evangelization. He was joined afterwards by Marshman and Ward, and the three planned for the occupation of all Northern India. Frederick VI., King of Denmark, sent word to them that he had taken their new college under his special protection, and expressed his great pleasure at the settlement of the missionaries in Serampore.

The forces of this mission radiated in all directions. The British government in India, with the Marquis of Wellesley at the head, was fearful of the Serampore press. It was thought that it would breed treason to the state, and orders were given for its suppression. But the objections were finally overcome, and the missionary work proceeded without embarrassment.

---

* Badley, article in *Central Christian Advocate*, June 25, 1887.

Martyn.

Henry Martyn, a chaplain of the East India Company, arrived in 1806, and began his brief but remarkable career in the valley of the Ganges. His success in philological achievements are, perhaps, without an equal. In less than two years after his arrival he had translated the New Testament into Hindustani, written a commentary in the same language on our Lord's parables, and begun a Persian translation of the New Testament. He was consumed by his passionate zeal for souls. He died in 1812, at the age of thirty-one, at Tokat, Asia Minor, on his way home from Persia to England. His body lies where he died, and his tombstone bears the following inscription, written by Lord Macaulay:

"Here Martyn lies! In manhood's early bloom
The Christian found a Pagan tomb;
Religion, sorrowing o'er her favorite son,
Points to the glorious trophies which he won—
Eternal trophies, not with slaughter red,
Not stained with tears of hopeless captives shed,
But trophies of the Cross; for that dear Name
Thro' every form of danger, death, and shame,
Onward he journeyed to a happier shore,
Where danger, death, and shame are known no more."

Martyn left behind an example which has been a singular force in leading many, in both England and America, to enter upon the missionary career.

Judson and Newell.

In 1812 two American missionaries, Judson and Newell, arrived in Calcutta. The British government, which had not yet learned that the Christian religion was a greater force to preserve India to England than the army itself, ordered their expulsion from the country. They were, however, permitted to go to Mauritius. After 1813, there were no further expulsions of missionaries. In due time we find Judson in Burma, beginning that career of patient and unremitting labor which has made his name illustrious in the annals of the Church universal. With the year 1830 the period of missionary limitations in India came to an end. The Bishop's College in Calcutta and the Baptist College in Serampore had been doing invaluable work, each in its own way, towards translating the Scriptures, establishing schools, and building up a Christian life among the native populations. The British government had learned that its interests in India lay in the same path with the evangelization of the country.

Duff.

Alexander Duff, a young man fresh from the University of Edinburgh, arrived in Calcutta, and immediately began to labor. He conceived the idea that there were still too many concessions to paganism in the old methods, and that the proper way to proceed was to make a new and public departure in the interests of a broad and thorough evangelization of India. He held that the native languages were too much used, and, therefore, that the natives should be taught English, and that it should be the fundamental tongue in teaching them. He opened his college in July, 1830, and boldly declared his policy—all the classes must be taught English, and the Scriptures must be taught daily, an hour, in the same tongue. It was a new measure, and shocked even missionary sensibilities. The learned Hindus resisted the measure. But Duff would not retrace his steps. All who came to his college must submit to his regulations. He began with five young men, but before the end of the first week he had over three hundred applications for admission.* His triumph was complete. The English government can never raise a monument high enough to Duff's memory, for to him mainly belongs the honor of securing the benefits of an English education to natives attending government schools.

Duff's career in India was remarkable. He had the daring of a great leader. He made several visits to Scotland and one to the United States. His eloquence, zeal, and thorough knowledge of pagan conditions in India made him irresistible in his plea for increased devotion to the cause of the evangelization of the heathen. He was the Peter the Hermit of our century. But there was this difference—Duff's crusade belongs to the high realm of permanent triumphs.

Results of Missionary Work.

The following may be regarded as an approximate result

* Sherring, "History of Protestant Missions in India," p. 106.

of missionary labors in India. The Rev. Dr. B. H. Badley, of Lucknow, is the leading authority on the statistics of missionary labor, and from his careful hand we derive our numerical statement.* There are thirty-six different missionary societies engaged in work in India. In addition to these there are at least ten private agencies.

No.	Names of Societies and Missions.	Began work in India.	Foreign Missionaries.	Native Ord'ned Agents.	Native Christians.	Communicants.
1	Baptist Missionary Society	1793	43	50	10,000	4,000
2	London " "	1798	47	44	55,029	6,221
3	American Board	1813	24	37	14,475	4,626
4	Church Missionary Society	1814	115	132	101,333	23,289
5	Gospel Propagation Society	1817	53	71	90,888	21,996
6	Wesleyan Missionary Society	1817	44	9	4,200	1,800
7	General Baptist Missionary Society	1822	8	9	3,393	1,259
8	Church of Scotland Mission	1828	17	3	1,306	396
9	Free Church of Scotland Mission	1828	32	10	1,598	1,527
10	American Presbyterian Mission	1834	36	12	1,743	1,000
11	Basel Missionary Society	1834	79	10	8,513	4,445
12	American Baptist Missionary Union	1836	27	55	64,500	28,127
13	American Free Baptist Mission	1836	6	4	1,085	558
14	Gossner's Missionary Society	1840	17	11	32,000	12,131
15	Leipzig Missionary Society	1841	25	12	13,589	4,130
16	Irish Presbyterian Mission	1841	10	—	1,418	302
17	Welsh Calvinistic Methodist Mission	1841	8	—	3,719	852
18	American Evangelic Lutheran Mission	1842	10	4	9,360	3,842
19	American Reformed Mission	1853	8	4	5,437	1,610
20	Moravian Mission	1854	3	—	36	11
21	American United Presbyterian Mission	1855	8	3	3,245	2,176
22	Methodist Episcopal Church Mission	1856	72	36	8,604	5,486
23	United Presbyterian (Scotland) Mission	1860	16	1	960	441
24	Danish Lutheran Mission	1861	6	—	481	80
25	Presbyterian Church of England Mission	1862	1	—	34	15
26	Hermannsburg Lutheran Mission	1866	11	—	800	300
27	Friends' F. M. Association "	1866	3	—	36	18
28	Indian Home Mission	1867	5	5	4,273	3,500
29	Canadian Baptist Mission	1868	9	3	4,500	1,870
30	German Evangelist Mission (U. S. A.)	1869	4	—	530	234
31	Scotch Episcopal Church Mission	1870	—	1	28	8
32	Orig. Secession Church of Scotland Miss'n.	1872	1	—	53	6
33	Canadian Presbyterian Mission	1877	5	—	126	72
34	Swedish Evangelical Mission	1877	8	—	34	16
35	American Free Methodist Mission	1880	1	—	—	—
36	Disciples of Christ Mission	1883	3	—	8	8
	Private and other Missions	....	26	4	2,421	1,152
	Total	....	791	530	449,755	137,504
	Increase since 1881	....	133	69	32,383	24,179

Including Burma and Ceylon the present number of foreign missionaries is 887 compared with 730 in 1881; foreign ordained agents, 768, against 674 in 1881. Travancore surpasses all other

* "Indian Missionary Directory," Lucknow and New York, 1886.

parts of India in missionary advance: out of a total population of 2,311,379 more than one fourth, 577,844, are Christians.*

Of the 791 foreign missionaries, 42 are sons (or grandsons) of missionaries, born in India; 25 of these are connected with American societies. The nationalities of the others are as follows:

England	275	
Scotland	78	
Ireland	17	
Wales	11	
Canada	23	404
United States		139
Germany		128
Switzerland		18
Sweden		11
Denmark		9
Others		40
Sons		42
Total		791

So far as ascertained (for even missionaries sometimes fail to answer circulars of inquiry), the American missionaries represent, as to nativity, the following states: Ohio, 19; New York, 16; Pennsylvania, 15; Massachusetts, 7; New Jersey, 7; Indiana, 6; Illinois, 7; Connecticut, 5; Maine, 4; Vermont, 3; West Virginia, 3; Iowa, 2; Wisconsin, 2; Kentucky, 2; New Hampshire, 2; Michigan, 2; Tennessee, 1; Minnesota, 1; Missouri, 1; California, 1; others, 33.

The years of service of the foreign missionaries are as follows:

Under 10 years	393
From 10 to 20 years	231
From 20 to 30 "	114
From 30 to 40 "	42
From 40 to 45 "	5
From 45 to 50 "	4
Over 50 "	2
Total	791

The veterans who have given upward of fifty years to India are the Rev. Geo. Pearce, of the English Baptists, who arrived

* Mateer, "Native Life in Travancore," p. 25.

in India in October, 1826, and is now living at Ootacamund, in South India, and the Rev. John Newton, of the American Presbyterian Mission, who was born in New Jersey in 1810, and

A KULI WOMAN, CALCUTTA.

arrived at Calcutta in February, 1835. Mr. Newton has spent most of the time at Lahor, his present station. Four sons, born in India and educated in America* (studying theology where their father did, at Allegheny, Pa.), have returned to India as missionaries. One has passed away to his reward; the others are still in the field.

Ceylon.

Number of stations (1881), 716; foreign ordained agents, 658; native ordained agents, 674; foreign lay preachers, 79; native lay preachers, 2988; churches or congregations, 4538; native Christians, 528,590; communicants, 145,097; contributions (rupees), 228,517; teachers, native Christian, 4345; teachers, non-Christian, 2539; theological and training students, 1377; Anglo vernacular schools, 472; Anglo vernacular pupils, 50,203; vernacular schools, 3703; pupils, 117,418.

Woman's work: Foreign and Eurasian female agents, 541; native Christian female agents, 1944; boarding-schools for girls, 171; boarding pupils, 6983; day schools for girls, 1281; day pupils, girls, 49,550.

Zenanas: Houses, 9566; pupils, 9228; total pupils, male and female (excluding Sunday-schools), 234,759; Sunday-school scholars, 83,321.†

This is an excellent showing, and represents an amount of faith and vigor which no imagination may depict. Between Ziegenbalg's arrival in Southern India and the present vast network of missions now extending over the country, there lies a period of less than two centuries of consecrated labor. The triumph is great, and there is abundant ground for encouragement that the time is not far distant when the gospel will reach every part of India.

Dearth of Missionary Labor.

There is danger, however, that these great achievements be overestimated. There are immense stretches of Indian territory which have not been reached, or, if reached at all, have been but scantily cultivated. We may take some examples in Bengal. Up to 1881 the district of Unao, with nine hundred thousand people, had never a missionary. The district of Burdwan, a

* See article in the *Independent* (New York), Oct. 28, 1886.

† Cf. "Statistical Tables of Protestant Missions in India, Burma, and Ceylon," for 1881. Calcutta, 1882.

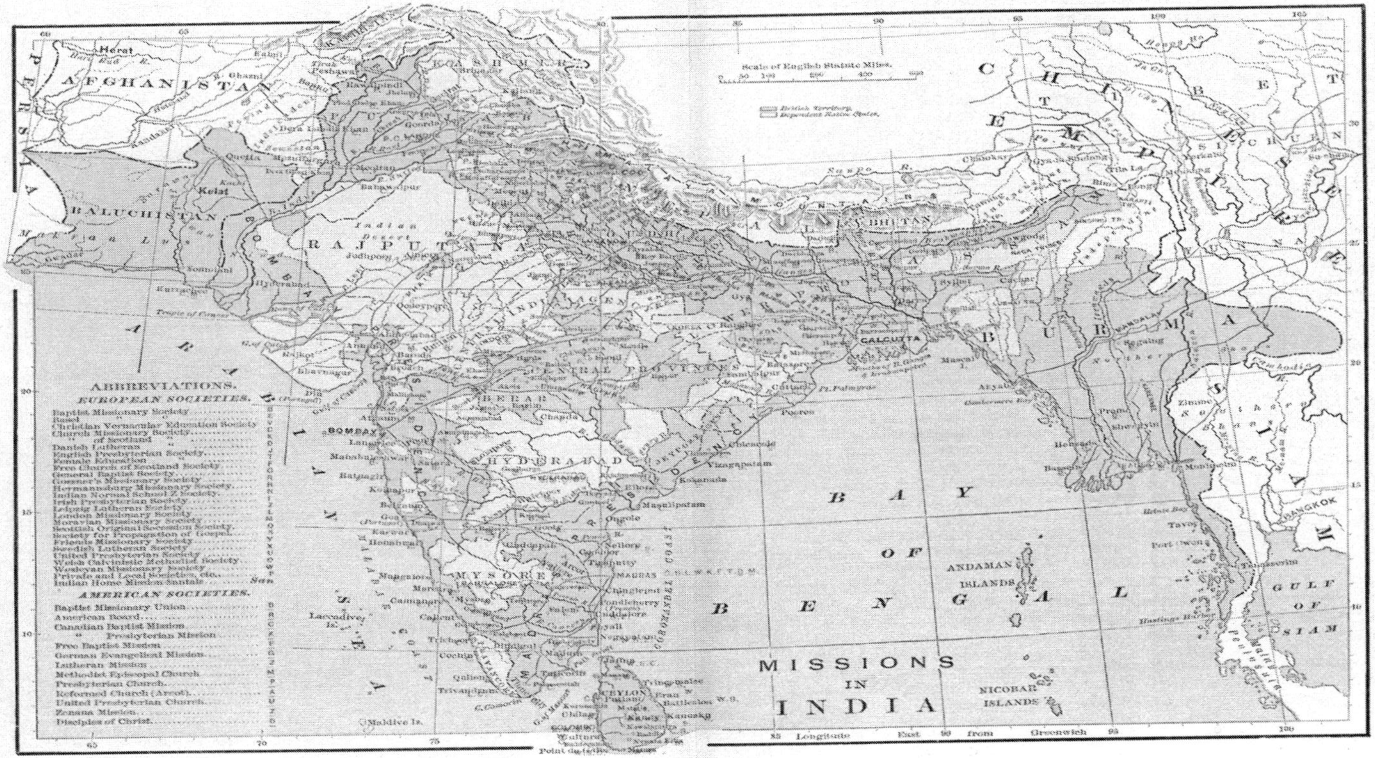

MISSIONS IN INDIA
ABBREVIATIONS.
EUROPEAN SOCIETIES.
Baptist Missionary Society
Basel
Christian Vernacular Education Society
Church Missionary Society
" of Scotland
Danish Lutheran
English Presbyterian Society
Female Education
Free Church of Scotland Society
General Baptist Society
Gossner's Missionary Society
Hermannsburg Missionary Society
Indian Normal School Z Society
Irish Presbyterian Society
Leipzig Lutheran Society
London Missionary Society
Moravian Missionary Society
Scottish Original Secession Society
Society for Propagation of Gospel
Friends Missionary Society
Swedish Lutheran Society
United Presbyterian Society
Welsh Calvinistic Methodist Society
Wesleyan Missionary Society
Private and Local Societies, etc.
Indian Home Mission Santals
AMERICAN SOCIETIES.
Baptist Missionary Union
American Board
Canadian Baptist Mission
" Presbyterian Mission
Free Baptist Mission
German Evangelical Mission
Lutheran Mission
Methodist Episcopal Church
Presbyterian Church
Reformed Church (Arcot)
United Presbyterian Church
Zenana Mission
Disciples of Christ
Scale of English Statute Miles.
British Territory.
Dependent Native States.
PERSIA
AFGHANISTAN
BALUCHISTAN
RAJPUTANA
BOMBAY
HYDERABAD
MYSORE
CENTRAL PROVINCES
BERAR
BHUTAN
BURMA
SIAM
CHINESE EMPIRE
ARABIAN SEA
BAY OF BENGAL
GULF OF SIAM
ANDAMAN ISLANDS
NICOBAR ISLANDS
CEYLON
CALCUTTA
MADRAS
BANGKOK
Herat
Quetta
Kelat
Maldive Is.
Laccadive Is.
Longitude East from Greenwich

hundred miles from Calcutta, on the East India Railway, contains an area of three thousand five hundred square miles, with one and a half millions of people. There is one missionary with nine Christian helpers. The Church has twenty-eight communicants. This district has been occupied by the Church Missionary Society since 1816.

The adjoining district of Bancoora contains about half a million of people. It has one missionary with ten Christian helpers. There are ten communicants. This district has been occupied by the Wesleyan Missionary Society since 1870. The district of Beerbhoom contains half a million of people, and has only three missionaries with nine Christian helpers. There are sixty-eight communicants. This district has been occupied by the Baptist Missionary Society since 1815.

The district of Moorshedabad contains about a million of people, and has only three missionaries with four Christian helpers. There are eighteen communicants. This district has been occupied by the London Missionary Society since 1824. The missionary workers are mainly occupied in Berhampur, with its population of twenty-seven thousand. But this district contains, besides Berhampur, one city with forty-six thousand persons, two towns with more than ten thousand, ten towns with over three thousand, fifteen villages with over two thousand, one hundred and forty-eight villages with over one thousand, five hundred and forty-seven villages with over five hundred, one thousand three hundred and seventy-three villages with over two hundred, and one thousand six hundred and fifty-four villages with less than two hundred inhabitants. This district, with its three thousand seven hundred and fifty-three towns and villages, is an occupied district, and has been so since 1824.

Jessor, containing four thousand two hundred and forty-seven towns and villages, has one missionary and five Christian helpers. Rangpur, containing four thousand two hundred and six towns and villages, has one missionary and four Christian helpers. Rajeshaye, containing four thousand two hundred and twenty-eight towns and villages, has only one missionary and seven Christian helpers.

It would seem that some such results as the following would indicate either an insufficient force or a providential indication to move out and permit other societies to enter. One district, with one million five hundred thousand people, has been occupied sixty-nine years, and the result is only thirty-five communicants. Another, with three missionaries, after seventy years, presents to-day but sixty-eight communicants. Another, with a million inhabitants, and three missionaries, presents but eighteen converts, after sixty-one years of labor.

Besides these feebly occupied districts, there are others, great and populous, without a single preacher. In British India the whole land is divided for administrative purposes into divisions and districts. A district usually contains from half a million to a million and a half inhabitants. In Oudh the districts average nine hundred thousand each; in Rohilcund, a little less. Now, taking the several governments, we have the following districts in which there are no missions:

Bengal, 10; Northern Provinces, 8; Panjab, 9; Bombay, 6; Central Provinces, 4.

To specify: Malda contains half a million of people, but has no missionary; Bagura has half a million, but no missionary; Pubna has nearly a million people, living in two thousand seven hundred and ninety-two towns and villages, but there is no missionary. These three districts, containing two millions of people, are but samples of many vast populous unworked districts throughout India. Let this, however, be noted: Here are three districts containing two millions of people, within a day's journey of Calcutta, in which no Church in all Christendom has a single missionary.

With such a picture, are not the laborers lamentably few?

Forms of Missionary Work.

It is difficult to enumerate the various forms of missionary operations. They are constantly increasing with the expanding work itself. The following may be regarded as the principal:

1. Schools.
2. Sunday-schools.
3. Preaching in churches.
4. Preaching in bazars and melas.
5. Bible translation and distribution.
6. The press—books, tracts, periodicals.
7. Training native Christians, industrial schools, agricultural projects.
8. Training native ministry, including selection, pay, testing character.

9. Woman's work. This is of broad scope, and has many branches of operation.
10. Medical work.
11. Apologetic instrumentalities: to meet present flank movements of the Somajes.

All Doors Open.

India is now open to missionary work. All the Indian gates are down; the bars are shattered into small fragments; the locks are ground into fine dust. Every stream sings a welcome to the evangelist of peace. The King of Nations is entering.

SHRINE AND TOMBS OF SWAMBHUNATH.

"... High as the herald star which fades in floods
Of silver, warming into pale gold, caught
By topmost clouds, and flaming on their rims
To fervent glow, flushed from the brink
With saffron, scarlet, crimson, amethyst;

> Whereat the sky burns splendid to the blue,
> And, robed in raiment of glad light, the King
> Of life and glory cometh!" *

The missionary often works on blindly, and his environment often leads him to disparage his own achievements. The late Rev. George Bowen, of Bombay, declared to Dr. Norman McLeod that in twenty-five years he had not made one convert to Christianity. But little he knew of his own great work. His "Guardian" was performing a service which was beyond calculation. From his great work, and his own spotless example, there will be harvests in the centuries to come.

One of the most significant signs of the Indian times lies in the fact that since the mutiny of 1857 England has learned that the Christian religion is the real, and only, basis of a permanent tenure of the country. In 1862 Lord Palmerston paid a tribute to the loyalty to the British government of the native Christians of India, and added: "It is not only our duty, but it is our interest to promote the diffusion of Christianity, as far as possible, through the whole length and breadth of India." The report of the Secretary of State and Council of India, 1871–72, says: "The government of India cannot but acknowledge the great obligations under which it is laid by the benevolent exertions made by missionaries, whose blameless example and self-denying labors are infusing new vigor into the stereotyped life of the great populations placed under English rule, and are preparing them to be in every way better men and better citizens of the great empire in which they dwell." There will be no lower attitude occupied by the government than is expressed in these strong words.

No missionary will ever again be warned off, as Judson was, from an Indian port.

* Edwin Arnold, "The Light of Asia," p. 113 (Lond. ed.).

CHAPTER XLVIII.

THE ROMAN CATHOLIC CHURCH IN INDIA.

In 1497 Vasco da Gama, after receiving absolution for himself and his crew, set sail from the Tagus, to find a new way to the Indies. Columbus had failed to find a western path; Vasco da Gama would see what he could do to find an eastern. Ten months afterwards he cast anchor off Calicut, and planted the Portuguese flag on Indian soil. Suddenly India presented itself as an inviting field for Roman Catholicism. Francis Xavier conceived the idea of converting to Christianity the Indian world. On May 6, 1542, he stepped ashore at Goa, and began those extraordinary labors which have made his name the synonym of heroism in all the communions of the Christian world. Even on shipboard he began his work of self-sacrifice. "He pillowed his head," says Kaye, "upon a coil of ropes, and ate what the sailors discarded, but there was not a seaman in that laboring vessel, there was not a soldier in that crowded troop-ship, who did not inwardly recognize the soul that glowed beneath those squalid garments. No outward humiliation could conceal that knightly spirit; no sickness and suffering could quench the fire of that ardent genius."* He made Goa his centre of operations, but visited various parts of the western and southern coasts of the peninsula. His method of work was simple, but very effective. His plan, as described by himself, was as follows: "I have begun to go through all the villages of this coast, with bell in hand, collecting together a large concourse both of boys and men. Bringing them twice a day into a convenient place, I give them Christian instruction. The boys, in the space of a month, have committed all to memory beautifully. Then I told them to teach what they had learned to their parents, household, and neighbors. On Sundays I called together the men and

---

* "Christianity in India," p. 17.

women, boys and girls, into a sacred edifice. They came together with great alacrity, and with an ardent desire to hear. Then I began with the Confession of the Holy Trinity, the Lord's Prayer, the Angelic Salutation, the Apostles' Creed, pronouncing them in their own language with a clear voice. All followed me in the repetition, in which they take an uncommon pleasure. Then I went through the Creed alone, pausing upon each article, asking whether they believed without any doubt. All in an equally confident tone, with their hand in the form of a cross on their breasts, affirmed that they truly believed it."

Xavier carried the Gospel, as he believed it, to the wildest tribes. Bercastel says, that by the year 1551 the number of converts along the fishing coast amounted to five hundred thousand.* In 1560 the Inquisition was established in Goa, and all the detailed arrangements for enforcing obedience to the decrees of the Church which were employed in Spain and Italy, such as inquisitors, qualificators, familiars, and jailers, were repeated on the far-off shore of India.

For three centuries and a half the Roman Catholic Church has been at work in India. A schism occurred, called the "Goa Schism," which long interfered with all positive advance. But that is now removed, and the Roman Catholic Church may be regarded as a unit in its system of work. The whole of British India is divided into vicariates apostolic, each vicariate being under a vicar apostolic, who is also a bishop in "countries of the unbelieving." For example, the vicar apostolic of Madras is bishop of Thermopylæ. Catechists are placed over large congregations which have no priest, who read prayers in the morning and evening, and conduct Sabbath services. When the catechist is ill, the people choose one of their own number to read.

Great attention is given to girls' schools. These are established throughout the country, and the education is conducted in a thorough manner. These schools have been so successful as to make important inroads on European and Eurasian families. Orphanages are established in many places, and agents go through the country for the purpose of securing places for those who are without any help. Higher education is cultivated. There are two very fine colleges in Calcutta and Bombay. The

* "Lettres Édifiantes et Curieuses," ix. 308.

SECTARIAL MARKS.

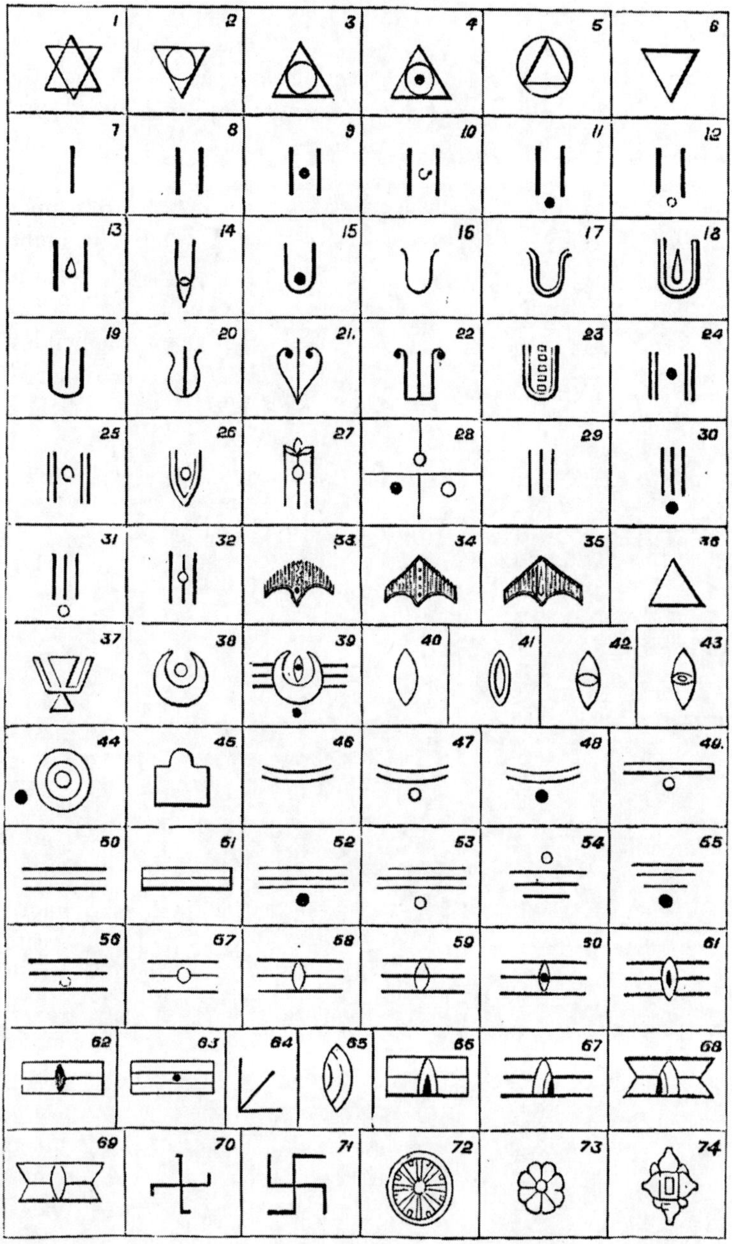

Nos. 1 to 5, Brahma, and the Trimurti. Nos. 6 to 35, Sectarial Marks of the Vaishnavas. Nos. 36 to 69, Sectarial Marks of the Saivas. No. 70, Mark of the *Sakti* sects. Nos. 71 to 74, marks of the Buddhists and Jainus.

present college in Bombay has a corps of sixteen European professors. These institutions open their doors alike to students of all confessions, and to Europeans and natives.

All the principal orders and offices of the Roman Catholic Church in Europe are represented in India. In addition to the vicars apostolic, the Roman Catholics of India have their archbishops, bishops, and a large priesthood of various nationalities—English, Irish, French, German, Belgian, Dutch, Swiss, Italian, and Portuguese.* They have cathedrals, churches, convents, chapels, and monasteries. The present numerical strength in India is about as follows:

Priests	835
Children in schools	45,171
Roman Catholic population	955,180

For Ceylon:

Priests	84
Children in schools	13,996
Roman Catholic population	203,609

The method of Roman Catholic work is modelled after Xavier's example, with such changes as experience has taught to be necessary. The missionary travels from place to place, and administers the Holy Sacrament to the people. He is received by the people with great demonstrations of joy, such as native music and banners, and is accompanied to the church. He then announces the length of his stay, and exhorts the people to profit by his presence, and approach the sacraments worthily. In the village visitation he gathers the people at 3 P.M., reads a Preparation for Confession, and leads in fervent prayer. Public doctrinal instruction is given, and realistic pictures of future rewards and punishments are held up before the people. The crucifix is held aloft, and the meaning is explained. The Act of Contrition is read, and vernacular prayers are offered. Confession begins, and continues until midnight. At sunrise the next morning the bell rings for Mass. After Mass comes Exhortation. In the afternoon the missionary receives visits from people who wish to become Christians. During the week or ten days of the

* Temple, "India in 1880," p. 167.

village visitation he baptizes, organizes, settles difficulties, and then leaves for another village, to repeat his work.*

The Roman Catholics in India differ essentially from the Protestant missionaries in their method of work. The Romanist enters into no argument against European infidelity, publishes but little except a few devotional books, does not attack with violence the pagan systems, does not visit the melas, or religious fairs, and speak to the people in miscellaneous throngs. His method is calm, conservative. He gathers the children, groups them into orphanages, never loses sight of his doctrinal system, and has a keen eye always on the increase of his flock. He looks after the poor, and teaches resignation. He never distributes a tract. Whenever he engages in controversy, he levels his pen against Protestantism. Having no family, the priest requires but little for his support, and does not have to return to Europe or America on account of the health of another. On the other hand, except in case of nuns, the Roman Catholic missionary loses all advantage of female workers and the example and influence of the Christian family.†

Have Roman Catholic missions been an advantage to India? On this point the Protestant missionaries are divided. We believe that any agency which prepares the pagan mind for casting off its idolatry is helpful towards the full truth. The greatest harvests of Protestants, so far, have been in South India, where the mission was begun by Xavier among the Tamils. No force which breaks the bond to polytheism is to be despised. The least spark of truth, on any shore, is better than none at all.

---

* Louis St. Cyr, "Catholic Missions in South India," pp. 78–80.

† "Missionary Conference of South India and Ceylon," vol. ii. p. 339. Calcutta, 1879.

CHAPTER XLIX.

AN INDO-AMERICAN ROMANCE.

One of the most romantic chapters in modern missions is the early connection between the missions of India and the Christians of New England. In Cotton Mather's curious little book, "India Christiana," published in Boston in 1721, there is as interesting a specimen of fraternal correspondence as can be found in the whole history of the Church. Ziegenbalg, the first missionary from Europe to India, had heard of Cotton Mather, who was at the time the leading representative of the Puritans of New England. Probably he arrived at his knowledge of him while a student in the Halle Orphan House. For Francke and Mather were at this time engaged in a correspondence, and it is not unlikely that Francke, with his warm evangelistic nature, spoke to his students about Mather's multifarious labors and marvellous authorship in Boston.

Afterwards, when Ziegenbalg was at work in India, he saw the need of learning from any quarter the best means of converting the heathen. He thought of Cotton Mather. He accordingly addressed a letter to him, in "Boston, West Indies," asking for advice and information as to his methods in dealing with the Indians of the West.

To this letter Cotton Mather replied in a lengthy epistle. He dated his letter Boston, New England, December 31, 1717. He concluded as follows: "My design was to Write a Letter, and not a Volume; 'tis enough to point at these things, without amplifications upon them. Reverend Sir, you plainly see, What we are; Joyned in our Minds, tho' parted by the Waters; one Soyle, though not one Soyle uniting of us. What remains is, that by Mutual Prayers to our most Merciful GOD and FATHER, we be helpful to one another. Live and prosper; always what you are and what you would be; Always Living to your Saviour; and not only very dear unto me, but also unto the whole Christian World, yea unto the Angels of GOD, unto whom you are a Spectacle." *

But Mather was not satisfied with sending words alone to his brother in the far-off East Indies. He also collected gold, from some young men (no doubt students of Harvard College), and books as well, and sent them with the letter. Both the letter and the money reached India, but were about fourteen months on the way. By this time Ziegenbalg had died, and it devolved upon his successor, Grundler, to answer the letter. He gave Mather a full account of the methods of work among the natives. I condense it as follows: We declare only one true God, who manifested himself in three persons. We consider man in his fourfold state: first, in his original blessedness; second, in his lost condition; third, in his penitent condition and a state of grace; and fourth, his state of eternal blessedness. We teach in both the Tamil and Portuguese languages. Catechists are employed, seven of whom are already in use. In their Biblical exercises they take a whole book of the New Testament, analyzing it and giving its thorough spirit and purpose. The exegetical exercise is an examination of the inward meaning of the special passage as brought out by the rules of interpretation. The theological exercise bears on the fundamental articles of faith. The catechists are instructed in all these, so that they may be able to teach the natives. The schools are free of all expense, and already eighty children are daily fed and taught. Both books and clothing are also provided them. The press is employed in printing the Old Testament in the Tamil tongue. We missionaries have our own paper-mill. It is said that there are two thousand Popish priests who go through the country endeavoring to win the natives to the Roman Catholic Church.† These, no doubt, were the successors of the missionaries first introduced by Xavier.

This letter was accompanied with some books, a translation of the New Testament into the Tamil language, and some small works, being the first-fruits of the mission press in India.

We, therefore, have three important facts showing the early relation between American Christianity and the mission field in

---

* "India Christiana," p. 74.

† Ibid., pp. 79 ff.

India: That there is every reason for believing that some of the first gifts from Anglo-Saxon Christians for the evangelization of India were from America; that one of the first full accounts of the methods of work in Indian evangelization sent to the Eng-

COTTON MATHER.

lish-speaking world was to New England; and that some of the first copies of books which came from the mission press in India and fell into Anglo-Saxon hands were sent to New England and were received by Cotton Mather.

CHAPTER L.

COUNTESS DUFFERIN FUND FOR FEMALE MEDICAL AID.

The new movement in behalf of medical aid for the women of India is one of the most important humane efforts of the present century. In far-reaching results it promises to be the greatest of all charities ever inaugurated in India, and one of the greatest in any land or age. Its origin has all the elements of a touching romance. In Punna, a city about a hundred miles from Lucknow, there lives a native prince—the Maharajah. In 1881 his wife, the Maharani, was suffering from a serious and lingering disease. Her case was desperate. It is contrary to all tradition and propriety that a male physician should enter a zenana, or lady's chamber, and make such diagnosis as might secure intelligent treatment. Besides, no European physician, or, indeed, any other European, lived in Punna. The prince had heard of Miss Beilby, a missionary physician living in Lucknow, and he sent for her to attend his suffering wife. Miss Beilby not only responded to his imploring appeal, but remained with her patient for several weeks. The Rani was restored to health through the missionary's skill and care. Miss Beilby was soon to return to England, to take her degree in a medical college. On the morning of her departure from Punna, she called at the palace to say good-by to her princely patient. The Rani was deeply affected. She had a great burden on her heart, and, dismissing all her ladies and attendants, said:

"You are going to England, and I want you to tell the Queen, and Prince and Princess of Wales, and the men and women of England, what the women of India suffer when they are sick. Will you promise me?"

The Rani was emphatic in confining her wishes to one thing—medical help for the suffering women of her dear India. But she was not willing that Miss Beilby should intrust the message to any one else; she must deliver it herself to the good Queen of England. Miss Beilby explained the great difficulty of seeing the Queen in person, and could give the Rani little encouragement that this could be brought to pass.

"But," said the Rani, "did you not tell me that our Queen

was good and gracious; that she never heard of sorrow without sending a message to say how sorry she was, and trying to help?"

The good missionary lady was willing to make the effort, but with slight hope of success in securing an audience with the Queen. When the Rani observed her readiness to do what she could, she asked Miss Beilby to write down the message at once.

"Write it small, Doctor Miss Sahiba, for I want to put it into a locket, and you are to wear this locket around your neck until you see our great Empress, and give it to her yourself. You are not to send it through another."

The locket and its precious message from the suffering heart of the Rani of Punna to the Queen of England were in safe hands. What will not a woman's heroism accomplish? In due time the knowledge of Miss Beilby's medical work in India, and of the Rani's message to the Queen, reached some of the ladies of her court. They communicated their information to the Queen, and she soon caused a message to be sent to Miss Beilby to visit her, and communicate in person whatever message she had to convey. The Queen listened attentively to all Miss Beilby had to say. The missionary handed the locket to the Queen. It was opened, and the little letter taken out and read. The Queen was profoundly impressed, and, turning to her ladies, said:

THE WALTER HOSPITAL, BUILT BY H. H. THE MAHARAJAH OF UDAIPUR, RAJPUTANA.

"We had no idea it was as bad as this. Something must be done for these poor creatures." She then gave Miss Beilby a message for the Rani, in reply to hers, and then added these words for all persons to whom Miss Beilby might speak on the sufferings of the women of India:

"We should wish it generally known that we sympathize with every effort made to relieve the suffering state of the women of India."

But the matter did not rest here. The Queen was not satisfied with the expression of a mere wish. Under the existing Gladstone ministry Lord Dufferin was appointed Governor-General for India. The Queen took pains to see Lady Dufferin before sailing, and impress upon her the importance of making some effort for bringing medical help to the women of India. Lady Dufferin gives the following simple statement of her parting visit to the Queen, and of the effect upon her own mind: "When I was leaving England, Her Majesty the Queen-Empress drew my attention to the subject, and said that she thought that it was one in which I might take a practical interest. From that time I took pains to learn all that I could of the medical question in India as regards women, and I found that although certain great efforts were being made in a few places to provide female attendance, hospitals, training-schools, and dispensaries for women; and although missionary effort had done much, and had indeed for years been sending out pioneers into the field, yet, taking India as a whole, its women were undoubtedly without that medical aid which their European sisters are accustomed to consider as absolutely necessary." *

I little thought, when I saw the magnificent reception given to Lord and Lady Dufferin on their entrance into Calcutta, and the military splendor surrounding them as they rode in state through the principal thoroughfares, amid the demonstrations of the vast multitude, what a burden was resting on Lady Dufferin's heart. The sorrows of the women of the country seem to have been constantly in her mind. Here is her own language concerning her feelings during the early part of her residence in the palace in Calcutta: "It seemed to me, then, that if only the people of India could be made to realize that their women have to bear more than their necessary share of human suffering, and that it rests with the men of this country and with the women of other nationalities to relieve them of that unnecessary burden, then surely the men would put their shoulders to the wheel, and would determine that the wives and mothers and sisters and daughters dependent upon them should in times of sickness and pain have every relief that human skill and tender nursing could afford them; and we, women of other nationalities, who are not debarred by custom or religion from employing doctors, and who have, in addition to medical aid, every variety of scene and oc-

* Article by Lady Dufferin in the *Asiatic Quarterly*, Calcutta, April, 1886. For my information concerning the details of the interview between the Maharani of Punna and Miss Beilby, and other incidents connected with the message to the Queen, I am indebted to a most interesting article by Mrs. B. H. Badley, in the Calcutta *Review*.

cupation to turn our minds from our own sufferings, we surely too should feel a deep sympathy with our less fortunate sisters, and should each one of us endeavor to aid in the work of mitigating their sufferings.

"I thought that if an association could be formed which should set before itself this one single object, to bring medical knowledge and medical relief to the women of India, and which should carefully avoid compromising the simplicity of its aim by keeping clear of all controversial subjects, and by working in a strictly unsectarian spirit, then it might become national, and it ought to command the support and sympathy of every one in the country who has women dependent upon him."

The idea of forming a national association for supplying medical aid to the women of India was the first practical effect of the Queen's wish. To Lady Dufferin belongs the honor of being the first to entertain it, and then of adopting prompt and wise measures for putting it into execution. She accordingly wrote to a number of the more prominent ladies of India, such as Mrs. Grant Duff, Lady Reay, Lady Aitchison, and Lady Lyall, and from them she received most encouraging support. She then drew up a prospectus, stating the need and her plan for its relief, which was translated into various languages and distributed throughout India. The society was formed bearing the name of the National Association for Supplying Female Medical Aid to the Women of India, and money collected was credited to the "Countess of Dufferin's Fund." The appeal was favorably received. The press throughout the country was unanimous in

HOSPITAL AND DISPENSARY BUILT BY H. H. THE MAHARAJAH OF DARBHUNGA.

approval, while the response from municipalities was equally encouraging. Certain objections, however, reached Lady Dufferin's ears. Here are her own words concerning some of them, with her half-satirical and pungent way of meeting them:

"The idea was indeed so kindly received that very few objections or unfavorable criticisms were made upon it. It may, however, be well to say something with regard to those that have come before me. A few persons maintain that the women of this country do see medical men professionally. In reply to this, I think I may safely say that they never do except in the last extremity, and that the doctor so admitted to a zenana enters with his head in a bag, or remains outside the purdah, feeling his patient's pulse, but unable to make any of the necessary examinations. Others simply state that the women do not want doctors at all, and that therefore any scheme for giving them medical relief is unnecessary and quixotic. To refute an argument properly, one should understand it, and I confess I do not understand this one. It seems to me simply to point to the total abolition of doctors, and to the extinction of medical science altogether. If women do not want doctors, then men can do without them. If the strong man, who has only ill-health, diseases, or accidents to fear, needs their services, surely the weak woman, who adds to all these liabilities the pains and troubles of childbirth, needs them too.

"I do not think, however, that, as a rule, men deny themselves medical advice; and I have even heard it whispered occasionally that a man thinks a good deal of his own little aches and pains, and can be somewhat nervous over an unaccustomed twinge. This may be a libel; but it is true that in India, as elsewhere, men have all that they require in the way of medical advice, while the women here have not, and the object of this scheme is to remedy an accidental injustice."

Such words as these present not only a full justification for the proposed object of the Association, but for the medical work which is now an important arm of missionary service on the part of all the societies. Besides, it must not be forgotten that for the very idea which resulted in the founding of the Association the whole Church is indebted to a lady serving under one of the English missionary societies.

The Association has now been at work about four years. Its objects are grouped into three great departments.

1. Medical Tuition. This includes the teaching and training in India of women as nurses, hospital assistants, and regular physicians for every department of medical practice. Lady Dufferin says that for the present the services of English and American ladies must be chiefly relied on, but that India must look to itself for a large, and even wholesale, supply of female doctors for the future.

2. Medical Relief. This includes (*a*) the establishment, under female superintendence, of dispensaries and cottage hospitals for the treatment of women and children; (*b*) the opening of female wards under female superintendence in existing hospitals and dispensaries; (*c*) the provision of female medical officers and attendants for existing female wards; (*d*) and the founding of hospitals for women where special funds or endowments are forthcoming.

THE DUFFERIN HOSPITAL, NAGPUR, BUILT BY THE CENTRAL PROVINCE BRANCH.

3. The supply of trained female nurses and midwives, for women and children in hospitals and private houses. This relates to women who have passed the stage of tuition, and who, whether native, European, or Eurasian, are qualified to undertake the duties of their profession; the Association will endeavor to place these in the ordinary manner, and there is nothing special to be noted on this point.

The National Association has received some criticism from some of the missionaries, who suppose that there is a measure of antagonism to their already flourishing medical work for women in India. Lady Dufferin has met with this objection, and gives reasons why the Association does not interfere with their work. She welcomes missionary societies to affiliation with the Association, and holds that in a country of such great needs there is work enough for all. The exact relation of the Association to the missionaries is as follows:

"The National Association cannot employ missionaries, nor can it provide hospital accommodation in which it is intended to combine medical treatment with religious teaching. It may, in certain cases, be glad to avail itself of medical missions as training agencies, and may occasionally attach an assistant to a mission dispensary in order to give that assistant the benefit of further training on leaving college under a female doctor's supervision; but in such cases it would have to be clearly understood that the assistant's duty would be strictly confined to medical work. No officers in the employ of the National Association can be allowed to exercise a missionary calling.

"The National Association does not undertake to provide funds for the travelling expenses or establishment of medical missionaries. While it is compelled to stand aloof from the medical missions, yet it has a philanthropic work in common, and has no wish to be considered antagonistic to them. The policy of the National Association with regard to them is one of non-intervention, and they should be left undisturbed in places where they are already established, except in the case of very large towns, where there is room for a second medical establishment, or when the municipality or the inhabitants of the district supply the funds necessary for obtaining the services of another female doctor; then it would be our duty to aid such a locality in procuring the desired medical assistance."

I do not doubt that such adjustments will be made, when the Association shall be fairly at work, as will be satisfactory to all the missionary societies. Indeed, it would be strange if the contributions for medical effort by the societies were not greatly increased, in time, by such development of sentiment as must result from the work of the National Association, and such emphasis be placed upon the need of medical help for the women of India as can be seen in the organization of a National Association with the avowed object of relief.

The National Association has already published three reports

—for 1886, 1887, 1888. These have been supplemented by an excellent little volume by Lady Dufferin herself.* Branches are organized in Bengal, Madras, the Central Provinces, the Panjab, and the Northwest Provinces. Local committees are constituted all over the country; and not only Englishmen, occupying prominent positions as officers and civil servants, but leading Eurasians and native rulers and scholars have espoused the cause with great enthusiasm. Lady Dufferin's appeal for a collection in honor of the Queen's Jubilee, to be appropriated to the medical care of the Indian women, met with a magnificent response. These sums are likely to increase every year, and the whole country to be covered with a network of affiliated associations. In some sections the enterprise is taking the shape of permanent endowment, so that to continue and develop the institutions will not depend at all on annual subscriptions, but on a certain and fixed revenue. In Rajputana, for example, two princes gave $190,000, which completed the endowment of the permanent fund of that country for the medical care of women. Down to the present time the total amount received by the Central Fund is about seven lakhs, or $280,000.

In evidence of the kindly feeling of Lady Dufferin towards the women who serve the different missionary societies as medical missionaries, I may add that in her last report she publishes a directory of the female doctors practising in India. From this list it appears that there is a total of sixty-five, and that of this number nineteen are from the United States.

---

* "Record of Three Years' Work of the National Association" (London, 1889), p. 22.

CHAPTER LI.

THE CRADLE OF MISSIONS IN NORTH INDIA.

LITTLE Serampore is fragrant with missionary memories. Ziegenbalg, Schwarz, Schulz, and others had represented the Danish and German missionary societies in the south. Then, wherever the English soldiers had gone, there were chapels of the Church of England, where services were held, but rather to keep up the old ecclesiastical associations than from any determined and aggressive spirit to make India a Christian land. But Serampore

BAPTISM AT NATIVE CHAPEL, SERAMPORE, THE FIRST NATIVE CHURCH IN NORTH INDIA.

has a profounder spiritual significance, and its memories reach deeper than any other spot in that wonderful land. It represents the first English purpose to bring to pass, in the realm of Christian life, what Clive and Hastings achieved by military and civil triumphs.

The day when William Carey walked up the bank of the Hugli, and fixed the site for a home in Serampore, was as important for India as Clive's victory at Plassey. It meant the determination of Anglo-Saxon Christians to plant the cross in every part of India. Without the band at whose head Carey stood, and without the Christian life which they were the means of introducing, it is safe to say that all the fruits of Plassey would have been lost, and that the jewel of India now in Victoria's crown would never have found its way there. England, with all her debt to her brave soldiers in that land, owes a still greater one to her missionaries, to whom she has never given either peerage or estate.

Carey had nothing but discouragement when he wished, while yet in England, to link his fortunes with the evangelization of India. But the young shoemaker would not "sit down." He turned his face towards the burning sun. He was not permitted to work in Calcutta. Those were the days when the East India Company was paying millions to sustain the corrupt worship of false faiths, and there must be no interference with traditions. But the man had still the habit of not knowing how to "sit down." He conceived the happy thought of a movement in the rear of the hostile camp. If he was ordered out of Calcutta, there was this little town of Serampore, just fourteen miles back of the metropolis, over which the East India Company had no control. In the earlier part of the seventeenth century a little trading company from Denmark had bought the place, and still owned it. The Danish flag floated over it. Here Carey was safe. Here, too, came Marshman and Ward. If one will measure achievements by their results, and by their power to project themselves into the distant future, the triumphs of three missionaries throw into total eclipse the proudest deeds of any Roman triumvirate.

What is Serampore to-day? The answer is easy. In 1845 the English government bought the place of the Danish kingdom, and the Queen's flag has floated over it ever since. But before that date it had already done its work. Carey, Marshman, and Ward had established their college, had set up their printing-presses, had honeycombed the false faiths by their fearless exposure of their immoral monstrosities; had sent missionaries up the entire valley of the Ganges, and had scattered far and wide the Bible and Christian literature in the popular vernaculars. Before the great Carey's tired feet were permitted to walk the "starry plain," he had the joy of knowing that the gospel was preached in forty Indian languages and dialects. When Calcutta opened its gates for the missionary from every land, there was no further need of Serampore. It had fought its fight, and won a footing in the metropolis. The Serampore of to-day, therefore, is only a memory and an inspiration.

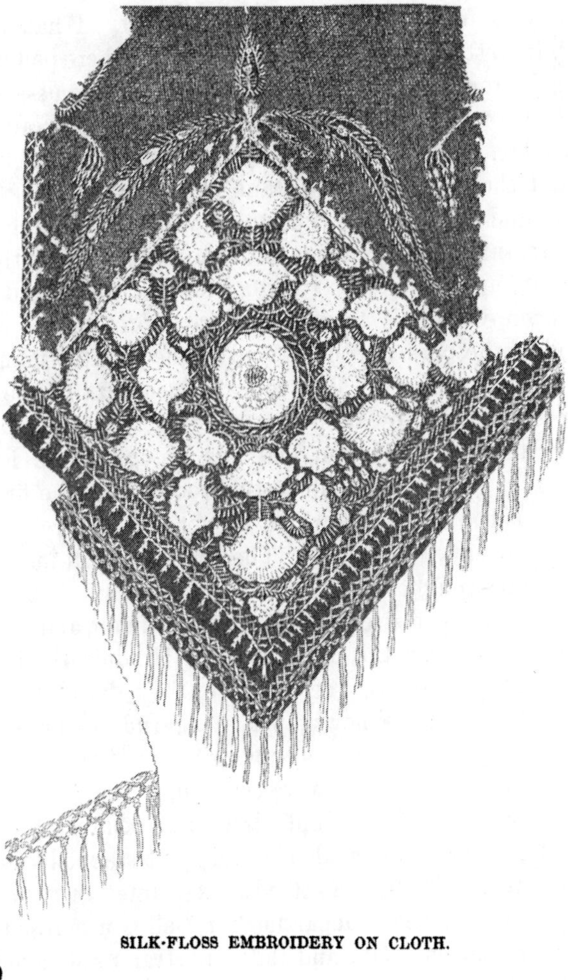

SILK-FLOSS EMBROIDERY ON CLOTH.

CHAPTER LII.

A WALK THROUGH OLD SERAMPORE.

Everything in Serampore recalls the past. I had no little difficulty in getting into the college building where had wrought side by side, for many long years, the three great missionaries—Carey, the poor cobbler; Marshman, the weaver's son; and Ward, the carpenter. There are but few students now. A little patience, and the sending to a distant part of the town, brought the keys; and I had ample time to inspect the building and its literary treasures. The college stands on the bank of the river, and from its upper windows I had a broad and beautiful view of the Governor-General's home at Barrackpore, on the opposite bank, and of the park beyond it, and of the country many miles up and down the Hugli. The roof of the piazza of the college building is supported by six pillars, of sixty feet in height. The imposing staircase is of iron, and was brought from England, probably as a gift. The main lecture-room is on the first floor. Above this is the large hall, which is over one hundred feet long and nearly seventy feet broad. The library is still undisturbed. The men who wrought here seem to have had upon them the spell of destiny. Each pen-stroke of Carey, Marshman, and Ward was a thunderbolt against the pagan wall of Hinduism. They had the power of prevision. For example, they dared to issue in March 31, 1818, a little newspaper in an Indian language, the *Sumachar Durpun*. That was the beginning of the large native journalistic productions which we see to-day.

Little souvenirs of Carey and his two associates lie here and there, as if the three immortals had only just stepped away from their desks to furnish new matter to the printer, or to say good-by to a young missionary departing for Delhi, or across the Bay of Bengal to Burma. Old and faded portraits still hang about the walls. Here are representations in oil of each member of the immortal missionary trio; Zoffany's portrait of Madame

Grand; and faded pictures of Frederick VI. and his wife, of Denmark.

Carey applied himself with great industry to the flora of India, and here are his botanical collections, a priceless treasure to the science of all time. The shelves abound in valuable books. Works in English constitute the least valuable part of the collection. The missionaries early learned that, to pull down paganism, they must first know what it is. Hence they collected rare Hindu and Pali manuscripts, on crude paper and on palm leaves, or in any shape in which they could find them. They brought them here, deciphered them, and then told the world the secret of their absurdities. The books now in this library which have grown out of the old and now dying faiths of India would be beyond price

THE COLLEGE AT SERAMPORE.

in the British Museum, or any other collection in the world. As bibliographical curiosities alone they are worthy of the closest study, for they illustrate exactly the old Indian methods of perpetuating letters. Sanskrit manuscripts are in rich abundance. Even Tibet has been made to yield some of its stores, for one finds on these shelves some fine manuscripts in the language of that country. Nor did these laborious and keen-eyed men forget the days of the great Mogul rulers, for here is the identical account of the apostles which the Jesuits presented to the Emperor Akbar. Those were the days in which to find literary gems. When these men first began to gather in India, it was easy to find rare treasures. The collectors have since scoured the country, and the glass cases in the great European libraries now contain what could be readily found and cheaply bought a century ago.

The old Danish church is at some distance from the college. It is small, and seats only about one hundred people, but abounds in memorials of the old times, when Christian missions were in their infancy in India. There are tablets in masonry of the three great missionaries. Lord Wellington, when only Arthur Wellesley, was a contributor to the building—probably the restoration of an older one on the same spot. But the missionaries are not buried here. The little cemetery where they lie is in another part of the town. Here is Carey's epitaph, written by himself:

WILLIAM CAREY,
Born 17th of August, 1761,
Died 9th of June, 1834.

A wretched, poor, and helpless worm,
On Thy kind hands I fall.

As a picture of unselfish labor on the part of three men, I know of no parallel to their mutual understanding. Here is a part of their stipulation: "Let us give ourselves up unreservedly to this glorious cause. Let us never think that our time, our gifts, our strength, our families, or even the clothes we wear, are our own. Let us sanctify them all to God and his cause. . . . If we give up the resolution which was formed on the subject of private trade when we first united at Serampore, the mission is from that hour a lost cause."

These men were in demand for outside labors, and drew large salaries. For thirty years Carey was professor in the Fort William College, down in Calcutta, and received a salary of five hundred dollars a month for his duties there, and as Bengali translator to the government. But all his dollars went into the common purse for evangelizing the Hindus. The three men and their families ate at a common table, and drew from the common fund only the pittance of twelve rupees, or four dollars and eighty cents, per month, each, for his support. Everything went towards the support of the out-stations, casting types, and the translating and printing of the Scriptures. The expense to the Serampore mission for the Chinese version alone was over one hundred thousand dollars.*

* Malcom, "Travels in Hindustan and China" (London ed. 1844), p. 62.

I have before me two Reports of these missionaries. Each is a "first" one, and now a rare pamphlet in any missionary collection. One Report is of the Institution for the Encouragement of Native Schools in India. It was issued in 1818. It shows that there were already one hundred and three schools under the care of this central one, and that six thousand seven hundred and three children had been taught. The other Report is that of the college, dated 1819, and issued by the Serampore press. It gives an account of the methods of instruction, the subjects taught, and the broad field whence the students came. There was a full

THE TOMB OF DR. CAREY.

corps of professors, and thirty-seven students were in attendance. Endowment there was none. Müller, of Bristol, never raised his flag of trust higher than this: "On the subject of funds for the college, the committee frankly confess that, beyond a humble trust in the divine goodness, and a reliance on the generosity of the public, they have no dependence whatever." *

The omissions in these reports are more remarkable than any statements which they contain. Here was a grand opportunity to say something about the enormous ignorance of the people,

* First Report of the College, p. 13.

of the absurd cosmogony to be corrected, and especially of the gross superstition and inhumanity of the ruling native faiths. But not a word is uttered. Every sentence is as calm, though not as cold, as the icy cone of Mount Everest. No prejudice is awakened. But the one golden thread which pervades all is, India needs, and must have, and is sure to have, the saving Word of Life.

The many years during which these men labored together, and the beautiful brotherhood of intense Christian work, must have presented a rare picture of the division of cheerful labor. They grew tired—as did Wesley of keeping his accounts—of drawing a few rupees a month for their support, and in 1817 each drew only what he needed. Neither laid up any property for himself. Carey died penniless. Marshman was the last to fall, and Malcom relates that when he visited him, in 1836, he was sixty-nine years old, but still a hard worker: "His eye is not dim, nor his step slow. He leads the singing at family worship with a clear and full voice; preaches with energy; walks rapidly several miles every morning, and devotes as many hours every day to study as at any former period."*

A week after my visit to Serampore I enjoyed the hospitality of the home of Dr. Lazarus, of Benares. Mrs. Lazarus is a relative of the Marshmans, had spent much of her early life in Serampore, and gave me some facts which came under her own observation, in illustration of the life which the three brothers led. Carey never would lose a moment. He carried his work with him, no matter where he went. Every day he needed two hours to ride down to his lectures and translating in Calcutta. But he had fixtures so placed in his wagon that he could consult his books and write almost as conveniently as at home. He thus utilized these four hours a day.

Carey had his times. Whatever the weather, on the first day of every March he appeared in his full suit of white cotton. When the first of November came, he was just as certain to appear at breakfast in his black dress. These colors he never changed until the date came round again. Three cups of tea, three pieces of toast, and two eggs were his unvarying breakfast. One of his daughters, Dolly, married a Mr. Baker, and

* "Travels in Hindustan and China," p. 63.

Carey and his wife had a certain evening every week on which they went to the daughter's house and took tea with the family. It was his habit, when about leaving his own home, to say to his wife: "Grace, put some tea in a piece of paper, for you know Dolly's tea won't be good."

BIRD-OF-PARADISE.

CHAPTER LIII.

THE SCEPTICAL INVASION OF INDIA.

One of the most serious questions connected with the press in India is the presence of sceptical tendencies. There is a break-up of the old faiths throughout the country. The trend is towards either Christianity or infidelity. Many of the learned natives would rather see the infidel writings from England and America introduced into India than Christianity. There are six hundred native newspapers in India, all of which, with the exception of about six, are bitterly opposed to the Christian religion. The natives associate Christianity with the downfall of their ancient nationality, and the incoming of Western ideas. They welcome anything which will arrest Christianity. They have drifted away from their ancestral faith, and have not accepted another. They are without any religious desire or principle. That is the status of the average educated Hindu to-day.*

A parallel to the India of to-day is to be found in the universal disruption of religions of the Roman Empire in the first three centuries of our era. Happily, Christianity was aggressive enough to step in and take the place of the dying systems.

To India the most sceptical productions of the American and English press are sure to come. The infidel magazines reach the country by the first mail. Bradlaugh's writings are familiar to the people of Madras, just as Paine's "Age of Reason" is to the people of Calcutta and Bombay. Sir William Robinson says that Bradlaugh's writings are doing more harm than all the absurdities teeming from the native press. The *Free Thinker's Text-Book* and the *National Reformer* are eagerly read. The *Philosophic Inquirer*, published in Madras, is a thoroughly sceptical serial. It makes the "*National Reformer* its prototype, Bradlaugh its hero, and Annie Besant its heroine. It

* Slater, Paper in "Miss. Conf.," vol. i. p. 122 ff.

produces some of the foulest impieties of the West." A rich citizen of Madras spends a large sum every year in importing French and English works, and distributing them among his countrymen. One of these, the "Bible in India," a translation of Jacolliot's books, tries to prove that the Hebrew and Christian revelations have their origin in Hinduism.

Mr. Slater says that he has met, in his visits, with Mirabeau's "System of Nature," carefully underlined, as the only book in the possession of the native. The owner said he believed in, and troubled himself about, only what he could see. Even foreigners aid in this wretched business. A Madras army surgeon has been employing himself in delivering lectures to a Hindu literary association in favor of the Positive Philosophy. He gave two hours, on Sunday afternoon, to this work. When sceptical difficulties in connection with the Bible were brought to him, he said as much against revelation as he could. Even societies are being organized to reproduce and propagate the sceptical writings from England and America. An important one exists in Lahor, while another has its headquarters in Benares. Societies in England which are free-thinking find a ready harvest in India. The English Secular Society is a fair illustration. Its destructive work is thus characterized in the *Journal of the Transactions of the Victoria Institute*, London, for 1885: "It seems necessary to call attention to the *immense exportation by the English Secular Society* of quasi-philosophical publications of *an avowedly atheistic character not only to her colonies, but also to the great cities of the whole world.* These societies are also indirectly promoting the secularization of education in India and the colonies, even in schools founded by Christians for mixed education." In a circular signed by Lord Shaftesbury and others, dated June, 1883, was the following: "The literature of India itself is very inferior, and shoals of atheistic and infidel publications are every year being sent to India from England. It is the bounden duty of Christian men to counteract this evil by aiding to create a healthy Christian literature."

The natives who still adhere to the old Hindu faiths are loath to give up the struggle. When means are at their command they do not hesitate to use them to prop up the tottering systems. Native rajahs interest themselves in circulating Hindu tracts, and have adopted shrewd methods to carry on their work. The Rev. S. P. Jacobs reports that the country seems flooded with literature opposing Christianity; that the Calcutta Theosophical Society receives a large subscription from a Maharajah; and that the Madras Free Thought Tract Society, in addition to its tracts, supports a sceptical monthly. The following, from one of its tracts, is a high compliment to the aggressive spirit of the missionaries, and is also a fair illustration of the kind of logic used to support the decaying Hinduism: "How many hundreds of thousands have these *padres* [missionaries] turned to Christianity, and are still turning? How many hundreds of thousands of dear children have they swallowed up? . . . If we sleep as heretofore, in a short time they will turn all into Christianity without exception; and our temples will be changed into churches. So, if, as we see, no converts are coming into Hinduism, and every year multitudes are going over to Christianity, there will not be a single Hindu left." In Lahor 50 rupees are collected every month for preaching Islam in the open air. In Bombay 16,000 rupees are subscribed towards making converts to the same faith. Of the one hundred and three newspapers in North India, all but two are opposing Christianity. About the same relation exists in South India. Special agnostic papers are published by educated natives. Five Mohammedan papers join the Hindu in this form of antagonism.* The Rev. Mr. Craven says that he knows of one rajah who is printing just now, at his own expense, two million of Hindu tracts, and intends to distribute them at the larger fairs in North India. The pictures of the gods best known to the Hindu pantheon are even lithographed in Germany and England, and brought out to Calcutta, and sold for native worship. I bought a package of these highly colored and realistic representatives of the leading gods of the Hindu pantheon, and have brought them home as accurate proofs of how the Anglo-Saxon, unintentionally, helps to continue Hindu polytheism. Though bought in Calcutta, they were manufactured under the shadows of the Protestant churches of England. A recent Baptist mission report says: "There are printing-presses in Rangoon, one of them a steam press, owned and conducted by natives, which

* Jacobs, "Our Mission Press in Madras;" also, "India: A Safe Investment," 1888.

are devoted to the printing of a Buddhist literature, and cheap editions, put in attractive forms, are exposed for sale on pagoda

A HINDU MENDICANT PILGRIM.

platforms, at steamer landings on the river, and wherever people are likely to congregate in all parts of Burma." There can be no doubt that a merely secular education in India is harmful. Religious instruction must accompany all educational processes. "Doubts as to all revelation and religion," says Mateer, "and a general spirit of scepticism, are often produced by a merely secular education in the minds of Indian students. They experience a constant oscillation of ideas and opinions which puzzle and distress them, without seeing their way to accept the definite teaching and authoritative revelation of divine truth which the Bible conveys. 'If we believe in one revelation, or incarnation,' argue some, 'we might as easily believe in ten.' In India a purely secular education and an acquaintance with Western science are taking from the people their ancestral religion and destroying all faith. Infidelity, atheism, and universal scepticism are being introduced along with European literature and culture; and unless we hasten to give them the Gospel of Jesus Christ they will be cast adrift, without chart or compass, on a sea of doubts and errors."* England is making an educated India. But she is not making a Christian India. The five national universities and the seventy or more colleges of the State are not teaching Christianity. The Bible and its teachings are excluded. The Rev. Dr. T. J. Scott, of Bareilly, in an article on the "Moral Education for Young India," in the *Calcutta Review* (1888), presents a terrible arraignment against the connivance of the educational department of the government at the sceptical tendencies in the schools and colleges, and even shows that, in one case at least, in the support of moral teachings in the Panjab University the "natives have outrun the government." Dr. Scott, with withering logic, exposes the emptiness of the "neutrality" attitude in teaching, and proves that the moral education in the government schools and colleges of India is reduced to zero.

This is a matter the missionaries cannot control. They are driven to establish schools of their own. They see their need and the opportunity, and they will not be slow to use their power to the utmost.

The greatest need in India to-day is a colossal reinforcing of Christian publishing agencies. Where there is one press, with scanty support, there ought to be a thousand, with immense resources for publishing large editions of the most important religious works from England and the United States.

---

* "Native Life in Travancore," p. 401.

CHAPTER LIV.

THE SOMAJES OF INDIA.

During the last half-century there has sprung up in India an important departure from the old Brahmanic faith. The Hindus have always claimed that their system is not a fixed thing, but that it admits of enlargement, and adaptation to changed conditions. Hinduism holds to the idea of new light and great changes, answering to the development of the times and the growth of the race. The presence of Christianity in India, and of its growing power over the native mind, has been the great factor in causing discontent with the Brahmanic faith in its old and stagnant form. The new reformatory movement within the Hindu fold has a theistic, and not a polytheistic, basis. It has already undergone serious changes; but every change has only proven the dissatisfaction of the educated native minds with the old idolatry. Down to the present time there have been four distinct associations, each with its literature, apostles, churches, and zealous adherents.

I.—The Adi Brahmo Somaj.

This is the original society. It was established by the Rajah Rammohun Roy, who was born in 1780 and died in 1833. He formally inaugurated his movement by opening a prayer-hall in Calcutta, where he welcomed men of all creeds to worship the one true God. He gave a certain theological direction to the movement. But the first practical form for a permanent society was given by his successor, Debendra Nath Tagore, who in 1843 presented to the friends of the movement a solemn covenant, signed first by himself and then by the remaining adherents. By this they bound themselves to cultivate the habit of daily prayer and to give up idolatry.

In 1858 the Adi Somaj received its first great impulse, when a young man, Keshub Chunder Sen, then in his twenty-first year, joined the society. His brilliant and fertile mind, eloquent speech, boundless enthusiasm, and rich acquirements of European knowledge, fitted him for this new position. He soon rose to great influence, and imparted to the Somaj an enthusiasm which it had not possessed. Up to this time the Adi Brahmo Somaj had no missionaries. But Sen gave up his position in the Bank of Bengal, and others united with him, and they devoted their energies to advancing the new faith.* In 1861 he made a journey to Krishnaghar, and later created a great sensation in Madras and Bombay. In 1862 he was formally acknowledged as an Achargi, or Minister of the Somaj. Tagore was more conservative than his young companion, and though he was induced to throw off some of the accompaniments of the strict Brahmanic faith, he would not go the full length to which the brilliant and radical Sen was rapidly hastening. Embarrassments and differences arose. Finally, Sen presented the following ultimatum as a condition of remaining in the Adi Brahmo Somaj: That the external sign of caste distinctions, such as the Brahmanic thread, should no longer be used; that none but Brahmos of sufficient ability and good moral character, who lived consistently with their profession, should conduct the services of the Somaj; and that nothing should be said in the Somaj expressive of hatred or contempt for other religions. The ultimatum was rejected. The result was that Sen and his friends seceded, and laid the foundation of a new society—the Brahmo Somaj of India.

The theology and philosophy of the Adi Somaj underlie all the new systems. The founder, Rammohun Roy, was a diligent student of theology, and mastered the English, Bengali, Sanskrit, Arabic, Persian, Greek and Hebrew languages, with a view to study the sacred writings of Hindus, Mohammedans, and Christians in the original. He arrived at the belief that a union of all religions could be effected under a form of monotheism. He established and endowed a prayer-house in Calcutta, from which he excluded all idolatry, with the purpose of "promoting the contemplation of the Author and Preserver of the Universe," and strengthening the bonds of union between

* Article on Brahmoism, "The Progressive Somaj," by Ram Chandra Bose, in the *Indian Evangelical Review*, July, 1883.

men of all religious persuasions and creeds. "His creed was simple rationalism." "He strove to please everybody, and succeeded in pleasing no one."* He claimed adherence to Jesus "as the sole guide to peace and happiness;" as "the founder of truth and of true religion;" and as "the spiritual Lord and King of Jews and Gentiles." But he did not admit the divinity of Jesus, in the Scriptural sense. He was a unitarian, and constituted the Upanishads, and not the New Testament, the canonical scriptures of his association. His faith was a sad mixture of pantheism and monotheism. In attempting to reconcile all religions, he failed to find unity anywhere. His successor, Debendra Nath Tagore, made little improvement on the frail foundation which he found. Mr. Dall reports this: "On first visiting Debendra Nath Tagore, in 1855, I asked him whether he ever allowed the name of Jesus to be heard in his church?"

"No, never," he replied.

"And why not?" I said.

"Because some people call him God."

When Debendra Nath Tagore organized his church in Calcutta there was a formal announcement of the abandonment of polytheism. This is the covenant which he and his twenty friends signed:

"1. I will live devoted to the worship of that one supreme Brahma who is the creator, preserver, and destroyer (of the universe), the cause of deliverance; all wise; all pervading; full of joy; the good; and without form. I will worship him with love, and by doing things that will give him pleasure.

"2. I will worship no created thing, as the supreme Brahma, the Creator of all.

"3. Except on days of sickness or calamity, I will every day, when my mind shall be at rest in faith and love, fix my thoughts in contemplation on the Supreme.

"4. I will live earnest in the practice of good deeds.

"5. I will endeavor to live free from evil deeds.

"6. If, overcome by temptation, I perchance do anything evil, I will surely desire to be free from it and be careful for the future.

"7. Every year, and in all my worldly prosperity, I will offer gifts to the Brahmo Somaj.

"8. O God! grant unto me that I may entirely observe this excellent religion."

The creed is beautiful enough, but it is one of only high mo-

* Ram Chandra Bose, article "Brahmoism—The Adi Somaj," in *Indian Evangelical Review*, Calcutta, 1883.

rality. When Sen proposed to advance beyond it, and make important approaches to positive Christianity, his overtures were rejected, and he left the Adi Brahmo Somaj and founded the Brahmo Somaj of India, or, as often designated, "The New Dispensation." The present president of the Adi Brahmo Somaj is Rajinarain Bose. Debendra Nath Tagore, Jr., is a member of the managing committee. This society is constantly declining. Its aggressive character was lost with the departure of Sen. In both numbers and teaching it is losing its hold. Many of the persons who were its members, and signed its covenant, have disappeared as protestants against the Brahmo faith, and lapsed into idolatry or indifference. The four fundamental principles which the few followers still adhere to are the following: "That God alone existed from the beginning, and created the universe; that he is omnipotent, omniscient, immutable, benevolent, and supreme; that by the worship of him alone can the greatest good in this life and the life to come be obtained; and that to love him and do the works he loves constitute his worship."

II.—The Brahmo Somaj of India.

This association was organized in 1866, and went forth before the world as the Bharatvarsya Brahma Somaj—the Brahma Somaj of India. Sen became its secretary and the practical administrator of its affairs. There was no president, God alone being recognized as head.* A selection of theistic texts was published, taken from the sacred writings of the Hindus, Mohammedans, Parsis, Jews, and Christians. These, with the Brahma Sangit and Sankistan, or Hymns and Choruses, were used in the Somaj services. The following motto, from the Bhagavadgita, accompanied the texts:

> "As the bee gathereth honey from flowers great and small, so does the really wise man gather substantial truth from the chaff of all scriptures, great and small."

Two religious newspapers existing before the schism—the fortnightly *Dharma Tattva* (Religious Truth), and the weekly *Indian Mirror*, which Chunder Sen was allowed to take possession

---

* Slater, "Keshub Chunder Sen and the Brahmo Somaj," pp. 48 ff. Madras, 1884.

of, were utilized industriously by the new Somaj. The Society now addressed itself to great reforms, and, going far beyond the philosophical limits of the Adi Somaj, boldly invaded the sphere of religion. It made relentless war on the social evils of the Hindu system. Pamphlets of progressive character, in Bengali and English, were published and circulated widely. Female education was advanced; child marriages were condemned; widow re-marriage was advocated; and, directly through Chunder Sen's labors, in 1872, the government passed an act legalizing Brahmo and civil marriages. This last was the great social reform of Chunder Sen's remarkable career. As an evidence of the prompt invasion of the rigid caste system by the Brahmo Somaj, during nineteen months of 1876 and 1877 there were eighteen Brahmo marriages, of which ten were intermarriages between persons of different castes, and four were widow marriages. The bridegrooms' ages ranged from nineteen to thirty-seven, and the brides' from fourteen to twenty-six; while eleven of the eighteen brides were specified as "educated." From July, 1861, to August, 1879, there were ninety-three Brahmo marriages, thirty-five of the brides being widows.*

KESHUB CHUNDER SEN.

With the public appearance of Chunder Sen the reformatory or theistic movement passed from the narrow limits of the Bengali into the English language. Chunder Sen was very active with his pen. In 1865 he published his "True Faith," a devotional book, somewhat after the manner of Kempis's "Imitation

* "Brahmo Year Books," for 1877–79, edited by S. D. Collet, London.

31

of Christ." In 1873 he published his "Essays, Theological and Ethical," and in 1872 and 1873 his "Brahmo Pocket-Diary," after the style of the Birth-Day Text-Books in England and America. His lectures were attended by large numbers of interested persons. When they were printed, they went far beyond the audiences of India, and found their way to England and the United States. Christ was prominent in them. Every year Sen delivered a lecture in the Town-Hall of Calcutta, on the anniversary of the founding of the Brahmo Somaj, and the interest of both Europeans and natives was intense and widespread. His first lecture was delivered in 1866, in the Theatre of the Calcutta Medical College, on "Jesus Christ—Europe and Asia." It was an attempt to reconcile India to the gospel and person of Christ. Debendra Nath had said: "Theism is free. Popery was the first that robbed Christianity of its freedom, and, owing to its freedom, Protestantism has also lost its freedom. Let not the name of Christ enter into the Adi Somaj. Three hundred and thirty-three millions of gods and goddesses have been defeated by Brahmoism. Let us not be intimidated by another finite God."

Such was the feeling in the educated minds of all India. Even the most hopeful reformer re-echoed it. He proclaimed the divine unity, but repelled the very thought of the divine Christ. Chunder Sen made a protest against this, the vital point, in his creed. He declared that Christ was a divine character. Through him the thought has permeated the whole country. "This feeling was dominant over the national mind till Chunder Sen came and dispelled the error. From that day the antipathy to Christ began gradually to disappear, and now almost every school-boy that makes a speech refers to him as the highest of divine characters."* Now, if we analyze this divine Christ, according to the conception of Chunder Sen, much will be found that needs qualifying. While he progressed in his Christology down to the day of his death, we do not find that he at any time believed Christ to be more than the highest manifestation of deity, and not absolute deity himself. Chunder Sen held up Christ and his gospel as the "means of man's renewal," as "sent by Providence to reform and regenerate mankind;" that "it is the Catholic Church

---

* "The Liberal and the New Dispensation." February 3, 1884.

of Christ that is opened wide to all men without distinction; that "in Christ, Europe and Asia are to learn to find harmony and unity." But, strangely enough, this great reformer "never called himself a Christian, but a theist."* Christ was more to him than all other teachers combined, but not the one supreme God. In his lecture on "The Apostles of the New Dispensation,"† he says that his new dispensation—the theology of the Brahmo Somaj—is on "the same level with the Jewish dispensation, the Christian dispensation, and the Vaishnava dispensation through Chaitanya. It is a divine dispensation. Its distinguishing feature is its denial of a mediator. Fling away the sectarian small Christ, and let us be one in the large Christ of all ages and creeds."

In 1881 he inaugurated the New Dispensation with much ceremony; the Hindu, Buddhistic, Mussulman, and Christian Scriptures lying on a small table covered with crimson cloth; the silk banner, "crimson with the blood of martyrs," was fastened to a silver pole, and fixed in front of the pulpit. The creed of the New Dispensation, to take the place of the Thirty-nine Articles, published in 1879, was the following:

"One God, one Scripture, one Church.
"Eternal Progress of the Soul.
"Communion of the Prophets and Saints.
"Fatherhood and Motherhood of God.
"Brotherhood of Man, and Sisterhood of Woman.
"Harmony of Knowledge and Holiness, Love and Work.
"Toga and Asceticism in their highest development.
"Loyalty to Sovereign."

Chunder Sen, carrying out his eclectic system, performed certain ceremonies. On one occasion, the Hindu Hari, or Saviour, was invoked, and the Brahmos, in imitation of the followers of Chaitanya, joined the "Mystic Dance," with banners and music. At another time Chunder Sen performed the Fire Sacrifice, in imitation of the ancient Aryan worship, as the ceremony of conquering temptation.‡ On still another occasion, the Hindu arati (offering) ceremony, or evening meal, was performed,

---

* Slater, "Keshub Chunder Sen and the Brahmo Somaj," p. 61.
† Delivered in Calcutta, January, 1881.
‡ On June 7, 1881.

accompanied with burning incense, waving candles, numerous musical instruments, and the chanting of the arati hymn. The rites of foreign churches were not forgotten, but introduced and blended with Hinduism. The Lord's Supper and Baptism were performed, and adapted to Hindu life. From Romanism, the vows of continence and poverty were borrowed, as also the rite of the canonization of saints; while Comtism lent its system of dedicating each day of the week and year to a special cultus.*

Chunder Sen organized important Brahmo societies in various parts of India, and, wherever he went to lecture, he was heard with such interest as no religious reformer in India had been listened to in recent times. He visited England, and his audiences there were astounded at his eloquence and thoughts. He returned to India, and continued his work of theistic reform. In a short time his health failed, and he died at the early age of forty-five. His body was cremated on the same evening, amid an immense concourse of mourners and spectators. Since his death there has been an arrest in the aggressive power of the Brahmo Somaj.

Chander Mozumdar, the author of a brilliant work, "The Oriental Christ," had been Sen's chief adherent. I had the pleasure of an interview with Mr. Mozumdar at his home in Calcutta. Of his pure purpose, serious thought, and correct life there can be no question. His personal bearing and appearance have been strong factors in his successful career as the most powerful assistant to Sen. Any one who sees him must confirm the following portrait of him:

"Mr. Mozumdar is a man of remarkably fine presence. He is a little over the medium height, with black, flashing eyes, raven black hair, and a complexion of such a clear and beautiful tint that when one has seen it he wonders how, as judges of beauty, we can prefer the chalky whiteness of the English type. His face shows intelligence in every feature and line, and in conversation he is easy, pleasant, and dignified. We have called him a reformer. The ample outline of his form does not call to mind the Hindu devotee, who spends long years in preparation for absorption, and is forgetful of his physical wants."†

* Slater, "Keshub Chunder Sen and the Brahmo Somaj," pp. 111, 112.

† *The Independent*, New York, Nov. 1, 1883.

Mozumdar made a visit to the United States in 1883, where he lectured, and came into close relations with the Unitarians of Boston. He is in profound sympathy with Christianity, but does not acknowledge the divine character of Christ. He speaks of him only as "the Son of God, the manifestation of divine character in humanity; that character descends in Christ for the enlightenment, conversion, regeneration, and adoption of all men." In 1885, Mozumdar established in Simla *The Interpreter*, as the organ of his views. Of the mission of the Somajes, we read in it the following hopeful outlook:

"The truly worthy men among the different bodies of the Brahmo Somaj must fraternize some day. The three Somajes must exchange invitations to their respective pulpits. Nay, we even expect to find the day when men who do not profess the religion of the Brahmo Somaj, but whose spirit is the same as ours, shall be cordially welcomed to our churches and pulpits, to give us the advantage of their devotions and precepts. The present writer has been often invited by Christian ministers to conduct divine service, and deliver sermons from their pulpits to congregations whose views differ very materially from his own. There never was the slightest hitch or misunderstanding on such occasions, and will it be said that the universal religion of the Brahmo Somaj is incapable of such toleration? The Brahmo Somaj is undoubtedly a church, a community; but it is *not a sect;* it is open to receive good men, and good things from every church, every religion, every community."*

The "Apostolic Durbar," or governing body of the Brahmo Somaj, consisted of all the apostles and missionaries, a total of twenty-one members. These had control of the spiritual interests of the Church. They resolved to keep the pulpit vacant, and the presidential seat in the Durbar also vacant. They held that the dead leader's doctrine of the immediate presence and influence of departed guides made it unnecessary to fill the vacancy—that Chunder Sen was still present, and could have no successor. Mozumdar rejected this doctrine, and contended for his right to preach in the pulpit. This was not granted. Meanwhile, the Brahmo Somaj, while still publishing its periodicals under the care of Chunder Sen's son, every year

* *The Interpreter*, May, 1886, p. 5.

is adding to the uncertainty of the future of the New Dispensation.

III.—The Sadharan Brahmo Somaj.

This is a secession from the Brahmo Somaj, which took place in 1878, because of a serious difference with Chunder Sen. One of the distinctive characteristics of the Brahmo Somaj had always been a protest against too early marriages, child widows, and other social evils of Hinduism. But on March 6, 1878, Chunder Sen gave his daughter in marriage to the young Maharajah of Kuch Behar. By the notable Marriage Act, largely secured by this great apostle of a new reform, the minimum ages for the bridegroom and bride were fixed at eighteen and fourteen years. But both his daughter and the young Maharajah were beneath these ages. Immediately a great outcry was heard all over India. Chunder Sen had violated his own social creed. He had compromised with the old Hinduism from which he had rebelled. In vain he pleaded certain excuses. Twenty-nine of the Provincial Somajes united with the most of the members of the great central Calcutta Somaj, and formed a secession, which called itself the Sadharan, or Universal, Somaj. From that moment the Brahmo Somaj lost prestige, while the Sadharan Somaj, continuing adherence to the fundamental doctrines of the Brahmo Somaj, flung out its banner to the breeze and gained adherents in all quarters.

Chunder Sen justified his course by holding that the marriage ceremony was only a formal betrothal. But this was without real force, and the public judgment pronounced against him. It was a real marriage. Idolatrous practices were adopted at the marriage. But these were adopted without Chunder Sen's knowledge, and under his decided protest. His leading apology was, that he was inspired to consent to the marriage of his daughter at her early age. He had already given out broad hints that he possessed adesa, or inspiration. He repudiated the claim to be a prophet, but held that he was "a singular man." In consenting to the marriage, Chunder Sen held that he was acting upon the "actual will and commandment of God," and that he was "compelled" to act as he did. The propriety of the marriage, he declared, was decided by his own special light. Before the question of this marriage arose, Chunder Sen had exhibited a growing tendency to regard his doctrines as infallible truth. This had awakened serious opposition within the Somaj. When, therefore, the marriage took place, and he gave his consent to it, the time had come for many of his followers to withdraw from fellowship with him. It was a severe trial. He bore himself with becoming dignity. But nothing he could do had the effect of calming the storm.

Sivanath Sastri, speaking for the Sadharan Somaj, stated the mission of this new theistic society to be the following:

"1. To preach and propagate the idea of a personal God — the *Parama Purusha*, as in Sanskrit he is called, of a God who loves righteousness and hates sin.

"2. To preach and propagate, and also to teach by personal example, the idea of true spiritual worship—consisting of communion and prayer, as distinguished from the outward observance of idolatrous rites; which idea, if once properly grasped, will inevitably give rise to spiritual struggles.

"3. To divest conceptions of piety from the errors of sentimentalism and mysticism on the one hand, and asceticism and ritualism on the other; and thereby to divert the religious enthusiasm of the people to channels of practical usefulness, to fields of active philanthropy, and to the elevation of individual and social life.

"4. To seek to establish the grand but often forgotten truth of the brotherhood of man, by the overthrow of caste, and every other form of tyranny of class over class; the elevation and emancipation of women being an important step in this direction.

"5. To promote freedom of conscience, to kindle the sense of individual independence; thereby sowing the seeds of domestic, social, political, and spiritual liberty.

"6. To communicate to the body of the people, through the means of individual lives, a living and conquering moral energy, born of faith and earnest prayer, which will impart strength and vigor to the exhausted moral and spiritual nerves of the race, and will help them to be morally and spiritually regenerated."

The creed was declared to be the following:

"1. There is only one God, who is the Creator, Preserver, and Saviour of this world. He is a spirit, infinite in power, wisdom, love, justice, and holiness, omnipresent, eternal, and blissful.

"2. The human soul is immortal, and capable of infinite progress, and is responsible to God for its doings.

"3. God must be worshipped in spirit and truth. Divine worship is necessary for attaining true felicity and salvation.

"4. Love to God, and carrying out his will in all the concerns of life, constitute true worship.

"5. Prayer and dependence on God, and a constant realization of his presence, are the means of attaining spiritual growth.

"6. No created object is to be worshipped as God, nor any person or book to be considered as infallible and the sole means of salvation; but truth is to be reverently accepted from all scriptures and the teachings of all persons, without distinction of creed or country.

"7. The fatherhood of God and the brotherhood of man, and kindness to all living beings.

"8. God rewards virtue and punishes sin. His punishments are remedial and not eternal.

"9. Cessation from sin, accompanied by sincere repentance, is the only atonement for it, and union with God in wisdom, goodness, and holiness is true salvation."

The new Sadharan Somaj instituted a liberal order of government. It was not to be ruled by one mind, but by officers duly elected by their fellows. The general officers are four in number, elected annually. They act in conjunction with a general committee of forty, also elected annually, and a certain number of representatives of branch Somajes. This committee, in its turn, appoints an executive of twelve persons for the year. This republican form of government was most flattering to the native taste for independence. No one mind could control the body. A large prayer-hall, or church, capable of holding twelve hundred persons, was built in Calcutta, and opened for use in 1881. Various organizations were founded to promote the interests of this new and vigorous Somaj; the Students' Weekly Service; the Students' Prayer-Meeting; the Theological Institution for lectures and discussions; the Theistic Philanthropic Society, for the moral education and improvement of working-men by a night school and house visitation; the Brahmica Somaj, for Brahmist ladies; and the Bengal Ladies' Association, for the union of lady members and non-members; a city school, for the higher education of boys, and a boarding-school for Brahmist girls, which trains girls for the university examinations. Its organs are, *The Indian Messenger*, a weekly, devoted to religious, social, and educational topics; a monthly magazine for ladies; a monthly magazine for children; and a Bengali and English political and scientific weekly. The leader of the Sadharan Somaj is Sivanath Sastri, but care seems to be taken that no one man attain to a controlling influence. The first four missionaries were publicly set apart in 1880. A Missionary Committee has in hand the special work of training missionaries, who, after obtaining a certificate, go out preaching for one year as "probationers." The Executive Committee hold themselves responsible for maintaining the families and educating the children of the missionaries. In addition to regular missionary laborers, many persons engaged in secular occupations, including several Calcutta students, undertake preaching tours, and other means of spreading the faith. In Bengal alone, in 1884, there were ninety different Somajes, while others existed in other parts of India. In all the three Somajes—the Adi, the Brahmo, and the Sadharan—there existed, in 1879, one hundred and thirty societies or Somajes. By 1884, this number had risen to one hundred and seventy-three, with fifteen hundred enrolled members, and about eight thousand adherents. By the present date it is safe to say that this total has increased at least thirty-three per centum.* There are, from last accounts, twenty-eight periodicals representing these three Somajes, of which fifteen are in Calcutta alone.

IV.—The Arya Somaj.

We now come to the consideration of a Theistic Society which differs essentially from the three preceding Somajes, and, nevertheless, agrees with them in protesting against the current Hindu idolatry and all forms of caste. It is violently opposed to the other Somajes, and not less so to Christianity. No word of even cold admiration of Jesus Christ and his gospel is spoken by its apostles. It claims that the Hindu faith of modern times is a gross superstition. Idolatry, and caste, and all the grosser forms of existing Hinduism are simply corruptions, which have grown up through the ignorance and evil purposes of men. The Rig-Veda, the oldest of all the Vedas, never taught any such absurdities. Only the purest monotheism can be found in it. The Arya Somaj, therefore, proposes a radical reform of all the religious and social evils of India by returning to the primitive Aryan faith, as laid down in the earliest Indian Scriptures.

This new Theistic movement arose in Gujerat, in Western India. It seems to have had no outward connection with the

* Slater, "Keshub Chunder Sen and the Brahmo Somaj," pp. 82 ff.

revolution going on in Calcutta, and yet, if we could trace its origin fully, we have no doubt it would be found to be due to the Theistic agitations prompted by the three Somajes which arose in Calcutta. Its founder, Dayanand Sarasvati, was the son of a Gujerati Brahman, and was born in 1825. His early development was rapid, and out of the usual line. His father, a worshipper of the god Mahadev, taught the boy the same worship. But the son read so much, and so widely, that his mind began to rebel against the absurdities of polytheism. When twenty-two years of age he forsook his father's family, and joined a company of fakirs, or mendicant priests. He heard a celebrated teacher, Anand Sarasvati, who gave a new shape to his whole life. The young man adopted an austere life, spent eighteen hours a day in meditation, travelled from place to place, and taught the necessity of a life of search for *gyan* and *moksh*—knowledge and salvation. He sought to turn the learned teachers from their old doctrines, and to teach nothing but the Vedas, and so help him to lead his countrymen back to the primitive Theistic faith. Here he failed. He then resolved to change his policy, and by means of rich men began to establish schools. He founded four of these, where the professors were paid about twelve dollars a month, and the pupils were provided gratuitously with food, clothing, and books. The study of Sanskrit was the chief employment, and the object was to spread the knowledge of the Vedas. But here, too, he failed. He adopted, in 1875, his final method—to travel through the country, distribute books, preach, and establish branch Somajes. This method proved successful. At the time of his death, in 1884, Dayanand Sarasvati had established Somajes in Bombay, Calcutta, the Northwest Provinces, Oudh, Rajputana, and the Panjab. There are now, throughout India, two hundred and fifty Arya Somajes. These, with an average of fifty members each, would make twelve thousand five hundred members. This is a low estimate, as the Lahor Somaj alone has five hundred members, and Bareilly three hundred. The chief Somaj is at Meerut. It is composed of twenty-three eminent and learned professors, and to them all reports must come.*

---

* Neeld, "The Arya Somaj," Budaon (India), n. d., pp. 3 ff. This is by far the best work produced in the history of the Arya Somaj.

The following is the creed of the Arya Somaj:

"1. There is but one God. He is without body. Omniscient, happy, true, without beginning and without end, self-existent, omnipresent, holy, and we must worship only him.

"2. The Vedas came from the *Gyan* of *Ishwar*. They are without beginning, and were revealed to man through Rishis of ancient times.

"3. There are three things which had no beginning and will have no end, viz.: (1) God; (2) Souls; (3) Matter. Souls and matter came out from God, and are subject unto him.

"4. The four Vedas are the only authoritative books, and they came from God by verbal inspiration.

"5. Eternity is divided into four periods or ages—(1) Satyug; (2) Dwápar; (3) Treta; (4) Kalyug. The three eternal things *act* during these periods, and manifest themselves in the order of the ages as enumerated.

"6. God exists in two states, viz.: Nirgun and Sargun. When he is passive, does nothing, is in a comatose state, and no attribute can be affirmed of him, he is Nirgun, or without attributes. When he is active, does something, becomes manifest, and attributes can be affirmed of him, he is Sargun. When in the state of *Nirgun* he came under the influence of *máya*, or ignorance, and through that influence became Sargun, then the universe became manifest and souls became conscious.

"7. Sin can be affirmed only of that person who actually sins, and hence it cannot be said that all men are sinners.

"8. Prayer should be offered to God five times a day.

"9. Obedience to God and a life ordered in accordance with the Veda will procure *Mukti*, or salvation."

The Aryas hold that by obedience to the following ten principles, and a performance of daily duties according to the Veda, a person may attain to a better birth:

"1. God is the origin of all true knowledge and all discoveries which are from that true knowledge.

"2. God is the Creator of the world, is incorporeal, omniscient, omnipresent, happy, holy, and we should worship only him.

"3. The Vedas are the books of true knowledge, and it is the duty of Aryas to read them and teach them to others.

"4. We must always be ready to give up untruth and accept the truth.

"5. All our acts must be performed according to the Veda.

"6. The special object of the Somaj is to help others, in both bodily and spiritual matters, and to make such improvements or reforms as may be beneficial to all.

"7. We must live with love to others according to our religion.

"8. Advance must be made in knowledge, and ignorance must be banished.

"9. Aryas should rejoice not only in their own prosperity, but also in the welfare of others.

"10. Persons performing duties for the public good must be subservient to others. In duties which concern our own persons we should be independent."*

On the question of woman and marriage, now the uppermost social question of all India, the Aryas hold that Hindu widows should be permitted to remarry; that girls should not marry until they are at least sixteen years of age; and that women should be educated.

While all the Somajes have seized upon the press with enthusiasm, as a means of propagating their opinions, the Arya Somaj has been foremost in the use of it. They have copied the methods of the missionaries very closely. Their Catechism is modelled after these of the Christian churches. They have presses in Lahor, Agra, Muthra, Meerut, Bareilly, Allahabad, and other places. In the places where the members meet, books and periodicals are on the table. A Hindu translation of the Veda is issuing in Allahabad, in monthly parts. Monthly papers are issued in Meerut, Lahor, and Bareilly. I have before me some numbers of the *Arya Patrika*, published in Lahor, in 1887, in which public meetings are reported, contributions are acknowledged, and independent essays are given, on such subjects as "The Poverty of India," "What is Brahmoism," and "Love, Justice, and Propriety should guide us in our dealings with others."

The order of service of the Arya Somaj is as follows: The service is on Sunday, because on that day the public offices and courts are closed. The meeting is led by the most learned teacher. The services are opened and concluded with a form of prayer from the Veda. Songs are sung. The Veda is expounded. The whole service is a gross imitation of Christian worship. Women and children are enrolled as members, but women do not attend the services; but, if they wish to know what has been done, must ask their husbands to tell them. The following "Ode to the Aryas," printed on the cover of *The Catechism*, published by the Central press, is a fair declaration

---

* Om, "The Arya Catechism; or, The Indian Youth's Aryan Moral Companion," Meerut, 1886, p. 29.

of the spirit which animates all the members of the Arya Somaj, and is no doubt sung at their services:

> "We are the sons of brave Aryas of yore,
> Those sages in learning, those heroes in war;
> They were the lights of great nations before,
> And shone in that darkness like morning's bright star,
> A beacon of warning, a herald from far.
>
> "Have we forgotten our Rama and Arjun,
> Yudhishtar, or Bishma, or Drona the wise?
> Are not we sons of the mighty Duryodhan?
> Where did Shankar and great Dayabanda arise?—
> In India, in India, the echo replies.
>
> "Ours the glory of giving the world
> Its science, religion, its poetry and art.
> We were the first of the men who unfurled
> The banner of freedom on earth's every part,
> Brought tidings of peace and of love to each heart."

There is a branch of the Arya Somaj even in London. The hymn-book used in the service is entitled "Theistic Hymns." Nearly all the hymns are from Christian hymn-books. Among them are the following:

> "My God, my Father, while I stray,
> Far from my home on life's rough way,
> O teach me from my heart to say,
> Thy will be done."

And,

> "O God, our help in ages past,
> Our hope for years to come."

And,

> "Death blights not, chills not, but awakes
> The heart's immortal, pure desires,
> O'er the dark vale a glory breaks
> From heaven, to which the soul aspires."

And,

> "My God, my Father, blissful name!
> O may I call thee mine?"

But the Arya is eclectic. He borrows a gem wherever he can find a lending hand. Accordingly, in his Theistic Hymns, for use in the London congregation, are the following:

"The boy stood on the burning deck,
Whence all but him had fled."

And,

"Tell me not in mournful numbers
Life is but an empty dream."

And,

"There's a magical tie to the land of our home
Which the heart cannot break though the footsteps may roam."

And,

"India, thou best of the climes of the world,
Where victory attended thy banners unfurled!
O country of sages! O land of the brave!
Thou cradle of poets and the heroes' proud grave."*

* Comp. Forman, "The Arya Somaj: its Teachings and an Estimate of it," pp. 61, 62. Allahabad, 1887.

CHAPTER LV.

RELIGIOUS SIGNIFICANCE OF THE REFORMATORY MOVEMENTS.

Is this new uprising in India a spasmodic effort, without relation to the general thought of the people? Or is it a logical growth, and important to the life of India? Studied in any light, it is of great moral and religious significance. Men of such pure life and rich mental endowments as Rammohun Roy and Chunder Sen may be charged with that vanity, confined to no age or race, which takes its supreme pleasure in moulding the opinions and bending the purposes of men, and through them, as willing adherents, in founding a new social and religious structure. But there is a more just solution of such careers. That Dayanand, the least admirable of the Brahmic apostles and the most unfavorable to Christianity, was a deceiver, and playing a stage-trick, is denied by both the voluntary sacrifices of his youth and his steady preaching of theism in his maturer years. When India shall have become wholly Christian it will not be surprising if it shall appear that the bright day has been hastened, not alone by the sublime labors of Christian missionaries, with their pure Gospel from the Occident, but also, though in an inferior degree, by those grosser and weaker efforts from the very body of the Hinduism of the Orient. It is one of the historical glories of Christianity that, for its greatest triumphs, it not only marches to victory by virtue of its own irresistible potency, but that it transmutes all that is good in the hostile ranks to minister to the final achievement. There is every indication that the theists, who have laid the foundations of all the Somajes, are, like neo-Platonism and other predecessors of all Christian ages, build ing more wisely than they know.

The appearance of Rammohun Roy at the head of the whole theistic movement of the last half-century is not the first time that better thoughts, gathering around the finest elements of monotheism, have crystallized in distinct approaches to the Scriptural conception of the divine unity. As the Hindu goes back to the oldest hymns of his Vedas, he finds that they breathe the spirit of monotheism. Even the pantheism of India has its foundation in God's unity. The present Hindu idolater, when closely questioned, does not deny the oneness of the Supreme Ruler.* He holds that his many gods are only manifestations, incarnations, and material forms of the one God. Every now and then, in the better and purer periods of Indian history, a new emphasis has been placed on monotheism. Apostles of a weak form of theism have arisen and protested against the gross idolatry.

In the twelfth, thirteenth, fifteenth, and sixteenth centuries the Vaishnava reformers protested against the degradation of the original monotheistic faith. They inculcated a doctrine which was an approximation towards the Christian idea of God's unity and personality, as set forth in the first article of the Church of England: "The one Supreme God, of infinite wisdom, power, and goodness, the Maker and Preserver of all things," was taught clearly and forcibly by those four great reformers—Ramanuja, Madhava, Vallabha, and Chaitanya. But the apple of gold was set in a picture of spurious silver. That this one God could descend and become incarnate in warriors, thinkers, and even lower animals, was a fatal mistake. A Supreme God of many possible descents was no god at all. Reactions came on, and the last idolatrous state was worse than the first.

The great reformer of the sixteenth century was Kabir, one of the twelve disciples of Ramanand.† He set before himself the impossible task of fusing Brahmanism and Mohammedanism. He rejected both the Vedas and the Qurán; discarded idolatry and caste; preached the unity of God; and made brotherhood, based on love to God and the practice of good works, the spiritual bond of his disciples.‡ His followers came from both the Hindu and Mohammedan folds, and at his death he was canonized. Shortly after him arose, in the sixteenth cent-

* Monier Williams, "Religious Thought and Life in India," pp. 475 ff.

† Monier Williams places Kabir in the sixteenth century ("Religious Thought and Life in India," p. 476). Slater assigns him to the fifteenth century ("Keshub Chunder Sen," p. 21).

‡ Slater, "Keshub Chunder Sen," p. 11.

ury, the "Luther of the Panjab"—Nanak Shah. He founded the Sikh sect, which still exists, and has its stronghold in the Panjab. Govind, the tenth Sikh teacher, impelled by the persecutions of the Sikhs by the Mohammedans, so shaped the policy of his adherents that the Sikhs and Mohammedans have ever since been implacable enemies. Thus the brotherhood became as much a fiction as that of the Jews and Samaritans. Even the Mohammedans, who have never claimed any sympathy with idolatry, have attempted the same undertaking of reconciling the conflicting religions of India.

Of the five Mogul emperors, Akbar was in many respects the greatest. He was also the most tolerant. He was the Marcus Aurelius of India. He borrowed from all the faiths of which he knew, and thus set up his fabric of the divine monotheism on Hindu, Parsi, Mussulman, Jew, and Christian foundation. He was so eclectic in his opinions that the passion gave color to his matrimonial tastes, and this "guardian of mankind," as his subjects adoringly called him, was so impartial as to take one empress from the Hindu fold, another from the Mohammedan, and a third from the Christian.

All these efforts at producing a reaction against the idolatry of India were failures. All possible zeal and voluntary poverty were employed. In vain was it declared that the original teachers of Hinduism were monotheists. There was no basis of general truth on which to build. There was no Gospel from which to learn the true incarnation; no Christian Church to serve as a model; no consecrated Christian lives in which to see the practical lesson of the divine unity in human existence.

From the days of Nanak Shah and the great Akbar, in the sixteenth century, down to Rammohun Roy, there was no serious attempt to find in the Vedas a principle of divine unity and to preach it to the people. For three centuries the millions of India were destitute of a teacher in whom could be seen the faintest approach to one who had caught sight of a syllable of the divine oracles. It has been only in the present century, since the missionaries planted the banner of the cross in all the centres, and carried it into the very jungles, that a new race of reformers has arisen, and preached the abolition of caste, the brotherhood of all men, and the unity of God.

That there is variety in the theological bases of the four Somajes need not surprise. The three Somajes which arose in Calcutta have most affinity with Christianity. The leaders breathed the very atmosphere of the Gospel. They saw its preachers, churches, schools, and press. It was the faith of the conquerors and rulers of their country. Would these reformers ever have arisen without the practical lesson of the Gospel before their eyes? No. Take the rays from the Scriptures out of the words and work of all three, and there would be nothing left. The most eloquent periods of Chunder Sen were spoken of Jesus, while the greatest book produced by any of these theists—"The Oriental Christ," by Mozumdar—was an attempt to give to Christ an Eastern character. The Arya Somaj, which has little to say of Christianity, and speaks of it only to oppose, arose in a part of India where Christianity is less dominant. But even its very methods are borrowed from those adopted by the missionaries. After the manner of these missionaries, its seven itinerant preachers of the Veda go through the country, pitch their tents at the melas, or fairs, and preach three or four hours a day. They are establishing an Arya college at Ajmir, and already have an orphanage in Ferozepore, and are starting one in Bareilly. The president of an Arya Somaj proposed to the Rev. Mr. Neeld to join him in opening schools among the low-caste people of Budaon.

The plausibility of the arguments of the preachers of this most hostile of the four Somajes is so well conceived, so forcibly presented, and so safely guarded, that the common people are easily led astray. The methods employed by the Somaj teachers—their advocacy of schools and female education, their bold repudiation of all forms of idolatry—in a word, their strong emphasis on everything which the new theism has in common with Christianity—are in every way calculated to make the natives regard for a moment the cause as identical with Christianity.

The most specious of all the arguments employed by the preachers of the Arya Somaj, and by the great body of Hindu people and priests who are still in the toils of the old idolatry, is the claim that all the best forms of Christian civilization and of Western culture have their real basis in the eldest Vedas. No Hindu doubts the great superiority of the new age to any former one. He knows that without the Englishman his India would be as far in the background as it was a thousand years ago. But how has it all come about? To whom does India owe even the civilization of the Englishman and even the American? To none other than the far-back founders of his own faith.

The apostles of the Arya Somaj declare that every modern conquest over the great forces of nature was anticipated by their seers and foretold in their Vedas. It is difficult, even when they quote these precious promises, for a dull Western mind to see the appositeness of the prophecy. But that is the misfortune of the Anglo-Saxon's dull perception. Here is where Dayanand finds the Vedic formula which lies at the root of all medical science: "O God, by thy kindness whatever medicines

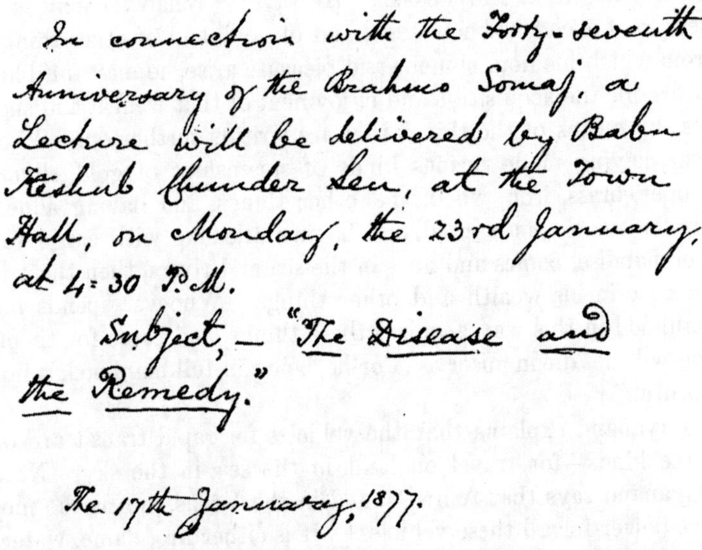

In connection with the Forty-seventh Anniversary of the Brahmo Somaj, a Lecture will be delivered by Babu Keshub Chunder Sen, at the Town Hall, on Monday, the 23rd January, at 4:30 P.M.

Subject,—"The Disease and the Remedy."

The 17th January, 1877.

A SOMAJ NOTICE.—FAC-SIMILE OF KESHUB CHUNDER SEN'S HANDWRITING.

there are, for us they are givers of ease; and for those who are injurious, evil, and our enemies; and with what injurious ones we keep hatred, for them they are injurious." Far journeys were known—so says the founder of the Arya Somaj—to the primeval teachers of his faith.

In the chapter "Concerning Travel," in the "Satyarth Prakash," Dayanand says that the Munis and Rishis and others used to tràvel in foreign countries. Viyash Muni, who lived five thousand years ago, and translated the Vedas, and his son Sukhdev, and their disciples, went to Patal—that is, America—

and dwelt there! One day the son asked the father for knowledge, and received for answer that he must go to Hindustan and ask the rajah. It is related that Krishna went to America and brought back Udalak Muni, to the sacrifice prepared by Rajah Udhistir. At another time an Indian rajah went to America, fought and overcame the American rajah, who gave his daughter in marriage to the conqueror. Dayanand declares that all the English knowledge of the railway, the steamship, fire-arms, and the telegraph has come from the Vedas, and that the English have only developed this knowledge received from the Aryan Vedas. In his chapter on "The Science of Travelling,"* he holds "this science of rapid transit in the sea, on the earth, and in the sky as taught in the Vedas." He says: "Whatever man is a desirer of excellent knowledge, and of gold, and of other things from which his nourishment and pleasure arise, he may fulfil his desire for the acquisition and enjoyment of that wealth and success by means of the things that are written further on. Whoever, having made various kinds of steamships of gold, silver, copper, brass, iron, wood, and other things, and having added fire, air, water, as wanted, and having filled up with cargo for merchandise, comes and goes in the sea and rivers, then there is increase in his wealth and other things. Whoever spends his manhood in this way acquires these things, and cares for them, and will not die in misery. For he, being in full manhood, is not slothful."†

Dayanand explains that the vehicles for rapid transit are of three kinds—for travel on land, in the sea, in the sky. Now Dayanand says that Ashwi, found in the Vedas, means the motive-power for all these vehicles! It is either fire, flame, water, wood, metals, horses, lightning, air, earth, day, night, sun, or moon! Therefore, we have the railway-car, the telegraph, the universal application of steam for "travelling." The same apostle of modern Hinduism finds in the Vedas a description of the division of the Indian railway carriage into six compartments; the speed with which it is drawn; the machinery for drawing and backing a train. He even describes a sky-vehicle. It is to rest on twelve pillars, must have machinery in sixty parts, which

* "Rig Vedadi Bhashya Bhurnika," pp. 191–200.

† Forman, "The Arya Somaj," pp. 50 ff.

must be fastened by three hundred large nails or screws. If, therefore, we are destined to be blessed with comfortable and safe flying-machines, the quick-witted Arya will be ready to say, "Did we not tell you so? Lo, it lies in the Vedas of our ancestors."

The Hindus not affected with the theistic heresy of the Somajes go further than Dayanand or any of the Brahmists. They hold not only that the Vedas contain prophecies of all modern inventions and discoveries, but that Brahma is a being of various incarnations. The application of steam is a recent incarnation, and therefore is a part of the Hindu system. When the railways were introduced into India the high-caste Brahmans would not ride on them. To travel in contact with one of lower caste, and especially with foreigners, was regarded as a mortal sin. The difficulty was great. The pundits rolled their eyes in ecstatic wonder. The waiting for reply was intense. At last it came, substantially as follows: "The Vedas prophesied the railway. Brahma has undergone a new, blissful incarnation. Hurry up! Get aboard." Therefore the most exclusive Hindu can now crowd into any railway of India or Burma, and from Bombay to Mandalay can coolly take his tramway ticket from the dog-paw of an Englishman or an American.

Taking the theistic movement, prompted by the four great Somajes, as a whole, it must be admitted that the missionaries are seriously divided in their estimate of it. Some regard it as a great evil, promising no good. But there are others who take a more hopeful view. They can see in the three progressive Somajes, especially, some elements of advantage to the good cause of the Gospel. The Rev. Mr. Neeld finds in even the grossest and worst Somaj, the Arya, some indications of help to Christian work. I believe the latter class are correct, and for the following reasons:

1. Everything which tends to break up the solidarity of the polytheistic mass of the Hindu faith must be advantageous to the spread of the Gospel. The whole history of the territorial expansion of Christianity shows that every disintegrating factor proved a blessing. It caused weakness, a loss of confidence, a fear that Christianity would find an entrance wherever an open door was left.

2. The reforms at which the four Somajes have aimed are not

only in harmony with missionary work, but actually parts of regular missionary operation. The education of girls, temperance, opposition to child-marriage, the founding of schools, and the printing of books and newspapers are alike parts of Christian enterprise and the theistic machinery.

3. The many discussions and publications of the preachers of the Somajes relate to European topics, and familiarize the native mind with the advance of Christian nations. Every new piece of information concerning any part of the Christian world, every recognition of a direct or indirect triumph of the Gospel, is only a new reminder of what the human mind achieves when blessed with the light of the Gospel.

4. The forms of service in all the Somajes are merely feeble imitations of Christian worship. Many natives who attend the theistic service see a world-wide difference between it and the idolatrous temple-service, and, being accustomed to the new order, can never again feel at home in an idolatrous temple. The estrangement is final and complete.

5. Through the emphasis of the Somajes on the Vedas it will yet appear to the whole Hindu mind that the Vedas are empty fables, and deserve to stand beside the myths of Hesiod and the visions of Mohammed. The awe with which the typical Hindu regards the Vedas is amazing. The Vedas are in Sanskrit, and not one learned Hindu teacher in a hundred knows that language. It is to him what the Greek and Latin are to the Englishman and American. Those who translate it, as Dayanand and others, do as they please with it. They make its *ashwi* mean steam, and its *patal* mean America, and the poor uneducated native must believe it. But others are translating the Vedas, and showing that even the Hindu translators have been only playing on the blind credulity of the natives. Amazing progress has been made by the missionaries, since the rise of the Somajes, in unfolding the true meaning of the Vedas. Dr. Martyn Clark, of the Church Missionary Society, has published, at Lahor, a most valuable series of pamphlets on the "Principles and Teaching of the Arya Somaj," in which he shows, by exact reproduction of the language of the Vedas, that the Arya Somaj cannot find authority for its principles in them, but that they teach idolatry and many of the grosser forms of the present polytheistic worship in

India.* Is he not right? Is it not safe to judge the tree by the fruit? Every temple in India is the natural child of the Vedas. Hence, by going back to them, it is only a return to the corrupt fountain of a corrupt faith. Had the Arya Somaj done nothing else than to bring the missionaries now laboring in India to take up the Vedas for a new study, not because they are a Sanskrit classic, but because of their theological absurdities, and subject them to the burning lens of Christian examination, its indirect and undesigned service would have been incalculable.

6. All the Somajes repudiate the temple. They build their own prayer-houses, or churches. Now the very sight of these new edifices is a reminder to every native passer-by that here is a structure in opposition to the temple. It is a drawn sword against the faith which underlies the Golden Temple of Amritsar and the holiest fanes of Benares.

7. The divergences among the Somajes are an open declaration of the fruitless search for unity even in a return to the Vedas. There are minor divisions among even members of the same order. When the leading teacher dies the Somaj is lost for a time. When Chunder Sen departed his Somaj lost all aggressive power. Since Dayanand's death some of his followers declare that he has come to life again. At this time there is a serious division among the Aryas on this very ground. The attacks of these Aryas on Christianity are becoming so violent as to affect even the persons of missionaries. They have stirred up mobs, who have assailed and beaten Christians. In Lucknow they have abused also the Mohammedans. Strange to say, the latter are now joining hands with the Christians against their persecutors, and say to the Aryan preachers, "You may speak

---

* Some of Dr. Clark's lectures are fine specimens of critical skill. Among them are the following: "The Origin and Age of the Vedas," "The Justice of God," "The Nature of God," "The Knowledge of God," and "The Vedic Doctrine of Sacrifice." All these are published in Lahore, and the first four in a second edition. These little works, unfolding the inner absurdities of the Vedas, and the absolute antagonism of them to the very doctrines which the Brahmas would draw from them, would be good reading for some of the English and American admirers of the early sacred literature of India, who profess to find in the Vedas a very fine, and about equal, companion-work to that other Oriental work, the Old Testament.

against Christians as much as you like, but not against Christ; we hold him a sinless prophet, and when you attack him you will have us as well as the Christians to oppose." *

8. The brotherhood of man preached by all the Somajes is an axe laid at the root of the old Brahmic tree. All the apostles of the four theistic societies declare relentless war against the despotic cruelty of the caste system. Every word spoken against this monster must, in the end, be helpful to the Gospel.

9. The public advocacy of the moral element in education in the government schools by the Somajes is in the very line of missionary operation. In a recent very able article on "Moral Education for Young India," in the *Calcutta Review*, by T. J. Scott, D.D., we find copious extracts from the *Liberal and New Dispensation* and the *Arya Patrika*, in which the government is severely attacked, not only for allowing infidel writings from Europe to be used in the schools, but for the general want of thorough ethical culture. Surely, it is no little significant that the leaders of the new Hinduism should advocate the introduction of the best ethical writings of Europe in the schools of India.

It must not be forgotten that the first stages of a movement of this radical character do not furnish the best opportunity for safe judgment as to final effect. When the Somajes shall have gained a larger following, and theism shall have become the central dogma of multitudes now in idolatrous bondage, it may come to the light that the Gospel shall reap a rich harvest among them. The theists have turned their backs upon the old faith. They do not incline to enter the Christian temple; but many of them are slowly advancing towards the outer court. Like Plato, Seneca, and Epictetus, they are unconscious searchers for the true light.

---

* Rev. B. H. Badley, D.D., in letter from India.

CHAPTER LVI.

THE OPIUM CURSE IN INDIA.

THERE is moving along the quay at Calcutta a long train of wagons, drawn by toiling, puffing bullocks. I am belated a little, and must hurry for the train, to spend my only day at Serampore. Our driver pushes his horses to their best, to get in advance of the line of wagons. By and by we pass them all, though the process has been slow. The wagons are evidently laden with the same ware, and are destined for the same point. Each is piled up with chests, all of equal size and appearance. They are on the way to the customs, to be inspected or to be shipped directly to China or other countries. What are the contents of those heavy chests? Each chest contains $133\frac{1}{3}$ pounds of opium. The Queen's government for India produces every pound. It provides the land, lends the money to the cultivator, receives and stores the whole amount, auctions it off at periodical sales in Calcutta to merchants who send it to them, and puts the profits in its own treasury.*

Has England ever made a greater contribution to the world's wretchedness? Formerly her opium went to China alone; now it girdles the world with a zone of sorrows. She even gives opium to her London children in Godfrey's Cordial, and to her invalids in Bauley's Sedative Liquor and Jeremy's Sedative Solution.†

The traffic in opium is the darkest blot on the page of Anglo-Saxon history in India. The more carefully we inquire into the methods by which the English took sole charge of the culture of the poppy plant, made a complete monopoly of the drug expressed from it, and then smuggled it into China, until they compelled that country to admit it as a legal import, the more

* "Traffic in and Use of Opium," p. 5. ———, 1882.

† Drury, "Useful Plants of India," p. 330. London, 1876.

surely is the conclusion reached that the whole transaction is devoid of a single mitigating circumstance. It must forever stand as a terrible crime against Christian civilization.

HISTORY OF THE TRAFFIC.

There have been three stages in the development of the opium evil in India. The first was the farming out the culture of the poppy to the highest bidder. The second was the smuggling of the opium into Chinese ports against the most rigorous Chinese laws, and even the death penalty for violation. The third was the downright compulsion of China to open her ports to the introduction of opium from India. These facts seem incredible, and yet each is supported by the clearest and most positive proof.

THE POPPY PLANT.

When the English went to India first, in the seventeenth century, they found that the culture of the poppy was largely a monopoly of the native Mogul princes. There is no doubt that the Mohammedans brought it with them from Arabia, and established it in India at about the same time that they began their memorable conquests in the valleys of the Indus and the Ganges. This early attachment of the Arab to opium accounts for the larger use of it by the Mohammedans of India than by the Hindus. Possibly, as the Mohammedan is interdicted by the Qurán from the use of ardent spirits, he rejoices in finding full compensation in the use of opium. The East India Company was not slow to perceive the chances for gain. It applied itself with consummate tact to the most direct methods of amassing wealth. They were careful to study the native usages, and, wherever it was possible to make them serve their purpose, to appropriate them. They no sooner saw that the culture of the poppy was already a native monopoly than they began to study the propriety of securing the same advantage. There was, however, some degree of caution at first. Not the Company as such, but some of the officers, on their own account, were the first Englishmen who cultivated the poppy and made money out of the opium from it. These were social servants in the Patna Factory.*

The opium bait was attractive. Why could not a company do what some of its agents were doing? If there was money to be made from the poppy, why should it not be done in a broad and public way? No moderate opportunities must be lost. The Englishman was in India for the purpose of trade only. Probably not one of the early English navigators or traders ever thought of the permanent occupation and possession of a foot of Indian territory. The whole curse of the Anglo-Saxon's planting of the poppy and cultivating it, and first smuggling it into China, and then forcing it upon the same country, grew with the opportunity. It was a terrible temptation, and was not resisted. But this must be said, that the latest chapter in England's encouragement of the opium trade is a natural result of the first tampering with the crime. The great wrong lay far back, with a few persons. History will take its deep revenge. Millions must sometimes pay the penalty for the far-back crimes of a few dozens, and many years of sorrow become the price for the crime of an hour.

The Trade in the East India Company's Hands.

The East India Company took the trade in opium out of the hands of the few civil servants of the Patna Factory, and used the proceeds to buy goods. But how should the Company make the wisest use of the new source of trade? What means would be the best to yield the largest revenue? It was a new matter, and required tentative measures. In 1773, the East India Company took the opium monopoly entirely out of the hands of the Patna Council, and leased the whole business to two natives for a fixed sum. It was found that the revenue was not satisfactory. Good husbandmen as the natives of India were, it was not clear that they could make the best return. The opium monopoly was put up at public auction. It must have been a wonderful scene when the public crier announced for the first time in

* "Reports of the House of Commons," 1783, vol. i. p. 70.

India the sale of the opium monopoly. The natives, no doubt, supposed that they could get the largest return from a plant with which they were familiar. They, of course, were on hand to bid for the monopoly. But the Anglo-Saxon was there too. He had calculated his chances. He knew just what he could do. He knew how much he would have to pay the natives to work for him; how many acres he would put in poppies; and how much of the drug he could reap for his harvest. So he bid against the native. The native became frightened at the boldness of his competitor. The Englishman outbid him. The native retired forever from his place as the manager of the opium culture of India, and the Englishman took his place. The stranger from a Christian land was to control the poppy and its poison, and get all the profit from the trade, while the native henceforth was to do all the heavy work of its cultivation.

Now it was intended by the East India Company that the opium monopoly should be continually sold at auction. For what purpose? They openly declared that they sold the monopoly to the highest bidder because this would correct an evil growing out of the monopoly. It would "prevent the British contractor from becoming doubly terrible to the natives when they should see that his contract was in effect a grant." * Here, then, was the comfort which came to the Company. They were not selling the monopoly of the opium production of India to the highest bidder. They were only making a grant!

But the auction method was not satisfactory. A new plan was adopted. The directors of the East India Company did, indeed, require that competition should be used; but the local government at Calcutta disobeyed the orders, and, with Warren Hastings at the head, in 1776, farmed out the monopoly directly to an Englishman by the name of McKenzie. The Company could cancel the arrangement with McKenzie, but they never did it. They contented themselves with reprimanding Hastings, the Governor-General, and his Council. Hastings had in his family one Sullivan, and it was important that this individual should be put in possession of funds. The method adopted to bring about this desirable result was successful. When the three years' contract with McKenzie for the opium monopoly

* Cf. "The Poppy Plague," p. 32. London, 1876.

had expired, this Sullivan became the fortunate possessor of it. There was no competition on his part. He did not need to trouble himself to propose to take it. He simply received the offer of it. He then sold his contract outright to a Mr. Benn, and he in turn to a Mr. Young. It is no wonder that the Committee in the House of Commons came to the conclusion that the contract was given to Sullivan for no other purpose than to supply him with a sum of money.*

With the taking of the poppy culture out of native hands, and the control of the monopoly in opium by the East India Company, the first chapter in the history of the great crime ends.

Opium Forced on China.

The next chapter is brief. It is the story of India, under English rule, getting such complete control of the opium trade as to regard it no longer as an article of merchandise, but of great revenue. The India market, however, was too narrow for such a result. It is clear that larger tracts of land were put under the cultivation of the poppy, and the consumption at home was not sufficient to exhaust the supply. But the genius of Warren Hastings was equal to even this emergency. The opium of the East India Company must be disposed of at all hazards. There had been already a small opium trade carried on between India and China, probably overland, through the passes of the Himalayas. The first supplies had been taken probably about the end of the seventeenth century.† But to Hastings belongs the rare honor of doing away with this slow method. He chartered a vessel, with the concurrence of his Council, for carrying opium to foreign ports, and especially to China. A small trade in the commodity had been carried on with Batavia, but the Dutch War had put an end to the market there. A new market must be found, and China solved the problem. But one vessel was not enough. Neither must the method be a mere incident. There must be a system. The outcome was, that the trade in opium to Chinese ports was undertaken by the government of British India. The first contract is a curiosity. Colonel Watson, an Englishman, was to carry the first regular shipload of

* Cf. "The Poppy Plague," p. 35. London, 1876.

† Ibid., p. 37.

opium. His vessel bore the appropriate name of the *Nonsuch.* He needed guns to protect his vessel, for opium was contraband in every Chinese port. The British government in India cast some cannon for the special purpose, while others were brought from Madras, a distance of seven hundred miles. Soldiers and medical stores were also supplied. Then came other ships.

Now, the iniquity of this beginning of the opium trade with China lies in the fact that it was purely a smuggling operation. China was doing all in her power to prevent opium entering the country. Her rulers and their advisers were resorting to all possible measures to keep the drug away from the people. It would seem that the men who represented the Chinese government could foresee, a century ago, the evils which China must certainly suffer should her people become corrupted by the use of opium. They declared that none of it should cross the frontier. Severe penalties were visited upon any violator. These penalties were increased from time to time. The whole power of the government was used to keep opium out of the country. Yet the English in India kept on sending it.

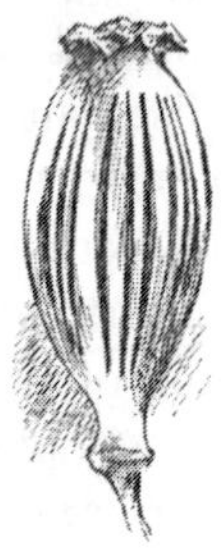

THE POPPY CAPSULE AFTER THE PETALS HAVE FALLEN, AND INCISIONS HAVE BEEN MADE.

In all English history there is not a more repulsive picture than that of the receiving-ships lying at Lin-tin as late as 1834. The Chinese succeeded in driving away the British trade in opium from Macao, and so the dealers drifted down to the mouth of Canton River, and anchored among the islands. Their vessels were safe here. They were well armed, and could resist attack from the Chinese, and could smuggle opium into the country. Thus Lin-tin became the depot of the opium trade for all China.

The English traders from India were trying to get opium into the country, and the Chinese doing their utmost to keep it out. And this became an affair of years. The clipper ships which brought the opium for China from Calcutta were the fastest on the Eastern seas. By the year 1834 the annual amount of opium brought from Calcutta had gone up from five thousand to twenty thousand chests. Meanwhile other ports for the enforced entrance of opium were established along the Chinese coast. The trade between India and China was confined largely to opium, and all the while China was fighting to keep it out. As a specimen of the large profit arising from the trade, a Mr. Innes, in 1831, disposed of three hundred and thirty thousand dollars' worth in one voyage. But Mr. Majoribanks, in the following year, was less successful. He took opium to new Chinese ports, but the people knew nothing of the drug, and refused to buy. The venture proved a failure.* Such was the persistence with which the English in India carried on the work of forcing opium upon the Chinese.

It must be admitted that the government in Calcutta made its deliverance on the illicit character of the trade in opium with China. Here is what the directors said in 1787: "It is beneath the Company to be engaged in such a clandestine trade; we, therefore, hereby positively prohibit any more opium being sent to China on the Company's account." This sounds well enough. But Warren Hastings went on with his measures, and the Company, while now and then issuing strong decrees against the illicit trade, continued to enlarge the cultivation of the poppy at home and the trade in opium abroad.

America's Share in the Crime.

But Americans are not without blame. The young and growing commercial spirit of the United States reached as far as those Eastern seas. The Chinese government published an edict in 1821, in which it gave an account of the recent seizure of the cargoes of one American and three English vessels at Canton for introducing opium in violation of the Chinese laws. One half of the cargoes of the vessels was confiscated as penalty. The Viceroy of Canton, finding that this seizure was a great affliction to merchants, remitted the penalty, but forbade the selling of the cargoes and the carrying away of any tea or rhubarb. Besides, a memorandum of these ships and their merchants was made, and they were prohibited forever from coming to Canton for trade.†

Here, then, we have the picture of England and the United States combining to force opium upon China.

---

* "The Poppy Plague," p. 55.

† Niles, *Register*, December 21, 1822.

In 1836 we find the first attempt made by a Chinese official to secure the legal entry of opium from India into China. Heu Naetse memorialized the Emperor to admit opium under a duty. His plea was that the imperial revenue would be enriched. But a member of the Imperial Council, Choo Tsun, opposed the proposition. The result was a vote of the Emperor's Council in favor of renewing the measures to keep opium out of the country. Violence against the illicit trade was resorted to. The opium ships were driven from Lin-tin in 1837. The emperor kept a close watch on his officers, and used all possible measures to keep out of the country the opium brought by English ships from India.

The final stage in the relation of the English government to the enforcement of opium upon China was brought about by war. It grew out of the death of a Chinaman in a quarrel with some English and American seamen. The Chinese felt aggrieved, and cut off supplies of food. Captain Elliot, of whom Gladstone said, in the House of Commons, that "he had completely identified himself with the contraband traffic in opium," began the war by firing the first shot. In 1840 a British fleet arrived, under Sir Gordon Bremer. The war continued nearly three years. England conquered, and the treaty of peace which she compelled was based on the following hard conditions: The payment to England of a vast indemnity within three years for meeting the expense of the war, the opening of five ports to British trade, and the ceding of the island of Hong Kong to the British Crown.*

The Chinese did all in their power to secure in this treaty the prohibition of the opium traffic. But the English would not consent. They wanted the opium trade to go on as before. The wicked trade promised too much gold to the Indian treasury to be sacrificed. Lord Palmerston put the matter on new grounds. Instead of demanding that opium be admitted to Chinese ports, he said he would leave it as a free-will offering from China. "Her Majesty's government make no demand in regard to this matter; for they have no right to do so." But the argument was unavailing. The Chinese Emperor would not yield. Opium, with all the humiliation and weakness of defeat upon China, was to be kept out of the country. All through the war opium

* "The Poppy Plague," pp. 75 ff.

had been introduced into China, and large profits made by the sales. But the Chinese convicted of dealing in the drug, or even using it, were severely punished. In Canton the violators could be seen in gangs of forty or fifty, with shackles on their hands and feet. It was, indeed, death for a Chinaman to trade in opium. But the merchants of India, and the government as well, were providing fresh supplies all the time.*

But one more war was needed to throw China open to the opium curse. The pretext soon came. A Chinese vessel had bought of the local British government at Hong Kong the right to carry the British flag. The Chinese officials knew she was a Chinese ship, and boarded her as a pirate. The English claimed her as belonging to their country. War broke out again. The English were once more victorious. China was compelled to pay again the costs of a war, and to suffer, in the two wars, the loss of thirty thousand lives. More ports were opened to English trade, and the Chinese government was compelled "by moral suasion, the force of which lay in an irresistible fleet and army, to legalize the importation of opium." England, therefore, in this wise, compelled China to accept her opium, and would not allow more than ten per cent. duty to be charged upon it. Thus it has come to pass that now 12,911,840 pounds of opium, or two thirds of all the opium produced in India, goes to China.

But the most remarkable act in this terrible tragedy is yet to come. In the treaty of Tientsin, between England and China, there was a clause by which each party should have the right to demand a revision of the commercial clauses. China was grieved over the opium which came from India. She wanted to prohibit the curse. Sir Rutherford Alcock says: "They were insisting and urging, by every argument they could adduce, the necessity of the British government consenting to the total prohibition of opium."† Sir Rutherford said afterwards that, had China even then declined to admit opium, she would have been compelled to fight England!

THE OPIUM CULTURE PRODUCES FAMINE.

The relation of the culture of the poppy in India to the hap-

---

* "The Poppy Plague," pp. 77, 78.

† "Report, East India Finance," 1871, Nos. 5870, 5865.

piness of the people is very close. The temptation is to plant the herb, for the profit from it is far greater than from any cereal. The cultivation of the poppy in Malwa results in from three to seven times the profit derived from wheat and other cereals, and sometimes from twelve to twenty times as much. The constant tendency is to put a larger acreage in the cultivation of the poppy. Now and then large tracts of country are visited with great famines. Experience has proven that in these very districts the poppy is most cultivated. Not enough cereals are cultivated to supply the people with food when any great flood, drought, or other calamity befalls the people. Behar, the very home of the poppy culture, for example, was visited by three great famines in eight years.

In 1883 the area of territory devoted to the cultivation of the poppy in Bengal was 876,454 acres. Any one can cultivate it who wishes, but the government, having still the monopoly, is the only purchaser. The native gets about three shillings and sixpence per pound. But the government must make its profit, and so it sells it at about eleven shillings per pound.* The profit, therefore, instead of going into the laborer's hand, goes into the treasury of Christian India.

The price of opium in India depends upon its range of prices in the Chinese markets. After all expenses are paid, the annual revenue to the government is upwards of 9,000,000 pounds sterling gross, and 6,000,000 pounds sterling net. It is levied in two ways: one, on the eastern or Bengal side, by opium made in state factories, from poppy cultivated under state supervision, and sold by auction at Calcutta, on the state account, to merchants who export it to China; the other on the western or Bombay side, by the export duty levied on opium made by private manufacture from poppy grown in native states.†

The missionaries are, to a man, persistent in their opposition to the production and sale of opium. Their crusade is destined to take wide range. Already a monthly magazine is devoted to this single object, and a vigorous society has been at work for some years past in the same interest. Motions to abolish the traffic have repeatedly been made in the House of Commons.

---

* "Encyclop. Brit.," vol. xvii. pp. 787 ff.

† Temple, "India in 1850," p. 239.

But the financial straits of the Indian government have for many years been such that neither party feels able to grapple with the problem. The first participation in the evil was simply for gain; but in process of time the revenue derived from opium became so large—namely, 8,500,000 pounds sterling—that the government now depended upon it. In other words, the Indian government has become entangled in its own chain, with which it thought to bind its helpless neighbor, China.

He who will begin a popular movement against the "grand government opium monopoly of India, unlimited," and arouse the English masses against it, will achieve a victory beyond that of Trafalgar and Waterloo. His name will take its place beside that of Clarkson, Wilberforce, Howard, and Florence Nightingale.

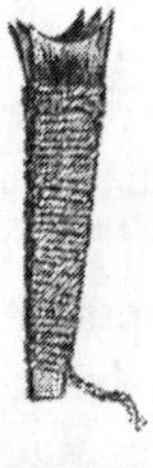

INSTRUMENT USED FOR MAKING INCISIONS IN THE CAPSULES OF THE POPPY.

CHAPTER LVII.

ÁPKÁ SHARÁB—YOUR HONOR'S FIRE-WATER.

It is an appropriate term by which the natives of India describe the intoxicating liquor which the people drink—Ápká Sharáb, or Your Honor's Fire-Water. They not only denote their contemptuous estimate of the fluid, but also the strong hand which furnishes it to the millions, at the rate of four cents a bottle.

Early Distillation.

We do not mean to say that intoxicating drinks had not been manufactured and used in India before the coming of the European. Indeed, the earliest records give proof that the people of the country understood the art of fermenting simple fluids, and drank them to intoxication. If in Noah's day the art was practised, and the sin committed, it need not surprise that the early history of all nations should reveal the same facts. The most ancient Hindu books, giving us information dating back three thousand years, inform us that the Aryans made an intoxicating fluid of the juice of the Soma, or "Moonplant," which they regarded as highly acceptable to their gods, and was therefore lawful for man. This drink was used in the later Vedic times. "It was made," says Macdonald, "from the juice of a creeper (*Sarcostomma viminalis*), diluted with water, mixed with barley meal, clarified butter, and the meal of wild rice, and fermented in a jar for nine days. The starchy substance of the meal supplied the material for the vinous fermentation, and the soma juice the part of hops in beer. Its effects on gods and men were those of alcohol."* The gods were invited to drink freely of it, and are represented as having been intoxicated by it. But we do not find that the drunkenness of a god was ever regarded as a virtue. On the contrary, it seems to have been

* "The Vedic Religion," p. 41.

considered rather an infirmity than otherwise. Rishi says to Indri: "Thy inebriety is most intense, nevertheless thy acts for our good are most beneficent." The Puranas, of still later date than the Vedas, represent Siva as drunken in his habits, and his eyes inflamed with intemperance. The Institutes of Manu recognize the practice of fermenting and using intoxicating beverages, and lay down regulations for the classes of distillers and vendors.*

The aboriginal races of India were acquainted with the same practice before the incoming of the Aryans. They have never lost either the art of distilling or the passion for drinking. They distil or ferment intoxicating liquors from the cocoanut, sago, date, and palmyra palms, from sugar and rice, and from the dried flowers of the *Bassia latifolia.*

The People of India Temperate.

Now, although the fermentation of liquors, and the drinking of them, were long practised, the great body of the people continued temperate. There does not seem to have been either any general craving for intoxicating liquors, or any large sale of them. Though made up of many races, and presenting a singular variety of languages, religions, intellectual strength, and social condition, no people of India, whether aboriginal or Aryan, were addicted to intemperate habits when Vasco da Gama first landed on their shores. This is easily understood. So far as the Hindus are concerned, their religious caste and social habits—with the exception of one low-caste sect—have in modern times prohibited the drinking of any spirituous liquor, while the Qurán requires total abstinence of every Mohammedan. In the earlier period of English rule, it was much easier to discover the original condition of the Hindus than at present, since the force of European example and the government excise have made it possible for all to drink. The testimony of Warren Hastings, who had excellent opportunities to witness the natives in their undisturbed condition, is therefore of the highest importance. He says this: "Their temperance is demonstrated in the simplicity of their food, and their total abstinence from spirituous liquors and other substances of intoxication."

---

* Mateer, "Native Life in Travancore," pp. 278 ff.

The manufacture and use of intoxicating liquors was discouraged by the rulers, both Hindu and Mohammedan. No Mogul emperor ever thought of reaping a profit from the manufacture, or did, what the English government now does, stand sponsor for the distillation and sale.* All intoxicating beverages were unclean things to a Mohammedan. None of the nobles under the Moguls used it; or, if so, in such a way that the fact has not gone into history. Akbar and some other rulers indulged, but we can well imagine that with the religious requirements against it, the people regarded such violation as an infirmity which received their pity or censure rather than their admiration. When the late Maharaja of Kashmir gave encouragement to Europeans to plant grapes and hops for wine and brewing purposes, the orthodox Hindus seriously considered whether he ought not to be put out of caste. But his sickness and death followed soon after, and the Hindus regarded his fate as Heaven acting for itself in this violation of the law of the "heaven-born" ruler.†

In 1787, the King of Travancore prohibited the use of cocoanut brandy under pain of confiscation of property; the drinking of ganja hemp and the use of opium were forbidden at the same time. Mateer, in stating this fact, however, supposes that, as this measure was not sustained a long time, the people must have been so addicted to the use of those drugs as to make it necessary to abrogate the law. We do not doubt that in some localities there was intemperance. But we claim that all the authorities go to show that no Indian government reaped an excise revenue from the manufacture and sale of any intoxicating liquor; that the religious castes and social customs were in favor of temperance; and that the vast body of the people were not only temperate by habit, but never acquired the passion for intoxicating drinks.

Canter Nisscher, who wrote about A.D. 1723, says of the Portuguese that they had no taste for strong drinks, but adds: "The Dutch, on the contrary, drink to such an extent as to expose themselves to the reproaches of the Portuguese and the natives; the English are liable to the same imputation."‡ The

---

* Gregson, "Drinking and the Drink Traffic in India," pp. 3, 4.

† Extracts from paper by Surgeon-Major Pringle, M.D., pp. 1, 2.

‡ Mateer, "Native Life in Travancore," p. 280.

French also were drinkers of lighter liquors. But the English were addicted to liquors containing more alcohol. We can well understand, therefore, the power of the example of the English when they gradually gained influence over both natives and foreigners. That example for evil has been increased in manifold ways since the entire political power of India has passed into their hands. Disguise it as we may, at the moment when the East India Company set up its first factory, and heard the jingle of its first rupee on the bottom of its treasure-box, India and Ceylon were occupied by races who were practically total abstainers from all intoxicating drinks.

We shall see directly what have been the effects of the English rule upon the country, not only in reaping a vast harvest from the furnishing of intoxicating drinks, but in implanting the passion for drink among the millions of the country.

The Distillation of Indian Liquors.

For our account of the distillation of Indian liquors, and the various kinds now used by the people, we must depend on Mr. Mateer. "The common fermented drink is called Kallu," he says, "or toddy" (Hindustani and Sanskrit, *tâdi*), the vinous sap of the palm, drawn in North Travancore from the cocoanut-tree, by the Ilavars and Chogans; in the South from the palmyra by the Shanars. It ferments after standing for a few hours in the heat of the day; and spoils, turning into sour vinegar in two or three days. Of this pleasant sub-acid drink the people say that a pint, or a pint and a half, will intoxicate a man. It is generally employed for yeast in making wheaten bread and rice-cakes. Arrack is an ardent spirit, transparent and colorless like gin, abundant and cheap throughout India. It is, properly speaking, rum, being distilled from palm-sugar with a small quantity of acacia-bark—or from the fermented sap of the palm. To distil spirits, the jaggery or unrefined sugar is broken up and put in water to ferment along with the bark for four days, then the whole is boiled in an earthen pot, the vapor being caught at the top in a tube of bambu and carried on so as to fall into another pot, or into some condensing-vessel placed in cold water. Distillation is effected in half a day. Sometimes the first product is redistilled. When manufactured from toddy, a quantity, say eight edungalies, is taken on the second day after being drawn from the trees, and put in a large earthen pot on an oven. On the top of this a small earthen pan, having three holes at the sides, is placed, and over this a brass pot containing cold water. The edge of the intermediate vessel is tightly secured with cloths so as to retain the vapor, and from a hole in one side a pipe is fixed to convey the spirits into a bottle. The cold water in the upper vessel, which is open to the air and used for condensing, is renewed from time to time as it becomes heated, until the whole quantity is distilled. Women generally attend to this work. Ten quarts of toddy will yield about two of proof spirits. A small quantity of the first product of the distillation must be thrown away, being sour and hurtful. The first bottle drawn will be first-rate arrack; the second bottle, second quality; the value respectively, twelve and ten chuckrams; total, twenty-two chuckrams, of which the profit to the distiller will be about five chuckrams. Less than a chuckram's worth will intoxicate some men. To make the very best arrack, toddy and arrack are mixed together and distilled. The people believe that it is in order to impart a strong intoxicating quality that the bark of Karinja (*Acacia leucophlaea*) is added; but Brandis, in his "Forest Flora," p. 184, says that it is added on account of the tannin it contains, in order to precipitate the albuminous substances of the palm-juice. On the east coast, spirits are commonly distilled from a mixture of rice-flour, sugar, and toddy, so that the government dues are fixed with some reference to the market price of rice. The spirits produced are not considered equal in purity and excellence to

CLIMBING THE TODDY-PALM.

those distilled from palm-juice or sugar alone on the western coast."*

The Government and the Liquor Traffic.

The entire relation of the British government in India to the use of intoxicating liquors presents a striking parallel to that of other countries in dealing with the same vice. How to make money out of a vice is the problem. The end to be reached is the filling of the treasury of the state. The method of reaching it is by putting a tax upon the liquor, or as it is called in India, "country spirits." The fallacy lies in supposing that there is a commercial advantage when the last analysis is reached. Is there money in the treasury? No; on the contrary, the state is worse off.* In order to see that the treasury is really undergoing a constant depletion, one must add the loss of physical labor, the destruction of domestic competence, the criminal costs, the reports of insanity, the abridged longevity, and an interminable catalogue of evils to the moral and religious life of the people. The tax on the use of liquor, like every bounty paid by a state for the existence of a vice and the committal of crime, is a losing process, whether in Calcutta, London, or Washington. India, in these terrible results, is like all other countries which reap a harvest from excise on intoxicating liquors. In her present condition she furnishes a fair warning to other countries which have been her teachers in vices hardly less than in virtues.

The excise regulations of the government of India began in Bombay in the year 1790. It was claimed that the people began to develop a taste for liquor, and that the cost of a quart of mowhra spirit, made of the juice of the palm, was so low—only a half-penny—that anybody could get drunk on it. Then the fallacy came at once to the front—tax, and therefore restrict. Put a tax on the tree, and the people will drink less. This was the outspoken argument, a good exoteric weapon in defence of the excise. The real argument was nothing of the kind. Tax the juice of the tree, and the government will have all the money it wants—that was the whole philosophy, and it has been steadily adhered to in India for a whole century. The

* Mateer, "Native Life in Travancore," pp. 279, 280.

object of the government has been to raise money out of the vice, and not to suppress the vice.

Two systems have been adopted by the government, which is the real purveyor of liquors to the people of India. The manufacture has not been allowed to everybody. Such important work must be conducted in such a way that fraud cannot be perpetrated—in other words, that every gallon of liquor distilled must be sure to pay its tax into the treasury of the empire.

The first method adopted was that of the Government Distillery. Its general name was the Sudder (Upper) Still system. There was one still, or only a very few, in the district. The arrangement was beautifully patriarchal. The government was the responsible proprietor of every distillery in the land. It built large sheds for the distilleries, provided all the necessary utensils for distillation and measurement, and set apart special police to watch the pandemonium. It was the owner of the machinery. Now, to do the work, there was a native contractor. He was closely watched. The amount turned out by each distillery was fixed by law. A duty was levied on still-head—that is, a certain rate was levied per gallon according to strength. Only a certain number of distilleries was permitted in each district. Then only a limited amount of London proof liquor was allowed to be produced from a certain amount of material. For example, the rule was that only two and a half gallons of proof spirits were to be manufactured from eighty pounds of *Mowah cassia latifolia.* The size of the stills was limited, and only pure liquor could be manufactured, and from wholesome material. The distillery was strictly watched by the government police, and the drink kept under lock and key. There were other safeguards, by which the output of liquor was comparatively limited. What was the result? The government did not make all the money it wanted for its general treasury. In order to carry on the government, six hundred and forty thousand pounds sterling were assigned to the Excise Department of Bengal, as its share to meet demands. But under the Government Distillery plan only from five hundred and fifty thousand to six hundred thousand pounds sterling had been raised for years. It seldom went beyond six hundred thousand pounds sterling. Now came the demand for six hundred and forty thousand pounds sterling. What was to be done? The old principle could not be worked up to that paying basis.

Now came a happy thought. The old Sudder system must be given up. It did not put money enough into the treasury. Mr. C. T. Buckland must go down to posterity as the brilliant man who was equal to this occasion. His genius evolved the Out Still system. He laid it before the government. It was adopted. The treasury soon had all the money it wanted. The Government Distillery was a ruin, and the Out Still was erected on the site. The new arrangement was introduced in the year 1876, but did not go into complete operation until two years had passed. But when once in full motion, it answered all expectations—except those of the friends of temperance. It filled the treasury to overflowing, but covered many a fair plain with drunkards.

Let us now look at this brilliant invention—the Out Still of New India. All the Sudder distilleries for country spirits must be shut up. The right to set up Out Stills, or stills outside government control, must be offered at auction to the highest bidder. He can distil what he likes, and as much as he likes, on condition that he keep his bargain with the government to pay the price at which he bought his right to distil. He buys for one year, just as he would hire a house. The auction is held by a district officer, near the magistrate's office, and superintended by a district officer or deputy magistrate, as the case may be. The government, in this way, is released from all expense and from all supervision.

The *Times* of India thus describes one of these government auctions: "Yesterday afternoon the Town Hall was the scene of a good deal of excitement. The last public auction sale of liquor licenses was held there by the Collector of Bombay. Parsis, Hindus, Goanese, and native Christians mustered in great force, the large hall being nearly full of men, women, and children. The first-class shops were put up first at the reserved price of five hundred rupees each, and, in spite of the moan made to government regarding the rigid laws that obtain with regard to spirit licenses, every shop fetched a considerable amount over the price fixed on it by government. Though there will be no sale next year, these prices will hold good for three years, as the licenses will only be renewed on payment of their value at this auction. After that, of course, the value will be assessed by the Ábkárí inspectors. Out of the fifty licenses put up, forty-nine were sold; the fiftieth was bought in, as the police objected to the locality. The sale will continue to-morrow, and for some days to come yet, as four hundred and fifty licenses remain to be sold. It is hardly worth mentioning that the government are turning a pretty penny by the rivalry of the bidders, for even here every caste seems to exult over the downfall of another. The sales are fetching more this year than they did this time twelve months ago."

Now, the direct result of this system is that the number of distilleries has been vastly increased. The people can now get all the liquor they desire. The Out Still is before all eyes. The increase in revenue is enormous. During the last five years there has been an increase in India's revenue from liquor of six hundred and sixty thousand pounds, or nearly twenty per cent. Such is the financial triumph of the Out Still.* No wonder the Commissioner of Revenue could exclaim in his report, for the joy of the government in London: "The expansion of revenue under this system has been *marvellous.*"

Now, it is but just to the government to say that it claims for its defence that there is no real increase in intemperance and the general consumption of intoxicants; that increased revenue is from an increased duty; that there has been increased vigilance on the part of the revenue officers; and that there is, under the Out Still system, less chance for fraud. But the testimony of tea-planters in Assam, of publicists, and of wise and observant missionaries long resident in India, is to the effect that the doubling of the revenue on liquor in ten years betokens increased consumption and drunkenness. The great increase in the report of consumption, in the number of stills, and in the revenue, cannot be accounted for on the government line of defence. The government never adopted the original plan of the Government Still, or the new Out Still to take its place, in order to lessen intemperance, but simply to increase its revenue. It gained its end. Besides, the special Bengal Commission was appointed, in 1886, for the express purpose of investigating this

---

* No. 166 of Government of India's Papers for 1887. Also, "Report of the Second Decennial Missionary Conference," Calcutta, 1883, pp. 433 ff.

very subject. It did its work thoroughly, and reached the conclusion of a vast increase in consumption. It declared that in Bengal, which is one fourth of all India, and contains a population of sixty-six millions, the quantity of liquor distilled and sold in 1874–75 was *one and a half million gallons.* The population at the utmost had increased eight or nine per cent., but the output and consumption of liquor increased one hundred and thirty-five per cent., and, in some districts, one hundred and eighty per cent.* Here we have the government against itself.

This very subject was the theme of an important debate in the House of Commons in March, 1888, during which the enormity of the government share in promoting intemperance—though we by no means claim such to be its motive—came out in strong light. Mr. Caine, a member of the House of Commons, said: "The fact is, the Indian government are in the position of licensed victuallers, who hold a monopoly of the liquor traffic, and are responsible entirely for the amount of the liquor that is sold and for the methods by which it is sold. . . . According to the evidence laid before the Commission, the Out Stills are frequented by large numbers of people, young and old, who are found often in a high state of intoxication, singing ribald songs and creating all kinds of disorder—in fact, the condition of things you would expect to find if uncontrolled and unchecked public-houses should exist in this country—in the lowest slums of London. . . . I contend that the whole tendency of the excise system is to increase the consumption, and that I have proved it to the hilt by the very documents which the government of India, misled by some mendacious official, has put forward to prove the contrary. The government are driving this license trade as hard as they can. Collectors find it the easiest way to increase their contribution to the revenue, and for years they have been stimulating the consumption of liquor to the utmost. If the government continue their present policy of doubling the revenue every ten years, in thirty years India will be one of the most drunken and most degraded countries on the face of the earth."†

---

* Ridley, "One Aspect of the Present Outcry against Foreign Missions," p. 9.

† "India and the Excise Revenue." Report of the Debate in the House of Commons, March 13, 1888, pp. 3, 7.

The most careful study of the Government Still system, contrasted with the Out Still system, leads us to conclude that the government safeguards against smuggling and other methods of concealment were much stronger and more numerous in the former than in the latter. The owner of the Out Still is not the government, but the highest bidder. He has farmed the job, just as a man farms the rents of a landlord holding an estate, and it is his interest to get all the money out of it he can. When he attended the auction, and his highest bid was accepted, his motive was purely financial, and not for the purpose of lessening intemperance. This motive, it is very supposable, controls all his methods.*

Is Intemperance in India Increasing?

To this serious question we are compelled to answer affirmatively. The proof is overwhelming that the temperate Hindus are gradually becoming a nation of drunkards. Roadside grog-shops are multiplying. Crime is fostered by them, and "the roads near by are made unfit for respectable people and unsafe for passengers."† In one well-known district in Bengal—that of Monghyr—the government distillery used to turn out five hundred gallons a day. Now, under the new Out Still system, the average is fifteen hundred gallons a day, or three times the former amount. The increased production means increased drunkenness and increased crime. Private drinking is now indulged in by nearly nine tenths of the Bengalis instructed in the English colleges and schools. Keshub Chunder Sen says: "So long as the men are in the University we can hold them, because they are not allowed to drink, but the moment they pass, away they go, and now the Sabbath day in Calcutta is simply a bacchanalian festivity for the educated Bengalis of the city. . . . Friends never meet nowadays without spirit being consumed. . . . Crime and immorality are also, in large measure, attributable to this cause. The instances of petty crimes and heinous offences committed under the influence of drink are of frequent occurrence, as may be proved by the criminal records of the country.

---

* The table in the Appendix (No. VI.) presents a comparative view of the receipts in India from excise duty on spirits.

† Pringle, "Extracts," etc., p. 3.

. . . It is, indeed, harrowing and painful to contemplate the extent to which sensuality, profligacy, and brutal revels on the one hand, and irreligion, blasphemy, and practical atheism on the other, are making ravages among all classes of the native community in consequence of the spread of drunkenness, and undermining the religious and moral life of the nation. . . . In short, the use of intoxicating liquor has done more than anything else to degrade the physical, moral, and social condition of my countrymen, and has proved a stupendous obstacle in the path of reformation." An English medical officer says: "The quantity of intoxicating liquor drank on holidays is incredible. In the course of practice I have met patients who have astonished me by describing their powers of drinking. One, a Mohammedan moonshee, asserted that he had finished a bottle of brandy and three bottles of beer at an evening sitting; another, a Kayasth a Vakil, that he had swallowed a bottle of brandy almost at a draught." The Rev. Frank Warne visited one of the out stills established by the English government, and says that "natives were lying all about, so drunk that they could not be aroused. The keeper of the out still, being rebuked for the sin of engaging in such business, coolly responded, 'The Christian English government commands us to do it, and takes rent for it; when the government says stop, we will stop.'"

The way in which the ever-increasing temptations to drink are breaking down all old religious restraints of the Hindus and Mohammedans is easily seen. The education in the schools has loosened the bands, and now come the vices of the civilized West. Native doctors say that delirium tremens is a common disease among their patients. Drunkenness is almost the invariable result of a native dinner-party. Indeed, liquor is being introduced into the zenana, and women are acquiring the passion. The Mohammedans are yielding, in spite of the Qurán. Scarcely a social meal takes place among the better class without European wines being used.* All barriers are falling down before the enlarging facilities for drinking. The rush is towards the still. When there was no tax on the palm furnishing the juice which served as a simple beer for the natives, the natives contented themselves with that. But now the government taxes every

* Gregson, "The Drink Traffic in India," p. 11.

tree which produces the juice. The people, having gotten the taste of the strong drink, now prefer it. It is quite convenient to reach the roadside groggery, and the liquor is furnished so cheaply that it requires but a small sum of money to drink at will. Nothing can give one a clearer idea of the illusions of intoxicating liquors than the way they blind one to his religious vows. The Shastras of the Nepali castes—the Bahun, the Khas, and the Thakuri—prohibit drinking, but these very people now indulge freely. "Their caste rules could restrain them from making intoxicants in their own houses, or from going to the other castes to procure them; but they have not sufficed to save them from the seductions of the government liquor-shops, whose keepers are only too willing to connive at secrecy, though even secrecy is now but little practised. Such cases generally commence with brandy obtained on the sly, or 'as medicine,' in the imported spirit-shops, and finish with 'country spirits,' taken in open and shameless defiance of religion and morality from the out-still shops."* The Rev. A. Turnbull, a missionary in Darjeeling, addressed a postal-card to the proprietors of the one hundred and ninety-nine tea plantations of the district, and inquired whether or not they considered the excise shops established by the government along every public road and in every private and public bazar a public evil, injurious to the local tea industry and to the material and moral interest of the tens of thousands of tea kulis. One hundred and forty-four replies were returned, and all except three were positive in their declaration of the curse of intemperance to the tea industry. One manager says ten per cent. of his laborers get drunk. The Brahmans of Darjeeling are breaking all caste by selling liquor in the bazar. Mr. N. L. Roy says: "The liquor traffic has corrupted the morals so that the laws of religion and the binding customs of society are being totally disregarded for the sake of strong drink. Why is it so? Because the temptations to drink are great—the facilities and opportunities for drinking are ample and daily increasing. And how should it be otherwise, since government is at the head of the drinking traffic? It defies competition with any other trade. I have been now eighteen years in Darjeeling. When I first came there was, to my knowledge,

* "The Traffic in Strong Drink" (Darjeeling), pp. 5, 6.

only one grog-shop; now there are nine such shops in one bazar."

Poresh Ram Patni, of Dinajpur, an honored native, thus describes the extreme present cheapness of liquor, and attributes the growing intemperance in large measure to that cause: "I remember the time when the out stills were first in use, many years ago. After that we had the Sudder Distillery system, and the shopkeepers were not allowed to distil liquor in their own houses. At that time it was only possible to buy liquor at a rupee a bottle. If you wanted half a bottle the man would charge you eight annas, and four annas for quarter of a bottle, and so on. Now that the out stills have been established, you can buy four kinds of liquor—the cheapest at two annas, the next at four annas, then at eight annas, and the last at one rupee a bottle. The lipuor we can now buy for one rupee is much stronger than that we could buy for the same price in former years. The bottle now sold for eight annas is equal to that we could buy for one rupee before."

Mr. J. H. Newberry, Collector of Rangpur, declares that the natives, when they drink at all, drink to excess: "Laziness, poverty, crime, and disease are the usual moral effects of excessive drinking. Natives of this country who drink any intoxicating liquor at all never seem able to restrain themselves to healthy and moderate drinking. They all drink to excess."

All these testimonies relate to the tea districts of India. The increase is equally great elsewhere, and equally destructive of the local industries. The Bengal excise commissioner makes the following important declaration: "There has been, undoubtedly, a very great increase of late years in the number of spirit-drinkers among the wage-earning classes, including those who cultivate land on their own account in addition to working for hire. This has been most marked in the Behar spirit-drinking tract, in the cities of Bengal, and in the centres of the jute-pressing, cotton and jute spinning, and coal-mining industries.

"The city of Monghyr rivals Patna in drunkenness, and the evidence taken at Jamalpur, even after the necessary deductions have been made for exaggerations and inaccuracy, proves that there has been a great increase of drinking among the workmen of that place." Mr. French, the manager of the Churaman Ward's estate in Dinapur, a man who has had fifty-two years' experience of the country, gives this evidence: "After forcibly describing the increase in drinking observed by him, he stated his belief that it is entirely due to the increased facilities with which liquor can be obtained at his very door. A deputation of the East Bengal Landowners' Association, who met the president of the commission at Dacca, stated to him that, in their opinion, the increase of drinking among the lower classes is in a great measure due to the shops being situated in markets and such-like places, and there can be no doubt that the selection of improper sites for shops has had much to do in most districts with the increase of drinking and drunkenness."

As to the quality of the liquor now served to the people of India by the government, there is but one opinion. It is a miserable decoction, adulterated and diluted, and can be sold at a profit for *two cents a bottle!* The natives can go to the grog-shop, and, poor as they are, are known to barter their smaller articles, such as shawls and umbrellas, for liquor. The liquor is anything but attractive in odor to the average European in India, and it now passes under the name of "Billy Stink." But, the passion for it being formed, the ill odor has no power to repel. It is a terrible arraignment which the Archdeacon of Bombay makes when he says of the English in India: "For every Christian we have made in India we have made one hundred drunkards."

Movements to Arrest Intemperance.

It cannot be supposed that such a great increase in intemperance could take place and move steadily forward without exciting profound attention, not only among the Christians of India, led by the strong missionary force, but by the English at home. The protest has gone from India to England, and now a sentiment is rapidly forming in the latter country which is giving great hope to all the churches represented in India. The debate in the House of Commons on March 13, 1888, was remarkable in every respect. Mr. Caine took up the cause of temperance in India, and proved that even the statistics had been manufactured, especially in the cases of Ahmadabad, the Island of Bombay, and Cawnpore. The debate was participated in by Lord Randolph Churchill, Sir G. Campbell, Sir J. E. Gorst, Mr. S. Smith, Sir Richard Temple, Mr. Boyce, and Sir J. Ferguson. Defence of the present system was made by some of the speakers. But the great array of facts presented by Mr. Caine was such that no amount of apology could mitigate the fact itself that the government, without intending to increase the traffic and intemperance, is nevertheless the real author of the astounding growth of the passion for intoxicating drinks and its consequent crimes.

In Darjeeling, where the tea plantations are a most important industry, there has been formed the Darjeeling Temperance Society, which is supported by prominent civilians, missionaries, and educated natives. It has issued a pamphlet giving an account of an anniversary held in June, 1888, and containing addresses by influential speakers and a large correspondence from tea planters, testifying to the increase of intemperance and to the responsibility of the government for it. An influential native writer, Dinshaw Edulji Wacha, has published a large pamphlet, showing the injurious effect of the present policy of the government in preventing crime from intemperance.* The British Soldiers' Association is an important organization in India, which has resulted in the signing of the pledge of total abstinence by ten thousand soldiers in the Indian army. Perhaps of all the organizations now operating for lessening the crime of intemperance in India, the Native Races and Liquor Traffic United Committee, of London, is the most important. It publishes valuable documents, sees that the public is well informed, and is using all proper methods to influence English opinion in favor of temperance in India.

The missionaries in India are alert in this important work. There seems to be no dissenting voice that the crime of intemperance is rapidly on the increase. All the churches are interesting themselves. When union conventions are held, the discussion of the subject forms an important part of the programme.

One of the most hopeful of all the signs is, that the natives themselves are arousing, with great energy, against the growth of intemperance. Gyan Chandra Basak, a prominent Bengali of Calcutta, has become a pioneer in the production of a native temperance literature by preparing, in Bengali, an excellent hand-book of temperance. So far it is the only vernacular work on the subject. It abounds in strong points, and makes the sta-

* "Indian Ábkárí Administration" (Bombay, 1888).

tistics of drink do their full work. He is a member of the Calcutta Band of Hope, which already has a membership of one thousand. It is safe to say that, if the natives had the power of local self-government, they would break up every still in the country. Their religion, with all its traditions, is against the drinking of intoxicants. Some of the native princes are unwilling to give any endorsement to any system for collecting excise from the sale of liquors. The Prince of Mysore has not yet allowed the Out Still to be auctioned off in his dominions. The late Rajah of Travancore, a highly intelligent man, said he "could not understand the English people. They held a great many meetings, and had a very strong political agitation against the opium traffic; if it was wrong to get money out of it in India, it must be equally wrong to get revenue out of intoxicating liquor in India. Why is it not just as criminal to degrade Hindus as it is to degrade John Chinaman? Why is it not just as wrong to send brandy and whiskey to Calcutta as to send opium to Shanghai or Hong Kong?" *

There is in Bombay a native Temperance League, whose special object is to arrest the growth of drunkenness among the Marhattas in Bombay and Western India in general. A native gentleman of Bombay, who seems to be connected with no society, is laboring as an individual in the interests of temperance in the Colaba district of that great city. Mr. Gregson, wishing to find out his motive for his crusade, inquired:

"Is it against the government?"

"No," was the reply.

"Do you threaten the people with violence?"

"No."

"Do you obstruct them in going to the shops?"

"No; my only reason is that I do not want the vice of drunkenness to spread among my countrymen," was his grand reply.

The native Indian writer is a master in the art of arranging English authorities and example in England against English example in India. An illustration of this keenness of criticism may be seen in the manner by which a native author, Wacha, introduces a fact in English history, supported by no less an author than Lecky, in his "History of England in the Eighteenth

---

* Quoted from Gregson, "Drinking and the Drink Traffic in India," p. 10.

Century," in condemnation of the present wholesale reaping of financial profit by England in India from the revenue from intoxicating liquors, and in proof of the groundlessness of the government's plea that restriction of the liquor traffic is a real barrier against increased intemperance. Lecky says: "By the year 1736, so frightful was the drunkenness, that even the sluggish parliament under Walpole was moved to strong measures; a duty of 20*s.* a gallon was imposed on all spirituous liquors, and a license of £50 a year was required for selling them in less quantities than two gallons. But these measures, which would have well-nigh extirpated gin-drinking could they have been enforced, were overstrained. The consumption of spirits, indeed, sank from 5,394,000 gallons in 1735, to about 3,000,000 in 1737; but at the cost of violent riots, and soon a clandestine retail trade arose, very lucrative and very popular, till in 1742 no less than 7,000,000 gallons were distilled. Then the law swung from one extreme to the other, and in 1743 the duty of 20*s.* was reduced to a penny, the license of £50 was reduced to 20*s.*, but neither drunkenness nor even clandestine selling yielded to this new mode of treatment. . . . At last, in 1751, wise and practicable measures avoided the excess of the law of 1736 and the defect of the law of 1743. . . . These laws were not beyond the capacity of the nation, and although not extirpating the chronic evil of spirit drinking and drunkenness, allayed the acute malady of the previous thirty years, and caused a notable diminution in the consumption of spirits, in drunkenness, and in disease."

The Results.

The effects of intemperance are the same the world over. Crime and poverty fatten on the vice, but there is a difference in countries. The evils of intemperance magnify in the ratio of the unevangelized state of the people who are cursed by it. The self-restraint possessed even by people living in a Christian land, and yet themselves not practical Christians, is one of the most patent of the indirect effects of the Christian religion. The atmosphere of Christian life has its effect on all who breathe it. But in such a great conglomeration of races as India presents, where the number of Christians is very small compared with the entire population, the general effect of the easy access to intoxicating liquors by every kuli in the land must be terrible. The missionaries are united in their testimony of the invasion of their hard-won little Christian folds by the growing vice. The Rev. H. Onasch, of Ranchi, in the district of Lohardugga, for example, makes the following report of the danger to his work among the aboriginal people of Chota Nagpur:

"Having been now for more than seven years here, and having plenty of opportunity to see the natives in their villages, I with a sorrowful mind state that drunkenness among Christians, Hindus of all classes, and Mussulmans is increasing rapidly.

"Referring to the native Christians of my own Church here, I will prove my assertion from the annual statistics since 1880, which I still have with me, viz.:

"In 1880, among 29,000 Christians: habitual drunkards, 41; moderate drunkards, 160.

"In 1881, among 30,000 Christians: habitual drunkards, 79; moderate drunkards, 163.

"In 1882, among 30,000 Christians: habitual drunkards, 61; moderate drunkards, 356.

"In 1883, among 30,000 Christians: habitual drunkards, 250; moderate drunkards, 274.

"Though we missionaries have done our best to check the evil, and though we have been successful in many cases, yet we have not been able to obtain a satisfactory result. Now if people under the Word of God and under Church discipline show an increase of drunkenness, how much more will this be the case with those who are under no obligation whatever; and it is, indeed, deplorable to observe how drunkenness affects the non-Christian Kols both in their moral and material condition. They are daily to be found in large numbers drunk in their houses, in the public places of their villages, such as the weekly village or town bazars, near government distilleries, and on the roads. A few instances will confirm what I say. In February last I came along the road from Kalamati to Ranchi. At the government distillery, at Topadana, a large number of Hindus and non-Christian Kols were sitting near the distillery, and nearly all of them in a more or less drunken state. The Chaukidar from Hatya was among them, and, on seeing me, came up to my cart and tried to stop me from going. I reached Doranda before sunset. Passing through the government distillery, I observed a large number of men, women, and children, sitting and drinking liquor. I stopped and looked at them, and found most of the men drunk and quarrelling, and thirteen women in a state of intoxication."

There is, however, not a mission field in India to-day which is not endangered by the growing intemperance. The Syrian Christians are cursed with the vice. The Roman Catholics are indulging in the same way, "even children learning early to drink, going with their parents, and getting a little from them." *

The Hill tribes, which are the descendants of the races conquered by the Aryans, and have ever remained more impervious to foreign influences because of their gross life and dense ignorance, are particularly affected by habits of intemperance. The liquors which they drink, and are growing fonder of all the while, kill with astonishing rapidity. The indigenous races have neither self-respect nor the power of self-discipline. They drink until they are drunk. The wayside shop, with the signboard, "Wines and Spirits Sold Here," means certain death to them.

An army surgeon, of twenty years' intimate knowledge of India, in a paper read before the Colonial Temperance Congress in 1886, wrote thus: "Twenty years' personal observation in the Northwest Provinces has demonstrated to me the appalling fact that the entire race of hereditary owners of the soil have all been swept off by drink. Brandy or government rum is what these poor creatures take to when the taste has been lighted up; and it is certainly a subject for thoughtful consideration that, while we in this country are rejoicing at the reduction of the excise revenue in Great Britain, what are we to say of the gradually increasing liquor revenue in India." †

What wonder? A penny's worth is all that is needed to intoxicate, madden, and wreck. Even if a poor native has no money, he can manage to get liquor. He can get it on credit, and mortgage his few possessions, if so be he can quaff the in-

---

* Mateer, "Native Life in Travancore," p. 284. This author furnishes some sad proofs of the invasion of the Travancore congregations by intemperance, and also some beautiful illustrations of the rescue of natives from the habit by becoming Christians. See pp. 284, 285.

† Ridley, "One Aspect of the Present Outcry against Foreign Missions," p. 8.

toxicating cup?* Then the back door—that invention of the saloon-keeper in Great Britain and the United States—is made to do its full work, if the proprieties prevent ingress by the front door.

Now, dark as this picture is, which we have unwillingly been compelled to draw, there is no real ground for discouragement. The gospel has never been carried to a country without at the same time, if not earlier, the transportation of the vices of the land which sends the truth. Already the missionaries are awake to the danger. The English people are becoming aroused to it. The real rulers of India did not hold council in Calcutta, or enact laws in the Westminster House of Parliament, but are the broad commonalty of the British Isles—or, rather, are the whole Anglo-Saxon race. The Indian conquest will be complete alike over the evils of false faiths and the vices which still grow, as tares among the wheat, in Christian lands.

---

* Gregson, "The Drink Traffic in India," pp. 45, 48.

BLACK TOWN, CALCUTTA.

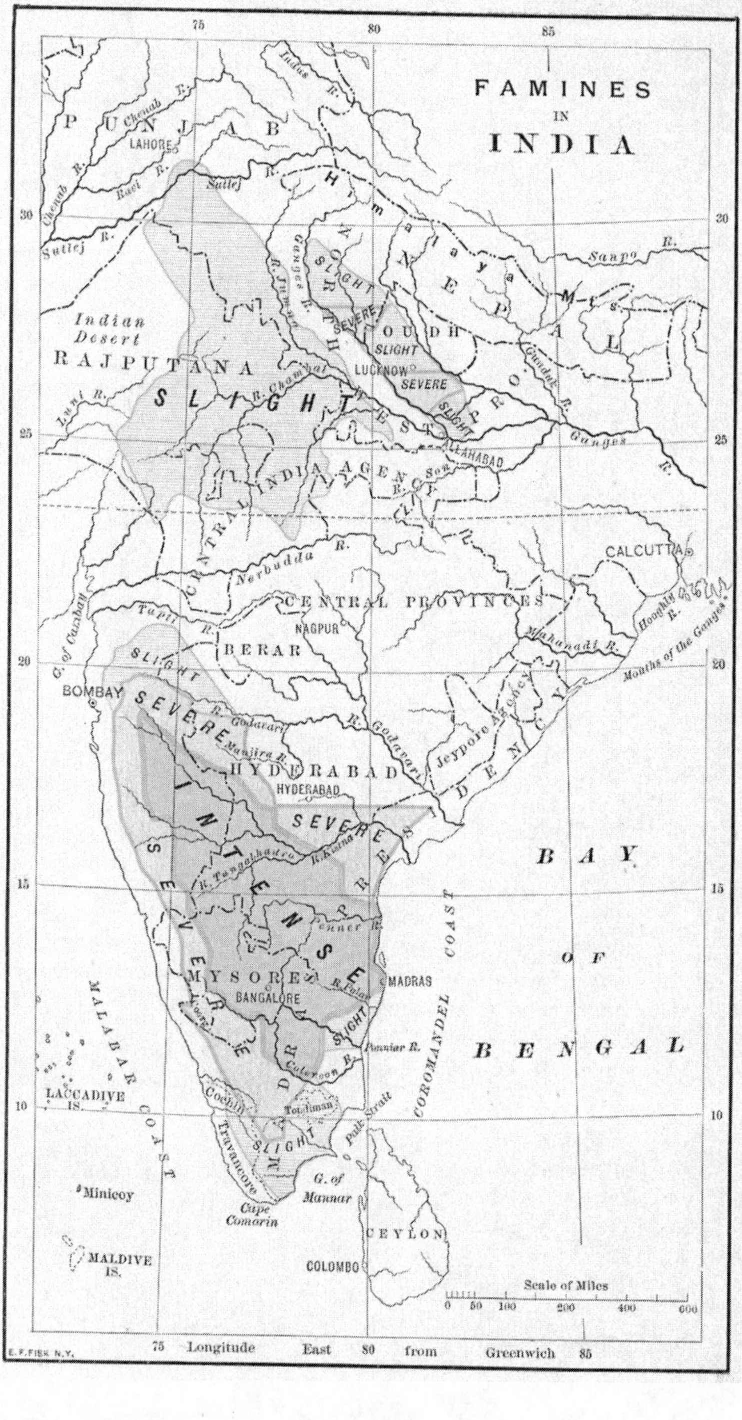
FAMINES IN INDIA
PUNJAB
LAHORE
RAJPUTANA
Indian Desert
SLIGHT
SEVERE
OUDH
LUCKNOW
ALLAHABAD
NEPAL
CENTRAL INDIA AGENCY
CENTRAL PROVINCES
CALCUTTA
NAGPUR
BERAR
BOMBAY
HYDERABAD
INTENSE
MYSORE
BANGALORE
MADRAS
BAY OF BENGAL
COROMANDEL COAST
MALABAR COAST
LACCADIVE IS.
Minicoy
MALDIVE IS.
CEYLON
COLOMBO
Cape Comorin
G. of Mannar
Palk Strait
Scale of Miles
75 Longitude East 80 from Greenwich 85

CHAPTER LVIII.

FAMINES OF INDIA.

ONE of the most appalling of all the evils from which India has suffered has been its famines. There are no adequate data for calculating the poverty and loss of life which have come from this one scourge. When the people of a district suffered

A HARD SWIM FOR IT.

the loss of their crops because of want of rain, they regarded the visitation as a direct mark of providential displeasure. Their gods were angry, and what could be done? Here is a picture of the famine of 1770. "All through the hot season," says

Hunter, "the people went a-dying. The husbandmen sold their cattle; they sold their implements of agriculture; they devoured their seed grain; they sold their sons and daughters, till at length no buyer of children could be found; they ate the leaves of the trees and the grass of the fields, and in June it was reported that the living were feeding on the dead. Two years after the dearth, Warren Hastings made a progress through Bengal, and he states the loss to have been at least one third of the inhabitants, or probably about ten millions of people. Nineteen years later Lord Cornwallis reported that one third of Bengal was a jungle inhabited only by wild beasts."* It was of this same famine that Lord Teignmouth wrote:

> "Still fresh in memory's eye the scene I view,
> The shrivelled limbs, sunk eyes, and lifeless hue;
> Still hear the mothers' shrieks and infants' moans,
> Cries of despair and agonizing groans,
> In wild confusion dead and dying lie.
> Hark to the jackal's yell and vulture's cry,
> The dog's fell howl, as midst the glare of day,
> They unmolested on their victims prey!
> Dire scenes of horror, which no pen can trace,
> Nor rolling years from memory's page efface."

It is estimated that in the famine of 1770 not less than ten millions of people perished. The greatest famines which have desolated India have occurred in the years 942, 1631, 1770, 1837, 1866, 1876–78. In the last great famine (1876–78) no less than sixteen millions of people were sufferers, by either death, disease, or insufficient food.† Gradually the government is getting control over the famines. It spares no labor or expense to bring relief. By means of the railways it furnishes quick transportation of provisions to the suffering people. In a single decade —1873 to 1883—the government expended seventeen million five hundred thousand pounds sterling on famine relief alone. The Rev. George Bowen says, truly: "Famine, this deadliest of Indian plagues, has now become all but impossible in consequence of the facilities afforded by the improved communications of the country."

* "England's Work in India," pp. 22, 23.

† Digby, "The Famine Campaign in Southern India," 1876–78, vol. i. p. 69.

Formerly, help was borne to a famine-stricken or pestilential district by slow and primitive means of transportation. The relief was scanty at the best, and many thousands died without help from any quarter. But now all parts of the land are brought into close relationship. England found India carrying its treasures of produce in a bullock cart, but now she stretches out her railways and canals, which, as arteries, sustain the life of the many millions.

INUNDATION OF THE INDUS.

CHAPTER LIX.

THE INDIAN INDUSTRIES.

One of the most interesting departments of the study of India lies in connection with her industries. Through the tour of the Prince of Wales in India, Europe has become acquainted with many of the industries of the country to which it was formerly a comparative stranger. Many gifts were presented to him, and

WOOD-CARVERS AT WORK.

some of them were of such exquisite workmanship and rare value that they excited the admiration of all who have seen them. On his return he gave permission that they be exhibited in various parts of the British Isles, and in every instance they awakened profound admiration. In addition to the interest excited by these gifts, the attention paid to India by the managers of the South Kensington Museum, where there is a large collection of objects illustrating the arts and industries of India, has contributed largely towards our acquaintance with both the ancient and modern life and employments of the people.

ANCIENT SPECIMEN OF WOOD-CARVING.

The traveller in India is amazed at the special industries peculiar to each locality.* Wood-carving is done in many places. Not only is the rich native's furniture often a triumph of the carver's art, but the very house itself, especially the façade, dating from the Mogul period, exhibits rare skill and taste. Wages are always low.

* Birdwood, "Industrial Arts of India," vol. i. p. 137. This, with Watson, "The Textile Manufactures and the Costumes of the People of India," London, 1867, will supply all necessary special information on the industrial life of the people of India.

For example, the skilled wood-carver receives at most six or seven cents a day. In most of the Hindu arts each city has its specialty. One kind of brass work is manufactured at Benares, and an entirely different kind at Moradabad. Cawnpore has long been illustrious for its leather-ware. The rich pottery of Jaipur is known throughout the length of India, and is now easily distinguishable in Piccadilly and Regent Street. Each place has an industry peculiar to it, which we must believe has come down from distant times. I have often been impressed, on looking at some striking ware, to observe the readiness with which a European resident in India would say where it had been made. The various fabrics worn by ladies are seldom produced in one large place, but are derived from many, and often very distant from each other. Each town has acquired its celebrity for its special ware, and every interest prompts to continue it.

Dacca, for example, has been celebrated for its muslins for twenty centuries. They were brought from India to ancient Rome, and were worn by the wealthy Roman ladies, as they walked along the Forum or lingered in the balconies overlooking the Tiber, while the Cæsars were yet ruling the great empire.* These fine, soft muslins are still made by the slow and simple contrivances managed by the hands and feet of the Indian artisan. They are sent abroad, and reach the markets of what was only savage Germania and Britannia in the days of Tacitus.

Alexandria was founded by Alexander for the special purpose of being an entrepot for Oriental trade. De Lesseps, by his construction of the Suez Canal, has carried out to practical fulfilment the very idea which Alexander the Great had when he built at the eastern end of the Mediterranean the city which to this day is his best claim to immortality. Long before the beginning of the Christian era there cannot be a question that Indian products found a market in that multiform city. Abu Fazl says that, in his day, the arts and sciences of India were three hundred in number.

Among the more prominent industries the weaving of rugs and shawls may be mentioned. The contrivance is very rude and primitive, but the products are exceedingly rich. The patterns are as intricate as they are beautiful, and some of them are of great antiquity. There is little doubt that rugs woven to-day in the valley of the Ganges, and shawls woven in Kash-

* Ker, "The Land of Ind," pp. 222, 223.

mir, are reproductions of patterns already old before the Aryans poured down in dense masses from their home in the table-lands of northwestern Asia. Many of the jails of India are centres for the weaving of fine rugs. The convicts are, in this way,

GOLD-BROCADE WEAVERS.

made serviceable to the state. There is great demand for the rugs woven in the jails. In Agra I saw a long row of "lifers," or prisoners for life, who were chained to each other by the feet, engaged in weaving a magnificent rug for Queen Victoria, and another row weaving a rug for the ex-Empress Eugénie, the latter probably as a gift for an altar. I found that in both Agra and Ahmadabad there was a scanty supply of woven wares on hand. Dr. Tyler, the superintendent of the jail at Agra, told me that orders must be given months in advance, in order to secure a good rug.

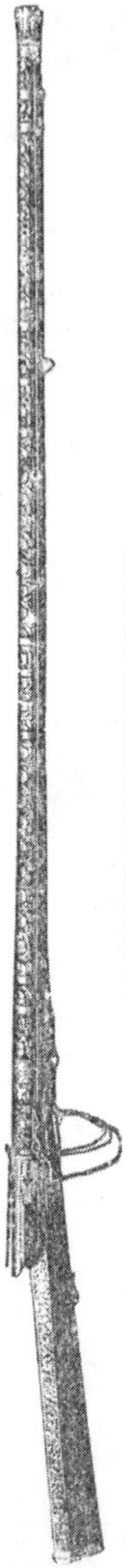

GUN-BARREL, DAMASCENED IN GOLD.

Paper is manufactured in different parts of India. The Serampore paper is now the favorite for general printing. Perhaps the paper longest known in India is that made in the Himalaya Mountains, from the inner bark of the *Daphne Cannabria*. The weaving of cotton goods has been carried on from remote times, for even the Rig-Veda speaks of the "weavers' threads."

The Portuguese found sealing-wax in use during the early part of their residence in the country, or in the year 1563. The silk industry was probably imported from China, but it has been long in existence in India. However, the people of India much prefer the weaving of wool to that of silk. Lacquer work was observed by Dampier in the 17th century, and was described in his account of his Indian journey. Calico-printing was practised by the ancient Hindus. Encaustic tiles, enamels, pottery, bleaching, printing in gold, brocades, engraving, gold wire, stuccoing, mosaic in fine jewelry, and the making of glass, first colored and then colorless, were known to the people of India from remote times. The leather work of Kashmir and Cutch descend from ancient days. Gold thread is still spun and twisted in Trevandrum. The use of alloys, in the treatment of the precious metals, is ancient, and is still practised with marvellous skill. One has only to linger awhile in the native bazar of Lucknow to see how successful has been the transmission of this ancient industry. The ancient Hindu knew well the proper combination of carbon with iron for the production of perfect steel. No blade of steel has ever surpassed that made in the humble forge of the ancient Hindu.

The tendency in these later days is towards the introduction of improved industrial machinery, and the doing away with the slow and laborious methods in use from time immemorial. In Travancore the most of the thread used in the country for indigenous looms is the coarser English cotton-twist. The native dealers procure it, and it is furnished cheaper than a similar quality can be supplied at home, and is more easily and evenly woven.* It is admitted free of duty. All the weaving in Travancore is done on private looms. There is now no special tax on looms, and hence the census takes no note of the whole number of looms. But the census reports of sixty years ago in Travancore alone gave the whole number of these household looms as four thousand one hundred and seventy, and the number of workers on them as eight thousand six hundred and eighty-seven. In former times the silks of Europe were made in the humble homes, while the little cottages along the shore of Lake Zurich produced the first silks introduced by the emigrants from

NECKLACE, PANJAB.

* Mateer, "Native Life in Travancore," ch. xxii.

Lombardy. But the simple looms, in Europe as in India, are constantly giving way to the combined work in the factory.

Where cotton cloth is introduced into Travancore from England, however, the cost is about one fourth more than the retail price in England. It must be admitted that while the tendency everywhere in India is towards the introduction of improved machinery, the disposition is everywhere growing to make use of European fabrics. One has only to see the large supplies of European goods in all the large towns, and the large number of the better classes clothed in European clothing, to be convinced of the fact that it is only a question of a little more time and money before the population of India will be clad in European dress.*

The most recent tables—twenty-fifth and twenty-sixth—of the Indian Statistical Abstract, contain the following description of the area actually under cultivation, the area at present uncultivated which might be cultivated, and the proportions of the different crops. The total acreage of India, according to the Survey Department, is 480,667,094 acres. Deduct 116,615,483 acres, the area of the feudatory and tributary states, and of other districts for which agricultural returns are not obtainable, and with which the figures do not deal, and we get 364,051,611 acres as the area of British India for agricultural purposes. Of this less than half, or 152,834,640 acres, is actually under cultivation, including 22,725,391 acres of current fallows. Of this 166,492,-458 acres which is uncultivated, rather more than half is fit for cultivation, and the remainder is not available for that purpose, so that an area of 80,000,000 acres in British India still awaits the husbandman. The area under forests, which is not included under either cultivatable or uncultivatable land, is 40,185,729 acres. The distribution of crops is as follows: rice, 23,114,662; wheat, 19,883,040; other food grains, including pulse, 71,439,218; tea, 226,412 (almost wholly in Assam); cotton, 9,852,654; oil seeds, 7,678,382; indigo, 1,034,889. It thus appears that there is practically unlimited scope, so far as area is concerned, for the increased cultivation in India of crops which are mainly intended for export, such as wheat, cotton, indigo, tea, coffee, and other products.

* See Appendix No. VII. for Official Census of the Trades and Occupations of the People of India.

In Ceylon the acreage of crops is reported as follows: tea, 150,000; coffee, 100,000; rice, 700,000; other grains, 150,000; cocoa-nuts, 450,000; other palms, 130,000; cinchona (quinine tree), 35,000; cacao, 13,000; cinnamon, 35,000; fruits and garden produce, 300,000. This acreage comprises but one fourth of the total area of Ceylon. Three fourths of the island are still jungles for wild elephants and other beasts; mountain ranges which have never yet produced a crop; and dark haunts for human beings who are as degraded and primitive as the cave-dwellers of Chihuahua.*

* Bishop C. H. Fowler, Correspondence of *Christian Advocate* (N. Y.), April 11, 1889.

THE SUPERB BIRD-OF-PARADISE.

CHAPTER LX.

POVERTY OF INDIA.

One of the first impressions made upon the traveller in India is the extreme poverty of the people. The people abound. In walking through the streets of the larger towns, the multitudes prevail. Go where one will, there are human beings. The average population to the square mile is two hundred inhabitants. In one district (Burdwan) there are six hundred people to the square mile. The people are poorly clad. A cotton-cloth around the loins is the entire costume of many millions. One cannot help halting and observing a little group of natives taking their meal. It is of the simplest quality, all vegetable or farinaceous. The question arises, How do the people exist on such simple and scanty fare? Yet they do exist. Starvation takes place only in time of famine. The average annual income of each inhabitant in India is difficult to determine. One authority says it is seven dollars and a half. Bishop Thoburn, who has lived in the country thirty years, says that the average wages for a man and his family, is five cents a day, and under favorable conditions, two dollars a month. Rice is the chief meal of the laboring classes. Besides rice, the people eat cakes of coarse meal made of millet. The poor never eat meat, or bread made of wheat. It is safe to say that ten millions of the people of India never sleep under any other covering than the open sky.

Compared with that of other nations, it would seem that the low rate of wage-earning is beneath the power of endurance. In England the average income per inhabitant is one hundred and seventy-five dollars; in France, one hundred and thirty dollars; in Austria, eighty dollars; in Spain, sixty dollars, and in Russia, forty-five dollars.

That many of the people of India are underfed is universally admitted. Sir William Hunter says that forty millions go

COMPARATIVE TABLE OF CROPS IN INDIA.

DIAGRAM A.

Showing the Areas of Crops cultivated in the following Provinces.

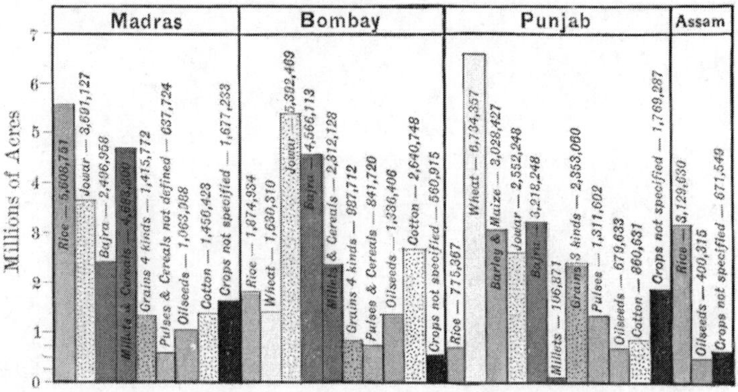

The areas of Crops in Madras, Bombay, Punjab, North West Provinces and Berar are given in full. — The returns from Assam, Oudh, Central Provinces and British Burma are incomplete in details.

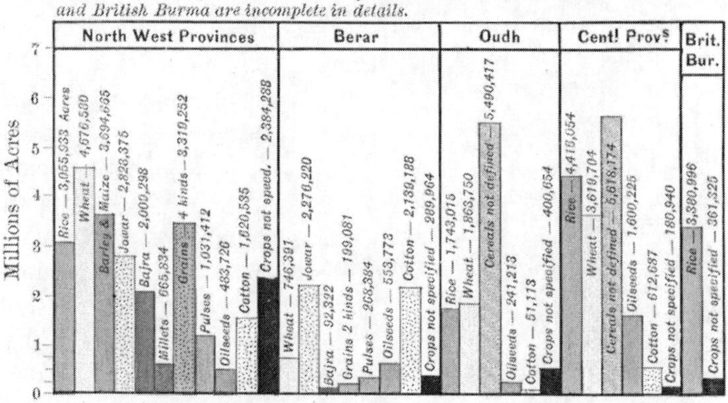

DIAGRAM B.

Showing Cultivated, ▭ Culturable ▭ and Unculturable ▭ areas ▭ indicates the portion for which returns are unavailable.

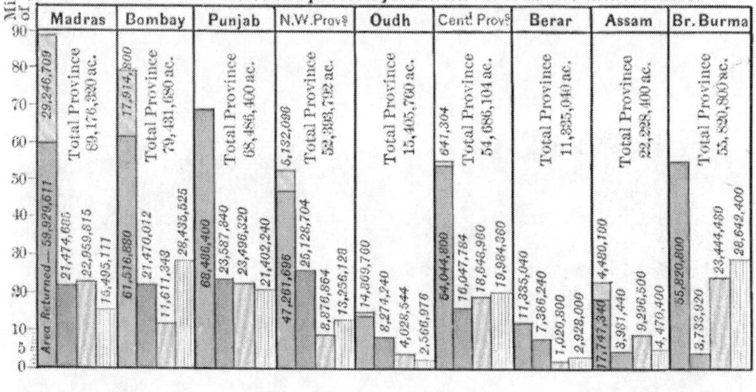

WOMEN WEAVING.

through life with too little food. This is probably a low estimate of the number. Sir Charles Elliot, Chief Commissioner of Assam, says: "I do not hesitate to say that half of our agricultural population never know from year's end to year's end what it is to have their hunger satisfied."

Some of the causes of this extreme poverty of the millions of India are not difficult to discover. The history of the country, until the English became the rulers, has been one long warfare. The highest use of the citizen was estimated to be in the ratio of his capacity to bear arms. To build up the individual man; to find employment for him; to see that he supported his family; and to secure his prosperity, as the highest function of the ruler, was never taken into the account. How many men could the leader kill in battle was the important question. The business of the average Hindu and Mohammedan was the use of deadly weapons. When great battle-fields, as Panipat more than once, were covered with many thousands of the slain, this was regarded only as the price which had to be paid in order to go into the next war with greater advantage and brighter hope of victory.

Much of the money belonging to the State was in the form of jewels or precious metals. These were stored in great subterranean vaults, as in Golconda, drawing no interest, and to be used only in organizing great schemes of new warfare. They were as useless as the surplus in the United States Treasury, and the ground of less political wrangle. The knowledge of the amount and place of concealment of these treasures was known to only the ruler, and a very few of his most trustworthy counsellors. When the ill fortunes of war brought out this stored wealth, the great amount of it surprised the conqueror. Clive must have been astounded at what his eyes saw, when he triumphed over the native kings. Nana Sahib's wealth was measured only by the cart-loads. Only within a couple of years great stores of treasure have been discovered beneath the ground in the palace of Gwalior. The treasures of the Marhattas, the highway-robbers of the late Indian history, almost defy our powers of credence. In addition to the countless wealth already brought to light, we can safely take for granted that the amount still concealed is immense.

Sir Henry Maine finds the great cause of India's present poverty in these concealed treasures. He says: "The true secret of the poverty of India, from which she is slowly recovering, I take to be the desolation caused by the war and brigandage of about two thousand several chiefs, while the Mogul dominion was dissolving. I think India during the reign of Akbar and Jahangir was probably as rich as the Western World thought, but its carefully hoarded capital was destroyed in the same way as the accumulations of the Roman Empire." Sir Richard Temple confirms this judgment. "The historical accounts of the plunder, realized after military or political catastrophes, may seem fabulous, but are nevertheless well founded, despite rhetorical exaggeration. There never has been a country where wealth was so much concentrated, or so little diffused, as the historic India. Hence the traditional ideas of Eastern wealth have indefinitely exceeded the reality. Besides these central accumulations of goods and property, there must have been much wealth collected in divers lesser places. No economist can study the story of the Marhatta conquests, wherein statecraft was chiefly devoted to the organization of plunder with unparalleled skill and audacity, without wondering how the country could have endured visitations so long protracted and so oft repeated. Here is proof, however, of the national habit of collecting, hoarding, and secreting property. Descriptions of accumulated wealth occur in the histories of the wars of the present generation; for example, the verified accounts of prize at Haidarabad, in Sind, in 1842, at Delhi, Lucknow, Kirwi, and other places during the war of the mutinies. During many years past, even up to this very day, the dacoities, or gang-robberies, which occasionally break out, tell the same tale of wealth collected in rural as well as urban homes, to an amount which might not otherwise have been suspected."

Now what do these hidden stores of precious stones and gold and silver prove? That the governments of India regarded concentrated capital as the real possession of the State, and not as properly the distributed possession of the individual subject. To acquire sufficient property, under the Mogul rule, to live in ease and comfort, without being in some way connected with the court, must have been next to impossible. The same may be said to apply to the Hindu courts existing before the Mogul rulers. War was the normal condition of the countries governed. The wealth of the land was really poured into the general treasury. The Hindu subject was only a machine for money-getting in the scanty periods of peace and money-snatching in the general time of war.

Other causes are clear enough. Among these is the great amount of wealth bestowed on the construction of places of worship. Then, the mosques and temples once built, the service in them was supported by great endowments. Further, the revenue applied to the support of the rulers was immense. There seems to have been no limit. Each ruler was only one man in the midst of a great horde of military chiefs, nobles, courtiers, and counsellors. All these grew fat from the public treasury. Palaces abounded. No caprice of the ruler or his friends was left ungratified. The nation was fairly exhausted to satisfy every lust. Even death put no stop to the certain and steady current of the people's earnings into the vaults of the palace. Tombs in memory of the dead were built, some of them by enforced labor, which were equalled only by the palaces of the living. No Roman emperor was ever honored with such tombs as were erected to some of the Mogul rulers. The Taj Mahal, erected to the memory of an empress, whether estimated by the wealth of its materials or the labor expended in rearing it, surpasses by far any known tomb in memory of a Cæsar.

Now these causes of India's poverty are slowly passing away. The government is economically administered. The earnings of the people are not spent on the construction of places of false worship, or for the support of the service in them. The interests of the native millions are steadily kept in view, and honesty characterizes every part of the management of the affairs of the empire.

The greatest present cause of poverty is to be found in the need of a sufficient and proper cultivation of the soil. India possesses all the needful climates. Her soil is rich. Much of it is still virgin soil, despite the many millions of the people. Take the presidency of Madras as an example. The arable area in that one presidency is 72,858,000 acres; but the portion which is actually cultivated is only 26,580,000. The rest is *poramboke*, or uncultivated land. Of the land under cultivation only twenty per cent. is irrigated. "The unirrigated and dry land is eighty per cent. Of the latter, a very large part consists of the worst of soils. The tillage on these soils is also very poor. Our native plough stirs, but does not overturn the soil, and seldom penetrates to a greater depth than three inches. There is also no such thing as after-cultivation, or hoeing. As to our irrigated land while it is under crops, it receives very little attention beyond watering and weeding." *

In addition to the small amount of cultivated land all over India, compared with land which could be cultivated, we must not forget that down to this day there is no science of agriculture throughout the country. There has really been no opportunity to develop such a science. Long periods of peace, security of person and crops, and a ready market, are all great boons which India, with all her treasures, has not yet possessed. Even the English have not, as yet, had the opportunity to do this important work. Their mission so far has been to acquire, solidify, and prepare for a great future this immense people. Even the elementary work of rotating crops has never been understood by the natives. The most which the India farmers understood, just here, is "the general principle that the soil should not be exhausted, but beyond allowing the land to be fallow, and raising during a portion of the year some vegetables from an insignificant area, they know of no established and scientific system of rotating the crops."

The attention of the government, and of the English people resident in India not connected with the government, but in sympathy with the development of all the material interests of the land, is now being devoted to the need of a larger area under cultivation, of a better understanding of agriculture as a science, and of better agricultural machinery and methods. Agricultural schools and colleges are springing up. In Madras the Saidapet College of Agriculture, and the Government Experimental Farm connected with it, are good beginnings. An excellent agricultural journal is published by the students of the Saidapet College. Constant progress will be made in developing, not only the productiveness of the soil and the enlargement of its area, but a taste for agriculture and a knowledge of its

* K. Sundararaman, article on "The Poverty of India," in *Christian College Magazine*, Madras, October, 1887. We acknowledge with pleasure our obligation to this paper, by a well-informed native writer, for important information on this interesting theme.

laws. The government has given abundant proof that it has its eye on this great source of national prosperity, and will spare no needful outlay for the attainment of its object.*

One of the means employed by the government to cultivate a taste for better agricultural methods among the natives is the agricultural exhibition. One recently held in Kathiawar, inaugurated by Colonel Nutt, was very successful. It was the eighth time a similar exhibition had been held in the same place, but was of larger scope than any preceding one. English residents, native chiefs, and large numbers of the general population were in attendance. There were exhibits of horses, cattle, sheep, and other animals, besides fruits, grains, manufactures, and an important collection of articles made by women. Lectures on agricultural subjects were delivered at stated times on each of the three days that the exhibition lasted. A series of ploughing-matches concluded the exhibition.

Much is to be done for the natives in correcting false ideas of wealth and many wrong social ways. For example, when a marriage ceremony takes place, the family of the bride will spend an amount of money out of all proportion to its means. The Nách girl or the musician must be paid for, an extravagant amount of silks and of other valuable cloths is bought, and many jewels are purchased. The father of a bride contracts a large debt for a marriage ceremony.

The passion for acquiring jewels, instead of available property, seems to continue. It is probably an inheritance from the earlier generations of the unsettled times. "I maintain," says Sundararaman, "that in *every* family in this country there is a disproportionate amount of the fortune of the family locked up in the form of jewels. There are families which can boast of 50,000 rupees worth of jewels, and often this amount is exceeded. It is a very ordinary thing that over a third of the possessions of a family which has an estate of 10,000 or 15,000 rupees should be locked up in jewels. Even in the poorest families, there exists this disproportion of jewels to possessions. When Messrs. Orr & Sons put forth their advertisements in the *Hindu* regarding Hindu ornaments, they are said to have realized in the very first month a sale of over 20,000 rupees."

* On the special pains taken by the government to improve the agriculture of India, see *Encyclopædia Britannica* (9th Edinb. ed.), vol. xii. p. 752.

The native of India has arrived at one great idea—that he can invest nowadays with comparative safety. There is no rapacious ruler to snatch away his earnings. He is beginning to lay up a little. Immense treasure, in small amounts, is now transmitted between natives by the post-office. Investments are constantly increasing. Many of the natives are taking shares, with the English, in the establishment of commercial enterprises. Some of the ancestral industries are reviving, and adapting themselves to the new mechanical contrivances for larger production. The increase of the foreign trade reveals a large development of native as well as foreign industry and enterprise. Thirty-three years ago the foreign trade of India amounted to only $250,000,000. Now it amounts to $700,000,000, the export trade of which amounts to $400,000,000. With the growth of agriculture, the enlargement of the earlier industries, the improvement of business habits, and the development of a commercial taste, the imports will be less needed. Why should India import cottons from Manchester, or cutlery from Sheffield, or pottery from Staffordshire? She was producing all these wares in great beauty and fineness when the Briton was dancing in savage glee around the rude circle of Stonehenge. She can do it again, though the Briton has gone to Westminster, and has produced Hampden, Shakespeare, Bacon, and Milton, and new civilizations beyond many seas.

CARVING ON THE BUDDHIST TOWER AT SARNATH.

AGRICULTURAL SHOW AT WADHWAN, KATHIAWAR, INDIA.

CHAPTER LXI.

BENARES THE HOLY CITY.—MORNING SCENE ALONG THE GANGES.

"ARE you going to Benares?" and "Have you been to Benares?" are questions one often hears during his tour in India. The Anglo-Indian never thinks you have seen the country well unless you have cast your shadow upon the holy Ganges at Benares.

This city is the central sanctuary of all Hindu worship, the metropolis of Hindu trade, and the fountain-head of Hindu learning. In tender associations to the Hindu mind, no spot approaches it. To have been born in Benares is a life-long blessing, and to die on the bank of the Ganges is the highest aspiration alike of prince and peasant. If a Brahman in any part of India has seen the Monkey Temple, or the Golden Temple, and laved in the Ganges at Benares, he is ever afterwards more highly esteemed by his townsmen, while it is a glad day in any rajah's palace, wherever he may live, when a new cask of water from the far-off sacred river is announced.

THE ORIGIN OF BENARES.

No one has determined the time of the origin of Benares. It was some time during the period when the Aryans held full sway in the country, and before any of the present faiths had been dreamed out. It first appears as a great Indian centre, but of the stages through which it passed we know nothing. It was over six centuries before our era, or 638 B.C., when Sakya Muni halted here, on his way from Gaya, and expounded his religion. Even then Benares was probably the home of a very busy population, or there would have been no attraction to that reformer to begin his work here. The great writers of the Hindus here wrote their works, and from this sacred centre sent them out on their mission to the Hindu world. No success could be hoped for if their thoughts did not first find expression under the same sun which smiled upon Benares.

The Brahmans do not like the name Benares, which Wilson, in his Sanskrit Dictionary, says has the meaning of "best water." They call their holy city Kasi, the Magnificent, for such it is in all their thoughts. A cheap little guide to the city in Hindustani, for sale by any little knot of Hindus, and written by a priest, gives in grave language the reason why Benares is the most sacred place in the world.

"It is commonly thought by Christians, Mohammedans, and others who are unacquainted with the truth, that this holy city of Kasi rests upon a portion of the earth. But such an opinion is altogether erroneous, as it has been revealed to us by the gods, and as our senses are at times permitted to discover. The world itself, since the days of its creation, has remained supported upon the thousand heads of the serpent Ananta (eternity), and so it will continue to be upheld until the command of Brahma shall be proclaimed for it to be forever enveloped in the evils of that interminable deity. Now, when the judgment takes place, the city of Kasi, with a circumference of ten miles from its centre, will alone remain firm. For it rests upon the heads of Ananta, but is fixed upon the three points of the trident of Shiv, or Mahadev, to whose care it will be intrusted. All who now die within its walls are blessed, and those who are found within it on that eventful day shall be blessed a thousandfold. Ages before the Mohammedan conquest of this city by the Sultan Mohammed, which happened in the seventh century; ages before it was made subservient to the Patans, which was a hundred centuries earlier; ages before Kasi was the second capital of the Hindu kingdom of Kanauj, which was the case a hundred centuries before that; ages before history has any record, Shiv built this wonderful city—of the purest gold, and all its temples of precious stones. But, alas! the iniquity of man contaminates and destroys the beauty of everything divine. In consequence of the heinous sins of the people, the precious materials of this sacred place were deteriorated, and eventually changed into stone, by permission of the founder Shiv. . . . Lately, the excesses and wickedness of the inhabitants are again increasing, and now the indignant Shiv is beginning to display his anger by turning the stone edifices into huts of mud and thatch."

GHATS.

This is the Brahman's conception of Benares. It is the city of his faith. Its vilest waters, its most malarious sinks, its decaying weeds, are alike sweet and dear to him.

I had ample time for my visit to this most remarkable place. Dr. Lazarus met me at the station, and entertained me at his beautiful home. His cultivated wife and daughters made my visit delightful as it passed, and charming as a memory. They took me to all the points of interest, introduced me to persons whom it was a pleasure to know and now to remember, and accompanied me to the station, when leaving for Allahabad.

Morning Scene Along the Ganges.

No scene in Benares can equal the strange panorama presented by the bank of the Ganges in early morning. Our *choti hazari* was finished betimes, and we drove off through the English cantonment, then into the narrow streets of the dense native city, and came to a halt on the bank of the smiling and busy river. Here we took a little boat, and ascended the deck, where we found chairs. The rowers barely touched the water. We simply glided slowly along with the current. It was the time of devotion. There are stairways at frequent intervals, leading from the water's edge up to the temple portals.

The multitude are already out, bathing or getting ready to bathe, or robing themselves again, the bath being finished. There must be several thousands in all. Some are far out in the water, their heads just above the surface of the sacred stream, and their eyes fixed upon the eastern sky. They do not move a muscle, but are lost in meditation. No stranger's face or sudden splash has any effect upon them. They are as fixed as the sacred pipul-trees upon the banks. Others have their holy Vedas before them, and slowly turn the worn leaves. Their faces wear a pleased expression, as though they know the promises are fulfilled now and here. Others recline upon the stepways up the ghats, the bright sun pouring its welcome heat upon their bared heads. Many are pilgrims, and their joy is great, as they walk out into the sacred stream, and halt, and put their heads beneath its surface, for the first and only time, after the pilgrimage of perhaps a thousand miles. Not a few, perhaps, of these have measured the whole distance of their wandering by their own bodies, their method being to lie upon the ground, stretch out the hand as far as possible, mark the spot which it can reach, and then get up, put their feet at that place, lie down again, and so repeat the measurement. A great many of the bathers have brass water-jars with them, which they fill for use through the day, if living in Benares, or, in case they live at a distance, for carrying to their far-off homes.

Every minute presents a new scene. Here, at an open space, is the expiring fire where a body had been burned, and the little mound of pale ashes in the centre is all that is left of the beloved. The portals of temples on the river front are filled with outgoing or incoming worshippers. Occasionally a splendid private home comes into view—a Hindu prince's house, which he has bought, and is now occupying, until the silver cord shall be loosed. The Brahman who dies on the banks of the Ganges has the shortest path to heaven.

Sacred bulls roam everywhere, no hand injuring one of them, and all of them fed by reverent Hindus. They can stop and munch at anybody's strawpile or doorway, and are always welcome guests. Many people are eating their simple morning meal, as though this place, by the river-bank, makes holy any dish. Priests are to be seen in the midst of the multitude. It is said that out of the total population of 600,000 in Benares, 80,000 are officiating Brahman priests.

The fakir is the most ostentatious of the priestly class. He sits by the roadside, covers himself with dirt, lives on alms, mumbles his prayers, and holds his face towards the blazing sun. Here, on the bank of the Ganges, is many a fakir. They lean on the incline of the ghats, and are well out in the water, or rest on a boatside, and seem lost in contemplation. Their faces are seldom cheerful. They are pictures of filth and despair. The women of the upper Hindu classes are not to be seen just now. They have all gone home. They left their houses early in the morning, say at four, were borne in palanquins to the bank, entered their richly ornamented boat, and were rowed out in the middle of the stream. The boat, by a peculiar construction, has a lattice-work for the water to run through. The bottom is firm, and here they take their bath, unobserved by any eyes, and are speedily rowed back to their palanquins, and are borne homeward by fleet-footed kulis.

But not all the rich are thus early. Some have only just arrived, and will soon be off again. Their journey has been long and painful. The rest of life, they know, is short. But it must be sweetened by a bath in the sacred river, and sacrifices of flowers in the temples of Benares. The joy which overspreads many a face, as the holy water laves it for the first time, can

ELEVATION OF TEMPLE OF VISHWESHWAR AT BENARES.

be seen in a moment. It is the fulfilment of the hopes of a life-time. Is the water cold? Yes. I could not endure the shock three minutes, yet these people seem to be accustomed to it. However, there is many a trembling form. It is the religious associations which make all pain an ecstasy.

Infanticide.

In former times the drowning of female children was a common incident in this busy morning scene. The following picture is true to history:

"Zeida hath laid her basket down,
Her offering to the sacred river;
No tears even yet her eye doth own,
But every feeble limb doth quiver;

"And sobs each like a dying gasp,
Burst from that agonizèd breast,
To which, with strong and straining clasp,
The hapless babe is pressed.

"A smile across its features plays
Unconsciously—and now another,
Answering the miserable gaze
Of that most wretched mother."

* * * * *

"A thrill of anguish shook her frame,
Then a brief frenzy o'er her came,
The thin veil from her head she tore,
And the poor infant round and round
In the soft gauzy folds she wound,
That soon its struggles might be o'er.

"And with quick steps, though each one sank,
In the green, oozy river bank,
Down among the reeds she cowered.
There gently laid the fated child,
And, o'er it, from her basket, piled
Green leaves, and blossoms showered,
Then pressing both hands to her head,
As if in agony of fear
Its dying shriek to hear,
Nerved by despair, with frenzied speed she fled."

Drifting with the Ganges.

We halt now and then, to take in more fully the strange morning scene in the Ganges at Benares. Palaces, bearing the names of all the principal native rulers, line the bank. Towers, lattices, porticoes, spires, and minarets, of all colors, form a matchless panorama of Oriental splendor.* Every moment the panorama shifts. But in each case there is animation. The scenes upon the forty-seven stepways, or ghats, which lead up from the river's edge to the terrace along the upper bank, are at once

A WINDOW IN BENARES.

bewildering and revolting. One face I can never forget—an aged man, absorbed, with eyes fixed upon the sun, as though hoping that he might be wafted that moment from the Ganges to the celestial city. Brahmanism and Mohammedanism exist

* Temple, "India in 1880," p. 35.

side by side here. We drift with the current until we come opposite the tall minaret built by the great Aurangzeb.

When the Mohammedans captured Benares, three centuries ago, they mutilated many of the temples, but did not prohibit Hindu worship. Their policy in India was more liberal, perhaps, than on any other conquered field. While permitting many of the Hindu temples to stand, they planted their own mosques, and reared their minarets, in close proximity. The mosque and minarets of Aurangzeb, on the bank of the Ganges, at Benares, however, stand on the site of a temple of Mahadev, or Shiv, or, as he is commonly called, Siva.

View from a Minaret.

The minarets are of singularly graceful proportions, and no view of the busy scene along this river in early morning is complete which does not include the prospect from the balcony at the top of one of them. We turn towards the bank, step ashore, pick our way through the busy bathers, and ascend the one hundred and twenty steps of the ghat to the platform of the mosque. Sacred bulls crowd about us, as though the lords of this creation. Dogs, too, abound, and are sure of their rights. They are a mangy herd, and I took pains to keep as far from them as possible.

The ascent to the top of the minaret is by a stairway, which, with the steps up the ghat, makes the whole distance from the surface of the river to the balcony of the minaret two hundred and fifty feet. The air within the minaret is stifling, and I am very glad to reach the balcony and feast my eyes upon this wonderful picture.

Benares lies at my feet. The green and smiling English part of the city stretches like a horseshoe about it, each end resting upon the bank of the Ganges. Far out in the country the fields are beautiful and of varied colors. The curves of the river, above and below, are exceedingly graceful. All along the bank, at my feet, there is a world of life and variety—people from all Hindustan wading, floating, or resting in the water, or scattered up and down the stepways of the ghats. Temples of all sizes now come out into new splendor within the native city. The narrow streets run in all possible directions, without the least regard to angles or points of the compass.

CHAPTER LXII.

A RIDE THROUGH BENARES.

At the foot of the minaret we found our carriage in waiting, and began to thread our way through the street of the brass-workers to the Golden Temple. It is dedicated to Shiv, the poison god, because Shiv swallowed the poison when the gods churned the ocean. The temple is a square, with three towers above it, a dome at each of the three corners. The towers are of stone, over which are copper plates, and over these again are gold plates, the latter giving the name to the temple. The quadrangle, constituting the temple proper, is thronged with worshippers.

The Well of Knowledge.

Near by is the celebrated Well of Knowledge. Here Shiv is supposed to reside. The stench of this well is intolerable. There is a shop near by where flowers are sold for offerings to the god. Every worshipper buys some of them, and comes to the well and casts them in. Then there are others constantly standing about the well, drinking the filthy water, as though it were nectar. The flowers fall into the well, and there decompose, and the water is thus made filthy and poisonous. It is surprising that such water does not produce almost instant death. Pilgrims come and go all the while, but no pilgrimage to Benares the Sacred is complete without at least one precious draught from the Well of Knowledge. There are natives beating gongs near by; fakirs lounging about, covered with dirt; begging monks of all ages; and a throng of pilgrims, constantly walking over the wet quadrangle to the holy well, drinking, dropping their coins, casting in flowers, and then moving slowly off, as if they had had one view of the eternal city, and must now go out into the gross world again. For offence to all the senses, I never saw a scene equalling this. I became faint because of the dense and corrupt odors of the spot, and we hurried away.

A common object of attention is the sacred cow. Here and there one moves along, stops at a bazar front, and gets some food, none daring to deny the intruder a wisp of straw or hay. The bull, throughout Bengal, bears heavy burdens, but his life is held to be sacred. Observant travellers claim that the na-

SCRAMBLING FOR PEAS.

tives feed him sparingly, and yet get all the labor out of him possible, without endangering his life.*

We drive next to the Monkey Temple. Here is a place where the monkeys are the principal object of interest. We have no sooner come to a halt than they slip softly out from their places of concealment behind trees or houses, and leap gleefully

* Jacolliot, "Voyage au Pays des Fakirs, Charmeurs," p. 124. Paris, 1881.

about. They are in great numbers, and appear to expect something to eat. However, as we are only Christians, we have failed to supply ourselves with provisions for the filthy but sacred brutes. Many of the monkeys live in the hollow of an old tree near the temple. They scamper about all parts of the temple spaces, and appear to have undisturbed access to the whole consecrated place.

While Benares is the centre of Hindu worship, it early became a field for Christian missions and education. I have nowhere seen a more beautiful school for native girls than here. Mrs. Lazarus was acquainted with the ladies in charge, and I had the opportunity to visit all departments of it. The girls range from about three to eighteen years of age, and are all, to the number of five hundred, instructed in the various branches of an English Christian education. The ornamental work, such as embroidery, is beautifully executed. This school occupies a large building in the heart of the native city. Between that on the one hand, and the offensive temple service on the other, it is not difficult to tell which will win in the long race of the future.

Queen's College.

Queen's College is a fine institution, founded in 1847, in part by private subscription and in part by government aid. It is well located, in a broad open space, and its appointments are comfortable and attractive. The lecture-rooms, library, and archæological collection compare favorably with any institution of similar grade in England or America.

Old Sarnath.

If we do not know the age of Benares, how shall we arrive at that of the city which preceded it? About four miles in the country from the city of to-day there are remains of two great towers, whose mode of construction and general shape prove them to be memorials of a time long anterior to any of the most ancient structures which have thus far been discovered in Benares. The group of houses near which they stand is called Sarnath, and a drive thither occupied an afternoon. Here Miss Lazarus was my wise and patient guide. Long before we reached the place the higher of these towers stood out prominently, and when we came in full view of it, and rested within its shadow, it was clear, from the remarkable belts of carving, that we were in the presence of one of the oldest memorials in all India.

Here, in this ancient Sarnath, we came across the traces of the Buddhism of the India of the distant times. This was the Deer Park at which Buddha arrived on leaving Gaya, and, attaining to Buddhahood, where he began his public ministry. The great tower was designed to commemorate some act, or a spot, to which special sanctity was attached at the time, but of which there is now no record. It was originally of immense size, and ornamented with great care. Whether it was part of a great building, whose traces are now entirely gone, no one knows. But this much remains—an immense tower, one hundred and twenty-eight feet above the plain, with a diameter of ninety-three feet. The lower part is of stone, and the upper of brick. There are broad faces around the lower part, in which are niches, where images of Buddha probably stood. Around the whole are fillets, of singularly beautiful and symmetrical patterns. These fillets are worthy of the closest study. The very sections which make up one fillet repeatedly change, and yet so closely do the two which join resemble each other that one barely observes the transition.

The patterns belong to a very remote period, and will, in time, help towards the determining of the exact age of the tower. The upper part of the tower was either never finished, or has been injured, and so long ago that it has the appearance of a great structure falling to pieces of itself.

The Chinese Buddhist pilgrims of the fourth and seventh centuries visited Sarnath, and described the two towers, but without throwing light on the purpose of either. The later of the pilgrims states that the kingdom of Varakasi, or Benares, was six hundred and sixty-seven miles in circumference; that in the city there were thirty Buddhist monasteries, which supported three thousand monks; that the great tower was built by Asoka; that the Deer Park monastery was divided into eight parts, and contained palaces; that each of the niches in the tower held a statue of Buddha in embossed gold; that west of this was the tank where Buddha bathed; and that, farther along, was the tank where he washed his monk's water-pot; and, still farther, the one where he washed his clothes.

We went within the wall enclosing the ancient monastery,

and examined every part. From there we proceeded to the smaller of the two towers, and clambered up the elevation on which it stands, and then to the top of the structure itself. The

BUDDHIST TOWER AT SARNATH, NEAR BENARES.

view of the beautiful country, and the city in the distance, was charming. The ride home through the English cantonment was delightful, and a fit close to my busiest day in Benares the Sacred.

CHAPTER LXIII.

A HALT AT ALLAHABAD.

Mr. Howard, an advocate of Allahabad, accompanied me to the chief points of interest in that "Holy City." That gentleman had come to India when a very young man, and was in Allahabad when the mutiny broke out. He was one of the many civilians who saw the danger, shouldered his musket, and did excellent service until the mutiny was conquered. It was a rare pleasure to have the society of a gentleman of such varied culture, and especially of such intimate acquaintance with the historical associations of the city and its fortifications.

The Allahabad of to-day is, in the Indian sense, a new city. About three centuries ago Akbar, greatest of the Moguls, founded both the city and fort. But this was by no means the first Allahabad. Here the Jamna and the Ganges form a junction. Each is a large river before the two unite. After the union the Jamna loses its name in that of the Ganges, and the great stream moves on with a majesty and power impressive in the extreme. There is no place in the whole length of the wonderful river to which such large bodies of pilgrims resort as on the plain outside the city where the rivers unite. A bath here has a peculiar sanctity, and must have had long before the Mohammedans crossed the Indus for the conquest of the region watered by the Indus and the Ganges.

If we look at the commanding location, the advantages for defence, and the delightful atmosphere, this must have been one of the earliest places in India to attract a population and to grow into a commercial centre. It first comes into notice in the third century before the Christian era, when Megasthenes, the Greek tourist, visited it. That industrious Chinese pilgrim, Hiouen Tsang, also visited the place, and makes mention of it in his travels. The old city was, perhaps next to Benares, the most sacred to the Brahman mind of any place in India. The peculiar ground of the sanctity was that Brahma here made sacrifices of the horse in memory of his having recovered the four Vedas from Shankhasur. When Akbar conquered the place, every attempt was made to give a Mohammedan color to the new city which arose upon the old. But the change of masters has made little change in faith. Of the one hundred and fifty thousand people, one hundred thousand are Hindus.

The sacred tongue of land where the two rivers combine is hallowed, and will remain so until the Brahman faith floats away

THE MAGH MELA, OR ANNUAL FAIR, AT ALLAHABAD.

before the Christian cross. It is estimated that at the Magh Mela, a religious fair, not less than from half a million to one million devout Hindus come from every part of the country to see it. Many people die on the way; others die while encamped on the plain, and still others on the way home.

Here I encountered the first strong reminders of the great mutiny of 1856 and 1857. Benares felt the shock, but did not suffer materially. What was the cause of the great difference between the places which suffered and those which did not? Why did not Benares and Allahabad run with blood, as did

Cawnpore and Lucknow, and, longest of all, Delhi? It was a twofold cause—generals, on the one hand, and English faith or no faith in the native soldiers, on the other. Wherever a general relied solely on the loyalty of the native troops, they betrayed him, and slew him and his countrymen. Wherever the general distrusted them, and had them so officered and distributed, and so armed that their ammunition and arms could be taken from them, he was master of the situation, and little or no blood was shed. Because Wheeler, in Cawnpore, placed full confidence in his sepoys, not only did he fall, but the city was converted into a butcher's pen, at the mercy of Nana Sahib. Allahabad came very near being a scene of like bloodshed. A mere incident saved the day. Captain Plunkett believed in the native soldiers, and allowed them their guns. But Captain Birch begged Colonel Simpson to reclaim the guns, as they were wanted in the fort. The sepoys refused to allow the guns to be brought to the fort, and were making off with them. Then the Oudh cavalry, also natives, were ordered to stop them; but the cavalry sided with the sepoys.

This was a fearful crisis. Shots were fired; fifteen English officers fell, and confusion reigned supreme. Off in the fort there was a body of Sikh soldiers. These Sikhs had been conquered in the northwest by England, and some were now employed as soldiers. It was a question what they would do. It was feared they would join the sepoys and the Oudh cavalry. But to the surprise of all, they did no such thing. Their officer, an Englishman named Brasyer, had their affections, and he drew up his stalwart Sikhs, and had them ready to fire. The sepoys were ordered to give up their guns. They wavered a moment. The pause was fatal to them. They began to fear the levelled muskets of the Sikhs. They surrendered their guns, and Allahabad was saved to the English.

Meanwhile the jails had been opened by some sepoys, and out came the convicts, with clanking chains, which the natives could not unlock. These people went from one English house to another, and set fire to them, and caught every English man, woman, or child they could find, and then cut them to pieces and cast them into the flames. It was pandemonium. But it lasted only a short time. The victory had been won at the fort, and to the small band of English soldiers and Sikhs now came the brave volunteers of Allahabad. Englishmen who were only civilians, but who kept guard at the fort night and day, had learned in a few days how to use arms of every size. The triumph of the English at Allahabad constitutes one of the brightest pages in the history of British heroism in that land.

Mr. Howard conducted me to the esplanade of the fort, where I enjoyed a charming view of the country for many miles, and where I could see at my left the confluence of the Jamna and the Ganges. The dark water of the former is soon lost in the light water of the latter. The Ganges, after receiving the Jamna, is one mile and a half in width. There are many places at the fort where I could walk, and enjoy a different view at each point. The terraces, towers, double walls, parade-ground, and comfortable officers' quarters form a most pleasing picture of a life far different from that which ruled here in the old times, when Akbar reared the fort, and, later, when the Emperor Jahangir had his palace here, and dispensed rude justice amid all the splendor of a Mogul court.

The Asoka Pillar is one of the most interesting historical monuments in India. It represents a class, now almost gone, of finely polished shafts, of granite or other durable stone, which date back nearly to the beginning of the Christian era. They contained Asoka's edicts, and were set up in various places throughout the country, as convenient means for promulgating laws. But when the land was overrun by new conquerors, the latter made use of the vacant faces of the pillar to record their own triumphs. This pillar in Allahabad is the best preserved, and by far the finest, which I saw in India. Generally, the Asoka pillars are in several fragments, and, though erect, are supported and braced by iron bands. In the present case, after the inscription of Asoka there is another by Chandra Gupta, and still another by the Emperor Jahangir. This last is a record of the date of the emperor's accession to the Mogul throne.

When near the Pillar of Asoka we visited the celebrated Akshai Bar, or Imperishable Fig-Tree. We descended a few steps, and found ourselves in an underground passage. After going thirty-five feet in one direction, the chamber makes a turn to the left, and extends thirty feet farther. Here, in the darkness of this place—and it is as hot as it is dark—there is the trunk of a fig-tree, which has neither roots nor branches, and yet throws out leaves. This is owing to the moisture which prevails in the place, and so long as any sap remains in the log there is an occasional appearance of leaves. The Hindus have a rare gift for turning any phenomenon into religious uses. So they have made a most holy sanctuary of the place where this worthless object is. The hundreds of thousands who come to the Mela every year must, of course, see the Akshai Bar before going home, and bring offerings to Shiv, whose statue is in the middle of the cave. When the log of the fig-tree gets dry, and can produce no more leaves, it is secretly removed, and another immediately substituted for it.

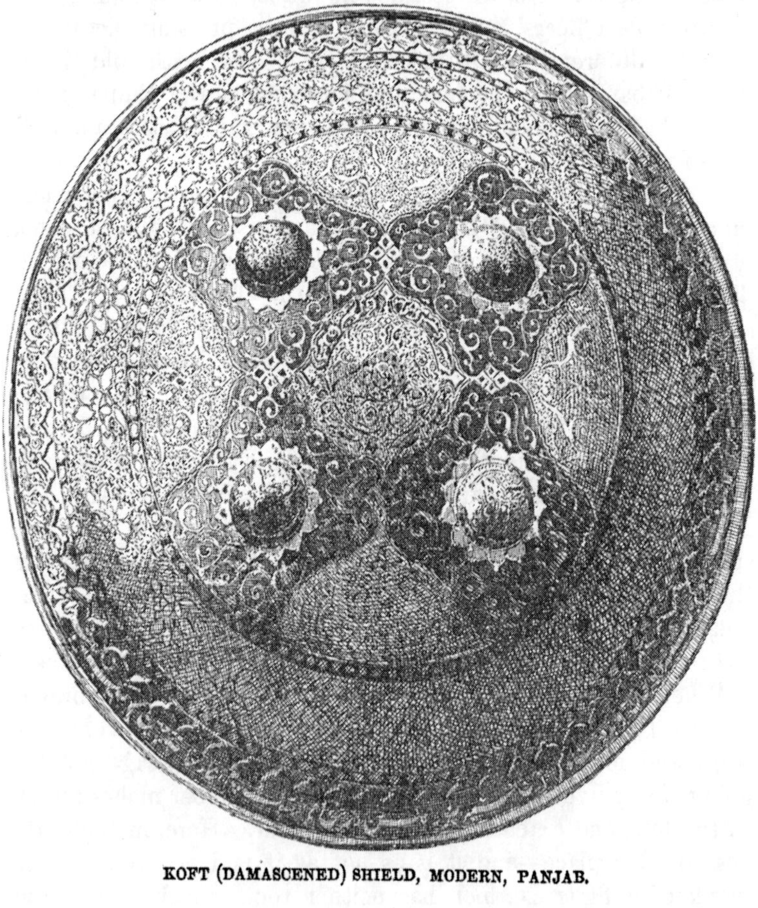

KOFT (DAMASCENED) SHIELD, MODERN, PANJAB.

CHAPTER LXIV.

CHRISTMAS IN CAWNPORE.—CHRISTIAN WORKERS.

My arrival in Cawnpore was in the midst of Christmas festivities. The English residents in India do not forget the Christmas associations of their mother country, but convert their Indian homes into scenes of festivity. The churches are decorated. The houses are all aglow with joy. Gifts come over from England, and go far and wide to the dear ones scattered over India, Ceylon, and Burma. This time of unusual joy is chosen for the great festal occasions in the schools. The native mind is profoundly impressed by the general gladness, and there are no happier people than the native Christians, to whom Christmas comes with a welcome which means far more to them than all their former pagan festivities. All the ecclesiastical bodies and the various missionary societies share in the gladness. The Christmas celebration in India, therefore, combines the domestic memories of England and the United States with that sacred significance of the great event which unites the Christian churches of all lands.

My Christmas in Cawnpore furnished an excellent opportunity to see the brotherhood of missionary workers, and to observe, in miniature, the triumph of the Gospel over the dying faiths of India. Cawnpore is, possibly, not in advance of some other Christian centres. But I soon found abundant evidence that the missionary advance here was far beyond my most sanguine anticipations. What would the immortal Henry Martyn, who lived in Cawnpore awhile, say if he could only see the transformation which has taken place since his humble beginning? If the people far away in the West, who have contributed largely to Indian missions, could see the many thousands who attend the Christmas services in Cawnpore, the multitude of native Christians, with their great company of teachers, and the thousands of children in the schools, they would be amazed and delighted at their Christian attainments.

All the churches at work in Cawnpore are succeeding finely. Here I met a friend of former years, the Rev. G. H. McGrew, D.D., who, with his West Virginia fibre, has wrought with a

GATHERING CHRISTMAS DECORATIONS.

steadiness of will and scholarly enthusiasm which were not surpassed by even a Marshman. He was busily engaged on a new edition of his "Makhzan i Ilm i Ilahi," or "Compendium of Theology." When I saw him taking ill-clad Hindu children by the hand, and patiently listening to their questions, I knew, even better than before, that a theological training, of itself, never unfits a man for the highest ministry among the needy, and for sacrifices to build them up into a beautiful life. Mr. McGrew had charge of the native Methodist Episcopal Church in Cawnpore, and before his return to America, in 1885, brought to completion the handsome new edifice in the busiest and most populous street in Cawnpore. The building would be an ornament to any American city. The Rev. Mr. Neeld had supervision of our Industrial School. He had already a good grasp on the language, and knew well the native mind. Here is a problem which is being rapidly solved by him and other missionaries in India — how a Hindu boy or girl can get an education, and earn it during the process. The young people in the school are all natives, but with as quick wits as ever battled with a spelling-book in any language. They work in English factories part of the day, and study the rest of the day, except such time as is given for recreation. By this system they not only secure a Christian education, but pay for it as they go. The Rev. Mr. Maxwell was the successful pastor of our English church. I had the pleasure of being present at a special Christmas service arranged by him, where every part was a beautiful and touching reminder of the usual Christmas exercises in the home-land.

Christmas was a busy day. Early in the morning, long before daylight, I heard the voices of a choir of young natives, who had come within our compound, and were doing all in their power to remind us of the joy of Christmas-tide. These were Christians, but there were many who performed little offices of respect for the day who were not Christians, and whose whole life, as either Mohammedans or Hindus, had been a violation of Christian teaching. They were tradesmen, servants, and others, all in some secular way related to the Christians and English-speaking people of Cawnpore. In the years past they had caught the meaning of the Anglo-Saxon's love of the day. They had observed the gladness. They had seen the happy children, and had learned why they valued the day. They knew it was the best and gladdest of all the year in the far-off lands of Christendom. Hence they were intent to do what would please the English-speaking people about them. Thus they became happy and great-hearted too, as another Christmas dawned.

THE SUCCESSFUL ROBBER.

They came with gifts of fruit and other trifles, to make even happier the English homes in Cawnpore.

I went with Mr. McGrew to a place where materials were collecting and work was beginning for a new missionary building. In two minutes the turbaned old native ran off into the grove and brought back fresh oranges, plantains, and other fruits, and lavished them upon us. Mrs. Neeld was receiving dishes and baskets of fruit and flowers, and other things, all day, borne by dark Hindu and Mohammedan hands. A close criticism would say that these people expected a full return in presents for all these things. Suppose they did. What if they thought that in one way and another they would get back tenfold for all they had brought? Even this was a tribute to the Anglo-Saxon's sense of gratitude. It was much for even a pagan to see the English gladness on this day, and to recognize it. His century and a half of contact with Anglo-Saxons had taught him why the heart of the Christian was happy when Christmas came. Of course, he knew the English hand never leaves itself a final debtor to the Indian. Touching, indeed, were these many heathen tributes to Christianity. Flowers and fruits were lavished upon the Europeans of Cawnpore, during this glad Christmas day, by people who had never dreamed of renouncing their idolatry. Even fresh leaves from the sacred peepul-tree were hung before the doors of the mission-buildings, as one way of paying a compliment to the faith which had brought the missionaries to that Eastern land.

The Industrial School had its Christmas celebration. Prizes were distributed for the most studious and industrious, while smaller gifts were made to every one of the scholars. It was a happy group. All were neatly clad. The most wonderful scene was the universal Christmas celebration, in the large Memorial School building. About twelve hundred children, besides many adults, were present. The head masters and teachers accompanied the young people. The girls were on one side of the hall, and the boys on the other. The girls might well congratulate themselves that they were there at all. Only Christianity would allow them to come on such an occasion and enjoy a public festivity. All the Indian faiths have trampled on womanhood these long ages.

The singing of the immense congregation of children was in Hindustani, and was very beautiful and varied. American melodies accompanied the Hindustani words. There were addresses, dialogues, musical performances, and all the belongings of a beautiful native Christian festival. There were a few seats, and they only for Europeans and Americans. The twelve hundred young people sat as flat on the floor as toads. It is their way. They are brought up to do it, and enjoy it. Clad in their bright colors, with their holiday smiles on, and waiting for the prizes and gifts of sweets and other things connected with the happy hour, certainly no happier company ever gathered together beneath the Indian sky.

I spent my last evening in Cawnpore with a company of Christian workers connected with all the communions of Cawnpore. Miss Easton, who had charge of the Young Ladies' Seminary, was my kind hostess. The hours I spent beneath that roof, in conversation with those noble workers for Hindu evangelization, are among the most delightful memories of my Indian winter. A part of our Christmas dinner, notably the oysters, was from the United States. The oranges were growing abundantly out in the grounds of the seminary, while roses of many varieties, and other plants, shed their fragrance along the pathways, and made glad and unique the Christmas hours.

The seminary is situated immediately on the Ganges. The flow here is rapid, and the river is very broad and deep. One acquires a strange liking for this wonderful Ganges. It grows dearer every day. I have crossed it over and over again, and have been rowed on it, and have wandered along its banks at leisure, and it at last became a friend. I always went to it, when within convenient distance, and sat upon the sward, and gazed upon its sacred waters. It is a river of humors and moods. It never greets you twice just alike. At no spot, in all its long flow, is it more nearly at its best, or does it wear a sweeter smile, than when it flows past Cawnpore.

CHAPTER LXV.

REMINDERS OF THE MASSACRE IN CAWNPORE.

One would never suppose, from these pictures of peace and beauty in Cawnpore at Christmas, that here were enacted the most brutal scenes in the terrible mutiny of 1857. Circumstances combined to make this place the very heart of the rebellion. A short distance up the river there is the village of Bithur. Here lived the last scion of the great Marhatta confederation. His name was Dandhu Panth, but commonly called Nana Sahib. He was the adopted son of Baji Rao, the last Peshwa, or king of the Marhattas, and the inheritor of his houses, lands, jewels, and other property. He had been adopted by the Peshwa in 1832, and had been trained to regard himself as a prince. A few years before the mutiny the old Baji Rao died, and the government, under the lead of Lord Dalhousie, declared that the dignity of the Peshwaship now ceased, and that Nana Sahib would inherit only private property. The pension and the royal salute were now withdrawn. All appearance of royalty ceased.

Nana Sahib's Revenge.

Nana Sahib resolved on revenge. The one hundredth anniversary of the Battle of Plassey was chosen as the day for retribution against the longer rule of the English in India. In the eye of the natives Nana Sahib represented the old royalty of the powerful Marhattas.* For four years he had tried to get the Board of Directors to reverse their decision, but they refused. Nana was quiet, but he thought only of revenge, and waited, close at hand.

But his nearness to Cawnpore was not the only ground of the weakness of the English position. The commanding officer of the English troops was the aged General Wheeler. He was a

---

* Lee, "The Indian Mutiny. Events at Cawnpore," p. 1.

simple-hearted man, and had but little fear of the mutiny of his native troops. Then, too, he was anxious to avoid giving to the natives any proof of suspicion of them, and, instead of having the English families take refuge within the magazine enclosure, he intrenched himself, and called the English people within his lines, and prepared for defence.

The Prison Pen.

But here he was practically helpless. The mutineers fired in upon his scanty force, killing alike men, women, and children. Wheeler's intrenchment was a narrow space. I could easily see its outline—a line of small stones, fifty yards apart, marking the exact dimensions. The whole space was only two hundred yards square. Outside the intrenchments was a well, into which the poor besieged people had to throw their beloved dead, at night, or at such moments as the dead could be borne to it, in intervals of merciless firing from Nana's troops. Cholera and small-pox had broken out within the enclosure, and there was no room for burying the dead. Two hundred and fifty bodies were thrown into this well during the three weeks of the investment. It is conjectured that as many as five hundred more bodies were otherwise disposed of, being buried by the mutineers or devoured by jackals.

The provisions were now scanty. The torrid heat was intense, there being no shelter for the beleaguered. Further resistance was hopeless.

Only a very few of these English people were soldiers. The most were civilians, ladies, and children. They were the families and friends of English people, either residing or visiting in India. They had, for the most part, been accustomed to all the refinements and luxuries of delightful homes. Now they were suddenly thrown upon the mercy of bloodthirsty natives. That they should die rapidly, under such exposure, was natural. But many were shot down by the sepoy sharpshooters from surrounding buildings.

Nana Sahib's Trick.

One day a note was received by General Wheeler. It was from Nana's own hand: "All those who are in no way connected with the acts of Lord Dalhousie, and are willing to lay down their arms, shall receive a safe passage to Allahabad." Here was an offer to the English to furnish boats to them to take them all down the Ganges to Allahabad, if they would surrender all their arms and ammunition. Wheeler thought it a very good offer. Some said, "No. We will live or die where we are." But Wheeler told them that the ammunition and provisions were nearly exhausted, and that the cholera and small-pox prevailed, and that the offer ought to be accepted. He carried his point over all the remonstrances. Twenty-one boats were loaded with the English sufferers, but all ran aground except one, which glided out into the stream. A few of the wretched English captives were still left on the river-bank, there being no boats for them. So soon as the twenty-one boats had been laden with the fugitives the sepoy mutineers, who were concealed on either bank, opened fire on them, knocked the boats to pieces, and let into the deep and swift Ganges those whom the shot had spared. Many struggled to the shore, but were killed or captured on reaching the bank. There were four, however, who escaped—the only ones who survived, to tell the tale of unparalleled cruelty.

GENERAL HAVELOCK.

Meanwhile the only boat which had escaped from the ghat ran aground a mile farther down the river. Here the people who were aboard, after desperate resistance, led by Major Vibart, were captured, and carried back to join those who had been taken at the ghat. Then the whole body were carried to Nana Sahib's headquarters and confined in two small rooms. Here, for two weeks, they suffered untold indignities. When Havelock approached Cawnpore they were transferred to another house, nearer the native city. There, the day before Havelock's victorious troops entered Cawnpore, the captives were cruelly slaughtered by Mohammedan butchers from the city, the sepoys having refused to do such revolting work. These men, with knives and swords, cut down the English prisoners, the fatal work taking from five in the morning until half-past ten. Three of those butchers fell prostrate by their efforts, overcome by the heat, the stench, and the sight of so much blood.

When Havelock reached this wretched place, then silent as the tomb, it took his men four days to bury the dead, either by putting them into the well or digging graves for them.

The English Revenge.

I learned here a most effective way of impressing the native mind with the majesty of English rule and the certainty of punishment. It seems that General Neill had the best chance to administer punishment. When he took the prisoners captured from Nana into the prison where the great massacre had taken place, the blood lay thick and clotted. General Neill had the whole floor marked off into squares. Then he made his captured sepoys clean it all up. He afterwards had them tied to the muzzles of his guns and shot into fragments. When the news of this method of dealing with the sepoy murderers spread abroad among the native population, it created the utmost consternation. Perhaps no one thing which took place during the mutiny produced a profounder impression on the native mind than this. The touch of Christian blood was a breaking of all caste, and, to the Hindu mind, a sending to immediate perdition every one who had done it.

Nana, with his main army, escaped. Nothing was heard of him until April of the following year, 1858, when General Grant's brigade captured a part of his army while retreating up into Nepal. His prime-minister, Azim Ullah, was killed by a round shot at a fortified village in Oudh.

The Capture of Nana Sahib's Treasures.

When the English were once more in full possession of Cawnpore, they went to Bithur to see if they could get possession of Nana's treasures. In his palatial compounds there were eleven wells, and it was believed his wealth had been concealed in one of them. The surmise was correct. An aged man told the soldiers which well contained the treasure. The water was drawn up. Then the bricks were taken out, and the treasure was at last reached. Seventeen bullock cart-loads of gold and silver treasure were taken from the well. Each cart, with its precious burden, attended by a special guard, was drawn to Cawnpore, and then to Calcutta, and afterwards shipped to England. This slow march of captured treasure through the country inspired the natives with an inexpressible awe. No secret was made of the

EXECUTION OF THE SEPOYS.

burden in the bullock-carts. It was England in possession of Hindu wealth. The military leaders performed another piece of effective strategy. They caused the guns taken from the Mogul chiefs in the siege of Delhi to be rolled all the way down from that city to Calcutta, and had them stopped in every town and village, to give the people an opportunity to see this strong proof of English power to overcome a great mutiny.

The fabulous stores of Nana's treasures suggest a theme of wildest romance. The Marhatta chiefs, risen from obscurity, had gained some of the most important victories ever won on Indian plains. Much wealth, in curious vessels of gold and silver, and in priceless gems, which had been in imperial hands for ages, fell into their hands. But India's princes always knew where to hide their wealth, and when the Marhatta power declined, the last scions of the royal family kept the place of the treasure a secret. It had been borne from place to place, and was held as a financial basis for a possible restoration of the former power. But it fell into English hands. So to London it must go, that no native of India might cherish the delusion that it rested anywhere on Indian soil, or could be brought into use again, to add splendor to a native court, or equip a native army, or buy a province.

The English had better success with Nana's treasures than with Nana himself. They never captured him. The story of his later fortunes is surrounded with mystery. It is supposed that when his cause became hopeless, by the English capture of Delhi, he went off into the jungle, and fell either by his own hand or by the wild beasts.

Scene of the Butcheries.

I spent an afternoon in going over the beautiful grounds which were once the scene of the cruelties and butchery perpetrated upon the English people. The desolate grounds of 1857 are now a picture of rare beauty. The whole region is converted into beautiful gardens, where shrubbery and flowers combine to form a scene of surpassing loveliness. The eye can see nothing but tropical luxuriance. Winding paths, clumps of rare flowers, and surprising combinations of foliage and colors, make a scene of varied and harmonious loveliness. Through the openings in the shrubbery one can see, in the distance, the now peaceful Ganges, hurrying on towards the sea, its sacred waters still cool from their cradle in the glaciers of the Himalayas.

The most notable object in these delightful gardens is a little octagonal Gothic structure, which crowns a mound of earth. In the centre of the building is the marble figure of an angel, by Marochetti. The arms are folded across the breast, and in each hand a palm is held. This edifice, with its beautiful angel, stands directly over the well into which the bodies of the slaughtered English had been cast, as their only possible grave, by the hands of their cruel enemies. Over the arch are these words: "These are they which came up out of great tribulation." Inside, over the entrance, one reads: "Erected by the British Government, MDCCCLXIII." Then comes the story of the massacre: "Sacred to the perpetual memory of a great company of Christian people, chiefly women and children, who near this spot were cruelly murdered by the followers of Dandhu Panth, of Bithur, and cast, the dying with the dead, into the well below, on the VIth day of July, MDCCCLVII."

Not far from this structure, with its angel, is a little cemetery. Flowers and shrubs abound everywhere, but thick among them are the tombstones to many of those beloved ones who were butchered, or died from disease, during the mutiny.

Twining Wreaths.

The Memorial Church is a large and beautiful structure. All around it are tablets in memory of the dead, who fell in the massacre. For tributes to the departed, it is more a tomb than a church. When I entered it, to examine it closely, I saw a group of young English ladies engaged in twining wreaths and making bouquets, to hang about the tombs, or lay on the slabs, as tributes to the dead. I observed one young lady in particular. She was working industriously, with piles of evergreens and flowers about her. I was attracted to her, because of the peculiarly serious expression on her face. Who is she? What disturbs her? I soon learned. There was one grave for which she designed her wreaths and flowers. It was that of General Wheeler, whose encampment had been on the very spot where this church stood, and who met his death by sepoy hands. His tomb is one of the most prominent in the church.

This young lady, with sad face and busy fingers, now making Christmas wreaths and bouquets for the aged hero's grave, was none other than the hero's own granddaughter.

CHAPTER LXVI.

LUCKNOW—THE HEART OF THE MUTINY.

FROM Cawnpore to Lucknow the distance is nearly fifty miles. The territory over which the road passes is full of interesting historical associations of British rule in India. The tragedy of Cawnpore was sooner ended than that of Lucknow; and, when the mutineers in the former city had been put to flight and death, the British troops hastened on to Lucknow, to close the agony of the suffering English people by a sharp and sudden attack on the mutineers. The conclusion cannot be resisted that the heroic patience and valorous bearing of the men, women, and children imprisoned in the Residency in Lucknow saved India to England. English domestic love and patience won the fight. Had the mutineers been able to enter the Lucknow Residency, and slaughter the heroic band there, they could well have overcome Havelock, who was hastening to their rescue.

When I reached Lucknow it was no picture of war which greeted my eyes. I had seen nothing in Cawnpore, with all its memories of blood and torture, but images of Christmas-tide. It was quite the same in Lucknow. The Anglo-Indians continue their festivities as long as possible. I found Christmas beginning in Calcutta, and it had been going on ever since. First of all came the anniversary exercises in the Centennial High School, then under the presidency of the Rev. Dr. Waugh, but now of the Rev. Dr. Badley. It was a beautiful scene—native girls and boys intent on a Christian education. The exercises were in Hindustani. The most suggestive feature of the programme was an enthusiastic oration by a native Hindu on the glories of the Battle of Plassey. Here was a young Hindu, in whose veins there was no English blood, declaring the inestimable benefit conferred by Clive on the civilization of the world by conquering this Hindu's ancestors at Plassey! It was just about the same as if a young Frenchman of our day should deliver a pane-

THE IMAMBARA AT LUCKNOW.

gyric on the English victory at Waterloo. This young Hindu, however, told the strict truth.

One of the overlooked factors which aided in securing victory to the English in India, during the mutiny, was the bravery of some of the native and European troops. Those who were true to the English fought with consummate daring. One of the East Indian soldiers, now a Christian minister, George Bailey, was as brave as any man who ever shouldered a musket. He is a conspicuous figure in clerical gatherings because of his coat made

THE MARTINIÈRE.

of the skin of a wild beast. The fame of his heroic deeds in Lucknow, against the mutineers, went far and wide. He was wounded and slashed in wild Indian fashion. But he outlived all, and has carried many rude scars ever since. He is now as brave a soldier of the Gospel as he was, over three decades ago, in defence of English supremacy in India.

The Martinière is one of the most notable of the large buildings. It was built by General Claude Martine, as a residence, and is said to combine more styles of architecture than any other structure in India. Martine was buried in the house, in a tomb under the central dome. His bones were scattered at the time of the mutiny, but were afterwards recovered and restored.

On Monday, December 31st, there was a picnic in the beautiful park, where the entire congregation of an English church spent the larger part of the day. There was a suggestion that I would be invited to ride there on an elephant. But I gave no encouragement to the proposition, not having forgotten my elephantine experiences in Haidarabad. On one large elephant in the procession were seated a fine Bible-class of young ladies.

One of my evenings in Lucknow was occupied in a visit to the charming home of Mr. Lewis Ingram. He, in addition to his legal duties, serves occasionally as a lay preacher. His wife was kind enough to exhibit some of the gold-and-silver-thread costumes which had belonged to her family for many years. She is a native of Delhi, and these rare objects gave me a good idea of the rich robes which the Mogul aristocracy wore in the days of their splendor. As a type of what Christianity can do for the home, of the happiness it brings with it, in far-off India, as well as in England and America, one might well stop before this door, and go no farther in his search.

BUDDHIST COLUMN FROM THE NAHAPANA GROTTO AT NASSICK.

CHAPTER LXVII.

MEMORIALS OF THE MUTINY.

THE historic Residency is not far from the house of the Rev. Dr. Waugh, where I was a guest. Whenever I had a few spare moments I went over to it, and always with a new delight. The leisurely visit with Dr. Waugh, when we strolled over every part of the picturesque ruin, and climbed to the top of the high tower, was enough for a general understanding of the famous place. But I wanted to catch the spirit of those wonderful events which had made the siege of Lucknow famous. The sun was in its bright, winter blaze. The vegetation was luxuriant, and of every possible color and fragrance. Here was a vast enclosure, where the English Resident, or representative of English authority, had lived in the bygone times. His palace was called the Residency.

Lucknow, being the fourth city in population in India, and the capital of the old kingdom of Oudh, was an important centre for English authority. The Residency was not only the English representative's palace, but the citadel of British rule. The great fortified mansion, with all its dependencies, covered a space twelve hundred feet wide and over two thousand long. The main edifice, though now only a picturesque ruin, can be seen in full outline. It consisted of a group of communicating buildings, having connecting halls, subterranean chambers, a great banqueting-hall, large rooms with lofty ceilings in both the first and second stories, and verandas, balconies, and jalousies in abundance. Before it was battered by the mutineers it had been a charming place. One could be as private as he might choose. In a moment he could walk out upon a balcony, or climb to the tower, or saunter among the sweet shrubs and luxuriant flowers, or hide himself in a kiosk among the vines, and while away his time over the last new book from London.

But the suggestions which push upon one at every step are

not of such a quiet time as this. You are at once confronted by an obelisk, with Persian and Urdu inscriptions, in memory of the native troops who fell at the siege in defence of the English people. Then come other monuments, in great numbers, in various parts of the ground—all of them telling the one story of Anglo-Saxon heroism and Indian rebellion. There is a graveyard, where many of the stones are inscribed to loved ones who fell here, in the Residency, during the siege. The building was of brick, and there is no material where shot and shell can combine to make a more striking ruin than when dealing with brick. The shot can pierce the walls, and leave its path behind, and the main wall still stand. I saw the holes which the balls had made as though it had been a very hailstorm of lead and iron.

The English do not rebuild the place, because, among other reasons, the native Indian can read here some lessons from the past for his guidance in the future. There is no need of a central citadel. The whole land is now English. Nature has grown wild in its freaks, and is covering rapidly the wreck made by war. The creepers have climbed over walls, dropped down on the inside of the old halls, and thrust themselves into doorways, while weeds and parasites in the lowest floor of the main building make their appearance again immediately after being cut off or pulled up by the gang of kulis ever on the watch. A careful eye still finds a flattened bullet now and then in the weeds and plaster of the inner rooms. In a room of the second story Sir Henry Lawrence died. He was born in Matura, Ceylon, a place noted for its diamonds. His mother used to say of her boy, "There's *my* Matura diamond."

Every room, if it only had a tongue, could probably tell of many a tragedy. The thousand souls—men, women, and children—who were cooped up here, never dared to put their heads out, except at imminent risk. Sepoy sharp-shooters, who had learned all they knew of guns, and had stolen even the guns themselves, from the English, stood off upon housetops and walls, and in the palms, and picked off an average of fifteen daily from the imprisoned people. The living had all they could do to bury the dead. When would help come? Perhaps never. No news came from the outside world. Those suffering people, now reduced in number and strength, had small supply of ammunition, and still less of food. They were on short allowance of provision.

All this was in the heat of an Indian summer. The air was still, and the heat intense, both night and day. The great banqueting-hall, which in former years had been the daily scene of luxury and festivity, was converted into a hospital. Piles of treasure lay in the subterranean vaults. But what was money in such an hour? The hospital was dense with a crowd of sick, wounded, and dying. Vermin swarmed on every hand. The flies infested every spot, and it was impossible to overcome them. But the sepoy assailants were not having an easy time; for the projectiles which they threw into the Residency, and were falling all about the English prisoners, proved that the regular ammunition was getting low. Blocks of wood, copper coins, fragments of iron, and even bullocks' horns, came whizzing within the walls. This was encouraging.

By-and-by a messenger stepped into the Residency with a letter. He had come the long distance between Cawnpore and Lucknow, and brought a letter from Havelock's own brave heart. The hero was on his way. He would be there as soon as he could. But he would have to fight every foot of the way. He could set no day, but was doing his best.

This was the first encouraging word. The prisoners took heart, and waited and hungered and starved. The tide of death never stopped. It was as fine a specimen of English heroism as ever blossomed under any sky. Havelock had a hard struggle. He knew the Indian methods well. But at last his guns were heard. The city lay between him and the Residency. He was in the rear of the assailants, who were now needed to protect themselves. After desperate fighting, he reached the Residency, only to be himself beleagued for nearly two months —from September 25 to November 17—when the besiegers were finally defeated by Sir Colin Campbell. Lucknow was now safe. The gateway of the Residency was thrown open. Deliverance had come. It was a time of gladness. The battle for all India had been fought and won.

I went to the great gateway of the Residency, and examined it minutely. It is surprising that the gate did not give way during the siege. It was beaten by the tempest of shot, and yet had stood. The bloody siege lasted four long months, or from July 2d to November 17th. The strange thing is, that any one was left to tell the story of the sufferings of the thousand who first went into the pen in the early summer. The beautiful cemetery, with its hundreds of loving and tender inscriptions to men, women, and children, tells the rest of the story.

I climbed to the top of the high tower. It has two landings, and one gets from each a good view of the surrounding country. As I reached the upper one, and looked out upon the peaceful paradise of to-day, I found that a Scotch Highlander had preceded me to the lookout. He was a stalwart young soldier, with kilt, tassels, and bright uniform, and was gazing upon the picturesque ruins and flowering plants and graceful palms, just below us, and out upon the city, and the distant palaces up the river. I could not see any trace of joy in his face. He was silent, and wore an expression which denoted intense feeling of not the most agreeable kind. The following was the substance of our interview:

"Beautiful scene, this," I remarked.

"Yes, it looks well enough."

"Those were desperate days which the brave English people spent in this Residency here," I rejoined.

"Yes, that they were, and the rebels got well paid," he answered.

"Of course, you were quite too young to know anything about it all."

"Yes. I know nothing of it from memory, but the wretches killed my father," he answered with a bitter emphasis. "They got well paid for it, afterwards. The men who did it got killed themselves."

"Then," I answered, "you have sad reason to remember this place; I am sorry it has such associations for you."

The young man relapsed into profound silence. His face became overspread with rage. He walked some time about the parapet, studied the topography of the place with great care, and then slowly took his way down the steps. He was entirely alone. He represents a class. Probably born in India about the time of the mutiny, he was taken to Scotland by friends, where he was educated, and later joined the East-India service, and now, for the first time, had a little furlough, which he was using to visit Lucknow and view the scenes which told him of his slaughtered father before he knew a father's worth. When the opportunity came for the sweet revenge no time was lost in embracing it.

There is a large garden, called Sikandra Bagh, in another part of the city, which had once belonged to an Indian princess. It is a square, of one hundred and twenty yards in extent. It is surrounded by a high wall. When Campbell met Havelock, and Outram was finishing the siege, it was now in order for the sepoys to seek shelter. A body of them looked upon this place as an excellent defence, and rushed through the broad portal, and entered it to the number of sixteen hundred and forty-three. When they tried to close the gate they could not do it. Four of the soldiers who were pursuing them, two Scotchmen and two Panjabi natives, followed so closely upon their heels that they stopped the shutting of the gates by almost superhuman strength. With their own bodies, well braced, they prevented it. But two were shot dead. The other two stood there, and were fairly crushed, but the bullets spared them. Just then the column in pursuit arrived. The sepoys saw their danger. It was now their turn to be in a pen. The wall was so high, and without a single aperture save the front entrance, that not one could get over it. The sepoys were face to face with the people whose countrymen, and even kinsmen, had been slaughtered by them. The tragedy was quickly enacted. Never were British soldiers hotter for blood. The sepoys were helpless. Every one of the sixteen hundred and forty-three sepoys was bayoneted on the spot.

I have no doubt that the father of the young Highlander whom I had seen on the tower of the Residency belonged to the Ninety-third Highlanders, who, with the Fifty-third Highlanders and the Fourth Panjabi Rifles, did this terrible work. The father had probably been killed in the early part of the conflict. But he and all his companions in death were now avenged.

I made the complete circuit of this pen of death. For an hour it must have been a pandemonium of bloodshed. The sepoys could only meet their fate without a blow. They surrendered to the cold steel of the Anglo-Saxon.

The associations of this awful place have been of such tragical character that at no time, since every foot of ground within the wall was drenched with blood, has there been any attempt to beautify it. Once a beautiful garden, smiling with the rarest and most fragrant plants, it is now a neglected place. Some parts of it have grown into mere jungle, with here and there an irregular mound, where the dead were tossed into rude pits.

Only this act of clemency was done as a precaution against pestilence. Probably this spot will be the last, of all the historical localities about Lucknow, to be graded again, and cultivated, and the great wall torn down, and become a fragrant garden or the site of a public building. As to a residence, I doubt if an Englishman in all India would consent to live upon it.

The Alam Bagh is a beautiful retreat, of five hundred square yards in area, about four miles from Lucknow. It is enclosed by a high wall. In the centre is a building, which, with the surrounding grounds, had once belonged to the Wajid Ali, who gave it as a home for one of his favorite wives. This place is beside the road leading from Cawnpore to Lucknow, and in the mutiny proved an important strategic point. The work of getting to Lucknow at all was Havelock's path to immortality, and when the Alam Bagh was reached his fame was complete. He died a few days after the relief of those who survived their four months' starvation and bereavement in the Residency. Very properly, the Alam Bagh has been chosen as Havelock's resting-place. His tomb, an obelisk thirty feet high, is here, amid the flowers. The inscription was written by his wife:

"Here rest the mortal remains of
HENRY HAVELOCK,
MAJOR-GENERAL IN THE BRITISH ARMY,
KNIGHT COMMANDER OF THE BATH,
Who died at Dilkusha, Laknau, of dysentery,
Produced by the hardships of a campaign
In which he achieved immortal fame,
On the 24th of November, 1857.
He was born on the 5th of April, 1795,
At Bishop Wearmouth, County Durham, England;
Entered the Army in 1815;
Came to India in 1823,
And served there, with little interruption,
Until his death."

"His ashes in a peaceful urn shall rest,
His name a great example stands, to show
How strangely high endeavors may be blessed
When piety and valour jointly go."

"This monument is erected by
His mourning widow and family."

This inscription tells only the general facts. There lies back of it a world of prejudice and opposition to Havelock. No man had been more thoroughly misrepresented than he. He was a Christian, and was so known throughout the army. This, perhaps, more than any other characteristic of the man, had made him an object of aversion to the military class in India. The prejudice was not without its effect in the distribution of troops. It was not designed that Havelock should have command of the troops in North India during the mutiny. He was out of the country at the time, in Persia, but he was needed. He came down the Persian Gulf to Bombay. When he reached there he was too ill to walk without help. The Rev. Dr. A. G. Frazer took him in his arms, and placed him in the small boat which bore him ashore. When he went north he met with nothing but opposition. When he entered upon the campaign, a poor invalid, who had spent his time in obscure stations, he was made a target of universal criticism. He knew the native movements well, and adapted himself to their habits. Hence, in making his advance, he moved ahead in the daytime, and in the night fell back a little. His progress was necessarily very slow, but he always kept the ground to which he fell back. That was the beginning of an advance from which there was no retreat. He knew what he was about. But no one else did. General Neill wrote most complaining, and even uncomplimentary, letters to him, and declared the folly of such a campaign. But Havelock was firm in his plans and work. He surprised both his enemies and friends. When he reached the Alam Bagh, outside of Lucknow, the day was fully won. His triumph placed him at the head of the leadership of India. For the combination of a far vision, sublime trust in God, and steady nerve while in great bodily suffering, the annals of warfare furnish hardly a parallel to Henry Havelock.

CHAPTER LXVIII.

A NATIVE PUBLISHING-HOUSE.

The natives of India are rapidly adopting Western methods. In no respect is that fact more apparent than in the publication of books and serials. From the time when Carey landed in Calcutta, in the last decade of the eighteenth century, and set up his printing-press in the little Danish suburb of Serampore, down to the present year, no Christian missionary has exhibited more energy and thrift than the Mohammedan and Hindu natives are now displaying in the distribution of their own literature. The most notable centre of this literary distribution which I found in India is the great publishing-house of Newal Kishore (the Son of a Weasel) in Lucknow. This city, one of the largest in India, is well situated as a distributing centre, not only for the whole valley of the Ganges, but for the entire Indian peninsula. Newal Kishore is, first of all, a school-book publisher. He seems to have the favor of the British government to a remarkable degree, and fills contracts for supplying books in the Indian tongues to schools in large portions of the Panjab. He is a Hindu, and makes no secret of it. But, with the publisher's instinct, he keeps his religion in the background. He never puts his faith at the top of his bill-heads. He is a broad man—broad in everything except Christianity, and it is not likely that the gospel has a more vigorous hater in the whole Gangetic valley than this wily man. But he is no bigoted professional. Bitter hater as he is of Mohammedanism, he seems as ready to publish books for the promotion of Islam as to issue apologies and text-books in behalf of Hinduism. Far be it from him to discriminate between the Qurán and the Ramayana. As to language, he likes the Urdu quite as well as the tongue of his fathers.

I had the opportunity to visit this establishment and closely inspect every part of it. It is not venturing much to say that, for variety of work, it is without a parallel in bibliographical history. My guide, who was furnished by the house, kept nothing back, either as to the departments of publishing or the modes of operation. All questions were promptly answered by him.

The Kishore publishing-house is situated on the Hazrat Gunge, the main street of the English quarter of Lucknow. The buildings are numerous, but low, mostly of one story, after the native fashion, and exceedingly plain. Many of them are mere sheds, where the work is done in full view from others on the premises. The roofs are of brick tiling. These buildings cover a great space, which is divided into many alleys and nondescript passageways, running at all angles with each other, and describing such curves as one can find in the denser parts of Lübeck or Nuremberg. I entered the premises by a long lane running at right angles from the main street. No one in passing along the street would suspect, unless he should turn into the lane, the number of men hard at work at the farther end, or the wonderful magnitude of their operations. The orders are constantly coming in from all India, and even from Afghanistan, Arabia, and Turkey in Europe. The many people engaged in carrying on this business have all they can do to fill the orders, and prepare for new ones on the way. Were the buildings covering such an area as this in Europe, and four or five stories high, yet turning out no more work than these primitive huts and sheds, their value could not be less than a half-million dollars. But the Rev. Dr. B. H. Badley, who has been kind enough to supplement by correspondence the notes which I made on the spot, informs me that, in Lucknow value, those many buildings and the ground covered by them would not sell for more than about forty thousand dollars. Not the least effort is made at ornamentation. The contrast between the beautiful premises of the Brockhaus establishment in Leipzig and that of Newal Kishore in Lucknow marks all the long distance between the "godly cleanliness" of Christianity and the dirt of Hinduism. One gets bewildered at what he sees. The huts have no wooden floors. Mother Earth is the common resting-place. I saw no woman's face; for, be it remembered, these are Hindu premises, and the women are at home and out of sight. The men and boys, in great numbers, sit on the earthen floor, in all possible postures, and carry on their work. They set type, read proof, and bind the sheets while sitting squat on the ground.

There is a great disproportion between the amount of type and the volume printed. While there is an immense quantity of type used in Kishore's house, the lithographing of a whole book is a favorite procedure. I have a copy of the Qurán, bought on the premises, which is one foot long and eight inches broad, and I am quite sure that not a type was used in the printing of it. The plates are lithographs, and of excellent finish. As this particular volume was intended to be illustrated in colors, the difficulty was to supply the cuts. This, of course, could have been met by a separate impression. But that is not Kishore's method. All these blanks are filled by colored illustrations applied by hand. These are quite rudely done, and yet the pictures are striking, and to an Oriental eye must be attractive. The Qurán which I bought has three hundred and seventeen pages, with numerous manual illustrations. It is bound in full leather. The price was only two dollars and a half.

But while a large portion of the work in this Hindu publishing-house is done upon stone instead of type, there is also an immense amount of the usual typesetting and casting. The Arabic and some of the Hindu tongues are very favorable for being etched on stone. The whole alphabet, in several cases, consists of curves, which can be easily executed by sharp tools. But when it comes to the Roman letters—and Kishore has his abundant uses for printing even English books—this shrewd publisher uses type, and his capable artisans know how to prepare plates from it quite as well as the English or American stereotypers.

There are several press-rooms. In one of them I counted twenty-one presses, all worked by hand. It was almost impossible to turn round in this crowded, stifling place. But each man knew his place and his work, and perfect order prevailed. There is one department where engraving alone is carried on. This is on both stone and hard wood. The etching-stone is brought from Germany, is precisely the same as that used by the Leipzig engravers, and is constantly imported in large quantities.

Nothing, however, is imported which can be produced in India. One would suppose that it would be safer and better to get the type from London. But Kishore has caught the trick of casting his own type, and here, in a special building, is the foundry where all his type is cast. One thing greatly surprised me—the absence of power-presses. The presses are all of English make, but down to 1884 they were still of primitive contrivance. I imagine that the cheapness of labor is the real solution of the question. In Lucknow skilled labor can be secured for about twenty cents a day. Book-binders get two dollars a month. Compositors in Lucknow work for from two to five dollars a month. Where such a state of things exists there is little motive for labor-saving machinery. But Kishore has recently made a new departure in the matter of power-presses, by getting a fine supply from England.

Much of the work in even the literary department of the Newal Kishore house is done on the premises. The only parallel to it I had ever seen was the Abbé Migne's establishment in Paris, where even the editors of the complete editions of the Fathers prepared all their matter beneath the same roof under which the compositors did their work, the pressmen completed it, and the packers sent off the great folios into every land. The only building in Kishore's house through which I was conducted that had a second story was the literary workshop. Here, by a not over-secure stairway leading up from the outside, I found a group of quiet, grave, and steady workers. They were the editors and revisers. They, like all Indians, sat upon the floor, and I must confess that they were the most dignified squatters whom it has ever been my privilege to meet.

AN INDIAN ARTIST.

The storerooms are one of the marvels in the Kishore house. The books are laid away in sheets in such vast masses that they occupy entire buildings, and reach from the floor to the rafters. These magazines are so closely packed that it was difficult to make my way through the catacomb. Neat placing there was none. The arrangement of the stock violated all the geometrical lines, and the dust was everywhere. Much of the matter was soiled, and many a spoiled sheet lay in the passageways, owing to careless packing. There is a great waste in this whole department. Too many copies are printed at once, for many of them have been lying, as I was told by my attendant, whole years in the same place. For these there had been a slow sale, or none at all. This is the department of a publisher's disappointments. But the work of superfluity seems still to be going on. Great masses of fresh sheets are constantly piled up, the new beside the old. Much of this stock is unsafe. There is no weather-boarding to the magazines, and the dampness, during the summer monsoons, must be fatal to a great deal of it. But the worst enemies of books in India are the white ants. They burrow during all seasons, and there is nothing which to these industrious parasites is more toothsome than printed paper.

The paper used by Kishore was formerly brought in great quantities from Serampore. But, latterly, paper-mills have been started in Lucknow, so that the Serampore ware is no longer in use. Nearly all the paper is slightly yellow, and is no doubt made of straw and rags. It is very tough, though not pleasing to the eye or agreeable to the touch.

In addition to Kishore's publications in books and pamphlets, I must not forget that he also supplies the natives with a daily paper. This is only one department of his house, and has its own set of compositors, pressmen, and editors. It is an easy-going affair, but pays well. If it did not, this astute provider of intellectual pabulum would drop it in an hour's time.

The kinds of books produced in this conglomerate establishment, in the heart of Mohammedan and Hindu India, are such as the millions demand. Just as I was making preparations for the translation of Kishore's Hindi catalogue into English, which I found some hesitation on the part of my attendant to furnish me with, I secured one in English, through the courtesy of the Rev. Dr. Badley. This, I believe, is the first time Kishore has given full publicity to the Anglo-Indian world of the issues from his press. And a mammoth affair it is, for it is a catalogue of about twenty-five hundred works, all issued from these low sheds. It is in large octavo, and occupies eighty-eight pages in titles alone, and twenty pages in a minute alphabetical index. While the typography is not a model of the printer's art, the arrangement and general character of the work make a thorough catalogue, which compares not unfavorably with that of Thacker, Spink, & Co., of Calcutta and Bombay, who stand at the head of the English book-trade of India. The scope of the issues is broad, including religious, educational, scientific, and legal books. The chief languages in which they are published are Sanskrit, Persian, Arabic, Urdu, Brij Bhasha, and English. But in addition to these must come many books in the subsidiary dialects.

No one can find fault with the price. Taking the Qurán as an illustration, I find the editions of so varied a character that they range in price, calculated in American currency, from twenty-four cents to ten dollars. But then the shrewd Kishore has also adopted the Bible Society's method of publishing in parts. The whole Qurán is divided into five sections, and four of them are sold at four and a half cents apiece, while the fifth is furnished at nine cents. The catalogue is careful to state in every case where the work is in the course of study in the government schools.

This last mention is an excellent advertising dodge. It is as much as to say: "See here. The English conquered us. They have given us great schools, and pay for their support out of the general treasury. But though our conquerors, they depend on us for supplying them with books. Now here are a great many which they use. I supply them to the schools. If such is the case, they must be very valuable. They would never have gotten in except by their worth. The English would have preferred their own books, but could not help themselves. *Ergo*, scatter these books everywhere. They go into the schools anyhow, but everybody ought to buy them." This, of course, is a very powerful argument, which, in the eloquent lips of a voluble colporteur at a *mela*, where fifty thousand natives may be present, must have an overpowering effect.

The English department of the catalogue is most interesting. There are thirty titles. There is no qualmishness as to the propriety of certain kinds of books. Anything goes down Newal Kishore's throat, if only it will bring money into his pocket. He publishes an "Imperial Fortune-Teller," but lest his patrons might think this a piece of Hindu superstition, he tells them this is only a translation into English from the German. He publishes tales in English from the Persian and other sources;

the "Arabian Nights," in parts, and also complete; English Primers (four cents apiece), Spelling-Books, Grammars (eight cents apiece), Letter Writers, Geographies, Cist's "History of India," Histories of Kashmir and Lucknow, School Dictionaries, an Almanac (four and a half cents a copy), and as a bit of choice patriotism, though nothing serious is meant by it, except to help the government use of Kishore's wares, Johnston's chromo-lithograph of her Majesty reviewing the Scotch Volunteers. As the Scotch were the people who, combined with Havelock's intrepidity, saved India to England by raising the siege of Lucknow, there is a special significance in this precious bit of stained paper, which one can buy for thirty cents.

Kishore is a competitor of the English type-founders. For, besides the use he makes of his own type, he manufactures Sanskrit and Nagri type for sale. Bookwork and miscellaneous printing are done by his presses, in addition to the issues on his own catalogue. On all cash payments for purchases of fifty rupees (twenty dollars) and upward, to one hundred rupees, he makes a discount of five per cent., and on purchases above one hundred rupees he raises his discount to ten per cent. In both cases he makes the transportation gratuitous. He expects parties who have no accounts to enclose stamps for replies. This enterprising publisher also makes public an offer to fill orders for goods of any kind which are for sale in Lucknow, and which he promptly despatches.

The number of men employed as pressmen, binders, messengers, bookkeepers, clerks, and in all other departments on the ground, is about twelve hundred. It is a great beehive, and yet everything moves on quietly. Evidently there are strict orders against all noisiness and wrangling, which one expects to find everywhere in India.

An important question is, how are these many publications to be brought before the public? The book-store, in the European or American sense, does not exist among the natives of India. The larger places have English shops, which receive the issues of the English press very promptly, and where orders are executed immediately. It seemed to me, however, that an undue advance was made on the London list prices, in view of the close connection by steamer between England and India. A package sent from London need not be rehandled until the Peninsular and Oriental steamer drops anchor in sight of the Malabar Road, in the Bombay crescent. But the English book-shop is altogether apart from the native stall. The Anglo-Indian does not care to handle the native books. He knows very well that his English is going to rule the world, and that in due time many of the dialects of India, and later the very languages, are going into oblivion before the triumphant march of the English tongue.

Now, the typical native book-shop is a booth in the bazar. It contains many elementary books, and some of the more advanced literature. But the premises are small, and usually confined to one room, a mere stall. The practical way by which the native publisher, like Kishore, gets his publications before the public, and secures a large sale, is by the system of colportage. The drummers circulate through the country very industriously, and know just where to go in order to secure the largest and best patronage. They are very quiet in their methods. What successful book-agent the world over does not know that too much talking is likely to spoil a sale? These men who represent the Kishore house go even beyond India. They cross over the Khaibar Pass into Kashmir. They know all the paths of the Afghan Mountains. They go down the northern slopes of the Himalayas, and thread the vales of Tibet. They gravitate down into the valley of the Tigris and Euphrates, and ply up and down the Persian Gulf. They are as much at home in Persian Teheran as in English Lucknow. They have even gone beyond the Asiatic limits, into Europe and Africa. In Cairo they are at home, while Constantinople gives them no scanty orders. The American drummer for the large houses of New York and Boston would have much to learn from the book distributors of Kishore, who knows his men, and keeps a careful lookout on each man's account.

There is broad significance in the efforts of Newal Kishore to propagate Hindu literature. He wants to control all markets not Christian. Were there no money in the business, he would immediately set his twelve hundred people adrift.

CHAPTER LXIX.

THE CURRENT LITERATURE OF INDIA.

THE growth of the indigenous literature is commensurate with the progress of education. The educated Hindu rushes easily into print. He enjoys nothing more than the effect of his thought on others. The issues of the Indian press show an annual total of about nine thousand publications.*

There are published in India 600 newspapers, 200 of which, mostly dailies, are in the Indian vernaculars.†

Bengal is, naturally, more prolific in literature than any other province. The capital, Calcutta, is the political centre. But there is more general intellectual activity there than in any other part of the Empire. The Bengali is a born writer. He is probably the youngest politician in the world. While yet a boy he begins to think on political subjects, studies English models, and very early gets before the world his notions as to how the government of India should become representative, and how the natives can best become factors in both legislation and administration.

The languages in which the many works published in 1886 are distributed, are as follows:

Arabic.	German.	Kannadu.
Arabic-Sindhi.	Gujerati.	Karen.
Assamese.	Hebrew.	Krukani.
Badugu.	Hindi.	Kurg.
Bengali.	Hindu-Sindhi.	Lankani.
Burmese.	Hindustani.	Latin.
Brij.	Italian.	Malayalim.
English.	Kachin.	Marhatti.
French.	Kanarese.	Marvadi.

* For minute literary tables, see Appendix No. VIII. Trebes is an excellent, perhaps the best, authority on Indian literature in its several historical stages. See his editions of Mann & Zachariæ, London, 1878, p. 179 et al.

† Lethbridge, "History of India," p. 119.

A MOSLEM SCHOOL.

Nepalese.	Prakrit.	Telugu.
Pali.	Sanskrit.	Tulu.
Panjabi.	Santali.	Turkish.
Pashto.	Sindhi.	Uria.
Persian.	Tamil.	Zend.

The variety of subjects treated in Indian literature is astounding. It reflects not only the polyglot character of the race-stems, but also the mixture of faiths. Among the books issued in 1882, in the Panjab, we find such a heterogeneous compound as the following: "The Little Office of the Immaculate Conception of the Blessed Virgin;" "Praises of Mohammed by his Followers;" "Attacks on the Prophet by the Christians;" "Stories of Krishna," and "Talismans from the Qurán." In the same region, the Northwest Provinces, there is one treatise on astrology and another on electroplating. In Burma the list of books includes a volume of songs in praise of the New Umbrella for the Dægen Pagoda. In the Central Provinces a collection of astronomical calculations was published, in an edition of five hundred copies. The Bengali publications comprise works on polygamy, the Brahmo discourses, and songs on the loves of Krishna. In Southern India a book in Kanarese has been published, in an edition of four thousand five hundred copies, reciting stories of Rama, Sita, and the Gopis. A gratuitous edition of one thousand and fifty copies of a work on astrology, in the Tamil, appears on the list of issues for 1882. Several other books on the subject are published, for general sale, among them one in an edition of four hundred copies. The latter is claimed to be an ancient work, two thousand years old.

Another Tamil work denounces Christianity, animal food, and intoxicating drinks. An edition of five hundred copies of this book appeared in 1882. In the same language appear two other works, of antagonistic tendencies—one a book of verses in favor of the Virgin Mary, and another a prose tale of a demon with a thousand heads. From the multitude of topics we may name: "Prayers to the Jain Saints;" "Exposure of Jugglers' Tricks;" "Seven Ways of Reading the Qurán;" the "Zoroastrian Scriptures;" "Genealogy of Brahman Families;" the "Mirror of Health;" a "Tract against Swindlers;" and a drama satirizing the tea-planters of Assam.*

* W. E. A. A., article in *Calcutta Review* (1875) on the "Native Literature of Modern India." See Trübner, *Amer. and Orient. Lit. Record*, 1875.

Among the works published in the year 1886 are the following: a book on Architecture, containing notes on the lucky and unlucky times for beginning a building; a "Biography of Faraday;" adaptations of Shakespeare's "Comedy of Errors," "Winter's Tale," and "Merchant of Venice;" Milton's "Paradise Lost;" "The Diseases of the Elephant;" "Cholera and its Cure;" a Marhatti version of Goldsmith's "Hermit;" the "Perils of Youth"—a work telling young men not to run off to Christianity or any other religion before examining their own; annotated editions of Goldsmith's comedies, "The Good-Natured Man" and "She Stoops to Conquer." There is a large increase of important missionary publications; of works by the Hindu reformatory associations, and of native attacks on infant marriages and other lingering abuses. Another important triumph must be added to the long catalogue of philological achievements of missionaries. In Bhamo, Burma, a "Kachin Spelling-Book" has been published by two missionaries. It is the first attempt to reduce the savage Kachin dialect to grammar.

A glance over the titles of the great mass of the native publications is sufficient to reveal the want of a practical character in the larger part of them. Ram Chandra Bose, an excellent judge of his own people, says of them: "The Hindus are the most dreamy people on the surface of the globe; and the literature of no other country as great as theirs confessedly is, appears at first sight so full of day dreams. The Hindu *geographer* does not travel, does not explore, does not survey; he simply sits down, and, perhaps under the influence of an extra dose of 'the exhilarating soma-juice,' dreams of a central mountain of height greater than that of the sun, moon, and stars, and circular oceans of curd and clarified butter. The Hindu *historian* does not examine documents, coins, and monuments, does not investigate historical facts, weigh evidence, balance probabilities, scatter the chaff to the winds and gather the wheat in his garner; he simply sits down and dreams of a monster monkey who flies through the atmosphere with huge mountains resting on the hairs of his body, and constructs thereby a durable bridge across an arm of interminable ocean. The Hindu *biographer* ignores the separating line between history and fable, invents prodigious and fantastic stories, and converts mere historical personages into mythical or fabulous heroes. The Hindu *anatomist* does not dissect, does not examine the contents of the human body; he simply dreams of component parts which have no existence, multiplies almost indefinitely the number of arteries and veins, and speaks coolly of a passage through which 'the atomic soul' effects its ingress and egress. The Hindu *scientists in general* set aside both inductive and deductive processes, and present their day dreams and nightmares as facts of accurate knowledge."

India is, however, rapidly arousing to the correction of her own errors. Take Hindu astrology as an illustration. This absurdity still holds many millions of Hindus in its strong arms. The sacred writings contain enough to make the people believe any nonsense. For example: "Krishna was born when the moon was in the Robini group of stars, and Krishna put his uncle to death. Therefore, whoever is born when the moon is so situated must be very unfavorable to his uncle." The entire life of the average Hindu is based on astrological assumptions. "Every act, every duty, through the entire round of domestic, social, mental, and moral life, whether employing a barber or entering into matrimony, must be explained and interpreted and engaged in by the aid of the astrologer. This is the tyranny of falsehood."*

A native author, Sir Madava Rao, has written a work in refutation of this nonsense, and challenges any one to produce a single illustration of astrological verity. Others will follow, in due time, in his footsteps.

We must not forget that the better style and quality of native publications, whether original or reprints, are gradually gaining the ascendency in every department. As examples we may mention the recent issue of Pope's "Essay on Man," an adaptation in Bengali; "Gil Blas," in Marhatti; and Shakespeare's "Julius Cæsar," in Marhatti. †

Many of the native publications classed as religious are purely controversial. They are attacks on Christianity. Both Hindus and Mohammedans are quite willing to attack Christianity in print. From the first, missionaries have indulged pretty freely in controversy. This spirit has been latterly on the decline, as

* The *India Witness*, Nov., 1887.

† The Missionary Conference: "South India and Ceylon," 1879, vol. ii. pp. 377 ff. A bibliography of Christian publications in the various missionary fields would be an important contribution to the history of general literature.

if the missionaries were now thinking the game hardly worth the chase. In some sections Hindus and Mohammedans have taken up the cudgel against one another. On the other hand, controversial works have been written, in a very hostile spirit, by rival sects within the same religious fold.

The languages in which the natives and missionaries produce their books and serials are determined by the territory. In the Northwestern Provinces the books are mostly in Persian, Urdu, Sanskrit, Hindi, and Arabic. In Bengal the native books are for the most part in Bengali and Hindustani. In Madras the Tamil, Sanskrit, Telugu, Malayalim, Kanarese, Persian, and Urdu prevail. In Bombay the mixture is even greater: Urdu, Persian, Arabic, Gujerati, Sanskrit, Marhatti, Kanarese, Sindhi, Pahlavi, and Zend.

One of the long-overlooked facts in Indian history is now coming to the light—the large place which woman has had in the development of a native literature. She has made for herself as large a place, in view of her depression, in Indian letters as in that of any Occidental country. Ahulya, Tara, Mandadari, Lita, Kunti, and Draupadi are as familiar in certain Indian circles as Olympia Morata, Renata of Este, George Eliot, and Elizabeth Barrett Browning are to intelligent people in England and America.*

---

* *Calcutta Review*, vol. xlviii. pp. 32 ff.; 91 ff.

CHAPTER LXX.

CHRISTIAN LITERATURE IN INDIA.

There has never been any timidity on the part of the Protestant missionaries in India in dealing with either the polytheistic faiths or the imported scepticism. The two great systems to be attacked are Mohammedanism and Hinduism. The Mohammedans, without having their ancient zeal and courage in propagating their opinions, are nevertheless ardently attached to them. They are never successful advocates of their tenets when they cannot use the sword. As this power is denied them in India, they are poor propagandists. Outwardly, they imitate their more liberal brethren in Egypt and Turkey, and even eat with Christians. The ordinary Mohammedan in India has borrowed from the Hindu the exclusiveness of the caste system, but it is a hopeful sign of the times that many of the more educated young Mohammedans are throwing away their scruples in this respect. In some places they even go further, and disregard the most positive rules of their religion by eating and drinking things forbidden alike to both Jew and Mohammedan. It is said that pork appears on the tables of some advanced members of the community, but when offered to guests offence is avoided by calling it "Chinese goat-meat."

The Mohammedans are beginning to take advantage of the schools, and print their full share of books and read the papers. But it must be admitted that no large class of indifferents has come into existence as yet. With people of such firm convictions no change can be expected in a few decades. But there are indications that point to more liberal ideas than have hitherto obtained. The Mohammedans of India are still smarting under the defeat in the mutiny of 1857. They are the conquered faith and people, and it cannot be expected that they should imbibe an early fondness for the ideas of their conquerors.* But

* Temple, "India in 1880," p. 130.

the missionaries have watchful eyes. Their presses are going night and day. Their operations are constantly enlarging. They know every antagonistic literary force, and measure it at its full value.

The first language of India in which Christian thought was expressed was the Tamil, the earliest cultivated of all the Dravidian idioms. This was the "Doctrina Christiana" of Giovanni Gonsalvez, who first cast Tamil characters in 1577. But the real beginning of the vast Christian literature which has been produced in India was with the productions of Ziegenbalg's press, about 1711. The first edition of the Scriptures, in any Indian tongue, was his Tamil version of the New Testament in 1715. The Old Testament followed in 1728. Between the first printed sheet of Ziegenbalg's little hand-press and the present works which come from the power-presses of the missions in Calcutta, there lies a wealth of Christian literature which no one can estimate.

As an illustration of the general missionary activity in publishing, we may say that in one year (1887) one mission, that of the Methodist Episcopal Church, published in Madras, under the charge of Rev. A. W. Rudisill, D.D., 500,000 pages of Tamil Christian literature. In Bengal alone, 10,000,000 tracts have been distributed since Carey, Marshman, and Ward began their work in 1800. During the last ten years, 10,000,000 copies of Christian publications in the vernaculars have been circulated in South India. The Madras Religious Tract and Book Society printed 7,500,000 publications in the native tongues, and in the last nine years it has printed 7,750,000 copies. One million copies have been printed by the Bangalore Tract Society in the last ten years. From 1838 to 1868 the three Tract Societies of Madras, Calcutta, and Bombay circulated nearly 10,000,000 copies of publications.

The Madras Auxiliary Bible Society has circulated, either in whole or part, 3,000,000 copies of the Scriptures. Down to 1874 the British and Foreign Bible Society had printed in Hindi and Urdu alone nearly 1,200,000 copies of the Bible. In 1870 the total of separate Christian publications in the various vernaculars of India and Ceylon amounted to nearly 4000 titles. Dr. James Mudge supposes that this number is now over 5000, those in Tamil leading with 1500; Hindustani (in its two branches,

Hindi and Urdu), 1000; and the other languages coming up to 2500.*

In 1873 the number of mission-presses was twenty-five. The number now can hardly be less than sixty. During the ten preceding years those presses had issued 3410 new works, in thirty languages; circulated 1,315,503 copies of the Bible, 2,375,040 school-books, and 8750 Christian books and tracts. This would be an aggregate of about twelve million copies of religious books. Dr. Murdock, however, thinks this too small a number, and believes that sixteen million books were printed in the decade closing in 1871. Dr. Mudge believes that, for the decade immediately closing, the total copies of religious publications must reach twenty million copies.

With all this great distribution of Christian literature, the disproportion between the circulation of books and the need of the people is still most alarming. Suppose the twenty millions of separate copies of Christian books to be now existing, and in one great pile, and that the two hundred and sixty millions of the people were to march up each to receive one, the apportionment would be only one little book for every dozen people. The need is terrible. The wail of the whole land is for the truth. The churches and societies in the Western Christian lands should adopt far more liberal measures to furnish India's millions with a sound and sufficient Christian literature. The passion for reading has struck every part of India. It is the universal mania. The people will have books and newspapers. It is for the Western Christian world to say what kind of reading it shall be.

It is matter of grave regret that not one of the leading missionary societies, of either Europe or America, seems to appreciate sufficiently the stupendous power of the press, and its incalculable possibilities, in either India or any other great Eastern mission-field. Only a few of the societies make direct grants to this department of missionary work. The missionaries are too often obliged to find their own resources, which, in consequence, are wretchedly limited. The question of a Christian literature for India is not to be settled in India, but in Anglo-Saxon Christendom.

---

* Article in *Independent*, New York, 1886. This gentleman was formerly a missionary in India.

CHAPTER LXXI.

AGRA AND THE TAJ MAHAL.

The Mogul palace was always built like a bird with outstretched wings or a tent with outrunning side-tents, as if the occupants were always on the march towards grander victories. This fugitive character of the royal residence also applied to the place itself. The Mogul emperors had no permanent residence. No will of the people was ever consulted. The sweet humor of the ruler himself decided where he should live and where his silver-tipped minarets, golden thrones, and tombs of marble and countless precious stones should bewilder every eye by their splendor. If Shah Jahân lived in Agra, it was reason enough why Aurangzeb should live in Delhi. There was a general revolution of place. The new man made the new capital. Hence the Moguls had several capitals—Fathpur Sikri, Agra, Delhi, and Lahor; or, as Milton puts it:

> "From the destined walls
> Of Cambalu, seat of Cathaian Can,
> And Samarchand by Oxus, Temir's throne,
> To Paquin of Sinæan kings; and thence
> To Agra and Lahor of great Mogul,
> Down to the golden Chersonese."

I was twice in Agra, once on my way to the Panjab, in the Northwest, and then on my return to Bombay. These two visits furnished the opportunity to visit the greatest of all tombs, the Taj Mahal, three times, with a fortnight's interval between the first and last visit. If one wishes to test the quality of an architectural monument, or any work of art, let him put a little time between his visits and see what the hours have to say. If there is a sense of monotony or familiarity, he may be sure there is something wanting in the object itself. But if at each visit he sees it in a new light, if it bears a different message back to him,

PALACE IN AGRA.

if he feels that something more is yet to come, and has been coming all the while, he may make up his mind that he is in the presence of a great creation.

On my first approach to Agra I saw the Taj to the left, about two miles off, with the Jamna flowing between the railway and the matchless structure. There it stood—the greatest tomb, the most elaborate and minute workmanship, the most nearly perfect specimen of combined marbles converted into flowers and fruits by inlaid precious stones, in the world. But I was disappointed. Its four great minarets, standing out as sentinels to protect the nestling domes, were not equal to the hearsay and descriptions. But I forgot several things—that I had been riding steadily for thirty-six hours, that it was early dawn, and, above all, that the Taj stands about twenty feet lower than the railway. With changed conditions one looks through different eyes.

Shah Jahân, one of the greatest of the Mogul emperors in both peace and war, had a wife who was his idol. She was the mother of his seven children. She lived for him alone, and he knew it well. To please her was his one study. She died in the southern country, and was brought home and buried in a corner of a magnificent garden on the banks of the Jamna. This garden had been a quiet place, enclosed by a high wall, where Shah Jahân and his family could enjoy a little retirement from the noisy court in the city. On festive occasions it also served as a place where imperial pageants were enacted. But from the moment when the beautiful empress was laid to rest beneath its palms, and the ferns hung their long fringes about her grave, there must be no more joy within that wall. She had said once, perhaps it was only a whisper to him, that she wanted him to build a marble palace for her which should eclipse all others the sun had ever shone upon, and should immortalize her name and his love for her. Perhaps he meant to do it. But the empress died, and too soon to see her dream of fame take shape in marble.

Yet her wish did not die. Shah Jahân, like his Mogul kind, resolved instantly, if he could not build a palace for her living, he would build a tomb for her dead. All those men sprang like lightning to their conclusions. They never mused, but hastened. All joy and song were banished from the garden. The best architect must be found. He came, perhaps from Italy, perhaps from France; but that is a secret. His name, even, has been lost, lest it might eclipse a little of the immortality of the dead empress. All lands must be searched for workers in stone. All mines must be threaded to make them yield the topaz, the goldstone, the amethyst, and all other precious stones which might give beauty and harmony to a marble surface by imbedding themselves in choice shapes, and make the marble only a background for pictures of broad and rich proportions. Persia and Kashmir must be ransacked for patterns of variety and beauty enough for the marble screens around the tomb. Then there must be no delay. Many thousands of workmen wrought at it, and yet, by all the quick methods known to even Indian despotism, it required twenty-two years to build the tomb. There is no knowing how much the Taj Mahal cost, nor how many people wrought at it. But it is known that when it was finished, in 1647, the remains of the empress were taken from their resting-place near by, and placed in the crypt in the centre of the building and directly beneath the dome. Immediately over the remains in the crypt, but on the main floor of the great mausoleum, the rich ornamental tomb was constructed. Below lies the empress. Beside her lies the man she loved. Shah Jahân in the latter part of his reign was dethroned by his son, and kept in close confinement in the palace at the fort. Here he spent his last years, and as he died he had at least one last privilege—he could look from the spot where his couch lay, through an open balcony, down to the bend in the Jamna where the domes and minarets of the Taj Mahal lifted their marble heights in air, and marked the spot where the wife of his best days lay. Her mausoleum was the last thing he saw.

However hard the fate a Mogul father suffered at his son's hands, death relaxed the stiffest grasp. Shah Jahân died a prisoner to his ambitious son Aurangzeb, but no sooner was the breath out of his body than the whole empire resounded with his praises. He was lauded in all proclamations, and swift messengers must go to the ends of the earth to tell how just and good the prisoner had been. Then no wealth must be spared to make his burial grand. Shah Jahân was laid away in the same mausoleum with his wife. So in building her tomb it came about that he built also his own. And the fact remains that Mohammedanism, with its curse upon woman, with its long enslavement of her, with its millennium of polygamy, has nevertheless built to a woman the most beautiful and costly mausoleum the sun has ever shone on. It is to the empress dead. There would be more hope for the accursed system if it would only do something for the woman living. With all its millions for a dead woman's tomb, Mohammedanism has never yet built one living woman's home.

One enters the enclosure through a great ornamental gateway. This of itself would be a handsome building, but it serves only as a poor inlet to the coming wonders. The ascent is by a stair-

GATEWAY OF GARDEN, TAJ MAHAL.

way to the second story, where there is a gallery. Here is the first good view of the Taj. Just below begins the garden, laid off in sixteen sections, stretching far back, and the whole forming a square of eight hundred and eighty feet. Each of the sections is appointed for a distinct class of vegetation—one for roses alone, another for ferns, another for palms, and then for other growths, until the sixteen are exhausted. Just opposite, as one stands on the lofty balcony of the gateway, there is seen at the farther end of the garden the Taj Mahal, resting on its vast marble platform of three hundred and thirteen feet square, and eighteen feet in height. On each side of the outer edge of the platform is a mosque, and at each corner rises a minaret one hundred and thirty-three feet high. The main dome of the mausoleum, which is in the centre of the marble terrace or platform, is fifty-eight feet in diameter and eighty feet high. At each corner of the mausoleum is a smaller dome, which gives completeness to this picture. The mausoleum itself would be a perfect square of one hundred and eighty-six feet, but the corners are cut off. This architectural device was resorted to, no doubt, to prevent the harshness that would come from the rectangles, but also to give the opportunity for those great niches, one above the other, where the shadows play hide and seek the livelong day. Straight through the garden, all the way from the gateway where one stands, to the Taj itself, there runs a stream of pure, clear water. This, with its twenty-three fountains and its central platform and fountain, gives a variety and movement to the whole scene, which at once take from the place all appearance of the tomb.

Everything one sees here, where stone is used, is of polished white marble. The bed and sides of the broad way down which the water runs; the splendid terrace on which minarets, mosques, and the wonderful central mausoleum stand; every part of the Taj itself, from the lowest step in the dark crypt to the topmost stone which covers the dome — it is all a wealth of spotless marble. One sees no wood, not even the precious sandal. Yet even the marble is not enough. All around the great central hall, beneath the immense dome, the lower walls are covered with rich reliefs, borrowed mostly from the flora that pushes itself out into numberless forms beneath this ever-shining sun. The lotus plays the most important part. Between the central hall and the main outer wall there is a broad way by which one goes entirely around the interior building. The inmost sanctuary, where the two great ornamental tombs rest, is shut off from the external walls by a wide way, and then by intervening screens of finely polished marble. No light falls from the dome, and all the light which comes into the burial-place is through these screens and small openings, which chasten the glare, and make one feel that he is in a place where the voice should only whisper, and the feet should take only slow and gentle steps. There is just the measure of light which is needed to produce the most subdued and softened effect.

So far all is marble. We have seen the rich reliefs all around the lower walls, where the vine and the lotus are most prominent.

But what about all the rest? If the whole building is of stainless marble, and one can find no wood or brass, there must be a coldness to this picture. The way to get rid of this difficulty was half performed when the sharp angles were cut off. An abrupt line can nowhere be found. Whenever one supposes he would come around to something harsh, he is disappointed. The very spot where the abruptness would begin has been chosen to prevent it. There is a curve, a fanciful turn in another direction, a willowy drooping perhaps, anything to take away the keen edge of monotony and coldness. Yet even a new turn to things is hardly enough. This would go far; but there must be something more, and richer, to ward off all possible danger.

Here is where the coloring comes in—the letting of the choicest foreign stones into this bed of the purest marble. You see this on all the outer walls of the Taj. These stones are thrust into the exterior walls with such profusion, such a wealth and waste, that one wonders why the display. But when you come to look at them as a whole, and see the design, or as ladies would say, the "pattern," there is not one too many. You could not spare a single bud from a rose or a leaf from a lily. These outer mosaics are all in keeping with the luxuriance of the outlying nature. They fall in with the palm, the fig, the cypress, and the peepul in the garden. They are like those great roses which now grow all about the spot where the body of the empress rested through the years while her mausoleum was being built.

But let us go within, where everything grows richer. The lattice of marble, which, as a wall, surrounds the two ornamental tombs, would be as chill as frost-work were it not for the brightening of its surface by the letting in of this world of botanic stones. Nothing known to the flora of Ceylon or India seems to have been forgotten. Those rarer plants which Baron Van Reede found out and put into the twelve great folio volumes of his "Hortus Indus Malabaricus," are here reproduced in the stones of corresponding colors. Look as closely as one may, he can hardly tell where the lines between the stones are, so minute is the workmanship, so deft the hand. All up the walls, in all the recesses, over all the doors, away up the posts of the enclosing screen of marble, over the archway by which one enters to the tombs, and then all along the tombs, from top to bottom, there run these luxuriant mosaics, until one is fairly lost in the very glare of their splendor. The stones are not over-minute, like the Roman mosaic, nor are they too large, like the Florentine. They are midway, and as to color they simply reproduce faithfully the wild irregularity of this wanton Indian nature. There is no sparing of labor. If a violet needed ten stones to give it the highest effect, the ten would be there. My friends, Prof. Foote and the Rev. Mr. Fox, and myself counted in one rose and its stem thirty-one separate precious stones. Here was a shading which was marvellous. It seemed that even individual stones had shading, so accurate was the selection and so skilful the placing. But no; the variety of color came from new stones. Each stone had a color of its own, and to produce another one there was a new stone let in.

One gets weary in a short time, and it does not answer well to hurry, or to try to see much at a time. My three visits had been well timed. The first was in the morning, when I was fresh, and had read the descriptions and was ready for the original. I went all over the garden; to the first tomb of the empress; into the crypt, and stood beside where her dust now lies; and to the main space where, right above the real tomb, the ornamental one is built. Then I wandered through the interior, and counted the colors of the foreign stones, and saw their fine work and the precious quality of the stone which was worthy of the work. Then I climbed to the top of one of the minarets, and saw the Jamna below, and its long sweep into the far distance towards the Ganges; and looked down upon the great marble bulb which goes by the name of a dome, with its little waiting domes standing about it, and then at the garden, the gateway, and the mosques at either side of the marble terrace. The verdure and bloom of the garden contrasted wonderfully with the glare of the marble world. The sun was in his full splendor. There was not a fleck of cloud. I could not rest my eye a minute upon either dome or on one of the supporting minarets without being dazzled. So soon, however, as I looked at the garden, and then at the purple stream of water that sang its way beneath the palms through the whole length of the garden, my eyes were rested for another survey.

My second visit to the Taj was in the twilight, when the voices outside were calming down, and the shadows were everywhere deepening. The fretted ceiling in the great exterior niches caught up the humors of the setting sun, and repeated them in their own recesses. No two were alike. There was variety everywhere. The interior great hall was as calm as the grave itself. The colors of the inlaid stone gave a friendliness and gentleness to the marble which made it something else than nature's densest frost. The long shadows of the minarets, falling like bars of lead across the white terrace of marble, and reaching far out on the sides, gave a certain weird aspect to the whole, which one would little suspect until he had seen it for himself. The garden took on its darkest shades, for there was no moon.

The superintendent conducted me about, and showed me now one object of interest and now another, which I had not seen before. Among other things he brought me to the oldest tree in the garden, which had stood there many a long year before Shah Jahân was born, or the father of his beautiful empress had set out from his Persian home to come down to India to join his humble fortune with the Mogul rulers of the Eastern world.

With these two visits I expected to see no more of the Taj. I then went northwest into the Panjab, but it so happened that I could conveniently stop on my return, and again be a guest at the home of Dr. and Mrs. Wilson. The bright nights of January were now upon us. "Would you not like to see the Taj by moonlight?" said Dr. Wilson. He knew very well what I would say.

The moon was at the full. The perfumes of the garden filled the air, and the shadows of palms and ferns gave relief to the pearly whiteness of the scene. The stream which flowed through the garden seemed of molten silver, and we walked along its margin, and watched the play of its little ripples with rare delight. We were the only visitors, and that dead silence reigned which pervades all Eastern countries immediately after nightfall. As we walked up to the great marble terrace on which the Taj stands, the scene was one of indescribable grandeur. The view by day, wonderful as it is, is far from repeated at night. Each hour seems to have its own way of revealing the Taj. The dome seems higher at night, as if a part of the very firmament, and in living companionship with the moon and stars. The four slender and richly carved minarets appear as stairways up to the cloudy realm. The Jamna appeared of wider and swifter flow. Its surface was serene, and it laved either bank so gently that the current could hardly be heard. No insects made chorus. The place was in the midst of a dreadful, grand silence.

The walls now shot out their splendor from the inlaid stones of varied hues and fabulous price. These many-colored stones, thrown into vine and fruit and flower by the artist's skill, and into texts from the Qurán, and climbing in delicate shapes up and about the matchless building, fairly blazed in the white moonlight. At certain angles the sight was painfully dazzling.

But within, the view was still more bewildering. The torch-lights shone through the marble lattice, and showed the pattern as the day could not. The goldstone and other precious stones, which ornamented the enclosure of the mausoleum, appeared with more distinction of color and finish of workmanship than at either of the other times I had seen them. It was a garden of cold splendor in stone. Dr. Wilson had a plan which I did not know before—that after we had walked around in the Taj awhile with torches, we should see the whole ablaze with Bengal lights. Suddenly they were let off, and the scene was totally changed. There was nothing that looked the same. That marvellous stone lattice, with its embroidery of precious stones, had again changed hue and effect. The walls swept on in graceful curves, and fairly lost themselves in the intense glow of the light. The marble reliefs, such as the palm and the lotus, stood out in such clear and shining outlines as to make one think for the moment that they were not supported by any background. The dome rose above all this varied beauty in a firm and solid sweep, and the Bengal light threw up its force to the very topmost point, and illuminated every block of the spotless marble.

The charm lasted quite long enough. It called one into new sensations. We walked out of the Taj, down the steps, through the garden, and under the great gateway. Soon we were out of reach of the perfumes and splendor of the world's greatest building and man's richest tribute to a woman's love and memory.

While the great Taj eclipses all other buildings in Agra, and indeed in all India, there are other structures in that city which are marvels of architectural finish and magnitude. Along the banks of the Jamna there stretches the great fort, whose high and massive wall encloses the Mogul palaces and the Pearl Mosque. Here, in calm and safe retreat, is the palace of the emperor Jahángír, in red sandstone. Its great corridors, its magnificent octagonal towers, its pillared halls with stone roof, its wonderful marble baths, its vaulted chambers, its monolithic cisterns

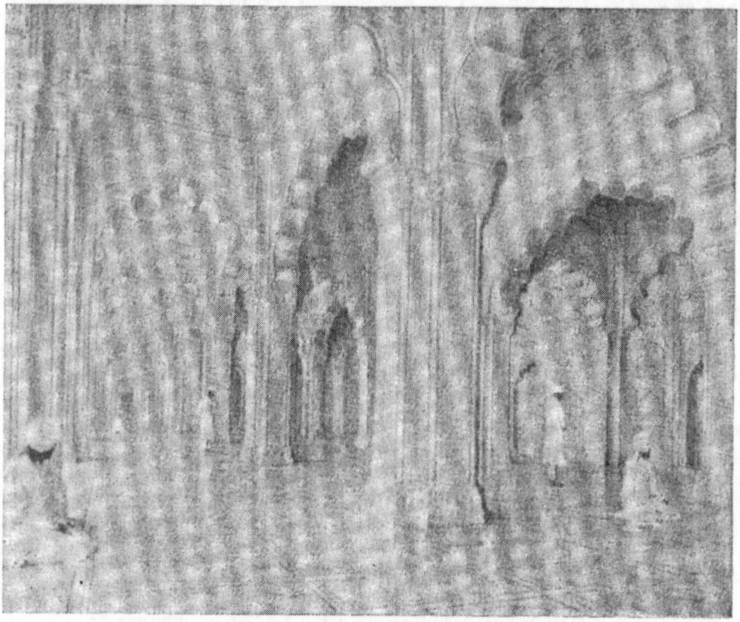

THE PEARL MOSQUE.

of light porphyry, its quiet marble nooks, and its pavilions for outlook over the stretches of the Jamna valley, make it one of the most magnificent monuments of Mogul splendor.

The Saman Burj, the palace of the empress, is concealed behind rich lattice-work in finest marble. Here is the Grape Garden, a square of two hundred and eighty feet, where the ladies of the court lived in all the luxuries known to the Mogul court in the days of its greatest splendor. Near by is the pavilion where Shah Jahân, a prisoner to his son, could look out, a mile to the eastward, and see the Taj, his tribute of affection to his beautiful empress. The Diwan i Khass, or Audience Hall, near by, is of richest carving, where flowers in red carnelian and other precious stones are inlaid in finest marble.

The Pearl Mosque, though not the largest, is perhaps the most beautiful in India. It is lined entirely with marble, veined with white, blue, and gray. At each corner there is an octagonal tower. In the centre of its court there is a marble tank. A marble cloister, supported by fifty-eight slender pillars, runs around three sides of the court. The central doorway is open, but the others are closed by screens of marble lattice-work.

The most remarkable place in the immediate neighborhood of Agra is Sikandra, the burial-place of the great Akbar. The very gateway is a triumph of architectural skill. At each corner of it there rises a white minaret, sixty feet high. The tomb of Akbar is surrounded by others, to various members of his family. The whole structure above and around this imperial dust is more like a palace than a tomb. Corridors, pavilions, marble lattice-work, and all the architectural devices known to the Indian architects of three centuries ago, are employed to perpetuate the memory of the great builder of the Mogul throne.

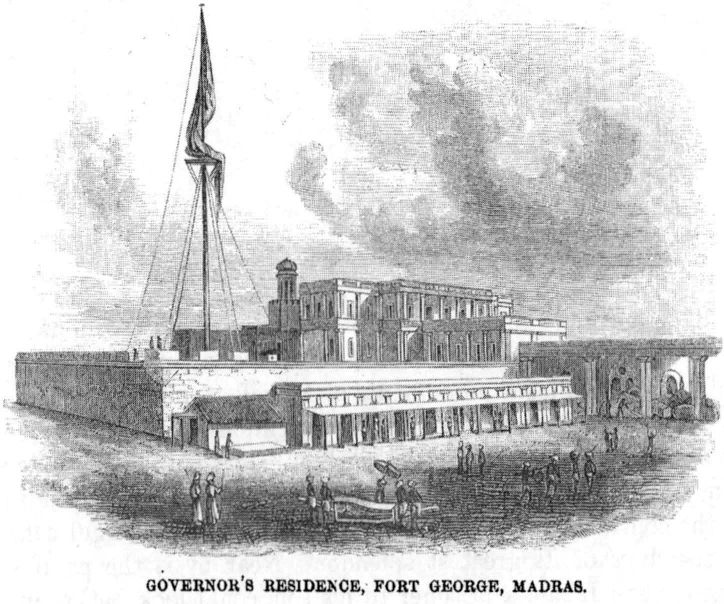

GOVERNOR'S RESIDENCE, FORT GEORGE, MADRAS.

CHAPTER LXXII.

DELHI, THE MOGUL METROPOLIS.

Delhi is a place which requires time to see well, and a careful study to comprehend its place in Indian history. My engagements were such as to give me both these advantages. In the dak bungalow, or post-inn, I found comfortable quarters. But I was interrupted, when not engaged in seeing the city, by a constant throng of vendors of ivory paintings, silver-ware, and many other things for which Delhi has been famous from remote times.

Then, too, there were other objects for sale, such as Kabul and Kashmir cloth and shawls, which were brought in great packages, and strewed all over my floor. By day and by night these vendors gathered about me, and several times I had to threaten to lock them in, if they did not pick up their wares and be off. But they never grew impatient. Whether one buys or not, it is all the same; they keep their equipoise. They watch your arrival at the train, and have messengers run after your carriage, to see where you make your lodgings. They are, besides, most faithful to the last. They will even follow you to the train, and, when you are seated in the carriage, they will come to the window and hold out, with reduced price, some object which they fancy you may be inclined at last to buy.

Delhi, more than any other city in India, represents the splendor and reign of the great Mogul emperors.

As a pillar, the Kutab Minar has no equal. As a mosque, the Pearl Mosque in Agra is rich beyond comparison. As a tomb, the Taj Mahal in Agra is, easily, without a parallel, while the palaces of Fathpur Sikri stand alone as memorials of kingly plans. But for general imperial splendor, Delhi surpassed them all. While there were times when other cities became capitals, according to the humor of the monarch, Delhi was, nevertheless, regarded as the general capital throughout the five reigns of the great Moguls. It was the largest city and the commercial centre, and abounded in the richest historical associations.

The origin of Delhi is lost in obscurity. The country about it is the scene of some of the greatest deeds recorded in the Mahabharata. The city first comes into prominence in the tenth century, as a magnificent capital, whose authority extended far and wide. Finally, the English traveller who went from Agra to Delhi in 1611 speaks of an Old Delhi even in that day. No city in India has had the benefit of a more thorough topographical examination. Many careful searchers, with pick and spade, have gone to work to make the multitudes of mounds tell their story. The result is—and to this conclusion all have come—that Delhi, the old and the new, covers an area of forty-five square miles, and that within this space are enclosed the ruins of seven separate cities. The style of architecture, the certain dates preserved, and the inscriptions, make this conclusion so strong that it cannot be disputed.

My first ride was to the fort. Here, as usual in India, we found palaces to be the chief buildings, while their defence was merely secondary. In every case one enters through a great gateway, and drives directly across broad grounds to the palace and throne of the Mogul emperor. There are no European analogies to the Indian notion of a palace. Everything must be open and airy. First of all, there is a central place, where the emperor sat on silken rugs, covered by rich canopies, and invited appeals from the common people. Far out, on either hand, stood his courtiers, in corridors or under other shading. I have seen a number of these very thrones; either a raised platform or a marble chair, where the great ruler sat and dispensed justice, without much intervention of minister or courtier. The Indian despot always took great pride in being seen by his people, and in administering justice without intermediaries. He would talk with the man himself who sought justice. The concealment of his person from all curious eyes was no part of his conception of splendor. He regarded it a mark of authority to appear at stated times before his assembled people, and hear complaints and settle disputes.

The Delhi palaces and all their belongings were contained in an immense parallelogram one thousand six hundred feet by three thousand two hundred feet. The buildings, great and small, were in marble and fine stone. The Diwan i Amm is a great open hall, where the emperor dispensed justice. The building is not high. You ascend by five steps to the hall itself, which is one hundred and eighty-four feet long, and open on three sides. The emperor's seat is a marble throne, with a marble canopy. Back of his seat, and forming the great background to this picture of splendor, is a wall which is ornamented with the fine and delicate mosaic work. The equal to this piece of mosaic, for variety and extent, can hardly be found in the world. The designs are of birds, and in semicircles, to conform to the sweep of the arch. Here are all the birds which one meets with in India. The natural colors, in fine stones, are as richly reproduced in this mosaic as in the folio plates to Audubon's "Birds of America." The attitudes and habits are even represented. Each bird is a study in itself. The calmer varieties are here portrayed as resting on twigs, or singing, or flying, or surprised and looking up, while the more muscular birds are described in the postures and acts which naturally befit them. All this is in precious stones. Besides the birds, there are mosaics, likewise in precious stones, of the fruits, flowers, and beasts known to India.

There is a door here by which the emperor used to enter, to take his seat upon his throne of administration. As one looks at it, and sees all this splendor in ruins, he almost asks himself the question, "What if Shah Jahân should now come out, and take his seat upon his marble throne, and beneath his marble canopy, and have the birds and beasts and flowers of all India crowd about him to do him honor, and hear the vast throng before him take up the loud acclaim of honor and praise, until all Delhi should be vocal with cheers, that the emperor has come out from his august silence and solitude, and now gives public justice to his people?"

In addition to the Diwan i Amm, or Public Hall of Audience, there was always the Private Hall of Audience, where none but ministers of state might venture into the emperor's presence. They had heard petitions, and had matters of grave import in charge, and this was now the tribunal to which they might come, and lay their affairs before the great ruler in person. It is almost in a line with the Public Hall, but is smaller. It, too, is of marble, with inlaying of gold and precious stones. It is ninety feet long and sixty feet broad. Three sides are open, and the roof or canopy is supported by six rows of pillars, at the top of each of which a group of arches meet. The following inscription is placed over the northern and southern arches:

> "Agar firdaus ba ru i zamin ast,
> Hamin ast, Hamin ast, Hamin ast."

Which, being freely interpreted, means:

> If on earth be an Eden of bliss,
> It is this, it is this—none but this.

Both the ceiling and the columns are ornamented in the richest coloring and designs known to Oriental art. It is believed that the ceiling was plated over with solid silver, but that it was stripped off by the Marhattas, and carried away, in 1760.

The Peacock Throne.

Here, beneath the wondrous canopy, stood the celebrated Peacock Throne, where the Mogul rulers gave forth their edicts for the government of India. It is thus described by Beresford:

"In this hall was the famous Peacock Throne, so called from its having the figures of two peacocks standing behind it, their tails being expanded, and the whole so inlaid with sapphires, rubies, emeralds, pearls. and other precious stones of appropriate colors as to represent life. The throne itself was six feet long by four feet broad; it stood on six massive feet, which, with the body, were of solid gold, inlaid with rubies, emeralds, and diamonds. It was surmounted by a canopy of gold, supported by twelve pillars, all richly emblazoned with costly gems, and a fringe of pearls ornamented the borders of the canopy. Between the two peacocks stood the figure of a parrot of the ordinary size, said to have been carved out of a single emerald. On either side of the throne stood an umbrella, one of the Oriental emblems of royalty. They were formed of crimson velvet, richly embroidered and fringed with pearls; the handles were eight feet high, of solid gold, and studded with diamonds. The cost of this superb work of art has been variously stated at sums varying from one to six millions of pounds sterling. It was planned and executed under the supervision of Austin de Bordeaux." *

* "Delhi," 1856.

The eyes of one of the peacocks were represented by two immense jewels—the *Koh-i-nur*, Mountain of Light, and the *Koh-i-tur*, Mountain of Sinai. When Nadir Shah sacked Delhi and broke up the Peacock Throne, he failed to find the great Koh-i-nur. The Mogul emperor, who was now disowned, did not seem to possess it. But a woman betrayed his secret, and informed the conqueror that the emperor still possessed it, and that it was concealed in his turban. As the bulk of the treasures was now in the conqueror's hands, and a treaty had been concluded, to make a search would violate all the proprieties. But a trick was employed. At a great ceremony, Nadir proposed to the dethroned emperor to exchange turbans with him, as a token of good faith. There was no time for reflection. The conqueror's turban was glittering with gems, and yet it would be worthless in comparison should the emperor's contain in its wreaths the coveted Koh-i-nur. The emperor could not decline his conqueror's proposition of good faith. The exchange was made. Later, when Nadir withdrew to his tent, and took off his turban, behold, he possessed the Mountain of Light—the Koh-i-nur!

This priceless diamond remained a long time in the Panjab, as a part of the Lahor treasury. When the Panjab was annexed to England in 1849, and the East India Company took possession of the Lahor treasury in part payment of the debt due by the Lahor government, a stipulation was that the Koh-i-nur should be presented to the Queen of England. When the East India Board met, the diamond was committed to the care of the illustrious John (afterwards Lord) Lawrence. He received it, dropped it into his waistcoat pocket, and forgot all about it. He went home, and on changing his clothes he threw his waistcoat aside. Some time after this, a message came from Queen Victoria ordering the great diamond to be sent immediately to her! Sir John Lawrence said to his brother, "Well, send it at once!"

"Why, you have it," replied Henry to John. John was astonished beyond description. But on finding his waistcoat, there lay the Koh-i-nur, in one of the pockets.* This was the greatest of its risks, and now it rests securely in Windsor Castle!

The ornamentation of this hall consists in part of richly colored inscriptions, in Persian, and so skilfully executed as to be a part

---

* *Leisure Hour*, London, 1887.

of the very artistic finish of the work itself. One would suppose these inscriptions to be only the lavish display of the painter's brush or the marble-cutter's fine chisel. Here is one of them:

> "Lovely angels, seeking pearls row after row,
> Come down to bless mankind, and fonts where flow
> Life's waters, which a crystal radiance show."

Over another arch one reads: "Praise be to God! What a mansion is this of many hues, and what a heart-delighting abode! I might call it a portion of Paradise, for even the holy-minded angels gaze on it with eagerness." In another place we read, with reference to Alexander's wall of steel, built so high that none could scale or cross it:

> "Higher than heaven we may find this fortress call,
> Which causes envy to Sikander's wall."

The imperial baths are still preserved in their original state. They consist of three great rooms, lighted through colored windows in the roof. The floor of each room is of white marble, inlaid with colored marbles of various designs, forming a whole of beautiful mosaic, as rich as a piece of Kashmir tapestry. The ceiling is also of slabs of white marble. Each room has, in the centre, a fountain, and one can see to-day the excellent arrangement, than which none are better in these later times, for a supply of hot and cold water. There is a solid beauty, a symmetry and real splendor, in them, worthy of the best of the Mogul emperors in his best mood.

Close by the Baths is the little Pearl Mosque, the Moti Masjid, where the emperor and his court worshipped. The entire building is of white marble. It has a façade of three arches, of the fine Saracenic curve. The door is of solid bronze. In the interior there is a severity and coldness that come from the simplicity of the finish. The Mohammedans, however much they may ornament their baths and palaces and tombs, are careful to have their mosques simple, and yet superbly solid and rich. They allow nothing which will suggest idolatry. There must be only the coldness of solid stone, no ornamentation with beast and bird. The most interesting object in this precious bit of architecture is the marble divan, or one might call it a throne, where the emperor reclined. This is hardly the place for it.

Possibly it has been brought into the mosque as the best way for its preservation. Its design is exceedingly graceful. It has been broken, by the fracturing centuries and dynasties, but all its parts are together, and in proper place. On a square in the magnificent marble floor, distinguished from all the rest, is the slab where the emperor always worshipped.

This little Mosque, with its marble couch, and then the wonderful Baths, are the best preserved of all the groups of imperial buildings within the wall of the citadel of the emperors who lived in Delhi.

MUSSULMAN WATER-CARRIER,
DELHI.

CHAPTER LXXIII.

THE ELDER DELHI.

One must go out upon the river-side of the palace and its dependencies in order to see the beauty and real charm of all the Delhis. Here is the Jamna, in its broad sweep and wild flow downward towards Allahabad, where it is lost forever in the Ganges. From the magnificent balconies and towers, and through the windows of the private apartments, the royal occupants could look out upon a landscape of great beauty and variety. There were no mountains, no succession of hills, no great display of varied scenery. But there was the river, and water was the joy of all Oriental hearts, from emperor down to the humblest bearer. The city, with its noises, lay in the rear of the citadel and the palace. When Aurangzeb, or any ruler, wished for calm and rest, all he needed was to come out on the river balconies, and see the quiet fields, the waving palms, the peaceful river, and flocks, as far out as the eye could reach.

But these emperors were seldom at home. Probably, if their days of calm and peace, spent here in this Delhi paradise, were summed up, it would be found that where they spent one here they spent fifty far away, on long and dangerous campaigns. All the Mogul palaces, though built at fabulous cost, were at best only brief dreams and hopes.

In order to visit the ruins of the elder Delhi, Professor Foote and I escaped from the crowd of vendors in our veranda, took carriage, and left our lodgings, early one morning, with a good guide. We left the present city by the Ajmir Gate, and soon found ourselves in the country, with here and there a mound which tells the story of the ruins of the former city, long before the Moguls had found a resting-place in India.

The country is well cultivated, and is rich and inviting to the tiller of the soil. Every now and then we passed the broken wall of the garden of some wealthy grandee, whose name is now

A STUDY OF RELATIVE VALUES.

forgotten. No doubt, in the far-gone centuries, this entire road was a royal way. The traces, on either side, are of former luxury and comfort. At about two miles from the present Delhi, on the left-hand side, we came to Jai Singh's Observatory. We left our carriage, and crossed the field to ascend it. Here is an inclined plane of stone, by which a stair led to the great astronomer's dial. There are several other structures which furnished facilities for taking astronomical observations. These buildings were constructed from designs by Jai Singh II., the learned Rajah of Jaipur, in 1724. He was the greatest astronomer whom India has produced. It was he who prepared the celebrated Tij Muhammed Shahi, or Tables of the Stars, which not only corrected all the previous astronomical calculations of India, but formed the basis for exact calculation in subsequent times. None of these astronomical buildings are now used. India now gets its astronomers and astronomy from the West. The buildings are only a shelter now for bats and goats, while wild weeds grow around the base of all their walls.

Kutab Minar.

In two hours we reached the traveller's bungalow, where we halted and took tiffin. We were but a short distance from the Kutab Minar. I had seen it so often in pictures, and it had stood out before us on our road from Delhi so prominently, that it seemed already like an old acquaintance. This immense tower, rising as gracefully as a reed from the river's bank, carries with it, like the Pyramid of Cheops, its own great mystery.

No one knows, and no one has explained plausibly, its purpose. It is neither minaret, tower, nor pillar. Yet it is all these in one. Here is a lofty structure, rising to a height of two hundred and forty feet and six inches, divided into five stories, and lessening from a base whose diameter is forty-seven feet and three inches, to a crowning platform whose diameter is nine feet. Once it was surmounted by a graceful cupola, but this was thrown down by an earthquake in 1803. If we add about thirty feet to the present column, and then surmount it by a cupola, we shall have nearly its original proportions.

But the abruptness of the upper part does not diminish the grandeur of this remarkable shaft. It is the loftiest piece of Mogul architecture which has ever been reared, or of which any trace exists. Its great charm is in the variety of its exterior. It is not one unbroken surface, but with its five stories, each of a style peculiar to itself, it forms a shaft singularly symmetrical, and at once majestic and graceful. The first three stories are of gray granite, faced with red sandstone. The remaining two are of the same material, but with bands of white marble. The flutings are a remarkable feature of this gigantic work. The base is a polygon, of twenty-four sides, and on this, and in harmony with it, rests the first story. Here the fluting is semicircular, alternating with the rectangular, the combination producing a most pleasing effect. It is a wonderful union of straight lines and curves.

SECTION OF KUTAB MINAR, DELHI.

The second and third stories reproduce, in the fluting, the style of the first—the second having only the semicircular fluting, and the third only the rectangular. The fourth story has no fluting, but is plain and circular. In the fifth story the semicircular fluting reappears. Around the top of each story there is a delicate balcony, which, instead of interfering with the general effect, adds to the beauty and impressiveness of the whole great structure.

If this great shaft were designed for a minaret, it certainly differs from all others known to Mohammedan art. The mosque here is not of such kind, or in such a place, that this could have served as a minaret to it. It has no defensive significance. It seems to be simply a great and noble shaft, which combines all the qualities of Mohammedan art, and serves as a memorial of the splendor of the Delhi of the twelfth century, long before the Mogul empire had startled the world with its despotic and barbaric splendor and its victories on many a battle-field.

The Hindu character of the architecture is striking. There are rich bands of engravings, containing sentiments from the Qurán, around three stories of the Kutab. They are Arabic, but in the Tughra character. In addition to the letters there is elaborate carving, of many exquisite designs, of pure Hindu intricacy and finish, and as rich as any of the tracery on the Sarnath temple in the rye-field of sacred Benares. The column is, perhaps, the finest triumph of Mohammedan architecture before it stood alone. It shows its Hindu dependence. The conqueror could not get along without the conquered, and hence, in his first bold flights, he made use of the wisdom of the men he had mastered. Later, however, he threw off all Hindu allegiance. His creations show no trace of the former masters of India.

I climbed to the top of the Kutab. It was a long and hard ascent, but at each landing I halted awhile, and went out on the graceful platform to rest.

The View from the Kutab.

Who will describe the view from this great height? Off, in a straight line, lies the Delhi of to-day, with its fort, its mosque, and its great wall. In another direction, where Humayun's tomb is, there is a still older Delhi than even the one where we now stand. It was Old Delhi, or Delhi Purana, before the first foundation-stones of the Kutab were laid. There flows the great Jamna, ever young, ever beneficent, despite the rise and death of the civilizations. No change takes place in the music of its waters. On they go, and still will go, from the Himalayas to the Ganges, and they will sing none the less sweetly when all India is Christian.

On every side, so far as the eye can reach, one sees the domes which cover tombs, mosques, and former abodes of the princes of the land. Decay is now the order of the day with them. Walls which begin to break are allowed to tumble to the earth. An old garden is not kept up. Nothing of small significance is restored, but is allowed to die. But valuable ruins are saved. England lets nothing important die in India. She has her men at hand, with pick and spade, and every restoring force, and brings all back to its former splendor. For instance, the base of the Kutab was covered with *débris*. The whole great creation was a bowing ruin when left by the earthquake. But it was worth the saving. Hence, England has taken care to have the *débris* cleared away, and the entire structure repaired, wherever a stone has been needed.

The Mosque in Old Delhi.

The mosque of Kutab al Islam was begun immediately after the Mohammedan capture of Delhi and the occupation of India. It was, probably, one of the first tributes of gratitude for the conquest of the Hindus. It was begun in the year 1191, and was completed in 1300. Of its kind it stands alone in India. You enter the spacious sacred enclosure through a majestic gateway of five arches. The court is four hundred and twenty feet long by three hundred and eighty-four feet broad. This is a cloistered space, with pillars of Hindu architecture. When the mosque was in its original state there were, it is supposed, twelve hundred pillars. Many now remaining are of every possible design. The variety of tracing, the wild freaks of the architect, the lavish introduction of all the curious and rich patterns known to the workers in silk and enamel, are here reproduced in stone and marble. They are to-day the pure and choice remnants of Delhi when it was only Hindu, before the Mohammedan scimiter had profaned the Indus or the Jamna. Hindu temples stood everywhere, beneath every shady palm, along the river at every bend, within every rajah's garden wall. But when the Mogul came, he changed all this. He tore down the images of men, and monkeys, and elephants, and peacocks, and gods. With heavy sledge he struck off the noses, and put out the eyes, and disfigured every face. "There is one God," he

TREES IN THE COURT-YARD OF THE MOSQUE.

cried, as he played the iconoclast. Then he took these same pillars, now destroyed for all idolatrous possibilities, and made them do service in his own mosques. There is an inscription over the entrance to the immense court which says that the pillars here used are made of the ruins of twenty-seven Hindu temples.

The Iron Pillar.

There is an iron pillar, in a court by itself, which is the most ancient of all the ruins in this early Delhi. It varies from the usual metallic memorials of the early days in that it is of solid wrought iron. Its height above ground is forty feet, and its diameter sixteen inches. But it has been ascertained that an important part, not less than twenty feet additional, is still below ground. It is believed by Prinsep and other antiquarians to belong to the third or fourth century of the Christian era. The Hindu tradition ascribes to this column the very origin of Delhi itself, for, when Anang Pal ordered it to be taken out of the ground, it was discovered that it was wet with the blood of the Serpent King. He did all in his power to place it firmly again in the earth, but failed. The pillar remained dhíla, "loose," and so sprang into existence the Delhi of all the later ages. There is a deep inscription, in six lines, in Sanskrit characters, which tells the history of this remarkable shaft.

On our homeward road we left the way by which we had come, and visited the Tombs of Humayun and of Nizam ud din Auliya. They are remarkable structures. Each tomb is not one building, but a group, where marble and other rich stones are brought into use in great profusion.

I afterwards climbed up a rough road to Indrapat, or Purana Qila. This is an old fort, within an ancient wall. It is a mere fragment of a ruin. But it marks the site of the most remote of all the Delhis. It is the worn and wasted fragment of the first city which stood in all this region. One can see to-day where the old gates once swung on their hinges.

But all the gates are closed or gone now, except one, that through which we went. We went along a rough and narrow lane, with beggars and the blind on either hand to greet us by their piteous cries for pice. We reached a beautiful mosque, and climbed up as high as we could, and then looked off upon the great valley of the Jamna. We lingered long in this abode of desolation. Near by, just across a narrow lane, is the ruin where Humayun kept his great library. But none of his precious volumes have been preserved. The books have gone with the reader, into oblivion.

A feeble old man was our guide about these lanes, and out in the open place overlooking the great vale. His mind was filled with images of departed glory. He was himself a part of his

A TOMB IN OLD DELHI.

sad story. Older ruins, but not a more striking type of the past, did I see that day than the aged man from whom I parted at the old imperial gateway, with its crumbling, but still glowing, ornaments of rich tiles.

CHAPTER LXXIV.

THE JAMA MASJID.—DELHI IN THE MUTINY.

THE rest of my time in Delhi was spent in the examination of objects of more recent date. I went again to the Fort, and saw the Halls of Audience and the Baths. The endeavor to see the precious little mosque once more was fruitless, for its brass doors were closed. Twice I visited the Jama Masjid, or Great Mosque. Here is a mosque, elevated, with its immense court, upon a broad platform. You reach the platform by three great stairways, which, because of the easy and graceful ascent, remind one of the steps by which the Greeks reached their Parthenon.

As I looked at these steps of the Jama Masjid, again and again, they made such an impression of majesty and grace as it was very difficult to account for. There is such a harmony between their length and height and angle of ascent, combined with the great structure into which they lead, that, as a mere pathway into a court and a place of worship, they are probably without a parallel in modern times. The steps narrow as they ascend, the lowest being one hundred and forty-nine feet and ten inches long. There are forty steps in all, each being eight inches high. "This mosque," says Temple, "built by the emperor Shah Jahân, . . . is probably the most beautiful mosque on a very large scale that has ever been seen in the world. Its vast dimensions, swelling cupolas, and lofty arches; its spacious court-yard, arcades, gateway, cloisters, and flight of steps produce ultimately an imposing effect. But even this is hardly perceived at first by the beholder, because his admiration is so riveted by the grace of its forms, the nicety of its proportions, the delicate adjustment of its component parts, and the harmony of its coloring. For the material of this noble structure the marble lends its brightness and the sandstone its finest red."*

---

* "India in 1880," pp. 40, 41.

JAMA MASJID, OR GREAT MOSQUE.

Here, as in many other mosques, special pains have been taken with the gateways. They are massive and imposing, and worthy of the mosque into which they introduce the traveller. The main doors are sixteen feet high, and are of wood, covered with heavy brass, which is richly ornamented with arabesques. The court is immense, three hundred and twenty-five feet square, and every part paved with stone. In the centre are a marble basin and fountain.

The mosque itself is two hundred and one feet long, and one hundred and twenty feet broad. It was built in the year 1658. Five thousand men wrought at it six years, in order to complete it. Its two minarets are one hundred and thirty feet high. From their top the best view of Delhi is to be had. In a little corner of one of the outer corridors there are some relics, which pious Mohammedans set great store by, such as a Qurán in Cufic, from the seventh century; another, written by the Imam Hasan; an alleged slipper of Mohammed, filled with jasmine; a block of stone, with a great footprint, claimed to be the impression of Mohammed's foot; a supposed hair of the prophet's moustache; and a piece of the canopy from over his tomb.

The Traces of the Mutiny.

Delhi will be forever associated with the Indian Mutiny as the very citadel of its strength. About this city of cities, where the traditions of Mogul splendor form only the newest chapter in the history of native rule, the natives of India have woven their finest threads of patriotism. The Hindu memory goes far back over the centuries, and all the currents of religion, romance, and military daring centre here. It is not surprising, therefore, that when Hindu and Mohammedan resolved upon throwing off British rule, they should think immediately of Delhi as their capital. This is precisely what they did. They planned that Delhi should be the centre of their restored royalty. Those old palaces should be clothed with their original splendor, if only the English could be driven out. The emperors should again walk the marble corridors, and once more sit in the Public and Private Halls, and dispense justice from the renewed Peacock Throne. Their beautiful daughters, like the sweet Lalla Rookh, should again be given in marriage only to kings, and be borne by only careful hands to Kashmir and other barbaric capitals.

A new Delhi should arise upon the ruins of the present. The Afghan should again be conquered. The Nizam, and every other native prince who had dared to help the English, should be hurled from his throne, as unworthy to be called an Indian. Not a trace of the Briton, or his Gospel, or his cannon, should be left, from the mountains down to Ceylon.

It was a great dream, but only a dream. The mutineers held Delhi with an iron grasp. The English could get it only by a siege. Their efforts to capture it lasted from June 8, 1857, to September of the same year. One attack after another was resisted with great bravery. The English knew that, unless Delhi should fall, their power in India would be at an end. There would be such a revival of the old national feeling that the natives could not be conquered. Hence, with full appreciation of the importance of the possession of this city, they spent every possible effort in that direction. The butchery of the defenceless English and their families, in cold blood, at the outset, showed the bitter feeling of the native mind. By careful combinations, though after repeated failures, the British troops, under General John Nicholson, took Delhi. I climbed up on the wall which joins at the Kashmir Gate, and saw the still clear traces of the havoc which was wrought by English shot and shell. Thirty years have not concealed the strong reminders of the bloody struggle.

But it was not shot and shell alone which did the work in this case. A body of English soldiers, right in the face of a terrible fire from the parapets, marched boldly up to the Kashmir Gate, rushed across the bridge, lodged powder bags against the gate, lighted the fuse, and blew open the gate itself. This last resort meant certain death to many an Englishman. Well they knew it, but they did not hesitate. The work was well done. Those who were left alive marched through the bloody opening into the city. On came the assaulting column in hot haste. Delhi was now sure to be again in English hands.

The fighting was not all over, however. But the city was held, and in two weeks more the English flag floated again from the gateway of the great fort. The final struggle was on the 23d of September, when brave John Nicholson, the general of the army, fell in the moment of victory.

Not far from the Kashmir Gate is one of the pillars of the

great Asoka. It has two pedestals, measuring together five feet in height. The pillar rises twenty-four feet above the pedestal.

After lingering long amid the weeds at the Kashmir Gate, and wandering over the still fresh and broken parts of the upper wall, I descended, and walked out to the English cemetery. Here I saw the plain tombstone to the memory of Nicholson. Many other graves of English soldiers and civilians are here. Some of the inscriptions are very touching. The Englishman's heart is never seen more clearly, and to its deepest depth, than in the tributes which he writes over his brother's dust in far-off India.

It was now midday, and the sun was intensely hot. I had no carriage, and none was to be found in the suburbs. But this was my only opportunity to go out into the country and see the Mutiny Memorial, a monument to the English heroes who won Delhi back to England, but died in the effort. The walk was exhausting, but the reward was ample.

The monument covers a hill which commands a great stretch of country. Seen at a distance, it presents a picture of great delicacy and beauty, and reminded me at once of the Waverley Monument to Sir Walter Scott in Edinburgh. The structure is an octagon, and has seven pointed windows, on which are inscriptions containing the history of the events—with the names of the fallen in battle—which led to the capture of Delhi. Nothing important is omitted. By going within, and ascending seventy-eight steps, I gained the top of the monument. Suddenly the broad and beautiful scene of Delhi and the outlying country came into view.

My previous wanderings in the city and its environs now enabled me to identify all the outlying parts which make up the Delhi of romance and history. This was my last view of the great city and its wonderful environment. I confess that I did not care for another, for fear this would be disturbed. Near by, just at the foot of the hilly crest whose crown is the Mutiny Memorial, I noticed a large body of native troops, undergoing drill, and commanded by English officers.

CHAPTER LXXV.

A TOUR INTO THE PANJAB.

In going northwest, into the Panjab, I was passing through the pathway of the Aryan conquerors of India. The Panjab is the latest India of England. Because of its frontier character, its unsettled condition, its varied and provincial life, and its barbaric antiquities, it is the least known of all the English possessions in Asia. Strictly speaking, with your back towards Europe, it is the front valley of the Indus. Everything has a meaning in India, and the Panjab is only another name for the Five Rivers which make the historic Indus. They rise far back among the western Himalayas, bring down their waters from glaciers twenty-five miles in length, and peaks twenty-six thousand feet high, and hurl their mighty torrent into one great current, which is thrown at last into the Arabian Sea. It is a fertile region, not less so than the Valley of the Ganges.

This Panjab is the open door, the only one by which the European of earlier days was able to descend upon the plains of India for conquest and a new home. The sea was not the path by which the old nations travelled for their mightier conquests. The desert and the mountain have been the road towards enemy and empire. When the river was reached, it was only to descend it awhile, and then leave its banks for the further campaign. The steaming Indian marshes have put to death more armies than hostile arrows ever struck. In the Panjab every foot of the land is a romance. No one knows how many armies have shivered in the winds of the hills of Afghanistan, and then pounced down through the Khaibar Pass into India, and overspread the country, until the people could rise and destroy the stranger within the gates. Whenever a European invader of Asia has reached well into the continent, his dream has always been India. That country has ever been, and still is, the pearl of all the Orient. Its perfect sky in winter, its plenteous rains

THE TIGER IN HIS LAIR.

in summer, its immense rivers, its boundless stores of wealth, and its enduring industries, which know no change, have made it the dream of every great conqueror. Many a one who invaded Syria and Persia and Arabia dreamed—even if he did not divulge his dreams—of India itself. He meant India always, even if, like Julian, he died before he reached it. Did Julian ever say that he had India in mind? Not that his biographers have told us. But his wars, his genius in arms, his love of letters, his vig-

BAITING THE TIGER.

orous campaign in Parthia, make us believe that his eye was on India, and nothing nearer, before he said on his last field, "Thou, O Galilean, has conquered, after all!"

The Panjab is Alexander's land. He had studied every part of it, and then reached it, at the head of his victorious army. Right where I am now writing his hosts marched by, and hoped to stay, and bequeath these rich fields to a Greek posterity. He found dynasties, old and strong before his own Macedonia had acquired a place on the world's map, and before the first stones of Priam's

Troy had been laid. Some of the kings of the region, with true Oriental suppleness, gave him a flattering welcome, and in Taxila, which still bears the same name it did twenty-three centuries ago, when he pitched his silken tent here, the kindly descendants of the old Turanian founders gave him a feast which lasted three full days. Alexander found the Aryans in full force in his forward march, ruling proudly and strongly, and having the same customs, and wearing turn-up shoes and loose robes of precisely the same style as the men and women who now move up and down these streets of Lahor, before my window. The Aryans had ruled in this country, on both sides of his pathway, almost as long before Alexander's day as he lived before ours. He found them just as determined to hold their own as the English have found their descendants, to their great cost, in these two latest centuries.

Long before reaching Lahor I could see the majestic outline of the Kashmir Mountains. They were as white as Mount Blanc's southern shoulder, over which I had climbed, in the far-back student days, from Aosta and Courmajeur. The Kashmirian panorama changed every few minutes, as our train moved along the curves. I was thinking of the romance of the region. Here it was that Lalla Rookh was borne tenderly to her new home, from her Delhi palace to the hanging gardens in the Vale of Kashmir the Blest. Here the English had gone up many a time into Afghanistan, to keep open the pathway to India, and shut out forever the Russian. Her diplomats and soldiers had played many a shrewd game, and hundreds of Anglo-Saxon nobles, nursed in English homes, had fallen by rude Afghan hands, and been left to bleach upon the plain.

Take Arthur Conolly as an illustration—living, and likely tortured down to the convulsions of death, in the filthy court of a Kabul prison.

I do not know a more affecting piece of bibliographical romance than that of his prayer-book, which he used in his last days, and whose story I have just come across in this very region. One day a prayer-book was found either by General Skobeleff, of Russia, or by a man who afterwards gave it to him. This was in Afghanistan. The book contained many of Conolly's notes, all along its margins, in careful writing. Skobeleff took pains to preserve the volume, and presented it to the London Geographical Society. The Society found its associations to be personal rather than general, and handed it back to its Russian owner. He then took care to learn of the kinspeople of Conolly, and so, one morning, in London, the book was handed to the servant, who answered the door-bell of Conolly's surviving sister. Think of the feelings of that sister, when she opened the precious packet and saw her dead brother's prayer-book! It had been twenty years since his dying hand had written his notes, and his spirit had gone up from an Afghan gibbet to its crown and joy. All these years his volume had wandered from one far-off bazar and owner to another. We talk often of the mortality of books. Is not their longevity a much more wondrous thing?

BRINGING HOME THE GAME.

CHAPTER LXXVI.

LAHOR—THE PANJAB CAPITAL.

No historian has been rash enough to fix a positive date for the foundation of Lahor. Its antiquity goes beyond all the records. One city after another has arisen on the ruins of its predecessor, and out yonder, under the ripe harvests, the old foundations are found in perplexing number. There cannot have been less than four Lahors, that of to-day being a mere parvenu growth, hardly older than four centuries; but still preserving the rich memorials of the rule and splendor of the Mogul conquerors. The first Lahor was probably an old city when Hiouen Thsang, the Chinese pilgrim, visited it, in the seventh century of our era. Hindu tradition, true to its habits, makes its origin divine, and declares that Loh, the elder son of Râma, was its founder. Its former grandeur was famed throughout the East. As one of the splendid capitals in early India, its name was known everywhere. Four centuries ago, Abu'l Fazl declared of it that it was "the resort of all nations." Shiraz and Isfahan were famous in the days of the undisputed sway of the Moguls, and yet a proverb of the day ran in this wise: "If Shiraz and Isfahan were united, they would not make one Lahor." Its fame had reached across both continents, and Milton found it in the old books, and so made wise use of it in his verse.

Ptolemy, in his geography (about A.D. 150), mentions a city along the banks of the Ravi, which is identified as Lahor, an identification the more striking because of the recent discovery of Aurakatis, also mentioned by him, about twenty miles from the present Lahor.

Lahor, as we see it to-day, is about the size of Cincinnati. Its wonderful architecture is of Mogul origin, and therefore comparatively recent. It was a great imperial city, and then guarded well the pathway from Afghanistan down into the valley of the Ganges. It is the Nuremberg of India. The great walls

OPEN-AIR RESTAURANT, LAHOR.

still surround it, and bristle with reminders of the great battles which were fought to their bitterest end on the historical plain of the Ravi.

The tomb of Anar Kali, "Pomegranate Blossom," is a beautiful memorial of the great Akbar's reign. It was erected in memory of the favorite woman of his court, and is remarkable for the magnificence of its sarcophagus. The English seldom change a Hindu ruin to other purposes. But here is an exception. They have actually converted this magnificent tomb into a little church, and banished to a dark closet, frequented by bats, the sarcophagus, "whose exquisitely formed words surpass anything of the kind in India." On the face and sides of the sarcophagus are inscribed ninety-nine names of God.

The Shalamar Gardens.

One night the Mogul emperor, Shah Jahân, had a dream of a garden like that of Paradise. He summoned his artists, repeated his dream of rare flowers, rich fruits, marble fountains, and cool pavilions; and ordered his visionary garden to be made a reality. The result was the Shalamar Gardens, which were laid out in seven divisions, representing the seven degrees of the Paradise of Islam. Of the seven only two remain, and they cover an area of eighty acres. Here are flowers, fruits, cascades, beautiful resting-places, terraces, and all the marvels of an Indian garden.* A tank is in the centre of the floral paradise. There are one hundred fountains in the first division of the garden, and two hundred rising from the tank itself. In the centre of the tank, or artificial lake, there is an islet, which is approached by a passage way.

On entering the portals of the great fort of Lahor, I found myself within an immense court, which is beautified by a splendid palace and a mosque of wonderful proportions. I saw no palace in India where it was so easy to identify each part, and its purpose, as here. In one place is the Takhtgah, or "Throne Place," where Akbar sat. In another is a clump of trees, where once stood the tomb of the holy man who used to warn the great emperor that he was mortal. Elsewhere there is the spot where the emperor heard his Arzbegi read the petitions of his people.

---

* Cf. F. D. Newhouse, Letters in *Western Christian Advocate* (Cincinnati).

Here is a rich marble pavilion on which a whole fortune of nine lacs was spent. But these scenes of splendor are wearying. One wanders through stately halls and lettered corridors, and out on verandas and balconies, until wearied with the splendor of this greatest palace of Lahor. English soldiers keep faithful guard over all. They have not the bearing of strangers, but are as deliberate and composed as if they were sauntering along the Thames embankment.

The Museum.

Some years ago an exhibition was held in Lahor, to which objects were sent from all parts of the country, in order to throw light upon the history, industries, and general life of the entire northwestern part of India. When the exhibition was over, a permanent museum in Lahore sprang out of it, many of the exhibits having been retained for that purpose. The result is a precious collection of Indian antiquities. The one in the South Kensington Museum is a mere toy-shop compared to this. While there are some collections in India which are larger, so far as natural history is concerned, there is probably not one which reveals so fully the India of the elder days, when its Oriental life was not disturbed by the intruding Portuguese or Frenchman or Englishman. Here, for example, is a stone with an inscription of the time of King Gondophares, two thousand years ago. Then there are pediments of pillars from a building of the ancient Taxila sculptures from the Usufzai country, where one sees the Greek influence of twenty-two centuries ago—such as the Phrygian cap and Macedonian cloak.

There are many coins, gathered hereabout, dating precisely from Alexander's day. Each city in the Northwest seems to have had its special industry, and in this museum they are all represented. Here are the damascened pottery of Gujerat and Sialkot, the vitreous enamel of Bhawalpur, the copper-engraved work of Kashmir, and the perforated metal work of Delhi. Then we have the gold and silk embroidery of Amritsar, and the coarse cloths of Kabul. An entire department is assigned to agriculture and the mechanical implements of the ruder India. The type of plough is here which the Indians were using in the valley of the Indus before Philip threatened Athens or Alexander was born. The kind of rope, the awkward rakes and hoes and pruning-knives, such as were in use before Alexander reached India, are here to be seen. Here is the floss-silk embroidery, on long curtains, literally covered with little mirrors, such as were used in the imperial halls of the Mogul palaces, and are still woven in the primitive looms of Amritsar.

Here is rough paper, made of bamboo and the bark of trees, just such as merchants wrote their letters on, and sent them by swift couriers up and down the valley of the Euphrates, many a long century ago. Here are monumental tablets, with worn inscriptions, reared by kings whose very names are forgotten in the rapid march towards the newer and the more practical. Here is a warrior's freak. It is a sword, with open steel handle, richly inlaid with gold and silver. It has a long hilt, and up and down its length run beautiful grooves, into which loose pearls are let, which glided back and forth as the sword was handled. But here in rich and great Lahor there is no dearth of emeralds, pearls, and diamonds. They were the playthings of kings and their wives. Special emissaries were sent out on long missions to search the world for the best. Many a life was wasted in the quest, and many a province was lost and won when the stake was one woman and a handful of diamonds.

HINDU POTTER, LAHOR.

CHAPTER LXXVII.

THE GOLDEN TEMPLE OF AMRITSAR.

We were met at the Amritsar station by a Christian native, the Padre Rajib Ali. He is a fine illustration of the power of Christianity to gather grand trophies from any false faith. He was formerly a Sikh, and a firm believer in the teachings of the Sikh Gurus. He came in contact with the Gospel, however, and resolved to accept it. He made public profession of the Christian faith, and was baptized by the Rev. Mr. Knowles. He now edits a Christian paper, which is doing excellent service in propagating the gospel among the Sikh people. The padre is tall, grave, serene, and in personal appearance as fine a specimen of the physical man as I have ever seen.

We were to see nothing in Amritsar until we had taken tiffin. This must be in the good padre's own house. His wife and daughter were in Calcutta, and we saw only his beautiful niece.

Amritsar, with its 134,000 people, and its important silk industry, is the most populous and wealthy city of the Panjab. Its chief interest lies in its religious associations. It is the centre of the Sikh faith, and has been the Jerusalem of the Sikhs from the time of the founding of their bizarre creed, in the year 1574. The Sikhs are a protest against the Hindu faiths. They start out with the idea that all idolatry is a crime, and for three centuries have stood up as strong foes of all the forms of Indian polytheism. Their Guru, or religious teacher, was Ram Das, and he was permitted by the Mogul emperor Akbar to found a city on this site. Hence, from here, as a sacred centre, the whole faith has grown, and Amritsar has become the shrine and glory of the Sikhs, wherever they are.

Special ceremonies are employed to admit into the mysteries of the Sikh religion. Some of the Sikhs do not seem to care whether their children are admitted or not. There is certainly no increase of adherents, and the probability is that the body is declining, and that the faith is cherished chiefly as a magnificent and precious treasure, more valuable as a memory than as a source of future strength. It is associated with the military splendor of the Sikh dominion in the Panjab.*

At the outer court we were invited to a seat beneath a tree. A servant of the temple came with slippers in hand for visitors. I had no hesitation in making the change, but was glad enough, after walking an hour in his bright slippers, on cold stone, to get back to shoes. One enters the sacred enclosure through the great gateway. Here, in an upper room, are kept the immense weapons which belonged to the Sikh chiefs when they were making warfare against the English for their faith and a home. These weapons are as ponderous as the heavy arms in Warwick Castle. What a story could these terrible instruments of death tell if they only had tongues! One can read in a nation's weapons the story of its life and work.

When the English came, and the Sikhs needed to be conquered too, it was the most violent conflict which India had witnessed since the days of Clive and his French opponents. It was a hand-to-hand encounter. The end was a compromise. Then came an alliance, but, of course, with the English at the head of the government. The Sikhs were left, however, with a measure of local rule, and with all their religious privileges undisturbed.

No wonder these Sikhs have put their death-dealing weapons in the gateway which leads to their sacred shrine. Theirs was the glory of steel. Out of the keen blade and heavy broad-axe they rose to existence and fame. Every page of their history is red with blood.

But we are only at the gate of the Temple of Gold. The scene is dazzling in this bright Oriental sun. The tessellated marble floor is cold to our slippered feet. The air is fragrant with many rich perfumes. The artificial and rectangular lake, in the midst of which the temple stands, reflects the images of the gnarled and ancient trees which surround it, while the houses send down their shadows in brotherly and fantastic combinations. The gate moves slowly back upon its hinges, and we make our slippered steps over the graceful marble bridge tow-

* Temple, "India in 1880," pp. 117, 120.

ards the Golden Temple, which stands upon a platform in the middle of the miniature lake. And here we pause.

This lake, according to the Sikh faith, is the Pool of Immortality. He who looks upon it lives. But he who bathes in it enters the Sikh paradise. Wherever a Sikh lives, and whatever sorrow he has passed through, a sweet and holy calm comes over his troubled soul the moment he sees this silver surface, and beneath it views the shadowy gold of his temple roof.

The lake is kept free from all impurities. It extends in all directions five hundred and thirty feet. It is surrounded by a marble pavement, twenty-four feet wide, and tessellated, the ground stone being of white marble, but varied with other marbles of alternate black and brown. All these marbles are brought from the far-off quarries of Jaipur. Along this rich and spotless margin there grow trees, beneath whose shade many a worshipper lies, or sits, as his humor pleases him. It is difficult to tell in some cases whether he sleeps or wakes. His face, in every instance, is a picture of calm joy. If asleep, he knows before he lost himself that he is near his sacred flood. If awake, he thinks of the Sikh heaven, where even the Golden Temple of Amritsar will be nothing compared to its great glory. On the outer margin of this surrounding marble pavement are charmed houses. Not every one may live here. The price of a house on the border of the Pool of Immortality is fabulously high. These houses have a style of their own, an individuality of taste being observed in the architecture of them all. They are kept scrupulously neat, servants watch the front at all times, lest something lie there which would disturb the sanctity of the environment. They are the homes of the Sikh nobility and chiefs, who come here from all parts to worship and to live. I suppose that, like the Hindus in Benares, it is the dream of their life to die within sight of the glittering roof of the Temple of Gold.

We now stand before the sacred shrine of the Sikhs. There are no images, not a single symbol of idolatry. The chief priest is seated on a rug of gold embroidery. He hands us each an orange, which it would not be courtesy to refuse. We ask him if we may see his sacred book—a copy of the Granth. With great courtesy he reaches beneath the low desk before him and draws out a package wrapped about with rich cloths. The sacred manuscript is unfolded, and he begins to read. The page

THE GOLDEN TEMPLE OF AMRITSAR.

is beautiful. The volume is kept with most religious care, and after a brief reading from only one page the priest wraps it up again in the cloths and puts it away in its usual place.

On another side of the main temple space, only a few feet from the chief priest, are the chanters, who sing the praises of the Sikh faith. Here are two expressions we heard:

> "The Hindu worships idols, and
> Therefore he is in error;
> The Mohammedan worships
> The prophet, and therefore he
> Is a false worshipper."

Then come many expressions descriptive of the attributes of the one and universal God. This chanting goes on all day. When one class get weary others take their place. Pilgrims come and go all the time. I noticed the rapt attention of some who had newly arrived. Their faces glowed with joy and bewilderment. Theirs had been a long desire. Now, at last, they see—perhaps for the first and the last time—the Golden Temple, of whose great glories they had heard from infancy. They fall flat upon their faces before they have fairly come within the shadow of the central hall, and lie motionless until reminded there is a nearer view and more to see and hear.

The ornamentation of the Golden Temple is exceedingly rich. There is no image of beast or bird. But the figures are taken from the forest and the garden—flowers and vines playing the chief part. Gold is the ruling color. It is laid on heavily. There are other colors, however, but of a deep, rich, and mellow shade, to harmonize with the gold and the sacred associations of the structure. We ascend to the next floor, where we come to a corridor, which extends completely around the temple. Here we look out upon the beautiful lake, and then at the high gateway, and the precious little connecting bridge, and the white and trim houses, with their venerable trees and marble pavements in front. It is a sight which has no parallel. All the sides of this Golden Temple are covered with richly painted verses from the sacred Granth. The temple is itself a book. I suppose there is not a word in the sacred volume which is not repeated here, in some part of this sacred structure.

Why is this the Golden Temple? And why, when you once

see it, does it remain a perpetual vision in your memory? First of all, because its upper roof is covered with a heavy plating of the finest gold. The elements have no power over it. There it has been shining on, from century to century, ever since 1581, the blazing sun reflecting its glory in the lake, and throwing its golden light fully on the eye of the pilgrim.

The roof itself is broken into several, there being first of all a central one, and then about it a number of others. The upper corridors and balconies have their roofs, the whole forming a

BEATEN WORK IN COPPER FOR THE "GOLDEN TEMPLE," AMRITSAR.

harmonious cluster about the one which covers the nave of the temple. There is, therefore, such a combination of golden surfaces of the varied roofs that the sun's reflection is intense. The result is an effect on the eye which, once seen, is never forgotten. The broad walls, and even the sides of the stairways, have the same rich shading which makes the Golden Temple of Amritsar one of the most harmonious architectural creations in India or the world. It is not of large size. But one must always take architecture in its combinations. With the gateway, the bridge, the lake, the surrounding houses, and the gnarled trees, the whole becomes more than a memory. It is henceforth a part of one's very self.

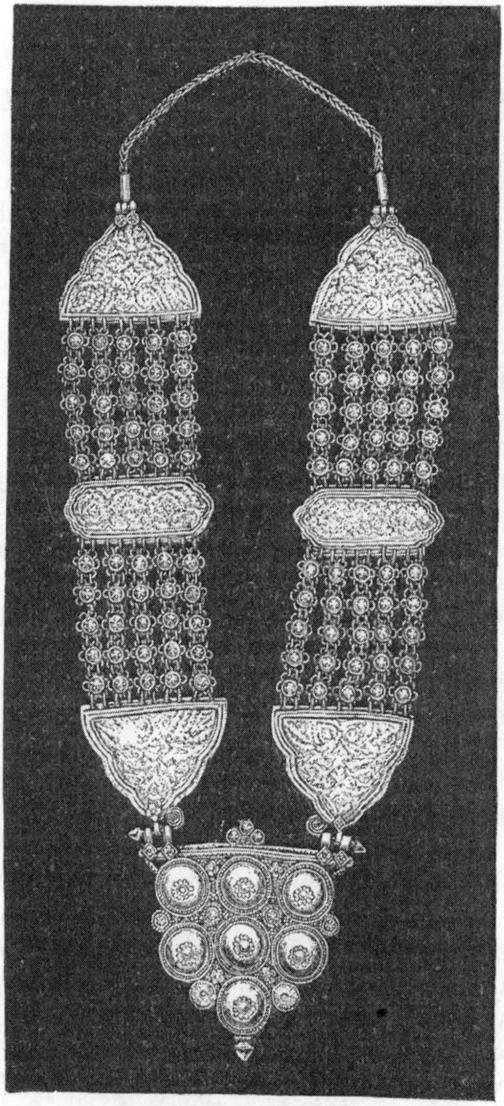

SILVER NECK ORNAMENT, SIND.

CHAPTER LXXVIII.

THE MOHAMMEDAN COLLEGE AT ALIGARH.

THE Mohammedan is fixed. He is hard to reach. He makes no promises. The Hindu is pliable, and is ready for change. Knowing this difference in the races, I was quite well prepared for Hindu adaptations of English methods. But I was ill prepared for a formal, thorough, and elaborate grafting of English ideas on a Mohammedan stem. Of late years the Hindus have been getting ahead of the Mohammedans. The Hindu youths have surpassed the Mohammedan in all the competitive examinations, and are crowding them out. This fact has given rise to the impression now prevailing, that the Mohammedans are declining in wealth and numbers, while the Hindus are advancing. This, as much as anything else, has led Mohammedan thinkers to adopt reformatory methods to elevate their young people, and to adapt Islam to modern conditions.*

I had heard of the celebrated Mohammedan Anglo-Oriental College in Aligarh, and was anxious to see it. By cutting off an hour here and another there, and doing an improper amount of early rising and night riding, I gained a half-day, and spent it here.

This institution is an educational phenomenon. It is more—it marks a new epoch in the history of Islam. It is a great educational establishment, which has grown out of the brain of one man, Sayad Ahmad Bahádur, a learned and venerable Mohammedan. Much care was taken by him in paving the way for the institution. In 1870 a committee was formed for the diffusion and advancement of learning among Mohammedans of India. They offered three prizes for the best essays on the subject, and the result was to adopt a proposal for a college. Its aim was declared to be the popularization of the study of European

* Temple, "India in 1880," p. 113.

science and literature among the Mohammedans in general and among the higher classes of the Mohammedans in particular, and to form a class.

Sayad Ahmad differs essentially from some of his co-religionists. He regards Mohammed as only a man, with many infirmities and no superhuman inspiration. Perhaps, if closely questioned, he would make still further admissions. But when a Mohammedan once concedes that Mohammed was fallible, he brings down the Qurán from its lofty place of indisputable truth, and reduces it to a purely human book. He may have nothing to say as to the Qurán, but his view of the writer must disturb also the sacred character of his writings.

This learned and very highly esteemed man conceived the idea that Mohammedanism, in its present exclusive shape, has no future. It is fated, and deserves to die, if it will not undergo modern renewals. There is enough in it to save it, but the English ideas must be taken on board. By this process only can the vessel float. Now, to bring this about, a central and strong educational institution, with a broad and thorough curriculum, must be founded. There must be no scanty giving. Mohammedans, and such only as have caught the breath of the nineteenth century, must be invited to contribute to its endowment. In addition to giving largely of his own means, Sayad Ahmad went south to the Nizam's dominions, and secured large gifts from the Nizam and his prime-minister, the celebrated Salar Jang. He also took upon himself the great burden of securing means from English gentlemen. He made no secret of his purpose. He wanted a great college established for the education of Mohammedan young men the world over. He travelled by night and day. He threw his entire time and wonderful energy into the undertaking. The result is the present large college in Aligarh.

Sayad Ahmad wished no honors for himself. But he did desire to see his work a success. I had the pleasure of an introduction to him, in his own rooms, in the main college building. Here he lives, in the midst of the buildings which his own energy has reared, and in constant sight of the many young men who have come from every quarter of the Mohammedan world to secure an education. He is advanced in age. His face is a picture of benignity and manly vigor at seventy-five. His beard is long and snowy white. In manner he is gentle and courteous. In speech he is deliberate, but not slow. He has been prompted by a desire to elevate his co-religionists of the Mohammedan faith, and, now that the work is well begun, he is spending his last years in handsome rooms in the main building, and holds merely a nominal official position, as honorary secretary and member of the managing committee.

The real basis of existence of the college is the Mohammedan disinclination to attend the government institutions. The Hindus have not been opposed to the national schools, and are to be found in all the classes. They had been conquered by the Mohammedans, and were as willing to study English and such sciences as the English conquerors of the Mohammedans had brought with them, as to study Arabic or Persian. "The change of rulers made no difference to them, and they took to English as their ancestors had taken to Persian. But the Mussulman, who, notwithstanding the downfall of his race, had still sparks of ancestral pride in his bosom, looked with contempt upon the literature of a foreign race, opposed all reform, and ignorance contributed to encourage him in his opposition. He obstinately declined either to learn the English language or modern sciences, still looked up with veneration to those mysterious volumes which contained the learning of his forefathers, and reconciled himself to his position by a firm belief in predestination. The result was a great political evil. A large number of Hindus had acquired a knowledge of the English language and thus kept pace with the times, and some of them rose to the highest offices under the English government. The Mohammedans, on the contrary, remained stagnant, remembered with pain and sorrow the past power and prestige of their race, and still continued to worship the learning contained in Arabic and Persian literature. The surrounding circumstances grew too powerful for them, and they gradually sank in ignorance, poverty, and degradation." *

Here lies the whole secret of the distancing of the Mohammedan in India by the conquered Hindu. It is the old story of the final triumph of the conquered.

In 1877 the foundation-stone of the Aligarh College was laid

* *The Pioneer*, Allahabad, [illegible], 1875.

by Lord Lytton, Governor-General of India. In 1878 all the classes were in full operation. The college was affiliated to the Calcutta University up to the First Arts standard in the same year; to the B.A. standard in 1881; and in Law, in 1883. In addition to buildings, extensive grounds, scientific apparatus, and other general needs, it was supposed that five hundred thousand pounds would be needed to furnish an income for providing for the teaching staff and other current expenses. This sum, I imagine, has been either fully raised, or so nearly that no anxiety is felt for the future of the institution.

There are two departments to the college—preparatory and scientific. There are eighty scholarships, tenable for one year, and yet open for re-competition. They range from fifty to one hundred and twenty dollars in value. There are separate studies for the two Mohammedan sects—the Sunnis and the Shiahs. There are also thirty fellowships, which are conferred on the best of the honor men. The annual value of the fellowship is two hundred and forty dollars, and it is tenable for seven years. There are singular adaptations to the native mind, such as the cooking and eating regulations of caste, and the muezzins, or Friday calls to prayer. The Shiah dons will go to mosque three times a day; while the Sunni dons will not eat at the feet of an imam, or preacher, who knows the Qurán by heart. But these requirements are only for Mohammedan students. There are Hindus and a few Christians in attendance, and for them all the honors and emoluments of the college are as fully open as for the Mohammedans.

The management of the college rests on four committees—on instruction in languages and secular learning, on Sunni theology, on Shiah theology, and the managing committee, on which last rests the internal management of the college and boarding-house. On April 1, 1884, there were two hundred and seventy-two students in attendance. Of these, two hundred and one were Mohammedans, seventy Hindus, and one native Christian. Nearly all of the students are boarders. The examinations are semi-annual. Five students have already gone to England, and are in the two great universities, having finished the full course at Aligarh.

There are twenty-four persons in the board of instruction. The principal, Mr. Theodore Beck, is an Oxonian. He was very courteous, and accompanied me over the grounds, and into the students' rooms and the boarding-halls, and explained all the details of the institution. The salaries range from ten rupees, or four dollars, to six hundred and fifty per month. Principal Beck receives the latter amount, besides ample apartments. The income for 1883, from all sources, was nearly twenty thousand dollars. The annual cost of a student in the college classes, including board, is about two hundred and fifty dollars per year. For all other classes the cost is far below this figure. There is a small sum which each boarder must pay for medical treatment, ranging from two dollars and a half to nine dollars, according to the grade of class.

The students come from every Mohammedan quarter. The valley of the Ganges furnishes the largest proportion, for here are the descendants of the Mohammedan populations which were built up by the Mogul emperors, on their invasion of the country. Then many students come from Southern India, the Nizam's dominions. But the territory lying between India and Europe is not without its representative. One student gives his residence as Constantinople. I saw a number of the students, and had the opportunity of conversing with them. An air of cheerfulness pervades the college. Chance led me to make inquiries of one, who was crossing the compound, as to where the principal's house was. He was very attentive, conducted me to the principal, and on the way explained, from a student's point of view, many things which I could not hope to learn from any officer. After leaving me at the door of the principal, that gentleman told me that my guide was the son of a Mohammedan prince, and a most worthy and industrious student. There was nothing in his manner or costume to indicate his princely belongings. But that is precisely what might be expected. The search for knowledge is a republican process, in whatever land one sees it.

I was greatly pleased with one feature of the Aligarh College. There is no concealment of the financial or other matters relating to its condition. The "Report of the Progress of Education in the Mohammedan Anglo-Oriental College at Aligarh" is the finest specimen of a financial statement, combined with minute data concerning the courses of study, which I have seen anywhere. It would be an excellent model for some of our American treasurers and other officers of colleges and universities, who imagine that the public have nothing to do with the details of financial management. Let the public know where money for a school comes from, and whither it goes, and they will intrust it with more. One of the curses of educational management in the United States has been its financial concealments.

While the general tendency of such schools as the Aligarh College is elevating in a moral sense, it is far removed from any Christian element. The Literary Club at Aligarh was founded by Sayad Ahmad. It was established originally by him at Ghazipur in 1864, and in 1866 was removed to its present habitat. Its theology consists mainly of negations, and is a curious medley: miracles are denied; the deluge never took place; all pilgrimages, except to London, Paris, or New York, are useless; bleeding animals should not be used for food, strangled animals being preferred, as the blood can then be eaten; polygamy is proper; resurrection is natural; there is no Mohammedan or any other heaven or hell, or a personal devil.*

The principal, from my conversation with him, led me to infer that Biblical teaching has no place whatever. There is but one Christian in the whole body of students. It is a question whether this is the result or the cause of the absence of the Bible. But the Mohammedans and Hindus can, alike, see that the college itself is a concession to Christian ideas. It was organized on purpose to introduce modern Europe into the heart of old and dead Asia. The newest ideas from the Tyndall and Huxley laboratory will, of course, come to the Aligarh College, but there will be many who will ask, "What but Christianity gave England its quickened thought?"

It is a question of only a few years when all the great schools, of every name, in India, will have a Christian basis. The pressure from the missionary institutions is already very strong, and is increasing constantly. The time is sure to come when from the India to which England has borne her gospel and constitution will come strong arguments for the Christian faith, to counteract some of the false teachings which are ever reappearing in Christian lands.

* For an excellent description of Sayad Ahmad, and the general influence of his system, see article in *Methodist Review*, January, 1891, by the Rev. Henry Mansell, D.D.

CHAPTER LXXIX.

THE RUINS OF FATHPUR SIKRI.

THE great Akbar pitched his tent for the night at the base of a lofty rock, which overlooked a stretch of country little less than fifty miles in diameter. This was in the year 1569, when he was returning from his triumph over the revolting Uzbeg nobles. His empress was with him. The night became a day, and many. On the crest of the lofty hill there lived fakir Selim, who called himself also "Chisti," in honor of his spiritual father, a native of the Persian village of Chist. Akbar took such pleasure in the fakir's society that he allowed himself to be persuaded to make the hill his home, and rear upon it, and all about it, palaces and mosques, and all the splendid structures which entered into the dream and state of an Oriental sovereign. Here a son was born to him, who took his place in history as the illustrious Jahangir. It is not surprising that Akbar and his empress loved this beautiful hill, and began to plan for its permanent occupation. The holy man had revealed to them the divine purpose, that it should become an imperial residence. When the Mogul ruler and his empress began to breathe the delightful air, and witness the beautiful landscape on every side, we may well imagine that they took pleasure in every plan for carrying out their ideal of a favorite and enduring home for themselves and their descendants.

The result of Akbar's plans is the Fathpur Sikri of history. To-day this city is as dead as Babylon. Yet it is safe to say that not in India, nor in any land, is there a more complete picture of royal splendor three centuries ago than one can now see in this magnificent city of death and the dead.

The ride to Fathpur Sikri from Agra is over a good carriage-road of twenty-two miles. My companions for the day were Mrs. P. T. Wilson, and a young friend of hers, a lady recently arrived from England. On the way out we passed the gardens of the Begum Samru, or, rather, of her husband, the German Walter Reinhardt, who died in 1778. This Samru was a desperate woman. She possessed the vices and desperate energy of the Oriental princess, and, to atone for her crimes, gave large sums of money for the founding of schools and a church. Near the garden is a cemetery, where the wife of the Emperor Jahangir was buried. Her tomb is a mere heap of ruins. The gardens were the scene of a terrible engagement between the English and the mutineers in July, 1857. The English were worsted in the fight, but the mutineers gained no permanent advantage,

CHIEF MOSQUE OF FATHPUR SIKRI.
(From Verestchagin.)

for, with their usual want of leadership, they failed to follow up their victory.

All along the road, on either side, there are beautiful trees and a finely cultivated country. The ground begins to ascend, and in the distance the great wall of Fathpur Sikri winds about the base of the palace hill, and climbs gently up its side. This wall was built by Akbar around three sides of his beautiful city of palaces. The fourth side seems to have been devoted in part to an immense body of water, where there was an abundance of fish, the catching of which was always a great amusement of the ladies and other members of the Mogul household. But there is no water now, and one sees only the general outline of the fishing-tank. The city wall, however, still stands. No city, not even Constantinople itself, has preserved a better wall than this dead capital presents to-day. Even the coping, with its perpendicular slits, where guns could rest, is entire for many a long reach. The city, as such, is nowhere to be seen. It is gone, and its site is occupied by fields and orchards and gardens. But the great imperial buildings which covered the hill still stand in silent splendor. One can see just where this city of palaces and of mosques once stood. It was all within the wall, one gate of which is three miles from the opposite gate. The city, then, was about three miles in diameter, with its outlying suburbs of lowly houses for the rude country folk. Heber recalls the resemblance of the wall to that of Oxford.* But he adds that, when looking at the magnificent quadrangle of the present Fathpur Sikri, measuring five hundred feet square, in size, majestic proportions, and in beauty of architecture, there is nothing whatever in Oxford comparable to it. With wonderful energy the Emperor Akbar, in the intervals of his wars, built up house after house, until many an acre was covered with palaces and mosques, and every other building that could add to the splendor of his name and power. His empress, his daughter, his two learned friends, must each have a palace and a court. There must be stables for his elephants and camels. When his favorites died, there must be mausolea of untold magnificence reared to their memory. Even to his favorite elephant there must be reared a memorial pillar, which stands to this day complete.

For fifty years this imperial city was the centre of Mogul power. Its name was the synonym of all that was splendid throughout the Oriental world. From its palace walls there rode messengers with imperial edicts which caused men to tremble from the vale of Kashmir down to the Vindhya Mountains and from Arabia to Burma. But the life of this wonderful imperial city was short. Whether it was the want of water, or the fakir's revelation that the emperor must not build a fort,

---

* "Narrative of Journey through Upper Provinces of India," Lond. ed., 1844, vol. ii. p. 14.

or that some unaccountable caprice seized Akbar's mind, we do not know. At any rate, within fifty years from the time when Akbar pitched his tent at the base of the hill, and began the city, it was a hopeless ruin, and even Akbar himself left it, and made Agra his capital. Its mission had been fulfilled. Death had settled in it. During the reign of Jahangir, the successor of Akbar, the city was declared by Finch, the traveller who visited it, as even thus early, "desolate, lying like a waste desert, and very dangerous to pass through in the night."

On reaching Fathpur Sikri from the Agra side, you enter through a magnificent gateway. The pavement is still smooth, from the wheels of three centuries ago. But there are no swordsmen to guard the gateway, and call out for a permit to enter the imperial portal. Only a few quiet vultures sit with folded wings and dull eyes, and look down upon the stranger. More splendid scenes their ancestors could look upon, in the centuries gone by, as couriers rode rapidly back and forth, and great pageants moved across the flint-paved courts below, when the multitudes went wild with joy. We drove across the first court, turned somewhat to the left, and halted in the space before the Daftar Khana, the record-office of Akbar, and now the bungalow for the entertainment of travellers.

To make even a hurried circuit of the buildings requires several hours. All the edifices are kept in excellent condition. The government has a good force of servants here, and they are under careful supervision. Wherever there is danger of a falling pillar, or any damage from time, or any other cause, the defect is immediately attended to. The courts and pavements are neatly swept. All the grounds are neat and clean. The structures are of red stone. The geologist would probably call it sandstone, but some of it is of such fine quality that it admits of a polish almost as finished as that of syenite. While the prevailing color is red, there is a variety of rich shades. The Indian climate is withering to the human body, but is kindly to the stone buildings. Nowhere have I ever seen more beautiful creations, which have escaped the ravages of both climate and warfare, than these immense buildings at Fathpur Sikri. When the emperor ceased to inhabit them, there was no further ground for a city. Its work was done. And in all the wars since then there was nothing to attract an army. It is not likely that a single shot of stone or iron has been hurled against wall or mosque or palace in Fathpur Sikri for three hundred years.

We took the buildings which lay nearest, and went through one after another, with not much regard to my guide-book or the venerable priest of the place who serves as cicerone. Akbar's khwab-gah, or sleeping-apartment, is reached by a stairway. It is a small room, only fifteen feet square, and is entered by a door on each of the four sides. Over the doors there are still legible the Persian inscriptions, beneath which the great king went to reach his sleeping-place. Great corridors run along each side of the building. But it is evident that they were only designed as places of promenade for the emperor and whoever might be permitted to approach his residence. Here one sees the ideal of an Oriental despot's residence. There must be, not one roof, beneath which the whole court should reside, but many houses, separated by courts and colonnades and gardens and groves and fountains. There must be plenty of space. There should be no intrusion when one wished to be alone. Each empress and favorite councillor had a separate establishment. Then, even for the officers of the emperor, there must needs be a separate palace. If he slept in one place he must dispense justice in another, and hold council in still another, and worship in a fourth, and bathe in a fifth, and meet his friends socially in a sixth. There must, by all means, be no monotony.

Near one of the palaces there is a large court, two hundred and ten feet long by one hundred and twenty feet broad, which is called the Pachesi, from its resemblance to a pachesi-board, the stones being so placed in colors that the Indian game of that name could be played there. One of the most elaborately carved palaces is that of Akbar's Turkish wife—for he was cosmopolitan in his selections—having a Hindu, a Turkish, and, it is believed by some, also a Christian wife. The pillars surrounding the palaces of the Turkish wife are both double and single, the corner columns of the outer being double, while the inner are single. There is no space which is not carved with rare and beautiful figures. The designs are of fruits and flowers, and therein are seen grapes, pomegranates, vines of all kinds, indeed, every fruit and flower known to the tropical world. These are carved with great delicacy, in relief, upon the solid stone.

There is variety of design everywhere. Few pillars are alike.

The sculptor gave a touch to one which he did not to another. The roof of the palace consists entirely of stone slabs, which project downwards, and extend far out beyond the walls. They thus form a screen from the sun. On looking up, on the under side of these projecting slabs which form the eaves of the palace, one finds that every inch is delicately carved. The figures are as finely cut, and in almost as good preservation, as the day when Akbar's artists took down their mallets and chisels from this finished gem.

HOUSE OF BABUL, IN FATHPUR SIKRI.
(From Verestchagin.)

On entering the palace the scene almost defies one's vision. Each wall is a study in itself. It is carved from floor to ceiling, while the ceiling itself is of solid stone slabs, and all their surface is covered by rich carvings in bold and beautiful relief. The whole palace, which really consists of but a single room, is a perfect gem of sculpture. But now it is only a desert place. Its most frequent visitor is the Christian missionary.

CHAPTER LXXX.

THE PALACES OF GWALIOR.

GWALIOR, as an illustration of the ancient Jain worship and architecture, is the most interesting city in existence. It lies at a distance from all the regular railway lines. The most convenient point for a visit is Agra, from which a slow and poorly managed branch road, of sixty miles in length, goes almost to the base of the great acropolis. On that lofty height the palaces and temples of Gwalior stand in all the eloquence of sculptured stone. To the student of Indian history this place has a world of meaning. Out of the level plain there rises abruptly this bold hill of about two miles long and an average width of a quarter of a mile. On one side the red sandstone cliffs are almost perpendicular. The surface of the great hill has been scarped in the long-gone ages, to make it the shapely pedestal for palace, temple, and troops. No large city ever shone here in the early sunlight. Only the royal, priestly, and military classes might live, in indescribable splendor, on this great height. The city of Gwalior lay below, just under the shadow of the beetling cliffs. There is still a city down there, while the masters live above, and look off on the charming landscape. But this time it is not the old Mogul masters. The English are here, and rule all. The smooth throats of their guns, which look over the long parapets of this wonderful acropolis, are of such iron eloquence that no disturbance ever occurs among the native thousands who sleep beneath them.

The mutiny of 1856 ran wild in Gwalior. It had a long and tenacious life. Perhaps it was the incomparable character of the fortress; or, possibly, the peculiarly hostile spirit of the native population, that accounts for the malignity of the opposition to English rule. But this much is certain, that long after Agra had surrendered, and even after the Delhi gate had been assaulted and battered to pieces, and the brave English troops rested not

THE PHUL-BAGH, GWALIOR.

until they reached the Mogul's palace, and feasted their eyes once more on the Peacock Throne, Gwalior still defied English arms, and even threatened to turn the tide in favor of the Sepoys. The little Presbyterian church in the plain below, about three miles from the base of the Gwalior height, contains tablets in memory of the butchered British soldiers. Then, at various points, there are three other cemeteries, all of which abound in little mounds, with memorial tablets, where the dust of slaughtered English soldiers rests. For the deliberate planning of the destruction of British rule, and for prompt and desperate measures to make the plan successful, no place in India surpassed Gwalior. It was a military centre for English troops, and yet so adroit was the scheme, and so well disguised was every rebellious measure, that the mutiny here was as sudden as a clap of thunder in a clear sky.

I left my luggage in the dak bungalow in Morar, and drove across the plain to the city of Gwalior.

The natives are a curious folk. Some of them are adherents of the old Jain faith, which is now declining, like all the other lesser false religions of India. It has many points of resemblance to Hinduism. It has its saints, looks forward to simple repose as the bliss of the future, and has such respect for animal life that it will not harm even the vilest reptile. Some of the Jain people, living in Rajputana, Gujerat, and Cutch, are among the most active and successful business men of India.*

Dirt prevails on every hand in the town below. The people, seeing I was a stranger, and from the West, were not very civil, and were little disposed to answer questions. I secured a guide, however, and began to climb the hill. No warder stands at the old gateway. The massive entrance is now as free as the very air. But one can see that the place had been carefully guarded in the old times. Whatever might be the force, it does not seem possible that these great gates could ever have been battered down. Yet the hour did come when even they yielded to British pressure. One gate, however, did not satisfy the sense of Mogul security. Should one be forced open, there must be still another beyond, with its bronzed keepers, to keep back the intrusive force. But should this yield, what then? Farther along

* Temple, "India in 1880," p. 119.

there was still another, and another, to the number of six in all—to guard the approach to the august king and fabulous treasure and awful temple.

I had never seen any parallel in India to this wonderful position. In addition to what nature had done, the lords of this great rock had shaved it and grooved it and perforated it to such an extent that it seemed to be a very part of the firm earth. It is India's Ehrenbreitstein. In the elder days the ascent was by steps, cut in stone, with horizontal resting-spaces between its flights. But in later times these steps have been removed, so that the ascent is now by an inclined plane. The constant climbing is no easy task, especially when one remembers that the sun shines all the year round on this great boulder, and so heats it that the reflected heat from the rock adds terribly to the direct rays of the sun.

I was amazed at one feature of this ascent. There are altars, and in one case a temple, hewn out of the solid stone. In the temple are altars and images carved with great care, and grown old and worn by the long roll and grinding of the wasting ages. The entrance to some of the altars is easy enough, only the deflection of a few steps from the main road being needed to reach their curious portals. But less easy is the way to others. I turned from the general road and followed little grooves in the side of the rocky hill, and crossed shaky and labyrinthine foot-bridges, and by and by reached the curious excavations where people worshipped in ages long since gone. Each one of these cave-altars has its sacred associations, its special deity to guard it, and its long and marvellous history. Flowers lie upon the pathway and on the sanctuary, which show how strong the hold of the past is on the pagan people of the present. The temple bears the name of the Shrine of the Four-Armed, having the date Samvat 933, which is equivalent to A.D. 876. There are colossal carvings along the side of the rock, some of single figures and others of groups, but all of hardly a later date than a thousand years ago. All are curious remnants of the Jain faith.

When the climb to the top of the hill is nearly finished, the broad road by which one has come brings him directly up to the portal of an immense palace. You enter the curiously carved vestibule, and find yourself within the precincts of what must have been one of the most magnificent palaces of ancient India. This,

FAÇADE OF THE PALACE OF PAL, GWALIOR.

however, is only one of six palaces. Their majestic and richly ornamented walls once adorned a good part of the whole plain of the acropolis. This lofty hill, with its foundations of firm rock, was too commanding and secure for one palace. Successive dynasties saw in it the best place in all their realm for a residence, and here they lived and reared their families, and down this worn way they marched to foreign wars.

The palaces are now in all stages of decrepitude and ruin. Here is the Mán Palace, which hangs on the verge of the precipice. It is also called the Chit Mandir, or Painted Palace, for all along its façade there once ran rich tiles, which the artists of the Mogul era knew how to make to perfection. This is a palace of grandeur and horrors. It is two stories below ground and two above. I was as curious to see the subterranean chambers as the upper. My guide was well acquainted with the place, and I was satisfied that he was giving me the full benefit of his knowledge. After completing the circuit of the first story below ground, I descended a gloomy, spiral stairway to the floor below. Every chamber had been cut out of the solid rock. All the foundations being of native stone, no hall or chamber could be made except by the pick. As to explosives, so far back was the time when these excavations were made that such a method of loosening native rock was not thought of. Indeed, gunpowder had, probably, not been invented at the time. In one of these lower chambers there is a central pillar of the native stone left by the diggers, which is exquisitely carved, and from its capital beautiful archways shoot out to all the angles of the room. It has the appearance of a Gothic chapel, and yet its builders probably knew no more of the Gothic arch and its luxuriant floral wreath than of the Coliseum. This was probably a special dungeon for peculiarly dangerous state prisoners. It is now the home of bats and vermin. No groan from these deep places could ever reach an ear above the ground. I was glad to get out of the awful place into India's dazzling sunlight.

Now this one palace must have been a thing of marvellous beauty in its day. Its outer walls are so nearly complete that one can see precisely what they once were. Along the edge of the precipice the front wall runs three hundred feet, while the breadth of the palace is one hundred and sixty feet. But this is no bare wall. It was of wild and varied beauty. From its windows the view upon the plain below was exceedingly bewitching. Little balconies of stone, finely carved and cut through into figures of delicate proportion, hung from the walls like jaunty tufts of richest lace. Here the members of the royal families, century after century, used to sit and catch the evening breath which always swept over this charming hill. The palace-wall has five round towers, with open domes for cupolas, and a battlement of open stone lattice-work running the whole length, and binding the towers into perfect union by the marble fringe. The rooms of this palace are as beautiful and rich as the outer adornments, and are arranged about two courts.

It was a habit of the Gwalior kings, whenever they built another palace, either in honor of a new wife or a new victory, or as a pleasant investment of money taken from a decapitated prince or two, to connect the new palace with the old by long galleries. The space on the Gwalior acropolis was none too large, and galleries supplied in a measure the dearth of roadways. There were many hundreds of people connected with each court, and we have only the palaces, the mere shells, to suggest the splendor in which they revelled.

The Palace of Vikram lies between two other palaces, the Karan and the Mán, and is connected with them by a narrow gallery of twelve hundred and ten feet in length. Over the great hall there rises a dome, whose support is furnished by eight springing ribs, four rising from pillars, and four from the angles of the building. The Shah Jahân palace also overhangs the cliff. Its proportions were vast enough to satisfy even a Mogul emperor, for it was over three hundred feet long, and nearly two hundred feet wide.

These palaces represent all the stages in the glory and decline of wonderful Gwalior. When the city at the base of the scarred and ornamental cliff arose, no historian can tell. But in the days when the palaces were in all their fresh and early beauty, the scene must have been bewildering. Here sat, in the cool stone jalousies, little groups of gay members of the court. Old warriors sauntered along the galleries, and told of battles won and of the capture of crowns whose gold frames were invisible beneath the banks of diamonds. All was quiet. The emperor must not be disturbed. But when he had slept out and made his appearance, there was a hush and awe which pervaded every place in all these splendid dwellings. The more distant drill-ground was every day the scene of magnificent display, and here the emperor would come out and take a hasty glance. This was his bit of machinery, by which he gained his gold and conquered provinces and chopped off royal heads. The morning sun blazed on these palaces, and the glare of the richly glazed tiles, whose figures revealed patterns long before grown old in Persia, was dazzling to every eye. The muezzin called to worship from the lofty minaret near by, and for a time all was silent in court, on parade ground, and in the palace halls. Nothing disturbed the stillness of the hour but the constant splashing of the marble fountains. The air was filled with the perfume of rare flowers, which grew in plenty on open swards and hung in frames from many a courtier's window.

This went on for long centuries, even before the Mohammedan broke in upon the royal silence here. Hindu kings had revelled in splendor on the acropolis of Gwalior. The place had grown from a wild waste, the lair of the tiger, the lion, and the boa, into a scene of splendor which vied even with the Fort and Taj of Agra, and the palaces of Delhi and Lahor.

Three Asiatic authorities try to account for the origin of this weird place. The bard Kharg Rai, living in Shah Jahân's reign, says that the city at the base of the hill was founded thirty centuries before the Christian era. But the more likely time is that of Fazl Ali, adopted by Hiraman, Tieffenthaler, Wilford, and Cunningham, who place the date at B.C. 275. The story of the foundation is that Suraj Sen, a Kachhwaha chief, who was a leper, and was out hunting, came upon this hill, and was very thirsty. A hermit, Gwalipa, gave him some water, which cured his leprosy. In return, the mighty hunter built here a fort and began his reign. The hermit gave him a new name, Suhan Pal, and told him that his dynasty should be on the throne as long as his descendants should be called Pal. This was the beginning of a line of eighty-three kings. But the eighty-fourth called himself Tej Kara, and so lost the kingdom. There are historical data of three dynasties—the Kachhwaha, the Parihara, and the Tomar. These were the Hindu rulers, but when the Mohammedan came and swept everything before him, Gwalior became a part of his possessions. It surrendered to the sultan Mahmud,

A.D. 1023.* He converted the palaces into state prisons. But in time the old splendor revived, and Mogul palaces repeated in even greater magnificence the imperial homes of the Hindus in the zenith of their glory. The Marhattas afterwards captured Gwalior, and defied all invaders.

---

* Meadows Taylor, "Student's History of India," p. 83.

A PILGRIM CARRYING RELIGIOUS RELICS.

CHAPTER LXXXI.

THE TEMPLES OF GWALIOR.

THE wonderful temples on the Gwalior acropolis fully equal the palaces as memorials of a distant past. Worship comes before thrones. The temples of Gwalior point to a much earlier date than the oldest palaces. The latter are grouped within a comparatively narrow space, and when one has passed beyond them, still following the main road which runs along the crest of the acropolis, he comes within the reach of the old, old temples. Everything reminds one of the gods. Here are eleven temples, which, like the palaces, are in all stages of decay.

The Teli Mandir is a fair illustration of the way in which the English keep up these priceless ruins. This temple is in the centre of the plateau, and is surrounded by a charming garden. I have nowhere seen a more beautiful suggestion of the Clugny Museum. Here, about the central structure, one does not find the venerable trees and the broken and picturesque surface which he sees in that calm and beautiful place in the heart of the Latin Quarter of Paris. But he has, in the Indian counterpart, great compensations. There are walks running out in various directions from the Teli Mandir, forming a piece of rich tracery, on which the eyes can feast for many an hour. The very vases at the angles, out of which grow plants of rare fragrance and beauty, are themselves fragments of temple urns, or the richly carved capitals of palace or fane, hollowed out to receive the burden of luxuriant flowers. Here is a Hindu goddess, converted into a standard for a rose to climb on. Then, all along the walks and out on the green sward, there are fragments of stone from the elder days, containing perfect inscriptions. Some of these tell-tale words recall times a thousand years ago, when the now ruling Englishmen was just emerging out of Saxon savagery. There are neat plates attached to every antique object, giving its name, origin, and the finder. Nearly everything lying about this temple, in this picturesque way, has been gathered hereabouts, either on the plateau or around the base of the hill on which palace and temple once stood in all their wild splendor. It is worth a sail to India to see this picture of fragments from ruins so arranged as to dazzle or enchant by their strange combinations.

But the greatest of all the points of superiority of this Indian Clugny above the French lies in the central edifice, the temple itself. It was never of vast dimensions. The taste of the age in which it was reared—say A.D. 800—was not towards great spaces, but massive walls, minute sculpture, and prominent height. The Teli Mandir is only sixty feet square, with a rich projecting portico of eleven feet. But the walls, which incline inward as they ascend, rise to a height of eighty feet, and then meet at a ridge of thirty feet in length. The thickness of the walls, the sweep of the great arches, and the exact and endless sculpture, are simply overwhelming. You stand on the threshold and look out upon the surrounding garden, with its wealth of perfume and beauty, and ancient Hindu statuary of gods and men. Chains, hanging in graceful festoons from posts made of ancient pillars, guard all.

The grounds, with their profusion of ruins and flowers, are a fit frame for such a picture as you are now to see. The doorway is thirty-five feet high, and the grave, calm god Garuda looks down in stone from the centre. The object of this temple, once dedicated to the worship of Vishnu, but since the fifteenth century sacred to Siva, seems to have been the embodiment of mirth. There, in relief upon the walls, are dancing and singing gods. The swaying palms in stone, the cheerful scroll-work, the thousand tricks of the long-dead sculptor, were all designed to add to the glory of this remarkable structure. No wood is to be seen now, and probably there never was a piece permitted to form a part of the permanent belongings of the temple. Only stone was worthy of the god. It must be such stone, too, as had a face hard enough to bear the images from nature, and the ruling creed which it was supposed would last as long as India itself.

Of all the temples, however, I was most impressed by the Sasbahu and Sahasra-bahu, or the mother-in-law and daughter-in-law. They stand together near the edge of the cliff. They are

COLOSSI OF THE OWRWHAÏ, GROUP OF ADINATH, GWALIOR.

sometimes called the "Temples of a Thousand Arms." One is larger than the other, and an inscription inside one of the porticoes places the date at A.D. 1093. But who knows the date? This temple is probably a new one, on the site of an older, built when Time was young. The larger temple is one hundred feet long and sixty-three feet broad. The top is now gone. The present height is only seventy feet, but when in a perfect state it must have been one hundred. One gets lost in wonder as he stands in front of this strange building. The temples of South India appalled me by their great spaces, their glittering pagodas, their wandering elephants, their crowd of worshippers, and the wealth of the shrines. But there was no grandeur in the architecture. The Gwalior temples are of a different order. The Mohammedan conquerors may have done some mutilation; but they have been forbearing, after all. One can still see, from the majestic ruin, what the temple was in the days of its grandeur. There is no petty architecture, no poor material, no common device.

On either side of the grand portal there are inscriptions dating from the primitive Hindu period. Even the doorsteps have been cut into rich tracery, a fit entrance into the central hall of the sacred building. On either side of the steps leading up to the great platform on which the temple stands there are nineteen figures, all in stone, as *portæ* to the fane. The temple is in two stories. The main lower hall has four immense pillars, on which the upper story and the pyramid which constitutes the roof are supported. Now, when we remember that here, as in the Teli Mandir, there is not a particle of wood, that even the beams and girders and floors are of hewn stone, the size of these four central figures must be enormous. Yet the sculptor and the architect must combine their wisdom to soften down the massiveness. There must be no clumsy effect. Hence these pillars, which are rectangular—for there are no curves here—are divided into perpendicular lines of carvings. On each one of these are twenty rows of these rich figures, running all the way from floor to capital. I counted, on the four sides of one pillar alone, sixty independent figures. Around the walls are bands of stone figures, the whole forming a luxuriance of carving such as one could hardly find a parallel to, even in India.

One wonders if, somewhere in this majestic temple, there is

not, by way of variety to the splendor, some calm and vacant space on pillar or wall. But no. There must be nothing lost. Each fragment of stone must tell its tale of faith and art. The spaces above are fairly alive with stone figures and rich carving. The ceiling of the lower story is concave, and is the interior of a vast dome. Now this dome is formed by belts of solid stone, the higher and narrower overlapping the lower and larger ones, until the highest point is reached. Each of these belts—and I counted twenty of them—is elaborately carved with figures, and done in the early period, when the Hindu imagination was wildest and most wayward, and the artist's hand ran out without restraint into the most ornate fields. Here, in the heart of the temple, is the *adytum*, and on the carved doorway which admits to it I counted no less than ninety-four figures. In number of designs, in minuteness of carving, and in delicacy of finish, they are a fitting culmination to this whole paradise of rare work in stone.

The mouldings, on every side, combine both beauty and strength. They are rich and bold, and at the same time as delicate as a piece of Genoese silver filigree. All ideas of clumsiness, which came to my mind when I saw these temples first in the distance, had now disappeared. What with the surfaces being filled with figures, and the massive pillars containing many, so cut as to have a heightening effect, the result must have produced in every one who lingered in this abode of Hindu art the impression that he was in the midst of as graceful and symmetrical a structure as human feet could walk over.

We now come to the third striking feature of this wonderful place. There are two main roads which lead to the top of the acropolis. Suppose there was a road ascending from the city side of Athens directly to the top of the acropolis, about midway its length. The ascent would be difficult, and so the road would have to be grooved along the native wall. This road, with the one already on the opposite, or country side, and running up where the Odeon is, would form a complete picture of the two roads which ascend to the plateau of the acropolis of Gwalior. Supposing we were to ascend the Athenian acropolis on the city side, and all along the road, cut deeply in the walls, were cave temples, where men worshipped when Hesiod had not yet touched his harp. This is a picture of the temple and altars along the road up which I had come to the top of the Gwalior acropolis. But what of the road on the other side? Now came another revelation—colossal figures, cut out of the solid, native rock, and left here. Some were mutilated by the Mogul emperor Babar, in the year 1527. But, for the most part, these figures still remain in their original completeness. I descended this road a long distance, and at every group of the immense figures I saw something new and entirely different from the rest.

These sculptures, cut out of the native rock, have no parallel even in India, either in number, finish, or size. There are five groups of figures. There are niches cut out of the perpendicular face of the rock, directly below the sharp edge of the plateau, and the figures are left in the middle of the niches. The native stone was cut away, and thus the figure came to its shape. I could easily get down from the road, and climb up to the feet of the figure, and go behind it. In some cases there was a natural stone bridge left in front of the figure, about even with the chest. This, no doubt, furnished a convenient scaffolding for the sculptor, and now it is the visitor's only pathway, by which he can get within touch of the upper parts of the great figure, and, by comparison, appreciate the enormous size of all these carvings.

There are twenty-one different recesses or cavities, in all of which the colossal figures still stand, either singly or in groups. I judge that there can hardly be less than seventy-five figures, of various sizes and symbolism. They range all the way from seven feet to thirty-seven in height. The largest figures are in a sitting position. The inscriptions and accompanying emblems fix exactly not only the date of their origin, but their significance. They were all made in the latter half of the fifteenth century, and are representations of the great pontiffs of the Jain faith. With the figure of each pontiff there is a shell, a lotus, a bull, a wheel, a horse, a goat, an antelope, a lion, a crescent, or some similar object, which was the sacred sign of the pontiff. These symbols are cut with the figures, so that one can tell whom the figures represent—whether Adinath, Nemnath, Supadma, Chandra Prabha, Mahavira, Kantanath, or some other one of the Jain immortals. The whole face of this side of the great acropolis is indented with these spaces, which were laboriously executed as fit niches where the leaders of the Jain faith might be kept in perpetual memory. The execution was rude and ponderous, but one must remember that for three centuries the storm of Mohammedan hate and the shocks of war have been beating about them. The wonder is, that even a single feature is left on one of these stone faces, and that the little bridges, whereon the sculptor stood, have not been knocked to pieces, to make complete the destruction of all memorials of the conquered race.

Here, on this historical spot, where the English have dislodged the Mohammedan, just as the Mohammedan had dislodged the Hindu, and as the Hindu had dislodged the Aryan races, the latest of all this long line of conquerors are the only protectors of the great surviving memorials of all the former races. Every race but the Anglo-Saxon has been destructive. One has only to see the Aztec destruction by the Spaniards in Mexico, and the Portuguese in India, on the one hand, and the preservation by the English of the Hindu remains in India, to mark the difference between the Saxon and the Latin. Had Clive never fought at Plassey, and Hastings never planned in Calcutta or Benares, there would be much less treasure for the antiquarian to-day. Throughout India the English government has paid great attention to the care of the architectural treasures of all the provinces. Excavations have been made, old walls have been followed, tumbling ruins have been supplied with braces and supports, and an air of brightness and comfort has been imparted to every part of the great structures. Conquered India owes to England the preservation of her own best ruins. Often the English officers have had antiquarian tastes, and have not only carried out the orders of the government, but have given their work all the wisdom and inspiration which come from sympathy with the purpose.

This has been manifestly the case with the Gwalior temples. It has been no slavish obedience to orders which has cleansed the buildings, and keeps them neat, and has surrounded them with gardens as rich as a piece of Teheran tapestry, but a cheerful seeking of the best ways to keep the treasures of the past, and let them have all the benefit of the sunlight of to-day.

I lingered long beside the parapet of the wall which surrounds the acropolis of Gwalior. After wandering up one ascending road and down the other, and among the labyrinths, and out along the galleries of the palaces, and then loitering in the grand temples, I was glad to drop down in a little niche in the wall, and look off upon the enchanting valley with its lengthening evening shadows. It was near sunset, and the valley and the distant hills were all ablaze with the evening glow. When there is no rising haze from the valley, one can see the immense temple of Sahamiya, thirty miles in the distance. Far away, too, were the red hills of Dholpur, while near by, just at my feet, lay the busy Gwalior of to-day. The air was deliciously cool, and made one quite forget the heat and weariness of the day. My driver had been unwilling to come up through the old gateways and make the climb to the plateau, and was waiting at the foot of the hill. I had now to walk the entire length of the acropolis, and descend to the first gate, where I had left him. But the sun by this time was powerless, and the walking was no inconvenience. I dropped awhile into each convenient seat along the wall, and enjoyed the evening scene upon the valley below. Each little curve in the wall brought its changes, while the varying glows of the sunset gave a wonderful coloring to the landscape. I found, at last, my patien, driver. His horses, having had a long rest, now scampered swiftly down the historic hill, and over the streets of the modern town, and then out upon the country road. I reached Morar in due time, and found that in my absence other guests had arrived at the little dak bungalow. But my room, having been secured already, was at my service. I learned that a strong effort had been made to spirit it out of my possession, but the presence of a little baggage in it had probably availed as proof visible of its occupation by an earlier visitor.

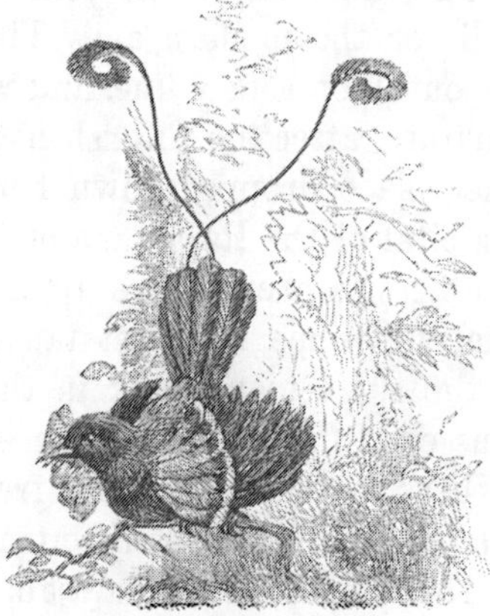

KING BIRD OF-PARADISE.

CHAPTER LXXXII.

JAIPUR—A RAJPUT CAPITAL.

On my way from the Northwest down to Bombay I had the opportunity of seeing traces of the old Rajputana civilization. The Rajput people resisted the Moguls with terrible earnestness, but in time were compelled to surrender.

Jaipur, the modern Rajput capital, could only be enjoyed by giving it a full day. I was lodged in the dak bungalow, about a mile from the station, and had excellent accommodations. My first object was a drive into the city, and then a general survey of its exterior. For a regularity and breadth of streets, and for a modern and Occidental business air, I had seen nothing in India similar to this place. It seems to have taken its type from Europe, and yet one does not require long to see that, though the city is thrifty, and laid out after European models, the people who did it are thorough Orientals. The life is Hindu, though the home is Western.

The books tell us that Jaipur was founded by the celebrated Maharajah Siwai Jai Singh II., in the year 1728. The modern date accounts well for the modern air. The truth is, the old Rajput life struck out upon a new line, and what was left of its wild and vicious nature, after the English had well overcome it, came from another place, dropped down here, built up Jaipur, and made it the capital of the Rajputana of these latest days.

The Rajput wildness is everywhere apparent. Here, in the gardens of the native prince, is a vast tank, where lazy crocodiles glide up to the surface and bask in the sun. The caged tigers are ferocious even for India. One great beast seemed so anxious to get a thrust at me that, in his frenzy, he caught the bars of his cage in his awful jaws, as if to tear them to pieces.

The palace of the prince, or Maharajah, is unusually lofty, the structure evidently being modelled after English ideas. But the carrying out betrays the Indian workman. Rich halls, beau-

A WEDDING PROCESSION.

tiful balconies, and such rugs as only Hindu fingers can weave abound everywhere. The audience-hall exceeds all other apartments in palatial splendor. It is broad, and constructed throughout of white marble. The same native taste is visible here as everywhere in India—love of beasts and all forms of animal life. But flowers are equally prominent. The Maharajah of Jaipur, like native princes everywhere in India, has a garden of such rare beauty as to bewilder any eye. It is half a mile long, and is adorned with fountains, graceful palms of almost every kind, and a wealth of plants at once rare, beautiful, and of finest perfumes.

I took special pleasure in visiting a collection of industrial objects, illustrative of the special wares of Jaipur and other parts of Rajputana.

But I was all the while intent on the ancient Amber—the renowned capital of this clan of the Rajput people. For this journey of five miles up a defile in the mountains the Rev. Dr. Humphrey had engaged two elephants early in the morning, and by noon we were informed that they were ready. We could go in carriages to Chandrabagh. Once there, we found our elephants in waiting for us. The howdah, adjusted to the back of my monster, was too loose for very comfortable locomotion. But I was informed that it could not turn over, and with that important communication I had to be satisfied.

The elephant is a docile walker. Your driver, while the beast lies flattened out and his riders are climbing up his sides, has perfect control of him. When the people are seated, and the driver would mount to his place above the neck, he simply puts his foot on the ear of the elephant, and with the next bound is in his position. Then the great piece of jelly begins to sway back and forth, and nothing but a firm grasp saves you from being thrown violently forward or backward, according to whether the monster is rising on his fore or hind legs. Then begins your regular motion. You hold on still, for you are not sure of your place. But after the waddling of, say, half a mile, and you get accustomed to the motion of your animal, and become interested in the strange sights which meet you in the world beneath, at every lunge of the elephant you get bolder, let go your grasp, and are ready to eat your lunch, or throw down pice to the moving crowd of native children, or read your guide-books. By the time I reached the palace gate I found myself holding on to nothing, and riding with as little concern as if the animal were only a Cairene donkey.

The road is lined with Hindu chapels, temples, and lowly dwellings. Everywhere there is a rich interlacing of shrubbery and trees. Two ancient forts, now in ruins, stand out to the left. They were probably the outer defences of the palace. But this is a mountain passage, and not wide. Hence resistance was easy enough. The Manta tank, with its lazy alligators, is on the left-hand side of the road. By and by we reached the old city of Amber. We were out of modern times, and suddenly thrust into the remote Rajputana past. Many a time the storms of war have swept this place and the mountain-sides. The stately palace crowns the top of the mountain. It consists of a group of buildings—all palaces. The city below might easily be taken, but so strong were the outer walls and great gates of this wonderful group of royal houses that the capture of them was a most difficult task. These buildings have run their race, and, now that the English influence is felt in Rajputana, the native princes have ceased their fighting, and the ruler of Jaipur lives in quiet down in the new city.

The old Amber palace owes its historical interest to the feuds and bloodshed of the eight centuries that lie beneath the leaning walls and waste of bygone architecture which rest on the lofty hill.

The Rajputs are a peculiar people. If we except the savage hill-tribes, they are the nearest existing approach to the Aryan conquerors of the original tribes in the far-back ages. Seven centuries ago, when the Mohammedans of Persia pressed down upon India, and were, at last, successful in uprooting the old Hindu life, they found the Rajputs in possession of the whole of Northwestern India. The word Rajputana is not the name by which the natives call this broad territory. Their name is Rajasthan, or the Country of the Chiefs. These people ruled over a country stretching from the valley of the Indus eastward along the Ganges, and southward far down towards Central India, and westward well in sight of the Indian Ocean. But they were not one people in rule. It was a confederacy of clans, similar to the Germans in the time of Cæsar, and the Scots in the time of Bruce. The process was simple. The chief of a sept, or clan, reached his throne by killing others weaker than

DETAILS OF ORNAMENTATION OF TEMPLE OF KHANDARIA,
KHWAJRAO, SOUTH OF PANNA, IN BUNDELKHAND.

himself. He was on guard all the time, lest a heavier axe might fell him. In time he acquired a reverence strong enough to have his son succeed him, provided there was gold enough to bribe every fighter into his interest.

But what should be done if there should be three or four sons? Only one could rule. Yet the rest must have a place. One would go in one direction, and another elsewhere, and begin the killing process. By and by there would be success, but often failure. In time, the great territory was overspread with these septs, where blood-letting was the order of the day. There was time to build splendid palaces and populous cities. But it was the interest of all to keep the septs rather small. Each knew that if one became too strong and large it would lead to the absorption of the rest. All the great cities of the Gangetic valley, and those far to the northwest, almost to the Afghan line of our day, were built up by the Rajputs, and occupied by one clan or another, as their capitals and commercial centres. But when the Mohammedans came with hot blood and furious speed, they swept the clans, one after another, before them, and drove them down to the centre of India, where they came to a halt, and made a second line of defence, because of the granite fastnesses which they seized upon and where they built new capitals. Lyall says: "The first Mussulman invasions found Rajput dynasties ruling in all the chief cities of the North, and over the rich Gangetic plains eastward to the confines of modern Bengal—at Lahor, Delhi, Kanauj, and Ayodha. Out of these great cities and fertile lands the Rajput chiefs were driven forth southward and westward into the central regions of India, where a more difficult country gave them a second line of defence against the foreigners. And this line they have held not unsuccessfully up to the present." *

But we have reached the bruised and battered gates of the Amber palace.

We are now walking over the stones where kings and courtiers and soldiers had walked for many a century. The chief palace was the home of the Minas clan. But this clan was in deadly feud with the Kachhwaha clan. Fortune turned in favor of the latter, and they drove out the Minas, and took their country

* "Asiatic Studies," pp. 182, 183.

and the palace. This was in the year 1037, and for nearly seven centuries, or until 1728, the Kachhwaha Rajputs feasted here, and swept down the gorge and out into the plain, in bright steel armor, and brought back rich spoils from many a battle-field. But when at last the greatest of all the conquerors came, the Englishman, the Kachhwaha Rajput saw that his day of resistance was over. He now played the diplomat, and said, "Here is an enemy it is of no use to resist. We will be his friend."

This logic was easy, cost no blood, and saved the Rajput throne. These Rajput princes are still in power—or the semblance of it—to the number of eighteen. There were twenty in all, but the English absorbed Ajmir and Marwar. The remaining eighteen are separate and independent states, but under English protection, and with a watchful English Resident near by, in every case.*

A RAJPUT HINDU, FROM MARWAR.

The Maharajah still comes up to the old palace on special occasions. In the great court across which we walked he sits in state at the Dashara feast. A regiment of soldiers stand around the court, and one hundred buffaloes and five hundred goats are slaughtered on the spot, as a sacrifice to Shila Devi. A flight of steps leads up to a public audience-hall, where there is a broad marble platform, whereon the august and scarred kings sat in ancient times. There are pillars at each end of the platform, and beyond them small rooms, with lattices, behind which the ladies might sit and watch the court pageants. The roof is supported by two squares of pillars, numbering thirty in all. Some of the pillars are of the red stone from the mountains near by, but the rest are of white marble.

We passed from one splendid hall to another, then up winding stairways into other chambers, all decorated richly, in the

* Pope, "Text-Book of Indian History," p. 28.

highest art known to the times. The Rajput, like all the Hindus, despised uniformity. Even his stairways must not be like each other. Little balconies must part company somewhere, if only in the unlikeness of a frail panel of filagree in marble. The usual Oriental fondness for minute mirrors is seen, when little disks, no larger than a four-anna piece, are grouped into arches and backgrounds, and throw reflections in myriads on every eye.

The Rajput had an eye to the picturesque. He was careful to have his windows so adjusted that the finest prospect could be enjoyed. From some of the balconies and windows in these palaces the prospect is wondrously beautiful. One can look down the gorge through which we had come, and see Jaipur spread out at its foot, and then the great plain sweeping far off into the distance, until it meets the horizon. All was peaceful enough now, but there had been times when anxious eyes looked out from these same windows for swift messengers, to bring news from the far-off battle-fields.

The view of the mountain-peaks, in another direction, brought out what I could not hope to see from the back of my elephant—gray old towers here and there, on the hill-tops, which date from the feudal times of Rajputana. Each has its own story, but the most of them are lost to the memory of man.

By descending the stairway, and crossing the court, we came to the white marble walls of the Jai Mandir. The panels are profusely ornamented, some with mosaics and others with flowers in relief. The opposite palace is the Sukh Nawas, or Hall of Pleasure. Here is some of the trickery which was common in the elder days to take away the monotony of palace life. In a small and dark room, away from the more splendid halls, there is a painting of a goose and a space, made to represent a fire-place. It is not a fire-place, however, but only a channel for an artificial stream of water, which was made to flow at proper times. The doors are of sandal-wood, with inlaid figures in ivory. "The whole is a charming retreat in sultry weather," says Eastwick. "The stream runs into an octagonal basin with fountains in the middle of the garden. The walls of this room and of the two vestibules are adorned with reliefs representing vases and urns for sprinkling rose-water, of various colors."*

* "Handbook of Punjab," p. 150.

I went from one building to another, and everywhere there were memorials of former grandeur. The very baths, of finest marble, were still entire and of great splendor. Here, as the centuries went by, these palaces had echoed with the wail of woe and the shout of joy. All phases of human life had been enacted here. But now the halls are deserted, except by the curious visitor from across the sea, or the rarer visit of a Rajput prince. The luxuriant creepers climb about the walls, and thrust their fingers into every crevice, and far up to the gay balconies. Nature, the young and the enduring, dallies with the marble creations of man the pilgrim.

We descended the last stone stairway, and found our elephants in waiting. Soon they dropped on their knees, and we climbed to our places on their backs, and were borne down the hill towards our carriages.

We were compelled to hurry, for our dinner was waiting for us at the dak bungalow. Even that had to be a hasty meal, for we must catch the evening train southward. We had no sooner reached our inn than we were beset by a crowd of vendors of garnets and other stones, both polished and in the rough. The mountains about Jaipur are very rich in such precious minerals. The articles consisted of cat's-eyes and other attractive stones, some of them solitaires and others arranged in strings, and as pins and rings. I saw two beautiful necklaces of light-colored garnets, which attracted my attention. They would just suit two little necks I knew of in Rome. The vendors saw that I was fascinated, threw their glittering wares into the carriage, now in rapid motion, and ran up for their money. Of course, I had to buy.

CHAPTER LXXXIII.

A DAY IN AJMIR.

THE Hindu city of Ajmir abounds in most interesting historical associations. Like Jaipur, it was once the capital of a Rajput clan, but has now lost its independence. No native Maharajah holds the semblance of a court. The origin of Ajmir belongs to the gray past. If one wishes to see a city which was already ancient when Mohammed was born, and where the Aryans had built and lived long before the Hindus had taken on their modern organization, let him come to Ajmir and drive through one of the five gateways which pierce the stone wall, and meander through its narrow streets, and see the quaint homes of the packed thousands.

The city lies in a plain. On a hill, rising abruptly from the plain, stands the celebrated fort Taragarh. This hill dominates the far outlying region. The temptation to build a fort on it was too strong to be resisted, and so firmly were its walls planted, and so steadily did all the defences grow with the centuries, that the history of this single fort is almost an epitome of the complete story of the great confederation of Rajputana states. Whenever the invaders of India gained a new foothold, their ambition centred in this castellated height. Those who could capture and retain it might well expect to control the whole of Central India. When the Afghans, under their king, Shahab-ud-din, entered India, at the end of the twelfth century, they marched straight on towards Ajmir and captured the great fort. But it was recovered after a short time by the Rajputs. The Moguls captured it again, and held it firmly; and in the seventeenth century it took its place with Agra, Delhi, and Lahor, as an imperial residence. But the Rajputs, although conquered, were not obliterated, and in the great collapse of the Mogul empire they took back their hill and its fort, which from time immemorial had been identified with the fortunes of their fathers. But the Marhattas, the fierce people who were preying on the Mogul empire, could not bear to see this stony fortress in Rajput hands. Hence they made a bold strike for it, and won it. But the fortress, with the city of Ajmir, was ceded to the English by the conquered Marhatta chief Sindhia, on June 25, 1818. Now, from the lofty crest of the great fort the English flag floats.

When Ajmir became an imperial residence of the Moguls, its power, already great, extended still more widely. The Rajputs are celebrated as the fiercest warriors of all India. Their deeds of heroism have gone into all Hindu literature and have floated into all the channels of Indian thought. For victory over terrible odds, and for ready death when the impossible could not be won, their fame is not surpassed by the prowess of Hermann of Germany or Harald the Fair-haired of Norway. Ajmir, when it fell at last into Mogul hands, received the special favor of the new chiefs. They seemed to regard it as their strongest point for defence on the southern side. The English caught knowledge of it, and to this far-off place James I. sent Sir Thomas Roe as embassador to the Mogul emperor, and to his account we are indebted for the many beautiful glimpses of the undisturbed Indian life of two centuries and a half ago.

The Rajputs were no sooner conquered, and Ajmir captured, than the work of transformation began. The Mohammedan now busied himself to brush aside the Hindu life and especially the faith, and to establish here, on his southward march, all the splendor of mosque and service which he had left behind him in Persia first, and then in Lahor, Delhi, and Agra. All that was needed in Ajmir was a good pretext for a magnificent mosque. This was furnished in the life and death of Khwaja Mayud-uddin Sanjar Chisti. He was of saintly character, and died in a little chapel in the year 1235. Here on this spot must the great Ajmir mosque be reared. Temples there were already in great number, such as were built in the early days, when forced labor was the usage and the crime. But they were Hindu buildings, and could well be subsidized to add splendor and beauty to the mosque. The legend is, however, that the mosque was built miraculously, in two days and a half. Hence its name, Arhai din Ká Jhomprá, or "Hut of Two Days and a Half." When a modern miracle is concerned, the question of materials is not im-

THE PALACE OF THE SETHS, AJMIR.

portant. The main hall of the mosque contains three hundred and forty-four pillars; and as they are nearly all of Hindu architecture, and have been introduced here from use else-

BULLOCK FEEDING IN THE STREET.

where, it is safe to accept Fergusson's opinion, that these pillars represent the spoils of not less than twenty or thirty Hindu temples.

In entering a mosque I have nowhere been met with so bitter and offensive a spirit as here. So repellent was the manner of my guide, and so threatening withal, that I not only feared that I would not be permitted to see the interior of the celebrated building, but that I might be treated with violence. Perhaps there were no officers near by, to watch the native insolence. Whatever the cause, it gave me a fair opportunity to see what sort of a spirit the Mohammedan can manifest towards an Anglo-Saxon when he has the power. These precincts are peculiarly sacred, and I suppose that the memories of former Mogul splendor here are not forgotten by the half-robed worshippers in the Hut of Two Days and a Half.

After putting on flannel slippers I ascended a flight of steps, and then passed through the "Heat Expanding," a lofty gateway of about one hundred feet high. This admits to a court, where, on the saint's anniversary day, the multitude are feasted. There are two great caldrons, which keep their place the year round. One of these holds 6400 lbs. of rice and 2400 lbs. of oil. To this are added raisins enough to give a flavor to the whole. The other caldron is filled with 3200 lbs. of rice, 1600 lbs. of sugar, and 480 lbs. of butter, with a proper proportion of raisins and lemons. On the day when the public feast is given, the entire court is filled with a multitude of people. The caldrons, however, furnish a supply for all.

The mosque is of less interest than the rich screen. This singular object is not only the glory of the court, but a gem of great renown throughout the Mohammedan world. It consists of seven arches, the central one rising to a height of nearly sixty feet, and lateral ones of less dimensions. They form, together, a picture of wondrous beauty. The screen is of stone. There is a combination of Kufic and Tughra inscriptions, with architectural decorations, in such delicate and skilful ways that the scene is bewildering. The architect, who is supposed to be Altamsh, the builder of the great mosque in Delhi, has thrown such light and beauty into this picture in stone that it is a marvel of Moslem grandeur and Hindu wealth of ornamentation. Fergusson says: "As examples of surface decorations the two mosques of Altamsh, at Delhi and Ajmir, are probably unrivalled. Nothing in Cairo or in Persia is so exquisite in detail, and nothing in Spain or Syria can approach them for beauty of surface decoration. Besides this they are unique. Nowhere else could it be possible to find Mohammedan largeness of conception combined with Hindu delicacy of ornamentation, carried out to the same extent and in the same manner." *

I entered the great mosque by the majestic central arch. Here a most inspiring scene is presented to the eye. Pillars of the finest workmanship, and of all the Hindu orders, stand up to the right and left, and in front, and support a ceiling of recessed compartments, which add vastly to the grand effect. Cloisters stand back to the sides of the mosque. The ornamentation is of the finest kind known to the most glowing days of Hindu art. The work is as delicate as a cameo. No slip of the hammer or chisel can be found. It is all so deftly wrought by unerring hands, and with such overwhelming power, that one cannot help thanking the triumphant Moguls for preserving, though for a mosque, the forest of rich pillars which had been doing service in Hindu temples, probably, for a couple of centuries before the conquerors feasted on their beauty, and their strong will brought the beautiful sculptures into the new service. The variety of the designs in the figures on the pillars, but more especially in the recessed ceiling, is amazing. Nothing was allowed to be repeated. It must all be beautiful, but it must be a beauty from which diversity dared not be absent. The spaces are enormous. The entire exterior dimensions are two hundred and fifty-nine feet by fifty-seven, while every art is employed to make the worshipper feel that he is in a much larger building than this. To ornament these great spaces, and give a rich decoration to the many pillars, was a triumph of the patience of genius for which even India, which surprises at every step, has few parallels.

A loitering along the shore of the Pushka Lake, famous alike in Brahman, Rajput, and Mogul annals, and an evening service, with an interesting congregation, completed my day at Ajmir. The Rev. Mr. Hard, who was my companion during my stay in Ajmir, accompanied me to the railway station. The train arrived at a late hour in the night, and I was glad to find an empty compartment for my ride towards Ahmadabad.

---

* "Hist. Architecture," p. 513.

CHAPTER LXXXIV.

AHMADABAD.

I REACHED Ahmadabad early in the morning, and had ample opportunity to examine the city and its ancient buildings in the suburbs.

About the latter half of the sixteenth century, Ahmadabad was one of the largest cities in Western India. In the splendor of its architecture and the wealth of its citizens, it was the Hindu Florence. From 1573 to 1600, it was "the handsomest town in Hindustan, perhaps in the world." Sir Thomas Roe declared it "a goodly city as large as London." When the Mohammedan conquerors broke through the Indian gates, and reached this superb city, it is probable that they found a wealth of Hindu art, a finish and minuteness of decoration, and a breadth of architectural plan which had not met their gaze before.

But nothing daunted, the Moguls began to convert this Hindu city into a Mohammedan metropolis. They reared mosques with a lavish use of gold, and with a boldness of design which it was hoped would far outshine the Hindu temples. In some instances, it seems, when the temple served for a good foundation, they reared their mosques and poised their graceful minarets on the very site of the former places of worship, and made use of the rich patterns in wood and stone to complete the decorations in honor of Mohammed's faith. But in other cases they chose new places, and began on foundations quite their own.

As a result, Ahmadabad is now a mixed city. The new and the old lie in closest brotherhood. The English rule has broadened some of the streets, and given a thrift and cleanliness which had not existed. But the two civilizations, Hindu and Mohammedan, are to be seen to-day in strange combinations. The waste of war has been slighter here than in most places which I have visited. The patient Hindu carver did his work so well that his Mohammedan conqueror was glad to spare it, and vex

RANI SIPRI MOSQUE, AHMADABAD.

it into service for his mosque and private house. One beautiful house, therefore, is the creation of one race, while its neighbor may be that of another.

I drove first into the suburbs, and halted at the tomb of Shah Alam. This man, who died in 1495, was the son of a Mohammedan saint, who arrived at great fame as the spiritual guide of Mohammed Begada. When he died no pains were spared to make his tomb a fit memorial of him. Even to this day it is an exquisite piece of sepulchral architecture. The tomb of Shah Alam is only one—his family lie about him, in a house which might well be called a palace of the dead. You stand upon a floor of alternate tiles of white and black marble, and look up to a dome whose under surface is radiant with gold and precious stones. There are, about one tomb, three double-sliding brass doors, each with three panels of close work, which are of such delicate workmanship that one might well imagine them made in some fabulous smithy, where the forgers had a delicacy of final touch not known to men.

The frame in which the doors are set is of white marble, and this, with other marble supports, is inlaid with pearl. Such of the marble as serves for screens is also inlaid with pearl, and pierced with instruments so fine that the spaces left appear to be a piece of frail and delicate lace instead of stone. The tombs are divided from each other by finely wrought screens, where the Hindu ornamentation seems to have been preferred to the Moslem.

The tomb is really too small a thing for the typical Mohammedan to spend his time upon. He is a child of the desert, and must have great spaces about him. He is no lace-weaver. In threading a needle and making fine stitches, and forming close meshes with silk as fine as cobwebs, the Hindu is master. But the Mohammedan is a great architect. His sculpture has spread from the Ganges to the Pillars of Hercules, and has thrust some of its most notable qualities into both the Gothic and the Classic. He rears on a large scale. His majestic domes and towering minarets and bold arches prove him the man of great plans.

The mosques of Ahmadabad are of splendid proportions and exquisite finish. The Rani Sipri, which was built in 1431, is a piece of rich and imposing architecture. The two minarets, about fifty feet high, have zones of fine Hindu work, reaching from the pedestal to the topmost gallery. They stand out alone, as warders to mosque and tomb. The stone lattice which encloses the tomb is composed of many patterns, each beautiful, and executed in the finest style. There is nothing in the elaborate wood-carvings of old Lübeck which exceeds the rich designs, wrought in stone, which one finds here.

The most splendid mosque, however, is the Jama Masjid. It was built soon after the Mohammedan conquest, and was designed to eclipse all other buildings in Ahmadabad. There is a corridor which has thirty-six pillars on each side. The façade to the mosque has a great central arch, and five smaller ones on each side, or eleven in all. The roof rises in one large central cupola, with fourteen cupolas grouped about it. The minarets were once large and imposing, but at least half of each has been thrown down by an earthquake. A forest of pillars, two hundred and sixty-four in all, rises at regular intervals, and supports the roof of graceful domes. Near the mosque, and within the spacious sacred enclosure, is the mausoleum of King Ahmad Shah. The beautiful portico, of eighteen pillars, is a fit introduction to this tomb of the founder of the mosque. Two other sarcophagi are near it. All of them are of finest white marble, with reliefs of Indian flora.

Magnificent as all these sacred edifices are, the finest piece of work to be found in Ahmadabad is Sidi S'aid's mosque. One side of it forms part of the wall which includes the jail buildings of the city. The jail itself was not built for the purpose which it now serves. Once it was a palace, occupied by nobles from Delhi. Then it became an arsenal, and, last of all, the provincial jail. The mosque of Sidi S'aid was converted into an office, but the windows could not be allowed to remain open. They were, therefore, walled up. To this fact these five windows owe their preservation. They are of stone, and for minute and delicate work they are without an equal even in India. Fergusson says: "It would be difficult to excel the skill with which the vegetable forms are conventionalized just to the extent required for the purpose. The equal spacing also of the subject by the three ordinary trees and four palms takes it out of the category of direct imitation, and renders it sufficiently structural for its situation; but perhaps the greatest skill is shown in the even manner in which the pattern is spread over the whole surface. There are some exquisite specimens of tracery

DETAIL OF RANI SIPRI MOSQUE, AHMADABAD.

in precious marbles at Agra and Delhi, but none quite equal to this."*

I looked at these windows with amazement. Here is a great central tree of stone, with branches running out in greater and lesser curves, all graceful and some interlacing, until every part of the arch is filled with branch and leaf. Then, behind and of equal height, is a magnificent palm, at whose topmost frond there rests a piece resembling the front of a diadem. All this

PERFORATED WINDOW, COPIED IN TEAK FROM THE WINDOW IN YELLOW SANDSTONE IN THE SIDI S'AID MOSQUE, AHMADABAD.

is in stone. But the sunlight and the monsoons of the centuries have not injured it. Surely no chisel ever made rude stone relate a more beautiful tale in stone than this.

But everywhere in Ahmadabad one sees the minute splendor of the former times. Here, for example, is a private house where a balcony still stands which tells of the grand days. Some nobleman lived here then, made rich because he had done much

* "History of Architecture," p. 533.

slaying while on the conquering path from the Northwest. It is a massive bracket, stuck against the wall, and swelling out into beautiful framework and wall and pillars, and a fretted roof which hangs down and over the entire balcony, and terminates in a piece of as fine work in stone and wood as ever left the dark rooms of the weavers of Brussels lace. Sometimes a shop is entirely modern, excepting a finely carved door or window, which recites its idyl of the grand days when the Mogul had not yet heard of the barbarian from the little island in the North Sea. Wherever one goes, it is the same—temple, mosque, and private dwelling, all telling the same story of the old splendor. There are single doors in Ahmadabad, where naked children play in filth, and where the battle of all the inmates is for bread, which would dazzle and bewilder the keenest searcher for the beautiful and rich in manual art.

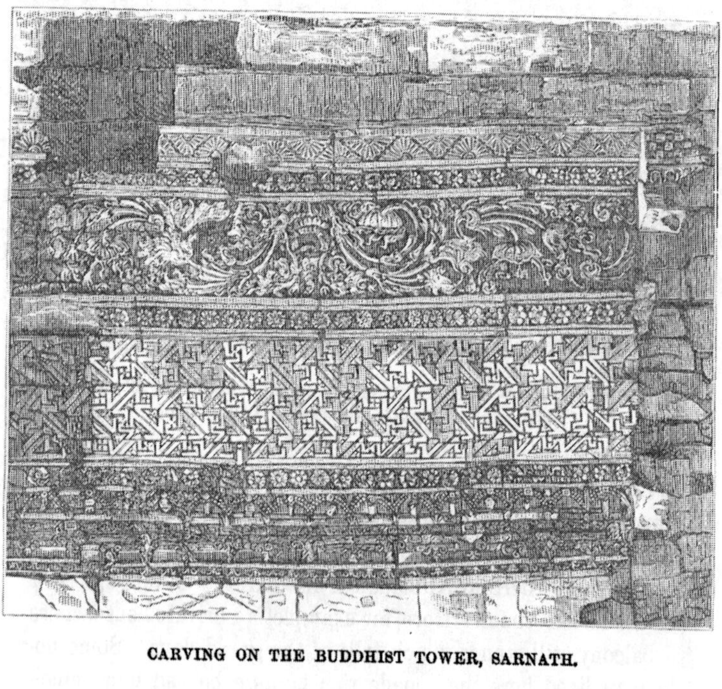

CARVING ON THE BUDDHIST TOWER, SARNATH.

BALCONY IN AHMADABAD.

CHAPTER LXXXV.

BASSEIN—A DEAD PORTUGUESE CITY.

History.

The story of the Portuguese in India is a touching bit of wild religious romance. It is now an old affair, its very memories being almost blotted out by the large later drama of the Saxon conquests and the recent firm and wise rule. The Portuguese went to India for wealth. The idea of general conquest was never fully in their mind. But no sooner had they gained a footing along the western coast, at Goa, Chaul, and Bassein, than the missionary idea even superseded the passion for gold. Francis Xavier determined to win for the Jesuits in this land what had been lost by the Reformation in the heart of Europe. The scope of his plans was broad, while his energy hesitated no more in the presence of the pagan millions of India than if they had been a few scores of Mexican Aztecs. When he gained permission from the pope to establish missions on the Indian coast, he meant to supply to the rest of his Church enough square roods to make full amends for those which Luther had torn from it in Central Europe.

What was India in those days? An unknown land. Its boundless jungles had not yet been disturbed by the gun and dog of the European hunter. There was native splendor beyond all conception of the Occidental world. The tribes could destroy each other, and the great nations of Europe knew nothing about it. The Mohammedan, after many centuries of desperate effort, had at last crossed the Indus, and swept down its valley and that of the Ganges, and filed over the table-land to the south of them, and reached the narrowing of the peninsula, and laved in the equatorial surf at Cape Comorin. He built up the great Mogul empire, which was now beginning to show signs of decay. The Portuguese trader came during this stage of decadence. His thought was for gold, and to take it back to Portugal and live behind his gilded jalousie in splendid idleness in his far-off Lisbon home. With him came the Jesuit missionary. Brazil is a strong American proof of how the two men combined for a complete conquest. Nay, there was sometimes added a third—the knight. Put these three together, and you have the whole secret of the Brazilian conquest. The same applies to the Spaniard in Mexico. The sailor, the soldier, and the priest, by a strong triple alliance, broke up the old life of the Aztec and the Inca, and built up that Spanish politico-ecclesiastical system which has only come to dissolution in our day. In the Indian case there were only two Portuguese characters, the sailor and the priest. The courtly knight—except Albuquerque and a few others—stayed away, except as governor and aide, to administer law in the name of the king. The romance was not wild enough to attract him.

Goa was the great centre of this new Portuguese life in India. It lies about midway between the harbor of Bombay and Cape Comorin, and in the old days was a natural outlet for the productions of that broad and rich country which constitutes the Mysore. During the present century the railroad system of India has left Goa quite in the rear. It is a city of great ruins. It is only a memory. Just now, however, there are indications that the fine harbor will be utilized as a point of departure for a new railway for a new piercing of the Mysore. But if Goa rises as a commercial city once more, it will be at the expense of the great Portuguese memorials. The ruined cathedrals and monasteries must soon disappear. No one can now conceive the former importance of Goa as a great Jesuit capital. It was a European fashion for long years to make rich gifts, from every part of the Roman Catholic world, to the institutions of Goa. Prince and peasant in Europe were induced to send thither their offerings, in the belief that nowhere was there a more promising field for the conversion of millions. One after another there arose in and about this vicinity buildings which would have adorned the broadest streets in Lisbon. Schools arose like mushrooms. Native children were gathered in from the outlying country, crucifixes hung about their necks, and they were taught the whole ceremonial of the mother Church. Students to a great number were in quick training for the priesthood. Xavier went up the coast to Bassein, then down to the Cape, and up the coast of the Bay of Bengal, and, not satisfied with his Indian achievements, went to China and Japan, and gathered in communicants by the same methods which he had adopted in Western India. A single sermon and a dash of water made the Hindu a Christian—in name.

The first collapse of Goa as a missionary centre came with the conquest of the Portuguese by natives. But there was still a hope that with the now rising French power in India there

THE CITADEL GATE.

might be a Roman Catholic restoration, and a new field for Jesuit operations. Yet France, while Romanist, nevertheless does not put her political machinery at the mercy of her priesthood. She lets her priests take care of the ecclesiastical life. Goa, in the case of final French occupation, might continue its work of propagandism, but the Church would have to look after the work and foot all the bills. But the final collapse came when the battle of Plassey was fought, and Clive gave India to England. This sealed the fate of Goa. Its harbor now shelters only an occasional ship. The streets are grass-grown. The once majestic churches are now piles of hopeless ruins.

Bassein was to Northern India what Goa was to the southern region. Its field was even more promising, for the territory which it commanded was broader, and embraced the two greatest valleys of all Asia. Xavier had his keen eye upon it, and three times visited it, and kept up a correspondence with the ecclesiastical leaders of the place. He came in the wake of the founder of Bassein as a centre of Portuguese authority in India —Nuno da Cunha, who ruled here from 1529 to 1538, and whose praises were sung by Camoens:

> "Then the fierce Sampaio shall be succeeded by
> Cunha, who the helm long time shall wisely guide;
> The lofty towers of Chalé [Chaul] he shall raise on high,
> While famous Dio shall tremble when by him tried.
> Strong Baçain [Bassein] shall not his artillery deny,
> But not without bloodshed; Melic with humbled pride
> Shall see her superb palisades down-torn,
> And not less because the work of the sword shall mourn." *

While Bassein was a commercial and political centre, and was held by Portuguese troops, and strongly fortified, it was still stronger as a base of ecclesiastical propagandism. The religious idea dominated over all. The absorption of all the hoarded wealth by the Church, and the city in which the Jesuits really subsidized the military power of the Portuguese in India to strengthen their position, form a most entertaining chapter in the Indo-European life of two centuries ago. Bassein is an island, hugging the shore closely, about thirty miles north of Bombay. The Portuguese fortified it by running a great wall around it, with towers and projections and all the appliances for long defence. It was honeycombed with secret chambers for stores in case of siege. From its parapets one could see at a great distance vessels approaching the coast, while from its peculiar relation to the land an enemy from the interior could be resisted with every hope of success. This island, with its bold headland, pushed its nose boldly out into the sea, tempted its owners to fortify it, build upon it, and prepare to hold it for all the ages to come.

The relations of the Portuguese to the Mogul rulers of the

---

* "Lusiad," canto x., lxi. (Mitchell's version).

North were anything but fixed. But these rulers conceived the idea of using the Portuguese as allies against other intruders. Now friendly and now hostile, these Moguls, who sat on jewelled thrones and made the whole Eastern world tremble at the mere mention of their names, found it to their advantage, after long meditation, to have such daring sailors as the Portuguese in alliance with them. The sailors could be carriers of their goods and the fruits of their soil to the Western markets. They could check the newly coming English too, who were just now exhibiting so decided a taste for Indian life and a suspicious love of Hindu adventure. Hence, when the Portuguese would build up Bassein, and make it a strong fortress for war and an ecclesiastical centre in peace, the Moguls had little to fear. They let them go on without disturbance. In due time, however, the Marhattas appeared, and they saw no use for the Portuguese in India. They resolved on their departure, and hence conquered Bassein, in the year 1739, as the key to their whole position. The Portuguese had dominated there two hundred and ten years, but had now fired their last gun. The strife of the Marhattas with the English was long and bitter. They were at last conquered, however, and, after holding Bassein seventy-nine years, surrendered it to the English in 1818, when it was incorporated with the Bombay presidency.

Visit to the Ruins.

I reached the railway station from Jaipur about three o'clock in the morning. There was not a place where I could find even fair accommodation for the rest of the night. In most of the Indian stations one can secure a room, where he may spread his bedding. But there was no room for a weary traveller this time. I was referred to a bungalow a few hundred yards from the station. On going there, and being shown the room, it had a woe-begone appearance, and was far from inviting to even the most sleepy occupant. There were too many crevices, and I feared insects large and small. I returned to the station, and half sat and half reclined until the broad daylight. After a frugal breakfast, I engaged a bullock-cart for the four miles and a half to old Bassein.

There are no springs to the typical bullock-cart, and your best position is to sit on the bottom of the contrivance. My two little bullocks started off in frisky style, and in an hour I was within the narrow and winding streets of the town which has grown up outside the old one, and yet must have had its beginnings even during the existence of the original Bassein. The scenery from the station to Bassein proper is charming. Fields of rice and various other grains stretch out on either hand. Here and there was a pond, which was all radiant with the sacred lotus in full flower and fragrance. One of the most conspicuous objects on getting fairly into the village was a ruined church. Its walls and roof were entire, but it was in wretched condition. Its windows were a curiosity, the first I had seen in India where the panes were of the pearl oyster-shell, cut thin, and about an inch and a half square. This was the Portuguese window. The labor of making great windows of such small pieces of shell, neatly cut and smoothed, was immense. At least one half the light was obstructed by the shell-slats, and when one adds to this the wooden framing for the shells, there must have been a considerable addition to the semi-opaqueness. But then this is India, and it is always a study to keep out the glare of the sun.

I soon left the town behind, and came upon rising ground by a winding road, through a thick grove of mango and peepul-trees. Off to the left stood the grim ruins of the old fort. I had now crossed the bridge, and so had passed upon the island of Bassein, which is about four miles long and two miles broad. This, nearly three centuries ago, was a very paradise of Portuguese enterprise and luxury on the one hand, and of Jesuit worldly wisdom on the other. Ruins were now on either hand. It was hard to tell which destructive force had been the stronger —time, or the merciless Marhattas. Any way that I might turn brought me face to face with some vast ruined cathedral. Now it was only the bare walls without ceiling or roof, and then I found myself walking over the marble slabs, with nearly effaced inscriptions, which covered the dust of Portuguese ecclesiastics and hidalgos. The dead underlay the entire nave and choir of one church after another. Some of the towers leaned at threatening angles, and yet in several cases it seemed safe enough to climb to the top of the wall and overlook this weird scene of ruin. There were arches which rose in graceful curves from one side of the portal to the other. Yet, at the keystone, there was often a depression which made it wise to get from beneath it. Occasionally, the central part of the wall had fallen outright, and left the jagged ends of the ruin on either hand.

Great pains had been taken to ornament the choir. Here was an elaborate sculpture, only fragments of which could be seen in scattered pedestals and capitals, and bits of the carved shafts. Where the walls had been less disturbed by the ravages of war and the elements there still remained tablets in mem-

CATHEDRAL OF ST. JOSEPH.

ory of ecclesiastic or civic officers whose lamp of life had died out here, far away from the dear Portugal which they left behind.

The Cathedral of St. Joseph is one of the most nearly complete of all the old churches. The great square tower which forms the portal still stands, and has to this day its gallery at the top, and even the ornamental work about its balustrades. Over the entrance one reads, in Portuguese, the still perfect inscription in stone:

"In the year 1601, being Archbishop Primate, the most Illustrious Sr. Dom Frei Aleixo de Menezes, and Vicar the Rev. Pedro Galvas Pereira, this Matriz was rebuilt."

This tower is an inviting point for a curious ascent. Da Cunha in his History tells us that he tried it, but in finding two steps crumbling beneath his feet he was compelled to beat a hasty retreat. No ruin in Bassein gives one a fairer idea of the splendor of these edifices when the Portuguese held undisputed sway here, and Goa and Bassein wrought hand in hand for bringing the millions of India beneath the Jesuit's crozier. Here were belfries which had sent out their sweet chimes over land and water in the days long gone by. Then there were lancet windows, calm side chapels, richly carved archways, and majestic pillars the entire length of the nave, all of such lavish wealth of sculpture and ornament as would have delighted Lisbon itself. The rebuilder of this cathedral died in Goa; but because of his relation to Bassein his remains were transferred here, as we learn from the following inscription on a black tombstone in the chancel to the right of the high altar:

"To this grave are transferred the bones of Pedro Galvao, Servant of the Lord, who managed and enlarged this temple. Died at Goa on the 19th of March of the year 1618."

The Church of St. Antonio was in its time one of the most imposing of the entire group on the island of Bassein. It seems to have been built by Fra Antonio do Porto, who figured largely in the Jesuit operations for the conquest of India. He destroyed two hundred Hindu pagodas, built eleven churches, and converted ten thousand one hundred and fifty natives to Christianity. The Franciscan church, or monastery—for it seems to have combined the two qualities—was, however, the grandest of all these ecclesiastical structures. It divided with that of St. Francis, in Goa, the honor of having chief authority in India. Several other churches were affiliated with it. The lateral chapels in the ruin are still to be recognized, and contain tombstones bearing the following touching inscriptions;

I.

H. M. Counsellor, died on the 24th of
August, 1558, and his wife, Dona
Luiza da Silva, and of his heirs.

II.

Here lies Dona Francisca da
Miranda, wife of Manoel de
Melo Perreira, Founder of this
Chapel, and her daughter Ines de
Melo, and her grandson Luis de Melo.
She died on 10th November, 1606.

III.

Grave of Dona Giomar da Aguiar, widow of Alvaro de Lemos. May he be with God! Died on the 11th March of 96 [1596]. Hers and her sons.

IV.

This tombstone was placed by
Dona Ira de Barredo for her
Interment in the grave of her husband
Antonio Tello de Menezes, who
Died on the 26th October, 1676. This
Grave was purchased by Manoel de
Carvalhar Pereira and his heirs. Our Father.

V.

In the reign of the most high and puissant
King
D. Joao de Portugal III. of the name.
When the Viceroy D. Affonso de Noronha was
governing India,
Son of the Marquis of Villa Real, and when
Francisco
De Sa was Captain of this fortress and of the
city
of Bassein. This bastion was founded under
the name of San
Sebastian on the 22d February,
In the year 1554.

I was bewildered with this wonderful scene. From one view I went to another, expecting to find that in some cases at least these relics of the Portuguese past would repeat themselves. But in no instance was this the fact. Each had its well-defined individuality. Where a cathedral had a supporting monastery, the space covered by the latter, as with the Franciscan and Jesuit monasteries, was at once imposing and immense. The old paths where the monks walked were quite obstructed by the tangled creepers. Many walls had lost their perpendicular, and now and then had tumbled to the ground, but it was easy to see the entire outline. The sacred edifices were in all stages of decay. Some were such complete ruins that not even a memorial tablet was longer in place, but had tumbled into the mass of stones and been broken into small pieces. Even the palaces of the General of the North and the Captain of Bassein were utter wrecks, only the broken walls and bastions and trembling portals remaining to tell of the former splendor of the place, and its importance in the eye of Portugal and of the daring and never-resting Xavier.

In one section my guide became doubtful of his way, and we proceeded with uncertainty. We were in a thick jungle, and could see only a short distance ahead of us. The path was overgrown, and I was intent on getting out of the tangled vegetation. All at once we emerged into the clear sunshine, which revealed a great cathedral, far gone as to wall and campanile. I strolled along the old nave, looked at its displaced tablets, and clambered over the roots and knolls which surround its immense walls.

One feature of this strange place surprised me more than any work of the Portugüese priest, governor, or factor. I mean the prodigies of vegetation. The custard-apple, the mango, and the peepul-tree grow here with a wild luxuriance which positively defies description.

Just within the walls where Portuguese hidalgos sat with their wives and children, and listened to the gospel according to Rome, and made confession, amid all the wealth and pageantry for which the Portuguese rule in Bassein was famed, there now grow tall and heavy trees, their topmost boughs higher even than the walls, and hanging down the exterior of the walls, and meeting the branches of the trees of less sacred growth. Trees have taken root on the walls themselves, and in each side of the wall, and sent down their long roots into the crevices of the rocks and struck the earth, and then twisted the very walls out of place, and grasped whole masses of solid rock, and now hold them in firm embrace. The creepers, not slender vines, but gigantic trees, have thrust their roots beneath the very walls of the cathedrals, and shot out their arms into the lancet windows, and gone up the sides of the campanile, and expanded into broad umbrellas, which hang over every side of the carved balcony, as though to hide it from the glare of the sun.

No woodman's axe is here. Nature, beneath this prodigal Indian sky, grows with a lavish and rapid splendor, and defies all the patience of the architect, and hides the finest toil of the sculptor's chisel. These vines spare nothing. Where the tree

CHURCH OF THE FRANCISCANS.

cannot penetrate the mass of rocks, its roots run down either side of bastion or wall until they reach the earth, and then penetrate it with such force that the severest monsoons of May and summer do not destroy their perpendicular. These trees do not seem to die, but to live on and grow larger, and send out their branches with such a wild luxuriance that they enter any window and climb over any precipice.

Then, in addition to the trees of creeping proclivities, one sees the cocoa-palm everywhere. It has no vines, but it still asserts its rights. It stands alone, and may grow beside a cathedral portal, and fan the archway with its bold fronds. The dead leaves lie in all directions, but they have only given place to still larger ones, which are beautiful and vigorous in their new growth. The smaller shrubbery is made up of many a species. It would require a very close examination of the botany of India to identify them. But here in Bassein they make a jungle such as I did not see even in Ceylon. The tendency everywhere, except with palms, is to vines. The strings from the trunks shoot off at all angles, catch upon larger shrubbery, grow into a tangled mass, and, instead of being stifled and coming to a halt, strike out again, find new holding-places, and grow into even larger masses. The soil becomes a thick mould, and is infested with any number of reptiles, which here in Bassein find only an occasional traveller to disturb their composure. Beneath some of the cathedrals there are secret passages, and in their best days it is most likely that all the larger ones were connected by underground paths.

One cannot help thinking, while wandering amid this scene of desolation, of the old Portuguese days. The Governor-General of India, who lived here, was supported by an immense salary. He had his rich retainers and numerous household, who lived in such splendor as none in Portugal besides the royal family had ever witnessed. Then the bells sent out their chimes from these many campaniles, and the congregations gathered for worship, and all the elaborate ritual of Romanism was conducted with a splendor and leisure quite in keeping with the hopes for the occupation, some day, of all India. The ladies, each with several attendants, coming from the splendid homes which surrounded Bassein on the water-front, were attired in the richest silks and adorned with the rarest jewels which the India of that day could supply. The music had lost none of its sweet melody by coming the long distance from Portugal. It was cultivated on Indian soil as a special agency for winning the Hindu to the new faith from the West.

At a given time, once a year, the Passion Play attracted universal attention. It was arranged in such a way as to appeal alike to the fears and hopes of the natives. Da Cunha thus gives the origin of it, as a means for impressing the Hindu mind, and at the same time to animate the Portuguese residents to new consecration for the conversion of India's millions. He says: "The history of 'Santos Passos,' or 'Passion Play,' at Bassein, is extremely curious. It originated with the Jesuits. The 'Santos Passos' were first performed in the church with the Jesuits' College of the Holy Faith at Goa, as a sequence to an event of religious revival in 1551, when the pope, in compliance with the request of St. Francis Xavier, granted a general jubilee for India, the first ever celebrated in this country.

"A Jesuit by name of Gaspar Berzeo, then established a society

MONASTERY OF THE JESUITS.

of the so-called 'disciplinantes,' whose business it was, while the preacher raised their religious emotions to the pitch of insanity, to chastise themselves with scourges which, in some instances, had little iron blades attached to them, so as to make incisions into the skin deep enough to allow the blood to flow. Sometimes the theopathy of the faithful, as is usually the case, was of so catching a nature that whole congregations were found busy in the process of flogging themselves. In some instances the voice of the preacher, who had in the meanwhile worked himself up to a frenzy, was quite drowned in the whack and thwack of the lash and stripe. The hysteric penitents, of course, fainted; but then there were the Jesuit brothers always ready by their side to help them into another room, where consolations were liberally dispensed to them. The sermon of the Jesuit preacher was generally in the text, 'Multa flagella peccatoris,' and at the end of it a crucifix was held out to the contemplation of the entranced congregation, when the hardy disciplinantes began their work of self-torture. This enthusiasm, however, could not last long, and soon gave place to the so-called 'Santos Passos,' or 'Passion Play,' performed in successive stages in weekly parts during the course of Lent, which, having begun in the Jesuits' Church at Goa, spread, as if by infection, in a very short time to every Roman Catholic communion in India. It was brought first to Bassein by the Jesuit Fr. Melchior Nunes Barreto." *

It is a curious question in ethnography, what has been the fate of the Portuguese descendants in India? The conversion to Christianity was never fundamental, and there is a much wider difference between the present race of Portuguese and the English Christians than between the native Hindus and the Portuguese. The Portuguese intermarried with natives, and in time almost all the Iberian characteristics of feature and form disappeared. The matter of faith and language alone remained. In the steamer by which I went from Colombo to Tutikorin. the whole deck was filled by these Portuguese Christians of to-day. I could not have discovered that they were Christians at all but from the crucifix which hung from their dirty necks. They had all the thriftlessness of the lower Hindu castes, and were ignorant in the extreme. Yet they were so-called Christians, and the direct offspring of the Portuguese missions planted by Francis Xavier around the Indian coast, from Bassein in the northwest around to the Cape, and then nearly up to Madras on the Bay of Bengal.

There are many of these Portuguese in Bombay, a race of themselves. All the waiters in the hotel where I lodged are of the same race. They are people who never rise above a very

---

* Da Cunha, "Notes of the History and Antiquities of Chaul and Bassein," pp. 249, 250.

low level. "They are extremely ignorant," says Da Cunha, "nor have they any talent worth developing for anything useful, except, perhaps, the lower walks of handicraft, such as carpentry, cotton-weaving, or the curing of hams." From the day when Bassein was conquered, there has not been a single literary or scientific celebrity among them. The highest in the class are but clerks in English and Parsi offices, where they carry on the mechanical work of copying. Occasionally a pamphleteer or two put in their appearance, but their productions are written in excessively bad English or equally bad Portuguese.

Of vernaculars, except, perhaps, a little colloquial corrupt dialect of the Marhatti, the present Portuguese know nothing, and appear to have renounced them from the day of their conversion to Christianity. These people are as much despised by the dominant race as by the Hindus. As for the moral character of the hybrid race, it may be summed up in the following dictum, which has been found true elsewhere—they have inherited the vices of both their parents, and the virtues of neither. There is no descendant of any high-class native among them. This fact is best proved by their physiognomy, which is, in short and general outline, a receding forehead, small eyes, prominent cheekbones, nose sunk at the root of wide nostrils, large mouth, and thick lips. In the more depressed classes and those addicted to drink, the expression of the face is scowling and unsteady. Another proof of their low descent is the spite and hatred they bear from the very bottom of their heart against high-class natives, who, from their natural shrewdness and superior intellect, seem destined to domineer over them.*

This unfavorable judgment applies with equal truth to the mongrel population which live in tents outside the old wall of Bassein. It would be difficult to tell the Portuguese Christian from the native Hindu. Their plane of life is quite the same. The Portuguese Roman Catholic here, and all over India, is a poor commentary on the character of the first converts under Xavier. They have churches here and there, but of such quality is their service that one finds it but little above the average Hindu worship. I examined carefully one of their cathedrals now in use in Tutikorin. In tawdry adornment, in poor and gaudy appeals by glaring and

* Da Cunha, "Notes," etc., pp. 250, 251.

coarse frescoes, and in the gross prominence given to the Virgin, I never saw, even in the obscurer parts of Italy, this so-called sanctuary surpassed.

The question forces itself upon one, as he walks away from the marvellous ruins of former Portuguese glory in Bassein: "What if those people were to-day dominant over the two hundred and fifty millions of India?" A strange Providence has ordered otherwise. Had the masters conducted themselves properly, and been fair types of the Christian colonist, there is no likelihood that they would have been disturbed. Their influence would likely have extended throughout the great valleys of both the Ganges and the Indus. But neither Hindu nor Mohammedan could see unselfishness in their measures. Theirs were the greed for gold, pride for the Church, and a lust for hasty and numerous converts. Therefore, when the Marhattas conquered Bassein, and paved the way unwittingly for the final triumph of the English, they were only helping India to her certain Protestant destiny.

FAÇADE OF A GROTTO OF KANHERI.

CHAPTER LXXXVI.

WHAT HAS ENGLAND DONE FOR INDIA?

English rule over India is not a case of hard conquest and commercial advantage. We think of Clive's terrible deeds and Burke's pictures of the crimes of Warren Hastings. We go still further back, and reflect upon the vicious parts of the policy of the East India Company during its long history. We come down to the present, and think of the government complicity with the trade in opium and the manufacture of liquors. But there is a broader view, which we are compelled to take if we would justly compare the India of to-day with what it was two centuries and a half ago. Even after discounting the wrongdoing of every English officer and administrator in India, and the connivance of the government at idolatrous practices, there still remain incalculable advantages to the country, which must be placed to the credit and honor of the Anglo-Saxon in India. These advantages cannot be attributed to the natural development of the natives, to the constant pressure of European ideas, or to the general force of our modern civilization. They are the direct result of the conquest of the country by England and of her subsequent rule over it.

First of all we must name the gradual unification of the country. The picture of Germany before the war with Austria, in 1866, which was the first blow for unification, is only a faint European parallel to the divisions of India before the conquest of the country by English armies. It is the purest fiction that there were ancient dynasties, which the English broke up. The land was one great tangled skein of races, languages, and recent governments. Century after century rolled by, and still the strife of war and bloodshed went on. Through the mountain gateways of the North there poured down daring armies into the plains of India, which showed no mercy, but swept away thrones and laws and cities, and ruled for a while, each being in time displaced and ground into powder by its successor. For seven centuries these cruel invasions went on, and India lay at the mercy of the strongest. This process was in full force in the eighteenth century, when six invasions upon the peaceful people took place in twenty-three years.* On the first of these later invasions, in 1738, when the Afghan conquerors reached Delhi, men, women, and children were hacked to pieces in the streets. Mill, father of James Stuart Mill, and most philosophical of all the historians of India, says of this massacre in Delhi: "With the first light of the morning, the invading leader, Nadir, issued forth, and, dispersing bands of soldiers in every direction, ordered them to slaughter the inhabitants, without regard to age or sex, in every street or avenue in which the body of a murdered Persian should be found. From sunrise to midday the sabre raged; and by that time not less than eight thousand were numbered with the dead. During the massacre and pillage the city was set on fire in several places."

The history of the great Mogul empire is one uninterrupted chapter of bloodshed. At the death of the Emperor Aurangzeb, in 1707, it reached its final expansion. It had no power to preserve its vitality. It was a loose mass, ready for any strong hand to break it into pieces. Its spoils were fought over by Afghans, Jats, Sikhs, revolting viceroys, rebellious governors, and military adventurers at large.† The Marhattas were the strongest force. They poured down from the mountains on the western coast, and carried desolation before them. They spared neither sex nor age, and the terror of their name was felt by every native of the country from Bombay to Calcutta. Not only were the English the first strong hand which had the power to stay the tide of Marhatta desolation, but to close up the two northern gateways against further invasions. It was the peaceful termination of a current of incoming freebooters which goes back of Marhatta, Afghan, Mogul, and Persian invasion, to the remote mythical period, when the Aryan came down from the northern gateways, when "Parasurama cleared the earth twenty-one times of the Kshatriya caste, and filled five large lakes with their blood,"

---

* Murdoch, "India's Needs," pp. 13, 14 (from Hunter, "England's Work in India").

† Lyall, "Asiatic Studies," p. 189.

and when the great Indian epic, the Mahabharata, began to be woven, and to unfold its unparalleled tale of the strife of races and the death of nations. Even the sea contributed its invaders. Pirates from the Burmese coast crossed the Bay of Bengal, pressed up the rivers, and carried desolation and death to the people. On the western coast the piracy was still more terrible. Whole fleets plied along the shore of the Indian Ocean, and levied such extortions as enabled the wealthy rajahs to sustain luxurious courts by the gains.*

The first and only force which arrested this struggle of ages in India has been England. The process of transition was long. Never has the Anglo-Saxon race had a more difficult problem to solve than, not merely to conquer, but to hold and set in motion the forces for a homogeneous Indian nation. The work was in rapid progress when the mutiny of 1857 broke out. This was the last disintegrating spasm. When the English army conquered the mutineers, a new bond, the strongest yet made, held the native races together. From that time to the present every step has been towards a united people. The old causes of internal separation are constantly disappearing. The Indian is beginning to feel, for the first time, that he is not the member of a tribe, but of a race; that he is not a soldier in sept, but a rightful owner of the broad soil; that he is not the slave of a rajah, but the citizen of a nation.

Crime is now rapidly decreasing. The frequent ebb and flow of conquest and oppression brought in a great amount of crime, which no laws could punish. The will of the ruler decided life and death. The laws themselves were the instruments of the strong to crush the weak. Even the sanctities of the Brahmic faith were utilized by wilder spirits to acquire gold by robbery and rapine. In India there were one hundred robber or "predatory" castes in the last century.† They were devoted to the worship of certain deities, and went out in bands, with a spear as their weapon. They attacked homes by night, and applied torture in case of resistance or concealment of treasure. Sometimes the robbers assumed the proportions of an army, in which case there was no thought of territorial possession, but solely of getting possession of the wealth of others. The Pindaris had no

* Hunter, "England's Work in India," p. 11.

† Ibid., pp. 15, 16.

modest purpose, but went in hordes of twenty thousand horsemen, and spared no class. The Thags were professional murderers. They worshipped the goddess Kali, or Devi, and, until the English broke them up, had plied their fiendish craft for many centuries. Death was always their object. They must kill in order to rifle the body safely. They always claimed the protection of the goddess. They had their leaders, their formulæ for admission into the murderous fraternity, and their watchwords. When once the crimes of Thagism were brought to the attention of the British government, the death-knell of the infamy was struck. Lord William Bentinck put Colonel Sleeman in charge of the difficult task. This officer, with his assistants, completely fulfilled his mission, and brought Thagism to an end, which had existed and spread desolation in India for twenty centuries. Hunter thus describes his meeting with one of the last of this old robber fraternity:

"Some time ago I was taken to visit the principal jail of the Indian provinces. At parting, when I was thanking the governor of the prison for all he had shown me, he exclaimed:

"'Ah, there is one thing more we must not forget to see.'

"He took me to a well-ventilated, comfortable room in the jail hospital, where, lolling upon pillows, reclined a reverend, white-bearded man.

"'This,' he said, 'is the last of our *thags.* He alone survives of the batch which we received twenty-five years ago!'

"I found that the miserable strangler had been for fifteen years enjoying himself in the hospital, the object of much solicitude to the doctors, and his life carefully prolonged by medical comforts, as an interesting relic of the past." *

Dacoity, or gang-robbery, was another form of crime which has required great energy on the part of the government to suppress. As late as 1879, in the Dekhan, it broke out with great violence, where the robbers sheltered themselves in the mountain fastnesses. Major Daniels, of the English army, distinguished himself by his extraordinary labors for its suppression. Sati, the crime of Hindu widows burning themselves on the funeral pyres of their husbands, was associated with the solemnities of the popular faith. To suppress the crime required

---

* "England's Work in India," p. 19.

the greatest possible energy of the government. It is now entirely eradicated, not only in the country directly under English rule, but also in the native states.

The inhuman crime of female infanticide, which has prevailed in India, has been very difficult to overcome, in spite of the prohibition of both the Qurán and the Vedas. The Rajputs and the native tribes have been most addicted to it. The first attempt to suppress it was in the eighteenth century, by Jonathan Duncan and Major Walker. They have been followed by others in the present century. In 1853 Lord Lawrence held a durbar at Amritsar, where the feudatory chiefs of the Panjab and the trans-Satlej States signed an agreement engaging to expel from caste every one who committed infanticide, and to adopt fixed and moderate rates of marriage expenses. Unquestionably the great expense which the bride's father must incur has had much to do with the prevalence of infanticide. Take the Rajputs as an example. The father of the Rajput bride has had to make gifts of money, clothes, jewels, and sweetmeats to the bridegroom's relatives, and, when the wedding comes, to pay enormous fees to the Brahman priests and the bhats, or minstrels. In the case of some rajahs these expenses for having a daughter who became a bride have gone up to the enormous sum of one hundred thousand pounds sterling.* To guard against such heavy expenses, the father has been in the habit of putting the infant daughter to death by giving her a pill of tobacco and bhang, or smearing opium or the poisonous datura over the mother's breast.

While the crime of infanticide has greatly decreased, the statistics of population furnish some suspicious facts. There is not the slightest reason to suppose that the proportion of boys and girls should not be equal in India, as in other countries. Yet in Oudh the excess of boys is seven per cent., in Bombay eight per cent., in the Northwest Provinces twelve per cent., and in the Panjab sixteen per cent. In 1870 a law was passed requiring special police regulation for towns where, because of the disproportion between boys and girls, there was suspicion of the practice of infanticide. In one tribe of Meerut, for example, there were found eighty boys under twelve years of age to only

---

* Smith, article in "Encycl. Brit.," vol. xiii. (9th ed.), p. 3. Bacon, "Oriental Annual," 1839, p. 92.

eight girls. In the Bengal population, the ratio is one hundred boys to eighty-seven girls. This disproportion is proof that, despite all the earnest measures of the government, the crime still prevails.

But a great end has been gained in concealing the crime from the public gaze. The first step towards the extinction of a crime is its banishment into darkness. The English purpose to exterminate infanticide is one of the many instances in which the Hindus owe to their conquerors a debt they can never pay, for teaching them the lesson of humanity to themselves.

Child marriages are an evil which will still survive for some time. According to the census of 1881, the number of Brahman widows above nineteen years of age in all India was 54,000. There are 80,000 Brahman widows under thirty. Neither child widow nor adult can marry again. Nearly all the Brahman girls are married between seven and ten years of age. If this state of things exists in the one class of Brahmans, what must be the number of child-widows of all classes throughout India? But the native Hindu mind, and notably Sir T. Madava Rao, is beginning its protest against this domestic crime. In due time the government will remove the curse of compulsory widowhood.

In view of the stringency with which crime is punished in India, the number of offenders is constantly decreasing. Notwithstanding the increase of population, there were in 1882 twenty-five per cent. less prisoners in the jails of India than there were in 1867.* Even the native princes are watched, and England is careful to see that her feudatory rulers have no such power as was exercised before she entered India. For example, under Hindu and Mohammedan rule the native ruler could appropriate, if he chose, all the revenue for his personal enjoyment, and could take away the life, liberty, or property of any of his subjects. Under English rule this license no longer exists. The native prince is subjected to essentially the same righteous regulations which govern the territory directly under English rule.

The salutary influence of the English government has even reached the evils existing among the aboriginal Hill Tribes. For example, it was found that, among this neglected class, the

* Murdoch, "India's Needs," pp. 18, 19.

debtors were converted into slaves. This class was promptly released by government order. Another class of slaves consisted of persons who had been captured in war. These, too, were liberated by the English rulers.*

All India is now a neighborhood. The arrival of the English mail is anticipated almost to the hour. Quick transportation is everywhere the rule. Bishop Heber required six weeks to go from Calcutta to Dacca by boat. Now the same journey is made in twenty-four hours. He required nearly three months to go from Dacca to Allahabad, a distance of seven hundred miles. The same distance can now be covered by any one in three days, by steamer and railway.† He spent nearly half a year, or from June 15th to November 27th, in going from Calcutta to Almora:

"Then on! Then on! where duty leads,
My course be onward still;
O'er broad Hindostan's sultry mead,
O'er bleak Almora's hill."

The same distance can now be travelled in four days.

Sanitary measures have been adopted. Before the English supremacy there was no attention paid to the laws of health. The rulers and the nobles had immense wealth, and could live in luxury. For the life of the millions there was no thought. The two fundamental questions were, to get men for the army, and to grind out a revenue for the support of the government. Whether the people were comfortable or not, whether they were long-lived or not, were concerns left entirely to the people themselves. When the English entered upon the rule of the country, they looked after the sanitary condition of the humblest, and the increased longevity is the proof of the success of their efforts. The Sanitary Department is one of the distinct parts of the administration of the government. A sanitary commissioner is attached to each local government, and under him are several grades of medical officers. Above all these there is a general sanitary commissioner, connected with the general government, and to him sanitary reports must come from all parts of the empire. The three great cities of Calcutta, Ma-

* Lewin, "The Wild Races of Southeastern India," pp. 87, 91. London, 1870.

† Buckland, "Sketches of Social Life in India," p. 7.

dras, and Bombay are supplied with water-works, which in each case are triumphs of engineering skill and of care for dense populations. These water-works are equal to those of the great cities of Europe and America. The same care is taken for the supply of wholesome water in the smaller towns throughout the country.* Many millions of pounds sterling have been expended on the sewage system—a problem hard to solve, especially in such flat surfaces as Calcutta and Madras. The government has further shown its solicitude for the improvement of the health of the people by issuing small manuals on sanitary science for their use in schools, and for general circulation.

In close relationship with this most praiseworthy care of the people by the government, the prevention and cure of disease must not be forgotten. The English, when they found themselves permanent occupants and rulers of the country, had to deal with a great mass of people whose chief occupation had been to find rice enough to keep themselves alive. The national life during the Mogul rule, being one of warfare and perpetual alarm, no intelligent care was bestowed on the treatment of disease. Whenever a plague invaded the country it ran its race. The people were at its mercy. Millions were swept away by it. The proverb common in parts of India, that "a mother can never say she has a son until he has had the small-pox," carried with it a terrible truth. The ravages of this disease were appalling. It is still terribly devastating, many thousands dying annually from this one cause alone. The natives used to parry it somewhat by inoculation, and they still have a prejudice against vaccination. But the government prohibits inoculation, and requires vaccination, without cost to the people. It employs vaccinators, and requires official returns for their work. Other diseases are watched carefully, and their violence brought to the minimum by the persevering efforts of the state.

Wherever the popular worship is concerned, it is next to impossible to guard the health and life of the people. For example, the many thousands who drink the sacred water from the Gyan Kup, or Well of Knowledge, in Benares, take into their bodies as corrupt a fluid as the idolatry or ingenuity of man could well compound. To make the people cease drinking the

---

* Temple, "India in 1880," pp. 322 ff.

filthy water would be an assault on the faith of the people which would shake the empire to its foundations. But the time will come when even in India it will be proven, not only that "cleanliness is next to godliness," but that it is a part of that new godliness which is sure to overspread the country. In order to mitigate the ravages of fever, the government has taken special pains to introduce quinine throughout the country. Plants have been brought from South America, and plantations are already producing supplies for the people. The price of quinine is very low throughout India.

The liberty of the expression of opinion is now universal. The Bengali, fond of expression and of writing under the shadow of the Government House in Calcutta, can write what he pleases about any officer in the land, from the humblest citizen to the governor-general himself.

A national Congress has been formed by the natives for all India. It meets annually, and aims at still larger political liberty, and still further social reform. It has among its members Hindus, Mohammedans, and even native Christians. It does much talking, and declares for a national parliament, with Indian representatives. This Congress is doing more than all other native forces to develop a national, but not disloyal, feeling among the native population. Literary societies and debating clubs are springing up in all the centres of population. The government watches all these evidences of native aspiration, and is gracious and patient in the extreme. Sometimes a stormy and fearless native makes a good point against the government, which, we may well suppose, is not forgotten, and in due time will bear good fruit. For example, Syed Mohammed Husain shows a glaring inconsistency in the matter of duties and home production, when he says: "We export wheat, and pay highly for making it into biscuits, vermicelli, and macaroni. We produce sugar, and pay again for manufacturing loaf-sugar. We produce tobacco, and pay again for bird's-eye. We export hides, but pay again for saddles, harness, patent-leather, boots and shoes. For patent-leather we pay four or five times as much as we received originally for our hides."*

---

* "Our Difficulties and our Wants in the Path of the Progress of India," p. 71. London, 1884.

India now sells far more than she buys. Every year the export of her staples exceeds her imports by 21,000,000 pounds sterling. The old native rate of interest in the rural regions was 37½ per cent. Now the native in the country, if he has land to pledge, can borrow at one third of that rate. Seven per cent. is regarded by the Calcutta merchant as a good investment.*

Many of the early industries, which existed when England took possession of the country, have been developed within the last few decades to remarkable proportions. The cotton of India being found inferior to that of the United States, the government has introduced American cotton-plants and American laborers, and already India is becoming one of the greatest cotton-producing countries of the world. She is rapidly learning the art of converting the fibre into woven fabric. A familiar picture still is the humble weaver, slowly working away with hands and feet at his primitive loom, which has probably undergone not the least change since the Rig Veda was first written on palm-leaves. But the English loom, and that carried by steam, is now taking the place of the few rough sticks and cords of the old household loom. The Indians are learning the secret which our Western States have already learned—to save the cost of transportation by producing its own manufactures. I visited an immense cotton-factory in Cawnpore, where steam and all the improved machinery of Europe are used. Englishmen manage the business, but the natives perform the manual labor.

The development of the natural resources of India by the English has been remarkable. Millions of arable acres have been added to the productive power of the soil. One section alone, 13,000 square miles in area, has been brought under the plough, and now produces 18,000,000 pounds sterling in cereals. The earth itself has been penetrated, and made to yield its hidden wealth for the enrichment of the masses. Coal-beds have been discovered in Western Bengal, in the Central Provinces, in the Panjab, and even in Burma. The coal-mining, though still in its infancy, already employs fifty thousand men, exclusive of their families, and Sir Richard Temple reckons the total annual output of the colliers at a million of tons.† The coal imported

---

* Hunter, "How India is Governed," p. 43. † "India in 1880," p. 303.

from England is six hundred thousand tons annually. But the native coal is continually taking the place of the English. Already the East Indian railway uses the Bengal coal, which costs but two rupees (eighty cents) per ton, while the imported coal costs fifteen rupees (six dollars) per ton. Iron ore is found in several parts of the country, and in due time we may expect to hear of large smelting and foundry works. The diamonds of Bundelkhand, the pearl fisheries of Bahrein, the opals of Ajmir, and the rubies of Burma, will continue to supply in no small measure the world's markets of precious stones.

India is no longer the prey of Western ambitious powers. It is a solid part of the British possessions. It knows, because it sends its troops, that England cannot fight a battle in Europe without its help. The expansion of education among all classes of people, the physical care of the helpless classes, the subtle bond of the English language, the development of the soil, the utilizing of the mineral wealth, the opening of the country for the incoming of Western ideas, and, greater than all combined, the breaking down of all doors for the free spread of the Gospel, make the India of the last decade of the nineteenth century a perfect contrast with the India of the first decade of the eighteenth. England has never achieved grander victories on Waterloo or at Quebec than those which belong to her quiet and peaceful administration of India. The day has not yet dawned when it is possible to measure the whole magnitude of England's service to the millions of India. Generations must elapse before this can be done. When the hour does come, it will be seen that the Englishman has never been wiser or more humane on the Thames or the St. Lawrence than on the Ganges, the Indus, and the Godavari. The real fact is, not that he has conquered the country, but that he has discovered it, and now governs it by as generous laws, and as even justice, as he rules over the millions within sight of his parliament at Westminster.

"Is it no blessing," asks the Rev. George Bowen, for many years a resident in India and a careful observer of its development, "that the Hindu of to-day has a much grander and better world to look out upon than his father had? The whole world, to his fathers, was *Mlechcha*, defiled, barbarous, beyond the pale of intercourse, abhorred even by the gods, who reserved their incarnations and manifold favors for the people of this country. Now, the educated Hindu thinks it a privilege to visit the Occident and become acquainted with the marvels of civilization and art. Once the sympathies of the Hindu were cabined, cribbed, confined, shrivelled up to the confines of his own caste; now what is to hinder their expansion to the ends of the earth, and the comprehension of all nations in his fellow-feeling?" * We can hardly expect a Frenchman, with his memories of the great failure of France to acquire India, to be overjust to the English presence. Yet the following is the tribute which a French scholar pays to England in India: "Neither in the Vedic times, nor under the great Asoka, nor under the Mohammedan conquest, nor under the Moguls, all powerful as they were for a while, has India ever obeyed an authority so sweet, so intelligent, and so liberal." †

Looking at the India of to-day, and comparing it with what it was before Vasco da Gama turned his vessels thither, and with what it was when Portuguese, Dutchmen, and Frenchmen contended for it, we may say with safety that England has been a blessing to the helpless continent. England has conquered India. But it has been less a conquest by steel and gunpowder than by all the great forces which constitute a Christian civilization.

---

* *Bombay Guardian.*

† Barthélemy St. Hilaire, "L'Inde Anglaise; son État Actuel son Avenir," p. 154.

APPENDIX

APPENDIX.

NO. I.

PRINCIPAL DATES OF INDIAN HISTORY.

I.—PREHISTORIC PERIOD.

B.C.

1600. Settlement of the Aryans in tract between Saraswati and Ghaggar rivers, one hundred miles northwest of Delhi.
1400. Arrangement of the Vedas by Vyasa.
1400–1300. War described in the Mahabharata.
1308. Invasion of India by Sesostris (mythical).
1200. Rama's Invasion of the Dekhan.
800. The date of the Institutes of Manu.
543. Death of Gautama, or Sakya Muni.

II.—SEMI-HISTORIC PERIOD.

518. Persian invasion under Darius Hystaspes.
500–400. Pandya kingdom of Madura founded.
330. Herat founded by Alexander the Great.
327. Invasion of India by Alexander the Great.
302. Mission of Megasthenes.
260–220. Asoka, the great patron of Buddhism.
104–76. Buddhistical books of Ceylon.
57. Era of Vikramaditya, King of Ujjain.

A.D.

100. Sah Dynasty of Gujerat.
399. Travels of Fa-Hian.
629–645. Travels of Hiouen Thsang.
800–1400. Puranas.
1009. Birth of Ramanuja.
1186–1206. Mohammed of Ghor.
1206–1288. First Slave Dynasty in Delhi.
1217. Chengiz Khan. First Mogul irruption.
1294. First Mohammedan invasion of the Dekhan.
1398. Timur (Tamerlane) in Delhi. Second great Mogul invasion.

1482. Baber.
1486. Bartholomew Diaz.
1498. Vasco da Gama.
1505–1508. Francisco Almeyda, first Portuguese viceroy.
1508–1515. Alfonso Albuquerque, second Portuguese viceroy.

III.—Mogul Period.

A.D. 1524–1857.

1524. Baber founds the great Mogul empire in India. He is the first of the six great Mogul emperors.
1527. Conquest of the Rajputs by the Moguls.
1530. Humayun, second great Mogul emperor.
1540. Francis Xavier in India.
1542. Birth of Akbar.
1556. Accession of Akbar, the third Mogul emperor.
Akbar's Conquests:
- 1567. He conquers his own feudatories.
- 1572. Subdues the Rajputs.
- 1573. Conquers Gujerat.
- 1586. He conquers Kashmir.
- 1592. Annexes Bengal, Behar, and Orissa.
- 1592. Conquers Sind.
- 1594. Conquers Afghanistan.

1580–1656. Downfall of the Portuguese.
1583. First English in India.
1594. The Dutch in India.
1600. Incorporation of the British East India Company.
1605. Accession of Jahangir, the fourth Mogul emperor.
1627. Accession of Shah Jahân, the fifth Mogul emperor.
1631. Portuguese driven out of Bengal.
1658. Aurangzeb, sixth Mogul emperor.
1664. The French in India.
1683–1707. Aurangzeb's war in the Dekhan.
1702. Birth of Haidar Ali, of Mysore.
1707. The Sikhs nearly exterminated.
1725. Birth of Robert Clive.
1732. Birth of Robert Hastings.
1744. Clive lands in India.

IV.—The English Period.

A.D. 1748–1889.

1748. Lawrence lands in India.
1756. Massacre of the Black Hole.
1757. Battle of Plassey, India secured to England.
1783. Peace of Versailles. Dutch possessions become English.
1786–1793. Cornwallis second governor-general.
1793. Lord Teignmouth third governor-general.

1818. Death of Warren Hastings.
1840–1842. The Opium War.
1853. Opening of the first Indian railway.
1857. Sepoy Mutiny breaks out.
1858. The conquest of the Mutiny. India safe under the English crown.
1877. Queen Victoria is declared Empress of India.*

V. — Governors and Governors-General of India under the East India Company.

A.D. 1758–1858.

1758–1767. Lord Clive.
1767–1768. Harry Verelst.
1769–1771. John Cartier.
1772–1785. Warren Hastings.
1786–1793. Lord Cornwallis.
1793–1798. Lord Teignmouth.
1798–1805. Marquis Wellesley.
1805–1806. Lord Cornwallis (second term).
1806–1813. Lord Minto.
1813–1823. Marquis of Hastings (Earl Moira).
1823–1828. Earl Amherst.
1828–1835. Lord Bentinck.
1836–1842. Lord Auckland.
1842–1844. Lord Ellenbrough.
1844–1847. Lord Hardinge.
1848–1856. Earl of Dalhousie.
1856–1857. Earl Canning.

VI.—Viceroys of India under the Crown.

1858–1861. Earl Canning.
1862–1863. Earl of Elgin.
1864–1869. Lord Lawrence.
1869–1872. Lord Mayo.
1872–1876. Lord Northbrook.
1876–1880. Lord Lytton.
1880–1885. Marquis of Ripon.
1885–1888. Lord Dufferin.
1888. Lord Lansdowne, present incumbent.

---

* Graham is an excellent authority on the minute periods. See "Genealogical and Chronological Tables Illustrative of Indian History," 2d ed., London, 1880.

NO. II.

AREA AND POPULATION OF THE PROVINCES, EXCLUSIVE OF THE 153 NATIVE STATES.

Provinces under the direct Administration of	Area in Sq. Miles.	Divisions.	Districts or Counties.	Inhabited Houses, 1871.	Population 1871.	Population on Feb. 17, 1881.	Density of Population to Square Mile.	
							Census of 1871.	Census of 1881.
The Governor-General.								
Ajmir	2,710	—	2	93,464	396,889	453,075	146	167
Berar	17,728	—	6	491,349	2,227,654	2,670,982	125	151
Kurg	1,583	—	1	22,900	168,312	178,283	107	114
Two Governors.								
Madras	140,430	—	22	5,892,179	31,385,820	30,839,181	224	220
Bombay (with Sind and Aden)	126,453	4	25	3,254,371	16,349,206	16,454,414	129	129
Three Lieutenant-Governors.								
Bengal	155,997	9	52	10,461,113	60,733,078	66,530,127	389	427
{North-western Province,	81,748	7	37	6,316,452	30,781,204	32,699,436	376	400
{Oudh	24,213	4	12	2,413,710	11,223,150	11,407,625	463	471
Punjab	107,010	10	32	4,015,476	17,611,498	18,850,437	164	175
Four Chief Commissioners.								
Central Province	84,208	3	18	1,674,291	8,173,824	9,805,149	97	118
British Burma	87,220	3	19	629,256	3,154,470	3,707,646	36	42
Andaman and Nicobar Islands	3,285	—	2	—	25,945	30,000	8	9
Assam	55,384	1	11	712,934	4,124,972	4,815,157	91	106
Total square miles of Provinces	887,969	—	239	35,977,459	186,356,022	198,441,512	210	223½

AREA AND POPULATION OF INDIA, BRITISH PROVINCES AND STATES, AND FOREIGN POSSESSIONS.

Provinces and States.	Provinces.			Native States.			Total.		
	Square Miles.	Population.		Square Miles.	Population.		Square Miles.	Population.	
		Census of 1871.	Census of 1881.		Census of 1871.	Census of 1881.		Census of 1871.	Census of 1881.
Government of India.									
Ajmir	2,710	396,889	453,075	—	—	—	2,710	396,889	460,722
Berar	17,728	2,227,654	2,670,982	—	—	—	17,728	2,227,654	2,672,673
Kurg	1,583	168,312	178,283	—	—	—	1,583	168,312	178,302
Mysore	—	—	—	30,500	5,055,412	4,186,399	30,500	5,055,412	4,186,399
Central India	—	—	—	89,098	8,360,571	9,200,881	89,098	8,360,571	9,200,881
Rajpootana	—	—	—	130,994	10,192,871	11,005,512	130,994	10,192,871	11,005,512
Haidarabad	—	—	—	80,000	9,000,000	9,167,789	80,000	9,000,000	9,167,789
Baroda	—	—	—	4,399	2,000,225	2,154,469	4,399	2,000,225	2,154,469
Andaman Islands	3,285	25,945	30,000	—	—	—	3,285	25,945	30,000
Bengal	155,997	60,733,078	66,530,127	47,440	2,328,440	2,603,492	203,437	63,061,518	69,133,619
Assam	55,384	4,124,972	4,815,157	—	—	—	55,384	4,124,972	4,908,276
British Burma	87,220	3,154,470	3,707,646	—	—	—	87,220	3,154,470	3,736,771
{ N. W. Province	81,748	30,781,204	32,669,436	5,125	636,543	744,424	86,873	31,417,747	33,443,917
{ Oudh	24,213	11,223,650	11,407,625	—	—	—	24,213	11,223,150	11,407,625
Punjab	107,010	17,611,498	18,850,437	114,742	5,370,096	3,861,683	221,749	22,981,594	22,712,120
Central Province	84,208	8,173,824	9,805,149	29,112	1,049,710	1,700,000	113,042	9,223,534	11,505,149
Bombay	126,453	16,349,206	16,454,414	66,408	6,784,482	6,941,631	191,847	23,133,688	23,396,045
Madras	140,430	31,385,820	30,839,181	9,818	3,247,689	3,001,436	150,248	34,633,509	33,840,617
British India	887,969	186,356,022	198,441,512	607,636	54,026,039	54,567,716	1,494,310	240,382,061	253,140,886
French Possessions	....	....	....	..	....	....	178	285,022	280,381
Portuguese Possessions	....	....	....	..	....	....	1,086	444,617	444,987
Total of all India	....	....	....	..	....	....	1,495,574	241,111,700	253,866,254

NO. III.—PRINCIPAL INDEPENDENT NATIVE STATES.

NAME.	Area in Square Miles.	Population.	Revenue.
			£
Kashmir	68,000	1,600,000	823,200
Kapurthala	1,650	470,000	170,000
Mandi	1,200	135,000	36,500
Chamba	3,216	140,000	19,000
Suket	420	45,358	6,775
Bahawalpur	22,000	500,000	200,000
Pattiala	5,412	1,650,000	440,000
Jhind	1,236	311,000	65,000
Nabha	863	300,000	65,000
Kalsia	155	62,000	13,000
Maler Kotla	165	46,200	28,000
Faridkot and Dujana	700	95,000	90,000
Loharu and Patandi	335	43,000	14,700
Nepaul	54,000	2,000,000	1,000,000
Sikkim	1,550	7,000	700
Bhutan	2,000	60,000	—
Udaipur	11,614	1,161,400	64,000
Jeypore	15,250	1,995,000	475,000
Jodhpore	35,670	2,000,000	250,000
Bundi	2,300	224,000	80,000
Kota	5,000	450,000	200,000
Jhallawar	2,500	226,000	160,000
Tonk	2,730	320,000	110,000
Karauli	1,870	124,000	50,000
Kishungurh	724	105,000	130,000
Dholpur	1,600	500,000	110,000
Bharatpur	1,974	743,710	287,500
Alwar	3,000	778,596	230,000
Bikanir	24,000	300,000	102,032
Jessulmere	12,250	75,000	10,000
Serohi	3,200	55,000	11,000
Daugarpur and Banswarra	2,500	250,000	45,000
Pertubgurh	1,460	150,000	60,000
Shahpoora	1,200	133,000	30,000
Gwalior	33,119	2,500,000	1,200,000
Indore	8,015	635,400	500,000
Bhopal	8,200	769,200	268,340
Dhar	2,500	150,000	80,000
Dewas	2,576	121,800	60,000
Jaora	872	85,500	79,930
Rewa	13,000	2,035,000	250,000
Tehri	2,000	195,000	90,000
Dattia and Sampthar	995	288,000	140,000
Baroda	4,399	2,000,000	1,150,000
Kohlapore	3,184	802,690	304,720
Sawunt Wari	900	190,814	29,400
Kutch	6,500	500,000	130,000
Hyderabad	98,000	10,500,000	2,000,000
Mysore	27,070	5,055,000	1,029,900
Travancore	5,630	2,311,380	535,000
Cochin	1,360	598,350	130,850
Cooch Behar	1,306	532,565	100,000
Manipur	3,000	126,000	5,000
Tippera	3,867	74,242	18,690
Rampore	945	507,013	146,400
Garhwal	4,180	150,000	80,000
Total	522,362	47,133,218	13,695,637

NO. IV.

The following table shows the number of candidates who came up from each province, the number passed, and the percentage of successful candidates for the years 1885 and 1886:

ENTRANCE EXAMINATION.

PROVINCES.	1885.			1886.		
	Number of Candidates.	Number passed.	Percentage.	Number of Candidates.	Number passed.	Percentage.
Bengal	2980	1070	35.9	3172	913	28.78
Assam	110	40	36.36	99	39	39.39
Northwest Provinces and Oudh	724	208	28.72	715	237	33.14
Rajputana	22	8	36.36	27	9	33.33
Jaypur	16	6	37.5	11	2	18.18
Panjab	102	34	33.33	67	28	41.79
Central Provinces	201	50	24.87	190	70	36.84
Central India States	64	21	32.81	45	9	20
Nepal	2	—	—	—	—	—
Burmah	58	13	22.41	51	23	45.09
Ceylon	38	13	34.21	16	7	43.75
Total	4317	1463	33.88	4393	1337	30.43

The number of candidates who failed in one subject only is subjoined:

English	501
Mathematics	323
Second Language	96
History and Geography	9

NO. IV.—*Continued.*

NUMBER OF CANDIDATES AT UNIVERSITY EXAMINATIONS, AND THE NUMBER PASSED, IN EACH YEAR SINCE 1857.

Year.	Entrance.		First Examination in Arts.		Bachelor of Arts.		Master of Arts.		License in Law.		Bachelor in Law.		Doctor in Law.		License in Medicine and Surgery.				Bachelor in Medicine.				Doctor in Medicine.		License in Civil Engineering.		Bachelor in Civil Engineering.		First Examination in Engineering.		License in Engineering.		Bachelor in Engineering.	
															First Examination.		Second Examination.		First Examination.		Second Examination.													
	No. of Candidates.	No. passed.	No. of Candidates.	No. passed.	No. of Candidates.	No. passed.	No. of Candidates.	No. passed.	No. of Candidates.	No. passed.	No. of Candidates.	No. passed.	No. of Candidates.	No. passed.	No. of Candidates.	No. passed.	No. of Candidates.	No. passed.	No. of Candidates.	No. passed.	No. of Candidates.	No. passed.	No. of Candidates.	No. passed.	No. of Candidates.	No. passed.	No. of Candidates.	No. passed.	No. of Candidates.	No. passed.	No. of Candidates.	No. passed.	No. of Candidates.	No. passed.
1857	244	162	—	—	—	—	—	—	—	—	—	—	—	—	12	12	—	—	—	—	—	—	—	—	—	—	—	—	—	—	—	—	—	—
1858	464	111	—	—	13	2	—	—	—	—	19	11	—	—	40	24	—	—	—	—	—	—	—	—	—	—	—	—	—	—	—	—	—	—
1859*	1411	583	—	—	20	10	—	—	—	—	20	3	—	—	31	12	—	—	—	—	—	—	—	—	—	—	—	—	—	—	—	—	—	—
1860	809	419	—	—	65	13	—	—	—	—	22	10	—	—	31	13	—	—	—	—	—	—	—	—	—	—	—	—	—	—	—	—	—	—
1861	1058	477	163	94	39	15	1	—	7	8‡	17	8	—	—	16	7	20	14	—	—	—	—	—	—	10	6	—	—	—	—	—	—	—	—
1862	1114	477	220	99	34	24	3	—	16	8	13	9	—	—	33	18	17	7	—	—	—	—	1	1	18	14	—	—	—	—	—	—	—	—
1863	1307	690	272	149	35	25	7	6	19	9	15	9	—	—	35	16	19	14	—	—	—	—	2	2	—	—	—	—	—	—	—	—	—	—
1864	1396	702	321	151	66	30	8	3	1	1	22	19	—	—	42	22	25	11	—	—	—	—	2	—	10	5	—	—	—	—	—	—	—	—
1865	1500	510	446	202	82	45	15	11	7	5	17	17	—	—	34	14	20	18	2	2	—	—	1	1	5	2	—	—	—	—	—	—	—	—
1866	1350	638	426	131	122	79	18	15	17	13	22	11	—	—	35	10	26	20	5	5	—	—	—	—	9	—	—	—	—	—	—	—	—	—
1867	1507	814	388	188	141	60	39	22	17	14	36	28	—	—	44	17	18	15	2	1	2	2	—	—	6	6	—	—	—	—	—	—	—	—
1868	1734	892	423	202	212	99	25	15	10	3	72	51	—	—	45	6	13	11	2	1	4	3	—	—	3	2	—	—	—	—	—	—	—	—
1869	1730	817	520	225	174	77	29	18	32	13	98	61	—	—	61	27	20	19	3	2	2	2	—	—	7	4	1	1	—	—	—	—	—	—
1870	1905	1099	540	233	210	98	32	24	26	18	87	74	—	—	56	42	7	5	4	4	1	1	—	—	9	3	—	—	—	—	—	—	—	—
1871	1902	767	507	204	212	84	39	35	27	12	83	52	—	—	58	38	29	27	2	2	2	1	—	—	12	2	1	—	—	—	—	—	—	—
1872	2144	938	560	220	232	100	32	24	58	17	100	26	—	—	68	29	42	27	2	—	5	3	—	—	14	7	2	1	—	—	—	—	—	—
1873	2544	848	539	305	242	126	30	20	93	44	137	88	—	—	77	31	48	23	1	—	4	2	—	—	18	2	4	1	—	—	—	—	—	—
1874	2254	966	533	193	212	92	57	32	65	46	103	79	—	—	113	34	47	36	6	4	2	1	—	—	22	2	2	—	—	—	—	—	—	—
1875	2373	838	575	182	217	90	38	18	—	—	71	40	—	—	155	31	42	13	11	7	1	—	—	—	16	6	4	3	—	—	—	—	—	—
1876	2425	1355	756	344	281	73	38	24	—	—	86	54	—	—	171	70	55	9	14	9	5	3	—	—	12	5	9	3	—	—	—	—	—	—
1877	2720	1166	791	253	287	144	49	31	—	—	83	61	2	2	196	46	60	28	23	9	8	7	—	—	24	8	10	3	—	—	—	—	—	—
1878	2617	1098	923	267	228	68	62	28	—	—	61	29	—	—	104	60	91	34	22	17	10	7	—	—	21	5	7	1	—	—	—	—	—	—
1879	2697	1069	1040	320	323	91	48	28	—	—	84	47	—	—	46	16	91	19	14	7	9	7	—	—	21	—	5	—	—	—	—	—	—	—
1880	2793	1666	983	398	319	112	52	32	—	—	89	47	—	—	18	4	111	65	29	14	17	7	1	1	27	10	4	3	—	—	—	—	—	—
1881	2937	1409	968	364	352	155	56	37	—	—	90	37	—	—	2	—	47	17	32	11	15	9	—	—	12	6	—	—	—	—	—	—	—	—
1882	3111	1458	1300	446	358	105	79	32	—	—	109	69	—	—	3	—	31	10	38	12	21	10	—	—	7	2	—	—	—	—	—	—	—	—
1883	3591	1785	1495	698	480	197	83	44	—	—	120	96	1	1	—	—	19	4	40	12	18	7	—	—	18	3	2	2	5	1	—	—	—	—
1884	—	—	673†	334	501 249†	229 127	86	64	—	—	93	52	1	1	4	—	7	1	38	21	21	9	—	—	9	—	—	—	10	5	—	—	—	—
1885	4317	1463	906	437	428	307	61	34	—	—	143	77	1	1	9	3	5	3	27	13	20	11	—	—	5	2	—	—	4	—	1	1	—	—
1886	4393	1337	1466	762	869	452	101	70	—	—	208	119	—	—	3	1	9	5	30	12	32	23	—	—	—	—	—	—	11	2	3	1	2	1
1887	—	—	—	—	—	—	—	—	—	—	223	152	—	—	21	11	26	18	—	—	—	—	—	—	—	—	—	—	—	—	—	—	—	—

* Two Entrance Examinations in 1859. † Supplementary Examinations. ‡ 6 of these were candidates for the B. L.

NO. V.

The following tables present the extent to which the applicants for University degrees in the various provinces are distributed among the faiths of the whole country :

BENGAL.

Religion.	Number of Candidates.	Number Passed. First Division.	Second Division.	Third Division.	Total.
Hindus	2812	152	381	263	796
Mohammedans	205	7	35	9	51
Christians	109[1]	25[2]	22[3]	3	50
Others	46[4]	1	8[5]	7[6]	16
Total	3172	185	446	282	913

ASSAM.

Religion	Number of Candidates	First Division	Second Division	Third Division	Total
Hindus	88	6	15	14	35
Mohammedans	6	—	1	2	3
Others	5	—	—	1	1
Total	99	6	16	17	39

NORTHWEST PROVINCES AND OUDH.

Religion	Number of Candidates	First Division	Second Division	Third Division	Total
Hindus	520	17	93	56	166
Mohammedans	115	6	20	12	38
Christians	74[7]	13[8]	13[9]	4	30
Others	6	2	1	—	3
Total	715	38	127	72	237

RAJPUTANA.

Religion	Number of Candidates	First Division	Second Division	Third Division	Total
Hindus	20	—	6	—	6
Mohammedans	5	—	2	—	2
Others	2	—	1	—	1
Total	27	—	9	—	9

JAYPUR.

Religion	Number of Candidates	First Division	Second Division	Third Division	Total
Hindus	8	—	1	—	1
Mohammedans	1	—	—	—	—
Christians	1	—	—	—	—
Others	1	—	1	—	1
Total	11	—	2	—	2

[1] Of these 16 were females.
[2] " 4 "
[3] " 5 "
[4] Of these 5 were females.
[5] " 1 was a female.
[6] " 1 "
[7] Of these 19 were females.
[8] " 4 "
[9] " 3 "

PANJAB.

Religion.	Number of Candidates.	Number Passed. First Division.	Second Division.	Third Division.	Total.
Hindus	27	3	1	5	9
Mohammedans	10	—	2	1	3
Christians	28[1]	4	9	3[2]	16
Others	2	—	—	—	—
Total	67	7	12	9	28

CENTRAL PROVINCES.

Religion.	Number of Candidates.	First Division.	Second Division.	Third Division.	Total.
Hindus	167	12	28	19	59
Mohammedans	11	1	3	1	5
Christians	10	1	3	1	5
Others	2	—	1	—	1
Total	190	14	35	21	70

CENTRAL INDIA STATES.

Religion.	Number of Candidates.	First Division.	Second Division.	Third Division.	Total.
Hindus	33	—	5	3	8
Mohammedans	4	—	—	—	—
Christians	2	1	—	—	1
Others	6	—	—	—	—
Total	45	1	5	3	9

BURMAH.

Religion.	Number of Candidates.	First Division.	Second Division.	Third Division.	Total.
Mohammedans	8	1	3	—	4
Christians	19	4	5	1	10
Others	24	3	6	—	9
Total	51	8	14	1	23

CEYLON.

Religion.	Number of Candidates.	First Division.	Second Division.	Third Division.	Total.
Christians	13	3	2	—	5
Others	3	2	—	—	2
Total	16	5	2	—	7

[1] Of these 5 were females. [2] Of these 2 were females.

NO. VI.

RECEIPTS IN INDIA FROM EXCISE DUTY ON SPIRITS.

	1868–69	1869–70	1870–71	1871–72	1872–73	1873–74	1874–75	1875–76	1876–77	1877–78	1878–79	1879–80	1880–81	1881–82	1882–83	1883–84
	£	£	£	£	£	£	£	£	£	£	£	£	£	£	£	£
India General..	13,148	13,247	17,811	19,966	21,620	20,639	23,132	22,824	27,526	29,840	29,230	29,007	29,389	33,222	35,249	36,581
Oudh..........	64,924	68,620	69,319	57,872	50,703	55,236	64,891	59,631	57,262	24,350	54,969	74,641	82,664	95,855	116,802	127,447
Central Provinces..	71,806	66,956	72,201	76,906	73,366	77,920	87,432	92,446	95,975	96,018	98,063	95,014	105,753	120,458	131,276	148,776
British Burmah..	44,782	35,056	34,225	37,260	44,790	50,699	56,889	68,667	74,383	72,047	72,319	77,906	77,404	78,265	75,487	73,799
Assam.........	—	—	—	—	—	—	7,535	8,001	8,143	9,661	11,535	11,973	14,049	15,156	16,411	22,829
Bengal........	293,510	277,623	309,032	319,298	346,472	354,305	827,822	365,222	371,491	405,832	407,256	423,893	530,364	575,725	596,833	638,521
Northwest Provinces..	125,615	82,539	108,112	126,803	124,609	118,453	128,405	97,960	102,796	97,030	131,815	154,397	195,297	224,965	249,571	266,840
Panjab........	53,156	45,645	42,890	49,838	48,325	48,081	50,736	52,903	57,196	55,839	50,392	54,248	64,560	69,136	74,078	84,714
Madras Presidency..	490,843	570,021	580,265	570,892	640,556	632,032	628,719	665,024	596,583	514,606	623,262	627,142	601,587	636,900	636,624	633,091
Bombay Presidency..	328,147	326,346	320,752	304,976	305,590	320,947	334,076	341,414	356,777	359,864	351,220	378,161	416,189	478,824	558,392	571,565
Total....	1,485,931	1,486,053	1,563,607	1,563,811	1,656,031	1,678,312	1,709,637	1,774 092	1,748,135	1,635,167	1,830,061	1,926.382	2,118,256	2,328,506	2,490,723	2,604,163

· NOTE. — Since the paper from which the above is an extract was written, the government of India in their defence state that latterly this increase in the excise revenue has been due not to increased consumption and consequent drunkenness, but to the increased duty on liquor. This is doubtless true to a certain extent, but then, how has this taste for drink been roused and stimulated? By cheap liquor, and as the Bengal Excise Commission state, by temptation to drink in the facilities offered for doing this by planting grog-shops in improper sites for shops, especially "in the neighborhood of villages of aborigines and of factories, and other places where large bodies of the wage-earning classes are collected together." *Thus numbers now must have their drink, cost what it may*, and thus, as in Assam, "material prosperity" in wages flows largely into liquor channels, instead of, in the case of emigrants, being saved to take home.

February 16, 1888.

ROBERT PRINGLE, M.D.

NO. VII.

OFFICIAL CENSUS OF THE TRADES AND OCCUPATIONS OF THE PEOPLE OF INDIA.

Occupations.	Males.	Females.
Officers of National Government	580,185	6,352
Officers of Municipal, Local, and Village Government	791,379	17,764
Officers of Independent Government and States	133,285	865
Army	311,070	1,682
Navy	300	—
Clergymen, Ministers, Priests, Church and Temple Officers	601,164	94,251
Lawyers, Stationers, and Law-Stamp Dealers	31,628	10
Physicians, Surgeons, and Druggists	113,579	75,239
Authors and Literary Persons	32,177	3,464
Artists	10,347	584
Musicians	187,695	19,631
Actors	58,807	40,381
Teachers	166,356	4,345
Scientific Persons	11,494	127
Wives of Specified Occupations	—	471,774
Other Wives	—	3,321,366
Engaged in Board and Lodgings	27,970	14,515
Attendants (domestic servants)	2,149,029	651,965
Mercantile Persons	983,869	124,409
Other General Dealers	886,149	286,464
Carriers on Railways	61,031	1,157
Carriers on Roads	635,482	13,770
Carriers on Canals and Rivers	322,688	2,877
Carriers on Sea and Rivers	104,237	574
Engaged in Storage	64,667	2,157
Messengers and Porters	174,598	15,063
Agriculturists	19,210	15,866
Horticulturists	166,355	54,448
Persons engaged about Animals	754,512	235,830
Workers in Books	19,384	127
" Musical Instruments	3,146	568
" Prints and Pictures	1,005	79
" Carving and Figures	15,338	4,463
" Tackle for Sports and Game	4,101	1,283
" Designs, Models, and Dies	819	16
" Watches and Philosophical Instruments	2,963	57
" Surgical Instruments	1	—
" Arms	4,293	245
" Machines and Tools	52,095	9,979
" Carriages	11,963	235
" Harness	6,114	781
" Ships	16,913	358
" Houses and Buildings	808,712	27,741
" Furniture	9,343	797
" Chemicals	61,220	19,813
" Wool and Worsted	178,519	69,670
" Silk	51,085	34,355

CENSUS OF TRADES AND OCCUPATIONS.—*Continued.*

OCCUPATIONS.	MALES.	FEMALES.
Workers in Cotton and Flax	2,607,579	2,877,876
" Mixed Materials	52,286	52,621
" Dress	2,082,191	733,089
" Hemp and other Fibrous Materials	108,729	164,367
" Animal Food	640,521	449,205
" Vegetable Food	1,445,916	1,719,513
" Drinks and Stimulants	708,699	204,331
" Grease, Grit, Bones, Horn, Ivory, Whalebone, and Lace	37,107	70,889
" Skins, Feathers, and Quills	263,056	48,559
" Hair	943	344
" Gums and Resins	489,618	273,169
" Wool	235,318	179,560
" Bark and Pith	3,092	68,550
" Bamboo, Cane, Rush, Straw, and Leaves	403,375	277,375
" Paper	7,670	1,410
Miners	3,428	549
Workers in Coal	2,602	1,161
" Stone-clay	667,286	354,721
" Earthenware	569,128	259,839
" Glass	32,841	11,904
" Salt	63,011	23,922
" Water	227,673	198,758
" Gold, Silver, and Precious Stones	459,157	13,799
" Copper	11,019	461
" Tin and Quicksilver	10,419	461
" Zinc	139	32
" Lead and Antimony	992	155
" Brass and other Mixed Metals	123,165	6,605
" Iron and Steel	454,555	18,806
Laborers and others (branch of labor undefined)	7,248,491	5,244,206
Other Persons of Indefinite Occupation	426,109	33,873
Persons of Rank and Property not returned under any Office or Occupation	48,262	13,109
Persons of no stated Occupation	48,794,195	86,135,617

NO. VIII.—BOOKS AND PERIODICALS PUBLISHED IN INDIA DURING THE YEAR 1886.

[These tables are derived from selections from the Records of the Government of India, Home Department, No. ccxxxiii, Calcutta, 1887.]

1. BOMBAY.

Subject.	Original Works. First Edition.	Original Works. New Edition.	Republications.	Translations.	Total.
Arts	46	3	2	10	61
Biography	6	1	—	2	9
Drama	56	16	6	6	84
Fiction	26	9	6	24	65
History	14	12	15	2	43
Language	57	61	19	38	175
Law	4	4	10	6	24
Medicine	24	2	—	29	55
Miscellaneous	523	33	31	99	686
Poetry	91	16	220	9	336
Politics	3	—	1	3	7
Philosophy (including Mental and Moral Science)	23	3	31	17	74
Religion	10	1	69	16	96
Science (Natural and other)	28	28	1	3	60
Science (Mathematical and Mechanical)	12	12	1	1	26
Voyages and Travels	2	—	—	1	3
Total	925	201	412	266	1804

2. BENGAL (Books only).

Subject.	Books published in English and other European Languages.	Books published in the Vernacular Languages spoken in the Province.	Books published in the Indian Classical Languages.	Books published in more than one Language.
Arts	5	56	1	—
Biography	5	11	5	—
Drama	4	97	11	—
Fiction	3	109	5	—
History (includ. Geography)	24	92	4	—
Language	74	294	36	121
Law	36	52	2	2
Medicine	6	94	22	9
Miscellaneous	70	322	28	37
Philosophy	5	9	9	14
Poetry	22	164	13	2
Politics	3	1	—	4
Religion	33	331	57	148
Science (Mathematical)	15	59	—	1
Science (Natural and other)	5	36	—	—
Travels and Voyages	—	3	—	—
	310	1730	193	338
Total				2571

The distribution, according to language, is as follows:

Uni-linguals	1960
Bi-linguals	331
Periodicals	280
Total	2571

This vast number of publications in the one Province of Bengal was issued in twelve languages: Arabic, Asamese, English, Hindi, Mussalmani, Bengali, Nepalese, Persian, Sanskrit, Sontali, Urdu, and Uriya. The number of separate books in English was 310, and the number of copies distributed 370,127. The number of books in other languages was 2261, and the number of copies distributed was 4,486,573. During 1886 there were published in Bengal 66 magazines and periodicals, 11 of which were in English, and 55 in other languages.

3. MADRAS (Books only).

Description of Works.	Books published in English and other European Languages.	Books published in the Vernacular Languages spoken in the Province.	Books published in the Indian Classical Languages.	Books published in more than one Language.	Total.
Original Works	141	241	24	49	455
Translations	14	76	—	2	92
Republications	29	301	41	12	383
Total	184	618	65	63	930

4. PANJAB.

Subject.	Original Works.		Republications.	Translations.	Total.
	First Edition.	New Edition.			
Art	2	1	—	—	3
Biography	6	—	3	—	9
Drama	9	—	40	—	49
Fiction	5	1	9	2	17
History	18	5	3	—	26
Language	56	34	118	7	215
Law	28	—	5	80	113
Medicine	89	—	15	4	108
Miscellaneous	106	19	43	16	184
Poetry	89	4	431	1	524
Philosophy (including Mental and Moral Science)	1	—	2	1	4
Religion	271	1	242	16	530
Science (Mathematical and Mechanical)	27	8	21	8	64
Science (Natural and other)	4	—	3	2	9
Voyages and Travels	1	—	—	1	2
Total	712	73	935	138	1857

5. NORTHWEST PROVINCES AND OUDH.

Fifteen hundred works of all classes were published during the year 1866. This was an increase of about sixteen per cent. on the number of publications in 1885, and of nearly one hundred per cent. on the number issued in 1884. More books were written in Urdu than in any other language. Hindi works were the next most numerous. After this come the English, which increased twenty-five per cent. over the issues of 1885. Among the more notable publications is the translation in Urdu of an American lecture on Electrical Physiology.

6. CENTRAL PROVINCES.

Here one work only, a volume of poetry, was published.

7. BURMA.

Here 141 publications were registered during the year 1886. Of these 20 were in European languages, 111 vernacular, and 10 biglot. Under the head of Drama there were 23 works; History, 5; Language, 21; Law, 1; Miscellaneous, 23; Poetry, 19; Religion, 48; and Science, 1.

8. ASSAM.

In this province 11 books were published.

9. MYSORE.

Here 117 works were published, of which 64 were in the Kannada vernacular.

10. BANGALORE.

The total number published was 12.

11. HAIDARABAD.

Here were 17 works issued, 16 of which were in the Marhatti language and 1 in the Marwari. One was on history, one on language, and the remainder miscellaneous.

INDEX.

THE END.